Copyright Notice

Copyright © 2019 **PMP Exam Prep Book**™

All rights reserved. No part of this publication may be reproduced, distributed, or transmitted in any form or by any means, including photocopying, recording, or other electronic or mechanical methods, without the prior written permission of the publisher and/or author, except in the case of brief quotations embodied in critical reviews and certain other noncommercial uses permitted by copyright law.

For permission requests, write to the publisher or author an email.

Master of Project Academy, Inc.
244 Madison Ave, New York 10016
info@masterofproject.com

Printed in the United States of America
Publisher: Master of Project Academy, Inc.
ISBN: 978-0-578-57020-4

Author
Resit Gulec, MBA, PMP®, ITIL®

Contributor
Ugur Arif Taskol, PMP®, ITIL®, PSM®, PSPO®

Additional Copyright Information

This publication is a derivative work of *A Guide to the Project Management Body of Knowledge (PMBOK® Guide),* which is copyrighted material of and owned by, Project Management Institute, Inc. (PMI®). Unauthorized reproduction of this material is strictly prohibited. The derivative work is the copyrighted material of and owned by, Master of Project Academy, Inc. Copyright 2019

Trademarks, Service Mark and Copyrights

PMI®, PMP®, CAPM® and PMBOK® are registered trademarks of Project Management Institute, Inc. PMP Exam Prep Book™ is a trademark of Master of Project Academy, Inc.

References made throughout this publication to PMP, CAPM, PMI and PMBOK Guide are acknowledged.

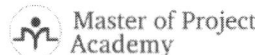

INFORMATION ABOUT PMP® CERTIFICATION	12
Why should I get PMP® Certification?	12
PMP® Certification Requirements	12
35 Contact Hours Project Management Education Requirement for PMP®	14
PMP® Exam Structure	14
SECTION 1 - ENVIRONMENTS IN WHICH PROJECTS OPERATE	16
Definition of Project	17
Why a Project is Initiated?	17
The Example of a Project	18
Definition of Operational Work	18
Definition of Project Management	19
Process Groups	19
Knowledge Areas	19
Definition of Program & Portfolio	21
What is a Program?	21
What is a Portfolio?	21
Interrelationships of Project, Program & Portfolio	22
Comparative overview of Project, Program, and Portfolio	23
How does project, program and portfolio differ in terms of management?	24
How is success measured in project, program, and portfolio?	24
Project Management Office (PMO)	25
Structures of PMOs	25
What does Project Management Office do in an organization?	25
Role of the Project Manager	27
Competencies of a Project Manager	27
Interpersonal Skills of a Project Manager	28
Objectives and Management By Objectives (MBO)	29
Objectives	29
Management by Objectives	30
Constraints	30
Organizational Process Assets	31
Enterprise Environmental Factors	32
Stakeholders	33
Example: Stakeholders of Golden Gate Bridge	34
Project Governance	35
Project team	35
Organizational Structure	36

Functional Organizations	37
Projectized Organizations	38
Matrix Organizations	39
Comparative Overview of Organizational Structures	43
Other Types of Organizational Structures	44
Advantages & Disadvantages of Different Organization Types	**45**
Advantages of Functional Organization	45
Disadvantages of Functional Organization	45
Advantages of Projectized Organization	46
Disadvantages of Projectized Organization	46
Advantages of Matrix Organization	47
Disadvantages of Matrix Organization	47
Project Management Process Groups	**48**
Lifecycle	**50**
Product Life Cycle	52
Project Life Cycle	52
Project and Development Lifecycles	54
Development Life Cycle Types	55
Project Phases	56
Phase Gates	57
Project Business Case	**57**
Benefits Management Plan	**58**
Tailoring	**59**
Lessons Learned	**60**
Quiz – Section 1	**62**
Answers	68
Mapping Game – Section 1	**69**
Answers	71
SECTION 2 – PROJECT MANAGEMENT PROCESSES	**74**
Project Management Processes	**75**
Initiating Process Group Activities	**78**
Planning Process Group Activities	**79**
Executing Process Group Activities	**82**
Monitoring & Controlling Process Group Activities	**84**
Closing Process Group Activities	**86**
Initiating Process Group	**87**
The major outputs of the initiating process group	87
Progressive elaboration	88
Assignment of the project manager	88

Business Case	88
High-Level Planning	88
The reasons to start the initiating process	89

Planning Process Group — 90
- The major outputs of the planning process group — 90
- Rolling Wave Planning — 91
- The reasons for starting planning process — 91

Executing Process Group — 92
- Meetings — 93
- Reasons for starting executing phase — 93

Monitoring & Controlling Process Group — 94
- The Reasons for Initiating the Monitoring & Controlling Processes — 95

Closing Process Group — 96
- The Reasons for Closing Processes — 97

Project Management Process Group and Knowledge Area Mapping — 97

Quiz – Section 2 — 102
- Answers — 105

Mapping Game – Section 2 — 106
- Answers — 107

SECTION 3 – INTEGRATION MANAGEMENT — 109

Overview of Integration Management — 110

Integration Management Processes — 111

Develop Project Charter — 112
- Project Charter Example — 112
- Benefits of Project Charter — 116
- Project Selection Models — 117
- Economic Value Added — 123

Develop Project Management Plan — 128
- Project Management Plan — 130
- Baseline — 131
- Requirements Management Plan — 133
- Change Management Plan — 134
- Change Control System — 135
- Configuration Management Plan — 136
- Configuration Management System — 136
- Process Improvement Plan — 137
- Summary of Steps — 137
- Project Documents — 139
- Project Management Plan Approval — 139
- Kick-Off Meeting — 140

Direct and Manage Project Work Process — 141
- Corrective Action, Preventive Action & Defect Repair — 143

Manage Project Knowledge Process	**144**
Monitor and Control Project Work Process	**145**
Perform Integrated Change Control Process.	**146**
Change Control Board (CCB)	148
Process for Making Changes	149
High Level Process for Making Changes	150
Close Project or Phase Process	**151**
Quiz – Section 3	**152**
Answers	159
Mapping Game – Section 3	**160**
Answers	161
SECTION 4 – SCOPE MANAGEMENT	**163**
Overview of Scope Management	**164**
Product & Project Scope	**166**
Plan Scope Management Process	**167**
Scope Management Plan	167
Requirements Management Plan	169
Collect Requirements Process	**169**
Tools & Techniques for Collecting Requirements	170
Requirements Documentation	174
Balance Stakeholder Requirements & Resolve Competing Requirements	175
Requirements Traceability Matrix	177
Define Scope Process	**178**
Project Scope Statement	178
Constraints and Assumptions	180
Create Work Breakdown Structure (WBS) Process	**180**
Rules for Creating WBS	183
Benefits of Using WBS	184
Relationship of Levels in WBS	187
WBS Dictionary	188
Validate Scope Process	**190**
The inputs of the Validate Scope process	191
The outputs of Validate Scope process	192
Steps of Validate Scope Process	192
Control Scope Process	**193**
Steps for Control Scope process	194
Quiz – Section 4	**196**
Answers	202
Mapping Game – Section 4	**203**
Answers	204

SECTION 5 – SCHEDULE MANAGEMENT — 206

Overview of Schedule Management — 207

Plan Schedule Management Process — 209
    Schedule Management plan — 210

Define Activities Process — 211
    Define Activities Process Example — 213

Sequence Activities Process — 214
    Types of Relationships in PDM — 215
    Types of Dependencies — 217
    Leads & Lags — 218
    Benefits of Network Diagrams — 219
    Sequence Activities Process Example — 220
    Important Points About Estimating — 221

Estimate Activity Durations Process — 222
    One-Point Estimation Technique — 223
    Analogous Estimating (Top-Down) — 224
    Parametric Estimating — 224
    Heuristics Estimating — 225
    Three Point Estimating (PERT Analysis) — 226
    Three Point Estimating PERT Analysis Example — 228
    Estimate Activity Durations Process Example — 228
    Reserve Analysis — 229

Develop Schedule Process — 230
    Critical Path Method (CPM) — 232
    Critical Path Method (CPM) Exercise — 234
    Notes about Critical Path Method — 239
    Schedule Compression (Fast Tracking & Crashing) — 240
    What-if Scenario Analysis — 241
    Resource Leveling — 242
    Critical Chain Method — 243
    Agile Release Planning — 244
    Project Schedule — 245
    Schedule Baseline — 247
    Develop Schedule Process Example — 247

Control Schedule Process — 248
    What are the activities in control schedule process? — 249
    Re-estimating — 250

Quiz – Section 5 — 251
    Answers — 256

Mapping Game – Section 5 — 257
    Answers — 257

SECTION 6 – COST MANAGEMENT — 260

Overview of Cost Management — 261

Plan Cost Management Process — 262

Cost Management Plan	262
Life Cycle Costing & Value Engineering	264

Estimate Costs Process — 265
- Types of Costs — 268
- Inputs to Estimating Costs — 269
- Estimating — 270
- Contributors to Creation of Estimates — 271
- Accuracy of Estimates — 272

Determine Budget Process — 273
- Determine Budget Process Example — 275
- Cost Baseline & Project Budget Components — 276
- What to Do After Determine Budget — 278

Control Costs Process — 279
- Progress Reporting — 280
- Earned Value Management — 283
- Earned Value Management Exercise — 283
- Variances in Earned Value Management — 284
- Variances in Earned Value Management Exercise — 286
- Forecasting in Earned Value Management — 287
- Forecasting in Earned Value Management Exercise — 290
- Important Notes About EVM — 292

Quiz – Section 6 — 294
- Answers — 301

Mapping Game – Section 6 — 302
- Answers — 303

SECTION 7 – QUALITY MANAGEMENT — 305

Overview of Quality Management — 306
- Terms About Quality — 307
- Quality Theorists — 308
- Concepts of Quality Management — 309
- Differences of Quality Management Process — 310

Plan Quality Management Process — 312
- Tools & Techniques Used in Quality Management Processes — 313
- The 7 Basic Quality Tools (7QC Tools) — 317
- Outputs of Plan Quality Management Process — 326

Manage Quality Process — 326
- The Tools and Techniques used in Manage Quality process — 327
- The Outputs of Manage Quality process — 328

Control Quality Process — 328
- Terms & Concepts About Control Quality Process — 329
- Outputs of Control Quality Process — 331
- Tips About Quality Management Processes — 331

Quiz – Section 7 — 333
- Answers — 338

Mapping Game – Section 7 — **339**
    Answers — 340

SECTION 8 – RESOURCE MANAGEMENT — 342

Overview of Resource Management — **343**

Roles & Responsibilities — **345**
    Role of the Project Sponsor (Initiator) — 346
    Role of the Project Team — 348
    Role of the Stakeholders — 350
    Role of the Functional Manager — 350
    Role of the Project, Portfolio & Program Manager — 351

Plan Resource Management Process — **352**
    Inputs for Plan Resource Management Process — 353
    Organization Charts & Position Descriptions — 354
    Resource Management Plan — 357
    Staffing Management Plan — 358
    Resource Histogram — 359
    Recognition & Rewards Systems — 360

Estimate Activity Resources Process — **361**
    Estimate Activity Resources Process Example — 363

Acquire Resource Process — **364**
    Inputs of Acquire Resource Process — 364
    Tools & Techniques Used in Acquire Resources Process — 365
    Virtual Teams — 367
    Halo Effect — 369

Develop Team Process — **369**
    Team-Building Activities — 370
    Tools & Techniques Used in Develop Team Process — 372

Manage Team Process — **374**
    Tools & Techniques Used in Manage Team Process — 375
    Powers of the Project Manager — 377
    Conflict Management — 378
    7 Common Sources of Conflicts — 379
    Conflict Resolution Techniques — 380
    Important Terms & Topics — 381
    McGregor's Theory of X and Y — 382
    Maslow's Hierarchy of Needs — 383
    David McClelland's Theory of Needs — 384
    Herzberg's Theory. — 385

Control Resources Process — **386**

Quiz – Section 8 — **387**
    Answers — 396

Mapping Game – Section 8 — **397**
    Answers — 397

SECTION 9 – COMMUNICATIONS MANAGEMENT — 400

Overview of Communications Management	**400**
Potential Dimensions in Communications Management Processes	401
Effective Communication Skills	402
Plan Communications Management Process	**404**
Number of Communication Channels	405
Communication Technology	406
Communication Models	406
Communication Methods	408
Communications Management Plan	408
Manage Communications Process	**410**
Monitor Communications Process	**410**
Quiz – Section 9	**412**
Answers	415
Mapping Game – Section 9	**416**
Answers	416

SECTION 10 – RISK MANAGEMENT — 419

Overview of Risk Management	**420**
Risk Management Concepts	422
Plan Risk Management Process	**424**
Risk Management Plan	426
Identify Risks Process	**427**
Tools & Techniques for Risk Identification.	428
Risk Register	429
Perform Qualitative Risk Analysis Process	**430**
Outputs of Perform Qualitative Risk Analysis Process	434
Perform Quantitative Risk Analysis Process	**434**
Tools & Techniques for Quantitative Risk Analysis	436
Outputs of Perform Quantitative Risk Analysis	440
Plan Risk Responses Process	**441**
Risk Response Strategies for Negative Risks	442
Risk Response Strategies for Positive Risks	444
Contingent Response Strategies	444
Outputs of Plan Risk Responses Process	445
Important Notes about Plan Risk Responses	446
Implement Risk Responses Process	**447**
Monitor Risks Process	**448**
Quiz – Section 10	**451**
Answers	460
Mapping Game – Section 10	**461**
Answers	462

SECTION 11 – PROCUREMENT MANAGEMENT — 464

Overview of Procurement Management — **465**
   Procurement Concepts — 465
   Project Manager's Role in Procurement — 467
   Centralized-Decentralized Contracting — 469

Plan Procurement Management Process — **470**
   Fixed Price Contracts — 471
   Cost Reimbursable Contracts — 473
   Time & Material Contracts — 476
   Terms & Concepts about Contracts — 477
   Tools & Techniques Used in Plan Procurement — 480
   Procurement Management Plan — 482
   Procurement Statement of Work — 484
   Procurement (Bid) Documents — 485
   Source Selection Criteria — 486
   Other Terms & Concepts About Procurement — 488
   Noncompetitive Forms of Procurement — 490

Conduct Procurement Process — **491**
   Tools & Techniques Used in Conduct Procurements Process — 491
   Outputs of Conduct Procurements Process — 496

Control Procurements Process — **496**
   Tools & Techniques Used in Control Procurements — 498
   Closing a Procurement — 499
   Key Outputs of Procurement Processes — 501

Quiz – Section 11 — **503**
   Answers — 510

Mapping Game – Section 11 — **511**
   Answers — 512

SECTION 12 – STAKEHOLDER MANAGEMENT — 514

Overview of Stakeholder Management — **514**

Identify Stakeholders Process — **516**
   Tools & Techniques Used in Identify Stakeholders — 517
   Stakeholder Register — 519

Plan Stakeholder Engagement Process — **520**
   Tools & Techniques of Plan Stakeholder Engagement — 521
   Stakeholder Engagement Plan — 523

Manage Stakeholder Engagement Process — **524**

Monitor Stakeholder Engagement Process — **525**

Quiz – Section 12 — **527**
   Answers — 529

Mapping Game – Section 12 — **530**
   Answers — 530

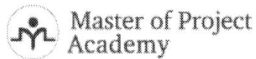

SECTION 13 – SAMPLE PMP® PRACTICE EXAM 532

SECTION 13 – SAMPLE PMP® PRACTICE EXAM ANSWERS & RATIONALES 571

Information About PMP® Certification

Before we dive into the details of knowledge areas, it is better to know details of PMP® and CAPM® certification.

Why should I get PMP® Certification?

PMP certification is the most recognized professional certificate for project management profession around the world. Many of the employers seek PMP certification in project management positions when they are hiring. Also, they seek PMP certification as a prerequisite for their current employees when they are promoting their employees to project management positions.

Based on several surveys, PMP certification holders command ~20% higher income than their uncertified counterparts. Therefore, importance of the PMP certification has grown rapidly in recent years.

PMP certification itself does not prove any competence or experience. But, PMP certification warrants at least a certain level of knowledge on project management area. However, PMI's PMP application process and audits seek for relevant experience and education requirements to be a PMP very strictly. Therefore, companies or organizations give very high credit to PMP certification compared to other certificates in the industry.

Strict process of PMI to check PMP certification requirements is the foundation of this high credit given by employers. Because, an employer will know that a PMP certification holder met the strict PMP certification requirements which proves a certain level of project management knowledge and practice.

PMP certification is not an easy sit and pass exam. There are PMP eligibility requirements that every PMP certification aspirant must meet. Let's see these PMP certification requirements now.

PMP® Certification Requirements

You might wonder why there are requirements for PMP certification. There are two fundamental reasons for this. The first main reason is project management is a serious profession that requires communication with several stakeholders throughout the project. While delivering a scope of work, project managers must be careful about communication, attitude and how to manage expectations of different people. Otherwise, the project delivery might fail. Therefore, having a solid project management experience is one of the requirements for PMP certification.

The second main reason for having requirements for PMP is project management requires solid theoretical knowledge on project management techniques. There are knowledge areas that a project manager has to be proficient in order to pass the PMP certification exam. These knowledge areas are tested in different project management process groups. In order to pass

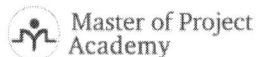

the PMP certification exam, a PMP candidate must score above a certain level from these project management process groups.

Because of these two reasons, requirements for PMP exam include PMP experience requirement and PMP education requirement. PMP experience requirement will show that the PMP candidate has enough soft skills to sit for the PMP exam. PMP education requirement will show that the PMP candidate has enough theoretical background to manage a project.

Following table summarizes the PMP certification requirements that a PMP aspirant must meet to apply for the PMP exam.

Education Level	Project Management Experience	Project Management Education
Bachelor's Degree (4 years of College/University Education)	4,500+ hours (equivalent to 3+ years of experience)	35 contact hours
Secondary Degree (High School or 2-year pre-undergrad education)	7,500+ hours (equivalent to 5+ years of experience)	35 contact hours

In order to apply for PMP certification, you need to have at least a secondary degree, for instance a high school or equivalent education level. If your highest attended education level is secondary degree, in order to apply for PMP certification, you need to satisfy following three PMP certification requirements.

1-) 5 years of project management experience (7,500 hours)
2-) 35 contact hours of project management education.

Note that, project management experience point in PMP certification requirements does not seek for active management of a project. Participating in a project environment also counts for this 5 years of experience requirement. However, 7500 hours of these 5 years, which makes around 3.5 years, need to be spent of leading and directing projects. Again, this doesn't mean that you should have enrolled in a project as a project manager. A leading or directing role can be supervisor of a junior team member or team members, team leader of a group, assisting project manager in some of the project management activities etc.

If your education level is a four-year degree or above, you should be looking for following PMP requirements. If your highest attended education level is a four-year degree or above, for instance bachelor's degree or equivalent, master's degree, doctorate etc. in order to apply for PMP certification, you need to satisfy following three PMP certification requirements

1-) 3 years of project management experience (4,500 hours)
2-) 35 hours of project management education.

Note that, project management experience point in PMP certification requirements does not seek for active management of a project. Participating in a project environment also counts for this 3 years of experience requirement. However, 4500 hours of these 3 years, which

makes around 2 years, need to be spent of leading and directing projects. Again, this doesn't mean that you should have enrolled in a project as a project manager. A leading or directing role can be supervisor of a junior team member or team members, team leader of a group, assisting project manager in some of the project management activities etc.

35 Contact Hours Project Management Education Requirement for PMP®

Regardless of your education level, you must attend in a 35 contact hours project management education to be eligible to sit for PMP exam. There are several education providers for PMP certification exam. However, you must be careful when selecting your PMP training.

PMI expects you to attend in a 35 contact hours instructional PMP course. So, following only a book or studying by yourself through PMP resources will not satisfy PMP certification requirements. You must attend in an online (self-paced or instructor-led) or in-person PMP classroom training.

Once you satisfy the PMP certification requirements, you can proceed to create your profile in PMI website and apply for the PMP exam.

PMP® Exam Structure

There are 200 multiple-choice questions in PMP exam. Total duration of the exam is four hours. 25 out of the 200 questions in the exam are not scored and used by PMI for quality control purposes. However, you will never know which of these 25 questions. They come randomly during you take the PMP exam.

Following table summarizes the PMP exam structure.

Number of Questions	Duration	Style
200	4 hours	Multiple Choice

There are different types of questions in the PMP exam. Situational, interpretation, formula, definition, knowledge and ethics questions will appear during the PMP exam.

Section 1

Environments in Which Projects Operate

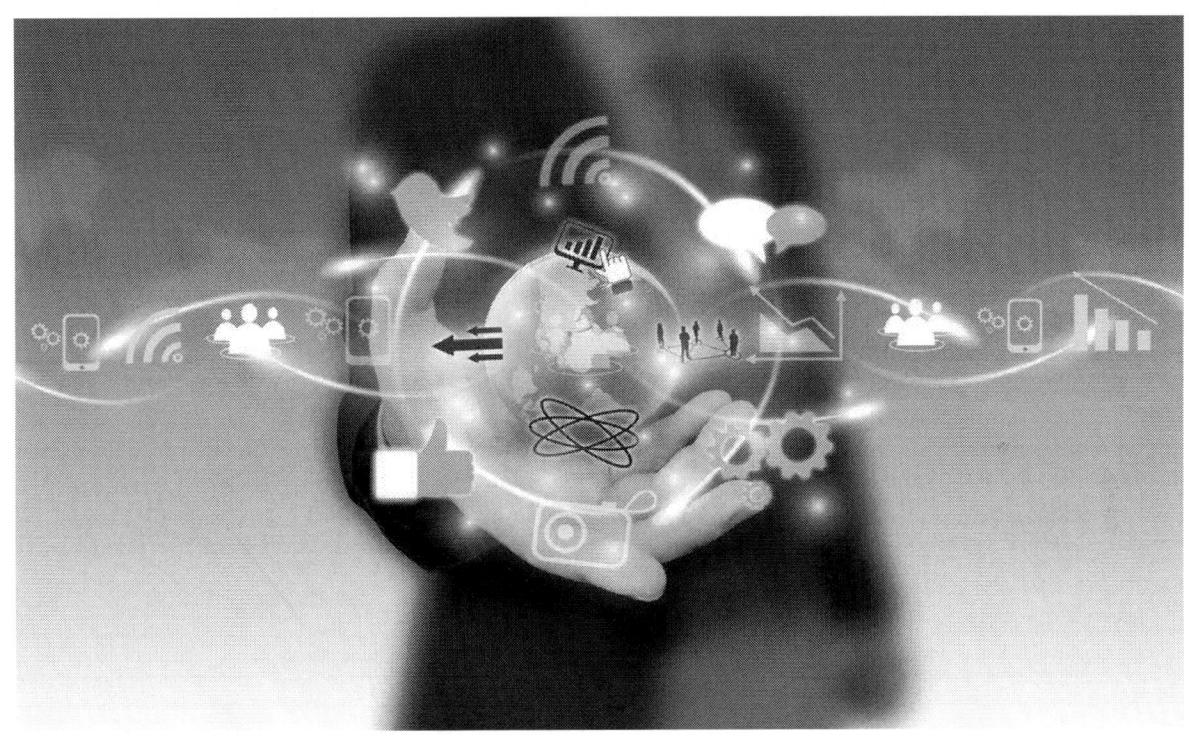

Section 1 - Environments in Which Projects Operate

Before you step into the details of project management, you must understand the foundations of project management and critical terms about project management. If you are familiar with project management, you might have heard about what you will learn during this section. However, keep in mind that, what you must know for PMP® exam might differ from what you know from "practical" project management.

What will you learn in this section?

- Project
- Operational Work
- Project Management
- Program
- Portfolio
- Project Management Office (PMO)
- Objectives
- Constraints
- Stakeholders
- Organizational Structure
- Life Cycle
- Project and Development Lifecycles
- Project Phases & Phase Gates
- Business Case
- Benefits Management Plan
- Lessons Learned

There is always a misconception between project and operational work. Although some operational work might look like projects, there are differences between them. There is a hierarchy between project, program, and portfolio and a role of the project management office and project manager.

Every activity, operation, action will have an objective in a company. Similarly, projects have their own objectives and constraints that affect the progress of the project critically.

Stakeholders are the people or organizations who may be affected by a project and the organizational structures are important in terms of the approach of a company to the project management. There are three different types of organizational structures in organizations and all have advantages and disadvantages.

There is a life cycle of a project and this helps project managers to focus on different aspects of projects at different times easily. As well, there is development lifecycles. There are several differences of predictive, iterative, incremental and adaptive lifecycles. Depending on the project nature, one of the project lifecycles is adapted when managing the project. Projects are divided into phases. These phases include related activities of a project and in order to complete a phase, predetermined phase gate rules must have been completed.

The Business case is the reason why projects are initiated. Benefits management plan covers the benefits that will be gained once the project is completed. Lessons learned documents constitute very precious knowledge and experience database for a company.

Generally, in this section, all the above mentions and the critical project management terms, definitions and their purposes will be described in detail.

Definition of Project

Project is a temporary endeavor with a beginning and an end. This is important. The project should have a beginning and it should have an ending. A project cannot go over time periodically.

> *Projects are temporary endeavors which create unique product, service or result.*

Projects should create a unique product, service or result. If it is not unique, for instance, if you are producing the same product in an assembly line, then you are not working on a project.

Why a Project is Initiated?

The most common project initiation reasons are listed here:

- **Market Demand:** A project might be initiated due to market demand. For example, women drivers prefer to use smaller cars in traffic. Due to this market demand in the last years, car manufacturers are producing small cars, especially for women. Producing a small car for women might be the reason for a project for a car manufacturer.

- **Strategic Opportunity/Business Need:** There might be a harsh competition in the sector. For example, in the smartphone industry, there is a harsh competition between Samsung and Apple. Two rivals try to beat each other. They release new versions of their smartphones with extended features and functionalities frequently. This might be a reason for a project in Samsung or Apple.

- **Social need:** Food is a basic need of humanity. There are several African countries fighting with hunger. In order to provide food for the children in Africa, UNICEF might start a project and this would be an example of social need.

- **Environmental Consideration:** Water and air pollution are becoming major problems in big cities around the world. Several cautions are taken and several projects are initiated to reduce air and water pollution in cities around the world. For instance, green buildings, buildings that generate their own electricity or reuse the water are examples for this category.

- **Customer Request:** There are several service companies and vendors in the market. For instance, for a telecom operator, Ericsson, Nokia, and Huawei are examples of major telecommunication vendors. When a mobile operator asks for a new system in their network, this would be an example of customer request from a vendor point of you.

- **Technological Advance:** A new project can be initiated in order to do an existing activity or process better. For instance, if a new machine will increase the production speed in a factory, in order to take advantage of this technological advance, a new project might be initiated to integrate this new machine.

- **Legal requirement:** Consider that, there are problems in regulations of miner stations in a country. In order to improve the conditions of the mineworkers, the government has released some regulations and each mine station employer has to obey these rules by the government. In order to improve these conditions of the miner stations, the mine stations may want to start a new project.

Although these are the major reasons for project initiation, there might be other cases that can start projects in organizations.

The Example of a Project

Consider "the construction of the Golden Gate Bridge of San Francisco" as an example of a project.

The project is started in 1933 and ended in 1937. It has a beginning and an ending. It was temporary. It did not take until today to build this bridge. Besides, the Golden Gate bridge has been built only once and it is unique in the world. There is not any identical Golden Gate bridge in somewhere else around the world.

Definition of Operational Work

Operational work is the most of the work performed in organizations. User registration in a company, fixing the technical problem of a customer, giving support on the phone to a customer, providing a new laptop to a new employee are all examples of operational work done in a company.

Operational work differs from the project in terms of being **ongoing** and **repetitive**. The results of the operational work are not unique or they do not have a definite end. For instance, a company must support its customers and this will be an ongoing activity as long as the company continues to provide its services and products to its customers.

> Operational works are "ongoing" and "repetitive".

As an example of the operational work: The yearly maintenance of the Golden Gate Bridge is an example of operational work.

Maintenance happens every year and most probably certain steps and processes are repeated on a predefined interval on the bridge to check whether the bridge is safe.

Therefore, maintenance of the Golden Gate Bridge is not a project.

Definition of Project Management

Project management is the application of knowledge, skills, tools, and techniques to project activities to meet the project requirements. There is a scope of a work that needs to be done, a timeline that the customer expects it to finish and of course, there will be quality requirements.

> Project management ensures that the scope of the required work is delivered on time as per the quality requirements.

Project Management profession is growing rapidly in recent years. The main reason for this is the competition in the market. Because the faster you deliver, the better you take the position. The cheaper you produce, the more competitive your product will be. The project management mainly aims to deliver a scope on time, on budget and with agreed quality. This is why project management is a growing profession in recent years.

Project Management follows a systematic process. For each topic and area, **project management has processes that have inputs, tools and techniques and outputs.** These ensure to deliver successful results respectively.

Process Groups

Each process of project management will be discussed in the further sections.

Knowledge Areas

Process of project management belongs to the knowledge areas. There are 10 knowledge areas in project management. These are:

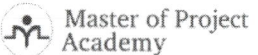

- Integration Management
- Scope Management
- Schedule Management
- Cost Management
- Quality Management
- Resource Management
- Communications Management
- Risk Management
- Procurement Management
- Stakeholder Management

Integration Management: Integration management mainly aims to control all processes and cohesive execution of the project in accordance with all project management processes.

Scope Management: Scope Management mainly aims to define the boundaries of the work that will be delivered in the project and helps to protect this scope until the end of the project.

Schedule Management: Schedule Management mainly aims to complete the project on time.

Cost Management: Cost Management targets to deliver the agreed scope based on the planned budget.

Quality Management: Quality management helps to ensure that the project meets its quality requirements.

Resource Management: Resource Management mainly aims to manage people and other resources of a project. Conflict resolution, staff planning, coaching, etc. are all done as part of human resource management. However, there will be other tools, equipment and vehicles you will use to complete the project. These are all managed under the resources management knowledge area.

Communications Management: There will be several stakeholders in a project. Each stakeholder will have a varying interest to the project and each stakeholder will require a different set of information. Communications management knowledge area ensures effective and efficient communication in a project.

Risk Management: Risk Management ensures to keep the up to date status of risks and their response strategies if those risks occur. Its main objective is being prepared for unexpected situations during the project.

Procurement Management: Projects require purchasing or leasing of tools, equipment, resources or people. This is under control of procurement management.

Stakeholder Management: People, groups or institutions that might be affected positively or negatively from the outcome of the project are stakeholders. Stakeholder management aims to treat each stakeholder accordingly to meet the balance of stakeholder requirements in a project.

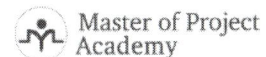

Definition of Program & Portfolio

What is a Program?

A program is a group of projects. Several projects can come together to constitute a program, however, these projects should be interrelated. Programs are constituted in order to manage interrelated projects better. If projects somehow do not relate to each other or do not affect each other, then there is no need to group these projects under a program.

> A program is a group of interrelated projects.

Example of a Program

As an example, consider there is a program of "Manufacturing of a new version of an Airbus plane", and under this program, there can be several projects such as avionic systems, communication systems, entertainment systems, security system, etc. All these projects are interrelated with each other because the airplane will be completed only if all these systems are merged and works properly.

What is a Portfolio?

A portfolio is a group of programs to achieve a business goal. In order to achieve a strategic objective of the company, several programs can come together to constitute a portfolio.

Although a program might not be directly related to another program, if it is serving for the same business goal, these programs can be grouped under the same portfolio. For the programs under a portfolio, it is important to serve for same business goal.

> A portfolio is a group of programs to achieve a strategic objective of the company

Example of a Portfolio

Consider that Airbus will develop three new airplane versions in six years.

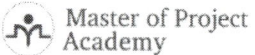

The development of each version of these airplanes can go independently from each other and these programs can be grouped under portfolio.

What is the strategic goal of this portfolio?

To be the world's most passenger-carrying airplane company. This strategy might be for beating Boeing in the market for instance.

Interrelationships of Project, Program & Portfolio

The interrelationship of project, program and portfolio will be shown over an example.

Consider the "six-year airplane manufacturing portfolio of Airbus" as a portfolio example from our previous examples. This portfolio includes three programs, which cover manufacturing of three different versions of Airbus airplanes.

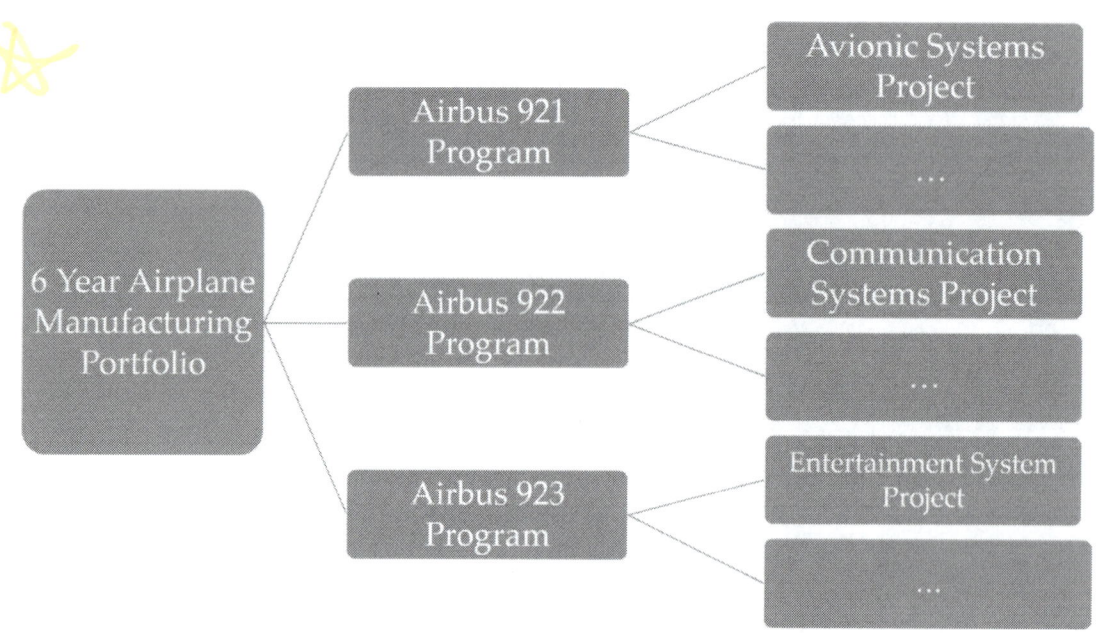

Airbus 921 program, Airbus 922 program and Airbus 923 program. Note that, these three programs serve for the same strategic business goal but they do not interfere or they do not depend on each other.

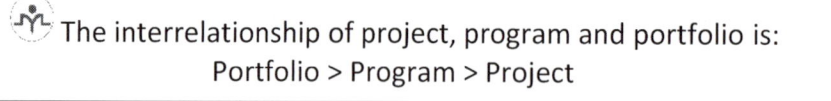

The interrelationship of project, program and portfolio is:
Portfolio > Program > Project

Under each program, there are interrelated projects. The examples are given in avionics systems project, communication systems project and entertainment system project for each program. Same projects might be the input for different several programs as well.

Comparative overview of Project, Program, and Portfolio

Look at how project, program, and portfolio differ from each other in terms of scope, change, planning, management, success and monitoring.

Organizational Project Management			
	Projects	**Programs**	**Portfolios**
Scope	-defined objectives -scope is elaborated throughout the project life cycle	-relatively larger scopes -produces more important benefits	-serves for an organizational scope -organization's strategic targets determines scope
Change	-changes are inevitable and managed through processes	-changes can come from inside or outside of the program	-changes can come from internal sources or from external environment
Planning	-high-level information is used and detailed plans are created	-overall program plan is created and high-level plans are created at the component level	-Processes are created and communication is critical
Management	-Project managers manage the project team	-Program managers manage the program staff and project managers	-Portfolio managers manage the portfolio staff, program managers and project managers
Success	-measured by produced product/service -time, budget, customer satisfaction are key metrics	-Realization of the program objectives	-return on investment, benefits realization
Monitoring	-Project managers monitor & control products/services	-Program managers monitor the program components – overall goals, schedule, budget and benefits	-Portfolio managers monitor strategic changes, resource allocation, performance results and risks

In terms of scope, projects have more definitive and narrower tasks.

The scope is progressive throughout the project lifecycle. This means, new change requests might come from the customer or business and this might affect the scope of the project.

However, programs have a larger scope, and provide benefits that are more significant. Because **several projects come together for a program**. Therefore, the program's scope will be bigger respectively.

In the portfolios, the scope is more different. Instead of what needs to be done, strategic goals or business vision of a company defines the scope of a portfolio. Projects deal with the changes that might affect their project. These changes often happen internally.

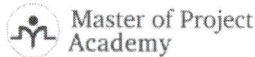

Program managers deal with both internal and external changes. For instance, a change or risk that is happening in one of the projects under the program might affect each other since they are interrelated. Therefore, the program manager must look broader.

Portfolio managers continuously monitor changes in the broader internal and external environment. Because **the portfolio serves for a strategic goal of a company** and a market or economic change might affect the portfolio as well.

In terms of planning, project managers progressively elaborate high-level information into detailed plans throughout the project lifecycle. The planning of a project includes detailed work package planning, detailed task planning which includes tasks that can be completed in a few days or even in hours.

In the programs, program managers develop the overall program plan and create high-level plans to guide the detailed planning at the component levels. **The programs do not dive into details of planning.** They keep track of whether components within a project have been completed or not.

In portfolios, portfolio managers create and maintain necessary processes and communication relative to an aggregate portfolio. Instead of a task and component monitoring, portfolio planning deals with whether the strategic goal or business plan will be achieved.

How does project, program and portfolio differ in terms of management?

Project Managers manage the project team and ensure that the project objectives are met.

A program manager manages the program staff, for instance, program assistant, and project managers under the program.

Portfolio managers manage the portfolio staff and program managers.

How is success measured in project, program, and portfolio?

Success is measured by product and product quality, timelines, and budget in projects. If the agreed scope is met in agreed quality, on agreed time and budget, projects are considered successful, however, in programs; all projects under the program must meet their objectives, timeline and budget respectively.

For portfolio, success a bit different. **If projects and programs help to achieve the business goal of the portfolio, then portfolios are considered as successful as well.**

The last point is Monitoring. Project managers are the ultimate observer of projects health. In programs, program managers are responsible for the progress of programs and they need to take proper preventive and corrective actions if there are risks that might affect the program.

For portfolios, the portfolio manager must monitor whether the portfolio keeps going towards the strategic goal that has been determined. If there are any internal or external risks that might affect the portfolio, the portfolio manager must act respectively.

Project Management Office (PMO)

Project management office is abbreviated as PMO. The main role of this department is centralizing the overall project management of the company.

A company executes several projects at a time. Project Management Office ensures the successful management and coordination of these several projects with its processes and tools.

Information, documents, coordination and management are done mainly with the help of Project Management Office department. Depending on the size of the company, the number of projects and size of the projects, size and hierarchy of the department might change as well.

Structures of PMOs

There are fundamentally three structures for Project Management Offices;

1. **Supportive:** Supplies templates, best practices, training, lessons learned…etc. Acts as a repository. (Low degree of control)
2. **Controlling:** Supports and requires compliance with tools, methods. (Moderate degree of control)
3. **Directive:** Directly manages the projects. (High degree of control)

Supportive: Supportive PMO supplies templates, best practices, training, lessons learned documentation, etc. to the other departments and projects. This type of PMO actually acts as a repository of the company. This PMO structure is like an archive of the company and gives information and documentation when necessary but it does not have a solid control on projects.

Controlling: Controlling PMO supports and requires compliance with tools and methods. They follow whether required documents are submitted in a project, or relevant steps are executed based on the processes, etc. This type of PMO has a moderate degree of control in projects.

Directive: Directive PMO manages the projects and it is the sole accountable from the success of projects. They do have a strong position in the company and a relevant authority respectively. Directive PMO has the highest degree of control among other types of PMO.

What does Project Management Office do in an organization?

- PMO may **manage interdependencies between projects**. There might be several projects ongoing in a project and one project might affect each other. For instance, Project A might be started only if Project B finished. These kinds of or even more complex interdependencies of projects are managed by PMO.

- PMO may **help providing resources to the projects**. When there is a new project, PMO assigns the project manager of the project. Alternatively, if the PMO is directive, all project resources of the company might be reporting to the PMO. For instance, software developers, analysts, test engineers, etc. In this case, PMO will be responsible for constituting the overall project team structure.

- PMO may **terminate projects**. If PMO sees that the objectives of the project will not be met anymore, it can discuss with the business or customer to terminate the project.

- PMO may **monitor compliance with organizational processes**. In order to initiate a project or close a project, several processes within an organization might be executed. For instance, if you will need a tool or equipment for a project, this will require procurement. To purchase this tool or equipment, processes of finance department might be executed. PMO will initiate and follow it in this case.

- PMO may **collect the lessons learned documentation from projects**. Projects experience several situations that show the weaknesses and strengths of the company. These should be documented and collected by PMO. These must be used in future projects to improve weak points or take preventive and corrective actions for the problems encountered in a past project.

- PMO may **provide templates**. A project requires several documents such as planning template, budget template, risk register template … etc. In order to have a standard type of documentation, PMO may provide templates for the projects.

- PMO may **provide guidance**. If a project faces a problem or if there is a conflict that needs to be escalated, PMO will guide in this case.

- PMO provides **centralized communication about the projects**. Coordination and management of projects in a company are centralized in PMO therefore; PMO may provide centralized communication about the projects as well.

- PMO may **be part of the change control board**. Change control board approves whether a change will be implemented in a project. As the department managing and coordinating projects, PMO may be part of the Change Control Board respectively.

- PMO may **be a stakeholder**. A stakeholder is a person or organization who might be affected positively or negatively from the outcomes of a project. By its nature, since PMO is managing and controlling projects, it will be a stakeholder as well.

Other lots of tasks and activities are done by PMO in a company.

Role of the Project Manager

The project manager is the person assigned by the organization to lead the team that is responsible for achieving project objectives.

Roles and duties of a project manager might change depending on the organization but project managers play a vital role in the success of a project. They act as a single point of contact most of the times whenever information is required from a project.

> A project manager is the ultimate accountable of a project's success

Depending on the type of organization, the project manager can report to three types of other managers.

- Functional Manager
- Program Manager
- Portfolio Manager

Functional manager: Functional managers are responsible for resources for a specific domain. For instance, if software developers of a company are under the software development line, then the software development line manager is a functional manager in this case. Depending on the PMO and project management structure of the company, project managers might report to functional managers.

Program Manager: Project managers might report to a program manager if their project is part of a program.

Portfolio Manager: They might report to a portfolio manager if their project belongs to a portfolio.

The main role of the project manager is, he **acts as the link between strategy and team.** A company has objective, strategies, and vision. In order to reach its goal, several projects are executed in a company. A project is a part of the overall success to reach a business goal.

In this respect, the project manager will guide its team to reach its project objectives and respectively the project will help to achieve the overall success of the company in its business goals and objectives.

Competencies of a Project Manager

A project manager should have the following competencies:

> Knowledge (about project management)
> Performance (how he applies knowledge)
> Personal (behavior, skills)

Knowledge about project management: Project management includes several knowledge areas like integration management, scope management, time management, people management, etc. In order to manage a project successfully, the project manager must have this competence.

Performance: Knowledge or theory without practical implication is not that much valuable. You might know the project management theories and knowledge areas very well, however, if you cannot perform them well on the field when executing a project, your project will suffer most probably.

Personal: A project manager spends 90% of his time with communication. This can be either written, face-to-face or informal. Therefore, a project manager must know how to reach people and how to encourage them to perform better.

Interpersonal Skills of a Project Manager

A Project Manager must have several interpersonal skills but the most important ones are listed here.

- Leadership
- Team building
- Motivation
- **Communication**
- Influencing
- Decision Making
- Political & Cultural Awareness
- Negotiation
- Trust building
- Conflict Management
- Coaching

> - The topmost skill that a project manager must have is **Communication**.
> - A project manager spends 90% of his time with communication

Communication: If you are not good at communicating with other people, this will automatically affect your project success. You can be a perfect software developer, perfect civil engineer or a perfect test engineer. Unless you do not have good communication skills, even if you have very good knowledge of project management, it will affect the success of your projects.

Leadership, team building, motivation, influencing, decision making, political and cultural awareness, negotiation, trust building, conflict management and coaching are other interpersonal skills that a project manager should have to manage projects better.

Objectives and Management By Objectives (MBO)

Objectives are what needs to be achieved as a result of the project. Each project will have unique objectives.

For instance, a new feature development can be a project objective, increasing revenue or decreasing costs can be a new project objective, or producing a new product can be objective of a project.

Golden Gate Bridge construction project was our project example. Objectives of this project can be:

- The bridge must have 6 lanes in total, 3 for each side.
- The bridge must carry at least 2,5 million kilograms
- It must resist an at least 8.5 Richter scale earthquake.

Constructing a bridge, which will be connecting two sides of a city, will have several other objectives. Note that if objectives of a project cannot be met, that projects will be considered as failed.

> If you have lots of requirements, then most probably you will have lots of objectives.

Objectives

- **Projects** are considered as **done, once objectives are met.** Therefore, the project manager must monitor project objectives and if there are any risks that can cause not meeting any of the objectives, then preventive and corrective actions should be taken accordingly.

- A reason for terminating a project before completion is that the project objectives cannot be met. If the Golden Gate Bridge could not have carried 2.5 million kg, that would be the reason for the project to be failed.

- **Project Manager** is the ultimate **accountable of meeting project objectives.** Therefore, Project Manager must keep track of objectives and ensure that project activities, tasks and deliverables will help to meet project objectives.

- Quality activities are for checking whether the project meets its objectives. For example, consider the Golden Gate Bridge project. After the construction finishes, you cannot open it directly to the traffic right? You need to test whether it will carry the traffic. Therefore, quality activities are for ensuring to meet project objectives.

- There is a trade-off between requirements and objectives. If you have many requirements, then most probably you will have many objectives.

Management by Objectives

Management by objectives is a management philosophy that ensures to complete a work, task or activity by managing the objectives that will bring you to the completion. Management by Objectives philosophy has three steps:

1. **Establishing clear and realistic objectives.** This is important because subjective objectives will not be sufficient. "We will produce a very good car". Is this an objective? No. Because good, bad, fast, slow are all subjective. A very fast car can be very slow for another driver. Therefore, the objectives must be quantitative. "We will produce a car that will reach 100 km/h in 8 seconds". This is an objective because quantitative values are determined.

2. **Periodically evaluating if project objectives are met.** Projects might take for months or even years to complete. Sometimes, several resources can work on a package for a long time. Therefore, you need to check the outputs of the work being produced whether it meets the project objectives. Otherwise, your product or deliverable might deviate from what you desired to get in the beginning.

3. **Implementing corrective actions if there are problems.** You set the objectives, work started to complete the project but there are problems in the middle of the work and you see that the objectives will not be met. You need to take corrective actions. This can be inadequate personnel in your project team, quality of the materials or a tool missing, etc. Whatever the reason is, you need to find the problem, fix the root cause.

Constraints

Constraint means a limitation or restriction by dictionary definition. It is similar in project management as well. Projects have constraints and the project manager must manage these constraints.

There are seven common constraints of projects. These are **Cost, Scope, Quality, Customer satisfaction, Risk, Resources and Time.**

Generally, there is a trade-off between these constraints. If you improve positive aspects of a constraint, this will bring a negative aspect on one of the other constraints.

For example, in order to reduce the delivery duration of the project, or in order to deliver project earlier than the scheduled time, you need to put extra resources to deliver the same amount of work in a shorter time. This means an increased cost or if you will not put extra resources, you need to reduce your scope to deliver less work in a shorter timescale.

If you try to deliver more with the same amount of resources but in a shorter timescale, this will cause to deliver your deliverables with faults, which means less quality. This will also lead to a decrease in customer satisfaction in the end.

 One impact on one constraint might affect all other constraints in the chain.

Therefore, once you are trying to change one of the constraints in a project, you have to keep an eye on what will be the impact of this change on other constraints.

Organizational Process Assets

Organizational process assets are:

- Plans, processes, policies, procedures and knowledge bases specific to and used by the performing organization.

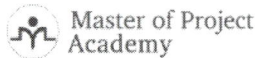

- For instance, project plan template, security policies, procurement procedures and company knowledge base are all categorized as organizational process asset.

- Organizational process assets include the lessons learned documentation from previous projects and historical information about the company. Therefore, it acts as the archive or repository of the company.

- Many documents, policies or procedures are under organizational process assets. They are used as input to most planning processes. For instance, if the company is trying to initiate a new project which is very similar to a project they finished in past, looking to lessons learned documentation of the past project will bring many insights during the planning of a new project.

- The corporate knowledge base is used for storing and retrieving information from this knowledge base when needed. This corporate knowledge base includes lots of useful information not only about the projects but also about many other topics such as how to get a work visa for a new country, how to fix a defect in software, tips on making more efficient meetings, etc.

Enterprise Environmental Factors

Enterprise environmental factors are inputs to many processes in Project Management.

Conditions that are not under the control of the project team that influence, constrain or direct the project are categorized as Enterprise Environmental Factors.

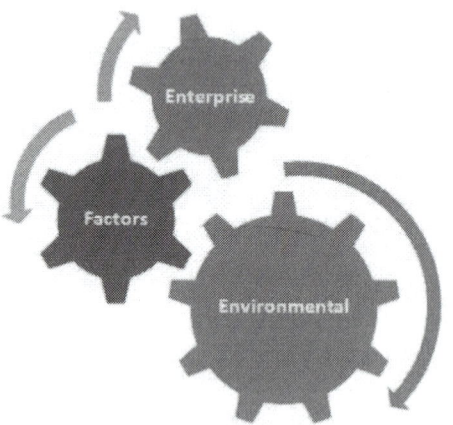

Enterprise environmental factors are input to most planning processes. It is better to give some examples for Enterprise Environmental Factors to illustrate these factors better in your mind.

- Organizational culture, structure, and governance
- Government or Industry Standards
- Political Climate
- Marketplace Conditions

- **Organizational culture, structure and governance is** an example for Enterprise Environmental factor. Because as a project manager, you cannot affect the management of your company or management hierarchy of your company. However, the approach of your management and hierarchy in the company directly affects project management in a company.

- **Government or Industry standards:** For example, if you want to produce health product, e.g. a blood pressure monitor, this must be in compliant with the standards of World Health Organization (WHO) and if you will market this product in the USA, it needs to be compliant and approved by FDA. Since these standards will affect your project scope, these are considered as Enterprise Environmental Factors as well.

- **Political climate:** Political climate is very important for projects. For example, if your project will be executed in a country that has an embargo, most probably you will have procurement issues. Alternatively, during the execution of a government project, the country of your company and your customer's company started to have a diplomatic crisis. This might affect your business as well. Therefore, a political climate is an important Enterprise Environmental Factor.

- **Marketplace conditions:** If you are working in a company, which is having an economic crisis, this affects the revenue of your company directly. Respectively, your projects might be affected as well.

Stakeholders

Stakeholders are people whose interests may be positively or negatively impacted by the project. **Anybody who can benefit or who may be distracted by the outcomes of a project are classified as stakeholders.**

Stakeholders include all members of the project team. Because as a direct contributor to the project, they directly affect the project.

Identifying stakeholders, understanding their relative degree of influence on a project, and balancing their demands, needs and expectations are critical to the success of the project.

A factory construction project that is expected to produce water and air pollution in a city. This will cause a big resistance from the residents of the city. There might be even protests and actions from the city management to stop the project. Therefore, stakeholder management is a very important aspect of project management.

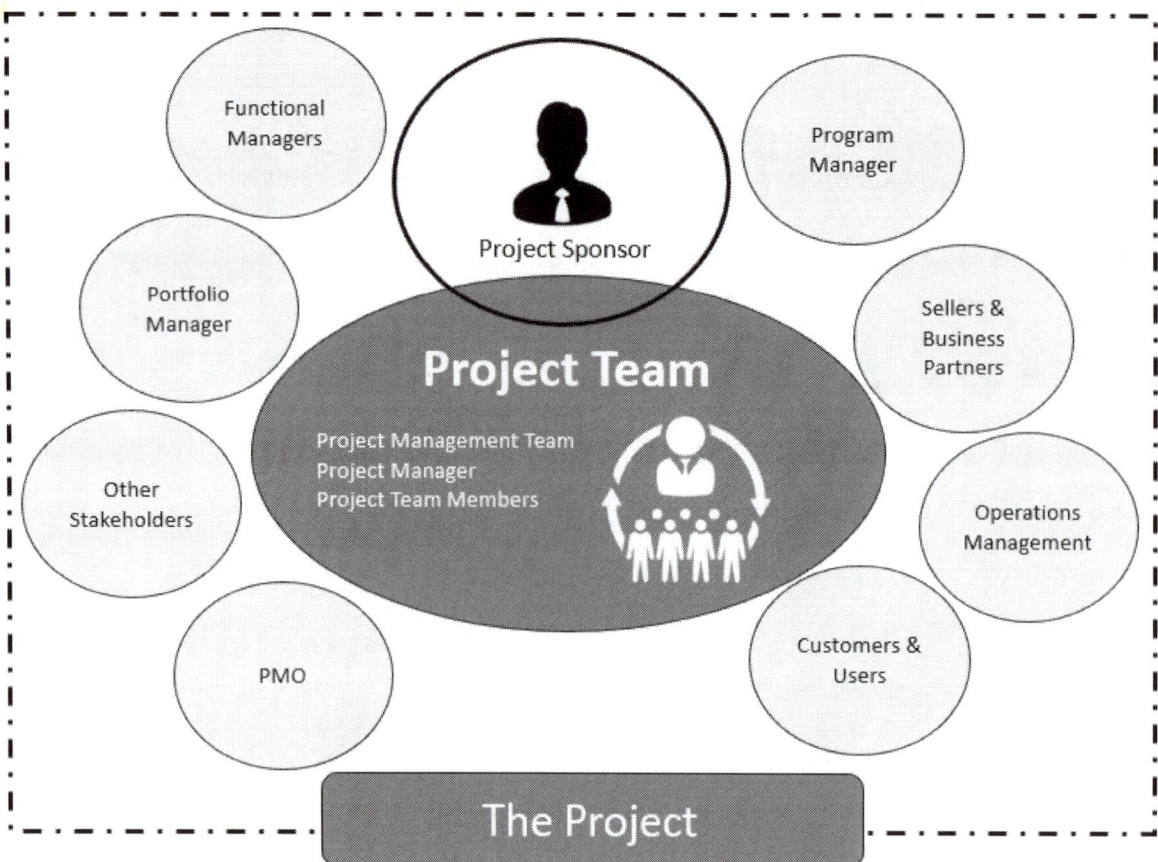

This figure illustrates the project team, sponsor and other organizations or people that can be stakeholders of a project. The project team is an inner circle. **The stakeholders in the project team are the internal stakeholders and the other stakeholders in the grey areas are external stakeholders.**

For example, portfolio managers, program managers, project management office, operations management, functional managers, sellers, business partners, customers, users are all external stakeholders of a project. Sponsor is on the intersection of internal and external stakeholder area. Because the sponsor is the spokesperson of the project supports, the project financially and protects the project from external risks.

Example: Stakeholders of Golden Gate Bridge

- All workers, the project team are stakeholders of the project as the internal stakeholders when the bridge was being built.

- Government is a stakeholder as the sponsor of the project. Because the government or management of the city finances the construction of the project. Any risk or problem that could have

happened during the construction of the project would affect the government as well.

- Sea transporters between the two sides of the bridge. Because they were making money with these transfers but with the construction of the bridge, most people or carrier companies might have switched to pass the bridge instead of using a Ferry for instance.

- People residing closer to the bridge are stakeholders as well. Their properties became more valuable or maybe they had been distracted because of the construction.

There might be several other stakeholders of a project but this list is just to illustrate stakeholders better in your mind.

Project Governance

Project Governance provides the project manager and team with structure, processes, decision-making models, and tools for managing the project. It gives all the necessary things to the project manager to manage a project. For instance, how to control the budget, how to control schedule etc. are all defined in the processes included in the project governance.

Project Governance involves stakeholders, procedures, standards, responsibilities and authorities. It does not include only tools, processes or models. The Stakeholders, procedures, standards, responsibilities, etc. are also part of the project governance.

> Project governance as a whole package assists in reaching project success

Project team

Project Manager and the group of individuals who perform the project work is called the project team.

A contributor cannot be considered as a project team member. For instance, the sponsor supports the project financially but he is not a member of the project team actually.

Team members must be assigned with a project activity and perform their work respectively.

A project manager is the leader of the team and the project manager must have the highest authority in the project.

> Project manager is a member and the leader project team

Because the project manager is the ultimate accountable of a project's success. Therefore, he should be able to direct project team members and to do this he should have the highest authority within the team.

Organizational Structure

The organizational structure of a company affects which department is powerful, which department has more decision taker, which departments are weaker etc.

Organization structure is one of the main factors affecting projects in an organization. Depending on the market conditions, competition, industry and history of the company, companies can adopt different organization structures at different times.

There are three types of organizations in terms of project management in a company.
- Functional
- Projectized

- Matrix

Functional Organizations

Functional organization structure is the most common type of organization in the industry. Many multinational and big companies in several industries adopt it.

In a functional organization structure, people are grouped by areas of specialization. For instance, marketing professionals are grouped under the marketing department; human resources professionals are grouped under the human resources department, technical people are grouped under IT department, etc. Depending on the size of these groups, managers, directors, vice presidents lead these groups.

If a department will need information or will initiate a request from another department, this is transmitted through the head of these departments. For instance, if marketing department needs a new software that will segment their customers and ease their marketing activities, head of marketing department will communicate with the head of IT department, and ask for this software request.

In functional organizations, team members do both project work and departmental work. For instance, if a software engineer in the IT department is assigned to a project, he has to complete his assignments in the project. On the other hand, if there are defects or problems that need to be resolved which is under the responsibility of the software department, he has to deal with these as well.

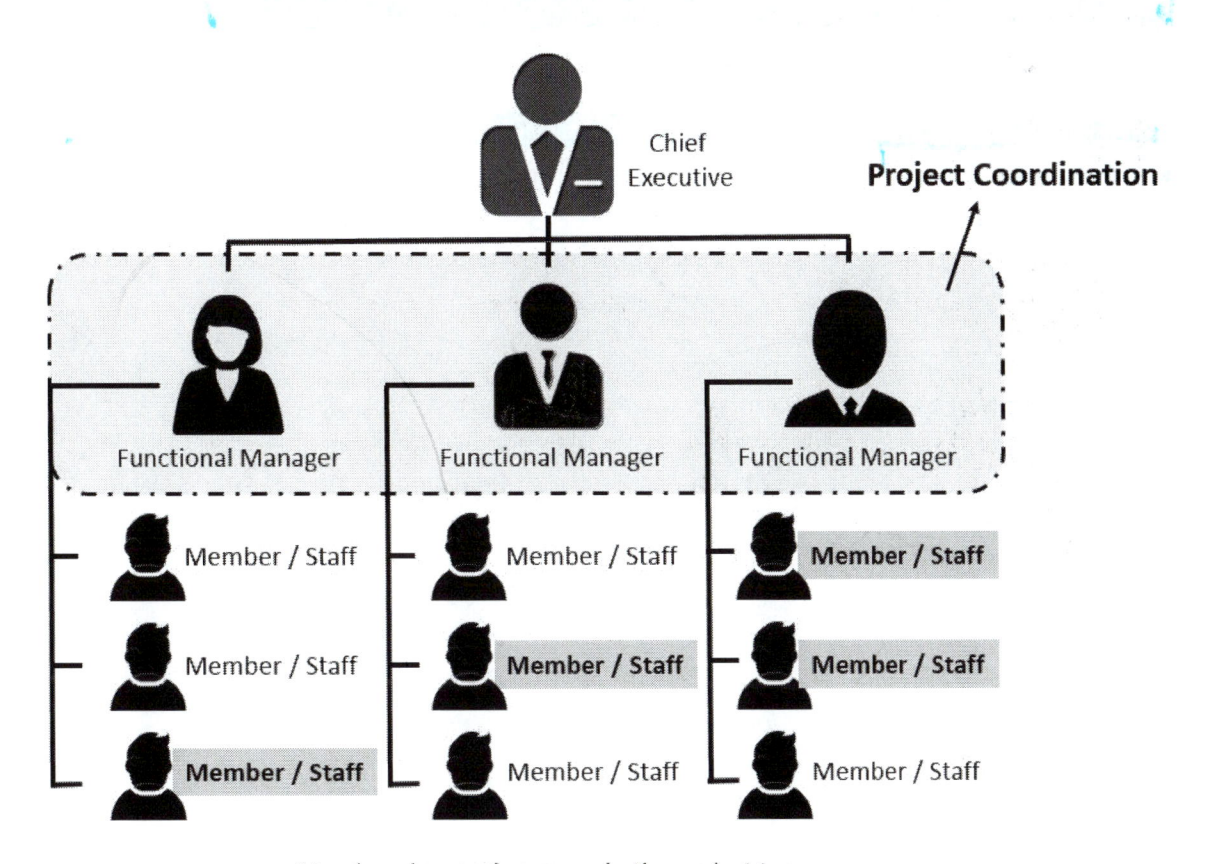

Members in gray boxes are in the project team

This is an example of the blueprint or organization chart of a functional organization structure. Gray backgrounded staffs are engaged in project activities and white backgrounded staffs are dedicated to departmental activities.

> In Functional organizations, the project coordination is done over the functional managers of each department.

Staffs from different departments work in a project in functional organizations. They turn back to their departmental work when their assignment in projects finish.

Projectized Organizations

- In projectized organizational structures, the entire company is organized by projects. The resources of the project are fully dedicated to the project activities.

- Project Managers have control of projects. Resources only report to the project manager and the project manager has the ultimate control of resources.

- There are not any departments so resources do not belong to a department. They report to their project managers only.

- When the project is over, the project resources either are assigned to a new project or need to find a new job.

> In Projectized organizations, the project manager has the ultimate control of resources.

This is an example of the blueprint or organization structure of a projectized organization. Staffs backgrounded in gray are engaged to project activities. They all belong to project activities; there is not any other alternative. Project coordination is done over each project.

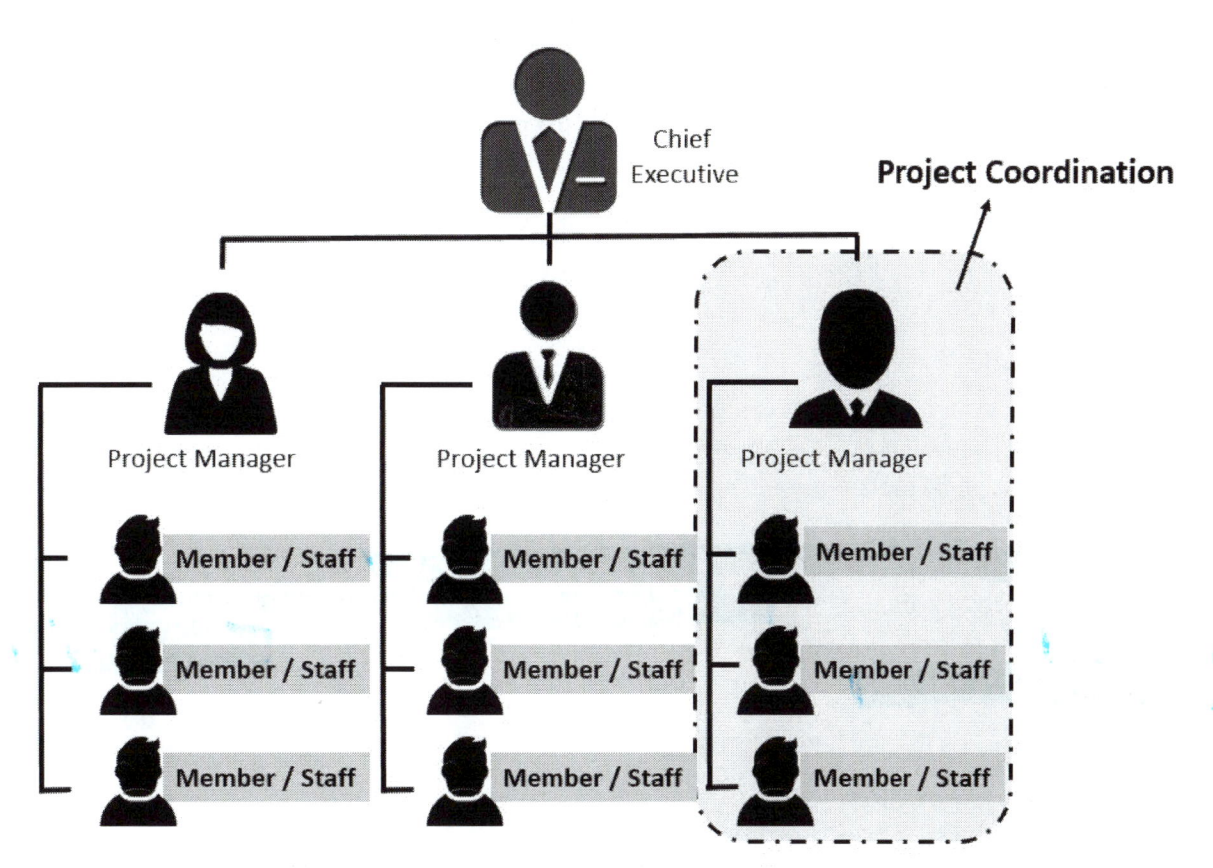

Members in gray boxes are in the project team

Matrix Organizations

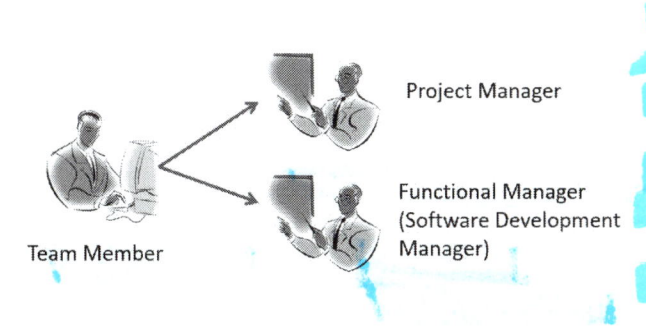

Matrix organizational structure attempts to get strengths of projectized and functional organization.

Projectized organizations ensure the dedication of project resources to the project therefore; projects have a higher probability of success.

Functional organizations ensure the sustainability of the organization since the resources turn back to their departments once the project is over. Therefore, Matrix organizations aim to get the benefits of these two organizational structures.

In Matrix organizations, team members report to their project manager and their functional managers. Because their actual managers are their functional manager but if they are assigned to a project, they will be reporting to their project manager as well. Consider a software engineer. If he is not working on a project, he will be reporting to his functional manager, for instance, a software development line manager. Once the software development line manager assigns this software engineer to a project, this engineer will start to report the project manager as well.

> In Matrix organizations, the power of the functional manager and project manager varies in different matrix organizations

Matrix organization is divided into 3 sub-categories.

- Strong
- Balanced
- Weak Matrix

The below figure shows how the power of the functional manager and project manager switches in each type of matrix organizations.

Strong matrix organizations are closer to projectized organizations. Therefore, power resides more on the project manager. Weak matrix organizations are closer to functional organizations. Therefore, power resides more on functional managers. Balanced matrix organizations are in the middle and power of functional and project managers are equal.

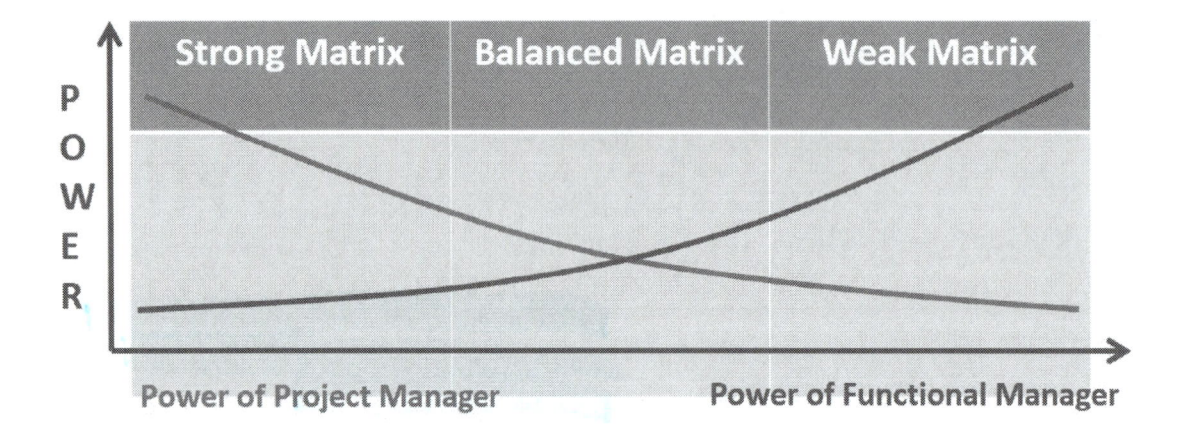

POWER

| Strong Matrix | Balanced Matrix | Weak Matrix |

Power of Project Manager | Power of Functional Manager

In weak matrix organizations, project managers generally have two roles.

- **Project Expediter:** Project expediter acts as a staff assistant and communications coordinator. They cannot take any decision. They do paperwork of the project, deal with the administrative issues such as bureaucratic communication between departments, etc. They do not have any influence on the project resources.
- **Project coordinator:** Project Coordinator acts like project expediter, but has some power and can take some decisions. They have slightly higher power and influence over the project compared to project expediters.

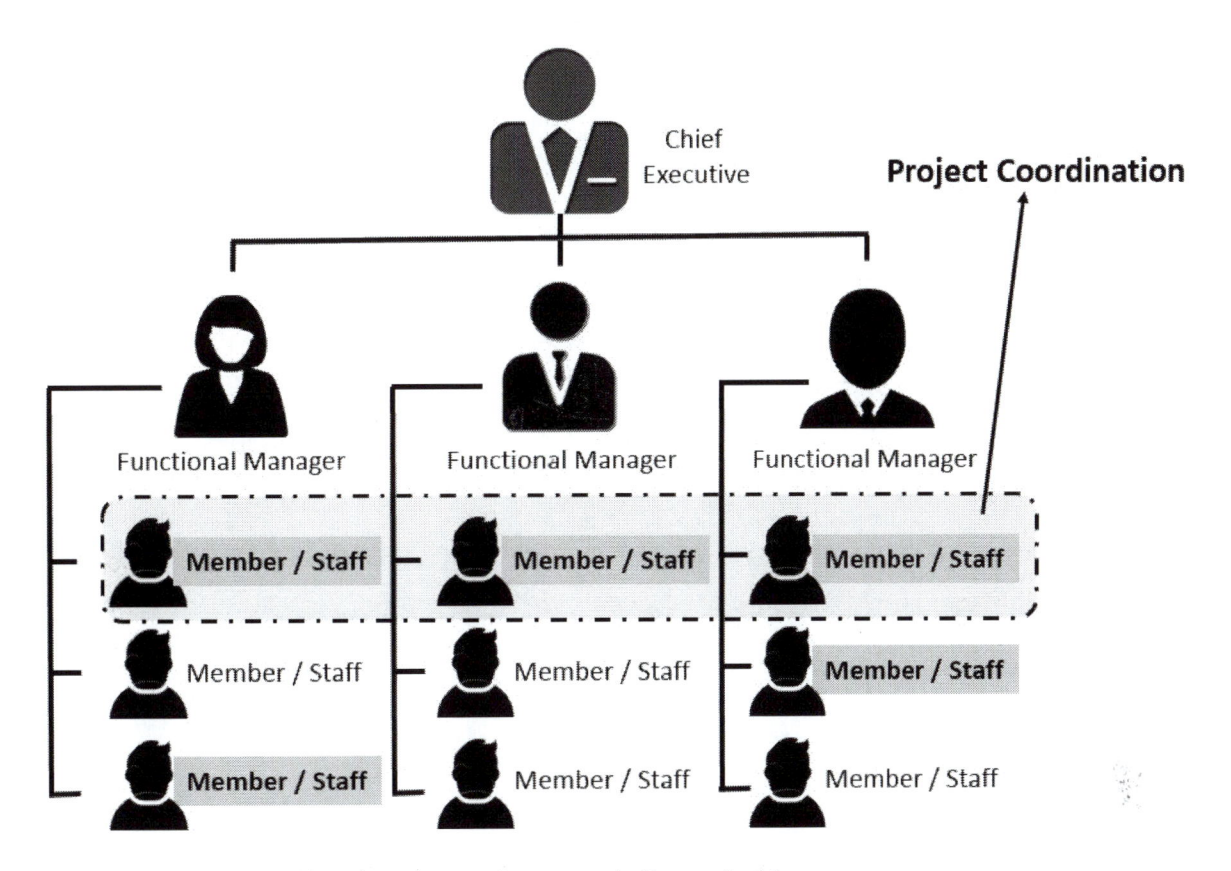

Members in gray boxes are in the project team

It is a blueprint example of a weak matrix organization.

Gray backgrounded staffs are assigned to projects and reporting mainly to the functional managers. Project coordination is done over the assigned staff maybe with the help of a project expediter or coordinator.

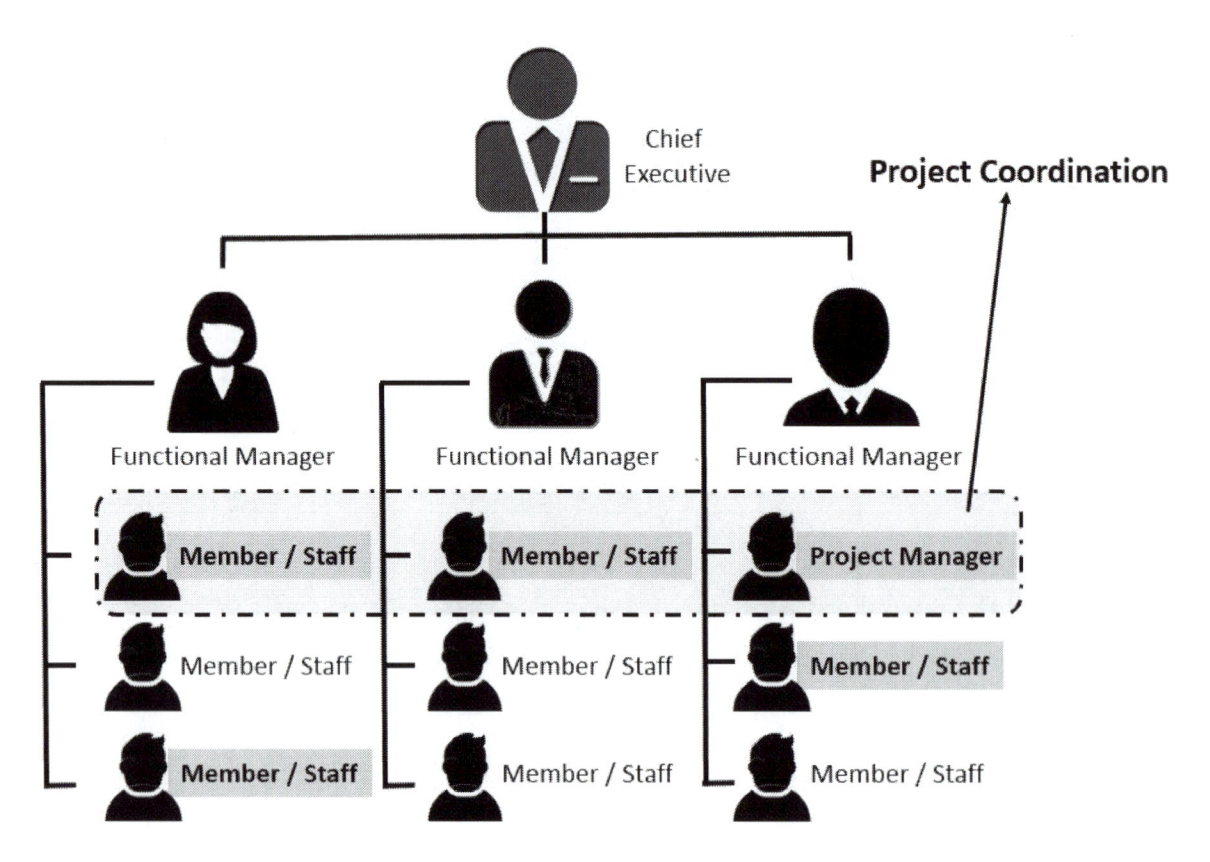

Members in gray boxes are in the project team

It is the blueprint example of a balanced matrix organization.

Gray backgrounded staffs are assigned to projects. Project resources, including the project manager, report to their functional manager, however, the project coordination is done with the control of the project manager. Functional managers also have power and influence on their resources.

Chief Executive — **Project Coordination**

- Functional Manager
  - Member / Staff
  - Member / Staff
  - Member / Staff
- Functional Manager
  - Member / Staff
  - Member / Staff
  - Member / Staff
- Functional Manager
  - Member / Staff
  - Member / Staff
  - Member / Staff
- PMO Manager
  - Project Manager
  - Project Manager
  - Project Manager

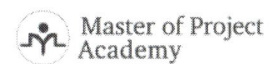

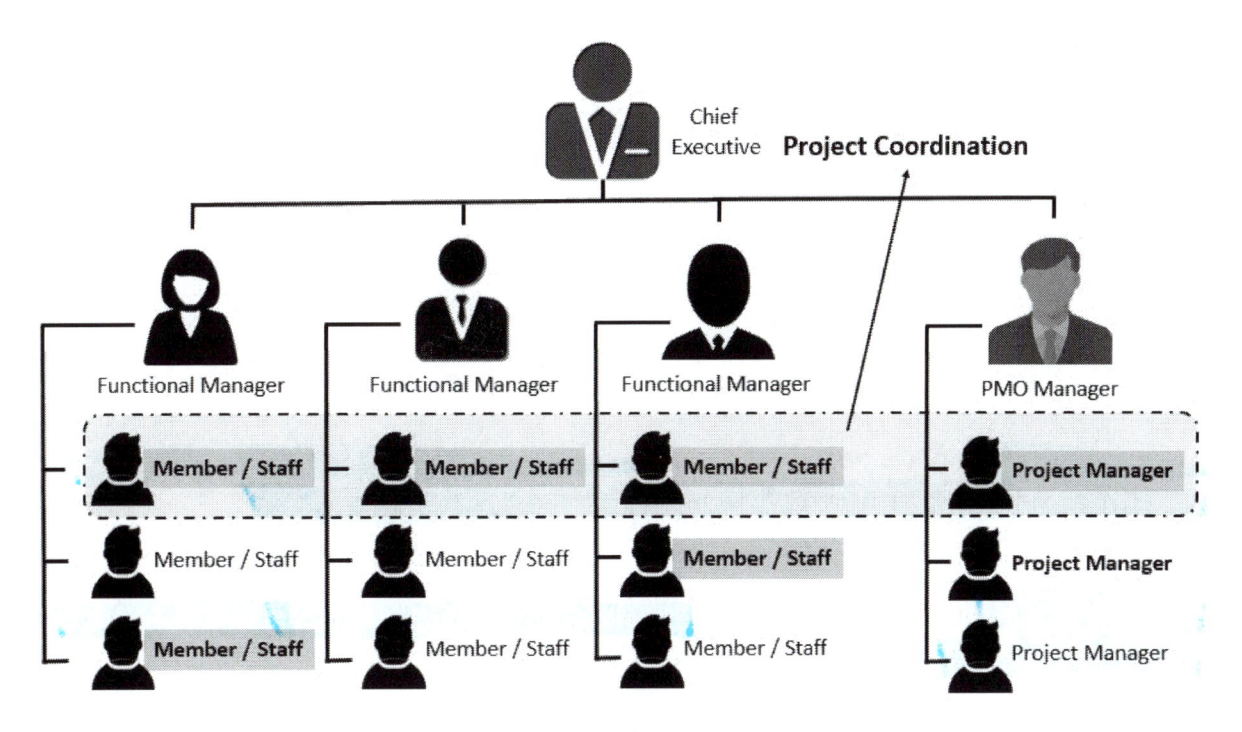

Members in gray boxes are in the project team

It is the blueprint example of a strong matrix organization.

Gray backgrounded resources belong to a project. The project manager coordinates and manages these resources and project activities. The difference from the balanced matrix is, project managers report to the managers or project managers, for instance, the head of project management office. In a balanced matrix organization, the project manager reports to a functional manager.

Comparative Overview of Organizational Structures

	Functional	Matrix Weak	Matrix Balanced	Matrix Strong	Projectized
Project Manager's Authority	Little/None	Low	Low-Medium	Medium-High	High-Full
Availability of Resources	Little/None	Low	Low-Medium	Medium-High	High-Full
Who manages the project budget?	Functional Manager	Functional Manager	Mixed	Project Manager	Project Manager
What is the Project Manager role?	Part-time	Part-time	Full-time	Full-time	Full-time
Administrative Staff	Part-time	Part-time	Part-time	Full-time	Full-time

The table above, Project managers authority, resource availability, who manages the project budget, project managers role and how project management administrative staff works are compared and listed on different organizational structures.

Project manager's role, resource availability, control of the project manager on the project are highest in projectized organizations, while the functional manager's is the lowest. In functional organizations, Project manager's role, resource availability, control of the project manager on the project are lowest in functional organizations.

Matrix organizations keep the power and influence of functional and project managers in balance.

Other Types of Organizational Structures

1. **Organic or simple:** In this organization type, people work side-by-side in the same office. Generally, the operation manager or owner of the work manages the team. The project manager has little or no authority on the team.

2. **Multi-divisional:** The organization is structured based on products, processes or geographic regions, etc. The functional manager manages the team in this type of organizations and project manager has little or no authority.

3. **Virtual:** People from different locations work for the same project. The project manager has low to moderate level of authority in these types of organizations.

Organizational Structure Type	Work Groups Arranged by:	Project Manager's Authority	Project Manager's Role	Resource Availability	Who does manage the Project Budget?	Administrative Members
Organic or Simple	Flexible – people work side-by-side	Little/None	Part-time or Project Coordinator	Little/None	Owner / Operator	Little/None
Multi-divisional	Product, processes, portfolio, program, region etc.	Little/None	Part-time or Project Coordinator	Little/None	Functional Manager	Part-time
Virtual	Network and contact points with other people	Low-Medium	Full-time or Part-time	Low-Medium	Mixed	Full-time or Part-time
Hybrid	Mix	Mixed	Mixed	Mixed	Mixed	Mixed
PMO	Mix	High-Full	Full-time	High-Full	Project Manager	Full-time

The table shows the other five types of organizational structures. Note that, PMO resembles project, program or portfolio management office in an organization.

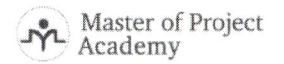

4. **Hybrid:** This is actually a mixture of different organizational structures. For instance, a balanced organization but people working for the project are in a virtual form, meaning that working from different locations. Project manager has a mixed level of authority in these types of organizations.

5. **PMO:** PMO refers to portfolio, program or project management office of the organization. Project managers in PMO have a higher level of authority and PMO rules the project management practices in the organization.

Advantages & Disadvantages of Different Organization Types

Advantages of Functional Organization

- **Management of specialists is easier in functional organizations:** The resources specialized in an area report to the same manager who knows the domain or area as well.

- **Team members report to only one supervisor:** This reduces the conflicts or contradictions of reporting to both project and functional manager.

- **Similar resources are centralized in groups:** For instance, software developers belong to the IT department, sales specialists belong to the sales department, etc. This ensures the sustainability of the organization, knowledge and expertise remains in the department although projects are completed.

- **Functional organizations define clear career paths for the staff:** Because the staff belongs to a department specialized in an area. Improving skills, knowledge and competence in that specialization can be proposed as career path for the resource. For instance, for a software developer working in a software development department, developer, senior developer, expert developer, and architect can be a career path as long as he improves his skills and competence.

Disadvantages of Functional Organization

- **People place more emphasis on their functional specialty to the detriment of the project:** Because their ultimate manager is their functional manager.

  Although they are assigned to a project, they take the direction of their functional managers more seriously compared to a project manager's direction.

- **No career path in project management:** This causes project management to be underestimated by the staff. Affects the success of projects respectively.

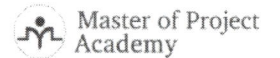

- **Project manager has little or no authority:** Because staff mainly reports to the functional manager and therefore, the project manager does not have that much power and influence on the project team.

Advantages of Projectized Organization

- **Efficient project organization:** Because all resources of the project are dedicated to project tasks and assignments. This dedication automatically increases the focus and motivation of team members for the success of the project.

- **Loyalty to the project:** Member of the project team are more loyal in projectized organizations. Because their ultimate manager is the project manager. The success of the project directly depends on the team members and this increases the loyalty to the project respectively.

- **More effective communications than functional:** More effective communication is ensured in projectized organizations compared to other organizations structures. Because team members are dedicated to a project and their existence in the organization is solely for the project they are working for. Project teams work in the same location and even in the same room in projectized organizations. This increases the effective and efficient communication among the project team.

Disadvantages of Projectized Organization

- **No "home" when the project is finished:** The most important disadvantage is there is no "home" for the project resources once the project is finished. Since there are not departments for the resources based on their specialties, if there will not be a new project, resources are released at the end of the project. This causes lack of professionalism in disciplines. Consider a software engineer worked in a project. At the end of the project, if he leaves the organization, his know-how will be lost as well. This causes the organization to lose professionalism in disciplines.

- **Lack of professionalism in disciplines:** Tools and resources of a project belong to only one project in projectized organizations. Consider that a project needs a testing tool to complete its quality assurance activities in a project. If the same tool will be needed for a second project in the organization, a new tool needs to be aligned for the new project team since the existing tool solely belongs to the first project team. This causes duplication of the same testing tool for the second project and means additional cost for the organization respectively.

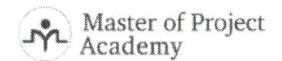

- **Duplication of facilities and job functions:** Another disadvantage of the projectized organizations is duplication of facilities and job functions.

- **Less efficient use of resources:** Projectized organizations use resources less efficiently. Since project, resources are dedicated to a project, even if a resource is not 100% utilized, that resource cannot be allocated on another task. Consider that project assignments of a software engineer take 4 out of 5 days each workweek. He is 80% utilized. Although he has enough time to do additional work, since he is fully dedicated to the project, this unutilized time of the resource cannot be used, unfortunately.

Advantages of Matrix Organization

- **Highly visible project objectives:** What needs to be achieved to complete a project successfully are clearly defined and understandable by the project team.

- **Improved project manager control over resources:** Team members of the project are reporting to the project manager as well and this gives respective authority to the project manager.

- **More support from functional areas:** Resources are grouped based on their specialties. In case of a lack of technical knowledge, resources can consult their senior colleagues or managers within the same functional domain.

- **Maximum utilization of scarce resources:** If a software architect needs to support a project for only 2 days, he can be assigned to other projects or activities for the remaining days of the week.

- **Better coordination:** Matrix organizations enables better coordination, better horizontal and vertical dissemination of information.

- **Better horizontal and vertical dissemination of information:** Every resource belongs to a function and he has a functional manager. If he is assigned to a project, he reports to a project manager as well. This structure strengthens the dissemination of information and better coordination of the staff.

- **Team members maintain a "home":** Even if they are released from projects, they turn back to their department and do departmental work. Alternatively, when a new project is initiated, they can be re-assigned to new projects.

Disadvantages of Matrix Organization

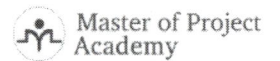

- **Extra administration is required:** There will be two managers of a resource: functional manager and project manager. In addition, there will be several resources from different functional disciplines in a project. This will bring additional administration for sure.

- **More than one boss for project teams:** For each resource, there will be two bosses: functional and project manager.

- **More complex to monitor and control:** Because there are several disciplines and there will be several resources from these several functional departments in a project. This will require management and coordination of different functional managers. Therefore, it is more complex.

- **Tougher problems with resource allocation:** The main reason for this is, there will be many projects needing resources from a single functional department. For instance, for the software projects of a company, software engineer resources will be requested from the software development department. If there will be many projects to initiate, this will cause resource allocation problems respectively.

- **Needs extensive policies and procedures:** Since there will be many functional departments and resources, in order to avoid conflicts, these need to be supported with the policies and procedures. For instance, how to request a resource for a project, how to prioritize projects if they ask for the same resource, how to release a project team member etc. needs to be documented clearly to avoid any misunderstanding between the departments.

- **Functional managers may have different priorities than project managers:** this causes higher potential for conflict. Consider that a department has its own works and a project manager is requiring a new resource from this department. The functional manager will not want to assign a resource to the project since he wants to complete the departmental work first. These kinds of conflicts may arise in matrix organizations.

- **Higher potential for conflict:** Functional managers may have different priorities than project managers and Matrix organizations are the most common organization type in the industry. Because these organizations give, fair power balance to both the functional manager and project manager. This enables a more sustainable and healthier corporate environment.

Project Management Process Groups

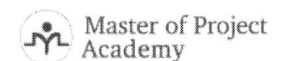

Project management process has five process groups mainly. These are

> - Initiating
> - Planning
> - Execution
> - Monitoring & Controlling
> - Closing

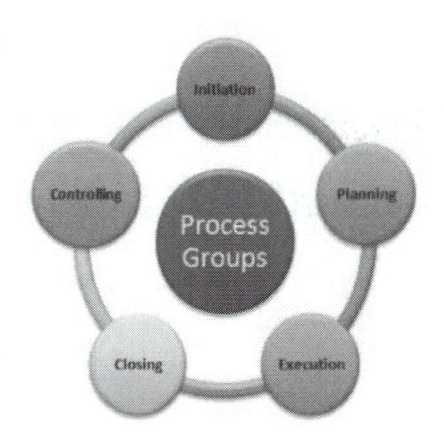

The lifecycle can change from project to project, or it may change depending on the industry, however, project management process groups are the same.

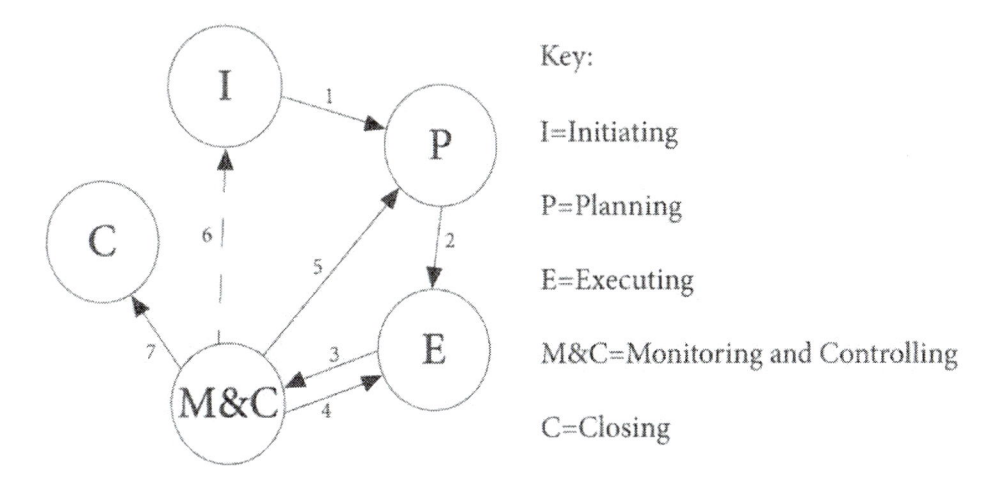

This figure shows the interrelationship of each process group with each other.

Key:
I=Initiating
P=Planning
E=Executing
M&C=Monitoring and Controlling
C=Closing

Initiating process group triggers the Planning process group. After documents and steps are ready to initiate a project, planning phase starts. **Then, the planning process group triggers execution process group.** After proper planning of the project, the execution phase starts and this is the phase, where most of the project work is delivered.

Monitoring & Controlling process group is the only process group that interacts with all other four process groups. Because this process group checks whether the project is going as planned and whether everything is ok.

Closing process group helps to complete and close the project after all objectives of the project are met if the project has been terminated in the middle.

> Executing processes help to deliver the actual work, outputs, and deliverables of a project.

Processes under these process groups are initiated and executed in each project.

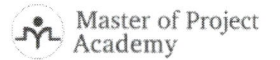

Lifecycle

Lifecycle is a progression through a series of differing stages of development.

Lifecycle actually defines steps or phases that each product or project goes over its lifespan. With the help of these common lifecycles, expected expenditures, activities or general progress of the projects can be estimated.

As an example, a generic project, no matter in which industry it is executed, it will include four major phases. First starting the project, second organizing and preparing, third carrying out the work, and closing the project.

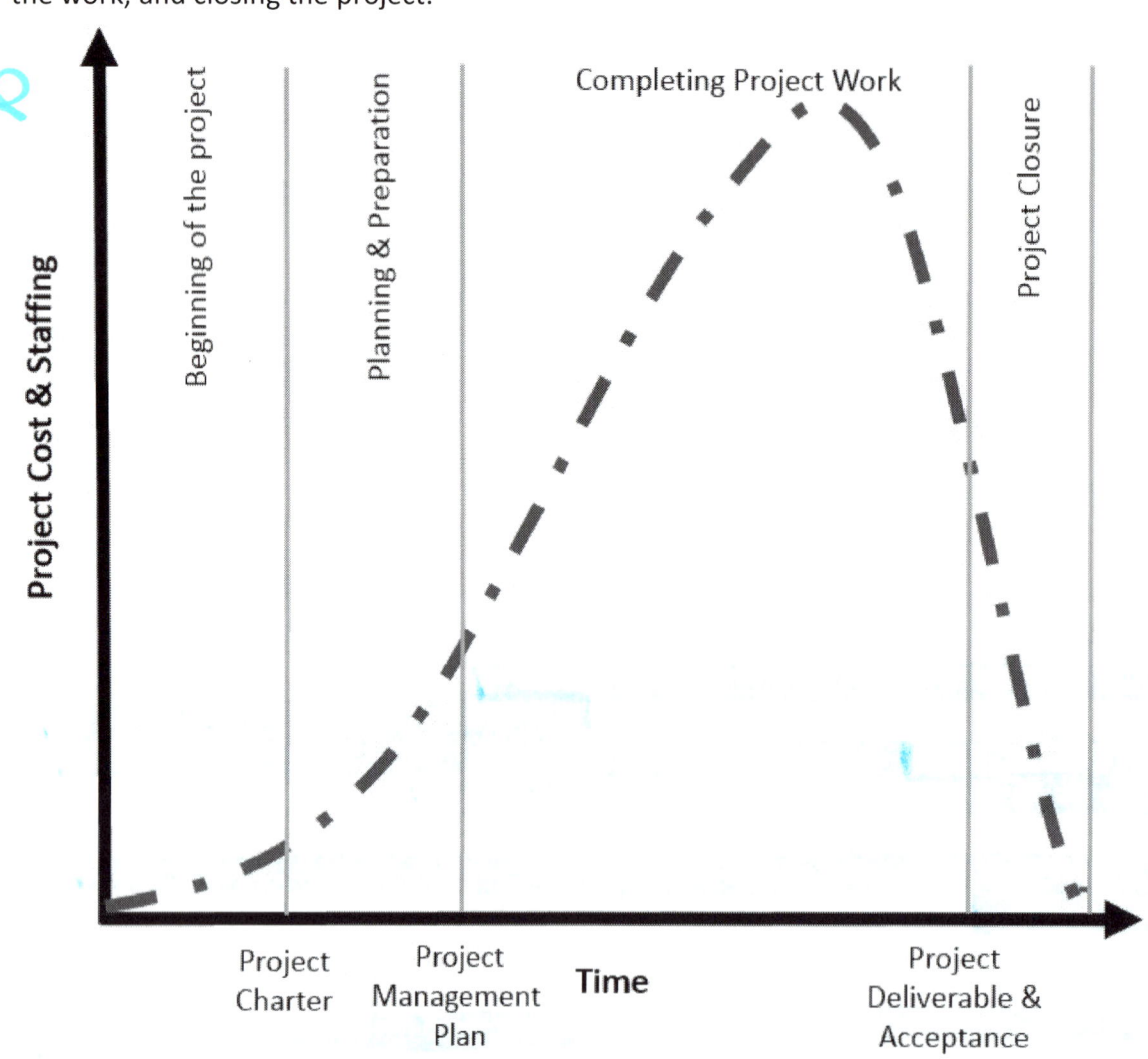

In the figure, these four phases of a common project lifecycle are shown. The figure also includes the major deliveries at the end of each phase of the lifecycle.

At the end of the 1st phase, starting the project, project charter will be produced. At the end of the 2nd phase, organizing and preparing, the project management plan will be produced. During the 3rd phase and at the end of the 3rd phase, deliverables of the project will be produced. In the 4th phase, closing the project, project documents will be archived and the project will be closed.

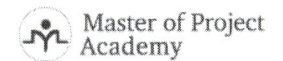

This common project lifecycle also depicts how cost and staffing level changes in a project over its lifecycle.

During starting and planning, cost and staffing level are lowest. Expenditures and resource usage are maximized during 3rd phase: carrying out the work. Then starts to decline in the 4th phase since the project is closing.

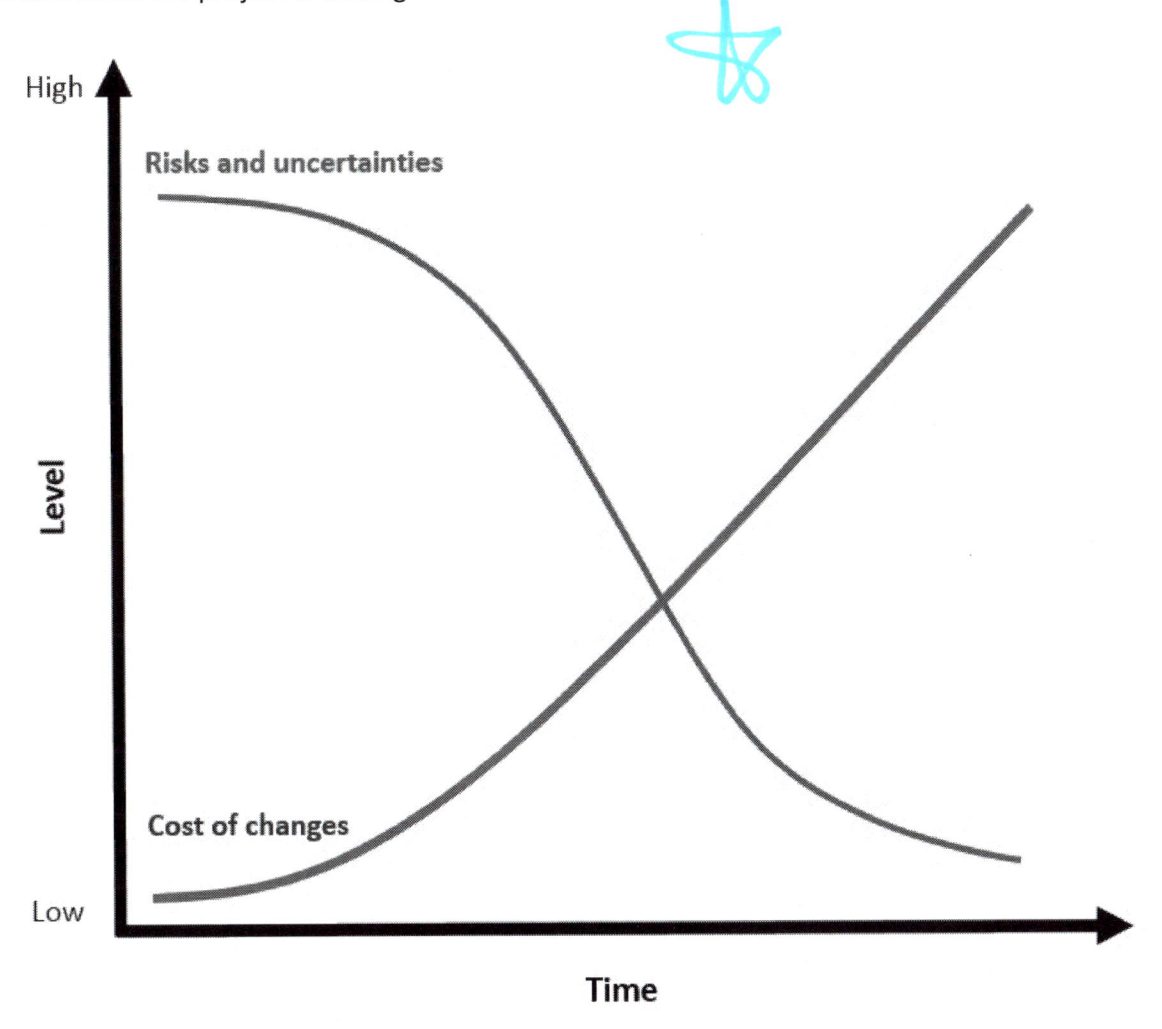

For instance, the graph shows how cost of changes and risk and uncertainty in a project changes over project time.

Cost of changes is lower in the beginning because most of the work has not been done or delivered yet. Therefore, if you change something in the project, it is expected that the cost of this change will be lower compared to a change that you will make in the future. Because, as long as you started to deliver project work, it will be harder and costlier to make a change in the later phases of the project. Because you have to do rework and maybe start from the beginning to revise the work you did until that date.

Similarly, Risk and uncertainty of a project are highest in the beginning. Because you do not know, exactly what you will face and how they might affect your project. However, as long as the project progresses, risks will be either eliminated or overcome and uncertainties will disappear respectively.

Product Life Cycle

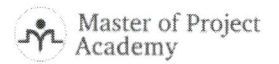

Product lifecycle starts from the conception of a new product to its withdrawal and it can require many projects to be delivered over its lifecycle.

For instance, consider an old version of iPhone. Does Apple still produce it? No.

However, starting from the conception until the end of life, several projects might have been executed to improve.

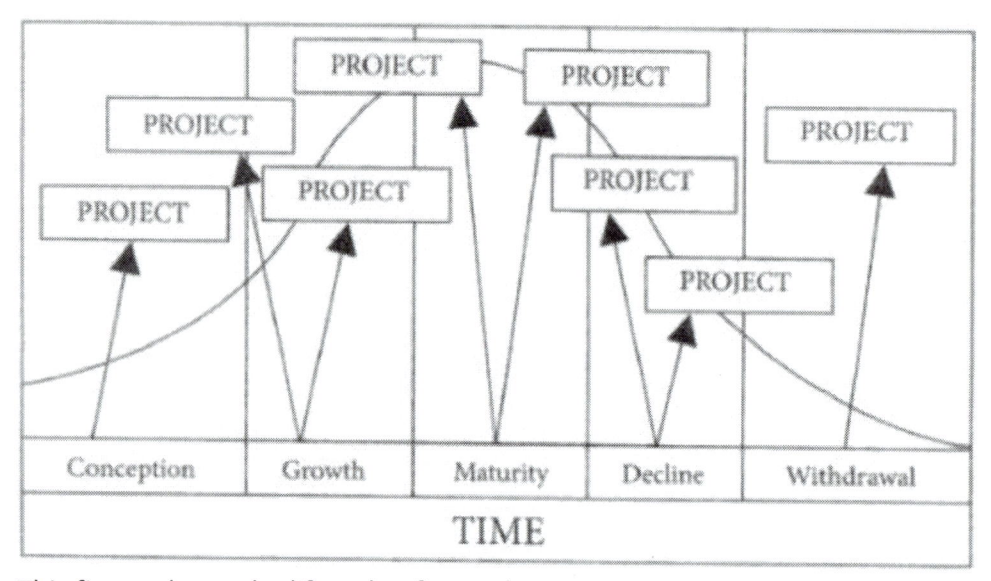

This figure shows the lifecycle of a product.

In the figure, it starts with conception, then it grows in the growth phase, then it reaches its maturity phase where it is expected to make the most revenue. Then in the 4th phase, its market demand starts to decline but still new projects such as fixing software issues can be initiated to support the product. In the 5th phase, the product is withdrawn and no more projects are planned and initiated once a project reaches its end of the lifecycle.

Although this is a generic lifecycle of a product, there can be exceptions for some products that would never decline.

For the different projects at different phases of this product lifecycle, such as,
- A project of "determination of customer's need" that can be initiated in the conception phase of the product lifecycle.
- A project of "analysis of competition" that can be initiated in the growth or maturity phase of the product.
- A project of "improvement of product features" can be initiated during the growth phase.

Project Life Cycle

Project lifecycle changes depending on the industry or organization's preferences.

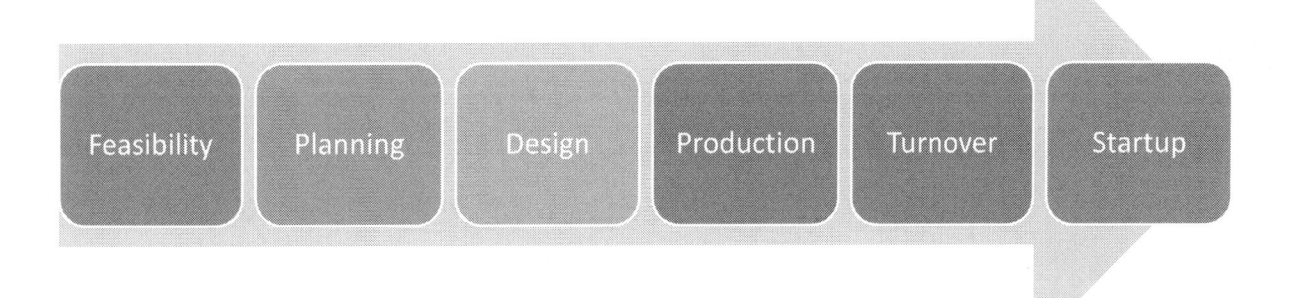

Feasibility → Planning → Design → Production → Turnover → Startup

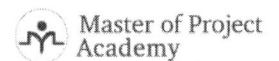

For instance, project lifecycle of a project in the construction industry will differ from a project in the IT industry.

Project lifecycle of a project in the construction industry will have Feasibility, planning, design, production, turnover and startup phases respectively.

However, in an IT project, project lifecycle will have high-level design, detailed design, coding, testing, installation, conversion and turnover to operations phases respectively.

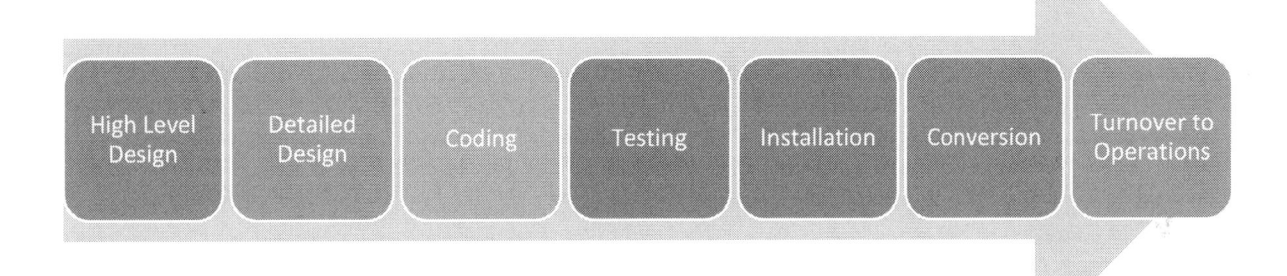

High Level Design → Detailed Design → Coding → Testing → Installation → Conversion → Turnover to Operations

Project Life Cycle in a Small Project

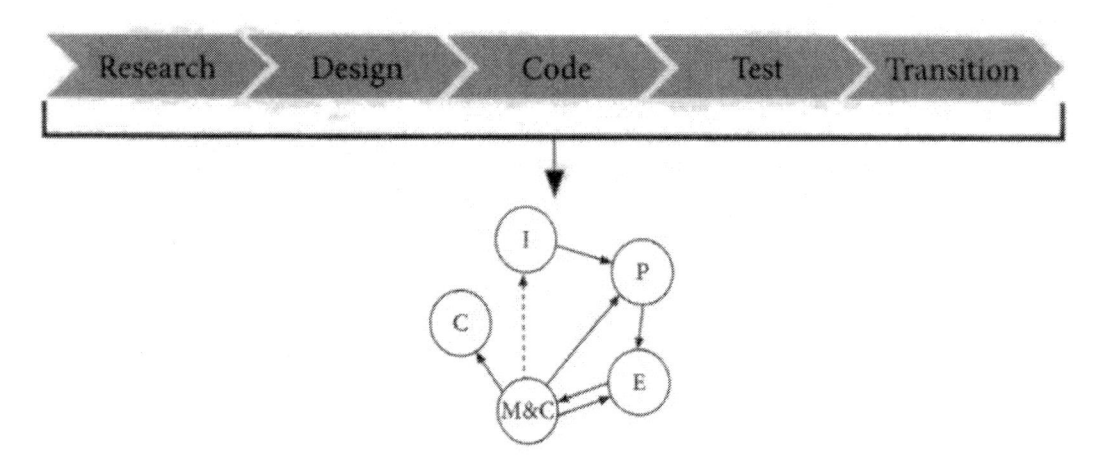

Research → Design → Code → Test → Transition

For a small project, all phases can be planned as a whole project.

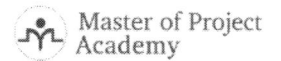

Project Life Cycle in a Large Project

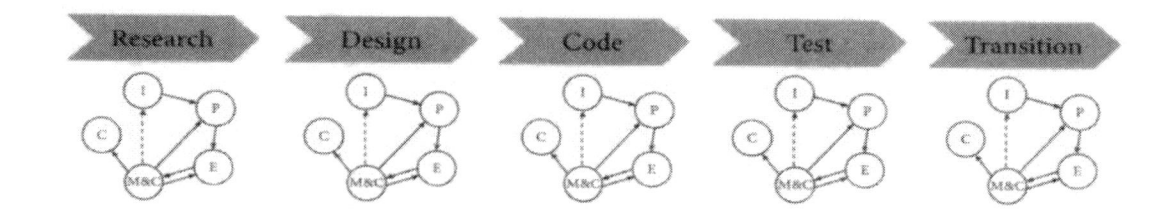

However, if there is a large project and if each phase of the project is big enough to consider as a separate project, then these projects management process groups are initiated and executed separately in each phase of the large project.

Project and Development Lifecycles

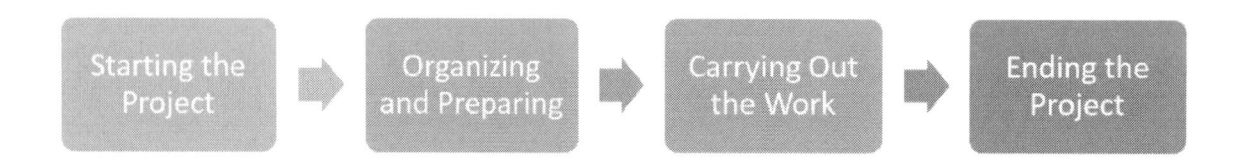

A project lifecycle is the series of phases that a project passes through its start to its completion. Project lifecycle actually provides a basic framework about how to manage a project. There is generic project lifecycle that every project can be mapped into. It has four phases, which were discussed before.

These are starting the project, organizing and preparing, carrying out the work and ending the project phases respectively.

Starting the project is the first phase. During this phase, a business case will be the reason to initiate the project. As mentioned previously, a market need, technological advance, regulation rules, etc. might be the reason to start a project. Once the project is started and charter is approved, the planning phase starts.

During the organizing and preparing phase, requirements of the project are detailed, scope documents are prepared, budget and schedule planning and many other aspects of the project are planned. Once the project plan is finalized, execution starts.

While carrying out the work phase, the project team works to deliver the scope of the project. Project scope is delivered as per the project management plans prepared in the previous phase. If there will be deviations from the plan, corrective and predictive actions will be taken to get back on track.

The fourth and last phase of the generic project lifecycle is ending the project. In this phase, all scope must have been completed and delivered to the customer. Customer accepts the final delivery officially and project closure activities are done during this process.

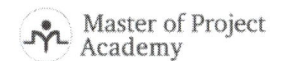

While this is the generic project lifecycle that can be mapped to any project, there might be specific lifecycles for each industry or organization.

For instance, a software development project can have phases like analysis, technical design, software development, testing, user acceptance tests, deployment, etc.

Project lifecycles can be either predictive or adaptive. However, in a project lifecycle, generally, there is one or more development lifecycle, which is directly related to the development of the product or service.

Development Life Cycle Types

Development lifecycles can be predictive, iterative, incremental or hybrid.

- **Predictive (Waterfall):** Predictive lifecycle is actually the traditional, waterfall project management lifecycle. **Project scope, time and cost are determined during the early phases of the lifecycle.** During the rest of the project, if changes arise or if the deviations from the plans occur, project management plans and documents are adapted to re-plan the rest of the project.

- **Iterative:** The project scope is generally determined early in the project lifecycle. However, time and cost estimates are modified progressively as the team knows more about the details of the project. In some cases, because of the context or uniqueness of the project, it might be hard to estimate costs or time for the activities of the project. In these cases, although the project scope is clear, the project team does the cost and time estimation throughout the project as their understanding of the product increases. There might be several iterations to finalize the end product of the project. However, each iteration must give an added or improved functionality compared to the previous one.

- **Incremental:** Incremental lifecycle produces deliverables through a series of iterations. The important point here is, these deliverables must be delivered in a predetermined period. For instance, if increments are determined to be delivered in every two weeks, the project team must be adding new functionalities or improving existing functionalities during this predetermined period. Project is finalized once the final increment delivers all required functionalities.

- **Adaptive (change-driven):** Adaptive or Change-Driven lifecycles can be agile, iterative or incremental. The overall scope of the project is determined at the beginning of the project. However, which of the requirements or functions that will be delivered in each increment is determined just before each iteration starts. For instance, if the project is the development of a website, which will have 42 screens, at the end of the first iteration, the project team might plan to deliver the first three screens. Note that, these three screens must be usable and testable at the end of the first increment.

- **Hybrid:** Hybrid lifecycle is a combination of the predictive and adaptive lifecycle. For some projects, although there might be parts or deliverables that can be easily estimated and planned, there might be some parts that will not be easy to estimate. In this case, predictive lifecycle can be used to deliver well-known requirements while adaptive lifecycle is used for evolving requirements.

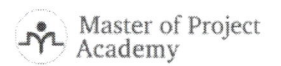

The project management team to choose the best lifecycle type for the project. After going over the requirements and expectations of the customer, the project management team should choose the optimum project lifecycle type that matches the characteristics of the requirements of the project.

Project Phases

Project Phase is a collection of related activities that will result in a meaningful deliverable once the activities in that phase are completed.

Phases of a project lifecycle can be described by a variety of attributes. These can be a name, number, duration, resource requirements, and entrance or exit criteria to a phase.

When dividing a project into phases, generally, work done in the phase gives the name to the phase.

Phases of a Software Development Project

The typical phases of the project lifecycle will be
- Analysis
- Technical Design
- Software Development
- Testing
- Deployment
- After-live support

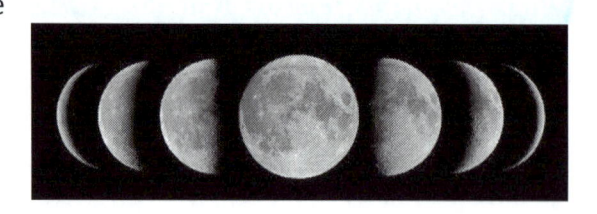

During analysis, project requirements are gathered and detailed. Analysis documents is prepared and project team develops the software accordingly.

Then, the technical design phase starts. During this phase, software architects and engineers work on technical solution about how they can ensure the project requirements as per the analysis document.

After the technical design, software development phase starts. Software engineers develop the services, technical aspects and technical solution as in the technical design.

Once the development finishes, test engineers will test the functionalities and features of the developed software. If there are any bugs or missing requirements, these are raised during the testing phase and project team fixes the issues.

Once the testing passes successfully, the software will be ready for deployment. Software is deployed and end customers start to use the product.

When the product is live, especially right after the deployment, unexpected issues might arise. After-live support is for this case. The project team works on rising issues to solve the issues immediately.

These are phases of a software development project. Each industry and even each organization can have its tailored phases for projects.

> The end of a phase and start of a new phase in a project is referred as a Phase Gate.

Phase Gates

Phase gates are held at the end of a phase. During phase gates, project performance and progress are compared against the project baseline.

Business case, project charter, project management plan and benefits management plan documents are revisited to check whether the end of phase results meet with these documents. If there are any conflicts or missing aspects, these must be corrected. Otherwise, the phase cannot be completed.

Generally, corporate companies define predetermined phases for different types of projects they have. For instance, phases for marketing projects, phases for technical projects, phases for integration projects, etc. A governance role in the organization, not in the same hierarchy with the project manager, inspects the phase success at the end of each phase.

For instance, once a project manager reports that the analysis phase is completed, the team or person responsible to check and assess whether the requirements to finalize the analysis phase is complete. Usually, this is done over a checklist. It covers actions like, whether the analysis document is complete, whether the analysis document is approved by the customer, whether the sponsor reviewed the analysis document etc. If the phase control passes successfully, the next phase in the project lifecycle starts.

Project Business Case

> Project Business Case and Project Benefits Management plan are two business documents of a project. These two documents are prepared before the project starts.

Project management activities and planning must be done based on the project business case and benefits management plan. The project manager must ensure that project management activities will be compliant with business case and benefits management plan.

The project sponsor is generally accountable for the preparation and management of the business case document. Because the ultimate owner of the business case which is the reason for starting the project is the project sponsor. Since sponsors are generally executive or high-level people, a different person might prepare this document on behalf of the sponsor. However, accountable will be project sponsor in any case. The project manager might provide recommendations during business case preparation and updates.

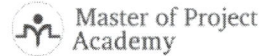

Business case document reflects why the project is initiated and benefits that will come at the end of the project. For instance, if the project is a marketing project that will reach a new prospective audience for the company, the benefit of this project can be extending the customer base of the company. This kind of reasons why the project is initiated and the benefits of the project are covered in the business case document.

Since the business case document covers the reasons of why the project is initiated and expected benefits once the project is completed, management of the company evaluates this document among other several business documents, which are in the portfolio of the company.

Based on the evaluation of the business cases, some projects might be deferred or canceled based on the budget constraints of the project or because of more urgent projects that must be executed first.

Business case covers:

- **Business needs:** Business needs document covers the main reasons for initiating the project. Business problems that will be solved or opportunities that will be maximized with the project are described in this section. Stakeholders who are affected with the project are identified and listed in this part of the business case document and high-level project scope is described.

- **Analysis of the situation:** Analysis of the situation part covers the identification of risks, success factors, root causes of the problems and how this project will meet with the organizational strategies, goals and objectives.

- **Recommendation:** Recommendation part of the document covers constraints, assumptions, dependencies, etc. It may include an implementation approach covering milestones, dependencies, roles and responsibilities.

- **Evaluation:** Evaluation covers how the benefits that will be delivered with the project will be measured.

Benefits Management Plan

The benefits management plan is another business document of a project, which defines the processes for creating, maximizing and sustaining benefits provided by a project.

Benefits management plan describes how and when the expected benefits will be delivered throughout the project. It also provides approaches about how to measure benefits.

The benefits of a project can be the actions, behaviors, products, services or results that provide value to the sponsoring organization.

Benefits Management Plan covers:

- **Target benefits:** Target benefits are tangible or intangible expected benefits of the project once it is completed. If there will be financial benefits, these are expressed as well.

- **Strategic alignment:** Strategic alignment covers how the project benefits align with the business strategies of the organization. For instance, if the company is aiming to reach two million-dollar revenues by end of the quarter, if this project will help to reach this goal, this is mentioned in strategic alignment heading.

- **Timeframe for realizing benefits:** Timeframe for realizing benefits describe when each benefit will be delivered throughout the project. Some benefits will be realized in short-term; some will be realized in long-term, etc.

- **Benefits owner:** Benefits owner is the accountable person for the monitoring, reporting, recording of the benefit.

- **Metrics:** Metrics describe how the benefits of the project will be measured throughout the project.

- **Assumptions and Risks:** Assumptions about the benefits and risks for realizing the benefits are also covered in the benefits management plan.

The benefits management plan is created before the project initiation and it is updated throughout the project. Realized benefits, changing risks or benefit owners, etc. need to be updated in the benefits management plan.

Tailoring

When you are managing a project, depending on the characteristics of the project, you should select processes, tools, techniques, etc. required to manage your project. For instance, if you will not purchase any material for your project, you might not need procurement processes in your project.

Some other processes in other knowledge areas might not be necessary for your project. You should not include those processes in your project management approach.

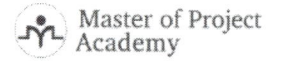

Selecting required processes, tools, techniques, etc. to manage a project is referred as tailoring. Tailoring can be done with the project team, sponsor, organizational management and other related parties with project management in an organization.

Tailoring is necessary because each project is unique. Not every process, tool or technique will be required for every project. You must be aware of the tools, techniques, processes and you should tailor your projects accordingly based on required tools, techniques, processes.

Lessons Learned

Lessons Learned documentation of a project includes:

- **What was done right:** The best practices applied during the project are recorded in the document. By this way, future projects get inspired from these best practices and have the benefit of these right implications.

- **What was done wrong:** Wrong decisions, wrong implementations, or impediments that caused project team to deliver slower outputs are all documented and what could have been done to not face these problems are all stored in lessons learned.

- **What would be done better**: if the project could be re-done. For instance, if the project had problems due to resource availabilities or planning weaknesses, these should be documented with the reasons.

Lessons learned should cover:

> Technical aspects of the project
> Project Management (WBS, risk planning, etc.)
> Management (communications, leadership)

- Technical aspects of the project include the schedule performance, cost performance and quality performance of the project. For instance, what was the planned budget and what is the budget at completion. What was the planned schedule and what is the completion schedule. These kinds of planned values and actual values must be included and variances should give an insight to the overall performance of the project.

- Work breakdown structure of the project, risk planning, schedule planning, cost planning, procurement planning etc. All management plans must be archived in the lessons learned documentation for future reference.

- Lessons learned documentation should give also recommendations on management, communications and leadership. For instance, if there were communication mistakes, these should be mentioned and what could have been done for better communication must be mentioned in the document.

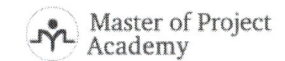

This figure depicts the role of the lessons learned and how it is improved with the help of new projects in an organization.

Before starting a new project, organizational process assets library of the organization is searched to check whether there are any useful lessons learned hints that can help in the new project. Then, useful hints are used during the new project. New lessons are learned throughout the new project and these are gathered throughout the project lifecycle. These new lessons learned are used in other current projects of the organization. At the end of the project, lessons learned documentation is finalized, and placed under the organizational process assets library of the organization in order to use in future projects.

Quiz – Section 1

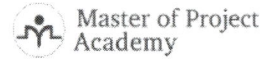

1- Which of the following is NOT characteristic of a Project?
   A) It has a beginning and an end
   B) Creates a unique product or service
   C) Temporary
   D) Repetitive and ongoing for years

2- You are working in a software company. In order to provide better quality in projects, your company is initiated an infrastructure renewal project. This is an example of which project initiation reason?
   A) Market Demand
   B) Technological Advance
   C) Customer Request
   D) Legal Requirement

3- Which of the following is an example for operational work?
   A) Extending a subway line with 2 more stations
   B) Manufacturing a new car with new features customized for women
   C) Sending password renewal e-mails every 3 months for each user working in a bank.
   D) Sending a satellite to space

4- Project management includes processes in order to manage and deliver a project successfully. Which of the following is NOT a process group of project management?
   A) Tracking & Reporting
   B) Initiating
   C) Executing
   D) Closings

5- Project management profession requires knowledge and expertise in project management knowledge areas. All of the following are project management knowledge areas EXCEPT:
   A) Stakeholder Management
   B) Procurement Management
   C) Budget Management
   D) Schedule Management

6- Which of the following about projects, programs and portfolios is NOT correct?
   A) Interrelating projects can be groups under a program for better coordination.
   B) All projects and programs under a portfolio must be related to each other.
   C) Programs and projects serving to same business goal can be grouped under a portfolio
   D) Unrelated projects cannot be grouped under same program

7- Project Management Office (PMO) centralizes the management of projects in organizations. Depending on the organizations, PMO can be in all of the following structures EXCEPT:
   A) Supportive
   B) Controlling

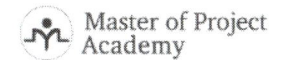

C) Directive
D) Managing

8- Project Management Office (PMO) in an organization may do all of the following in an organization except:
A) Test the functional requirements of products developed.
B) Provide guidance
C) Manage interdependencies between projects
D) Gather lessons learned document

9- Project manager reports to different people depending on the organization type. A project manager can report to all of the following EXCEPT:
A) Functional Manager
B) Program Manager
C) Senior Team Member
D) Portfolio Manager

10- All of the following are roles of Project Manager EXCEPT:
A) To lead the team to achieve project objectives
B) Perform the most critical tasks of the project
C) Using interpersonal skills while managing project
D) Linking the strategy of the project or organization with the project team

11- Which of the following is NOT required to exist in a Project Manager?
A) Knowledge about project management
B) Performance on applying project management methodologies
C) Personal skills to manage communication
D) Subject matter expertise on the technology used in project

12- Your company will hire a project manager for its Project Management Office (PMO) department. Hiring process of the company evaluates several aspects of the candidates. Which of the following is the MOST important aspect that needs to be assessed in a Project Manager candidate?
A) Team Building
B) Communication
C) Leadership
D) Coaching

13- Objectives of a project define what needs to be achieved as a result of project. All of the following about objectives are correct EXCEPT:
A) If 95% of the objectives have been met in a project, it can be considered successful
B) A trade-off exists between requirements and objectives
C) Meeting project objectives is under Project Manager's responsibility
D) Quality activities are done for checking project meets its objectives

14- Which of the following is NOT a common type of project constraint?
A) Time

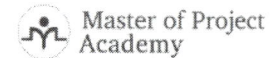

B) Resources
C) Technological Advance
D) Cost

15- Organizational Process Assets is input or output in most of the project management processes. Which of the following about Organizational Process Assets is NOT Correct?
A) Functional Organization structures do not need Organizational Process Assets in the company
B) Includes lessons learned documentation and historical information from past projects
C) Acts as corporate knowledge base for storing and retrieving information
D) Includes plans, processes, and procedures used by organization

16- You are working as a project manager in a smartphone manufacturer. There is a harsh competition in smart phone market and several patent conflicts are ongoing between the smartphone manufacturers in courts. This is an example of:
A) Stakeholder
B) Objective
C) Organizational Process Assets
D) Enterprise Environmental Factor

17- You are working as a project manager in a health products manufacturer. All of the following are examples of Enterprise Environmental Factors EXCEPT:
A) Structure of the organization
B) Budget provided for your new project
C) Standards published by World Health Organization (WHO)
D) Market conditions

18- Stakeholders are the people whose interests may be positively or negatively impacted by the project. All of the following about stakeholders are correct EXCEPT:
A) Requirements of all stakeholders' must be met in a project
B) Project team members are part of stakeholders
C) Stakeholders might have competing requirements with each other
D) Meeting expectations of stakeholders are critical to success of the project

19- Project governance provides the project manager and team with structure, processes, decision-making models and tools for managing the project. In this concept, which of the following is not an example of project governance?
A) Documentation of the organization for how to assign tasks to resources
B) Tool for requesting resources from line managers
C) Requirements of the customer
D) Source selection procedure of the organization for procurement

20- Organizations choose different types of organizational structures for their organization. Which of the following is not a type of organizational structure?
A) Functional
B) Line
C) Projectized

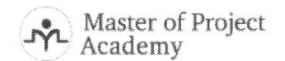

D) Matrix

21- Which of the following is NOT true about Functional Organizational Structure?
   A) People are grouped by areas of specialization
   B) Team members do project work and departmental work
   C) Information is exchanged through heads of regarding departments
   D) Least common type of organizational structure seen in market

22- You are working in a software company and your company has a projectized organizational structure. Which of the following is TRUE?
   A) People in resources will turn back to their departments after project finishes
   B) Functional managers have control of projects
   C) Company is organized by departments based on specializations
   D) Project manager has the ultimate control of the project

23- Organizations, which have Matrix type of organizational structures can, adopt three different types of Matrix Organizational Structure. Which of the following is NOT type of a matrix type organizational structure?
   A) Tight Matrix
   B) Strong Matrix
   C) Balanced Matrix
   D) Weak Matrix

24- Your friend is working in a weak matrix organizational structure in his company. When you discussed with him, he described that he does the paper work of the projects, acts as staff assistant and communications coordinator in projects. His role can be defined as:
   A) Project Assistant
   B) Project Organizer
   C) Project Expediter
   D) Project Coordinator

25- When you are talking to one of your friends who works as a senior architect in a construction project, he mentioned that they are assigned to projects and after project finishes, they return to their departments. In addition, he said that they report both to project manager and their department manager. Your friend works in a:
   A) Projectized Organization
   B) Matrix Organization
   C) Functional Organization
   D) Departmental Organization

26- All of the following are advantages of Functional Organization EXCEPT:
   A) More effective communication is ensured in projects compared to matrix or projectized organizations
   B) Team members report to only one manager
   C) Employees can have clearly defined career paths
   D) Similar resources specialized in similar topics are centralized

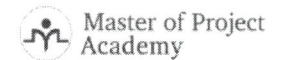

27- All of the following are advantages of Projectized Organization EXCEPT:
   A) Efficient project organization
   B) Loyalty to the project
   C) Most efficient communication compared to matrix or functional organizations
   D) Resources can turn back to their departments when project finishes.

28- All of the following are advantages of Matrix Organization EXCEPT:
   A) More support can be ensured from functional areas
   B) There is only one manager for resources
   C) Better coordination
   D) Better utilization of resources in the company

29- Which of the following is TRUE about project life cycle?
   A) Project life cycles can change depending on the industry or organization's preferences.
   B) All project life cycles have same 5 phases: initiating, planning, executing, controlling and closing
   C) Project management processes must be customized based on different project life cycles
   D) Project management processes are followed only once through a project life cycle

30- Lessons learned documentation includes what would be done if the project could be re-done. Lessons learned documentation could cover all of the following EXCEPT:
   A) Technical aspects of project
   B) Best practices experienced throughout the project
   C) Personal details of every project team member
   D) Mistakes done during project management

31- Which of the following is NOT true about lessons learned documentation?
   A) Must be collected and updated throughout the project
   B) Only best practices of the project should be mentioned
   C) Lessons learned documentation would be used in future in organization
   D) Once finished, lessons learned documentation is stored in organizational process assets library of the company.

32- Which of the following documents include feasibility study of a project about what kind of tangible and intangible benefits will be gained once the project is completed.
   A) Project Management Plan
   B) Project Charter
   C) Business Case
   D) Scope Document

33- Which of the following statements is NOT true about "tailoring" in project management?
   A) Good practice does not mean that all processes and techniques of project management should be applied in all projects.
   B) Selecting only the appropriate and required processes for a project
   C) Tailoring is a must since each project is unique
   D) Mapping each and every process of project management in new project.

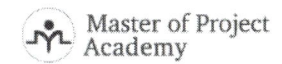

34- Benefits management plan is a business document of a project. Benefits management plan covers all of the following EXCEPT:
A) Resource List
B) Target Benefits
C) Strategic Alignment
D) Assumptions

35- You are starting a new project. Some parts of the project are very well predictable and can be estimated clearly. However, some parts of the project have unclear points that the project team feels uncomfortable to provide any estimation. Which development lifecycle best matches for this project?
A) Predictive
B) Iterative
C) Incremental
D) Hybrid

Answers

1 - D	26 - A
2 - B	27 - D
3 - C	28 - B
4 - A	29 - A
5 - C	30 - C
6 - B	31 - B
7 - D	32 - C
8 - A	33 - D
9 - C	34 - A
10 - B	35 - D
11 - D	
12 - B	
13 - A	
14 - C	
15 - A	
16 - D	
17 - B	
18 - A	
19 - C	
20 - B	
21 - D	
22 - D	
23 - A	
24 - C	
25 - B	

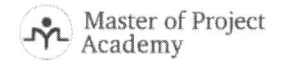

Mapping Game – Section 1

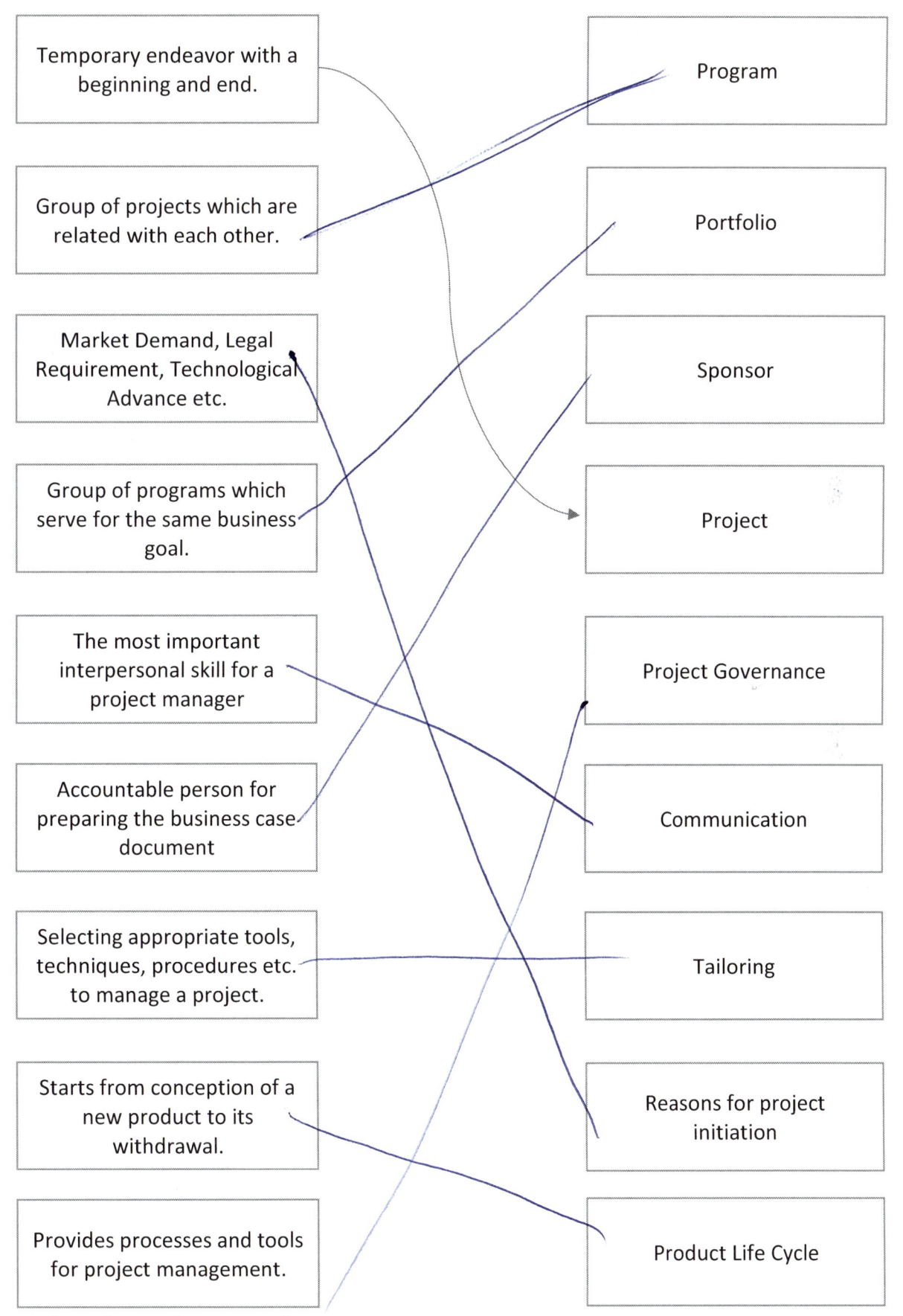

Left	Right
Temporary endeavor with a beginning and end.	Program
Group of projects which are related with each other.	Portfolio
Market Demand, Legal Requirement, Technological Advance etc.	Sponsor
Group of programs which serve for the same business goal.	Project
The most important interpersonal skill for a project manager	Project Governance
Accountable person for preparing the business case document	Communication
Selecting appropriate tools, techniques, procedures etc. to manage a project.	Tailoring
Starts from conception of a new product to its withdrawal.	Reasons for project initiation
Provides processes and tools for project management.	Product Life Cycle

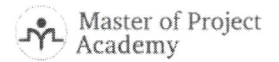

Left	Right
Held at the end of a phase for review of business case, Project charter, plans etc.	Disadvantages of Matrix Organization
Visible project objectives; Maximum utilization of scarce resources.	Advantages of Projectized Organization
The project manager has little or no authority.	Example of an operational work
Handling customer incidents which are received daily.	Disadvantages of Projectized Organization
Lack of professionalism in disciplines; Less efficient use of resources	Advantages of Functional Organization
Extra administration is required; More than one boss for project teams	Advantages of Matrix Organization
Similar resources are centralized and managed easier.	Organizational Process Assets
Efficient project organization; Loyalty to the project	Disadvantages of Functional Organization
Plans, policies, procedures and knowledge bases used by the organization.	Phase Gates

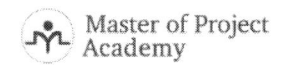

Answers

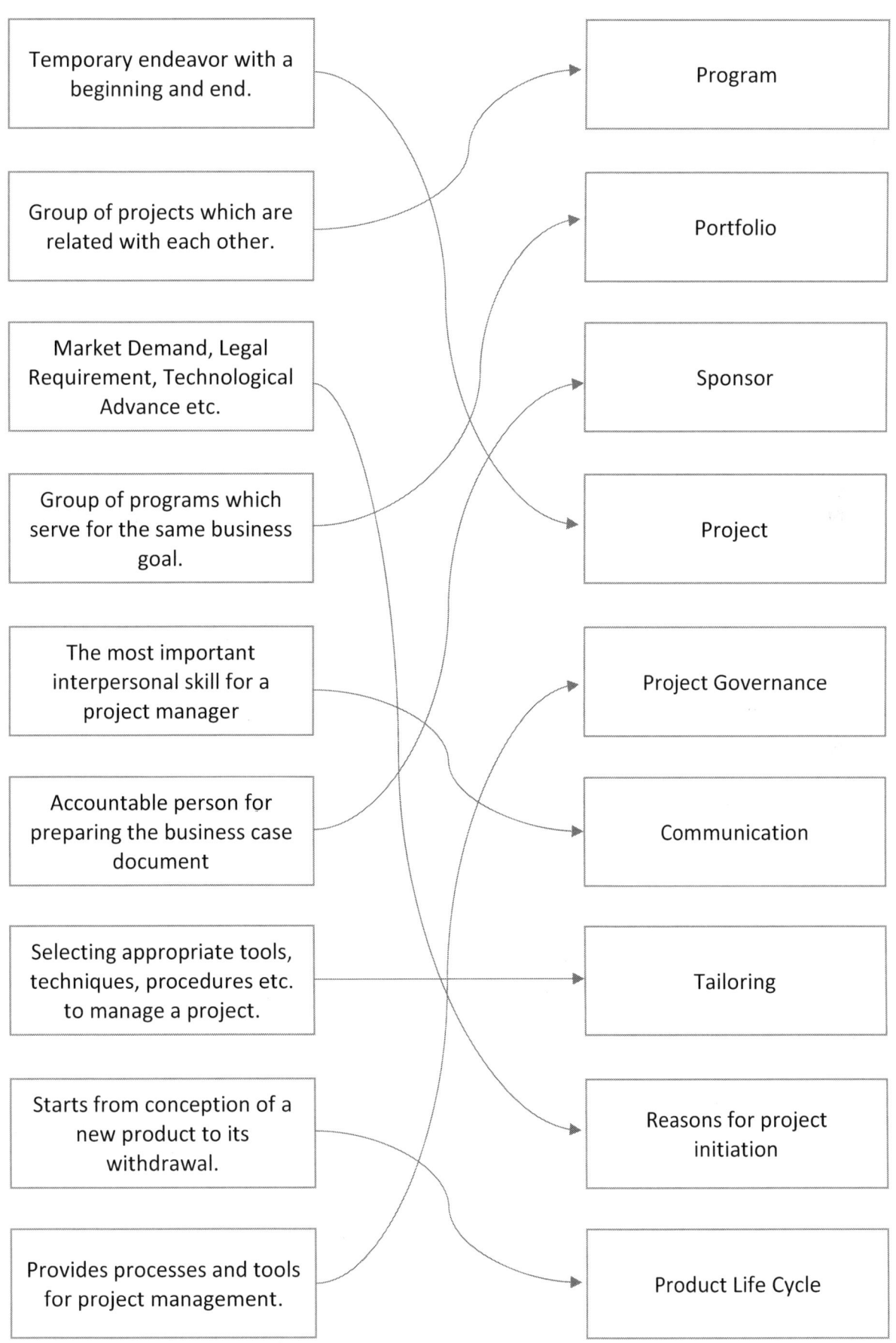

Left	Right
Temporary endeavor with a beginning and end.	Project
Group of projects which are related with each other.	Program
Market Demand, Legal Requirement, Technological Advance etc.	Reasons for project initiation
Group of programs which serve for the same business goal.	Portfolio
The most important interpersonal skill for a project manager	Communication
Accountable person for preparing the business case document	Sponsor
Selecting appropriate tools, techniques, procedures etc. to manage a project.	Tailoring
Starts from conception of a new product to its withdrawal.	Product Life Cycle
Provides processes and tools for project management.	Project Governance

PMI®, PMP®, CAPM® and PMBOK® are registered trademarks of Project Management Institute, Inc.

Left	Right
Held at the end of a phase for review of business case, Project charter, plans etc.	Phase Gates
Visible project objectives; Maximum utilization of scarce resources.	Advantages of Matrix Organization
The project manager has little or no authority.	Disadvantages of Functional Organization
Handling customer incidents which are received daily.	Example of an operational work
Lack of professionalism in disciplines; Less efficient use of resources	Disadvantages of Projectized Organization
Extra administration is required; More than one boss for project teams	Disadvantages of Matrix Organization
Similar resources are centralized and managed easier.	Advantages of Functional Organization
Efficient project organization; Loyalty to the project	Advantages of Projectized Organization
Plans, policies, procedures and knowledge bases used by the organization.	Organizational Process Assets

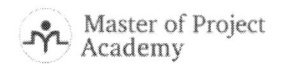

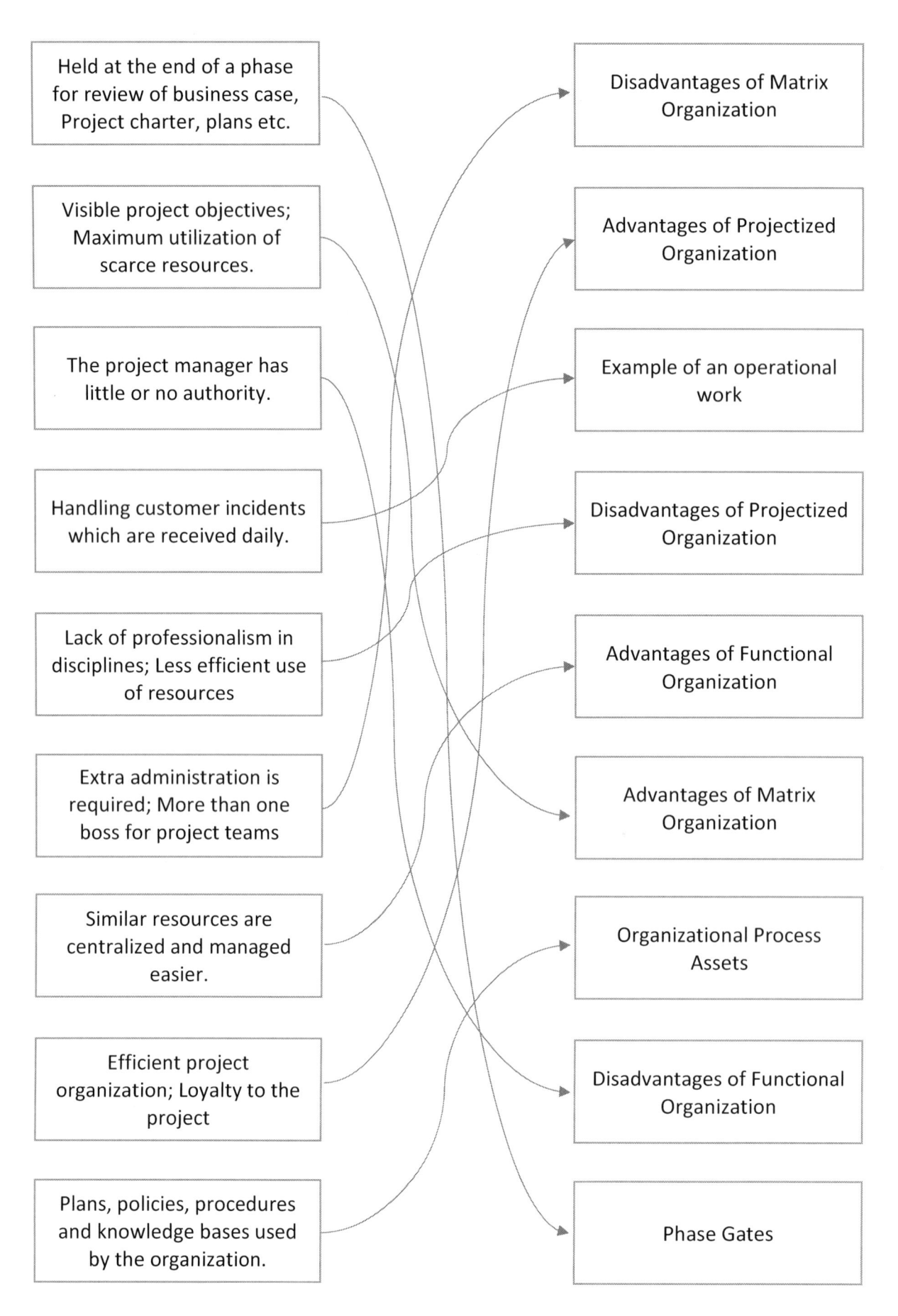

Section 2

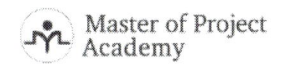

Project Management Processes

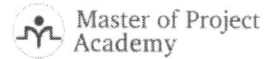

Section 2 – Project Management Processes

There are several processes in project management those help to manage a project in a structured and healthy way. For instance, what needs to be in hand to determine a budget, what needs to complete the schedule, how quality requirements will be determined etc. are all completed with the help of project management processes. During this section, we will be going over project management processes and process groups. Project management process of each knowledge area will be covered under the regarding knowledge area section of this book.

Throughout this section, we will go over the five project management processes group and the activities of these groups:

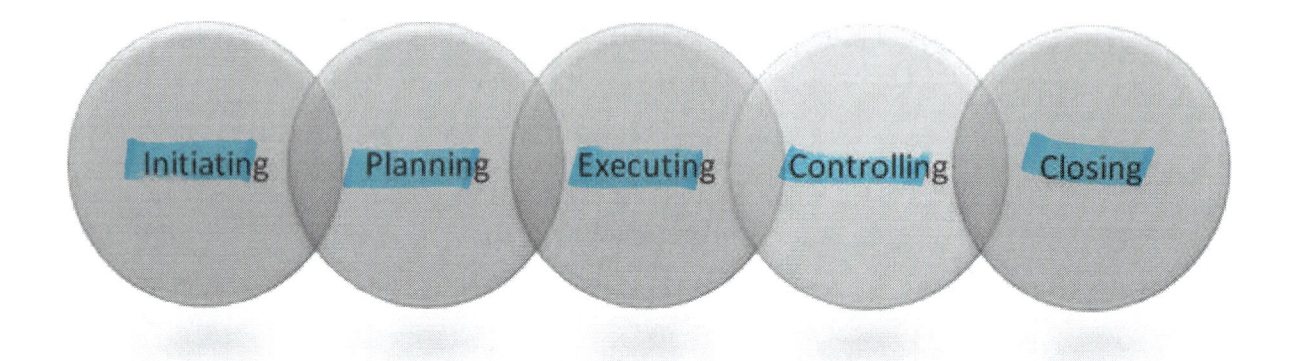

Initiating — Planning — Executing — Controlling — Closing

- **Initiating Process Group Activities:** These activities mainly help to initiate a project.

- **Planning Process Group Activities:** These activities ensure proper planning of the project.

- **Executing Process Group Activities:** These activities help in managing the project work and help in producing the work or deliverables of the project.

- **Monitoring & Controlling Process Group Activities:** These activities help successful progression of projects. Monitoring and controlling activities check whether the project goes as planned and whether there are deviations from the expected results. If there are deviations, project management aims to correct the variances to meet the project objectives.

- **Closing Process Group Activities:** These activities help to finalize project activities, document closing paper work and complete the project successfully.

During this section, we will be going over how these process groups are triggered, what are the major inputs and outputs of the process groups as well. At the end of the section, we will give project management process group and knowledge area mapping. We will list the processes of each process group and which knowledge area they belong to in a table.

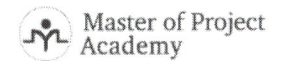

Project Management Processes

Project management processes define what to do when in a project. There are several activities from initiation to closure of a project and each activity has a sequential order as well.

- Can you purchase a tool that will be used in a project before the initiation of the project?
- No

- Can you assign resources of the project before completing the project plan?
- No

Therefore, the activities are defined in an organized and structured manner with the help of the project management processes. The Project management processes:
- define what to do when in a project.
- define what you need to do to manage the project.
- define what will be the inputs and outputs to complete an activity

For instance, determine project budget process will help project manager to understand what he needs to complete the budget estimation of a project.

There is a sequential process for managing projects:

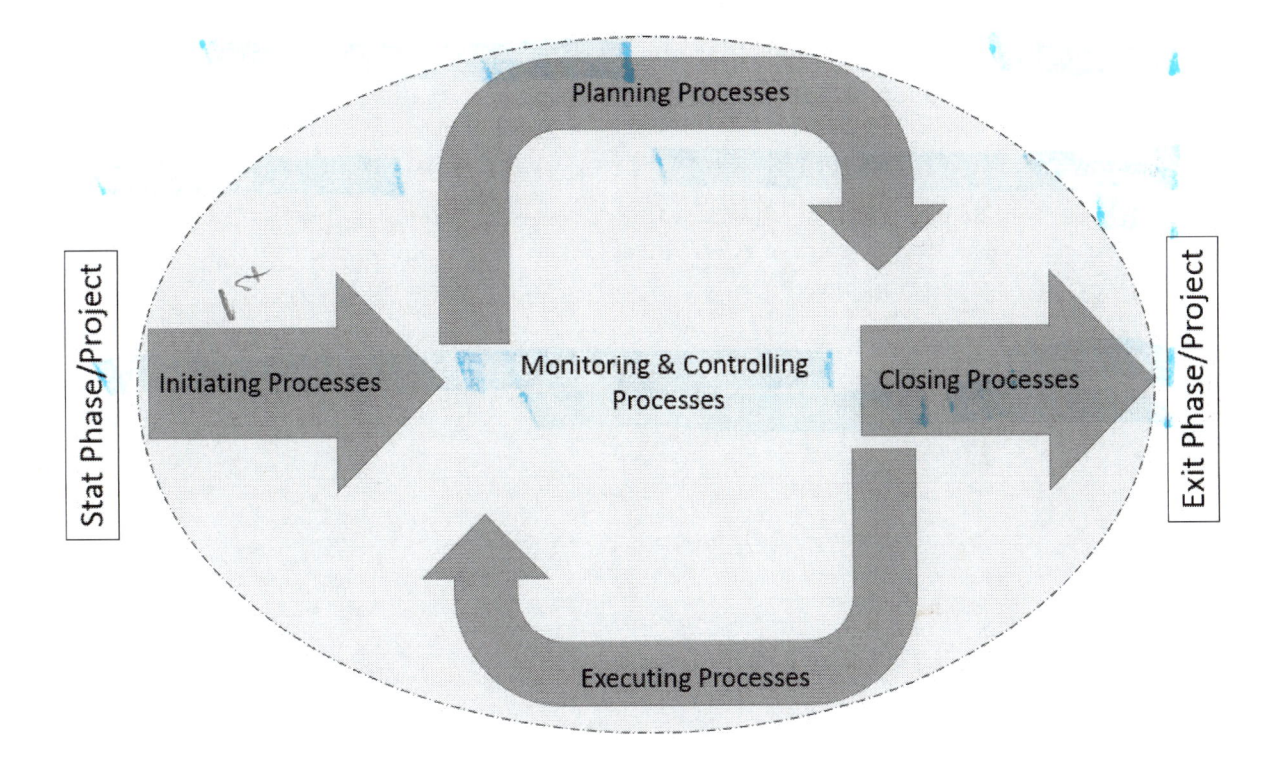

This figure illustrates the interaction of project management process groups with each other.

Entering phase is the start of the project. Once a project starts, **initiating processes** are triggered which help to initiate the project successfully. Then, **planning processes** will take place and project planning will be done. Once the planning finishes, **project execution** starts. During project execution, deliverables of the project are produced and delivered to the customer. As you see in the figure, **planning processes and executing processes are in a loop**. Because based on the actual outputs and actual results of the project, re-planning or re-adjustments might be needed to reach the project objectives. For instance, if the project is exceeding the budget that was planned in the beginning, corrective actions and re-planning must be done to correct these deviations. The last step is **closing processes**, which will help to complete the project. **Monitoring and Controlling processes** cover the processes of other four process groups. Because monitoring and controlling is done from initiation until end of the project. In order to complete a project successfully, project progress, metrics and measurements must be considered whether everything is happening as planned in the beginning.

1. **Initiating (Start):** At this stage, necessary business case to start the project is shaped. Then, sponsor of the project, who will financially support the project, will initiate the project start and project manager will be assigned to manage and coordinate project activities.

2. **Planning (Plan):** At this stage, end-to-end project planning is completed. This plan includes cost management, scheduling, quality management, resource management etc. details of the project.

3. **Execution (Do):** This is the stage where the actual project output is delivered. Project deliverables are produced and delivered to the customer at this stage.

4. **Monitoring and Controlling (Check & Act):** This stage actually interacts with all other stages. Because the main purpose of this stage is checking whether the project progresses as planned. If there are any deviations from the planned targets or metrics, regarding corrective and preventive actions need to be taken respectively.

5. **Closing (End):** At this stage, project activities are finalized, paper work to complete the project is finished. Lessons learned documentation is finalized and archived in the organizational process assets of the company.

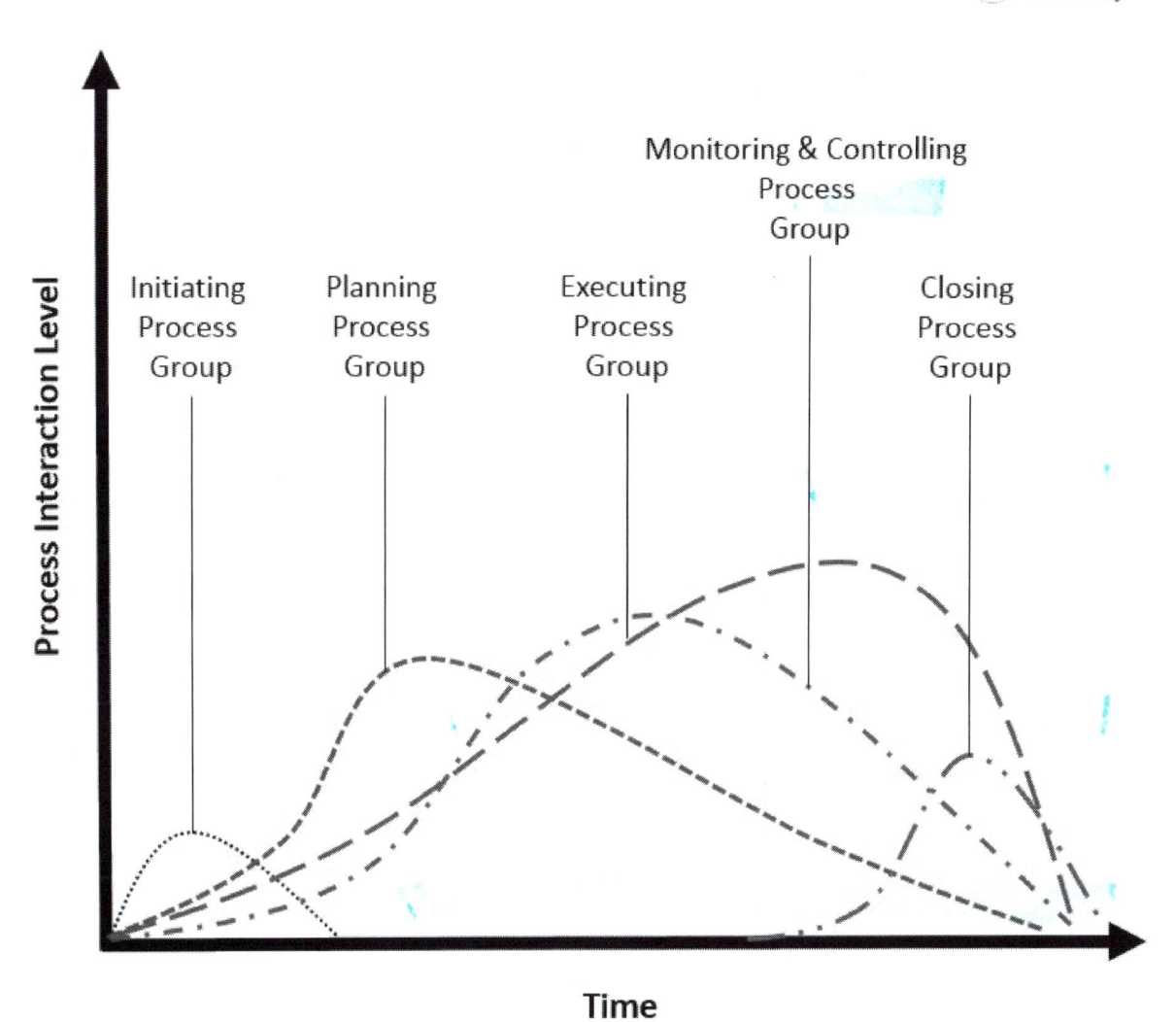

Process Interaction Level vs Time

Process groups shown on the graph:
- Initiating Process Group
- Planning Process Group
- Executing Process Group
- Monitoring & Controlling Process Group
- Closing Process Group

X-axis: Time
Y-axis: Process Interaction Level

This figure shows the level of process interaction over time in a project or in a phase of a large project. Initiating process group processes are active at the very beginning of the project and their level are lower compared to other process groups. Once the level of initiating process group starts to decline, level of planning process group activities starts to increase. Executing process group follows the planning process group and it reaches the highest level of interaction among all process groups. The last process group, which is towards the end of the project or phase, is closing process group. Monitoring and controlling process group has the longest duration in terms of process interaction in a project or phase. As mentioned already, the main reason of this is, monitoring and controlling processes check all other process groups whether the project is healthy and whether the project will meet its objectives.

Initiating Process Group Activities

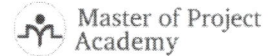

Initiating

Initiating process group activities mainly aims to initiate a project successfully.

It ensures that planning process group activities are triggered once initiation of the project is complete.

- **Select project manager:** Once a project is determined to be initiated, sponsor of the project who will financially support the project needs to trigger regarding steps and procedures. Assignment of a project manager to the project is one of the first steps since project manager will be the main responsible and coordinator of the project management activities.

- **Determine company culture and existing systems:** Organization structure of the company, tools, procedures and policies will affect how project will be progresses. For instance, if there is a procedure for assigning a task to a project team member, this needs to be determined during initiating.

- **Collect processes, procedures, and historical information:** Processes that will be used to manage the project will be gathered. If there had been a similar project in the past or if there are, lessons learned that might be used in the current project, these are searched in the organizational process assets of the company.

- **Divide large projects to phases:** If a project is very large, dividing it into smaller phases will ease to determine project objectives, management, and coordination, also monitoring, and controlling project activities. Therefore, big and long-lasting projects should be evaluated whether it is possible to execute these projects in phases.

- **Understand the business case:** Business case of a project defines why the project is initiated. At the end of the project, if the project does not serve for the reason that it was initiated for, project will be considered as failed. Therefore, while setting project objectives, business case of the project should be kept in mind all the time.

- **Uncover initial requirements and risks:** Customer requirements are collected and later in planning processes, these requirements are detailed. Similarly, project risks that are visible during the initiating stage should be documented and if there are any response strategies, those should be documented as well. Later in planning processes, project risks and their response strategies are evaluated in detail.

- **Create measurable objectives:** A project objective must not be subjective. For instance, "we will create a camera for a smartphone that will take good pictures". Is this a measurable objective? No. Because a good photo cannot be good enough for another person. However, if you set the objective as "we will create a camera for a smartphone that can take 32 Megapixels photos". This is measurable because 32 megapixels is a quantitative objective of the project.

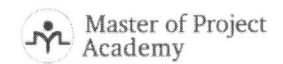

- **Develop project charter:** Project charter will be issued in detail in further notes. Project charter involves high-level information about the project. Sponsor is accountable for the creation of project charter but project managers can prepare the project charter in a project.

- **Identify stakeholders:** is another important activity of initiating process group. Powerful and influencing stakeholders might affect the project progress drastically. Therefore, stakeholder expectations and requirements must be documented and managed properly throughout the project for the sake of the project success.

- **Develop stakeholder management strategy:** Each stakeholder will have varying expectations and requirements from a project. Each stakeholder will require different approaches. Appropriate stakeholder management strategy must be developed especially for powerful and influencing stakeholders of the project.

Planning Process Group Activities

After the project is initiated, next step is planning.

Planning process group activities help to create planning documents of the project. We will list the planning process group activities one-by-one.

- **Determine how you will do planning:** Planning process group activities define how you will approach project planning as well. They help to create a proper project planning.

- **Finalize requirements:** Project requirements including scope, quality, cost, schedule etc. must be finalized at the beginning of planning. Because the overall project plan will be shaped based on the project requirements. If these requirements change, re-planning must be done.

- **Create project scope statement:** We will describe the project scope statement in our further notes in detail. Project scope statement defines what will be done during the project and includes major deliverables and outputs of the project.

- **Determine what to purchase:** During planning, tools, equipment or any other resources that need to be purchased or leased must be determined and planned. For instance, if there will be construction project, steel, wood, tools for construction etc.

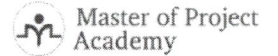

must be purchased. Some vehicles might be required and these vehicles might be leased instead of purchase. All these must be planned.

- **Determine team:** During planning phase, project resources that will be working throughout the project are determined. For instance, for an IT project, how many software engineers will be working? How many test engineers will be needed? Etc. are planned and determined during planning.

- **Create Work Breakdown Structure and Work Breakdown Dictionary:** Work breakdown structure is abbreviated as WBS. We will see the WBS and WBS dictionary in our further notes in detail. WBS actually depicts the hierarchy of project deliverables in a project. For instance, completion of login page, credit card payment page and transaction page can constitute a payment module work package of a website project. With several other work packages, a whole website can be completed. These kinds of hierarchies define the WBS. In addition, WBS dictionary is for giving detailed information for an item in the WBS.

- **Create activity list:** Activities that must be completed to finish a project are determined during planning phase. These activities must be as small as possible to assign a project team member. By this way, better management and coordination of the project can be ensured.

- **Create network diagram:** It is another planning process group activity. Network diagram of a project shows the interdependencies of project actives. Which activity must finish before starting on another activity, which activities have to finish together and similar interdependencies of activities are defined in Network diagram. For instance, before completing the software development of a web page, you cannot start testing. So, testing activity must start once the software development activity finishes. These kinds of relationships are depicted on the network diagram.

- **Estimate resource requirements:** During planning, how many resources will be needed, tools and equipment that are required and materials that will be used are estimated.

- **Estimate time and cost:** Projects are temporary endeavors. They should have a start and end. Based on the scope and quality requirements of the project, project schedule and budget that is required to complete this scope on determined schedule are estimated.

- **Determine critical path:** There are several activities of a project. There are interdependencies of activities as well. While some activates can be performed in parallel, some activities will depend on other activities to finish for instance. After the interdependencies and duration of the activities are determined, critical path of the project is determined. Critical path of the project shows the longest path in the network diagram from start of the project until end. Therefore, it defines the total project duration actually.

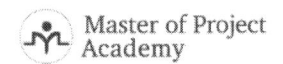

- **Develop schedule:** Schedule plan of a project shows which activity will start when. It also includes national holidays, annual leaves, public holidays etc. Schedule of a project includes start and end dates of each project activity.

- **Develop budget:** Budget plan of a project shows how much money will be spent for what in a project. It includes the expected payment dates and amount of money that will be paid to the sellers, vendors or partners etc.

- **Determine quality, standards, procedures & metrics:** What will be the quality objectives of the project? Are there any standards that the project must be compliant? ISO 9001 for instance. What will be the procedures to follow? For instance, what are the steps for leasing a vehicle from a vendor or what is the outsourcing policy of the company? In addition, what will be the metrics? Will you use US standards or UK standards? These should be determined during the planning processes.

- **Create process improvement plan:** Especially recurring processes needs to be improved throughout the project. Because there is always, room for doing an activity better. How to improve processes continuously should be planned.

- **Determine all roles & responsibilities:** Clear roles and responsibilities matrix is essential for the project success. This kind of a matrix will clearly show what is expected from who and clears out all ambiguities if there are any. Otherwise, assignments or activities that are not addressed clearly can cause conflicts and delays in projects.

- **Plan communications:** How will you communicate the project information with your stakeholders? For instance, weekly report will be sent to project stakeholders in each 2 weeks and executive directors will be informed through a 30 minutes meeting at the end of each month. These kinds of what kind of information will be disseminated to who and when are planned during planning.

- **Perform risk identification, qualitative and quantitative risk analysis and risk response planning:** Project risks that are visible in planning phase must be listed. These risks must be addressed with risk response strategies to reduce the impact of these risks when they occur.

- **Go back-iterations:** Project planning is iterative. Because an action or plan you did later might eliminate the validity of a previous action or plan. Therefore, progressive planning and iterations are done to reach the most appropriate project planning in the end.

- **Prepare procurement documents:** If there will be tools, equipment, materials or resources that will be purchased from external organizations, how to purchase these from vendors or suppliers must be documented. For instance, how will you select the supplier? What will be the conditions to make a payment to one of your suppliers etc.?

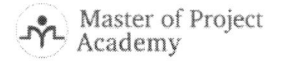

- **Finalize "how to execute & control" parts of all management plans:** At the end of the planning, execution and monitoring & controlling approach of the project must be concrete. These plans must be implemented to reach the goals of the project in the end.

- **Develop final PM plan and performance measurement baseline that are realistic**: Final project plan must be completed by the end of the planning phase. This plan should include measurable objectives and attainable cost and schedule targets.

- **Gain formal approval of the plan:** This is crucial. Once the project planning is completed, this plan must be approved by all project stakeholders. Project manager must be sure that everybody is on the same page about the project objectives and targets by the end of the planning phase. If there are disagreeing parties, these need to be clarified and revisions must be done. Otherwise, any party who does not believe in the created project plan or does not support the project plan brings a very high risk to the success of the project.

- **Hold kick-off meeting:** Kick-off meeting is organized by the project manager and critical stakeholders are invited to the kick-off meeting. Project plan is overviewed; project objectives, targets and outcomes are summarized to the project stakeholders.

Executing Process Group Activities

After the planning phase of a project, executing phase starts. During executing phase, actual outputs of the project and project deliverables are produced. Executing process group activities help to deliver project deliverables during executing phase.

During executing phase, actual outputs of the project and project deliverables are produced. Executing process group activities help to deliver project deliverables during executing phase.

- **Execute the work according to PM plan:** Project plan that has been completed and approved by the stakeholders by the end of the project planning phase is executed throughout the executing phase. Actions and steps planned in the project management plan are followed.

- **Produce product scope:** Output or the main deliverable of a project can be a product. Product scope is clarified in executing phase. This includes the features, characteristics, abilities etc. of the product.

- **Request changes:** Changes are inevitable in a project. Although the project requirements are finalized and project scope is determined during planning, customer or business might come with additional requirements or changes in existing requirements. These changes must be evaluated and managed properly.

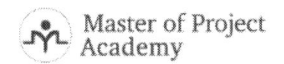

- **Implement only approved changes:** Changes are evaluated by change control board in projects. We will see the change control board and change management process in our further notes. Only changes that are approved by the change control board can be applied in a project.

- **Ensure common understanding:** During executing phase, project manager must ensure that project objectives are understood by each stakeholder and everyone is on the same page for the success of the project.

- **Use the work authorization system:** Work authorization systems are generally used to assign tasks or activities for project resources. Since this is the phase where the actual deliverables of the project are produced, activities or tasks of the resource are assigned by the help of work authorization system.

- **Continuously improve:** Better performance, better coordination, better management and better results should be aimed in projects. Therefore, continuous improvement of the processes must be aimed during the executing phase

- **Follow processes:** Processes that help to deliver project outputs are followed throughout the executing phase.

- **Perform Quality assurance:** Quality assurance is for checking whether the produced outputs are as planned in the beginning and meets the project requirements. For instance, if the project is producing a new version of a car, test-drives are planned to check whether car is safe enough to be launched and whether it is safe enough to drive in a live traffic etc.

- **Perform quality audits:** This is for checking whether quality requirements of the project are met.

- **Acquire final team:** Since this is the phase where actual project work is produced and end results are delivered to the customer, final project team that will perform the project activities is acquired. These resources are managed. Since there will be people performing project tasks and activities, these people must be managed through executing phase.

- **Evaluate team and project performance:** While the team is producing outputs, performance of each team member and overall project team performance must be evaluated. In addition, the project performance such as cost performance, schedule performance, quality performance must be assessed as well. If there are variations from the planned targets, correction actions must be planned respectively.

- **Hold team building activities:** Motivated people can bring success to a project. Therefore, team-building activities play vital role in project management to keep up the motivation of the project members.

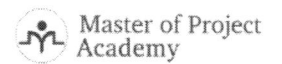

- **Give recognition and rewards:** Over performing or successful team, members must be recognized and awarded. This can be a bonus salary, additional vacation or a gift card etc. By this way, team members will be encouraged to perform better in project and this will bring better performance in the project respectively.

- **Use issue logs:** Issue logs store the problems or actions that needs to be taken by the people. Let us consider that you are working for an IT project. If your project members need an access to a database to work on their software development activities, this access request needs to be logged in the issue log. When the access is provided, issue must be resolved respectively.

- **Facilitate conflict resolution:** We will see conflict resolution techniques in our further notes. Since executing phase is the most active phase of a project in terms of project activities, it is more likely to have conflicts between people during this phase. Conflicts must be managed properly and resolved respectively to prevent any negative impacts that can cause in the project.

- **Send and receive information:** Project information is sent and received throughout the project executing phase. For instance, weekly, or monthly reports are generated to inform project stakeholders about the progress of the project. In addition, most of the project communication will take place during this phase since the major project outputs are delivered during this phase.

- **Hold meetings:** Meetings with managers, executives, and project team members are organized. This is mainly for giving information about the project and for resolving the issues or impediments if there are any.

- **Select Sellers:** During planning phase, procurement procedures and procurement plan is prepared. When the executing phase comes, what to purchase from which supplier or seller are determined.

Monitoring & Controlling Process Group Activities

Monitoring and controlling process group activities help to keep project on track. These process activities check whether the project is going as planned and whether there are any deviations from the baseline. During this heading, we will list the monitoring and controlling process group activities one-by-one

- **Act to control the project:** Necessary steps, control points and actions are taken to monitor and control the project. These actions provide if project is deviating from the planned baseline.

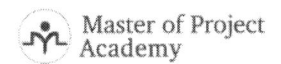

- **Measure performance:** In order to check whether the project is going well, performance must be measured. For instance, cost performance of the project will give an indication whether the planned budget will be sufficient to complete the project. Schedule performance of the project will give an indication whether the planned schedule and dates can be reached.

- **Determine variances and if they warrant a change request:** If there is a lot of variance from the baseline, for instance if it is expected that the project duration will exceed the planned duration by 20%, then regarding actions must be taken to meet the project targets.

- **Influence the factors that cause changes:** Changes are inevitable in a project. However, preventive actions can be taken to influence the factors that cause changes. For instance, detailed scope and requirement clarification with the customer will reduce the changes that will be coming from customer.

- **Request changes:** If there is a deviation from the planned values, then a change can be requested to meet the planned values again.

- **Perform integrated change control:** Changes in a project must be implemented in an integrated manner. Because a small change on one aspect of the project might affect the overall project. Perform integrated change control evaluates the changes and its impacts on the project. Then, a proper change implementation is planned to minimize the risk of changes.

- **Approve or reject changes:** Changes are evaluated by the change control board and if this board rejects the change, it will not be implemented. If a change is approved, project plan revisions must be done and change should be implemented properly.

- **Inform stakeholders of approved changes:** If the decision of the change control board is approving a change. This must be communicated to the stakeholders. Because, the previous plan, scope and targets have a change and stakeholders must be notified about this change.

- **Manage configuration:** Configuration of a project describes the meaningful and properly working combination of different modules or parts. In order to ensure healthy project progression, configuration is managed.

- **Create forecasts:** Monitoring and controlling process group activities create forecasts on what will be the budget of the project on completion, what will be the end date of the project if the project performs as it performed until now etc. These forecasts help to see how far the project is from its targets.
- **Gain acceptance from customer:** Once the project deliverables are completed, they are presented to the customer. If the deliverables meet the requirements agreed with the customer in the beginning, customer accepts the project and closing phase is triggered.

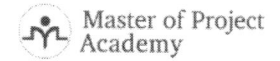

- **Perform quality control:** Quality control activities check the quality attributes of the delivered outputs. For instance, the product of a project might meet the budget and schedule targets. However, the quality requirements might not meet the customers' expectations. In this case, project will be considered as failed as well. Therefore, perform quality control is important.

- **Report on project performance:** Since forecasting and project performance is measured during monitoring and controlling, reports about the project performance to relevant stakeholders are sent during this phase as well.

- **Perform risk audits:** Risks may affect a project drastically. Therefore, each anticipated risk must be documented, and risk response strategies for each risk must be planned in case a risk occurs.

- **Manage reserves:** Reserves are planned to accommodate costs of risks and unexpected situations in projects. For instance, if the project budget is 100,000 USD, a 10% reserve can be planned to accommodate impacts of risks. Alternatively, if the project duration is 12 months, an additional 2 months can be planned as buffer to overcome any kind of risks that might occur during the project. These reserves are managed in monitoring and controlling phase.

- **Administer procurements:** Tools, equipment or resources can be outsourced from a supplier during a project. Administration of these purchases, outsourcing and leasing activities are done during monitoring and control phase of a project.

Closing Process Group Activities

Closing process group activities ensure the recording project documents, archiving in organizational process assets, making final payments, releasing resources and completing the project. We will list the closing process group activities one-by-one.

- **Confirm work is done as per the requirements:** Once the project is closing, all deliverables of the project must have been completed and delivered to the customer. Formal acceptance of the customer for the completed work is taken.

- **Complete procurement closure:** Since the project is closing, any remaining payments that needs to be made to the suppliers or partners are completed. Procurement steps are completed respectively.

- **Gain formal acceptance:** Formal acceptance of the project and project deliverables are taken from the customer. Usually, customer presents a written document, it can be an email or signed off document, which states that the project has been completed and they accept the outputs of the project.

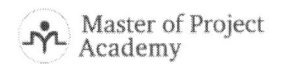

- **Complete final performance reporting:** Final performance of the project is calculated and recorded. These include cost performance, schedule performance, quality performance etc. For instance, whether the project has been completed under budget or if it could not be completed, how much did the project exceed the planned budget?

- **Index and archive records:** Collected documents are finalized. Final versions of the project management plans and all necessary documents about the project are archived in the company records.

- **Update lessons learned:** Lessons learned is collected and gathered from all stakeholders. Lessons learned documentation is stored in the organizational process assets of the company.

- **Hand-off completed product:** Once the project is completed, product of the project is handed over for the use of the end customer. Handover may need a predetermined period of assistance or some documents describing how to use or how to operate with the product.

- **Release resources:** After the project is completed successfully, all assignments of the project resources are closed, lessons learned inputs from the project resources are collected and then these resources are released respectively.

Initiating Process Group

Initiation phase of the project starts with authorizing the project and assignment of the Project Manager. A business case, market demand, social need etc. can cause the initiation of a project. After evaluation of the project, if the decision is to initiate the project, sponsor of the project authorizes the project and financially supports the project activities. The organization assigns a project manager for this new project.

The major outputs of the initiating process group

- **Project Charter:** It is one of the major outputs of the initiating process group. Project charter describes high-level information about the project. It includes sponsor information, high-level scope, high-level risks, business need, project manager information, etc.
- **Identified stakeholders:** It is another output of the initiating process group. Stakeholders are people or group who might be affected from the outcomes of a project. Management of powerful and influencing project stakeholders is crucial for a project's success. Stakeholder analysis and identification is done during initiating process group.

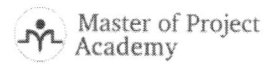

- **Strategy for Managing Stakeholders:** It is generated during initiating as well. After stakeholders are identified and analyzed, proper stakeholder management strategy is generated respectively. For instance, an executive director that will decide whether the product of the project will be launched or not is a very critical stakeholder of the project. These kinds of stakeholders must be managed closely and their expectations must be satisfied to execute the project successfully.

Progressive elaboration

Estimates, product scope and some other steps might start in initiating and iterated in planning process. Because as long as the project progresses and new information about the project is collected, more accurate and precise planning can be done. Therefore, re-planning is done throughout the project.

Project Management Plan is finalized in planning, detailed estimate, scope and some other points might be clarified during execution or monitoring & controlling. Because as long as the project work is accomplished, unclear points and ambiguities affecting to make precise and accurate plan will be eliminated.

Assignment of the project manager

Project manager is assigned early in the process. Because as long as a project is authorized, there will be many project management activities that needs to be coordinated and managed. Project manager will do these works for completing the project in a better way.

However, this is not the case in real world for many cases. Project managers are generally assigned when the project will start in real world. I have some experiences that project managers have been assigned when the project started as well. Therefore, although theory states that project manager must be assigned as early as possible once the project is authorized, this might not be practical in the real world.

Business Case

Business Case states the reason why the project is initiated. Therefore, business case of the project must be considered throughout the project in all stages. Because if the business case cannot be addressed with the completion, project will be considered as failed.

High-Level Planning

High Level Planning includes very high-level steps and deliverables of the project. Detailed planning is completed during planning phase of the project.

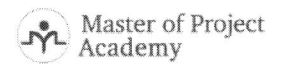

- **Creating high-level WBS:** It is completed in initiating phase. This high-level WBS includes major work packages and deliverables of the project. Detailed WBS is finalized during planning phase.
- **Order of magnitude estimation:** It is done during initiating process. Because there is very little information about the project, and with the limited information and high-level assumptions, it is not possible to make accurate and precise estimations. Order of magnitude estimation has a variance of 50%. This means, actual value of an estimation can reach 50% higher or lower of the estimation value.
- **High-Level risk identification:** The risks of the project are listed. If there are risk responses for these risks, these are documented as well. However, detailed risk identification and planning risk response strategies are done during planning.

The reasons to start the initiating process

There are three main reasons to start the initiating process:
- Business need
- Beginning a new phase of a project
- Re-evaluation of the business need

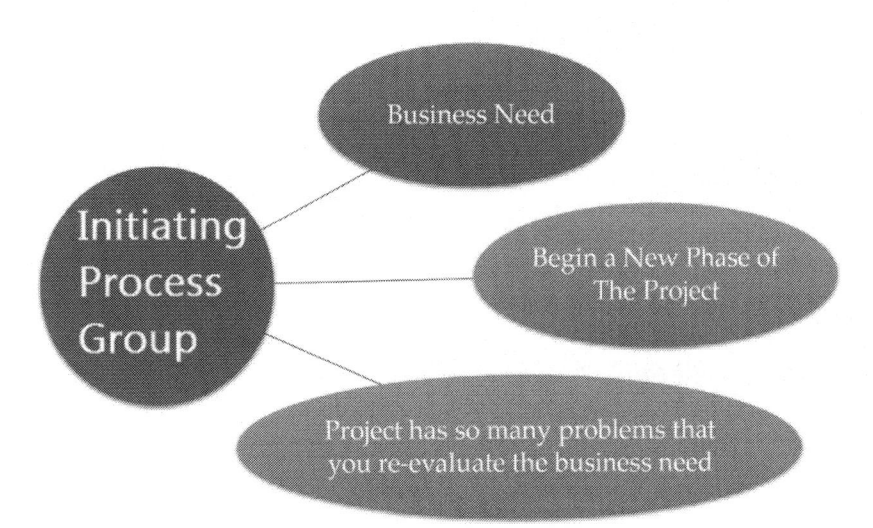

- **Business need:** Business need, market demand, social need etc. are the reasons for project initiation. After the evaluation of the business need, if the senior management of the company decides to initiate the project, project is authorized and project manager is assigned respectively to manage and coordinate the project.

- **Beginning a new phase of a project:** If the project is a large project and if there are many phases, initiating process group is triggered at the beginning of each phase.

- **Re-evaluation of the business need:** Initiating process group is triggered if there are so many problems or conflicts in a project and if the stakeholders start to criticize the business need. Because, if there are so many conflicts in a project, the reason why the project started might not be a valid case anymore. In this case, re-evaluation of the business case is done by re-initiating the initiating process group.

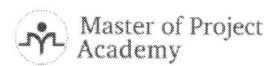

Planning Process Group

Planning processes ensure healthy planning of the project to ensure successfully meeting project objectives.

Planning enables walking through the project and getting it organized before it is actually done. Therefore, during the project planning, for each task, cost estimate, schedule estimate, interdependency with other tasks etc. are analyzed and an overall plan is produced. This gives an indication of what will be the overall budget of the project, duration of the project etc. By this way, regarding allocations are ensured within the company.

Resources, time, and money can be saved during "planning" and while the work is being done with the help of planning. Because planning ensures what you will need when. For instance, with the help of planning, you will have an overview of when will the testing start and you can negotiate with the test department manager accordingly to allocate test engineers when the time comes to testing in the project.

The major outputs of the planning process group

Result of the planning process group is project management plan and project documents. Note that, project management plan includes several other plans such as cost management plan, schedule management plan, quality management plan etc. These plans include detailed guidelines on how to manage different aspects of projects.

Planning Process Group = PM Plan + Project Documents

Planning is iterative, thus, result of each step may affect or cause changes to previous steps. Let us consider that you have two activities in your project. First activity is 5 days, and second activity is 7 days. The second activity is dependent on the first activity; it cannot start before first activity is finished. Let us assume that first activity is completed with a delay in 8 days. This will affect the start date of the second activity and revision and reiteration of the plan respectively.

Iterations start after Risk Analysis since final cost and schedule can be determined after Risk Analysis. Because, each risk has an associated cost to overcome the impacts of the risks once they occurred. These costs are planned and accommodated during planning phase, in the budget of the project.

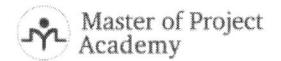

Risk Management can result in changing resources, when they are used, in what sequence activities are performed, and almost all parts of "planning". Because, based on the risks of the project, alternative and optimum solutions to minimize the occurrence possibility of risks need to be generated. This causes changes in planning respectively.

During planning, High Level of Confidence in Schedule requires more planning and Low Level of Confidence in Schedule requires less planning. This means, if you want to prepare a more accurate and precise plan that will have little variances, this will bring higher and more detailed level of planning. Because, precise estimations can be done only by spending more time on planning.

For instance, Effort you need to spend in planning when creating a schedule with +/-20% accuracy is less than +/-5% accuracy. Therefore, depending on the accuracy level you need, appropriate time for planning needs to be organized.

Who is involved in planning? Everyone! During planning of a project, each stakeholder might provide inputs. These inputs must be evaluated by the project team to develop overall project plan. While the inputs during planning comes from stakeholders, Project Management Plan and project, documents are compiled by the Project Manager. Therefore, the project manager is accountable for the development of the project management plan.

Rolling Wave Planning

Rolling Wave Planning is applied in project management. You might not be able to plan a phase of your project, for instance testing phase, installation phase etc. in detail until the phase is finished. Until you complete the all project activities, based on the actual results of the project, you need to revise the future activities of the project accordingly. This is called rolling wave planning.

The reasons for starting planning process

There are two main reasons to start planning processes in a project.

First reason can be the initiating process group activities have been completed and planning of the project can start. Second reason can be the changes, corrective and preventive actions that may require re-planning.

For instance, if there is an approved change, impact of this change on the project is reflected to cost management plan, schedule management plan etc. Because with the new change, it is very likely that the overall budget of the project will increase and project duration will increase.

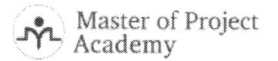

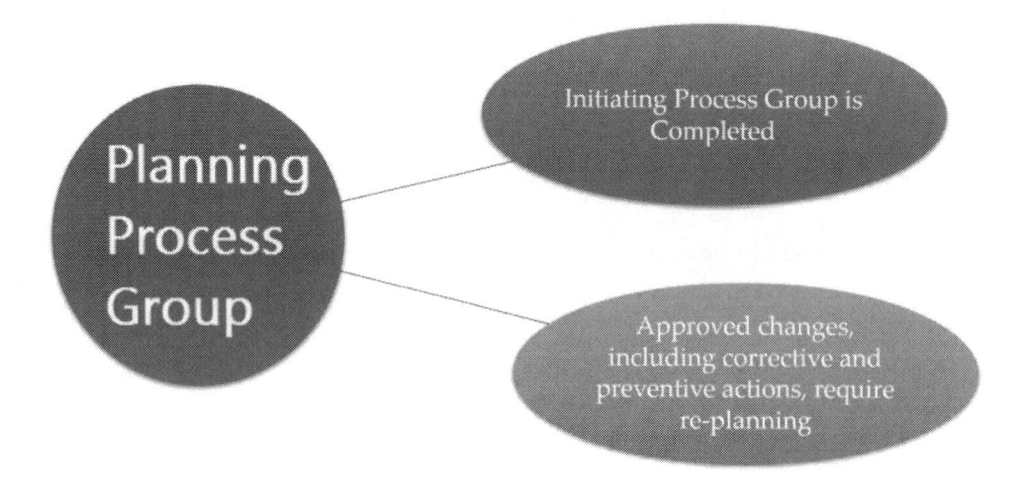

Corrective and preventive actions might require re-planning as well. Corrective actions are taken to rectify a deviation or problem occurred in the project. Preventive actions are taken to eliminate any risks that can affect project in a negative way. Therefore, the main difference of corrective and preventive actions is; corrective actions are taken to fix an occurred problem while preventive actions are taken to minimize the occurrence possibility of a negative risk. Both corrective and preventive actions might re-planning in a project.

Executing Process Group

Executing processes help to deliver the actual work, outputs, and deliverables of a project.

Executing phase of a project is the phase where most of the project activities are completed; project deliverables are produced and delivered to the customer.

Purpose of executing process group is to complete the work defined in Project Management plan and to meet project objectives. What to do when, order of activities, tools, materials and equipment that will be procured, budget that will be spent throughout the project etc. are all determined during planning. These plans are executed throughout the executing phase. If you have successfully planned a project, executing phase will go smoothly and you will be able to complete the project successfully. However, weaknesses in the planning will affect the execution of the project. These weaknesses can cause exceeding budget, delays in project activities, decrease in quality etc.

Executing processes focus on:
- **Managing people:** Majority of the project activities are handled by the project team. Project activities are assigned to project team members. Therefore, during executing a project, people in the team must be managed properly to complete project activities and finish the project successfully.
- **Following processes:** Steps of how to do what are described in processes and during executing process, these processes are followed. For instance, how to purchase steel

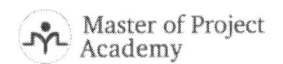

from the selected supplier for the construction project is defined in procurement management processes. When the time comes to purchase steel in the executing phase, regarding procurement management processes will guide on the steps that needs to be followed to complete purchase.
- **Distributing information:** Since majority of the project work is delivered throughout the project execution, progress information about the project is distributed to the project stakeholders frequently during executing phase. Meetings with the project team are organized to review status of the project; next steps in the project, problems and how to solve these problems etc. are all discussed during meetings.

Meetings

Meetings are important in executing process group. Different types of meetings can be organized and different level of information can be provided in each meeting during executing phase. For instance, meetings with the project team will have detailed discussion on project activities, particular problems etc. On the other hand, meetings with the senior management will have high-level information about the project progress, whether it is on track, on budget etc., and whether there are any high-level risks upcoming in near future etc.

During meetings,
- **Risks are reviewed:** If there is a risk that is expected to happen in near future, actions to overcome the impacts of the risk must be reviewed.
- **Contingency plans:** They accommodate the impacts of risks must be reviewed. For instance, one of your project team members might resign from the job in near future. In case he resigns, 2 weeks of handover period might be needed to new project team member that will take over the activities of resigning employee. These 2 weeks of handover might cost 10,000 USD for the project since. Contingency plan to recover this cost must be reviewed respectively.
- **Do not only discuss status or what is done:** Meetings are not only for giving information about the progress. What could have been done better, problems and alternative solutions, risks, and best practices that can ensure better performance should be discussed during meetings.

Reasons for starting executing phase

There are two main reasons for starting executing phase of a project.

First reason is project planning is completed. Once the project planning is over, project management plan is developed. Then, formal acceptance of the stakeholders is taken for the plan. Executing stage starts to perform steps that have been determined in the planning.

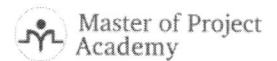

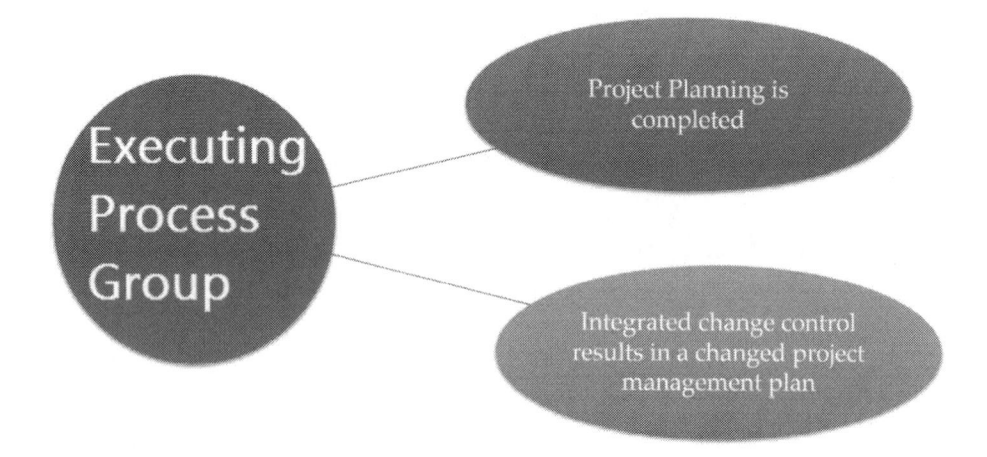

Second reason is, integrated change control can result in a changed project management plan. For instance, if there is a change request that has been approved by the change control board, this must be implemented. To implement this change, first, project management plans are revised accordingly. Then, executing processes are triggered to implement approved change in the project.

Monitoring & Controlling Process Group

Monitoring and controlling processes help to check whether the project is going as well as planned. These processes identify if there are any deviations in actual results from the planned values. For instance, whether the project is under budget, whether the project will be finished on time, whether quality requirements are met etc. are all checked and evaluated with the help of monitoring and controlling processes.

- **Measuring performance of the project to the project management plan:** It is the main objective of monitoring and controlling processes. For instance, if the overall project budget is 250,000 USD for a project and 6 months is the duration, monitoring and controlling processes check whether these budget and time targets will be met. These are just for examples. There are several other aspects that needs to be measured in a project and these are measured with the help of monitoring and controlling processes mainly.

- **Approving change requests:** Although scope is determined, plans are finalized and project management plan is developed, changes might arise during project execution. Because, as the project progresses, outputs and deliverables of the project are provided to customer. Based on the actual results, customer might come with new requests or change its existing requirements. These changes are evaluated by change control board and approving/rejecting change requests are done during monitoring and controlling phase.

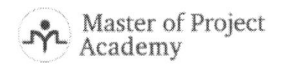

Recommended corrective and preventive actions: These are proposed with the help of monitoring and controlling processes. Based on the performance checks of a project, if there are negative variances from the planned values of a project, corrective actions must be taken to get back on track. For instance, if the current measurements of the project show that the project will be completed 2 months later than the planned date, appropriate actions must be taken to complete the project on time. Preventive actions are for taken for reducing the impacts of any risks that might affect the project.

- **Defect repair:** Produced product might not work as planned in the beginning. For instance, let us consider that you are working on a smartphone development project. Once the smartphone is produced, during tests, it is discovered that camera of the device does not shoot bright pictures as it was planned. This is actually defect of the product that is observed during monitoring and controlling phase, and must be fixed before completing the project.

- **Project manager is accountable for meeting the performance measurement baseline:** Performance measurement baseline includes budget, schedule, and quality etc. targets of the project. Meeting these targets are under the main responsibility of the project manager. Project manager manages the project team and stakeholders to meet these targets by the end of the project.

- **Project manager takes actions to correct any variances**: If there are any problems that is causing to meet project objectives, these variances must be corrected. For instance, if the total budget will be exceeded, how to find additional funds for the project must be checked.

- **Any deviations from the plan should be made up rather than requesting a change to the project to accommodate them:** If there is a deviation, before changing the targets of the project, whether this deviation can be handled by alternative solutions must be analyzed. Requesting change, asking for funds, extension of the schedule etc. must be the last options for accommodating deviations in a project.

The Reasons for Initiating the Monitoring & Controlling Processes

This figure below describes what reasons initiate the monitoring and controlling processes and in what cases monitoring and controlling processes trigger other process groups.

There are three main reasons to trigger monitoring and controlling processes. These are
- requested changes,
- work performance information and
- deliverables.

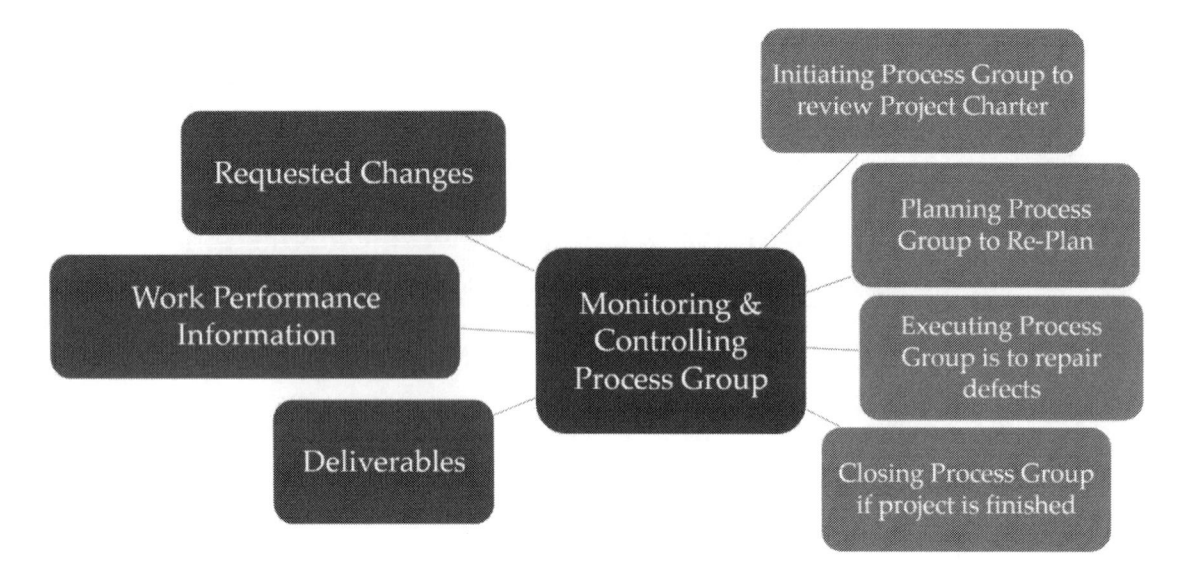

Moreover, based on the progress of the project, changes and deliverables:
- initiating processes can be triggered to review the project charter,
- planning processes can be triggered to revise planning,
- executing processes can be triggered to repair defects or implement approved changes and
- closing processes are triggered if all objectives of the project are met and results are as planned

Closing Process Group

Closing processes ensure the successful completion of the project.

Therefore, once the project deliverables are completed and delivered, accepted by the customer, closing processes take place to close the project.

- **Project is finished in this process group:** During closing phase, deliverables that needs to be completed, payments that need to be made to the suppliers, requirements check whether they all have been met etc. are done. Because, these are criteria for completing and closing a project.

- **Includes administrative activities:** Closing a project includes written approvals, documentation and communication with different parties. For instance, sign-off of the customer is acquired; payments to the suppliers are completed etc.

- **Final product is delivered:** During executing phase, all deliverables of the project might have been completed. When it comes to closing phase, final product must have been delivered and accepted by the customer.

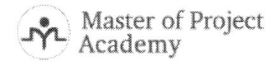

- **Celebration! Success must be appreciated and celebrated:** If project has been finalized and closed successfully, project team must be rewarded and this success must be celebrated. This will encourage all employees in the organization for future successes.

- **Report final project performance of resources:** Employee salary increases are determined mainly based on the employee performance in most of the organizations. Therefore, upon project completion, final performance of the project team members must be reported. Overall project performance of a project resource must be considered when promoting, determining salary increases etc.

- **Latest versions of Lessons Learned are compiled:** Lessons learned is gathered throughout the project but Latest versions of Lessons Learned are compiled during closing phase. After collecting inputs from stakeholders, and finalizing the lessons learned, this final document is archived in the organizational process assets of the company.

- **Formal sign-off and acceptance is acquired:** The most important step of the closing phase is getting formal sign-off and acceptance of the customer. Because, projects are initiated based on a business need and customer request. Therefore, if customer does not accept the final outputs and product, project cannot be closed.

- **Project is closed after getting final sign-off and administrative work are completed:** After getting final sign-off of the customer, there will be procedures and paperwork within the organization to officially close the project.

The Reasons for Closing Processes

There are three main reasons to trigger closing processes.

- **Project phase completion:** If there is a large project with several phases, in closure of each phase, closing processes are triggered.

- **Project completion:** The project objectives are met and closing the project

- **Project termination:** Project termination is actually closing the project since the project objectives will not be met anymore or the business case, which was the reason for initiating the project, is not valid any more. Even if a project is terminated, reasons for termination, last status of the project and documents must be archived in company records respectively.

Project Management Process Group and Knowledge Area Mapping

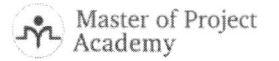

Project management processes belong to the process groups and knowledge areas actually. There are 10 knowledge areas in project management. During the rest of the book, each section will go through a knowledge area respectively. During those sections, processes that belong to the knowledge area will be described and explained in detail.

In this heading, we will only provide a mapping of which processes belong to which knowledge area.

Knowledge Areas	Project Management Process Groups				
	Initiating	Planning	Executing	Monitoring & Controlling	Closing
Integration Management	Develop Project Charter	Develop Project Management Plan	Direct and Manage Project Work Manage Project Knowledge	Monitor and Control Project Work Perform Integrated Change Control	Close Project or Phase
Scope Management		Plan Scope Management Collect Requirements Define Scope Create WBS		Validate Scope Control Scope	
Schedule Management		Plan Schedule Management Define Activities Sequence Activities Estimate Activity Durations Develop Schedule		Control Schedule	

Integration Management knowledge area is the only knowledge area that has processes in each five process groups (initiating, planning, executing, Monitoring & Controlling, Closing). These processes are:
1. develop project charter, *(Initiating)*
2. develop project management plan, *(Planning)*
3. direct and manage project work, *(Executing)*
4. manage project work, *(Executing)*
5. monitor and control project work, *(Monitoring & Controlling)*
6. perform integrated change control and *(Monitoring & Controlling)*
7. close project or phase. *(Closing)*

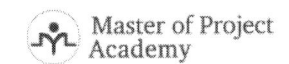

Main purpose of integration management knowledge area processes are execution and delivery of the project work end-to-end successfully.

Scope Management Knowledge area has six processes. Four of them belong to planning and two processes belong to monitoring and controlling process group. These are:
1. plan scope management, *(Planning)*
2. collect requirements, *(Planning)*
3. define scope, *(Planning)*
4. create WBS, *(Planning)*
5. validate scope and *(Monitoring & Controlling)*
6. control scope. *(Monitoring & Controlling)*

Scope management processes aims to control scope in a project and protects scope creep.

Schedule Management knowledge area has six processes, five of them are in planning and only one process belongs to monitoring and controlling. These are:
1. plan schedule management, *(Planning)*
2. define activities, *(Planning)*
3. sequence activities, *(Planning)*
4. estimate activity durations, *(Planning)*
5. develop schedule and *(Planning)*
6. control schedule. *(Monitoring & Controlling)*

Main objective of the Schedule management processes is completing a project on time without variance.

Knowledge Areas	Project Management Process Groups				
	Initiating	Planning	Executing	Monitoring & Controlling	Closing
Cost Management		Plan Cost Management Estimate Costs Determine Budget		Control Costs	
Quality Management		Plan Quality Management	Manage Quality	Control Quality	
Resource Management		Plan Resource Management Estimate Activity Resources	Acquire Resources Develop Team Manage Team	Control Resources	
Communications Management		Plan Communications Management	Manage Communications	Monitor Communications	

Cost management knowledge area has four processes. These are:
- plan cost management, *(Planning)*
- estimate costs, *(Planning)*

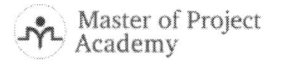

- determine budget and *(Planning)*
- control costs. *(Monitoring & Controlling)*

Cost management processes aim to complete the project under planned budget.

Quality Management knowledge area has three processes. These are:
- plan quality management, *(Planning)*
- manage quality and *(Executing)*
- control quality *(Monitoring & Controlling)*

Quality management processes ensure to meet the projects' quality objectives.

Resource management knowledge area has six processes, which are:
1. plan resource management, *(Planning)*
2. estimate activity resources, *(Planning)*
3. acquire resources, *(Executing)*
4. develop team, *(Executing)*
5. manage team and *(Executing)*
6. control resources *(Monitoring & Controlling)*

Resource management processes mainly aim to manage people, tools, equipment, vehicle etc. of a project.

Communications management knowledge area has three processes. These are:
1. plan communications management, *(Planning)*
2. manage communications and *(Executing)*
3. control communications *(Monitoring & Controlling)*

Several communications will take place in a project internally and externally. Management of information dissemination is done with the help of communication management processes

Knowledge Areas	Project Management Process Groups				
	Initiating	Planning	Executing	Monitoring & Controlling	Closing
Risk Management		Plan Risk Management Identify Risks Perform Qualitative Risk Analysis Perform Quantitative Risk Analysis Plan Risk Responses	Implement Risk Responses	Monitor Risks	
Procurement Management		Plan Procurement Management	Conduct Procurements	Control Procurement	
Stakeholder Management	Identify Stakeholders	Plan Stakeholder Engagement	Manage Stakeholder Engagement	Monitory Stakeholder Engagement	

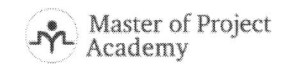

Risk Management knowledge area has seven processes. Since risks are evaluated mainly in planning phase, 5 out of 7 processes belong to planning phase.
1. plan risk management, *(Planning)*
2. identify risks, *(Planning)*
3. perform qualitative risk analysis, *(Planning)*
4. perform quantitative risk analysis, *(Planning)*
5. plan risk responses, *(Planning)*
6. implement risk responses and *(Executing)*
7. monitor risks. *(Monitoring & Controlling)*

Risk management processes mainly aim to reduce the impacts of risks to the project once they occur.

Procurement management knowledge area has three processes, which are:
1. Plan procurement management,
2. conduct procurements and
3. control procurements.

Main purpose of procurement processes is management and coordination of purchasing activities in a project.

Stakeholder management knowledge area has four processes. These are:
1. identify stakeholders, *(Initiating)*
2. plan stakeholder engagement, *(Planning)*
3. manage stakeholder engagement and *(Executing)*
4. control stakeholder engagement. *(Monitoring & Controlling)*

Stakeholder management processes help to manage expectations of project stakeholders during the project.

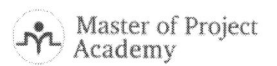

Quiz – Section 2

1- Which of the following is NOT a project management process?
   A) Initiating
   B) Starting
   C) Planning
   D) Execution

2- Which of the following activities does NOT happen in Initiating Process Group?
   A) Select the project manager
   B) Divide large projects into phases
   C) Create activity list
   D) Create measurable objectives

3- You have collected processes, procedures and historical information in your project, identified stakeholders and developed a management strategy for these stakeholders. In which process group are you in?
   A) Initiating
   B) Planning
   C) Execution
   D) Monitoring & Controlling

4- You are in planning process group in your project. All of the following are activities you will do in this process group EXCEPT:
   A) Finalize requirements
   B) Create a project scope statement
   C) Develop Schedule
   D) Manage People

5- Activities in planning process group must be followed in a sequence. Which of the following activities is done at LAST in planning process group?
   A) Determine what to purchase
   B) Estimate time and cost project activities
   C) Determine critical path
   D) Hold kick-off meeting

6- You are performing risk identification, qualitative and quantitative risk analysis and risk response planning activities in your project. In which process group are you in?
   A) Planning
   B) Closing
   C) Monitoring & Controlling
   D) Initiating

7- Your colleague in project management office is managing a project. During your discussion with him, he mentioned that he is performing quality assurance and audits. In which process group is your colleague in?
   A) Initiating

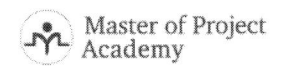

B) Planning
C) Executing
D) Monitoring & Controlling

8- All of the following activities are done in Executing Process Group EXCEPT:
A) Give recognition and rewards
B) Measure performance
C) Use issue logs
D) Select sellers

9- You are in the monitoring & controlling process group of your project. Which of the following is an activity that you should do in this process group?
A) Perform integrated change control
B) Complete procurement closure
C) Gain formal final acceptance of the project
D) Determine all roles & responsibilities

10- All of the following are activities done in Monitoring & Controlling Process Group EXCEPT:
A) Administer Procurements
B) Manage Reserves
C) Create forecasts
D) Hand-off completed product

11- Which of the following activities is done as LAST step in closing process group?
A) Confirm work is done to requirements
B) Update lessons learned documentation
C) Release Resources
D) Index and archive records

12- All of the following are major outputs of initiating process group EXCEPT:
A) Project Charter
B) Project Management Plan
C) Identified Stakeholders
D) Strategy for Managing Stakeholders

13- All of the following about project management process groups are true EXCEPT:
A) Project Manager is assigned as early as possible in the process
B) Project team is acquired in initiating process group
C) Business case is the reason why project started
D) High-Level planning is done in initiating

14- There are different reasons for initiating process to start in projects. Which of the following is an example of business need?
A) Analysis phase of the project has ended, and development phase will start
B) Customer requested new change requests during project execution
C) A car manufacturer started to a new project to produce a new car model for women

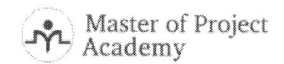

D) Problems occurred during project had to be resolved

15- All of the following about planning process group is true EXCEPT:
   A) Project Management Plan and documents are compiled by Project Manager
   B) Major outputs of the process are project management plan and project documents
   C) Planning is iterative
   D) Only project manager and executives of the company are involved in planning

16- Which of the following BEST describes "Rolling Wave Planning"?
   A) You might not be able to plan a phase of your project in detail until the phase is finished
   B) Planning is completed in planning process group
   C) Initial plans deviate maximum 10% throughout the project
   D) If planning is not possible in projects, execution can start directly

17- Which of the following project management knowledge areas have processes in all project management process groups?
   A) Integration Management
   B) Scope Management
   C) Stakeholder Management
   D) Risk Management

18- Organizing meetings are important during execution process group. All of the following about these meetings are true EXCEPT:
   A) Risks are reviewed
   B) Contingency plans for upcoming risks are reevaluated
   C) Tasks of each team member must be reviewed
   D) Agenda must not be only status or what is done

19- Performance of the project is measured in monitoring and controlling process group. All of the following about this process is correct EXCEPT:
   A) Project Manager is accountable for meeting performance measurement baseline
   B) If a project is deviating from baselines, customer must be informed immediately
   C) Project Manager takes actions to correct any variances
   D) Project Manager must prevent the reasons of changes in a project

20- All of the following are reasons for entering closing process group EXCEPT:
   A) A Project phase is complete
   B) Project has been completed
   C) Project has been terminated
   D) Market need

Answers

1 – B	11 - C
2 – C	12 - B
3 – A	13 - B
4 – D	14 – C
5 – D	15 – D
6 – A	16 – A
7 – C	17 – A
8 – B	18 – C
9 – A	19 – B
10 – D	20 – D

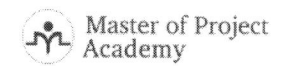

Mapping Game – Section 2

"Understanding the business case" belongs to which process group?	Executing
"Develop budget" belongs to which process group?	Everyone
"Index and archive records" belongs to which process group?	Project Manager
Who is involved in planning?	Initiating
"Measure performance" belongs to which process group?	Initiating; Planning; Executing; Monitoring & Controlling; Closing
The Five Process Groups	Monitoring & Controlling
High Level Planning is done in which Process Group?	Planning
"Perform quality audits" belongs to which process group?	Closing
Who is accountable for meeting the performance measurement baseline?	Initiating

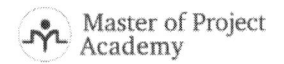

Answers

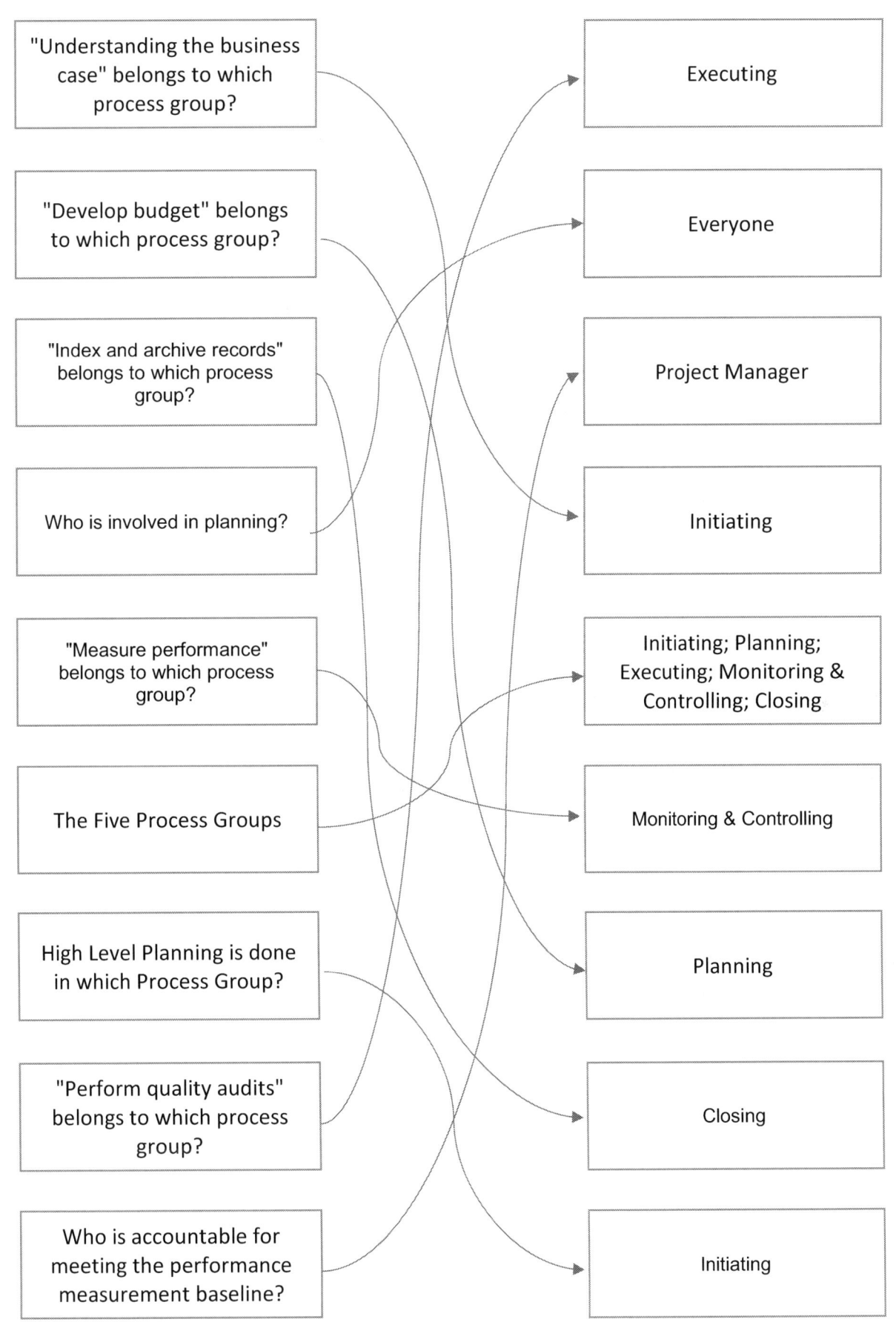

Left	Right
"Understanding the business case" belongs to which process group?	Initiating
"Develop budget" belongs to which process group?	Planning
"Index and archive records" belongs to which process group?	Closing
Who is involved in planning?	Everyone
"Measure performance" belongs to which process group?	Monitoring & Controlling
The Five Process Groups	Initiating; Planning; Executing; Monitoring & Controlling; Closing
High Level Planning is done in which Process Group?	Initiating
"Perform quality audits" belongs to which process group?	Executing
Who is accountable for meeting the performance measurement baseline?	Project Manager

Section 3

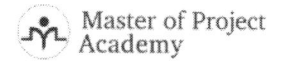

Integration Management

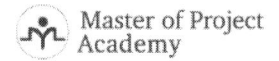

Section 3 – Integration Management

Integration Management is one of the biggest knowledge areas of project management. There are 5 process groups and phases in a project. There are lots of processes and activities that need to be managed and coordinated. This is done mainly by integration management. Integration management purposes to direct and guide project as a cohesive whole to produce meaningful outputs and meet the project objectives.

What will be our agenda throughout this section?

- **Overview of Integration Management:** We will describe what integration management aims and who does what during integration management briefly.

- **Integration Management Processes:** There are seven processes of integration management knowledge area and integration management knowledge area is the only knowledge area that has processes in each five process groups.

- **Develop Project Charter Process:** This process aims to produce the project charter. Project charter is like identity card of the project in the organization. It includes high-level information about the project and regarding information is gathered with the help of develop project charter process.

- **Project Selection Methods:** There can be several possible projects that can be initiated in a company. However, capital or investment budget is determined for a period, and based on these restrictions, companies try to select best projects that will produce more profitable and advantageous results. Project selection models help at this step. Project are evaluated mainly based on their financial aspects and optimum projects are selected for initiation.

- **Economic Models for Project Selection**: Economic Models help to evaluate different projects and select the best options respectively.

- **Develop Project Management Plan Process:** This process belongs to planning process group and aims to finalize project planning and project management plans.

- **Direct and Manage Project Work Process:** This process aims to perform the activities that will produce the deliverables of the project.

- **Manage Project Knowledge Process:** This process aims to use existing knowledge and create new knowledge to reach project objectives and contribute to organizational learning.

- **Monitor and Control Project Work Process:** This process checks whether the project is progressed as planned.

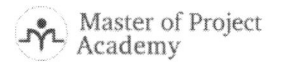

- **Perform Integrated Change Control Process:** This process ensures the change management properly in a project. Changes are evaluated by change control board and accepted changes are implemented with the help of this project.

- **Change Control Board (CCB):** Change control board evaluates the change requests and impacts of these changes in a project. A change is approved or rejected based with the evaluation of change control board.

- **Close Project or Phase Process:** Once the project delivered all its deliverables and projective objectives are met, project is closed officially with the help of Close Project or Phase Process.

Overview of Integration Management

Integration management ensures the management and coordination of all activities in a project. In other words, integration management helps in **putting all pieces of a project together into a cohesive whole**. Several activities, processes and people work in a project and this needs a proper planning to coordinate all these parts of a project.

Actually, integration management is the **reason for Project Manager's existence in an organization**. Because project manager manages and coordinates project activities in a project which is the same purpose of integration management as well.

During integration management, **team members perform the work**. Executing phase of a project is where project team members perform their activities to produce project deliverables. This belongs to integration management.

We have seen previously that sponsor financially support the project. **Sponsor also protects the project**. There might be internal and external risks that might affect a project. Since sponsor of the project is actually spokesperson of the project and initiator of the project, he must protect the project from impacts of any risks.

Project Manager integrates all pieces! There are several activities, stakeholders, processes, project team members etc. in a project. Project manager is the ultimate responsible of integration of these aspects to meet the project objectives. While doing this integration, project manager aims **Doing things faster, cheaper and fewer resources while meeting objectives.** Planning is done mainly to walkthrough the project activities until end, and producing a plan that will successfully deliver results with less resource and under a determined budget. Therefore, project manager ensures efficient and effective management of a project.

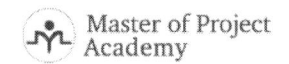

Integration Management Processes

We have seen the processes of integration management previously. However, it is better to see all integration management processes on the same sheet again.

There are 7 processes of Integration management.

1. **Develop Project Charter (Initiating):** This process aims to gather high-level project information to produce the project charter. This will help in authorizing the project in the organization. Then, planning phase will start.

2. **Develop Project Management Plan (Planning):** This process belongs to planning process group. This process will ensure proper planning of a project also it will help in producing project management plans such as scope management plan, schedule management plan, cost management plan etc.

3. **Direct and Manage Project Work (Executing):** This process belongs to executing process group. This process ensures the deliverables of the project to be produced. Main outputs of the project are produced and delivered to the customer during executing phase. This process mainly aims to deliver project deliverables.

4. **Manage Project Knowledge (Executing):** This process belongs to executing process group. This process aims to use existing knowledge in the organization and create new knowledge throughout the project. With existing knowledge and new knowledge, project team aims to reach the project objectives.

5. **Monitor and Control Project Work (Monitoring & Controlling):** This process belongs to monitoring and controlling process group. Plans are done, execution of the project starts. However, actual results will not be exactly as you planned no matter how well your project plan is. Deviations and variances from the planned values are measured with the help of monitor and control project work process.

6. **Perform Integrated Change Control (Monitoring & Controlling):** This process belongs to Monitoring & Controlling process group as well. Changes might be requested due to deviations or variances from the planned values. Alternatively, customer might require changes to the project, for instance, they can come with a new requirement or change their existing requirement. These change requests are evaluated by the Change control board with alternative solutions and impacts to the project. If changes are approved, these needs to be implemented in the project and perform integrated change control process ensures proper implementation of changes in a project.

7. **Close Project or Phase (Closing):** This process belongs to closing process group. Once the project is completed, if customer accepted the final product and signed-off the

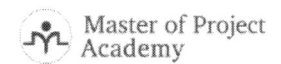

acceptance, if all project objectives are met, project can be closed officially. Alternatively, if it is a phase of a large project, phase can be closed. Close project or phase process aims to collect and archive all project documents, make all remaining payments to the suppliers etc.

Develop Project Charter

Develop project charter process, as it can be understood from its name, aims to produce the project charter. Project charter includes the high-level project information.

First part of integration management: In order to authorize a project officially, project charter must be produced. Project charter can be considered as the corporate identity of the project in an organization. We will see what a sample project charter contains during this heading.

Authorizes the project in an organization, it provides authority to Project Manager: Once a project is decided to be initiated, project sponsor is accountable for the creation of the project charter. Project manager is assigned to a project as early as possible. Once project charter is produced, this authorizes the project in the organization and gives authority to the project manager to manage and coordinate project activities.

Output of the process is Project Charter: Main purpose of the develop project charter process is gathering relevant information about the project and producing project charter respectively.

Project Charter Example

Remember our sample project: Golden Gate Bridge construction project.

We will list all major information about a project that can be included in the project charter. Note that, information we will give here are just for example and may not depict the real reasons or information about the project.

First thing that should appear in the project charter is **Project Title and Description**. Project title and description should give a very brief information about the project.

Project Title: Golden Gate Bridge

Project Description: Population of San Francisco is increasing and transportation need between two sides of the city increases in proportion. Sea transportation cannot suffice for the need over the recent years. This project will ease the transportation of vehicles between two sides of the city.

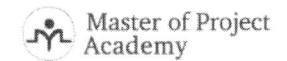

Project manager of the project and his authority must be declared in the project charter. For the Golden Gate Bridge project, John Winer has been assigned as the project manager.

Project Manager Assigned and Authority Level: John Winer will be the project manager of this project and he has the authority to determine budget, select team members, and approve/reject changes to project.

Note that, there may be several responsibilities of the project manager. At this part, only high-level information about what the project manager can does with his initiative must be listed.

> Business case of the project describes why is the project done and what was the case that caused this project to be initiated.

Business Case: The Golden Gate Bridge project is being done in order to solve the transportation problem of San Francisco between two sides. After the project completion, 80% of the vehicle transportation is expected to be done over the bridge, which will solve the transportation problem.

While this is a business case, there might be several cases for the initiation of the project. Business cases of a project must be included in the project charter.

Resource requirements of a project are planned during planning phase of the project and final project team is acquired during project execution. However, high-level resource estimation might be included in the project charter and if there are already assigned resources to the project; these are listed in the charter as well.

Resources Pre-assigned: Architects of the project are Gilbert Roberts and William Brown. Head Construction Engineer is Henry Chor. Other resources will be determined by the Project Manager.

Stakeholders of a project are people or group who may be affected positively or negatively from the outcomes of the project. Stakeholder management is a very critical activity in a project. Expectations and requirements of the stakeholders must be managed properly throughout the project. Especially powerful and influencing stakeholders must be managed closely. Stakeholders of the project are identified during initiation. However, as long as new stakeholders are identified in next phases of the project, stakeholder list and stakeholder management strategy of the project must be updated.

Some sample stakeholders of the golden gate bridge project can be:

Stakeholders:

- **Government:** Since this is a major project affecting the whole country, progress and outcomes of the project may affect the government. For instance, if a few construction

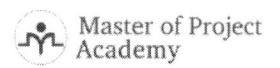

engineers die during construction, government may be criticized for the security preventions of the project and this might affect their political power over the citizens.
- **Residents:** Residents who are residing close to bridge area. Residents might be affected during construction because of the voice, pollution etc. After the project, their properties might gain additional value since they are close to the bridge. Alternatively, tenants might start to pay higher rental fees since value of the properties increased.
- **Project Team:** It is by default stakeholder of a project. Because they are performer of the project activities. Therefore, they will be directly affected from the outcomes of the project.

There can be several other stakeholders. We have just listed some stakeholders for the project.

Stakeholder requirements must be listed in the project charter. Note that, there might be competing requirements of different stakeholders. In that case, conflicts must be resolved and agreed requirement must be considered. For instance, one stakeholder might require eight lanes in total in the project while another stakeholder asks for six lanes and additional lanes for pedestrians and bicycles. Since these two requirements cannot be implemented at the same time, it must be discussed and final requirement must be written.

Stakeholder Requirements:

- The bridge will have 3+3 lanes and in total 6 lanes.
- Bridge must resist against 8.5 Richter earth quake
- Bridge must carry 2.500.000 kilograms.

There will be several other requirements of stakeholders in a project. These should be included in the project charter.

Product description and deliverables of the project are listed in the project charter as well.

Product Description / Deliverables:

Golden Gate Bridge is the end result or end product of the project.

And specifications of this product are

- Height: 227 meters
- Width: 27 meters
- Two legs of the bridge must be completed in first year.

Of course, there are several other specifications of the Golden Gate Bridge. We have just listed some product specifications of the bridge that might be included in the project charter.

Measurable project objectives are defined in the project charter as well. Project objectives define what needs to be completed throughout the project in order to reach project's goals.

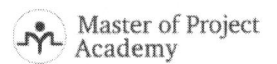

Measurable project objectives:

- Opening a new transportation channel between two sides of city.
- Ending the project in 3 years
- Completing the project with 200m USD budget.

Project Approval Requirements must be listed in the project charter. What items need to be approved, and who will sign-off the project is defined in the project charter?

Project Approval Requirements:

- Minister of Transportation will approve the Work Breakdown Structure of the project.
- Final project approval will be determined by the committee constituted for this project in Ministry of Transportation.
- Final project will be approved by Minister of Transportation on behalf of the Government. Additional acceptance criteria might be listed in the project charter about payments, delivery conditions etc.

High-level risks of the project must be listed in the project charter. We will see in further notes, but risks do not mean only negative impacts to a project. There are positive and negative risks. Positive risks are actually opportunities for the project while negative risks are potential threats for the success of the project.

High-level risks:

- Bridge will connect the two sides of San Francisco, which will increase the geopolitical importance of San Francisco. This is an example of opportunity or positive risk.
- Ease of vehicle transportation may cause to higher usage of vehicles, which can increase the air pollution. This is an example of Threat or Negative Risk.

Project Sponsor Authorizing This Project must be listed in the project charter as well. Note that, there might be several sponsors of the project. For instance, for the golden gate bridge example,

The Sponsor(s):

- Franklin Roosevelt, President of USA
- Angelo Joseph Rossi, Mayor of San Francisco
- Joseph Strauss, Head of Golden Gate Project Committee can be the sponsors who will be authorizing the project.

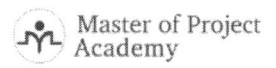

Benefits of Project Charter

We have seen what a project charter includes over our Golden Gate Bridge Construction Project example.

During this heading, we will go over the benefits of the project charter.

- **Without a project charter, Project Manager cannot be successful:** Because project charter defines the fences of a project. It includes business case, major stakeholders, what are the acceptance criteria, high-level risks, product specification etc. This information plays a vital role in the beginning of planning phase.

- **Project charter may be prepared by Project Manager but must be published by the sponsor:** Since project manager is assigned as early as possible in a project, project manager might prepare the project stakeholder in a project. However, creation of the project charter is under the accountability of the project sponsor. Nevertheless, in real world, project sponsor are very high-level people like executive directors, vice presidents, CEOs etc. Therefore, preparation and administration of project stakeholder might be done by the project manager. However, sponsor must publish once the charter is finalized.

- **Project charter is broad enough therefore; there is no need to change during execution:** As we have gone through, project charter includes very high-level information about the project. These are detailed throughout the project planning in the planning process group. Nevertheless, usually, there is no need to go back to update the project charter after initiating phase.

- **Project Charter recognizes and authorizes the project:** It includes high-level information about project and acts like the corporate identity of the project in an organization.

- **Project charter gives project manager the authority to spend money and commit resources:** After the project charter is approved, it is officially accepted by the organization. Budget and resources planned for the project can be used after this step.

- **High-level requirements of the project are defined in the project charter**: This constitutes a base for detailing the project requirements further during planning phase.

- **Project charter links project to ongoing work of the organization:** There might be several projects in an organization. Project charter outlines how the project will help in meeting strategic goals of the organization. Therefore, depicts the link between the project and other works of the organization respectively.

Project Selection Models

There can be several possible projects to initiate in an organization. However, it is not possible to execute every possible project in an organization. This is mainly because of budget and time constraints. Because executing every project will cost a lot. On the other hand, even if the budget constraint is overcome, it will be impossible to complete several projects due to market competition etc.

Therefore, organizations evaluate different possible projects before initiation and decide which projects to initiate respectively.

> Project Managers must know why their project was selected and how it fits into the organization's strategic plan.

Because, during planning, this is crucial to plan project activities to meet the project objective once the project is completed.

There are two common approaches for project selection. These are:
- **Benefit Measurement Methods:** Benefit Measurement Methods are Comparative Approaches. Comparative approach evaluates several projects based on their benefits, profits, revenue etc. Optimum project is authorized respectively.
- **Constrained Optimization Methods:** They are Mathematical Approaches. Mathematical approach takes many inputs about a project and these are modelled mathematically usually by the help of software programs. These programs outline possible outputs of the project mathematically.

Benefit Measurement Methods have four types of models. These are
- **Murder Board, which is a panel of people who try to shoot down a new project:** Participants in the panel acts as the devil's advocate and try to claim negative aspects that will come with the implementation of the project. Based on the results of the panel, if a project can defend these negative aspects, it is selected for initiation.
- **Peer review:** This method is used to evaluate projects based on the perspective of similar people in an organization.
- **Scoring Models:** This model scores candidate projects for each predetermined category. Projects with higher scores are evaluated for initiation.

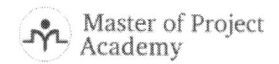

- **Economic Models:** Economic models are important because this is the most common approach used by many companies for project selection. We will go through the details of economic models through our next headings.

> Economic models are important because this is the most common approach used by many companies for project selection.

Constrained Optimization Methods have four models and these are:
- Linear Programming
- Integer Programming
- Dynamic Programming
- Multi-objective Programming.

Note that, we will not go through details of these models. I wanted to give you an overview of what are the project selection models that can be used by a company. We will go through the details of different economic models for project selection in our further notes.
Economic Models for Project Selection are:
- **Present Value:** This gives us the today's value of a money that will be paid or received in future.
- **Net Present Value:** This gives us the today's value of the sum of all transactions (inbound and outbound) that will happen in future.
- **Internal Rate of Return:** This gives us how much percent of the investment will turn back as revenue in future.
- **Payback Period:** This gives a duration that the project will cover the money invested with its revenues.
- **Benefit-cost ratio:** This ratio gives us whether the benefits of the project are higher than the costs.

Present Value

Present value is an economic model that calculates the present value of a money that will be paid or retrieved in future. Because a dollar today worth more than a dollar tomorrow.

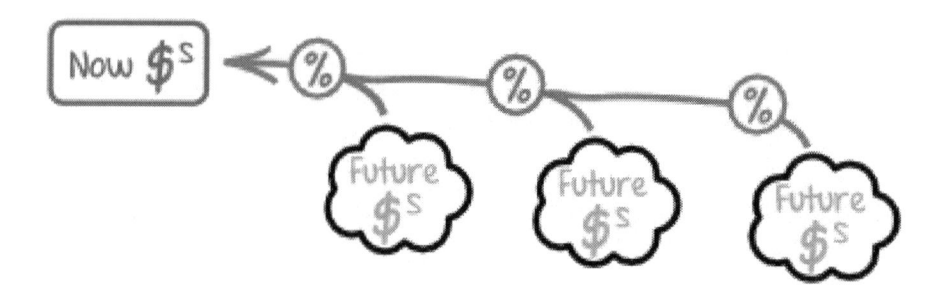

In other words, there is time value of money. Actually, the main theory on the background of this model is, if you have a money now, you can invest in different instruments. Like share of a company, interest etc. Therefore, if you invest your money in an instrument, you will have more money in future than you have now. Retrospectively, if you will receive a money or pay money in future, today's value of that amount will be lower.

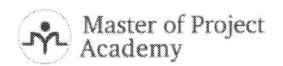

In addition, Present Value calculates the today value of future cash flows. Generally, interest rates are used for calculating present value. This is the formula of Present Value:

PV: Present Value
FV: Future Value
r: Interest Rate
n: Number of Periods

$$PV = \frac{FV}{(1+r)n}$$

Let us go over a sample scenario to understand present value model better. Assume that your project has three instalments.
- 1st Instalment: $100,000, that will be paid in the beginning of the project.
- 2nd Instalment: $100,000, that will be paid at the end of 1st year.
- 3rd Instalment: $100,000, that will be paid at the end of 2nd year.
- The Interest Rate is 10% per year.

Let us calculate the present value of these instalments now.
- Since 1st instalment is paid at the beginning of the project, its present value will be same with its actual value. It is $100,000.

$$\text{1st Instalment's PV} = \frac{FV}{(1+r)n} = \frac{\$100,000}{(1+0.10)0} = \$100,000$$

- Second instalment is paid at the end of first year. If we substitute the future value, interest rate and number of periods in the formula, we find that present value of the 2nd installment as $90,909.

$$\text{2nd Instalment's PV} = \frac{FV}{(1+r)n} = \frac{\$100,000}{(1+0.10)1} = \$90,909$$

- Third instalment is paid at the end of 2nd year. If we substitute the values in the formula, we find that present value of the 3rd instalment as $82,645.

$$\text{3rd Instalment's PV} = \frac{FV}{(1+r)n} = \frac{\$100,000}{(1+0.10)2} = \$82,645$$

- Briefly, although total money that will retrieved from the customer is $300,000 in total, since it will be retrieved over time, present value, or in other words, today's value of these installments is $273,554.

Total Cash flows = $300,000
NPV of Cash flows= $273,554

Net Present Value

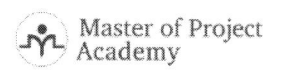

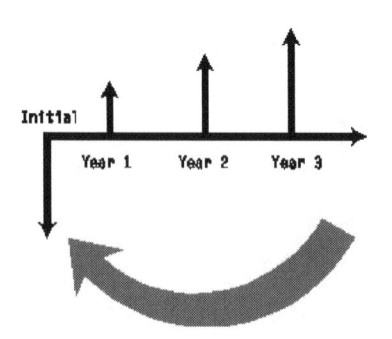

Net present value uses present value calculations, calculates total inflows and outflows of a project to calculate net results.

It is described as Present value of total benefits (revenue or income) minus the costs over many periods. Net present value is abbreviated as NPV.

If Net present value of a project is greater than zero, this means project will make profit. Therefore, projects with NPV higher than zero must be selected.

> If NPV > 0, then investment in the project is a good choice.

If there are lots of projects in the agenda of the company, Projects with higher Net present values should be selected. Because higher net present value means higher profit respectively.

> Projects with higher NPVs should be selected.

Consider our previous project example. Assume that you will have following costs in this project.

- 1st Cost: $90,000, in the beginning of the project.
- 2nd Cost: $120,000, that will happen by the end of 1st year.
- 3rd Cost: $40,000, that will happen by the end of 2nd year.
- Interest Rate is 10%.

If we substitute these cost amounts in the present value formula,

- Present value of the 1st cost is same as its actual value: $90,000. Because it accrues immediately.

$$1^{st} \text{ Cost's PV} = \frac{FV}{(1+r)n} = \frac{\$90,000\$}{(1+0.10)0} = \$90,000$$

- Present value of the 2nd cost is $109,091.

$$2^{nd} \text{ Cost's PV} = \frac{FV}{(1+r)n} = \frac{\$120,000}{(1+0.10)1} = \$109,091$$

- Present value of the 3rd cost is $33,058.

$$3^{rd} \text{ Cost's PV} = \frac{FV}{(1+r)n} = \frac{\$40,000}{(1+0.10)2} = \$33,058$$

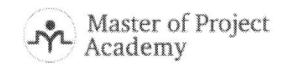

- Briefly, although $250,000 will be spent as project cost throughout the project, net present value of these payments will be $232,149.

Total Cost = $250,000
NPV of Total Cost= $232,149

Bring these cash inflows and outflows on the same table to see the net results.

Instalment	Nr of Periods	Instalment Amount	PV of Instalment	Cost	Nr of Periods	Cost Amount	PV of Cost Amount	NPV
1	0	$100,000	$100,000	1	0	$90,000	$90,000	$10,000
2	1	$100,000	$90,909	2	1	$120,000	$109,091	-$18,182
3	2	$100,000	$82,645	3	2	$40,000	$33,058	$49,587
		Total PV of Instalments	$273,554			Total PV of Costs	$232,149	$41,405

This table includes the present value of the instalments that will be retrieved and present value of the project costs together. 1st instalment's net present value is greater than the cost at the beginning. In total, net present value is $10,000.

2nd Instalment's present value is lower than the cost of that year. This results with -$18,182.

3rd instalment's present value is greater than the cost of last year. This returns a positive net present value as well.

If we sum up the net present value of all years, we find that while the project will receive $273,554, total cost that will be paid is $232,149. This makes total net present value as $41,405.

Since the total net present value is greater than zero, this project is profitable and can be initiated.

Internal Rate of Return

Internal rate of return is another economic model used in project selection. Internal rate of return is abbreviated as IRR. Explains how much percent a project will turn back. For instance, 12% of the investment will return in 2 years.

For instance, if $100,000 is needed for initiation of a project and if internal rate of return is 12% in 2 years, this means project will bring $12,000 profit by the end of 2nd year.

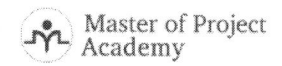

Calculation of the IRR is complex. Therefore, we do not give the formula of the IRR here. It is enough to know only that projects with higher IRR's should be selected. Because higher IRR means higher profit respectively.

> ✦ Projects with higher IRR's should be selected. Because higher IRR means higher profit respectively.

Payback Period

Payback period is another economic model for project selection. Payback period is the number of time periods it takes to recover investment of a project. Therefore, projects with shorter payback period should be selected.

> ✦ Payback period is the period that recovers investment of a project. Select projects with shorter payback period.

For instance, if a company invests 100.000$ for a project, and payback period is 6 months. This means, product or outcome of the project will bring 100.000$ in 6 months. Then it will start to make profit.

Briefly, payback period is the duration of when the project will cover the investments made to complete the project.

Benefit Cost Ratio

Benefit cost ratio is another economic model used for project selecting. This model estimates projects to determine what work should be done. In addition, an estimation of the benefits of the project is done. Then, benefits of the project are compared against the costs of the project. Here, the benefits can be considered as the revenue that will be gained from the outputs of the project.

- If **Benefit Cost Ratio > 1**, it means Benefits > Costs
- If **Benefit Cost Ratio = 1**, it means Benefits = Costs
- If **Benefit Cost Ratio < 1**, it means Benefits < Costs

Therefore, Projects with higher Benefit Cost Ratio should be selected. Because this means revenue of the project, or any other advantages that the project will bring is higher than the costs of the project. This will bring profitable or advantageous results respectively.

> ✦ Projects with higher Benefit Cost Ratio should be selected

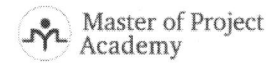

If Benefit Cost Ratio is less than 1, project should not be executed. Because the project will not generate profitable or advantageous results.

Economic Value Added

Economic value added is abbreviated as EVA. EVA is concerned with whether the project returns to the company more than its costs. For instance, if the project costs for $100,000 and if the company will have benefits that will have a value of $120,000, then the economic value added for this project will be $20,000.

EVA is the amount of added value the project produces for the company's shareholders above the cost of project.

> This added value might be either financial or intangible assets.

For instance, you can run a marketing campaign that will increase the brand awareness of your company. Although it might not directly bring revenue to the company, it might increase the brand value. Therefore, it will be considered as economic value added as well.

Opportunity cost

Opportunity cost is the opportunity given up by selecting one project over another. As we discussed already, there might be several projects that an organization can initiate. However, due to budget, schedule, resource constraints etc., some projects are selected over another.

Consider that there are two projects in your organization that the management is considering to initiate.

Net present value of project A is $200,000 and net present value of Project B is $150,000. Both projects can be initiated because they both generate positive Net Present Values. However, if only one of these projects would be selected, Project A looks more reasonable since it will bring higher net present value.

Moreover, if Project A is selected, then **opportunity cost of selecting Project A is $150,000.** Because, by selecting project A, Project B will not be initiated and therefore net present value of $150,000 with project B will not be gained.

Sunk costs

Sunk costs are expended costs. At a point during the project, sunk costs represent all money that has been spent until now in the project. For instance, if there has been spent $100,000 until now in the project, this is sunk cost.

Sunk costs are not considered when deciding whether to continue a troubled project. Because, that is the money that has been spent already.

For instance, project might have spent $200,000 while it was planned to be spent $100,000 for the work that has been accomplished until now. This is a big variance. Senior management of the company might evaluate to terminate this project due this cost variance. However, when considering termination, $200,000 spent already might not be considered. Because it has gone already. If the future works starting from now will bring benefits to the company, project can be continued respectively.

Law of Diminishing Returns

The most common way of increasing the productivity is increasing resources. For instance, two workers paint a house faster than one worker does. Alternatively, two machines can produce more products than one machine.

However, law of diminishing returns proposes that after a certain point, adding more input or resources will not produce proportional increase in productivity. The main reason of this might be due to extra coordination.

For instance, if two workers will paint the house, they need to do the work in a coordinated way. At some parts, they might intersect in same locations and this might affect their productivity.

> After a certain point, adding more input or resources will not produce proportional increase in productivity.

Think of a construction project.

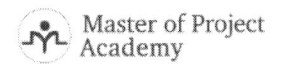

Number of Construction Workers	Constructed Area per day (m²)	Average Constructed Area per day (m²)
4	20	5.00
8	36	4.50
12	44	3.67
16	48	3.00
20	50	2.50

At the first column, you see number of construction workers increasing in each step. Second column shows the constructed area per day, and the third column shows average constructed area per day.

As you see, constructed area per day increases, but average constructed area per day decreases because there might be coordination issues and there might be management issues that you should consider when working with higher number of workers.

In addition, in the graph, on the right side, you see that there is not a linear increase of the area constructed per day while the number of workers increases. It bends over time when the number of workers increases. This is the law of diminishing returns.

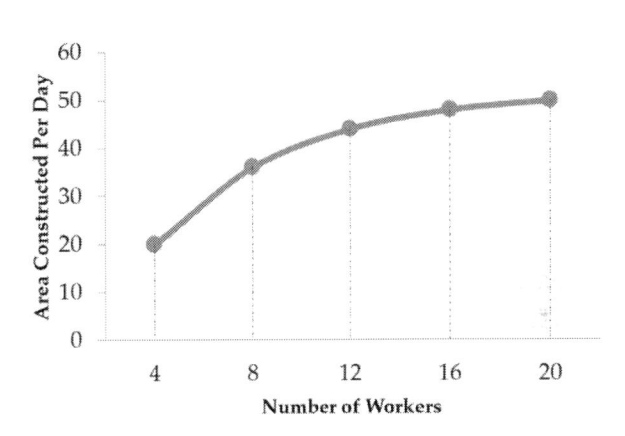

Working Capital

Working capital is calculated by:

> Working Capital = Current assets – current liabilities

This is a finance term and it is used as amount of money available to invest for a company. Assets include the liquid money, properties, shares, and any other investment instrument that can be used. Liabilities are actually debts of the company. These can be rental fees, payments to the suppliers, salaries that will be paid to the employees etc.

> Working Capital is the amount of money available to invest for a company.

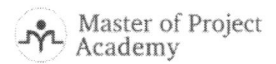

Depreciation

Large assets, for example equipment, vehicles purchased by a company, lose value over time. For instance, think you bought a brand-new car now. Will it have the same value after you use it for five years? Of course not. Value of the car will decrease during time and this is called depreciation. This is an example of depreciation. In order to calculate the current assets of a company, depreciation is considered.

> A tool, vehicle, equipment etc. that will be purchased now will not be able to be sold with the same value after some time.

Large assets, for example equipment, vehicles purchased by a company, lose value over time.

For instance, think you bought a brand-new car now. Will it have the same value after you use it for five years? Of course not. Value of the car will decrease during time and this is called depreciation. This is an example of depreciation. In order to calculate the current assets of a company, depreciation is considered. Because, a tool, vehicle, equipment etc. that will be purchased now will not be able to be sold with the same value after some time.

There are two common models used for calculating depreciation.

1. **Straight Line Depreciation:** In straight-line depreciation, it is assumed that, same amount of depreciation will happen in each year or each period.
2. **Accelerated Depreciation:** Value of the tool, equipment etc. depreciates faster than straight line. Depreciation is higher during the first years or periods in accelerated depreciation.

See the two types of depreciation over an example. Assume that your company purchased a bulldozer in order to use in construction projects. Purchasing amount is $300,000. This bulldozer will lose its value over time.

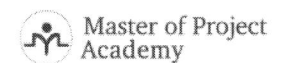

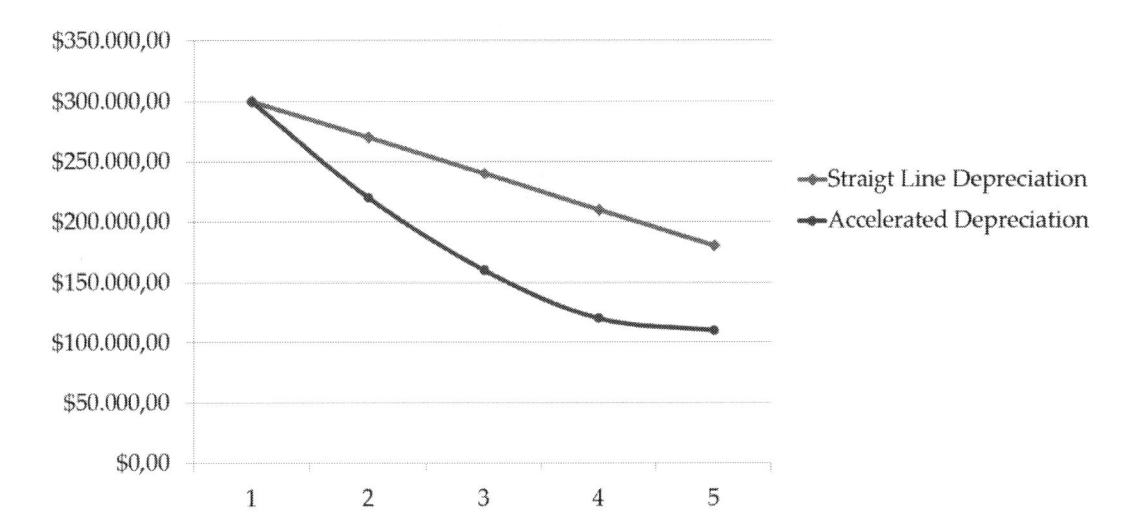

This figure shows how depreciation will happen in straight-line and accelerated depreciation models. Blue line represents the straight-line depreciation. Each year, $30,000 is depreciated from the value of the bulldozer.

Red line represents the accelerated depreciation. As you see, depreciation is higher during first years and lower in last years. Depreciation amount is $80,000, $60,000, $40,000 and $10,000 respectively.

Project Statement of Work (SOW)

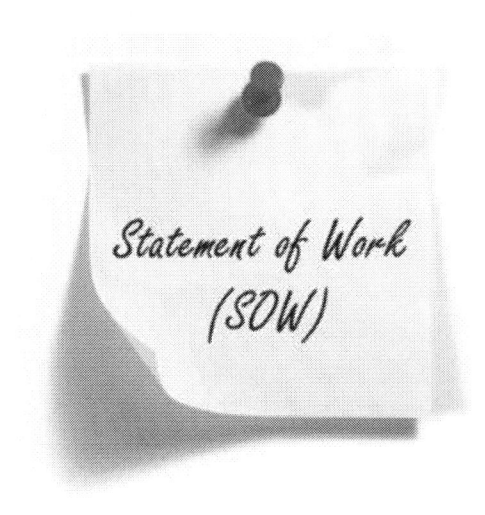

Project Statement of Work is abbreviated as SOW. **It is created by customer or sponsor and describes their needs, product scope, and how the project fits into their strategic plan.**

This document is widely used in the industry. If a company wants a product or service, the details of the product or service are documented in detail in the project statement of work. Based on the details of the service or product that is requested by the customer, several vendors or suppliers enters in bidding or offering to get the project.

Project Statement of Work is abbreviated as SOW. It is created by customer or sponsor and describes their needs, product scope, and how the project fits into their strategic plan.

This document is widely used in the industry. If a company wants a product or service, the details of the product or service are documented in detail in the project statement of work. Based on the details of the service or product that is requested by the customer, several vendors or suppliers enters in bidding or offering to get the project.

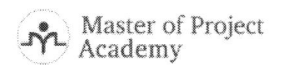

For instance, consider that a construction company will outsource the bathroom decorations of its projects to a vendor. The company writes in detail what kind of materials will be used, what will be the quality, what is the schedule requirements etc.

Based on these requirements, several bathroom-decorating vendors can make bids, and company can select one of these vendors for its project.

Charters with Work under Contract

All projects should have charters. As we have seen in our previous notes, charters describe the high-level details of the project. **However, there can be different charters for buyer and seller in a project.**

Consider a software project that is executed for bank. If you think from the seller's prospective, the seller is executing the project in order to make profit and to gain revenue from the bank based on the deliverables they will give to the customer.

Nevertheless, if you think from the buyer's prospective, which is the bank, they might be doing the project in order to take a strategical advantage, for instance a technological advance, which will differ their services from the competition.

Moreover, the purpose of the bank could be, getting the market leader position in the banking industry.

Develop Project Management Plan

Second process of integration management knowledge is: develop project management plan process. This process defines strategy for managing the project and the processes in each knowledge area. Project Management Plan of a project describes detailed planning of what needs to be done throughout the project to complete the project successfully and meet the project objectives.

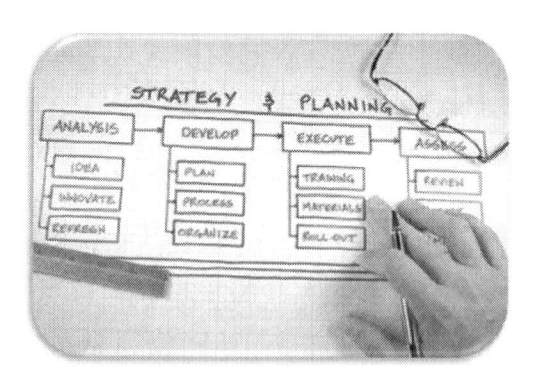

Project Management plan consists of project documents and management plans. A management plan is unique to each project to address its particular needs. For example, cost, risk, or communication of each project is unique. Therefore, unique management plans are required to manage several aspects of projects.

> Creation of management plans is an integral part of a project manager's job.

Creation of management plans is an integral part of a project manager's job. In order to develop an integrated project management plan, all management plans must be interrelated and compliant with each other. Cost management plan, schedule management plan, risk management plan, communication management plan etc. must be compliant with each other to constitute a reasonable and attainable project management plan. For instance, cost management plan describes what will be spent throughout the project. Schedule management plan includes the delivery dates of project deliverables. Human resource management plan includes the details of project team members etc. Cost management plan must include the payments of the project resources described in the human resource management plan and these payments must be done in accordance with the schedule management plan.

We will see in our further notes in detail that each knowledge area has a particular management plan. These management plans are prepared with the inputs of the project stakeholders. However, preparation of management plans and overall project management plan is under the accountability of the project manager.

> A management plan covers how you will define, plan, manage and control the project.

A management plan covers how you will define, plan, manage and control the project. For instance, cost management plan describes the expenses that will be paid throughout the project; risk management plan includes the risks of the project and risk response strategies for these risks in case they occur.

Management plans look forward in time and try to address management concerns. Because, planning means anticipating how certain set of activities will be done in future with the inputs of today and assumptions. With the information available, management plans are produced respectively.

As I said already, there are management plans for all knowledge areas: scope management plan, schedule management plan, cost management plan, quality management plan, human resources management plan, communications management plan, risk management plan, procurement management plan and stakeholder management plan.

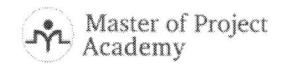

Project Management Plan

Project Management Plan integrates all knowledge area management plans into a cohesive whole. Scope management plan deals with the proper management of scope in a project, cost management plan deals with the expenses, human resource management plan deals with the management of project team members etc.

However, all these plans aim to focus the success of that regarding domain only. Cohesive success of all management plans can be ensured with the integration function of the project management plan.

> Project Management plan includes series of plans.

Project Management plan includes series of plans. This is mainly because of iterations and baselines. Because the actual work will not go as planned no matter how perfect your plan is. Based on variations, changes or actual work, re-planning and respectively re-iteration of the plans might be needed. These can cause to take new baselines in a project.

Project Management Plan includes:

- **Project Management plan includes Project management processes that will be used on the project:** There will be several processes like determine budget process, acquire team process, plan procurement process etc. These processes belong to knowledge areas and process groups as we have seen in our previous notes. Processes that need to be used throughout the project are included in the project management plan.

- **Management plans for knowledge areas:** There are 10 knowledge areas in project management and there should be a particular management plan for each knowledge area respectively.

- **Scope, schedule and cost baselines:** Baselines show the snapshot of the project at a certain time throughout the project. For instance, scope baseline shows what the scope of a project was, schedule baseline shows start and end dates of activities, project duration and completion dates, and cost baseline shows the expense plan of the project. Since there might be change requests or variations from the planned values in the project, new baselines might be taken and each baseline should be stored in the project management plan respectively.

- **Requirements management plan:** Requirements management plan includes how the traceability of the customer requirements from the customer until accomplishment will be ensured. It describes how to get requirements, how to track them throughout the project and how to deliver and get acceptance from the customer.

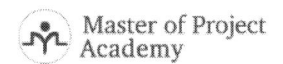

- **Change management plan:** Changes are inevitable in a project. Customer might come with new requirements or their requirements might change as long as they see the outputs of the project. Therefore, change requests might be initiated. How to receive a change request, how to evaluate affects, how to approve, who will be the change control board, how to implement an approved change request etc. are all described in the change management plan.

- **Configuration management plan:** Configuration management mainly deals with the versioning of project work. There will be several versions of components or documents in a project, and several. Consider that you have 2nd version of project management plan and this includes the 4th version of cost management plan, 6th version of schedule management plan, 1st version of procurement management plan. These kinds of versioning of project documents and other components are handled with the help of configuration management plan.

- **Process improvement plan:** If there are repeated set of activities, these should be done better in each next attempt during a project. Either the time to complete same activity shortened, or a weak aspect must be improved etc. How to improve these repeated activities and processes are described in the process improvement plan.

Baseline

Baseline refers to a snapshot of the project taken at a certain time. For instance, a baseline is taken once the project planning is finished, and later in the project, how far the actual results deviated from the plans are compared against the baseline. Alternatively, if a change request is approved, impacts to the cost, schedule etc. are revised in the plans and then a new baseline is taken.

Performance of the project is measured against the cost baseline. Performance measurement baseline is constituted with three different baselines: scope baseline, schedule baseline and cost baseline.

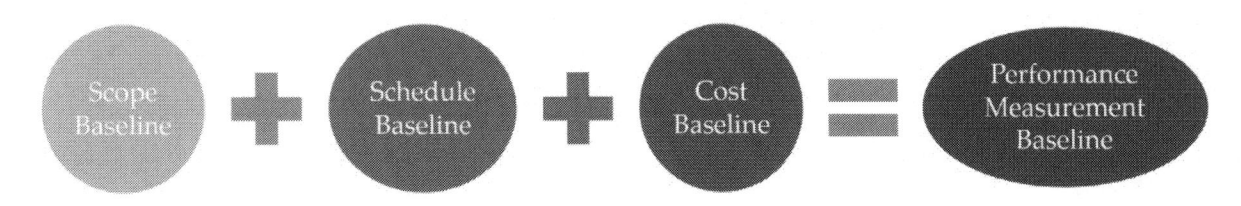

Scope Baseline + Schedule Baseline + Cost Baseline = Performance Measurement Baseline

- **Scope Baseline** includes project scope statement, Work Breakdown Structure, and Work Breakdown structure dictionary.

    - **Project scope statement** includes the work that will be done throughout the project and requirements of the work as well.

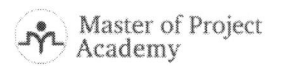

- o **Work Breakdown Structure** shows the hierarchy of the activities, components, and work packages that will help to compete the overall project work. For instance, consider the airplane-manufacturing project. Audio system, multimedia systems etc. are parts of the entertainment system, which is a work package. Other systems like avionic systems, communication system work package all together constitute the completion of an airplane-manufacturing project.
- o **WBS dictionary** provides detailed information about the items in the WBS.

- **Schedule Baseline** describes the agreed-on schedule of the project.
    - o Schedule baseline includes start and end dates of each activity.
    - o It provides milestones in the project and also duration of the project
    - o It includes completion date of the project.

- **Cost baseline** provides time-phased cost budget.
    - o The amount of money that will be spent throughout the project is detailed with the dates that payments will take place and amount that will be paid.
    - o Based on this baseline, company arranges it funding for the project respectively.

> Project manager must look into deviations from baseline when work is being done.

Because after the planning is completed, this plan is agreed on by all stakeholders and everybody expects that actual results will be as planned during planning. Project manager will check during project execution whether there is any variance from the cost baseline, schedule baseline or scope baseline. If there is a risk that will cause to exceed project budget, or if there is a risk that will cause project delay, corrective and preventive actions that will affect the project should be taken.

> Baselines can be changed but it should not be so easy.

Because baselines are for checking how well you could reach to your plans. If baselines are change too frequently, deviations or variance from the initial planning will be deceptive. Therefore, in real world, baselines are generally changed only if there is an approved change request or with the acknowledgement of the project sponsor.

> Changes to baselines can be formally requested during executing or monitoring and controlling process groups.

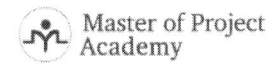

Baseline updates cannot be done easily once they are tied and agreed by the stakeholders. Because baselines will be the reference point to check project performance. Changing this reference point will cause misleading performance measurements respectively. Therefore, baselines are updated with an official request and with the approval of the project sponsor or customer.

> Changes are evaluated and approved in the Perform Integrated Change Control process.

We described this process in our previous notes. Changes are evaluated by the change control board with its impacts to the project. If a change is approved by the change control board, then impacts of the change are revised in the project plans first, and then change implemented respectively.

> Deviations from baseline are often due to incomplete risk identification and risk management.

If there is a deviation from the baseline, for instance if the cost of an activity or item is exceeding the planned values, or if an activity or work package is taking longer than the planned durations, then there might have been an unanticipated work or impact. This is mainly because of improper risk identification and risk management.

Requirements Management Plan

Requirements are mainly acquired from the customers of a project. However, all stakeholders will provide their inputs regarding their expectations from the project. Although all stakeholders and customer might propose requirements for the project, several requirements might not be approved in project scope after evaluations.

> Requirements management plan is part of scope management plan.

Since requirements of a project mainly define what will be delivered throughout the project, requirements management plan is part of scope management plan. Requirements of a project define the scope of the project and determines the project objectives as well.

> ⚡ Requirement management plan describes how requirements will be identified, managed and controlled.

There might be several requirements coming from several stakeholders especially during initiation and planning phase of the project. Some of these requirements might not be feasible or some of the requirements might be conflicting each other. Therefore, requirements are evaluated and only agreed requirements are tried to be accomplished throughout the project. During the execution of the project, it is checked whether determined requirements are ensured with the project deliverables. For instance, requirement traceability matrix we will be seeing in our further notes is a method for tracing which requirement has been met with which deliverable.

Change Management Plan

Although requirements have been determined and scope has been sealed, there might be new requirements of customers or existing requirements might change. Then, project plans are revised to accommodate these changes respectively.

- **Change management plan describes how changes will be managed and controlled:** Each change should be evaluated with its impacts and alternative solutions to implement the change. If a change is approved by the change control board, then it is implemented after project plans have been revised appropriately.
- **While evaluating changes negative effects of the changes should be limited:** Generally, changes affect a project negatively. They might either cause the budget to exceed planned values, or extension in the project duration etc. While evaluating a change, alternative solutions that can be implemented should be analyzed. The optimum solution that will affect the project at minimum should be considered.
- **Changes should not be undertaken lightly:** There might be a small change in a particular activity or in a small component of the project. However, this small change might bring severe impacts on other parts of the project. Therefore, impacts of the change should be examined and planned properly.

Change management plan includes:

- **Change control procedures:** For instance, who can initiate a change request, who can bring it to the change control board, who should analyze the impacts and who will review the impacts etc. are all defined with the procedures in the change management plan.

- **Approval levels for authorizing changes:** Change requests are approved by change control board but there might be different levels to pass to authorize a change. For instance, first the engineers in the change control board can analyze and give the first approval, then senior management reviews the impacts and gives the second approval for the change. If a change passes first and second approval levels, it might be forwarded to sponsor to give the final approval. These kinds of levels for authorizing a change must be documented in the change management plan.

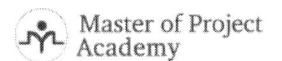

- **Creation of a Change Control Board (CCB) to approve changes:** Change control board consists of people who will review the impacts and possible implementation alternatives of a change. A change can be implemented in a project only if it is approved by the Change Control Board.

- **A plan of how changes will be managed and controlled:** It is detailed in the change management plan as well.

- **Who should attend meetings regarding changes are described in the change management plan:** For instance, project manager, technical leader and architect of the project must be present during change impact analysis meeting. Sponsor, engineer who made the change assessment, project manager and senior manager must be present during change final decision meeting etc. These kinds of who should attend to what must be defined in the change management plan.

- **Organizational tools to use to track and control changes:** Many companies use tools to track and control changes. For instance, PPM of HP or Jira of Atlassian are tools used for tracking a request within a company. It shows the details of request, initiator, history of changes, approval levels and who approved etc. If there are these kinds of tools in the company, these should be stated in the change management plan.

Change Control System

Change Control System includes standardized forms, processes, procedures, and software to track and control changes. How a change can be initiated, what kind of paper work needs to be initiated, how to pass different approval levels to get an approval for a change etc. are all defined in the standardized forms, processes and procedures of the project. There can be a software tool to manage changes in a company. These tools help to manage and coordinate changes especially in big corporate companies. A change is first initiated through this tool with the information of why the change is required, scope of change etc. History of change, who approved and who is the next level approver etc. can be seen with the help of these tools.

> Forms, processes, procedures and software tools that will help in managing changes in a company is all belong to the change control system.

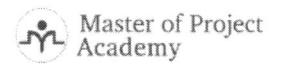

Configuration Management Plan

Configuration Management Plan defines how you will manage changes to deliverables and the resulting documentation, including which organizational tools you will use. In each change that will be made to the management plans, a new version must be taken.

For instance, first version of the scope management plan might be 1.0 and when a new update comes, it might be versioned as 1.1 and if a major update comes, it might be versioned as 2.0 etc. At a certain point through project, there will be several releases of each management plan and these will belong to a version of the project management plan as well.

For instance, project management plan version 1.3 includes scope management plan version 2.2, schedule management plan version 1.5, quality management plan version 1.1 etc. How to do this versioning, including numbering, when a new version will be published, when to take a new version of the project management plan etc. are described in the configuration management plan.

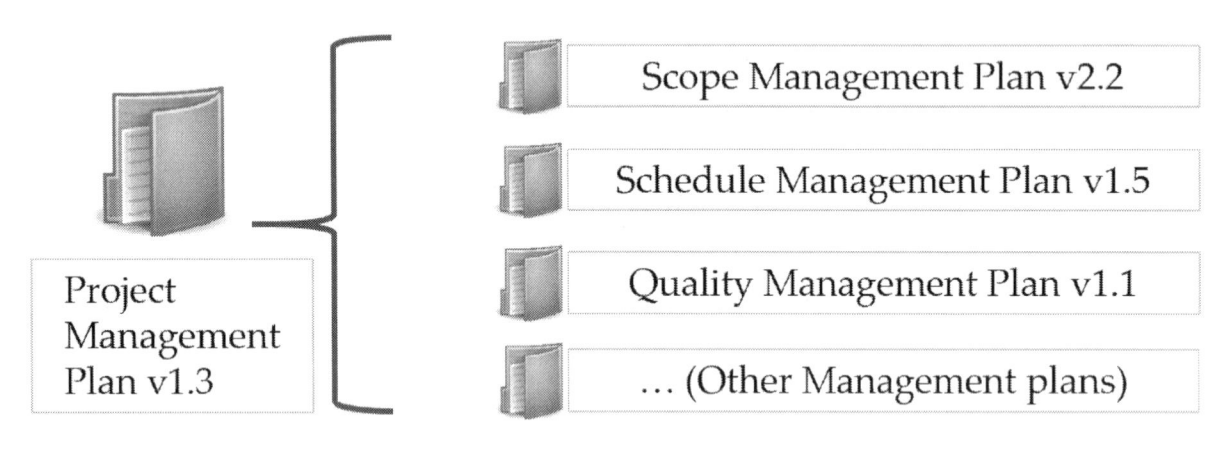

Project Management Plan v1.3
- Scope Management Plan v2.2
- Schedule Management Plan v1.5
- Quality Management Plan v1.1
- ... (Other Management plans)

> Configuration Management plan describes how to do Versioning of changes in a project.

Configuration Management System

Configuration management system helps in managing versioning of project management plans, documents and project components.

Configuration management system includes everything for versioning in a project.

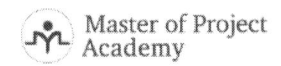

- **Configuration Management system may include Change Control System:** Because major cause of taking a new version for a component, document or plan in a project is a change. Therefore, change control systems might be under the configuration management system in a company.

- **Configuration Management system is Part of Project Management Information System (PMIS):** It contains organization's standardized configuration management tools, processes and procedures. These describe common rules, policies and procedures on how to do versioning in projects.

Process Improvement Plan

There might several processes of a company to manage project. **Project manager identifies existing processes to use on the project and may create some of his or her own.** For instance, scope management process, cost management process, procurement management process etc. of the company might be existing and these existing processes will be used by the project manager throughout the project.

However, new processes that do not exist in the company might be needed for the project. In this case, project manager must initiate to create a new process to deliver project outcomes faster.

For instance, consider that 100 PCs need to be installed during a project. If these PCs will be identical with each other, installation steps will be same for each PC. In order to complete these installations faster after first three installations, project manager should create a process to complete remaining installations faster. For instance, a document including set of steps to complete installation or a software script that will install applications automatically on each PC etc. can be developed to complete installations faster.

> How to improve existing processes and how to produce new processes depending on the project needs must be outlined in process improvement plan.

Summary of Steps

Develop Project Management Plan is a broad process and we have seen many steps until this point. This will be a good point to give a brief summary of what we have seen until now.

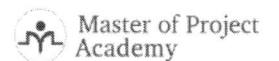

A project starts with a business need. Sponsor or Customer asks, "What do I want". There will be several answers of these questions and these will describe the project requirements. Based on the project requirements, objectives of the project are determined and project scope is defined. Project Scope Statement of work describes what is expected to be achieved by the end of the project.

A project manager is assigned to a project as early as possible.

With the project statement of work, project manager goes through companies' existing culture and systems, processes, procedures and historical info to identify stakeholders and prepare project charter.

Note that, creation of project charter is under the accountability of the project sponsor but project manager might prepare it. However, it must be published by the project sponsor. After project sponsor signs the charter, it is published by the sponsor. Once project charter is published, project is authorized and this will give authority to the project manager to proceed project management activities. Then, project develop project management plan process starts that will produce the project management plan of the project.

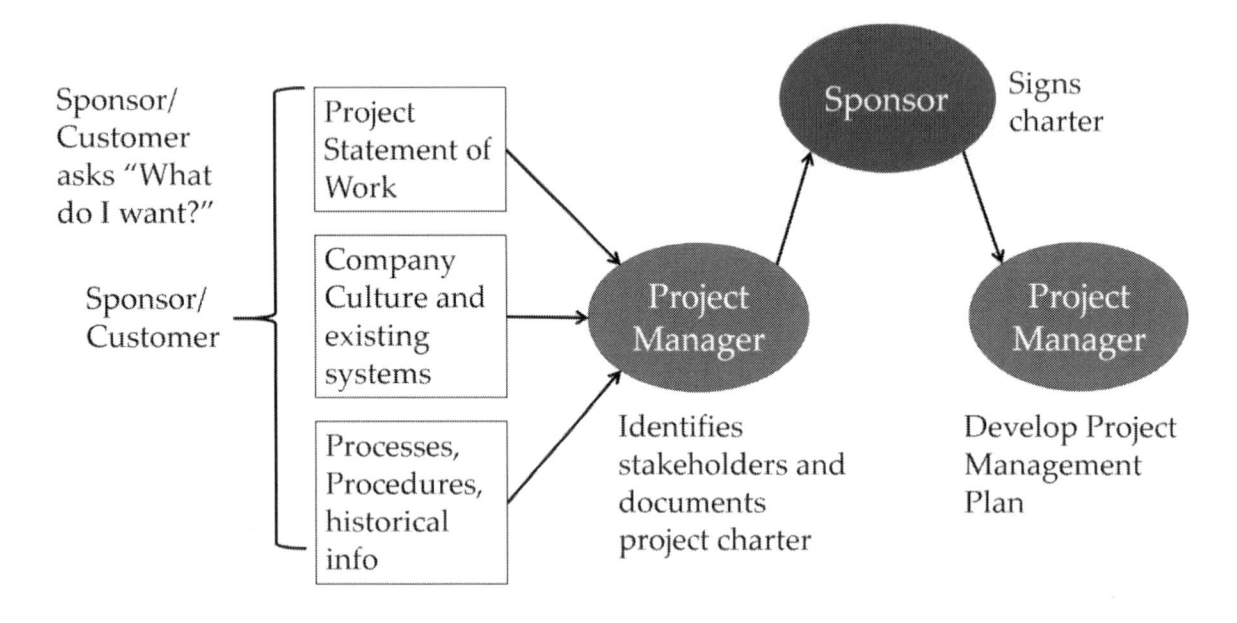

> Project Management Plan needs to be approved by all stakeholders.

Because, stakeholders might affect the success of the project if their expectations or requirements are not met in the project. Once project management plan is finalized, agreement of all stakeholders must be acquired.

Project management plan must be realistic. This means, it should include attainable targets. Consider a project activity that can be completed in 10 days, if you push your project resources to complete it in 5 days, this will be unrealistic. Unrealistic plans cause demotivation in the team since they will not be able to meet the targets. This will affect the project outputs drastically. For instance, demotivation may increase turnover of the resources, due to time pressure quality of the produced work might decrease and customer can be unhappy since the targets are not met. Therefore, realistic and formal plans should be produced.

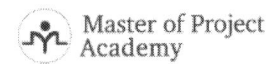

> ★ Everybody in the project needs to believe it can be done according to plan.

If the project targets are attainable, project resources will agree with the plan and will be motivated to complete the work.

Project Management plan is designed to be as complete as possible before executing process group begins. With the information available in the initiating, project planning is finalized. Then project execution starts. Project planning is an iterative and ongoing process throughout the project. As long as the actual results are seen, project plans are revised accordingly.

Project Documents

Any documents used to manage a project is called as project document. Requirements traceability matrix, RACI Matrix, Project charter, procurement papers, assignments sheets and several other documents are called as project documents.

Project documents might be updated during project. As long as new information becomes available or actual results of the project requires updates on other aspects of project, project documents are updated accordingly.

> ★ Project documents are not part of a project management plan.

They exist apart from the project management plans but they are critical for the success of the project as well.

Project charter, statement of work, activity list, quality metrics... etc. can be given as examples for the project documents.

Project Management Plan Approval

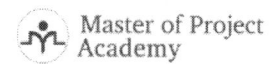

Project management plan must be approved by stakeholders. This is a critical step of the project because stakeholders especially the internal stakeholders will perform the project activities or support the project activities.

If the project management plan is not approved by them, when the time comes to get their support on the project, they might not perform their part since they were not agreeing with the plan.

Project Management plan must receive formal approval by:
- Management
- Sponsor
- Project Team
- And Other stakeholders

> This approval must be acquired formally from the stakeholders. This can be a signature on the project management plan, written approval through email or approval through a software tool used by the company.

Kick-Off Meeting

Kick-off meeting is meeting of all parties just before project execution starts. After the project management plan is finalized and approved by the project stakeholders, next step is starting to execute this project plan during executing phase.

To do this, customer, seller, project team, sponsor and other stakeholders of the project are invited to the project kick-off meeting, which is organized by the project manager. Generally, kick-off meetings have the highest number of participants among the other meetings of the project.

During the kick-off meeting,
- high-level information about the project is provided,
- project objectives are listed,
- major outputs that will be delivered throughout the project are announced and
- milestones of the project are listed.

> The main Purpose of the kick-off meeting is to make sure everyone is on the same page.

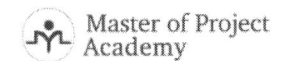

Because after this step, approved project management plan will be executed to meet project objectives and everybody should be clear about the objectives and how the project team will act to reach those objectives.

Direct and Manage Project Work Process

After the project management plan development, executing phase of the project start.

Direct and Manage project work process of the integration management mainly deals with successful management and coordination of project management plan activities to complete the project as planned and to meet the project objectives.

- **Direct and Manage Project Work Process is the integration part of executing process group:** There are lots of executing process group activities and processes under each knowledge area. Main purpose of the direct and manage project work process is coordinating these activities and processes to produce project outputs as planned.

- **Direct and Manage Project Work process involves managing people, doing the work and implementing approved changes:** Project management plan activities are performed during executing phase and this is ensured with the help of Direct and Manage Project work process mainly. If there are variances in the actual results from the planned values, change requests might be raised and if approved, these change requests are implemented with the help of direct and manage project work process.

- **Direct and Management Project work involves requesting changes and completing the work accompanying approved change requests:** If there is a variance that needs to be corrected or there is a defect, request change is done in this process. For instance, consider that your actual results show that you are 10% behind of the planned schedule, and you will exceed the project budget by $30,000 once you completed the project. These variances must be corrected and a revised plan must be produced to accommodate these variances. Alternatively, consider that, scope of the project is developing a custom software for a customer. During acceptance tests, customer finds an issue that does not meet their requirements. If this requirement was in scope but could not be delivered properly, this is called defect. These kinds of corrections for the project variances and defect repairs are implemented during direct and manage project work process.

Now, we will see what can trigger to start direct and manage project work process and what direct and manage project work process can trigger throughout the project.

```
                                    ┌─────────────────────────┐
                                    │  New Change Requests    │
                                    └─────────────────────────┘
                                    ┌─────────────────────────┐
                                    │  Deliverables           │
                                    └─────────────────────────┘
┌──────────────────┐                ┌─────────────────────────┐
│ Project Planning │                │  Work Performance       │
└──────────────────┘                │  Information            │
                       ╔═════════╗  └─────────────────────────┘
                       ║Direct and║
                       ║ Manage   ║  ┌─────────────────────────┐
┌──────────────────┐   ║ Project  ║  │ Implemented, previously │
│ Approved Changes │   ║  Work    ║  │ approved changes,       │
│ Corrective Actions│  ╚═════════╝  │ corrective actions,     │
│ Preventive Actions│               │ preventive actions, and │
│ Defect Repair    │               │ defect repair           │
└──────────────────┘               └─────────────────────────┘
                                    ┌─────────────────────────┐
                                    │ Updates to project      │
                                    │ management plan and     │
                                    │ project documents       │
                                    └─────────────────────────┘
```

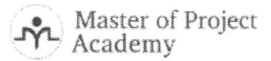

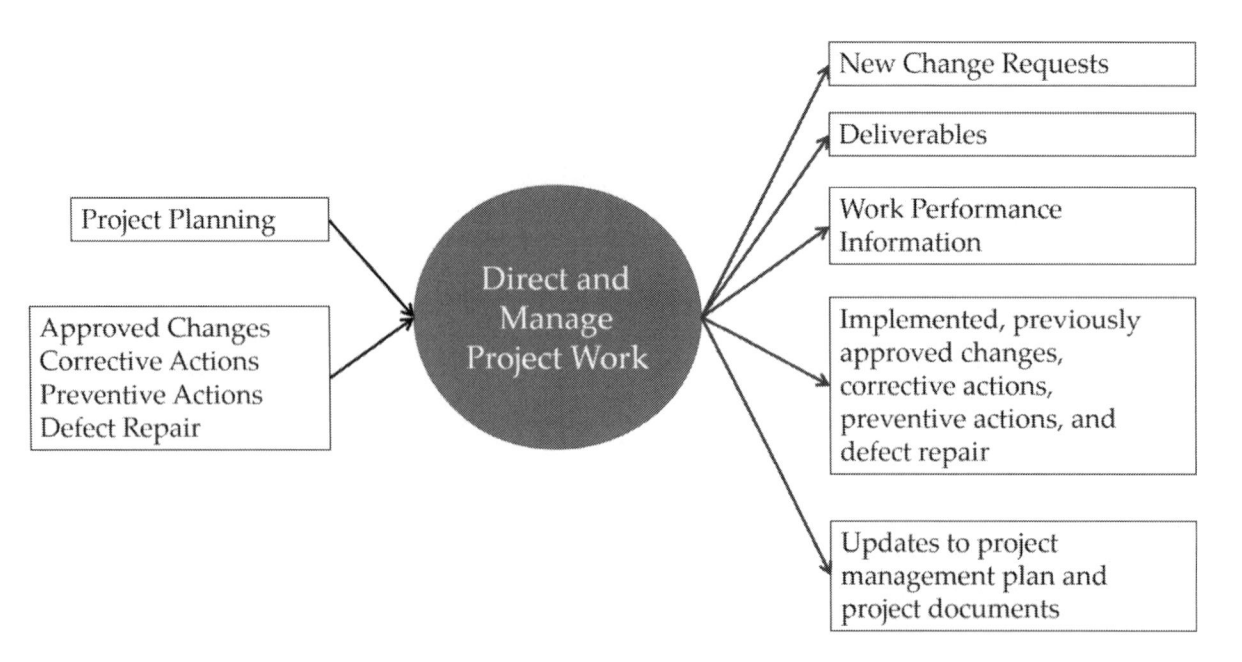

- **Completion of project planning is the major input for starting direct and manage project work process:** Because, once the project plan is finalized, executing phase starts to implement the project activities planned in project planning and Direct and Manage Project work process is triggered. This process will trigger other executing processes of other knowledge areas to complete the project work successfully.
- **Another input to start Direct and Manage Project work process is Approved changes, corrective actions, preventive actions and defect repair:** If a change is approved by the change control board, implementation of the approved change is executed by the Direct and Manage Project Work process. We will see corrective and preventive actions and defect repair in detail in our next heading. Briefly, corrective actions are taken for variance that happened already, preventive actions are taken for future risks to reduce their impacts and defect repair is done for the problems identified during quality assurance, for instance in testing.

What can be the outputs of Direct and Manage Project work process?
- **New change requests:** During executing project activities, customer might come with new requirements or their existing requirements might change. In this case, change request is submitted and evaluated by the change control board. If it is approved, then it is implemented in Direct and Manage Project work process again.
- **Deliverables:** The main purpose of the direct and manage project work process is producing the planned project deliverables and final product of the project.
- **Work Performance information:** While executing phase progresses and deliverables are produced, actual results will not be exactly as planned. Some activities might take longer to complete while some activities are completed earlier. On the other hand, some activities might be costly than the planned values while other activities will spend less money. These actual results and produced outputs are measured against the baseline with the determined metrics to check how well project is progressing.
- **Implementation of approved changes, corrective actions and defect repairs** are also outputs of Direct and Manage Project Work process.

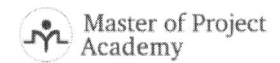

- **Updates to project management plan and project documents:** Based on the actual results of the projects, implemented corrective or preventive actions and defect repairs, project plans might require revisions. Because to meet the project objectives, future activities of the project must be revised based on the results of the actual results. This requires updates in project management plan and project documents respectively.

Corrective Action, Preventive Action & Defect Repair

You will hear corrective action, preventive action and defect repair too frequently in project management world.

Actually, we have gone over these terms in our previous notes. Nevertheless, during this heading, we will give details and samples for each of them to illustrate these better in your mind.

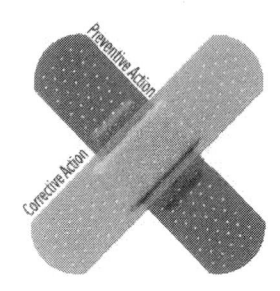

- **Corrective action**: It is an activity that realigns the performance of the project work with the project management plan. No matter how perfect your project plan is, you will have variances in project execution. Actual results will differ from the planned values. To meet the project objectives such as project budget and schedule, you need to take actions accordingly. Otherwise, you cannot meet the objectives.

   For instance, consider that you are managing a smartphone project. During monitoring and controlling, your performance results showed that project is 10% behind the planned schedule. In order to meet the project objectives, project must be completed on time if there is not a new requirement coming from the customer or if there is not an approved change request. To meet the agreed schedule, there is only one way. Future tasks of the project must be completed faster than planned to finish the project on time. To do this, you can request extra resources for the project and assign them to future activities to complete remaining scope in a shorter time.

- **Preventive Action:** It is an activity that ensures the future performance of the project work is aligned with the project management plan. What differs the corrective and preventive actions is, corrective actions are taken based on happened actual results while preventive actions are taken for a future anticipated risk.

   For instance, consider that one of the senior engineers in your project team might resign in 2 months and if he resigns, there will be knowhow loss and handing over his tasks to a new engineer will take time and this will affect the project schedule respectively. As you see, this is a risk but not happened. However, a response strategy must exist to accommodate the impacts of this risk if it happens. Preventive action for this risk can be know-how transfer from this senior engineer to other project resources and documenting the knowhow of this engineer to not lose the critical competence of the project.

- **Defect Repair:** It is an activity to modify a nonconforming product or product component. Once a product or deliverable is complete, it must be checked whether it meets the requirements. If there are problems with the product or deliverable, these problems must be fixed by the project team before handing over to the customer.

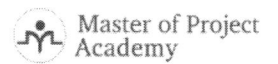

For instance, consider that camera of the smartphone that is developed in the project does not activate flash automatically when taking photos at night. If this was a requirement determined in the beginning, this must be fixed. This is called defect repair.

> Remember, the approved change requests in a project can be
> - Corrective Action,
> - Preventive Action or
> - Defect Repair.

Because change requests are submitted if there is a new requirement in the project, to correct the variances, prevent the impacts of any kinds of risks and fixing defects.

Manage Project Knowledge Process

Main purpose of the manage project knowledge process is **using existing knowledge in the organization and project team, and creating new knowledge to ensure a successful project completion.** An organization will have a corporate history from experiences and projects.

When initiating a new project, project team will use this existing knowledge. For instance, lessons learned from a previous similar project, actual completion durations of activities etc. will be very beneficial to use when planning the new project.

Throughout the project, when the project team is using existing knowledge and gaining experience, they will have new knowledge. This new knowledge will bring benefits to the project and organization as well.

> Main output of this process is lessons learned register.

Main output of this process is lessons learned register document. Lessons learned register is created very early in the project and it is updated throughout the project as new knowledge is created, experiences are earned and project team shares their thoughts. There is a common misconception about lessons learned documentation that, many people think that lessons learned documentation is prepared at the end of the project. This is not correct. Lessons learned documentation must be started early in the project and it must be updated throughout the project.

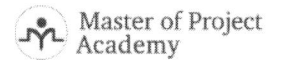

Knowledge can be explicit or tacit.

- **Explicit knowledge** can be documented using words, pictures, numbers etc. For instance, if a software developer knows how to write a code, and if he can document this, this is an example of explicit knowledge.

- **Tacit knowledge** is personal and cannot be documented easily. Based on the experiences, beliefs, insights and expertise, people earn tacit knowledge. When you ask a critical about what to do to a senior professional and junior professional, their approach will be different. Even if they have same theoretical experience and background, with the experience of years and tacit knowledge, most probably, senior professional will provide answers that are more reasonable.

> Knowledge management is making sure that the previous and new skills, experience and expertise will be shared among the organization.

Monitor and Control Project Work Process

Monitor and Control Project Work process mainly aims to check whether the project is progressed as planned.

If a variance is detected during monitoring and controlling, change requests are submitted to get back on track on the project.

- **Control function done from initiating until closing.** Because each step, each action, each process needs to be controlled. There are certain set of activities to follow in a project and these must be checked whether this sequence is followed in the project.

- **Results of the monitor and control project work process are Change Requests and updates to project management plan and project documents.** Because based on monitoring and controlling activities results, if there is a variance in the project from the planned values, this variance must be corrected. For instance, if there is a variance in schedule, it must be corrected to meet the project deadline. If there is a risk that might affect the project in future, its preventive action must be taken or if the produced outputs do not meet the project criteria, then defects must be fixed. These might be change requests as well and in order to implement these change requests, project plans and documents must be revised accordingly.

- **Change requests are evaluated in Perform Integrated Change Control process.** Because a small change in a project can have a high impact on other parts of the project. Perform integrated change control process evaluates a change, analyzes its impacts on the project and provide alternative solutions to implement the change. By this way, optimum way to implement a change is determined.

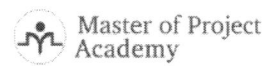

- **Monitor and Control Project work process involves monitoring performance measures.** In order to detect whether project is going as planned, these measurements are must. For instance, budget performance measurement of the project will show whether the planned budget can be met, schedule performance of the project will show whether the project will be completed on planned date etc. Actually, these performance measurements are inputs for submitting a change request. Because based on these measurements, if project is at risk of falling behind of the baseline values, changes are requested and implemented to get back on track.

- **Work Authorization System might be used in monitor and control project work process.** Work authorization system is mainly used to assign a task to a project team member officially over a corporate tool. If there are deviations in the start or end dates of project activities in the work authorization system, this might be an indication of variance that needs to be controlled within monitor and control project work process.

- **There will always be changes in projects.** Even if you make a perfect project plan, actual results will be different from the planned values. In order to align future work of the project work based on the actual results, change requests will be submitted.

Perform Integrated Change Control Process.

We have seen in our previous notes that there will be change requests in a project and these will be evaluated by the change control board. If the change requests are approved, these changes will be implemented in the project respectively.

- **The changes in a project are accepted/rejected/handled in Perform Integrated Change control process.** From submission of a change request until its implementation and closure, perform integrated change control process ensures the successful change management in a project.

- **A change in one of the constraints should be evaluated for impacts on all of the other constraints.** Consider that you are managing a software project. Assume that database of the project stores the members as account id, name and surname respectively. If a change request asks to change name and surname orders in the database, this might be a very small change from the perspective of database work. Nevertheless, if there are many other parts in the software, which is depending on this name/surname order, they will be affected and changes might be required on those parts as well. Perform integrated change control process aims to evaluate the impacts of a change end-to-end.

- **In order to evaluate the impacts of a change, it is necessary to have Realistic Project Management Plan and a complete product and project scope.** Because only a complete project plan and scope can include the interdependencies of activities or components of a project. With the help of these complete plans and scope, impact of a change can be evaluated properly on other parts of the project.

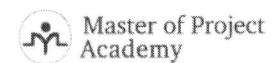

- **Generally, project manager should prevent the root cause of the need for changes.** Because, frequent changes cause frequent updates and revisions in the plan and this requires rework. Project targets and dates generally change by implementing a change request in the project. This might cause demotivation of the team as well. Because project objectives and target dates will change too frequently.

- **It is expected that companies have established procedures for managing and controlling changes.** Evaluation of a change and implementation in a project is a complex procedure. How to evaluate a change, how to analyze the impacts, steps for approving a change, how to implement an approved change etc. must be documented by processes, policies and procedures.

- **If there are lots of changes in a project, it will be impossible to coordinate the work.** Many change requests mean either the planning was not properly done or requirements could not be gathered and addressed properly. Because change requests come from the customers or if there is a variance in the project. If there are many change requests in a project, requirement evaluation and planning should be overviewed.

Project Manager should make sure to:

- **Work to obtain final requirements ASAP.** This is a very critical factor for the success of a project. Because requirements are foundations of the project scope. Once the project scope is determined, project planning starts. Therefore, incomplete or improper requirement gathering will cause an incomplete and weak planning respectively. The result will be several change requests during project execution.

- **Spend enough time in risk management to identify the risks.** Because risks are the primary causes of variances in a project. Each risk might be identified during project planning and a response strategy for each risk must be addressed. By this way, once a risk occurs, how to accommodate the impacts of risks will be ready and this will reduce the level of variances in a project.

- **Come up with time and cost reserves.** Once you planned the project, completed budget plan, schedule plan etc., you should bear in mind that actual results will not be as same as you planned. Especially if risks occur, these will cause additional costs and delays in projects. Therefore, once the planning is complete, project manager should also plan time and cost buffers for the impacts of risks. For instance, if a project will be completed in 1 year with a 1-million-dollar budget, time reserve for this can be 2 months and budget reserve can be 1 hundred thousand dollars. These cost and time reserves should be included in the final project plan.

- **Have a process in place to control changes.** Changes are inevitable in projects and how to submit changes, how to evaluate, how to approve and implement these changes must be clearly documented in processes.

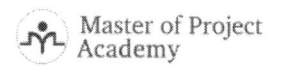

- **Follow the process to control changes.** While managing, coordinating and implementing changes, these processes must be followed to complete a change successfully.

- **Have a process and templates in place for creating change requests.** Submitting a change request might require a certain set of information to be provided. For instance, initiator of the change request, reason of the change, effects of change, history and flow of approval etc. This information will be required for each change request therefore having a template will ease to submit and progress changes in a project.

- **Have clear roles and responsibilities for approving changes.** Changes are evaluated by change control board but there can be different approval levels and, in each level, approval of different stakeholders might be required. For instance, first level analysis and approval can be given by the engineers, 2nd level approval can be given by the senior managers, 3rd and the last approval can be required from the project sponsor. These must be cleared out to manage changes smoothly in a project.

- **Re-evaluate the business case if the number of changes become excessive.** Lots of change request occurs if the requirements analysis and management could not be done properly or if the project planning was not done properly. Since business need is the initiator of a project, and source of requirements, in case there will be lots of change requests in a project, business need caused the initiation of the project must be re-evaluated.

- **Consider terminating a project that has excessive changes and starting a new project with a more complete set of requirements.** Lots of changes in a project will cause to lose track of the project, demotivation of team members due to frequently changing objectives and problems in performance measurement as well. Therefore, if there are lots of change requests in a project, terminating the current project and re-initiating a new project that will have concrete and complete requirements will be more reasonable.

- **Allow only approved changes to be added to the project baselines.** There can be several change requests in a project but after the evaluation of change control board, many of them might be rejected. Only approved changes must be implemented in a project. Respectively, only approved changes should be reflected in project plans, documents and baselines.

Change Control Board (CCB)

Change Control Board is abbreviated as CCB.

Many projects have Change Control Board. Because project will receive, change requests and these must be evaluated by change control board.

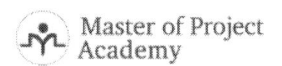

- **The change control board is responsible for reviewing and analyzing change requests.** Once a change request is submitted, this is analyzed by the change control board. Impacts of the change on the project are assessed. For instance, a new requirement coming from the customer might require additional 3 weeks' time to develop and $50,000 cost to fund the implementation. In addition, some technical impacts can be assessed and reviewed by the change control board as well. For instance, a customer request one of its databases to be accessible by public users, and this might be causing security issues by the company. These kinds of impacts are assessed, analyzed and evaluated by the change control board.

- **Based on the impacts and alternative solutions to implement the change control board approves or rejects changes.** Only the changes approved by the change control board can be implemented in a project.

- **Change Control Board may include,**
    - Project Manager,
    - Experts,
    - Customer,
    - Sponsor, etc.

Process for Making Changes

Changes in a project must be assessed, evaluated and implemented through a set of structured and planned activities.

During this heading, we will go through process for making changes. There are 8 major steps for making a change in a project. We will go over these 8 steps one-by-one.

1. **Prevent the root cause of changes.** First preventive action that must be taken against changes is prevention of changes. Because too much changes cause too much planning, management and coordination issues, demotivation of the project team members etc. Therefore, root cause of the changes must be eliminated in a project.

2. **Identify change.** Although you take all preventive actions, it is inevitable that your project will receive changes. Once change is received, it must be identified. Identification includes what is the reason of the change, what is the aim of the change, who initiates the change etc.

3. **Look at the impact of change:** After change is identified, impacts of the change are evaluated. These impacts include both to the product of the project and to the project performance. For instance, change in an existing requirement of a project might bring additional features to the end product. However, it might require $100,000 additional cost and 2 months' development time. These kinds of impacts are analyzed.

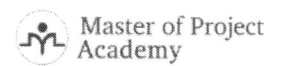

4. **Create a change request.** After change impact, analysis change request is submitted. Change request is submitted once identification and impact analysis are finished. Actually, change request submission authorizes a change officially.

5. **Perform integrated change control.** Perform integrated change control process belongs to monitoring and controlling phase of the integration management knowledge area. After a change is requested officially, this process ensures successful analysis of the change, evaluation and if it is approved, implementation respectively. There are 4 steps of perform integrated change control process:
    - **Assess the change.** The origin of the change request, the scope of the change and the main purpose of change are analyzed. Impacts of the change are evaluated.
    - **Look for options.** Identify the options for implementing the change. There can be different alternatives to implement a change request. These alternatives include alternatives from technical and project management point of you. The main reason of this is, finding the best implementation option that will affect the project least.
    - **After the change is evaluated, change is approved or rejected.** Impacts of the change are analyzed by the change control board and options to implement the change are reviewed. Based on the evaluation of change control board, change is either rejected or approved. Only approved change requests are progressed further to implement.
    - **After reject or approval decision, status of the change is recorded in the change control system.** By this way, evaluation history of a former change request can be seen in future.

Note that, the step number 6, 7 and 8 are executed only if the change is approved by the change control board.

6. **Adjust the project management plan, project documents and baselines.** If a change is approved, impacts of this change are updated in the project management plan, documents and baselines. For instance, if an additional $100,000 and 2 months' development time is required, these are updated in the project baseline.

7. **Manage stakeholders' expectations by communicating the change to stakeholders affected by the change.** An approved change will affect the product of the project, time plan, cost plan etc. Therefore, the impacts of the change and new objectives of the project must be communicated to the stakeholders appropriately after a change is approved and plans have been revised accordingly.

8. **Manage the project to the revised project management plan and project documents.** After the plans are revised to cover the implementation of the change as well, new revised plan is executed. This will ensure the successful implementation of the change as well.

High Level Process for Making Changes

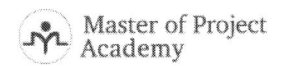

Remembering the eight steps for making a change might be hard. Therefore, we share a 4-steps process for making changes.

1. **Evaluate the impact.** When a change is received, how it affects the scope, product, cost, schedule etc. must be evaluated.

2. **Create options:** Several alternatives to implement the change must be assessed. This is important to identify the least affecting implementation option.

3. **Get the change request approved internally.** After the evaluation of the change, impacts, and alternatives to implement, change control board either accepts or rejects a change. Only approved change requests can be applied in a project.

4. **Get customer buy-in.** Changes will affect the final project product, budget, schedule etc. These updates in the project must be communicated to the project stakeholders respectively. Because knowing the up-to-date objectives of the project is a crucial success factory.

Close Project or Phase Process

This is the last process of integration management knowledge area.

Close project or phase process aims to finalize a project officially in an organization.

- **Focuses on closing out all knowledge areas.** Several processes and activities are executed in all other knowledge areas. Close project or phase process will ensure successful completion of these activities and processes as well. Main purpose is collecting all project documents, getting final acceptance, archiving documents and finalizing the project officially.

- **A project must be closed even if it stops or it is terminated.** Projects can be terminated if it is seen that the project objectives are no longer valid, or project objectives will not be met. Even if it is the termination, project closure must be done appropriately. Why the project is terminated, reasons of termination, last status of the project, last performance of the project, latest project documents etc. must be collected and archived in the organizational process assets library. This is crucial because when a similar project will be initiated, records of this project can be checked to get lessons from the termination.

- **Getting final approval of the overall project from customer.** A project can be closed only if the customer approves the final product of the project. Therefore, an official approval of the customer must be acquired at this process. This can be a sign-off, written approval, email stating the acceptance etc. Once the approval is acquired, project documents are collected archived and project is finalized.

Quiz – Section 3

1- Which of the following BEST describes the aim of Integration Management in a project?
   A) Providing a high-level overview of the project
   B) Linking strategy of the company with the project objectives
   C) Integrating Planning and Executing process groups
   D) Putting all pieces of a project into a cohesive whole

2- Project Charter is an output of Develop Project Charter process. All of the following about project charter is true EXCEPT:
   A) First step of integration management
   B) Created during planning and executing process groups
   C) Authorizes the existence of the project
   D) Provides authority to project manager

3- During creation of your project charter, you mentioned that "Kelly Watson will be the leader of the project, and she has the authority to send executive progress reports and manage the project budget". This defines:
   A) Project Title and Description
   B) Business Case
   C) Project Manager Assigned and Authority Level
   D) Resources Pre-assigned

4- You are working as a project manager in a construction company. In your new project, a new hotel is built nearby a lake. Who are the stakeholders of this project?
   A) Resident living close to lake
   B) Civil engineer working in the project
   C) Owner and sponsor of the project
   D) All of the above

5- You are working as a project manager in a smart phone manufacturer. During your meetings with your customer, you have noted the following:
a.   Smart phone must have an 8 MP camera
b.   Smart phone must support Wi-Fi and 3G
c.   Smart phone must not be heavier than 60 grams
These are examples of:
   A) Stakeholder Requirements
   B) Product Description
   C) Project Approval Requirements
   D) None of the above

6- You are working as a project manager in a software company. Which of the following can be a measurable project objective?
   A) Delivering a good software application
   B) Having an application which will have nice screens
   C) Completing project in 6 months, with a 500.000 USD budget
   D) Delivering an application with very few defects

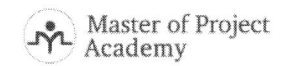

7- All of the following are benefits of project charter EXCEPT:
A) Links project to ongoing work of the organization
B) Having a charter eliminates the necessity of a detailed project plan
C) Recognizes the project
D) High-level requirements of the project are defined

8- Which of the following is NOT an Economic Model for project selection?
A) Present Value
B) Internal Rate of Return
C) Payback Period
D) Project Scoring

9- You have just started to your project. Customer made the initial payment, 50.000 USD after you started to your project and there will be two more 50.000 USD installments at the end of 1st and 2nd year respectively. If your company uses present value as project selection method and if yearly interest rate is 10%, which of the following is true?
A) Present value of the total project is less than 150.000 USD
B) Present value of the total project is 150.000 USD
C) Present value of the total project is more than 150.000 USD
D) Present value of the total project cannot be determined with the provided information

10- Your company is using net present value as economic model when selecting projects. Currently, three projects are evaluated:
a. Project A: NPV = 100.000 USD and project length = 6 months
b. Project B: NPV = 200.000 USD and project length = 2 years
c. Project C: NPV = 50.000 USD and project length = 1 month

Which of these projects should be selected?
A) Project A
B) Project B
C) Project C
D) Information provided is not sufficient

11- If your company uses Internal Rate of Return (IRR) as a project selection method, which of the following projects should be selected?
A) Project A with IRR = 4%
B) Project B with IRR = 9%
C) Project C with IRR = 11%
D) Project D with IRR = 13%

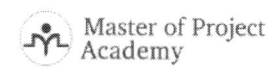

12- Payback Period is one of the economic models used in project selection. All of the following about payback period is correct EXCEPT:
   A) Payback period is the number of time periods to recover investment of a project.
   B) Projects with shorter payback periods should be selected
   C) Projects with longer payback periods should be selected
   D) If payback period is 3 months for a project where 100.000 USD has been invested initially, it will generate 100.000 USD revenue in 3 months after project has been accomplished.

13- In your construction project, a worker builds up 5 meters of wall in a day. Since this task has been delayed and needs to be finished as soon as possible, you decided to put another worker to work on building up this wall. When you checked again the status, you have seen that 2 workers started to build up 8 meters of wall in a day instead of 10 meters of wall. This can be explained by:
   A) Team ineffectiveness
   B) Opportunity Cost
   C) Demotivation
   D) Law of diminishing returns

14- Your company uses straight line depreciation when valuing vehicles and equipment. A truck that has been bought two years ago for 300.000 USD is now valued for 260.000 USD. What will be the value of truck after three years from now?
   A) 220.000 USD
   B) 200.000 USD
   C) 180.000 USD
   D) 150.000 USD

15- All of the following about Project Statement of Work (SOW) are correct EXCEPT:
   A) Created by customer or project sponsor
   B) Defines needs and product scope of project
   C) Includes resources of the project
   D) Describes how project fits to customer's strategic plan

16- Management Plans of project are created during Develop Project Management Plan Process. Which of the following is NOT true about Management Plans?
   A) Looks back in time to find problematic parts of the project
   B) Unique to each project
   C) Created by project manager
   D) Covers how the project will be managed and controlled

17- Project Management Plan integrates all knowledge area management plans into a cohesive whole. Project Management Plan includes all of the following EXCEPT:
   A) Processes that will be used in project
   B) Scope, Schedule and Cost Baselines
   C) Change Management Plan
   D) Lessons Learned Document

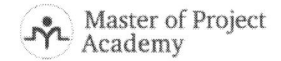

18- Performance Measurement Baseline is used to evaluate performance of the project during monitor and control process group. Performance Measurement Baseline includes all of the following EXCEPT:
   A) Risk Baseline
   B) Scope Baseline
   C) Schedule Baseline
   D) Cost Baseline

19- Scope baseline of a project includes all of the following EXCEPT:
   A) WBS
   B) WBS Dictionary
   C) Procurement Statement of Work
   D) Project Scope Statement

20- Three baselines of a project created during planning processes are scope baseline, cost baseline and schedule baseline. Which of the following is NOT true about baselines?
   A) Baselines help to see deviations during project execution
   B) All changes to project must be reflected in baselines as well
   C) Changes to baselines should be formally requested
   D) Deviations from baselines often occur due to incomplete risk management activities

21- Change Management Plan describes how changes will be managed and controlled. Change Management Plan includes all of the following EXCEPT:
   A) Change control procedures
   B) Risks of project
   C) Participants of change meetings
   D) Approval levels for changes

22- Which of the following is NOT a Project Document?
   A) Scope Management Plan
   B) Project Charter
   C) Activity List
   D) Project Statement of Work

23- Which of the following BEST describes Kick-Off meeting?
   A) First meeting of project manager after he/she is assigned to the project
   B) First meeting of project manager when requirements gathering started
   C) Makes sure everyone is on the same page before execution of project starts
   D) First status meeting of project after execution starts

24- Which process of the Integration Management Knowledge area includes managing people and doing the project work?
   A) Monitor & Control Project Work
   B) Perform Integrated Change Control
   C) Develop Project Management Plan
   D) Direct and Manage Project Work

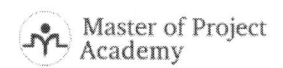

25- Which of the following processes' main output is the Lessons Learned Register document?
   A) Monitor & Control Project Work
   B) Manage Project Knowledge
   C) Develop Project Management Plan
   D) Direct and Manage Project Work

26- During execution of your project, you notified that work of software developers might be lost if server is corrupted. In order to avoid this problem, you have scheduled daily backups of the developed work. This is an example of:
   A) Corrective Action
   B) Preventive Action
   C) Defect Repair
   D) Risk Assessment

27- You are working as a project manager in a car manufacturer. Your customer required you to develop a car, which can reach to 100km/h in 10 seconds. During your tests, you have realized that car can reach to 100km/h in 10.5 seconds. You have to perform additional activities to reach this speed in 10 seconds. This is an example of:
   A) Corrective Action
   B) Preventive Action
   C) Defect Repair
   D) None of the above

28- Which of the following is an example for corrective action?
   A) Putting extra resource for an activity which is already late and getting delayed
   B) Planning activities for a problem that might happen in future
   C) Fixing a software problem occurred during customer acceptance tests
   D) Planning dates for project deliverables

29- One of the civil engineers in your construction project will leave the project at the end of the month. A new engineer will be joining the team and he will hand over what he did in the project through a documentation. Civil engineer writes down the details of the project in the hand over document. This is an example of:
   A) Tacit Knowledge
   B) Explicit Knowledge
   C) Know-How Knowledge
   D) Intuitive Knowledge

30- Which of the following can be an example of Approved Change Request?
   A) Corrective Action
   B) Preventive Action
   C) Defect Repair
   D) All of the above

31- Which of the following is NOT done during Monitor and Control Project Work Process?
   A) Implementation of an approved change request

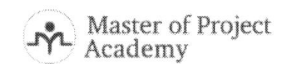

B) Control of the project from initiating to closing
C) Generation of change requests
D) Monitoring performance of the project

32- Changes are inevitable in a project. Changes are accepted, rejected and handled in which of the following processes?
A) Monitor and Control Project Work Process
B) Change Control Process
C) Change Management Process
D) Perform Integrated Change Control Process

33- Which of the following is NOT true about a project manager's role during integration management?
A) Spend enough time in risk management to identify the risks
B) Start the project as soon as first requirements have been obtained
C) Come up with time and cost reserves
D) Follow the process to control changes

34- Your project started to receive so many change requests and these change requests started to be excessive. Which of the following would be BEST action?
A) Evaluating every change request and deciding for every change request in status meetings
B) Escalating the issue to Change Control Board
C) Terminating the project and starting a new project with a complete set of requirements
D) Only doing the change requests that will not affect baselines

35- Which of the following is responsible for analyzing, approving and rejecting change requests in a project?
A) Change Control Board
B) Change Management Team
C) Project Management Team
D) Project Change Leaders

36- During your customer acceptance tests, customer wanted a new feature to be included in final product and raised a change request. You evaluated the impacts of the change request, which of the following is NEXT step?
A) Reject the Change
B) Get approval for the Change Request
C) Implement the Change if it does not affect your plans
D) Create options for implementing change request

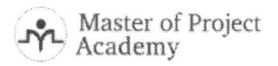

37- Close Project or Phase is a process of integration management knowledge area. Which of the following is NOT true about this process?
A) All project work must have been completed before entering this process
B) Final approval is got from customer
C) Focuses on closing all knowledge areas
D) If a project has been terminated, close project or phase process can be skipped

Answers

1 – D	21 – B
2 – B	22 – A
3 – C	23 – C
4 – D	24 – D
5 – A	25 – B
6 – C	26 – B
7 – B	27 – C
8 – D	28 – A
9 – A	29 – B
10 – B	30 – D
11 – D	31 – A
12 – C	32 – D
13 – D	33 – B
14 – B	34 – C
15 – C	35 – A
16 – A	36 – D
17 – D	37 – D
18 – A	
19 – C	
20 – B	

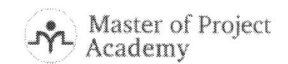

Mapping Game – Section 3

Left	Right
A document that provides authority to Project Manager.	IRR (Internal Rate of Return) Example
Today's value of future cash flows	Explicit
12% of the investment will return in 2 years	Examples of work performance data
series of phases that a project passes through from its initiation to its closure	Project Charter
actual cost, actual duration, and the percent of work completed. Examples	Tacit
knowledge that is personal and difficult to express	Autocratic
knowledge that can be readily codified using words, pictures, and numbers	Present Value
A decision-making technique	Project Life Cycle
It is used to forecast future performance based on past results.	Trend Analysis

Note: An arrow connects "actual cost, actual duration, and the percent of work completed. Examples" to "Examples of work performance data".

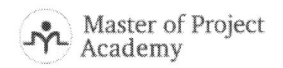

Answers

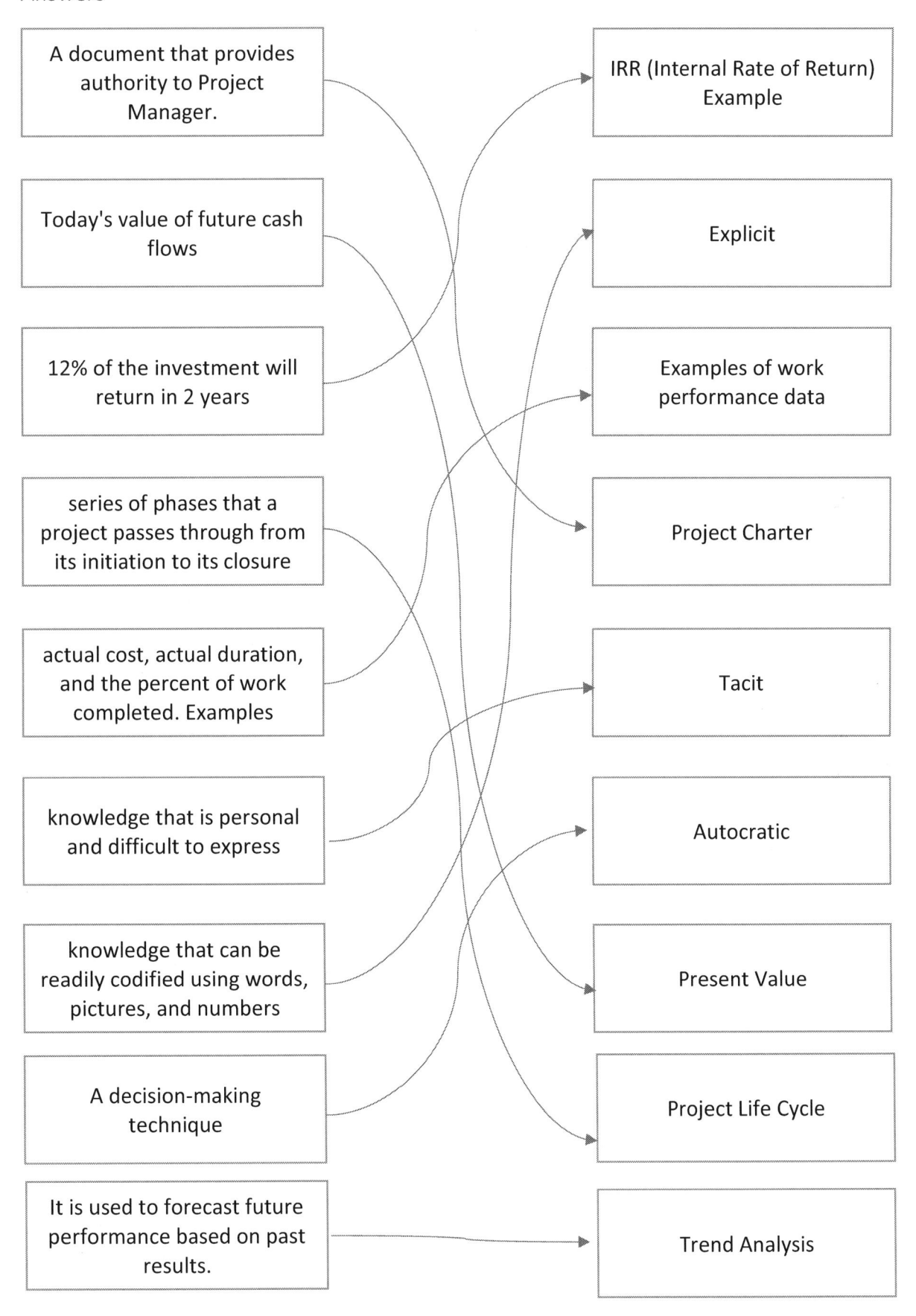

Left	Right (matched)
A document that provides authority to Project Manager.	Project Charter
Today's value of future cash flows	Present Value
12% of the investment will return in 2 years	IRR (Internal Rate of Return) Example
series of phases that a project passes through from its initiation to its closure	Project Life Cycle
actual cost, actual duration, and the percent of work completed. Examples	Examples of work performance data
knowledge that is personal and difficult to express	Tacit
knowledge that can be readily codified using words, pictures, and numbers	Explicit
A decision-making technique	Autocratic
It is used to forecast future performance based on past results.	Trend Analysis

Section 4

Scope Management

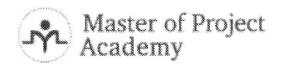

Section 4 – Scope Management

During this section, we will go through Scope Management Knowledge Area. Scope of a project defines what will be done and what will not be done throughout the project. Therefore, it draws the boundaries of the project and shows what will be delivered once the project is completed.

Project scope can include features of a product, quality and performance metrics, availability requirements etc. Since project schedule, project budget, human resource requirements etc. will all depend on the scope of the project that will be delivered, scope management is a critical knowledge area in project management. In real-life projects, many requirements, which were not, clearly gathered from the customer cause scope creep and deviation from the project targets respectively.

In this section, we will go through:

- **Overview of Scope Management Knowledge Area:** We will describe the scope management and important points about scope management.

- **Scope Management Processes:** There are six processes of scope management knowledge area, four of them belongs to planning process group and two of them belongs to monitoring and controlling process group. We will list these processes first, and then in further headings, we will describe each process in detail.

- **Product & Project Scope:** Product can be an output or end result of the project and we will describe the distinction between product scope and project scope.

After these descriptions, we will start to dive into scope management processes in detail.

1. **Plan Scope Management Process:** Plan Scope Management process is the first process of scope management knowledge area. How to manage, control and deliver the scope of the project is planned in this process.

2. **Collect Requirements Process:** Second process is Collect Requirements Process. Collecting requirements from the customer is actually foundations of the project scope. Because customer requirements or business needs initiate the projects and collect requirements process helps in collecting business and customer requirements from relevant stakeholders.

3. **Define Scope Process:** Define Scope Process finalizes the project scope. Although several project requirements can be gathered from several project stakeholders, some of these requirements will be invalidated through discussions, or some requirements will conflict with each other. This process will help in finalizing the project requirements and project scope.

4. **Create Work Breakdown Structure Process:** Work breakdown structure of a project describes the hierarchy of tasks, work packages and overall project work to complete

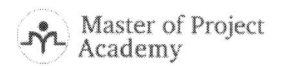

whole project scope. Create Work Breakdown Structure Process divides project scope into smaller work packages for better coordination and delivery.

5. **Validate Scope Process:** Once the project deliverables are completed, it needs to be checked first whether they meet the initial requirements. For instance, internal testing is done for a developed software to check whether it meets the desired functionality.

6. **Control Scope Process:** At the very end step, once a deliverable is final, it needs to be checked by the customer. Control Scope process aims to ensure that customer gets the final project deliverables as agreed in the beginning of the project. After customer checks, project is accepted and closed respectively.

Overview of Scope Management

During this heading, we will describe the scope management, common concepts about scope management, what gold plating is and high-level approach to changes in scope management.

> Scope management is the process of defining what work is required and then making sure all of that work and only that work is done.

Scope of a project defines what will be delivered throughout the project. Therefore, it directly constrains the schedule of a project, resource requirements, project budget etc. In order to complete a project successfully, scope management must be done appropriately and only the work in the scope must be delivered.

- **Scope must be clear and formally approved before work starts.** During planning, several business and customer requirements are gathered from project stakeholders. These requirements actually constitute the base of the project scope. Some of these requirements will be conflicting each other or some of the requirements will be eliminated after meetings. In the end, there will be a final project scope. This final scope must be agreed by all project stakeholders since it will describe what will be produced and delivered as the outcomes of the project.

- **Requirements are gathered from all stakeholders.** Consider that you are working on an e-commerce shopping website project. A stakeholder from marketing department might require being able to send vouchers to members if they did not purchase anything in last 30 days, product manager of the project might require the system to support up to 1 million members, security operations stakeholder might require the website to be HTTPS compliant and secure for transactions. We can give several sample stakeholder requirements like these. These actually constitute the scope of a project.

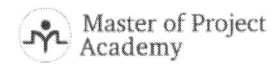

- **Requirements gathering can take a long time.** Depending on the project, number of stakeholders and complexity of a project, requirements gathering can take a long time. Because you need to get expectations of stakeholders, evaluate conflicting requirements and maybe you will need to organize several meetings to finalize your requirements. This can take a long time in a project.

- **While the project is completed, only the work in the project management plan should be done.** Because all your budget planning, schedule planning, resource planning, risk planning etc. has been done based on your agreed scope. If you try to deliver anything extra that is not in the scope, this will bring a risk to exceed your plans respectively. It is better to describe gold plating here.

> Gold Plating is delivering more than what is required in the scope.

- **Gold Plating:** Once you initiated a project, there will be new requests coming from the customer. Most of the time, customer will claim that what they are requesting is not a change request. As a project manager, you must be careful in managing the project scope and make sure that you will not be doing anything extra other than the agreed project scope. However, in some cases, project team performs extra activity and delivers extra work, which is not in scope of the project, and this is called gold plating.

  For instance, consider our e-commerce shopping website example. Your customer wants the system to work only in Chrome browser. However, if you also manage the work to work also in the Internet Explorer, or in any other browser, this is an example of gold plating. Because in your agreed scope, you must deliver a system that will work on Chrome but you do extra work to deliver internet explorer operability as well.

> Gold plating is not allowed.

- Gold plating a project is not allowed. Because you are doing extra work and this extra, work will bring extra effort, extra budget necessity, extra resource requirements etc. Therefore, Project manager in a project must prevent gold plating.

- **If there is a change coming from the customer, any change to the scope must be evaluated.** Change's impacts on time, cost, risk planning, quality etc. must be evaluated. For instance, making the e-commerce shopping website operable in internet explorer will bring extra development effort and test effort. This will bring additional cost and risk with it respectively. These must be evaluated by the relevant stakeholders and change control board must accept a change in order to implement.

- **Changes are not allowed without an approved change request.** After change evaluation, its impacts on schedule, cost, quality, resources etc. will be highlighted. If the change control board agrees to implement, then the change can be implemented.

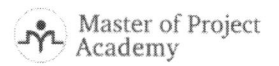

- **In order to prevent scope creep, the project manager must continuously determine what is in and what is not in scope of the project.** Because while you are managing a project, one of your project resources might be doing extra work. For instance, although it is not in your project scope, one of your software developers might be developing shopping cart function to work in internet explorer as well. This may cause him to delay his activity and bring extra cost. Project Manager must be aware of the project scope and prevent any scope creeps that might occur throughout the project.

We have already gone through the processes of Scope Management knowledge area. However, it is better to list all processes here again since we are giving an overview of the scope management.

There are six processes of scope management. Four of the processes are in planning process group and two of them are in the monitoring and controlling process group. These are:

- Plan Scope Management Process,
- Collect Requirements Process,
- Define Scope Process,
- Create WBS Process,
- Validate Scope Process and
- Control Scope Process.

Product & Project Scope

We have seen two terms until now too frequently: Product and project. What is product scope and what is project scope? How do they differ from each other? During this heading, we will describe the product and project scope.

Product Scope: Product Scope describes the requirements that relate to the product of the project.

For instance, if we consider our e-commerce shopping website example, supporting 1 million members, sending vouchers to inactive members, supporting 1,000 members concurrently, enabling secure transactions are all examples of requirements that are in product scope.

Briefly, product scope answers, "What end result is wanted?" question. Because product scope describes the features of the end deliverables of a project.

Project scope: Project scope describes the work the project will do to deliver product scope or product of the project.

In order to deliver e-commerce shopping website, you need to do scope management, cost management, resource management and many other activities. All of these activities to deliver the end results of the project successfully are considered as Project Scope.

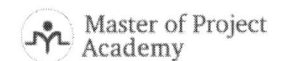

Example: Building a New Train Station.

Let us describe Product and Project Scope over a train station construction project example as well.

Project: building a new train station.

Product Scope: deliver a new train station that will have 4 railways, support the traffic of 3,000 passengers per day, including 2 waiting lounges etc. As you see, these are all features of the train station once the construction project completed.

Project Scope: works to be done to build new station. For instance, procurement of the materials, acquiring construction workers, controlling project budget, planning schedule and many more project management activities are in project scope.

Plan Scope Management Process

Plan scope management process is the first process of Scope Management Knowledge area.

Plan Scope Management process is the process of **creating a scope management plan that documents how the project scope will be defined, validated and controlled.**

Scope of the project will be shaped with the requirements of the customer and project stakeholders. Then, once the project produces outputs, these need to be validated whether the produced outputs meet the desired expectations. Throughout the project, scope must be controlled and project manager must prevent any scope creeps.

> Business case of the project describes why is the project done and what was the case that caused this project to be initiated.

Now we will see what these two plans include.

Scope Management Plan

Scope Management Plan describes how the scope will be defined, developed, monitored, controlled and verified. For instance, how to collect requirements of customer and project stakeholders, how to eliminate conflicting requirements, how to track whether the agreed scope is being delivered and how to verify whether the agreed project deliverables are produced are all detailed in the Scope Management Plan.

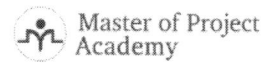

> Scope Management Plan is part of the project management plan.

Scope management plan is a major input to Develop Project Management Plan process. Because, scope of a project defines what will be done throughout the project. Based on the scope of a project, critical aspects of a project such as schedule, budget, quality and resource estimations are affected directly. Therefore, scope management plan, which will help to finalize scope of a project, is a crucial input for the Develop Project Management Plan process.

Scope Management Plan includes processes:

- **Prepare a detailed project scope statement:** Project scope statement describes the scope of a project at a very high level if you remember from our previous notes. Scope Management plan will guide on preparing a detailed project scope statement.

- **Enable the creation of WBS:** WBS is the abbreviation of Work Breakdown Structure. WBS shows the hierarchy of activities and work packages that will be delivered to complete overall project scope. For instance, an e-commerce shopping website can include several systems such as member management system, transaction management system, marketing system etc. Under these systems, there will be several work packages for instance, transaction management system can include shopping card function, credit card verification method etc. Respectively, these functions may require several activities to complete. Therefore, WBS of a project shows a blueprint of the work that needs to be completed throughout the project.

- **Establish how the WBS will be maintained and approved:** Once the WBS of a project is finalized, it needs to be approved by the project stakeholders before starting project execution.

- **Specify how formal acceptance of the completed project deliverables will be obtained:** As we described already, scope management plan includes also verification and validation of the project scope. Once project deliverables are produced, these are first tested by the project team and any defects that do not meet the agreed requirements are fixed. After these tests, produced deliverables must be checked by the customer and approved officially if they meet the agreed requirements in the beginning.

- **Control how requests for changes to the detailed project scope statement will be processed:** After the scope is finalized and approved by the project stakeholders, any change to the scope must be done through a formal change request process. Only approved changes by the change control board can be implemented in a project. Respectively, if there is a change, project scope statement must be revised accordingly and how to do this is documented in the Scope Management Plan.

Requirements Management Plan

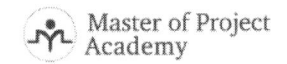

Requirements Management Plan describes how requirements will be analyzed, documented and managed. Requirements are the foundations of project scope. Stakeholder requirements are gathered, evaluated and finalized and then these constitute the foundations of project scope.

Requirements Management Plan includes

- **How requirements activities will be planned, tracked and reported:** Each requirement in a project must be documented and history of this requirement must be stored in project records. Even if a requirement is invalidated or eliminated during meetings, the reason for elimination or reference to conflicting requirements must be documented for future references.

- **Configuration management activities:** Configuration management of a project mainly deals with how the versioning of project documents will be done in a project.

- **Requirements prioritization process:** Depending on the size and context of the project, there can be several requirements coming from several project stakeholders. Many of these requirements might be conflicting with each other or some of the requirements will be more important than others. How to do this prioritization must be documented in the Requirements Management Plan.

- **Product metrics:** For instance, will you use European metrics or US metrics in your project? These will affect how you will record your quality assurance results and how you will report your project outputs to project stakeholders.

- **Traceability structure:** It is included in the requirements management plan. Once the requirements of the project are finalized, these requirements must be checked and tracked throughout the project whether they are met with the project deliverables. How to trace these requirements must be documented in the requirements management plan.

Collect Requirements Process

Collect requirements process is the second process of scope management knowledge area. In order to define scope, requirements of the stakeholders must be collected first and the main purpose of collect requirements process is gathering stakeholder requirements in a project.

- **Requirements are actually what stakeholders expect from a project or from the product of the project:** Requirements of the project stakeholders must be gathered in the project and managed properly. After requirements are finalized, these must be included in the scope and tracked throughout the project. In addition, how requirements are met with the project deliverables must be demonstrated to the project stakeholders to complete a project successfully.

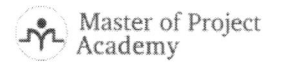

Example: E-commerce shopping website

Now, let us go over some sample project requirements, our e-commerce shopping website example.

> One of the requirements can be **System should take backup at 2:00 to 2:15 am**. Because it is expected to get the lowest traffic at, night on a web site and a stakeholder that will be related with the operations of this site can be asking for this requirement.
> Another requirement can be **1000 concurrent users should be able to operate on website without any service degradation.** This can be a requirement of the capacity manager. Based on the anticipated traffic, it might be required to support 1000 users concurrently in the website.
> In addition, the last requirement sample can be **Entry screen should be loaded in 2 seconds**. Speed of a website is crucial factor in the eyes of today's customer. Therefore, loading time of a website is a critical factor that is affecting customer experience and this can be a requirement from the customer service team.

Note that, there will be several requirements in a project and we just listed three of them here to illustrate requirements of a project in your mind.

- **High-level requirements of a project are defined in project charter:** If you remember from our previous notes, project charter is created in the initiating phase of a project. As long as high-level requirements of a project are determined, these are included in the project charter.

- **Collect requirements process involves more specific inputs:** New requirements will be received later and requirements will be gathered and finalized during planning.

Tools & Techniques for Collecting Requirements

Collecting Requirements is a crucial activity in project management.

Because, requirements of a project define the project scope. Any weakness in requirements management will cause scope issues respectively.

In order to collect requirements from project stakeholders, several tools and techniques are used. During this heading, we will be going over each tool and technique used in collecting requirements.

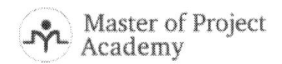

1. **Interviewing:** Interviewing can be done through a meeting, through a phone call or through e-mails. In this technique, Project Manager interviews the stakeholders to get their requirements. There can be a checklist, a list of questions in project manager or he can just ask to the stakeholders to express their expectations from the project in a free form. Project manager notes down and stores the requirements received from the project stakeholders.

2. **Focus Groups:** Focus group is used to get a specific set of stakeholders' requirements. For instance, you can organize a meeting with executive directors in your company to get their requirements first, and then organize a separate meeting with the functional managers to get their requirements. These are examples of focus groups.

3. **Facilitated Workshops:** In facilitated workshops, stakeholders with different perspectives are brought together. Consider that you will manage a software project. You can bring analysts, software developers, test engineers, operation team and customer together. Each group of project stakeholders will look to the project from their perspective and express their requirements. For instance, operation team will consider operational aspects, customer will express business requirements, and software developers will state the technical requirements.

4. **Brainstorming:** Brainstorming is actually a Group Think. Because several people come together to list requirements of a project. During the meeting, new ideas are generated from existing ideas. This helps to identify new requirements.

5. **Nominal Group Technique:** This is actually a technique to prioritize ideas rather than generating new requirements. In nominal group technique, meeting participants rank the most successful ideas. This helps to focus on more valuable or prioritized ideas first in generating project requirements. Nominal group technique is usually used in brainstorming meetings. Because there will be several ideas coming from several stakeholders. If these are not ranked, focusing the stakeholders on a narrower topic and finalizing requirements will be tough.

6. **Delphi Technique:** In Delphi technique, a request for information is sent to project stakeholders anonymously. Stakeholders list their requirements individually and send back these requirements. Then, these results and collected results are sent again to project stakeholders. Collecting requirements anonymously is mainly for not affecting stakeholders' decision based on the owner of the requirement. For instance, if a senior director and functional manager are sending their requirements, if the functional manager would know the requirements of the senior director, because of the hierarchical relationship, he can be affected from the requirements of the senior director. Resending requirements and getting back feedback goes until consensus is reached among the stakeholders.

7. **Idea/Mind Mapping:** This technique is actually a diagram of ideas or notes to help generate, classify, or record information. Ideas or parts of a project are drawn on the table, and new ideas or parts that can be in the project are generated.

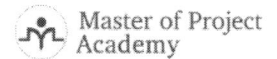

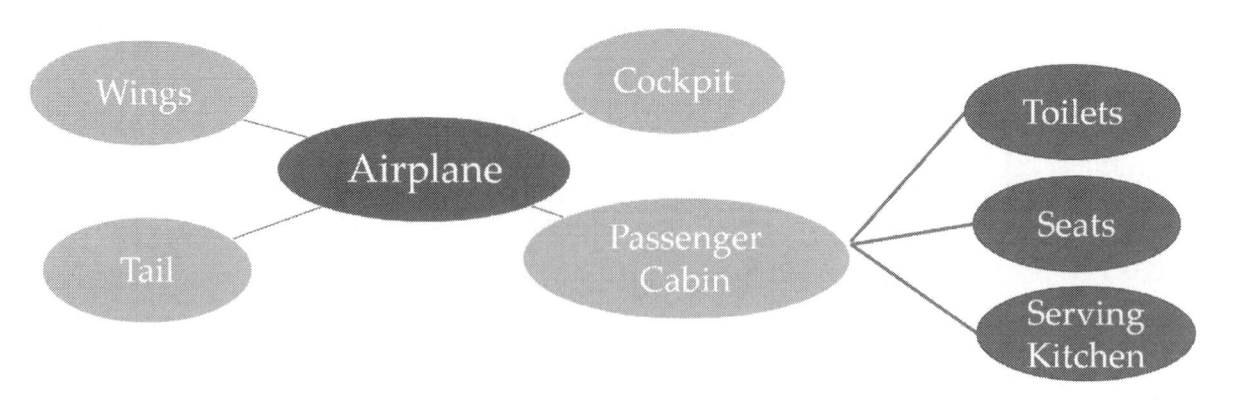

For example, an airplane will consist of parts such as wings, cockpit area, and tail and passenger cabin. When thinking about what can be in the passenger area, we can list toilets, seats, serving kitchen area etc.

8. **Affinity Diagrams:** In affinity diagrams technique ideas generated from any other requirements gathering techniques are sorted into groups by similarities. For instance, requirements about cockpit area, requirements about passenger area, requirements about tails etc. can be grouped.

   Affinity Diagrams technique helps to see additional scope or risks. Because, similar requirements will be seen together under same group, which will ease to see if there will be any more requirements, or if there are any further risks regarding a group of requirements.

   As you see, requirements or parts for each area of an airplane are listed in this figure. When we see this figure, you can think about several other requirements for each group and grouping helps to think about these new requirements. For instance, a new requirement for the passenger cabin can be tray tables.

9. **Questionnaires and Surveys:** Questionnaires and Surveys technique is used for large groups where there are several stakeholders that you have to collect their requirements. Consider that you have more than 200 stakeholders in a project that you need to contact and collect their requirements. Organizing a meeting or interviewing one-by-one will take a long time to finalize requirements. Preparing questionnaire and surveys and collecting requirements of several stakeholders will be easier with this technique in this case.

10. **Observation:** In observation technique, a potential user of the product is watched to identify requirements. For instance, in order to determine the user experience or most used features of an e-commerce shopping website, a consumer can be observed. Based on the steps that the consumer will take, project requirements can be identified or prioritized.

11. **Prototypes:** In this technique, model of the proposed product is developed and then this model is presented to stakeholders for feedback. Consider that a smartphone manufacturer will produce a new smartphone. In order to get feedback of stakeholders, features and functionalities from existing smartphones can be combined in a prototype. This prototype can be presented to a set of consumers to get their feedback.

12. **Group Decision Making:** In this technique, several opinions are evaluated in a group. There can be several requirements about a project and each stakeholder might express their own requirements. In the end, these must be evaluated whether these requirements will be in the project scope.

    There are four approaches in Group Decision Making technique.
    - ❖ **Unanimity:** In this case, everyone agrees with the idea that is being evaluated. Therefore, it is qualified to be in the final list.
    - ❖ **Majority:** In this case, more than 50% of the group agrees on a requirement. In order to put a requirement to the final scope, if this approach is applied, more than half of the group must agree on it.
    - ❖ **Plurality:** In this case, largest block in a group agrees on a requirement. For instance, if 40% of the group agrees, 30% of the group disagrees and 30% of the group does not have a decision, since largest part of the group agrees, the requirement will be qualified to be in the scope.
    - ❖ **Dictatorship:** In this approach, one individual makes the decision for the group on a requirement. For instance, if the Senior Director is in the group and if he has the privilege to approve or disapprove a requirement, regardless of what other participants think, Senior Director's decision will determine whether the requirement will be in the project scope.
13. **Benchmarking:** In benchmarking technique, company compares its actual or planned practices, to those of comparable organizations to identify best practices. Because a company must be profitable to survive in the market. In order to be profitable, it has to know the market dynamics, competitors in the market, its strengths and weaknesses against competitors. Projects must be initiated to take a position in the market accordingly. For instance, if Samsung benchmarks its test processes with the Apple's, this is an example of benchmarking. Because they are both in the smartphone and tablet market and they are rivals.
14. **Context Diagrams:** Context Diagrams actually give example of a scope model. They visualize how a system; function or product will work. By this way, scope becomes more understandable. Context Diagrams define how other users and systems interact with it. Context diagrams show steps that the customer need to do, steps that will be done by the process, actions that will be completed by the product, outputs of the system etc.

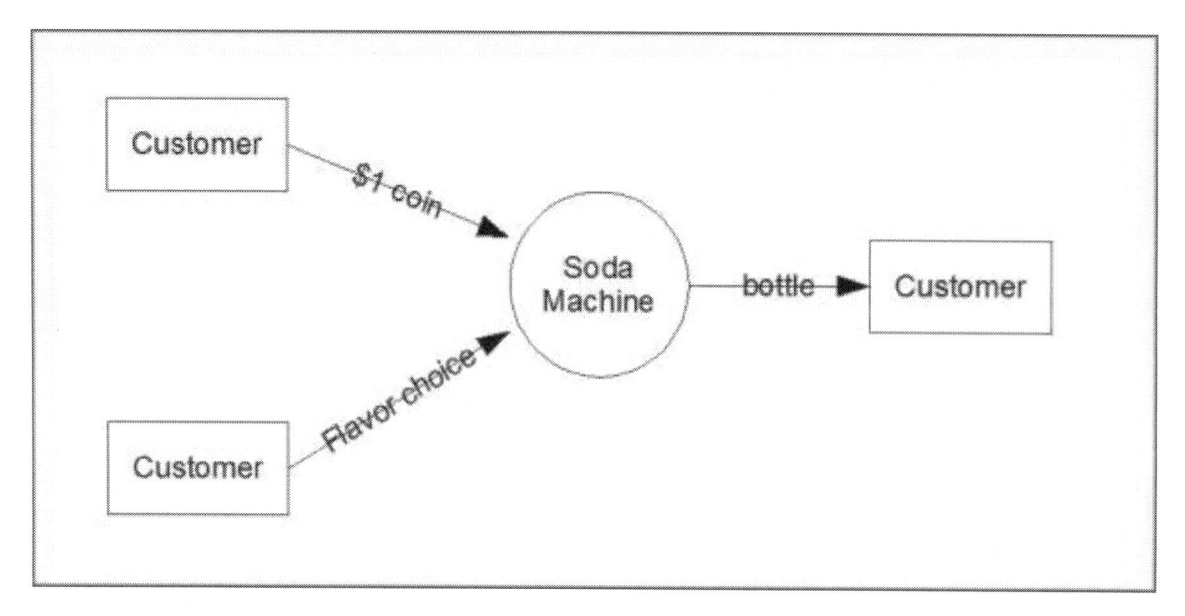

[Context diagram showing: Customer → $1 coin → Soda Machine; Customer → Flavor choice → Soda Machine; Soda Machine → bottle → Customer]

This figure shows a context diagram of how a soda machine works. As you see, customer first puts a $1 coin. Then he selects the flavor. Then the soda machine gives the bottle to the customer.

15. **Document Analysis:** In Document Analysis technique, existing documents are used to elicit requirements for the project. For instance, consider that Apple will produce a new smartphone version. Existing documents of older smartphone versions will be a basis for generating requirements for the new smartphone. Therefore, business plans, agreements, requests for proposals, application software documentation, use cases and many more documents can be source for generating requirements if you are using Document analysis technique.

Requirements Documentation

Several techniques can be used to collect requirements in a project. After requirements have been collected and finalized, they are documented. Because requirements are foundations of the project, scope and they reflect the expectations of project stakeholders. Requirements history, whether it is in the final list, or eliminated, which deliverable will fulfill the requirement etc. needs to be documented in order to meet all agreed requirements of a project once the project is completed.

Requirements documentation Includes:

- **Business Requirements:** Business requirements generally come from the customer of the project. They represent the product features, or what the end outputs of the project need to provide. Consider our e-commerce shopping website example. Developing a retail online shopping site that will get the 2% of the market in US is an example for business requirement.
- **Stakeholder requirements:** Any person, group of people, company or parties that will be affected positively or negatively from the project are project stakeholders. Each project stakeholder can bring a requirement to the project.

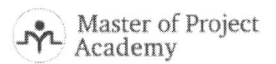

- **Solution requirements:** Solution requirements are actually technical requirements. For instance, during meetings with the software architecture team of the company, since the customer data of the e-commerce shopping website is critical, software architecture team can require to build a geographically backed up databases.

- **Project requirements:** These requirements are generally about schedule and budget. For instance, sponsor of the project might require to complete the project in 6 months and with a $1,500,000 budget.

- **Transition requirements:** These generally describe how to switch from an old system or product, to a newer one. For instance, consider that you are managing a database upgrade project. Since your site will be, live and since database will have critical customer data, how to switch off old database and how to activate new data on new database must be clearly planned. Otherwise, there will be service loss and this will affect customers.

- **Assumptions, dependencies, and constraints:** Assumptions, dependencies, and constraints are also included in requirements documentation. Project management is actually planning activities that will happen in the future with the information available today. While doing these, assumptions can be done. Consider a construction project. Weather conditions can affect a construction project severely. Therefore, planning can be done under the assumption that there will not be long-lasting bad weather conditions that will affect the project.

  Dependencies can be either internal or external. For instance, a software development project can be depending on the infrastructure implementation project and the software development project can start only after infrastructure implementation project completed. Alternatively, start of a construction project will depend on the procurements of the materials.

  Constraints define limits of the project. For instance, if the budget available for the project is $1,000,000, this is a constraint and you have to finish the project with this budget. Alternatively, if the company can assign only six software developers for your project, this is an example of resource constraint.

  Note that, assumptions, dependencies and constraints affect the success of project. Therefore, usually, assumptions, dependencies and constraints are put in contracts as well to make these legally binding.

Balance Stakeholder Requirements & Resolve Competing Requirements

Management of stakeholder requirements is crucial for the success of a project. Because there will be several requirements from several stakeholders and many of them might compete with each other. Especially, when requirements are competing with each other, resolution of the conflict must not make any stakeholder unhappy when his or her requirement is eliminated.

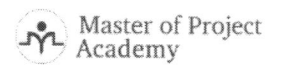

Balancing stakeholder requirements:

Make sure that the requirements meet objectives: Objectives of a project define where the project must be headed to. Once the objectives are met, requirements tied to those objectives must be fulfilled respectively.

Prioritize requirements: There will be many requirements coming from several stakeholders of a project. These must be prioritized and requirements with higher priority must be monitored carefully. Because these not meeting high priority requirements can cause even failure of the project.

Resolve conflicts between requirements: Consider that high-level planning of a project shows that project can be completed in 8 months with a $1,000,000 budget. However, the sponsor of the project asks to complete the project in 6 months. This brings additional $200,000 cost to the project since additional resources will be outsourced. Sponsor might not accept this additional cost but might push for reducing the project duration. This is actually a conflicting requirement example that needs to be resolved.

If there is any conflict with those of customer, the customer's needs normally take precedence: Because the end user of the product or outputs of the project are customer. Therefore, if a stakeholder requirement is conflicting with the customer's requirement, usually the customer's requirement will beat the other one.

If a conflict cannot be resolved, ask for management support: In some cases, requirements of powerful stakeholders might compete with each other. For instance, for a marketing feature development project in an IT company, Chief Marketing Officer can ask for the project to be completed in 6 months. The Chief Technical Officer can say that they can complete the project in 9 months due to technical and resource constraints. If you cannot resolve this conflict between these two powerful stakeholders, you can ask support of your management.

Resolve Competing Requirements

Competing requirements must be resolved smoothly. If resolving a requirement conflict will make any side unhappy, this might bring a risk to your project. Unhappy stakeholder might not support the project or he can underperform when you need his support in the project. Therefore, Project Manager should resolve competing requirements by accepting those which most match to:

- **Project Charter:** Project charter includes the high-level project scope, risks, requirements and information about the project.

- **Project Scope Statement:** Project Scope Statement describes what will be done during the project.

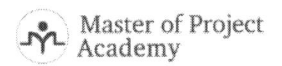

- **Constraints:** Constraints actually define the limits of the project. For instance, project budget or number of resources are constraints of the project. These will define the amount of work you can complete and schedule of the project as well.

- **Business need:** Business need is the reason for the project's existence. Therefore, when there is a conflict in requirements, it will be a good idea to check the business need of the project. The requirement that most matches to the business need must be qualified when resolving the conflict.

Requirements Traceability Matrix

We have seen in our previous notes that requirements in a project must be documented, tracked, controlled, validated and verified. Requirements traceability matrix helps to track the requirements over the life of the project to ensure they are accomplished. Requirements Traceability Matrix is abbreviated as RTM. Each requirement is written down in the RTM and its evolution, how it is fulfilled, which deliverable fulfills the requirement etc. can be seen in the RTM.

Requirements Traceability Matrix is usually in a form of table with IDs per requirement, source of requirements, responsible of requirement, status...etc. Most of the corporate companies have a template for Requirements Traceability Matrix and requirements are tracked over RTM throughout the project starting from initiation until project closure.

REQUIREMENTS TRACEABILITY MATRIX
<PROJECT NAME>

ID	Associate ID	Requirements Description	Business Needs, Opportunities, Goals, Objectives	Project Objectives	WBS Deliverables	Product Design	Product Development	Test Cases
001	1.0							
	1.1							
	1.2							
	1.2.1							
002	2.0							
	2.1							
	2.1.1							

This figure shows a sample requirements traceability matrix. As you see the top part of the document shows high-level information about the project. Project name, cost center, and project description or similar high-level information about the project. We know the project name and project description already but cost center is a new concept. In corporate companies, project costs are generally controlled with cost centers. Procured materials cost of resources, expenses are accrued in this cost center and budget provided by the sponsor is tied to this cost center. Finance team sees and reports inflows and outflows from this cost center and last status of the budget is controlled with the help of this cost center.

ID and associate ID are numbering to identify requirements in the requirements traceability matrix. Requirements description area gives detailed information about the requirement. For instance, the system must support 1,000 concurrent users at a time. Business needs, opportunities, goals and objectives column depicts the relationship of the requirement with these aspects of the project. Project objectives column shows which objective will help in fulfilling this requirement in the project. WBS deliverables column shows which deliverables of the project will fulfill the requirement. Product Design and Product Development columns show the requirements tie with the technical aspects of the project. For instance, two servers and four processors can be written here if these will suffice the 1,000 concurrent user's performance requirement. The last column, test cases, shows how this requirement will be tested once the regarding deliverables are completed. For instance, a test load tool can simulate 1,000 concurrent users traffic on the system to check whether this requirement has been fulfilled.

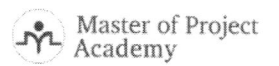

Define Scope Process

Define Scope process primarily concerns what is included and what is not included in project and its deliverables. Main purpose of the process is drawing the boundaries of the project, work that will be delivered throughout the project and major deliverables of the project. Define Scope process finalizes the project scope.

While defining scope, Define Scope process uses three main documents to define project and product scope.

Requirements Documentation: As we discussed already, requirements of a project shape the foundations of project scope. In other words, requirements come together and after evaluations, final requirements are used to finalize the scope of the project.

Project Charter: Project Charter outlines the high-level project scope, high-level risks, already assigned resources etc. Therefore, using project charter will help to define the scope in a project as well.

Risks, Assumptions and Constraints: Risks, assumptions or risks directly affect the outcomes of a project. For instance, if you are working in a high-possible earthquake zone in a construction project, you need to consider the risk of earthquakes and how they will affect your project. Maybe you need to use extra material that will increase your costs but make your building more resistible for earthquakes. Similarly, assumptions and constraints will affect the project scope as well. If there is a limited budget to complete a project, and if scope is very broad that will make impossible to complete the project with the available budget, this must be highlighted during planning. Either scope must be reduced or additional budget must be planned.

Product analysis is done to produce a detailed scope in the end. During product analysis, objectives and description of the product stated by the customer or sponsor are analyzed. After analysis, it is expected to reach tangible project deliverables. Because customer requirements or expectations are just explanations or statements. After evaluation, these must be addressed with project deliverables and once these are produced in the project, customer acceptance must be acquired respectively.

Project Scope Statement

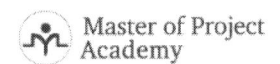

Project Scope Statement is the primary output of the Define Scope process. Because the main purpose of the Define Scope process is finalizing the project scope after reviewing and evaluating all customer requirements collected during Collect Requirements process.

Project scope statement officially states what will be done in the project. After Project, scope statement is produced, every project stakeholder must agree on this since it will be the detailed scope of the project and what will be delivered throughout the project.

Project Scope Statement, Work Breakdown Structure and Work Breakdown Structure Dictionary together constitutes the Scope baseline.

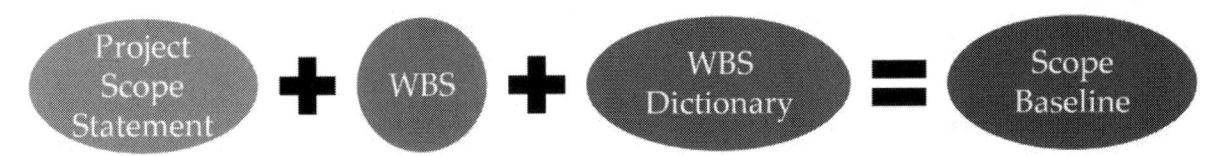

Project Scope Statement + WBS + WBS Dictionary = Scope Baseline

As we described before, work breakdown structure shows the hierarchy of project deliverables in a structured manner. In addition, Work Breakdown Structure Dictionary provides detailed information about each item in the Work Breakdown Structure.

Project Scope Statement is part of project management plan. It is not a management plan but it is a crucial document since it will outline the scope of the project in detail.

Project scope statement includes:

- **Product Scope:** Product is an output of the project and features, specifications, details about the product are described in the product scope. Therefore, since product is a project deliverable, product scope will be included in the Project Scope Statement as well.

- **Deliverables:** Project will produce deliverables throughout the project until all project scope is completed. Consider that you are working in an e-commerce shopping website project. The final product is end-to-end working e-commerce shopping website for sure. However, there will be interim deliverables such as login screen, category page, member profile screen etc. These interim deliverables can be tested by the customer before waiting the final product delivery. Since deliverables are smaller parts of the overall project scope, these are listed in the project scope statement.

- **Product Acceptance Criteria:** Product acceptance criteria shows in what conditions customer will accept the project. This is actually a handshake between the project team and customer that in what circumstances the customer will accept the final project and give acceptance. These criteria generally generated through requirements. For instance, if it is agreed with the customer in the beginning that the member login will be accomplished in less than 2 seconds, this is written in product acceptance criteria and when the e-commerce shopping website is ready for customer tests, if member logins are processed successfully in less than 2 seconds, customer must accept.

- **Project Exclusions:** What is not part of project must be written in project scope statement as well. Because in some cases, some project stakeholders might think some out of scope items in the project scope. Therefore, it is better to clearly outline critical points, which are not in scope of the project. Consider that you are working on installation of a new database project in an IT company and the scope is only installation and configuration. It is better to mention that migration of data from old database in out of scope. Because some stakeholders might consider that new database installation will cover also migration of data as well.

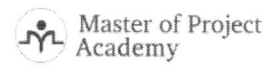

- **Additional risks:** Risks that might affect the project must be included in the Project scope statement as well as Constraints and assumptions. Constraints limit the dimensions of the project and planning is done based on these constraints and assumptions. If constraints or assumptions of a project does not go as planned, these will affect the project scope and other aspects respectively. Therefore, these must be written down in the project scope statement.

Constraints and Assumptions

Project constraints are factors that limit the team's options. Therefore, project planning must be done with considering constraints. These constraints can be project dependencies, or about schedule, cost, quality, human resource, technical etc. For instance:

❖ "Project must be completed in 6 months!" this is an example for project schedule constraint.

❖ "Existing system must not be interrupted from 12 am to 6 am". This is an example for a technical constraint. This constraint requires to not to touch the existing system for 6 hours from 12 am until 6 am. Therefore, when planning project activities, there should not be any activity planned for these slots in a day.

Assumptions are assumed true, but they might not be true during project execution. Planning is actually doing forecasting of future activities with the information available today. Therefore, making assumptions is unavoidable during planning. For instance,

❖ "Dedicated personnel from marketing team will support the team" is an example for an assumption. However, during execution, dedicated marketing personnel might not be available or might be available only 1-2 days a week. This will affect your project respectively.

❖ "Bugfix effort for each developed screen will not exceed 20% of the development effort for same screen." This is actually a common assumption made in software project estimations. However, in reality, if there will be many bugs after the software is developed, bugfix efforts can exceed 20% and this can cause project delays and exceeding budget.

Create Work Breakdown Structure (WBS) Process

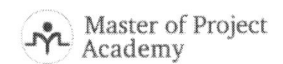

Work Breakdown Structure is abbreviated as WBS and Create WBS process mainly aims to produce the WBS of the project.

- **Create WBS process subdivides project deliverables and project work into smaller and manageable components.** This is mainly done for better estimation, better management, better coordination and better monitoring. Consider our e-commerce shopping website project. If we ask the team to give their estimates to complete the project, it will be very hard for the project team to provide their estimates. But if we divide the project into smaller parts such as Database, Screens, Services etc. and then also subdivide these major parts into smaller pieces such as login screen, payment screen, member profile screen etc. providing estimations, assigning activities, coordinating and monitoring the project will be easier respectively.

- **WBS provides a structured vision of what has to be delivered:** It includes major packages that needs to be delivered, and smaller deliverables that will complete these major parts respectively. By this way, smaller deliverables of the project can be visible to the project team.

- **WBS helps to better understand the project:** Because it is actually the hierarchy of project deliverables that will accomplish the completion of the project product. Therefore, WBS will show which deliverables will help to complete which part of the project work and how that will fit into project product respectively.

- **WBS shows hierarchy of deliverables:** By this way, it can be easily seen what needs to be completed to finish a work package in the project.

- **WBS can be organized by phases or major deliverables:** This means, if there is not a product in the project, and a service will be delivered instead, phases of the project can be broken down further as well. For instance, analysis, development, testing, integration etc. can be major phases of a project. Alternatively, if there is a product, there will be deliverables such as screens, databases, infrastructure etc. for a software project.

Now, let us go over a sample work breakdown structure.

WBS Diagram

Project Title: Aircraft System

Major Deliverables (Level 2):
- Project Management
- Training
- Data
- Air Vehicle
- Support Equipment
- Facilities
- Test and Evaluation

Work Packages (Level 3):
- Project Management: System Engineering Management, Supporting PM Activities
- Training: Equipment Training, Facilities Training, Services Training
- Data: Technical Orders, Engineering Data, Management Data
- Support Equipment: Organizational Level SE, Intermediate Level SE, Depot Level SE
- Facilities: Base Buildings, Maintenance Facility
- Test and Evaluation: Mock-ups, Operational Test, Developmental Test, Test
- Air Vehicle: Airframe, Engine, Communication System, Navigation System, Fire Control System

---

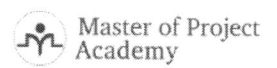

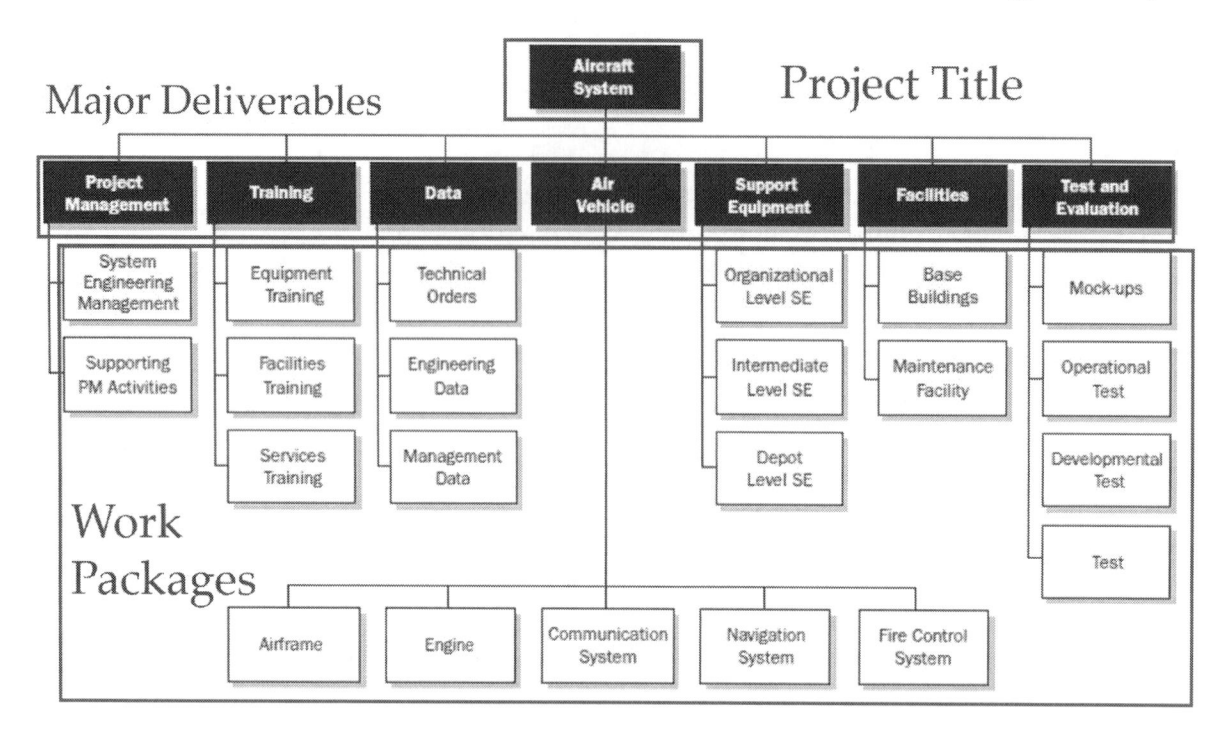

This figure shows a sample work breakdown structure for an aircraft-manufacturing project. As you see, **the final product is Aircraft System. That is put on top of the hierarchy**.

Then **in the second level, major deliverables and activities that constitute an aircraft system are shown**. These are Project Management, Training, Data, Air Vehicle, Support Equipment, Facilities, Test, and Evaluation. As you see, WBS shows both project management activities and product deliverables as well. For instance, Project management is actually not part of the product, aircraft system. Nevertheless, it is in the WBS.

Moreover, **in the third level work packages that are under each major deliverable are listed**. For instance, Air vehicle is a major deliverable and work packages that will complete this major deliverable are: Airframe, engine, communication system, navigation system and fire control system.

Moreover, for activities like project management and training, further activities and each training that needs to be delivered are listed. For instance, for training major deliverable, three trainings need to be delivered. These are Equipment training, facilities training and services training.

> Work packages consist of "nouns" instead of "actions".

As you can see, work packages are nouns such as technical orders, base buildings, operational test etc. Project activities are actually written in actions such as "complete the operational test" and this is not a convention used in WBS.

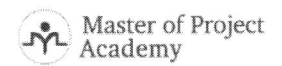

Rules for Creating WBS

Work breakdown structure of a project is actually a snapshot of project deliverables that will be completed throughout the project. Therefore, creation of WBS is crucial. There are rules for Creating WBS respectively. These rules must be followed when creating WBS of a project.

- **WBS is created with the help of the team:** Project team is informed about the project and product scope. Since project team will perform the project activities, they should provide breakdown of project deliverables respectively.
- **Each level of the WBS is smaller piece of the level above:** Remember our WBS sample we have seen in previous heading. Aircraft system was the product. In the second level, major deliverables of the product were listed. In the third level, work packages of these major deliverables were listed.
- **Some levels will be broken down to further than others will:** This means that while some branches can go up to further levels, some branches can stop at higher levels. For instance, a work package might have been broken down to third level while another work package might have been broken down to seventh level.
- **WBS includes only deliverables that are really needed:** Unnecessary activities or deliverables must not be in WBS of the project.
- **Work packages are reached when their deliverables meet the following criteria:**
- **Deliverables can be realistically and confidently estimated:** One of the major benefits of having a WBS is easing the estimation, management, coordination and monitoring project deliverables throughout the project. Therefore, once the WBS is created, deliverables must be smaller enough to estimate.
- **Deliverables can be completed quickly:** If a deliverable requires huge work, it might be better to consider breaking down further. Because bigger work packages or deliverables will be tough to manage, estimate and coordinate.
- **Deliverables can be completed without interruption:** This means, a deliverable must be small enough to not to depend on many factors to be completed first.
- **Deliverables may be outsourced or contracted out:** It is not wise to completely outsource an entire aircraft system development to a supplier. Nevertheless, navigation system or fire control system might be outsourced to a supplier.
- **After completing WBS of a project, project deliverables are entered into the project scheduling software:** These projects scheduling software tools help to define project activity dependencies, start and finish dates of activities etc. and help to complete an end-to-end project schedule plan respectively. Most common project scheduling software tools used in the market are Microsoft Project and Primavera.
- **Work Packages in WBS are divided further into schedule activities with the help of WBS dictionary:** Because, Work Packages are described as nouns only with a couple words. These work packages will require several activities to be performed to complete. Consider the aircraft system WBS. Engine was a work package under the air vehicle major deliverable. Engine of an Aircraft is still very complex to manufacture and activities that need to be performed to complete must be derived from the WBS dictionary.
- **After creation of WBS, levels are numbered for ease of location:** As you see in the figure, Project is divided into 2 major deliverables and these are numbered as 1 and 2 respectively. Then, work packages under each major deliverable is numbered as 1.1, 1.2

etc. for major deliverable 1 and 2.1, 2.2 etc. for major deliverable 2. As you see in the figure, some work packages are broken down to further levels compared to others as we expressed before.

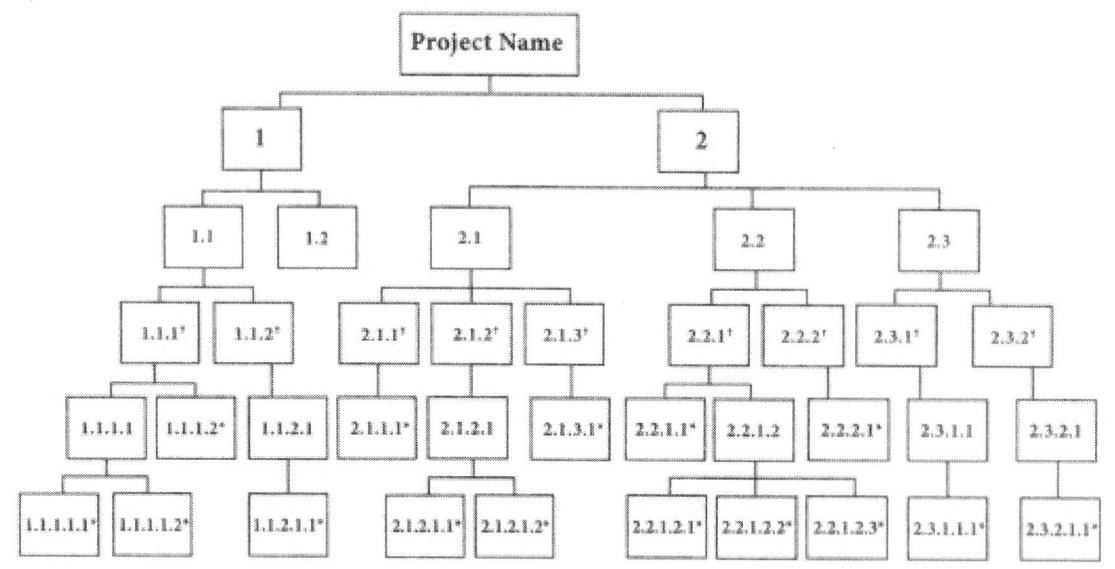

- **If your organization works on similar projects, WBS from one project may be used on another:** Consider smartphone manufacturers. They release new versions of same product frequently. For instance, Apple releases new releases of iPhone and Samsung releases new versions of its galaxy series. In each release, they bring new functionalities and features for sure. However, majority of other functions remain as well. Such as, camera, finger print systems, main case etc. Therefore, in each new release development project, existing WBS's of previous smartphone development projects can be used with some adjustments.
- **In addition, whenever there is a new project PMO should collect WBS examples and store it in the organizational process assets library:** By this way, in future, new projects can use these WBS examples when they are creating the Work Breakdown Structure of the project.

Benefits of Using WBS

Work breakdown structure of a project shows the hierarchy of the project work and deliverables in a project. Therefore, there are many benefits of using work breakdown structure. We will go over each benefit step-by-step.

- **WBS helps prevent work from slipping through cracks:** Since work breakdown structure of a project shows the project deliverables and work that needs to be competed in a project, it actually guides the project team on what needs to be done in an organized manner. By this way, unnecessary work or anything not directly in scope of the project are eliminated and helps the team to focus in the project scope only.

> WBS provides the project team members with an understanding of where their pieces fit into the overall project management plan

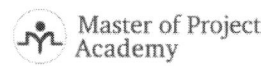

- **WBS provides the project team members with an understanding of where their pieces fit into the overall project management plan and gives them an indication of the impact of their work on the project as a whole:** Consider our Aircraft system WBS sample we have seen in previous notes. A project team member working on engine work package will be able to see how his activities will help to complete the overall project and product scope. If you consider that, there will be several project team members, WBS will help the project team to see how each activity or deliverable helps in completing the product and project scope.
- **WBS facilitates communication and cooperation between and among the project team and other stakeholders:** Since WBS shows the hierarchy of the project work and deliverables of a project scope, completed work, remaining work to be done; project team members working on same work package etc. can be easily communicated between project stakeholders with the help of Work Breakdown Structure. Since there will be several smaller parts under work packages, and these will be assigned to project team members, WBS will help in cooperation between project team members to complete project activities respectively.
- **WBS helps prevent changes:** Changes are inevitable in a project. However, preventive and corrective actions must be taken to prevent root cause of changes in a project. Changes happen because of unclear project scope or missing requirements in a project as well. WBS shows the breakdown of the project scope, work that needs to be performed and deliverables as granular as much in a project. Therefore, WBS helps prevent changes since it helps to clear project scope for all project stakeholders.

> WBS provides a basis for estimating staff, cost and time.

- **WBS provides a basis for estimating staff, cost and time:** This is a very important benefit of using WBS in a project. It is always hard to make estimations about staff requirements, cost and time for a big amount of work. There will be higher possibility of deviations in actual results if estimations are done over bigger work packages. However, if all work is divided into smaller parts, it will be easier to do estimation and deviation amount and possibility will be reduced respectively. Is it hard to make an estimation about whole aircraft system? Alternatively, breaking down the project work into smaller pieces and making estimation for each smaller part such as engine development, entertainment system integration etc. Of course, smaller pieces will be estimated easier and more accurately by the project team.
- **WBS is the foundation of the project:** Almost everything that occurs in planning after creation of WBS is directly related to WBS. This is a crucial benefit of WBS. Since WBS shows the snapshot of project work and deliverables to complete the project scope, it is actually the foundations of planning. Cost estimation, time estimation, resource estimations, schedule planning etc. are all done with the help of WBS. Therefore, WBS plays a vital role in project planning.
- **Project costs are estimated at work package level:** Since WBS shows smaller pieces of project work and deliverables, project cost estimation can be done at work package level. Then, cost of each work package level is sum up towards the first level of WBS to estimate

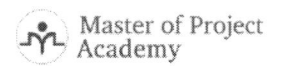

the overall project budget. We will see this in detail in our future notes during cost management knowledge area.
- **Risks are identified by work package:** Therefore, during risk planning, risks that are associated with each item in the WBS are outlined and all project risks are identified with the help of WBS.
- **Work packages are assigned to individuals or parts of organization:** Since WBS breaks down each work or deliverable into smaller pieces, it makes easier management, execution, coordination and monitoring respectively. Generally, each work package is small enough to assign to a project team member, or part of an organization for instance, assignment to training department, test team etc.

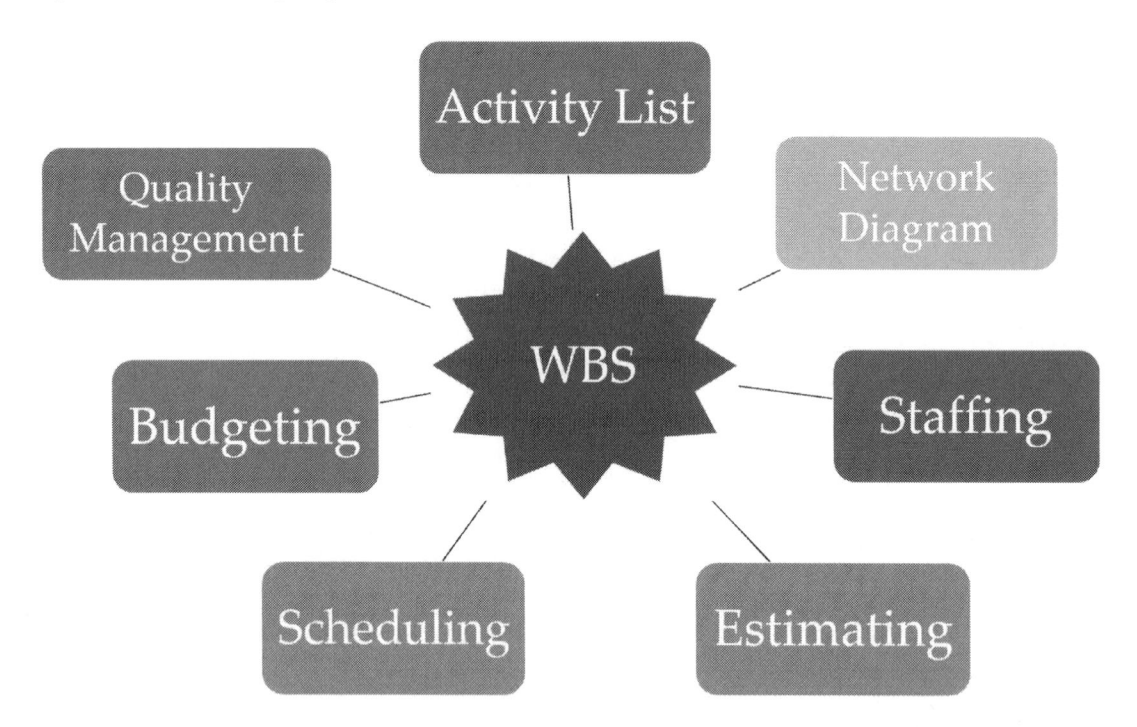

This figure shows which activities can be completed after the creation of Work Breakdown Structure in a project. As you see, WBS is at the heart of the many critical activities in a project.

- **Activity list** of a project shows which activities to perform throughout the project to complete the project scope. Since work, breakdown structure of a project shows the work and deliverable hierarchy of a project, activities that needs to be performed can be derived from the work packages under the WBS.
- **Network diagram** of a project shows the interrelationships of project activities. It shows finish-to-finish, finish to start, start to start and start to finish relationships of activities. For instance, if you are working on an e-commerce shopping website project, you cannot start the testing of activities before development of the activities finish. Alternatively, in a construction project, you cannot start to construct the building before procurement of materials. Network diagram shows interrelationships of all project activities and helps in determining the project schedule respectively. Since WBS shows the hierarchy of project work and deliverables, it will directly help in determining the project activity relationship and creation of the network diagram respectively.
- **Staffing** is actually determining the human resource necessity of the project. Since WBS will show the project work and deliverables, it will help to determine the

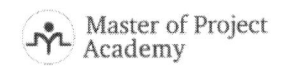

project staff who can complete the project activities. These include the competence requirements, number of staff, skill set etc.
- **Estimating** is done with the help of WBS as we stated previously. Since WBS shows a detailed outline and smaller pieces of work and deliverables that needs to be completed, WBS is used as a primary input in cost, time, resource and other estimations as well.
- **Scheduling** is also completed with the help of WBS. Scheduling actually finalizing start and finish dates of each activity and completing the start and finish dates of overall project respectively. After creation of network diagram and using the time estimations for each activity, scheduling of the project will be completed.
- **Budgeting** can be completed after finishing cost estimations of WBS items. Because project budget shows the total amount of money that is required to complete a project. After estimating cost requirement of each work package in the WBS, these estimates are sum up to find the total project budget.
- **Quality management activities** can be planned based on the WBS as well.

Work Breakdown structure can be used to:

- **Identify a scope change to the project:** There will be changes in a project, and since WBS shows the overall project scope and deliverables of the project, how the change in the scope will fit into the existing project scope can be identified with the help of WBS.
- **Evaluate the impacts of changes on scope:** A small change on a minor part of the project might affect several other aspects of the project. Since WBS shows the hierarchy of the project work and deliverables, a scope change on a work package might affect other parts related to that work package as well and this can be seen easily with the help of the Work Breakdown Structure.
- **Control scope creep by reminding everyone what work needs to be done:** WBS shows the overall project work and deliverables. Therefore, anything that is not seen in WBS will be out of project scope. If stakeholders are reminded to visit Work Breakdown Structure of a project frequently, this will help to keep stakeholder on the same table and prevent scope creep respectively.
- **As a communications tool:** Since it shows the relationship and hierarchy of project work and deliverables, communication and cooperation of project stakeholders can be done with the help of the Work Breakdown Structure.
- **Help new team members to see their roles:** When a new team member joins the team, overall project scope, project objectives and goals must be introduced to the new team member. WBS will be a good point to show all project work and project deliverables. By this way, once he is assigned with new activities, he will be able to see how his activities fit into the overall project scope with the help of the WBS.

Relationship of Levels in WBS

During our previous notes, we have seen how levels of the work breakdown structure is broken down. Actually, levels in the work breakdown structure corresponds to different terms. During this heading, we will see these terms and how they are associated with the different levels of WBS respectively.

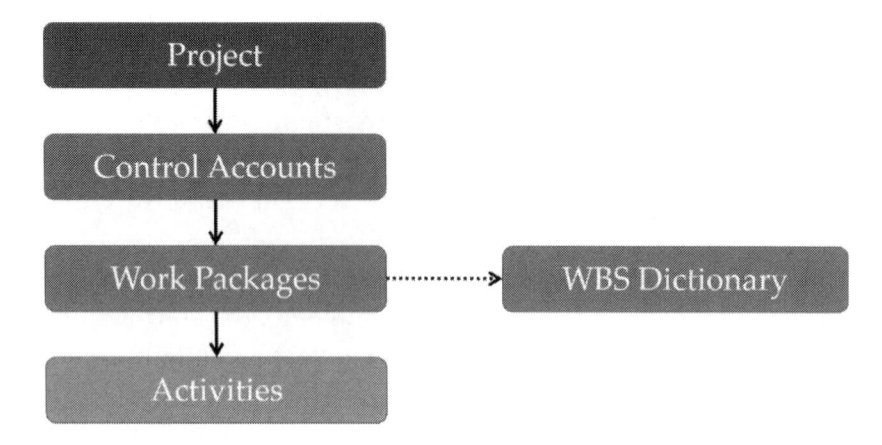

```
        Project
           ↓
    Control Accounts
           ↓
    Work Packages ········> WBS Dictionary
           ↓
       Activities
```

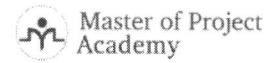

- **First and the top level of the WBS is project title.** In the end of the project, overall project scope will be completed; therefore, all project work and deliverables are under the project respectively.
- **Second level of the WBS is Control Accounts.** Control accounts are major parts, systems, phases or deliverables of a project. For instance, for a software project, Database System can be the control account level in the WBS.
- **Third level of the WBS is Work Packages.** Work packages come together to constitute control accounts. For instance, for the database system control account, work packages under this control account can be software application, servers, data structure etc.

Note that, work packages in a WBS must be small enough to manage, coordinate, execute and monitor. Since work packages are the very small part of a WBS that is deliverable to the customer, these must be explained clearly to the project stakeholders. To explain work packages in detail, Work Breakdown Structure dictionary is used. Work packages only state nouns and name of the deliverable. However, what needs to be delivered must be explained in detail and that is achieved by WBS dictionary. We will see a sample WBS dictionary in our next heading.

- **Moreover, the last level of the WBS is activities.** Actually, activities are the tasks that must be assigned to project team members to complete the work package. For instance, sample activities for the servers or software application work package can be:
    - Install database software
    - Configure database software
    - Integrate database server with other network components

WBS Dictionary

WBS dictionary is associated with the work packages in a work breakdown structure (WBS).

- **Work Breakdown Structure Dictionary provides a description of the work to be done for each WBS work package:** As we have seen before, each work package is depicted as nouns or with a couple of words in the WBS. In order to complete the project scope properly, it must be understood very well by the project stakeholders. Therefore, what needs to be done to complete a work package are detailed in the WBS dictionary.

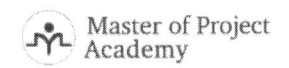

- **WBS Dictionary helps preventing the scope creep by defining the details of work package:** Since what needs to be done within, a work package is detailed in the WBS dictionary, project team members are illuminated with the scope and this helps prevent the team to do the unnecessary work or any work that is out of the project scope.
- **WBS Dictionary is a project document and it is output of the Create WBS project:** After the creation of WBS, each work package is associated with a WBS dictionary to describe what will be done in scope of regarding work package.

Now, let us go over a sample WBS dictionary and what it includes respectively.

WBS Dictionary			
Control Account ID #	Work Package #	Date of Update	Responsible Organization/ Individual

Work Package Description
Acceptance Criteria (How to know if the work is acceptable)
Deliverables for This Work
Assumptions
Resources Assigned
Duration
Schedule Milestones
Cost
Due Date
Interdependencies Before this work package After this work package
Approved By: Project Manager   Date:

As you see, top level of the WBS dictionary represents high-level information about the work package:
  - **Control Account ID** that the work package belongs
  - Work Package ID
  - Date of update
  - **Responsible Organization or Individual** who will complete this work package during the project.
  - **Work Package Description** area will describe what needs to be done in detail. It is actually the scope of work that will be done to complete the work package.
  - **Acceptance Criteria** area will describe in what circumstances or conditions the work package will be accepted. These are generally derived from the project requirements. For instance, login mechanism work package will be accepted if login of a member is accomplished in less than 2 seconds. This is a sample for acceptance criteria.
  - **Deliverables of this work** area describes the smaller pieces of deliverable under the work package that will be produced.
  - **Assumptions** are the things that are assumed true, but may not be true if you remember from our previous notes. If there is any assumption regarding the work package, this must be listed in this area.

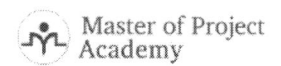

- o **Resources assigned** area shows the organizations or individuals who will perform the work package activities. There can be a department name, an individual name, supplier or all of them in this area.
- o **Duration** area shows how long it will take to complete and deliver the work package in the project.
- o **Schedule milestones** include the critical points that needs to be passed when delivering a work package. For instance, milestones for a work package can be installation completion, configuration completion and customer acceptance.
- o **Cost** area shows the total budget that must be allocated to complete this work package in the project. Cost of work packages in a work package are sum up to find the budget of control accounts and sum of the budgets of control accounts will result in determining the total project budget.
- o **Due date** area shows the final date that this work package must be delivered.
- o **Interdependencies** area shows dependencies that are predecessors and successors of this work package. These interdependencies are critical when constructing the network diagram of the project. Because, if there are any predecessors of a work package, you cannot start that work package before predecessors are completed. For instance, in a construction project, you cannot paint the interior area of the building before completing the main frame of the building. These kinds of dependencies must be listed in WBS dictionary.
- o **Approval details:** After a work package is completed, it must be accepted by customer and date of acceptance must be written here.

Validate Scope Process

5th process of the scope management knowledge area is Validate Scope Process.

Project team performs the assigned activities to complete the project scope and throughout the project, deliverables of the project are completed.

Once the deliverables are completed, they must be reviewed by the customer to check whether they meet the agreed requirements in the beginning of the project. A deliverable is accepted and mark as completed only if it is accepted by the customer after checks.

> Validate scope process is the process of formalizing acceptance of the completed project deliverables.

Validate scope process aims to organize frequent, planned-in meetings with customer or sponsor to gain formal acceptance of deliverables during Monitoring & Controlling process group.

Customer check and acceptance of the deliverables is a critical activity since the final acceptance of the project will be received from the customer. Frequent meetings to get customer acceptance are critical because if there are many deliverables in a project, and if you wait the end of the project to get acceptance, if there are any disputes in the deliverables, it will be hard to do rework and revise the deliverable accordingly. Therefore, deliverables of a project must be shown to the customer frequently and acceptance must be acquired.

Validate scope process helps to:

- **To show the customer that project is on track.** Consider that there will be 100 hundred deliverables in a project and the project duration is 2 years. Even if the customer will be reported about the project progress, as long as the customer does not see the outputs or deliverables, customer will not be 100% confident. However, if these deliverables are presented to the customer and the customer acceptance is acquired frequently as long as new deliverables are ready, customer will be more confident, reworks will be minimized, and project reporting to customer will be easier.

- **To find changes or issues during project rather than at the end.** Since customer will review the deliverables as long as ready, if there are any issues or problems with the deliverable, the project team will be able to fix the issues before the project deadline closes. However, if all deliverables are presented to the customer at the end of the project, and if there will be many issues to correct, project team might not deal with all issues in time and this can cause project delays respectively.

- **The customer either accepts the deliverable or makes a change request:** When a deliverable is presented to, the customer either accepts the deliverable or makes a change request. If the deliverable meets the requirements agreed in project scope in the beginning, customer accepts it. Alternatively, if there are problems and requirements are not met, defects must be fixed by the project team and the deliverable must be represented to the customer again. The last case is, even if the deliverable meets the agreed requirements, based on the evaluation of the deliverable, customer might come with new change requests. For instance, new functionality, new features etc.

The inputs of the Validate Scope process

- **Validated deliverables:** The work must be completed and there should be "validated deliverables". In order to check whether a deliverable met the initial agreed requirements, it must have been completed first. After a deliverable is completed, it is controlled in Validate Scope process.

- **Approved Scope:** It is another input of the Validate Scope process. Scope baseline refers the last agreed scope of a project by all project stakeholders. Validate scope process checks whether a deliverable meets its agreed requirements against the approved scope. Requirements, specifications, expectations, performance etc. of a deliverable is defined on scope, and once the deliverable is ready, these are checked.

- **Requirements Traceability matrix (RTM):** Requirements Traceability matrix is an input to validate scope process to show that requirements were achieved the validated deliverable. Requirement traceability matrix show the status of each requirement, track of requirement, and which deliverable will fulfill the requirement. Therefore, RTM will be an input for Validate scope process.

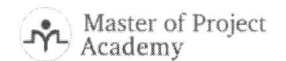

The outputs of Validate Scope process

- **Accepted Deliverables:** If the deliverable has been produced as per requirements and the customer approves this, deliverables are accepted by the customer.

- **Change Requests:** Deliverables might have met all requirements agreed in the beginning. Customer might come with new requirements since he sees a working deliverable now. These new requirements are initiated with a change request. If change requests are approved by the change control board, then the change request can be implemented by the project team.

- **Defects:** If the deliverables do not meet the agreed requirements, these needs to be fixed by the project team, and customer needs to check the deliverable again after the fixes.

- **Project document updates and work performance information:** After deliverables are completed and accepted, project documents must be updated and accepted deliverables must be marked in the project documents respectively. In addition, work performance information about the deliverable must be updated. For instance, whether it meet the budget forecast, schedule forecast, quality requirements etc.

Steps of Validate Scope Process

Let us go over the steps of Validate Scope process to give a better understanding.

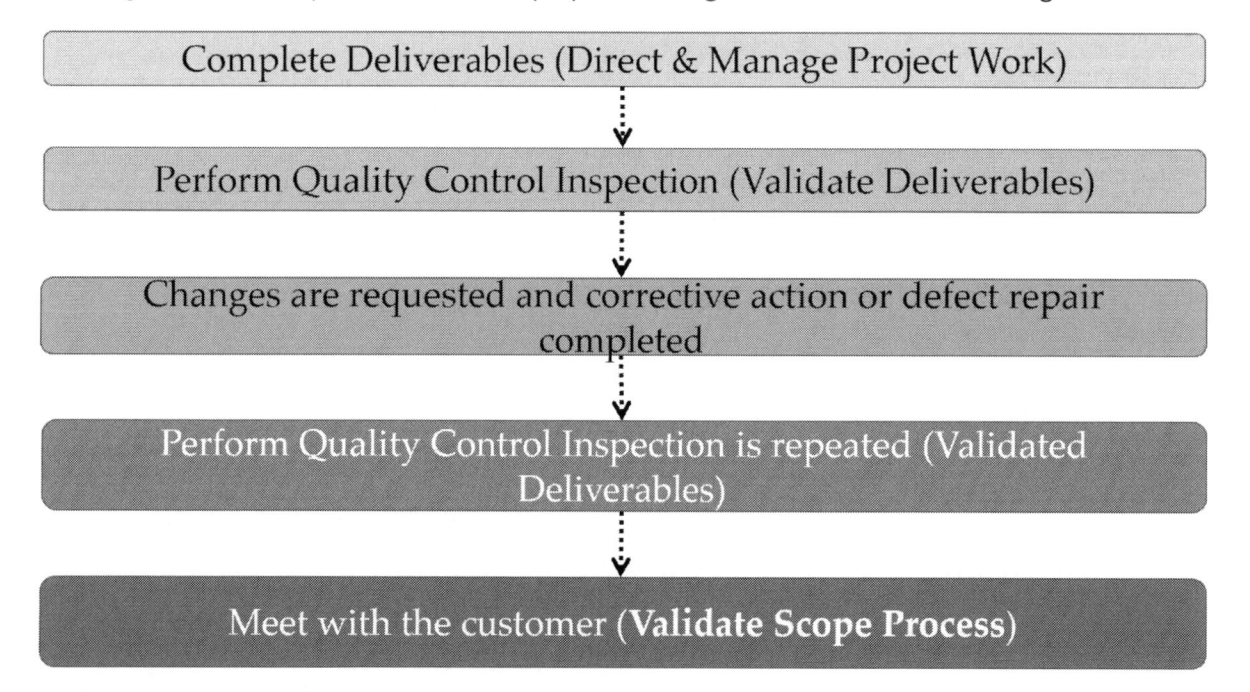

Complete Deliverables (Direct & Manage Project Work)
↓
Perform Quality Control Inspection (Validate Deliverables)
↓
Changes are requested and corrective action or defect repair completed
↓
Perform Quality Control Inspection is repeated (Validated Deliverables)
↓
Meet with the customer (**Validate Scope Process**)

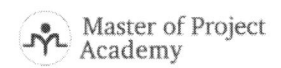

1. First deliverables of the project are completed during direct and manage project work process.
2. After the deliverables are ready, Perform Quality Control inspection step takes place. This is done generally by the quality control department of the company. For instance, consider that your project team completed a module of a software in a project. Test department will check before the customer whether the completed module works as per requirements.
3. After customer checks changes are requested by the customer or defects are fixed by the project team to meet the requirements.
4. After defects are fixed, deliverable is now ready for the demonstration. Perform Quality Control Inspection is repeated but this time, customer checks the deliverables.
5. After customer makes his tests, verifications and validations, project team meets with the customer. After customer, checks the deliverables there are two possible outcomes.
    a. First outcome is, if the deliverable meets the requirements customer accepts the deliverables.
    b. Second outcome is, changes are requested or if there are defects, these are reported to the project team for fixing. Note that, change requests will be evaluated by the change control board and only approved change requests will be implemented in the project.

Control Scope Process

Control scope process is the last process of the Scope Management Knowledge Area. Control scope process is the process of monitoring the status of the project and product scope and managing changes to the scope baseline. After scope is finalized in a project, it needs to be monitored throughout the project whether project activities will lead to successful delivery of project deliverables. Control scope process mainly tracks this in a project.

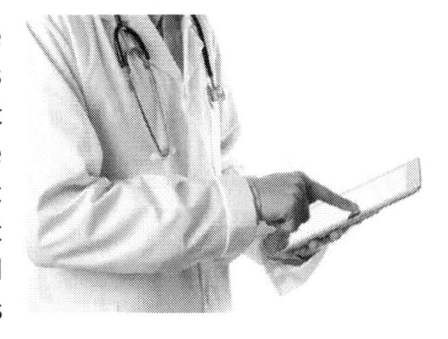

There will be changes in a project as well. If a change is approved by the change control board, it needs to be implemented in the project. Control scope baseline manages these changes to the scope baseline respectively.

Control Scope process does the measuring project and product scope performance and managing scope baseline changes. When delivering product and project scope, how these deliverables meet the initial agreed, requirements must be checked. If many gaps between the requirements and deliverable come into place during perform quality assurance and many defects are reported by the customer, these need to be corrected and regarding preventive actions to reduce number of defects, in future deliverables must be taken.

In Control scope process to control the scope, there are two main prerequisites.

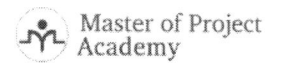

- **Scope definition must be clear.** Because, scope performance measurement will be done mainly on the sealed scope in the beginning. To do accurate and precise scope performance measurement, scope definition must be clear.
- **Work must be completed.** In order to check the results of a delivered work against the scope baseline, it must be finished first.

Steps for Control Scope process

There are five steps of Control Scope Process:

1. **Measure performance against scope baseline:** In order to check whether delivered work meets the initial agreed requirements, it is measured against scope baseline. Scope baseline stores the last and up-to-date scope of a project.

2. **Determine magnitude of variance:** After evaluation and checks, if the delivered work does not meet the agreed requirements and scope, level of variance is identified.

3. **Decide whether corrective/preventive action is needed:** After variance against the scope baseline is determined, this variance must be fixed. These can be defect repairs or preventive actions that will reduce the possibility of future scope variances.

4. **Updates to scope baseline, project management plan or project documents:** Depending on the corrective and preventive actions that will be taken to fix the variances and get back on track on the scope baseline, regarding documents and plans must be updated respectively.

5. **Impact of changes should be evaluated:** Output of the control scope process can be change requests. In order to assess the outcomes of the change request to the project, impact of changes should be evaluated. Because, change control board will determine to approve a change request by evaluating the impact of changes as well.

See how control scope process is related with perform integrated change control process.

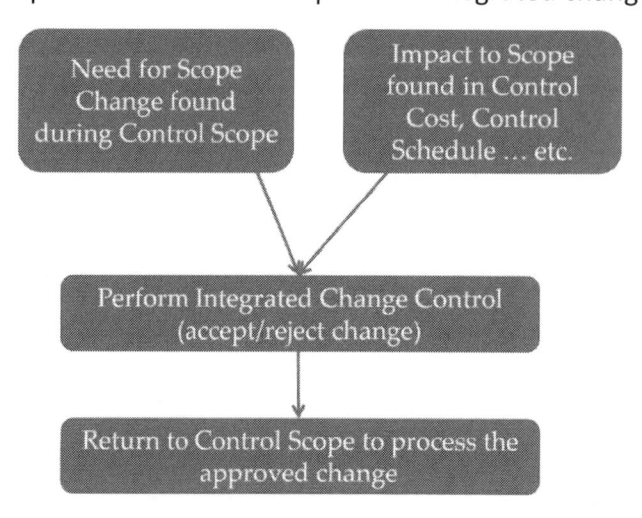

```
┌─────────────────────┐      ┌─────────────────────┐
│   Need for Scope    │      │  Impact to Scope    │
│   Change found      │      │  found in Control   │
│ during Control Scope│      │  Cost, Control      │
│                     │      │  Schedule ... etc.  │
└──────────┬──────────┘      └──────────┬──────────┘
           │                            │
           └─────────────┬──────────────┘
                         ▼
           ┌─────────────────────────────┐
           │ Perform Integrated Change   │
           │ Control (accept/reject      │
           │ change)                     │
           └──────────────┬──────────────┘
                          ▼
           ┌─────────────────────────────┐
           │ Return to Control Scope to  │
           │ process the approved change │
           └─────────────────────────────┘
```

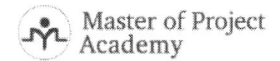

Need for scope change is found during control scope process. Deliverables and work completed in project must be checked against scope baseline. If there are variances in the completed work or deliverable, or if customer is requesting changes, these must be updated in the scope.

Alternatively, during other control processes of other knowledge management areas such as control cost, control schedule etc., impact to scope can be found. For instance, customer might come with an earlier delivery time compared to what was agreed in the beginning. With the same resources and budget, this can be possible only if the scope is reduced. This means an impact on the project scope.

These two reasons will initiate the perform integrated change control process. As we have seen during integration management knowledge area, changes in a project are evaluated based on a structured approach and only approved change requests can be implemented in a project.

Based on the outcome of the perform integrated change control process, if the change request is accepted by the change control board, control scope process will take the approved change request and implementation will take place. Regarding updates on project documents, scope baseline and project, management plans will be done respectively.

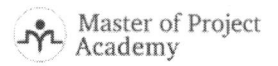

Quiz – Section 4

1- Scope Management processes define what work is required and then making sure all of that work and only that work are done. All of the following about scope management are correct EXCEPT:

    A) Scope must be clear and formally approved before work starts

    B) Requirements are gathered from all stakeholders

    C) Requirements gathering can take long time

    D) Small works do not exist in project management plan can be done if schedule is not affected

2- Which of the following is an example of gold plating?

    A) Developing a new feature which is not in requirements in product of the project

    B) Finishing the project under budget

    C) Finishing the project before deadline

    D) Correcting a defect occurred during acceptance tests

3- All of the following processes of Scope Management belong to planning process group EXCEPT:

    A) Collect Requirements

    B) Define Scope

    C) Validate Scope

    D) Create WBS

4- Requirements Management Plan is an output of:

    A) Collect Requirements

    B) Plan Scope Management Process

    C) Validate Scope

    D) Create WBS

5- How the scope will be defined, developed and verified is described in:

   A) Requirements Management Plan

   B) Scope Management Plan

   C) Content Management Plan

   D) Project Plan

6- Scope Management Plan includes all of the following processes EXCEPT:

   A) Creation of WBS

   B) Preparing a detailed project scope statement

   C) How formal acceptance will be obtained

   D) How budget for delivering scope will be spent

7- Requirements Management Plan includes all of the following processes EXCEPT:

   A) Configuration Management activities

   B) Product Metrics

   C) Defect List

   D) Traceability structure

8- You are working in a smart phone development project. You are in the Collect Requirements Process of your project. Which of the following is NOT a valid requirement?

   A) Must have a good quality

   B) Must have an 8 Mega Pixel camera

   C) Must have a Li-on battery

   D) Must be delivered in 6 months

9- Several tools & techniques can be used during Collect Requirements Process. Which of the following is NOT a tool & technique used in this process?

   A) Sponsor Meeting

   B) Interviewing

   C) Brainstorming

   D) Nominal Group Technique

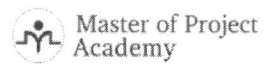

10- You are working in a software company. In order to collect requirements of your project, you sent an information request to several stakeholders anonymously. After collecting initial requirements list and combining requirements, you sent back the list again to participants. This is an example of:

A) Brainstorming

B) Facilitated Workshops

C) Affinity Diagrams

D) Delphi Technique

11- You are working in an automobile manufacturer. Your company is planning to produce a new car model in following years. In order to get the feedback of customers, the company showed a first version of the car model in Paris Auto show. This is an example of:

A) Group Decision Making

B) Analysis

C) Prototype

D) Questionnaires and Surveys

12- There might be competing stakeholder requirements in a project. During balancing stakeholder requirements, all of the following can be done EXCEPT:

A) Prioritization of Requirements

B) Requirement of a strong stakeholder should override a weak stakeholder

C) Resolving conflicts between requirements

D) Management support should be asked if a conflict cannot be resolved

13- During your project, you are aiming to track the requirements over the life of project to ensure they are accomplished. You should use:

A) Defect List

B) Requirements Traceability Matrix

C) Test Report

D) Project Plan

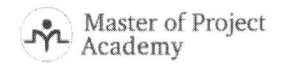

14- Which process of Scope Management is primarily concerned with what is and is not included in project and its deliverables?

A) Define Scope Process

B) Complete Scope Process

C) Collect Requirement Process

D) Validate Scope Process

15- During Define Scope Process, all of the following are used to define project and product scope EXCEPT:

A) Requirements Documentation

B) Project Charter

C) Cost Plan

D) Information about risks, assumptions and constraints

16- Primary output of Define Scope Process is Scope Baseline. All of the following are components of scope baseline EXCEPT:

A) WBS

B) WBS Dictionary

C) Project Cost Statement

D) Project Scope Statement

17- Project Scope Statement includes all of the following EXCEPT:

A) Roles and Responsibilities

B) Product Scope

C) Product Acceptance Criteria

D) Constraints and Assumptions

18- You are managing a telecommunication product integration project in a telecom operator. Which of the following can be an example of project constraint?

A) A personnel from operations team will support the team during project

B) Maximum concurrent users will not exceed 200 at a time

C) RAM of the equipment will not be used more than 80% at a time

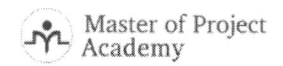

D) System backup must be taken between 2.15-2.30 every night.

19- Main output of Create WBS (Work Breakdown Structure) Process is WBS. All of the following about WBS is true EXCEPT:

  A) WBS is a structured vision of what has to be delivered

  B) WBS helps to better understand the project

  C) WBS shows the delivery dates of each deliverable

  D) WBS shows hierarchy of deliverables

20- There are some rules when creating WBS. Which of the following rules is NOT correct?

  A) WBS is created with the help of the team

  B) Each level of a WBS will be broken down to same level

  C) Each level of the WBS is smaller piece of the level above

  D) WBS includes only deliverables that are really needed

21- Using WBS brings several benefits in a project. Which of the following is NOT a benefit of using WBS?

  A) Helps prevent work from slipping through cracks

  B) Prevents procurement of certain items

  C) Helps prevent changes

  D) Provides a basis for estimating cost and time

22- WBS contains nouns instead of actions and details that need to be done regarding a specific deliverable. Which of the following completes WBS in terms of describing what needs to be done for each WBS work package?

  A) Scope Baseline

  B) Project Statement of Work

  C) WBS Detail List

  D) WBS Dictionary

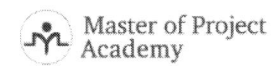

23- Validate Scope is the process of formalizing acceptance of the completed project deliverables. All of the following about this process are true EXCEPT:

   A) Final acceptance of the project is done during this process

   B) Helps to show customer that project is on track

   C) The customer either accepts the deliverable or makes a change request

   D) Frequent, planned-in meetings are done with customer to gain acceptance of interim deliverables

24- All of the following are outputs of Validate Scope Process EXCEPT:

   A) Accepted Deliverables

   B) Change Requests

   C) Closure of project if deliverable is accepted

   D) Work Performance Information

25- Monitoring the status of the project and product scope and managing changes to the project scope baseline is done during:

   A) Create WBS Process

   B) Define Scope Process

   C) Validate Scope Process

   D) Control Scope Process

Answers

1 – D	16 – C
2 – A	17 – A
3 – C	18 – D
4 – B	19 – C
5 – B	20 – B
6 – D	21 – B
7 – C	22 – D
8 – A	23 – A
9 – A	24 – C
10 – D	25 – D
11 – C	
12 – B	
13 – B	
14 – A	
15 – C	

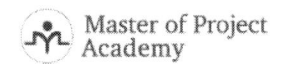

Mapping Game – Section 4

The features and functions that characterize a product, service, or result	User Story
Shows a business system and how people and other systems interact with it	Define Scope
Describes the stakeholder role, the goal and the benefit to them	functional and nonfunctional
process of developing a detailed description of the project and product.	provides a framework of what has to be delivered.
The 2 types of project life cycle	Context Diagram
The approved version of scope statement, WBS and WBS dictionary	Product Scope
describe the qualities required for the product to be effective.	Scope Baseline
What are the 2 solution requirement groups?	Nonfunctional requirements
The key benefits of "Create WBS" process	Predictive and Adaptive

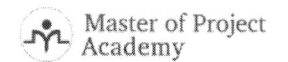

Answers

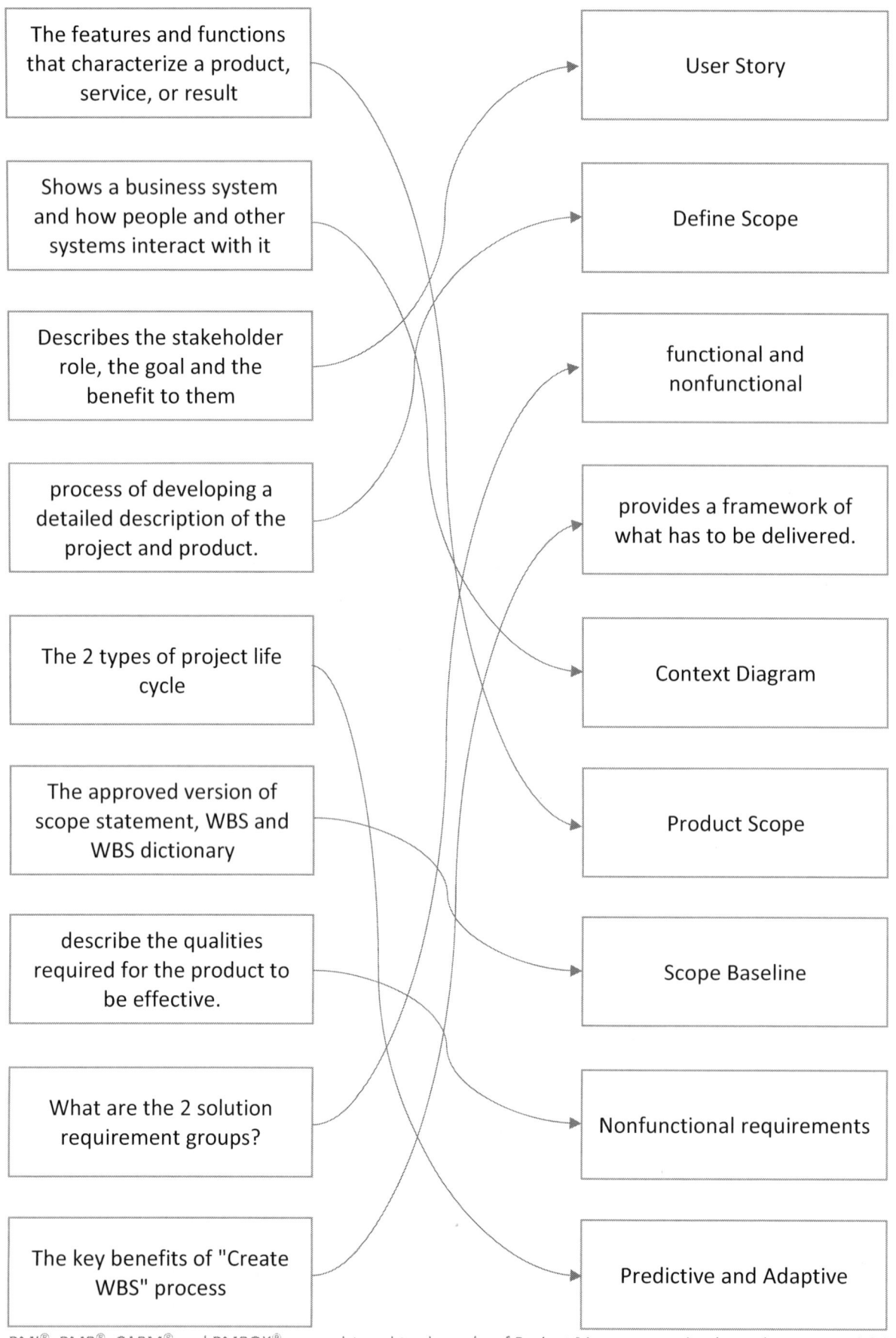

Left	Right (matched)
The features and functions that characterize a product, service, or result	Product Scope
Shows a business system and how people and other systems interact with it	Context Diagram
Describes the stakeholder role, the goal and the benefit to them	User Story
process of developing a detailed description of the project and product.	Define Scope
The 2 types of project life cycle	Predictive and Adaptive
The approved version of scope statement, WBS and WBS dictionary	Scope Baseline
describe the qualities required for the product to be effective.	Nonfunctional requirements
What are the 2 solution requirement groups?	functional and nonfunctional
The key benefits of "Create WBS" process	provides a framework of what has to be delivered.

Section 5

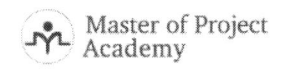

Schedule Management

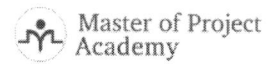

Section 5 – Schedule Management

Schedule Management Knowledge area is another important knowledge area in project management. Schedule management mainly deals with the relationship of the activities, start and end dates of the activities, overall project schedule and ensuring the timely completion of all project activities respectively.

During this section, we will go over the processes and content of Schedule Management Knowledge area:

- **Overview of Schedule Management knowledge area:** We will describe the schedule management and scheduling overview. We will list the processes of Schedule Management Knowledge area that we will go throughout this section.
- **Plan Schedule Management Process:** This is the first process of the Schedule Management Knowledge area. Plan Schedule management process is the process where all time planning activities of a project are organized. How to define interrelationships of activities, schedule compression techniques, time planning approach etc. are done in scope of Plan Schedule Management Process.
- **Schedule Management Plan:** Schedule Management plan describes how to set start and end dates of activities, how to plan overall project deadlines and how construct and manage schedule of the project respectively.
- **Define activities process:** This is the second process of the Schedule Management Knowledge area. In order to complete the schedule of the project, first, what needs to be performed during the project must be outlined. These are activities. Define activities process will help to figure out the activities that needs to be performed to complete the project.
- **Sequence activities process:** There will be many activities in a project but some of them will be depending on others, some will need to finish together or some will need to start together etc. We will see how interrelationship of activities are defined during Sequence Activities process.
- **Precedence diagramming method:** It is an important method used in completing overall project schedule.
- **Leads and lags:** Leads and Lags describe the amount of time that needs to be waited between activities.
- **Network Diagrams:** Network diagram of a project shows the overall activity relationship and paths from the start activity to the end of the project respectively. Therefore, network diagram is a critical element in project planning in order to complete the project schedule.
- **Estimate Activity Durations process:** In this process, activity resources provide their effort estimations for the activities they are assigned to. This is important to bottom-up the duration estimations of each activity and complete the project schedule respectively.
- **Tools & Techniques Used in Duration Estimation:** Several tools and techniques are used during estimation and we will go over each of them in detail.
- **Develop Schedule process:** In this process, information collected during previous processes are gathered and overall project schedule is completed. This includes the start and end dates of each individual activity in a project.

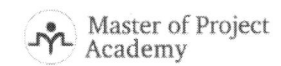

- **Critical Path Method:** It is the most popular method used in determining project schedule. We will go through Critical Path Method in detail with sample scenarios.
- **Schedule Compression:** Projects might face risks or some activities may take longer than planned. Alternatively, even if everything goes as planned, management or customer might come with a tighter schedule request. In that case, remaining activities must be completed faster than planned and this is possible with Schedule Compression methods. We will describe the Schedule compression in detail.
- **What-if scenario analysis:** It is used to anticipate future outcomes of the project based on simulations. These are generally executed with the help of computer programs.
- **Resource leveling:** It is done to optimize resource usage in a project and ensure fair workload in project team members respectively. We will go over Resource leveling in future notes as well.
- **Critical chain method:** It is a method to determine the overall project schedule and we will go over this as well.
- **Project Schedule & Schedule Baseline:** Project Schedule shows the start and end dates of each project activity and the overall project deadline respectively. Schedule baseline shows the project schedule snapshot of a project in order to compare actual results in future.
- **Control Schedule process:** It is the last process of Schedule Management knowledge area. Control Schedule process controls the project schedule against baselines and take corrective and preventive actions to keep project on track.

Overview of Schedule Management

Schedule Management includes processes required to manage the timely completion of the project. There are lots of stakeholders, several project team members and several activities that need to be performed in order to reach project goals and objectives.

> Schedule management ensures the coordination, sequence and timely completion of project activities to complete the project on time.

Project Schedule is the major output of the Schedule Management. Project Schedule shows the start and end dates of each activity, interrelationship of activities, and overall project start and end dates respectively.

This figure summarizes the scheduling overview. As you see in the right circle, there are lots of project information like WBS, activities, resources, durations, constraints, calendars, milestones, lags, etc. These bulk data provide detailed information on activity level but it needs to be processed to reach a complete project schedule. To do this, a scheduling method is used. Most popular scheduling method is Critical Path Method, which is abbreviated as CPM. CPM method shows the shortest duration to complete all project activities. We will go over the CPM in detail in our further notes.

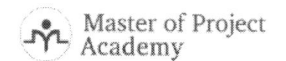

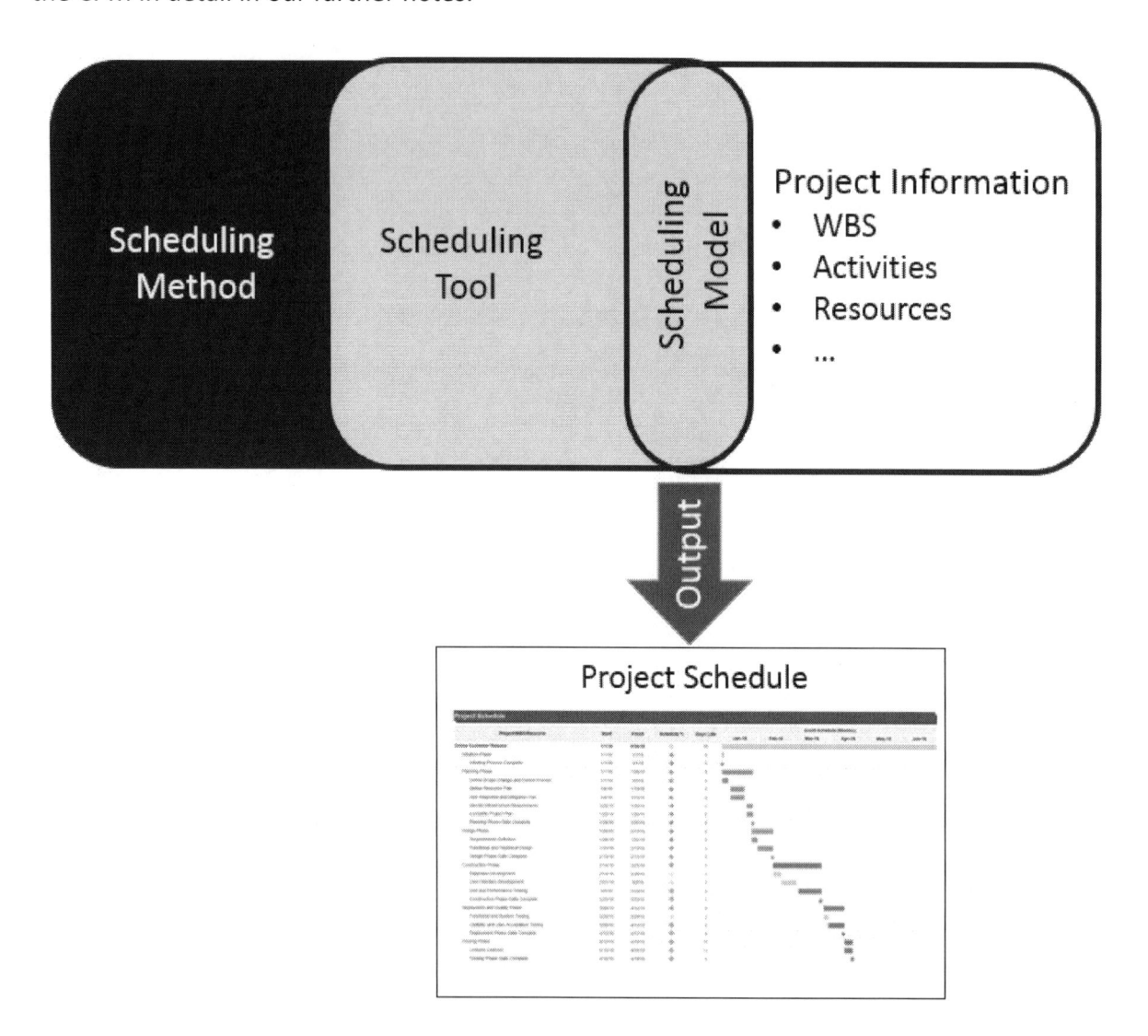

In order to use CPM, generally, a scheduling tool is used and these are usually computer programs. Most common scheduling tools in the project management world are Microsoft Project and Primavera. These tools help you to enter all project activities one by one, define interrelationship of activities, assign project resources, define calendars etc. and generates the overall project schedule.

Once the project schedule is completed, there are several alternative ways to present. Here, you see three common project schedule presentation methods:

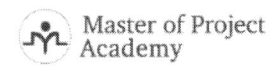

Project Schedule Presentation Samples

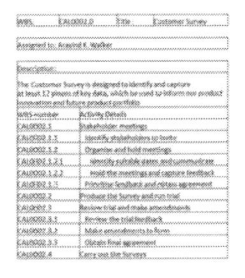

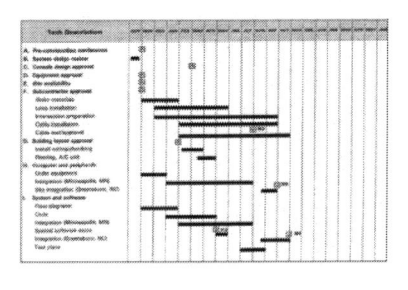

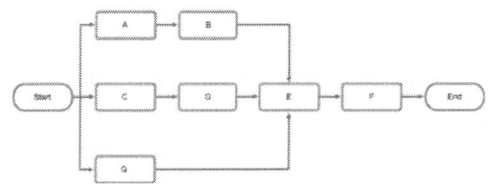

Activity List   Bar Chart   Network Diagram

- **Activity list** shows short description of each activity, start and end dates, and assigned resource respectively.
- **Bar chart** shows short description of each activity and relationships of activities with bars next to each activity.
- **Network diagram** shows each activity as a box and duration of the activity is placed on the box. Interrelationship of activities are shown with arrows.

We will go over these presentation methods in detail during our further notes.
- Schedule Management Knowledge area has six processes. Most of the schedule management takes place during planning, therefore five processes of Schedule Management knowledge area belong to planning process group and only one process belongs to Monitoring and controlling process group.

Processes of Schedule Management Knowledge area are:
1. Plan Schedule Management
2. Define Activities
3. Sequence Activities
4. Estimate Activity Durations
5. Develop Schedule
6. Control Schedule

We will go over each process during our further notes in detail.

Plan Schedule Management Process

First process of the Schedule Management knowledge area is Plan Schedule Management process. Plan Schedule Management is the process of establishing the policies, procedures, and documentation for planning, developing, managing, executing and controlling the project schedule.

> Plan schedule management process aims to ensure the timely completion of project.

- **Plan Schedule Management process provides guidance and direction on how the project schedule will be managed throughout the project.** Based on the information in the beginning of the project, activities are determined, resources that will be performing these activities are planned and durations of activities are estimated. Then, overall project schedule is constituted. However, regardless of your project planning accuracy, project actual values will differ from the planned ones. Once there is a deviation in the project schedule, necessary corrective and preventive actions must be taken to get back on track. Plan Schedule Management process provides this guidance when necessary.
- **Major output** of the Plan Schedule Management process is **Schedule Management Plan.**

Schedule Management plan

Schedule Management plan answers the following questions.
- **How will I create the schedule?** It includes the steps that need to be taken to create project schedule. For instance, how to determine project activities, how to assign resources to activities, how to do effort estimation, which scheduling method should be used etc. are all included in the Schedule Management Plan.
- **What tools will I use for scheduling?** For instance, if there is a pre-determined effort estimation model in the company, this must be included. Scheduling tool that will be used, for instance Microsoft Project, must be mentioned in the Schedule Management plan as well.
- **How will I go about planning the schedule for the project?** Creating the project schedule requires a planning as well. Determining project activities, assigning resources to activities, effort estimation, sequencing activities and finalizing the project schedule must be planned properly. This is included in the schedule management plan.
- **How will I effectively manage and control the project to the schedule baseline, and manage schedule variances?** Once the project schedule is created, schedule baseline will be taken. Nevertheless, changes and deviations are inevitable in a project. Project schedule must be readjusted based on approved change requests and schedule variance. How to do this is outlined in the schedule management plan.

What does Schedule Management plan include?

- **Scheduling methodology and scheduling software to be used on the project are included in the schedule management plan**. For instance, if critical path method will be used to determine the project duration, this must be documented in the schedule management plan. Similarly, if Microsoft Project is the tool that will be used for scheduling, this is included in the schedule management plan.
- **Establishment of a schedule baseline is included in the schedule management plan as well**. Schedule baseline is critical to check whether the project is going as planned and whether the project deadline will be met. Therefore, schedule baseline is included in the schedule management plan.

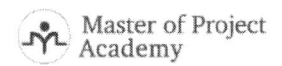

- **Identification of performance measures, to identify variances early is also included in the schedule management plan.** In order the check whether the project is going as planned and whether the agreed deadline will be met, performance measurement must be done. How to do this, frequency, methods that will be used when measuring etc. need to be included in the schedule management plan.
- **Planning for how schedule variances will be managed** must be included in the schedule management plan as well. For instance, if there is contingency budget that will be used to acquire and assign additional resources when there will be a schedule variance, this must be included in the schedule management plan.
- **Identification of schedule change control procedures must be placed in the schedule management plan.** When there is an approved change request, or when there is a variance, existing schedule usually needs an update. How to change the schedule and its procedures must be included in the schedule management plan.
- **How you will measure schedule performance and in what frequency must be outlined in the schedule management plan.** Weekly, monthly or in each 2 weeks? What will be the frequency of schedule performance measurement? What will be the metrics and tools to measure schedule performance? These must be in the schedule management plan.
- **Guidelines on how estimates should be stated must be in the schedule management plan.** After activities are determined and resources are assigned, effort estimation takes place. In order to ensure coherent estimation and reporting, units for estimations must be documented in the schedule management plan.
- **Variance thresholds must be included in the schedule management plan.** We will see the schedule performance index in our further notes. Schedule performance index shows whether a project is behind the schedule or ahead of schedule. Variance threshold defines when there should be a corrective action taken.
- **Type of reports for schedule.** Will you use bar chart, activity list, network diagrams or what are the other types of reports that you will use for schedule reporting? This must be defined in the schedule management plan.

Define Activities Process

Define Activities process is the second process of Schedule Management knowledge area. During define activities process, based on the determined scope, activities that must be performed to reach the project goals and objectives are defined.

Define Activities is the process of identifying and documenting the specific actions to be performed to produce the project deliverables.

These activities will be performed by project team members and they should be as small as possible in order to manage and project better.

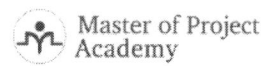

> ⚡ Well-defined activities are usually as small as to be completed in hours or in days.

Work packages are broken down to activities in order to better estimate, schedule, monitor and manage. Work packages show a small interim deliverable or work that needs to be completed. Nevertheless, activities are small parts of each work package and the work package can be completed by completing all activities belonging to it. Breaking down the work packages to activities will help better and more accurate estimation, management and coordination in a project respectively. Because each activity will be very small like installation of a PC, development of a simple screen, etc. Assignees of these activities will be more confident during estimation.

It is better to distinguish and highlight two important concepts here:

Creation of Work Packages is completed in scope of Scope Management knowledge area but these work packages are turned into activities in Schedule Management knowledge area.

Creation of Work Packages → Scope Management
Creation of Activities → Schedule Management

- **You need scope baseline (scope statement, WBS and WBS dictionary) for defining activities:** In order to define activities in a project, you need scope baseline. If you remember from our previous notes, scope baseline includes scope statement, WBS and WBS dictionary. Scope statement describes the high-level information about the scope of the project. WBS shows the work and deliverable hierarchy of the project and WBS dictionary provides detailed information about the work packages. Therefore, when defining activities under a work package, this information will be very useful.

- **You will define activities with your team:** Define activities process is completed with the help of the project team. Because, project team will perform the project activities and based on the project scope and determined work packages in the WBS, project team members will define the project activities that needs to be performed to complete a work package.

What are the outputs of Define Activities process?

- **Activity List:** Activity list includes the project activities that needs to be performed in order to complete the project scope. This list includes activity names briefly such as: install database, configure database, execute creation scripts etc.
- **Activity attributes:** It is another output of Define Activities process and complements the activity list. WBS id of the activity, predecessors or successors of activity, leads and lags are highlighted in the activity attributes of each activity.
- **Milestones:** Milestones are not an activity and generally not assigned to any resource. However, they reflect a significant point in project. For a software project, sample milestones can be: completion of analysis, completion of design and development, completion of tests, handover to customer etc.

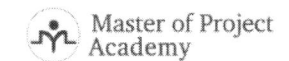

As we expressed already, milestones are significant events in project schedule.

- Milestones have zero duration and represent a specific moment in time. Since they reflect a moment, they are not assigned to a project resource or they do not have a duration.

- Sponsor of the project may impose milestones and milestones are included in charter. For instance, product launch is an important milestone and this can be imposed by the sponsor. There can be several milestones in a project but keeping the list short and showing the progress completions over these milestones will ease your progress reporting and communication with stakeholders respectively.

Define Activities Process Example

In our previous notes, we have seen the Define Activities process. Now, we will go over a sample define activities process. We will use this sample project in our further notes as well. Our sample project is Billing System Development for a utility service provider. It will include three major systems: Charging System, Database and Invoicing System. Invoicing system has one screen and one sub-system: invoice verification system.

Assume that you are defining the activities of invoicing screen work package. Activities of this work package can be
- Analyze invoice screen requirements
- Design invoice screen
- Develop invoice screen
- And test invoice screen

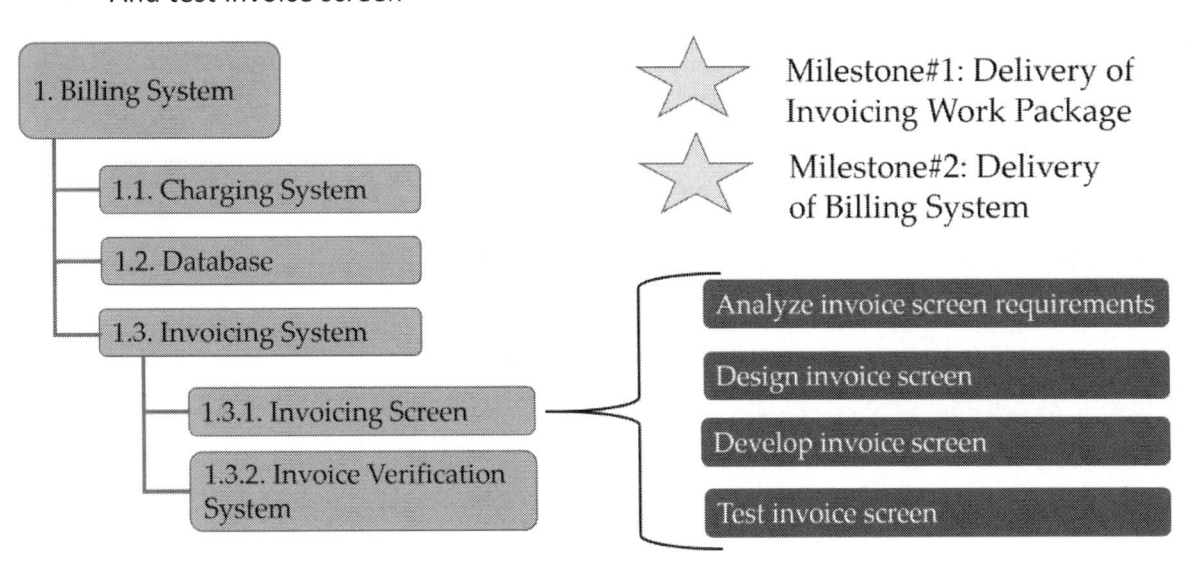

1. Billing System
    - 1.1. Charging System
    - 1.2. Database
    - 1.3. Invoicing System
        - 1.3.1. Invoicing Screen
            - Analyze invoice screen requirements
            - Design invoice screen
            - Develop invoice screen
            - Test invoice screen
        - 1.3.2. Invoice Verification System

⭐ Milestone#1: Delivery of Invoicing Work Package

⭐ Milestone#2: Delivery of Billing System

This means that, after completing these four activities, invoicing screen work package will be completed. These activities can be assigned to project team members. For instance, analyze invoice screen activity can be done by the analyst of the project, design invoice screen can be completed by architect or designer, develop invoice screen can be completed by software developer and test invoice screen can be completed by test engineer.

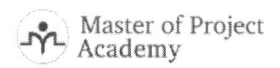

Moreover, sample milestones of this project can be Milestone #1 Delivery of invoicing work package and Milestone #2 Delivery of the Billing system. Depending on the sponsor's approach and project dynamics, there can be several milestones. We just wanted to illustrate how define activities process will take place in a sample project and provide sample milestones respectively.

Sequence Activities Process

After define activities process, activities that needs to be performed to complete the project scope are determined. However, these activities must be performed in a sequence. Some activities will depend on other once, therefore they need to wait before the dependent activity finishes, some activities will start together and some activities will finish together.

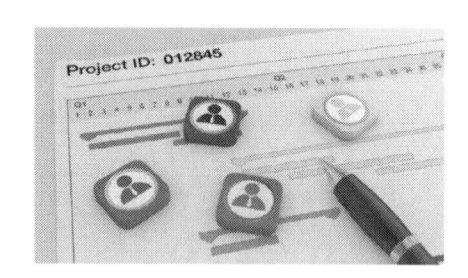

Therefore, sequence of the project activities must be formed. This is done with the help of Sequence Activities process mainly.

- **Sequence Activities is the process of identifying and documenting relationships among the project activities.** Therefore, the main purpose of the sequence activities process is finalizing the interrelationship of activities to complete a project scope and reach the project goals.
- **Key result of the Sequence Activities process is Network Diagram.** Network diagram of a project visualizes the project activities in boxes with activity ID and shows the interrelationship of activities with arrows.

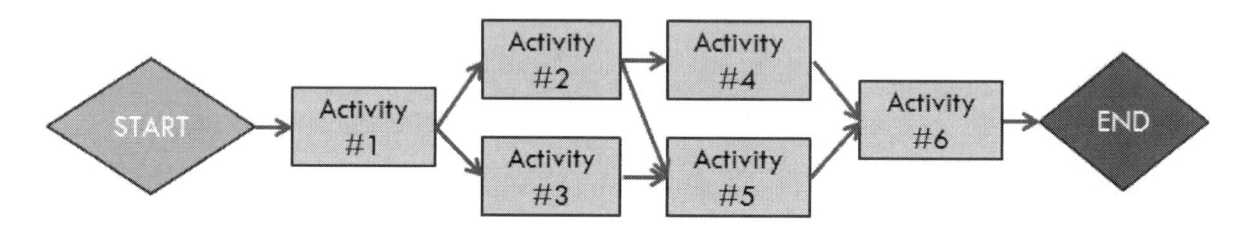

This figure shows a sample network diagram. As you see, after the start of the project,
- Activity #1 must start first.
- After Activity #1 finishes, Activity #2 and Activity #3 will begin.
- Activity #4 can start only after Activity #2 finishes.
- Activity #5 depends on Activity #2 and Activity #3 therefore; it will start only after these two activities are completed.
- The last activity, activity #6 can start only if Activity #4 and Activity #5 are completed.
- After activity #6 completion, project will end.

Note that this is just a simple and sample network diagram in order to show you how a network diagram is. In real-life projects, there will be many project activities and network diagram will be much more complex than this.

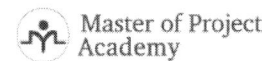

If activity durations are added in the Network diagram, critical path of the project can be seen as well. We will see the critical path calculation in our further notes. Network diagram is a critical input to determine the critical path of the project and if activity durations are placed on these activity boxes, these will help in seeing the critical path of the project as well.

Precedence Diagramming Method, which is abbreviated as PDM, is the most common method to draw network diagrams. During our notes, we will see the PDM method. PDM is also referred as Activity-On-Node and abbreviated as AON. This is because the activities are represented as boxes or nodes in the network diagram.

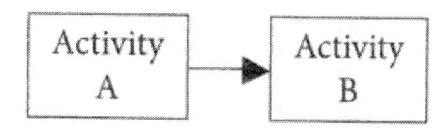

```
[Activity A] → [Activity B]
```

In Precedence Diagramming, method boxes represent the activities of the project and arrows represent the dependencies of these activities.

For instance, in this figure, Activity A is connected to Activity B with a forward arrow. This means, Activity B is depending on Activity A, and Activity B can start only after Activity A is finished. In other words, Activity A is the predecessor of the Activity B.

Types of Relationships in PDM

In order to complete the network diagram of a project with the precedence diagramming method 4 types of relationships between the activities are used. These are:
1. Finish-to-Start,
2. Start-to-Start,
3. Finish-to-Finish, and
4. Start-to-Finish.

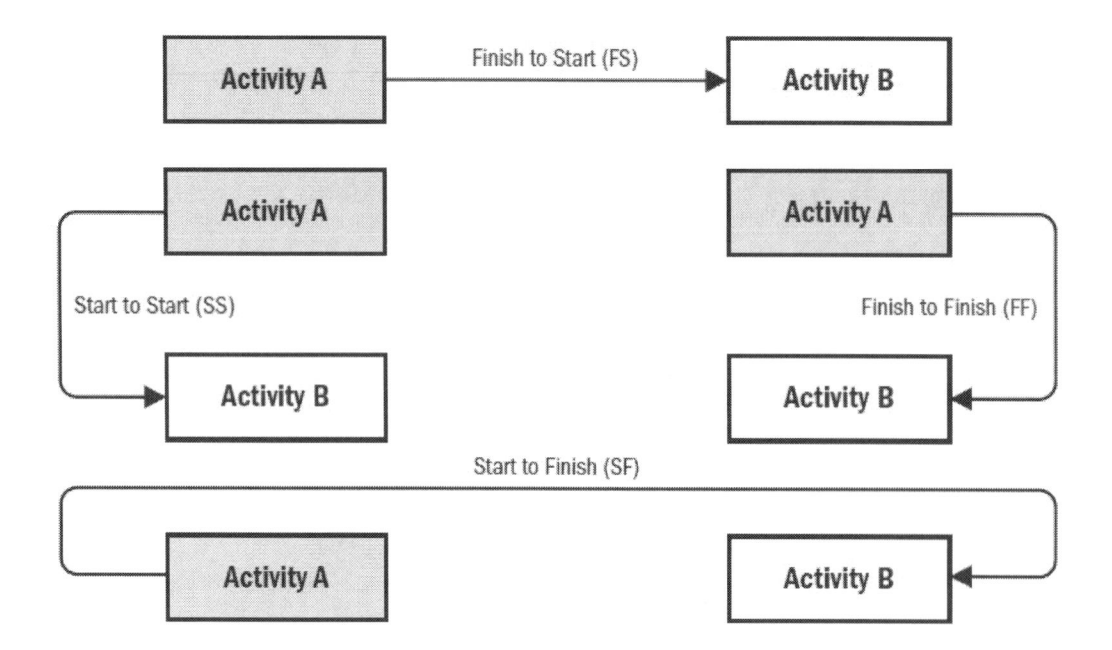

We will go over each type of dependency during this heading.

- **Finish-to-Start:** 1st type of dependency is Finish-to-Start dependency and abbreviated as FS. This is the most common dependency type used between activities. If an activity cannot start before a predecessor activity finishes, then a finish-to-start dependency must be between these activities.
  For instance, in a construction project, you cannot paint the building before you complete the construction. In a software project, you cannot start testing of a screen before it is developed. These are examples of finish-to-start dependencies in projects.

- **Start-to-Start:** 2nd type of dependency is Start-to-Start dependency and abbreviated as SS. This type of dependency shows that two activities will start together. For instance, in a construction project, building the mainframe of the construction will start with the procurement of materials. In this case, these activities will be shown as start-to-start dependent in the network diagram.

- **Finish-to-Finish:** 3rd type of dependency is Finish-to-Finish dependency and abbreviated as FF. This type of dependency shows that two activities in a project will finish together. For instance, in a software project, during tests, bugs will be found regarding the developed software. These bugs will be fixed by the software developers. Nevertheless, after that, testing team must re-check whether the bug is really fixed. Therefore, testing and bug fix activities are an example for finish-to-finish type of dependency in a project.

- **Start-to-finish:** 4th and the last type of dependency is Start-to-finish dependency and abbreviated as SF. Start-to-finish dependency is a very rare type of dependency in projects. In this type of dependency, Activity B can finish only after Activity A starts. These types of relationships can be used in just-in-time supply chain materials for example. Assume that you are working in a car manufacturing company and in your assembly line, you are using an electrical component for the cars, which is provided by a supplier. Say, there are 100 components in your warehouse. However, you have a threshold that if this number of components falls below 20, a new order should be placed to the supplier of the electronic component. In this case, there is a Start-to-finish dependency between the remaining number of electronic components in the warehouse and placing a new order.

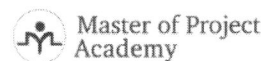

It is better to describe about GERT here. GERT is a modification to the network diagram drawing method allows loops between activities. This figure shows an example for the GERT.

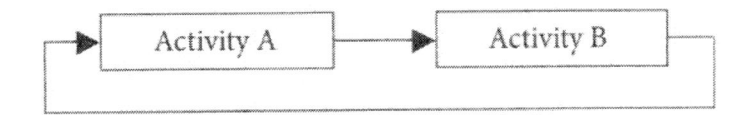

```
Activity A  →  Activity B
```

Activity B has a finish-to-start dependency to the Activity A. Activity B can start only after Activity A is finished. However, after Activity B is completed, activity A is re-initiated.

We can give the software development and testing as an example for this scenario. After software development finishes in a project, testing must start. During tests, bugs will be found. These bugs must be fixed by the software developers. Bug fixing and re-testing will continue until all bugs of the software will be finished. This is an example for GERT.

Types of Dependencies

We have seen the type of relationships in our previous heading. However, what are the types of dependencies between project activities?

There are 4 types of dependencies and we will go over each of them one-by-one during this heading.

1. **Mandatory Dependency (Hard Logic):** First type of dependency is Mandatory Dependency, which is known as hard logic as well. Mandatory dependency is inherent in the nature of the work. Consider a software project, and there is a screen that will be developed in scope of the project. Can you test it before the development finishes? Of course, no! Therefore, there is a mandatory dependency between development of the screen and testing of the screen in this case.

2. **Discretionary Dependency (Preferred, Preferential or Soft Logic):** Second type of dependency is Discretionary Dependency, which is known as preferred, preferential or soft logic as well. Discretionary dependency is determined by the project team and can be changed in order to shorten the project. Consider that John is a team member in the project and he has several activities. In order to complete the project earlier, you might change the order of John's activities. Activities remain same but the order changes. This is an example for the discretionary dependency.

3. **External Dependency:** Third type of dependency is External dependency. External dependencies come from outside of the project. For instance, in order to start your

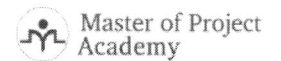

project, there is another project that must be completed first; this is an example of external dependency. Alternatively, if there is a government regulation that must be completed to continue the rest of the project activities, this is an example of external dependency as well.

4. **Internal Dependency:** Fourth and the last type of dependency is internal dependency. Internal dependency involves a precedence relationship between project activities. Consider that you are working in a construction project. Activities must be performed in order to complete the project. For instance, before the architecture team finishes the design of the building, construction work cannot start. This is an example of internal dependency. Alternatively, if there are several activities assigned on a project team member, he cannot start to new one before completing the previous one although there is not a mandatory dependency.

Leads & Lags

Leads and Lags are important terms in project management. You might have heard leads or lags previously. During this heading, we will go over leads and lags with samples of these terms as well.

Lead Time: The successor activity starts before the other activity finishes.

Consider a software development project. Coding of software development of a screen or function might start before its technical design finished. Technical designs of a screen or function in a software project will describe how the screen will be developed, buttons that will be on the screen, services it will use etc. If the technical design takes 20 days, after 15 days, most of the details about the technical design can be completed and the software developer can start to development of the screen with the certain parts. This will help to shorten the duration of the project since you will not wait to finish the all design.

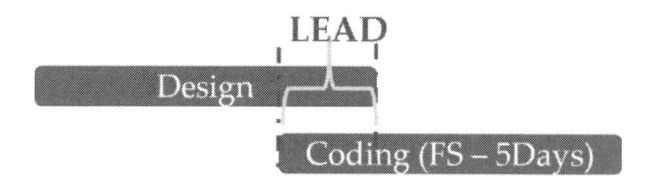

LEAD
Design
Coding (FS – 5Days)

In this scenario, these 5 days' time that will be before the design finishes when the development starts is called as lead-time.

Lag Time: The successor activity starts after the other activity finishes.

Consider a construction project. In order to start the construction, concrete will be prepared and poured on the foundations of the building. However, generally, after this concrete is poured, construction of the frame starts after a time, in our case after 3 days. This is mainly because for ensuring the hardening of the concrete for a safer construction.

```
         LAG
  ┌──────────────┐   ┌──────────────────────────┐
  │ Pour Concrete│───│ Constructing Frame (FS +3Days)│
  └──────────────┘   └──────────────────────────┘
```

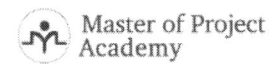

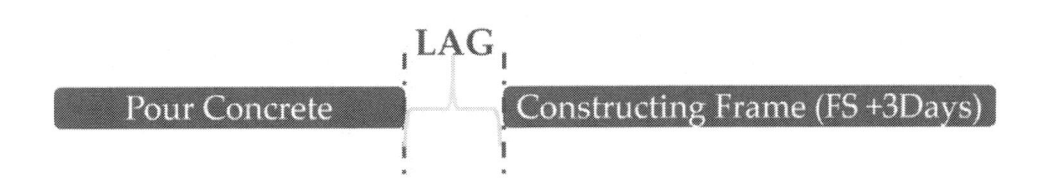

In this scenario, these 3 days' time that will be between the pouring the concrete and constructing the frame is called as lag time.

Benefits of Network Diagrams

- **Network Diagrams help justify your time estimate for project:** Since network diagram of a project shows how activities are interrelated with each other from the beginning of the project till end, it will be very beneficial for calculating the overall project duration. After the critical path of the project is determined, activities on the critical path will give us the total duration of the project respectively.

- **Network Diagrams aid in planning, organizing and controlling:** Since all project activities are shown in sequence with relevant interrelationships, the network diagram of a project will help the project manager and team during planning and organizing. Network diagram will be useful during project execution as well since it is a snapshot of the project activities tied with the dependencies.

- **Network diagrams show interdependencies of activities:** This is what we saw already in our previous notes. Since interdependencies of activities are visible in the network diagram, it will be easier to see which activity can start after which one, which activity depends on each other, predecessors and successors of each activity etc.

- **Network Diagrams show workflow of the project activities:** So, the project team will know the sequence of activities. At a certain point in the project, it will be easier to see in the network diagram what has been accomplished and the remaining activities and their interdependencies with each other.

- **Network diagrams identify opportunities to compress the schedule:** You may need to shorten the duration of the remaining activities in a project. This can be because your project is behind schedule and in order to complete the project on time, you need to compress the schedule. In this case, since network diagrams show the order of the activities and durations, it will be easier to focus on how to compress the remaining activities in the project.
- **Show project progress:** Since it shows the order of activities in a project and total path from the beginning of the project until end, it is a good instrument for showing the project progress.

Sequence Activities Process Example

Now we will see how sequence activities process can take place for our sample project. We have defined the activities of invoicing screen work package as: analyze invoice screen requirements, design of invoice screen, development of invoice screen and test of invoice screen.

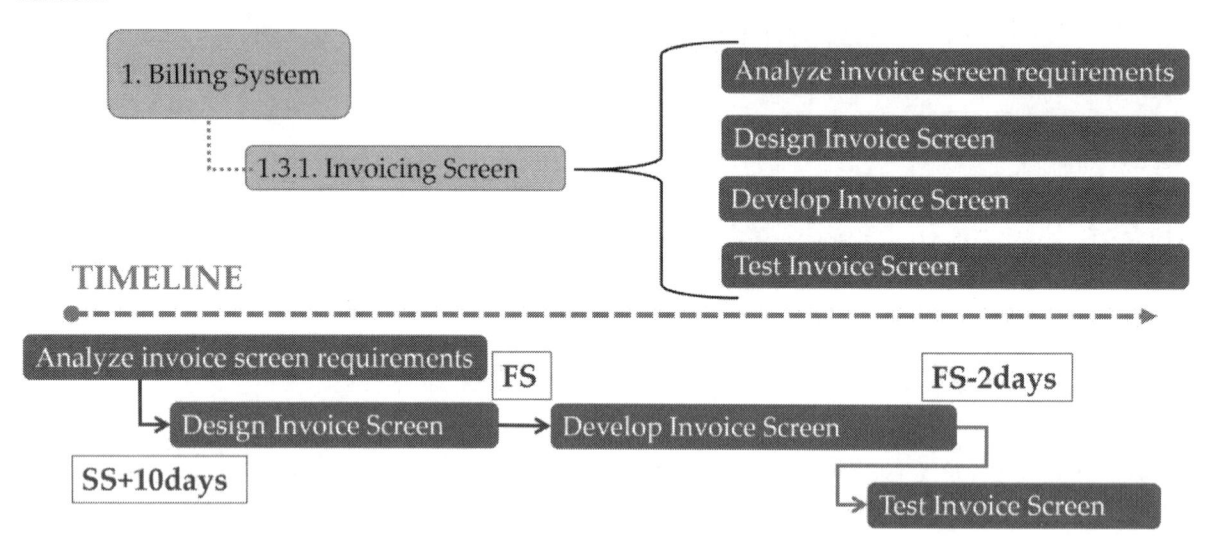

During sequence activities process, these activities must be planned in order to complete the project successfully. Activities will be starting from the beginning and will be ordered until end.

First two activities are
- analyzing invoice screen requirements and
- design invoice screen.

The relationship between two activities is *start-to-start + 10 days*. This means that, design invoice screen activity can start only after 10 days passed after analyze invoice screen requirements started. This is a general approach in software development projects that, design of the screens or features start after analysis comes to a level. Therefore, there is a time between each activity.

After design of invoice screen activity is completed next activity: develop invoice screen can start. Development of the screen will be performed based on the design and analysis output. There is a finish-to-start interrelationship between design invoice screen and develop invoice screen activities since development of the screen cannot start before analysis and design is complete.

Last activity is test invoice screen. After the development, screen must be tested before showing the final outcome to the customer or handing over to the customer. If there are any bugs or problems with the screen, these must be fixed appropriately. Test of the invoice screen can start 2 days before the development finish date. Because, let's assume that development of the screen takes 10 days, and after 8 days, it is expected that majority of the development is complete, and testing can start. In order to gain time in the project, testing can start 2 days before the development completion date.

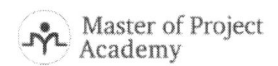

Important Points About Estimating

Estimating in a project is crucial. Because, based on the estimations, project schedule and duration are finalized. Company sets its objectives and alignment of other projects accordingly. Project stakeholders set expectations based on the determined deadline.

During this heading, we will go over the important points about estimating.

- **Estimation should be based on WBS to improve accuracy:** WBS shows the breakdown of the work that will be delivered throughout the project. It shows the work packages, work accounts etc. in detail. Therefore, while estimating, if estimations are done over the components of the WBS, this will lead you to a successful estimation of the project respectively.
- **Estimation of an activity should be done by the person doing the work:** This is very critical to get the buy-in and increase the motivation of the project team member. Estimation of an activity can change depending on the competence and experience of the team member. For instance, same activity can be completed in a shorter duration by a more experienced team member. Therefore, estimations must be given by the assignee.
- **Historical information from past projects is key!** Especially if there had been similar projects executed in the company, records of those projects will be very beneficial during estimation of the new project. Because, actual results from a similar activity that has been performed will be illuminating what will be faced during the similar activity in the new project as well. This will ensure realistic estimations and reduce possible variations respectively.
- **Schedule baseline should be taken in the beginning and should not be changed except change requests:** Because, schedule baseline shows the planned start and end dates of each activity in a project. When measuring performance of the project, these initial dates will be checked against the actual values and this will give the schedule performance of the project. In order to measure the variations and make necessary corrections to the project, schedule baseline must not be change except there is an approved change request in the project.
- **Changes should be requested when schedule problems occur:** After the schedule planning is complete, project execution will start. Actual values of the project activities will differ compared to the planned values. If there is a deviation in the schedule, corrective actions must be taken to get back on track in the project.
- **Project manager may periodically recalculate the estimate to complete, ETC, value:** We will see the estimate to complete during our further notes. Estimate to complete gives total budget that is needed to complete remaining activities in a project. Therefore, it is critical to know whether your planned budget will meet the estimate to complete value during the project. If there is a deviation, corrective and preventive actions must be taken to prevent any deviations.

- **There is a process for creating the most accurate estimate:** First, you need to breakdown the work packages into smaller activities. Then, assignees of these project activities will provide estimation for these activities. During estimation, different techniques may be used. These must be done in order to increase accuracy in estimation.
- **Project manager must meet any agreed-upon estimates:** Estimations are done to complete a project on an agreed budget, on an agreed time and on an agreed quality. The ultimate goal of the project manager is to manage the project work to complete and deliver project scope on time, on budget and with the agreed quality.
- **Estimates can be decreased by reducing risks:** If there are many risks in a project, appropriate budget and time that is needed to accommodate these risks when they occur must be planned respectively. These risk reserves will increase the budget and extend the schedule of the project respectively. Therefore, estimations can be reduced by minimizing the risks in a project.

Estimate Activity Durations Process

Till now, we have seen how schedule is planned in plan schedule management process, how activities are defined in define activities process, order of activities in sequence activities process.

- **The Estimate Activity Durations is the process of estimating the number of work periods needed to complete individual activities with estimated resources:**

After activity resources are determined, these resources estimate the activity durations. How long they need to complete an activity. Based on their estimations, overall project duration will be determined respectively.

- **During Estimate Activity Durations process amount of time that each activity will take places is estimated.** Based on the description and details of the task, assignee of the activity makes an estimation. Each activity duration is estimated similarly by the assignee of each activity.

- **Before estimation, if there are ambiguities or unclear points about an activity, estimation will have padding:** In order to understand this, let us see what padding is first.

- **Pad:** Pad is extra time or cost added to an estimate because the estimator does not have sufficient information about the activity. During estimate activity durations process, project resources make their estimations based on the current available information today. If there is not that much information about the activity, or if there are risks that may arise and cause the activity to take longer, this will cause padding during estimation.

- **Project manager should find ways to make each activity as clear as possible to make accurate estimates:** Any risks might be eliminated as much as possible. Unclear points or missing information about the activities must be cleared out to have a more accurate estimation from the project resources.

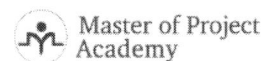

- **If there is a need for a pad, it should be addressed through risk management:** Although the project manager tries to eliminate risks, there might be still existing risks that must be considered. In this case, if there is a need for a pad, it should be addressed through risk management. Because, reserves to accommodate risks when they occur are planned during risk management activities. During Estimate Activity Durations process, project resource must consider only the activity duration if everything goes as planned.

One-Point Estimation Technique

Activity durations are estimated based on some techniques in a project. During this and following headings, we will go over alternative estimate activity durations techniques. First technique is One-Point Estimate.

- **In one-point estimate technique estimators submit one estimate per activity:** Estimator goes through the activity description and details. Based on the information available, he provides an estimation to complete this activity. For instance, "4 days needed to complete installation".
- **One-point estimates should be used for projects that do not require a detailed, highly probable schedule:** This means, if a precise and accurate schedule is not a must in your project, you can use this technique.

If you need a more detailed schedule in your project, one-point estimate technique can have negative effects on the project. These are:

- **One-point estimate technique forces people into padding:** Since there is limited information about an activity and you ask a fixed estimate for the project duration, estimator feels to say something although he might not be confident to provide an estimate yet. Thus, he tends to do padding in order to accommodate ambiguities during estimations.
- **Hides information about risks. Because, during estimation, assignee of the task provides an estimate based on available information:** However, in other techniques, for instance in PERT technique, three estimates are taken for an activity: optimistic, most likely and pessimistic. If there are lots of difference between optimistic, most likely and pessimistic values, this gives an indication about the risk level of the activity.
- **Creates a schedule that no one believes:** This is because of the nature of the one-point estimate actually. Since every assignee gives an estimate for the activities without detailed analysis or backing, this causes unrealistic schedules to occur respectively.
- **If activity is performed less than estimated, trust might be lost:** Say you have used one-point estimate technique in your project during Estimate Activity Durations process. One developer said, his estimate for a screen development is ten days, but after the actual results, you have seen that the developer completed his work in six days. For another developer, you discover that his estimation was 20 days, and he completed his task in 13 days. These kinds of early finish of project activities will make your customer to think about the precision of your estimates, because you have given a high estimate in the beginning, but your actual results show that the activities can be completed in shorter durations.

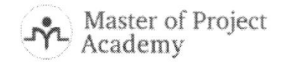

Analogous Estimating (Top-Down)

Analogous estimating is known as top-down estimating as well. In analogous estimating technique, if there are similar activities from previous projects that have been completed, new activities are estimated based on the actual values and experience earned from the previous project.

> - Analogous estimating can be done for a project or an activity.
>
> - So, the total project can be estimated if the whole project is similar to a project that has been completed before. Alternatively, it can be done on activity level.

See some examples for analogous estimating.

- Similar project took 5 months, this will take 5 months as well. In this case, if the company is initiating a new project that is similar to a project that has been completed, duration of the new project is estimated based on the previous project duration.

- Similar installation took 3 days before, this one will take 3 days as well. In this case, an installation activity will take place in new project, which is very similar to the previous project's installation activity. Therefore, same duration is estimated.

Parametric Estimating

Parametric estimating technique calculates projected times for an activity based on historical records, from previous projects or other info. It is actually a mathematical approach to find the estimation of a project activity. Parameters that might affect the duration of a project activity are determined, and based on these parameters, project activity durations are estimated.

Result of the parametric estimating technique is estimates based on measures like time to spend per line of code, linear meter or per installation. For instance, consider that you are managing a software project, in order to estimate the duration of project activities, time spent for writing a line of code is important. Based on this parameter, you can guess the duration of the other activities.

Alternatively, if you are managing a construction project, and if you know how long it takes to complete 1-foot square area to build, you can estimate the project activities duration with this parameter.

Parametric estimating has two approaches mainly:

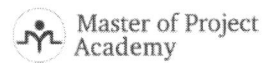

- **Regression analysis (scatter diagram):** In this approach, two variables are analyzed to see if they are related with each other. For instance, number of functions in a screen and number of boxed in a screen. These might give us about the complexity of a screen in a software project.

  Another example can be experience of the software developer and time to complete a screen. It is expected that time spent on the development of a screen should decrease as the experience of the software developer increases. Regression analysis is done to check whether these variables are related with each other.
- **Learning Curve:** This approach proposes that because of improved efficiency and experience, similar activities in a project should take less time in future in the project.

  For instance, if you are managing a construction project and there will be 100 rooms that needs to be painted, it is expected that painting 100th room will take less time than painting of 1st room. Because the workers will have more experience on the building and painting similar room. Similarly, a software developer is expected to develop a similar screen in a shorter time in a software project.

Heuristics Estimating

Heuristics is another estimation technique for Estimate Activity Durations process. In Heuristics technique, activity duration of an activity is estimated over an assumed rate, which generally comes from industry practices.

For instance, Rule of thumb 80/20 states that, 80% of the problems are caused by the 20% of the potential source of problems. By this way, you focus on those 20% to fix the majority of the problems in an environment.

Let us give some other examples about Heuristics technique.
- **In a Software project, industry practices say that design of the project will be 15% of the development work.** This is not a rule of god for sure. There might be exceptional and extraordinary software projects that goes beyond this ratio. For instance, if you are running a major infrastructure project in an IT company, it is expected that design work will be higher compared to a regular software project.
- **Similarly, testing of a software project is estimated as 25% of the development work.** Of course, this can vary depending on the software project dynamics. For instance, if you are testing a website on several smart phones and web browsers to check its responsiveness, this will take a long time in the project respectively.

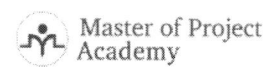

Three Point Estimating (PERT Analysis)

Three-point estimates or PERT Analysis is most common way to calculate activity durations in a project.

In PERT Analysis technique, Estimators of the project activities provide three estimates for each activity.

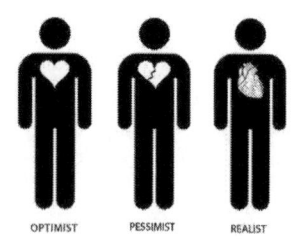

1. **Optimistic activity duration (O):** This estimation is provided for the best-case scenario. Estimator considers that everything will go smoothly during the activity and provides an estimation for this case.

2. **Most Likely activity duration (M):** This estimation is provided for the realistic scenario. We all know that there will be issues, problems in the project. Estimator considers probable issues he could face during the activity, and provides an estimation for this case.

3. **Pessimistic activity duration (P):** This estimation is provided for the worst-case scenario. Estimator considers all possible issues that could happen during the activity and provides an estimate that the activity could be finished in worst case.

After optimistic, most likely and pessimistic estimations for an activity are collected, there are two approaches in calculating PERT estimate.

1. First approach is Triangular Distribution. In triangular distribution, average of the optimistic, most likely and pessimistic estimations are taken and this represents the activity duration.

   > Triangular Distribution $= \dfrac{O+M+P}{3}$

2. Second approach is Beta distribution. In beta distribution, optimistic and pessimistic estimates are summed up with the four times multiplied value of most likely estimate. Then, result is divided into 6 and this represents the activity duration.

   > Beta Distribution $= \dfrac{O+4M+P}{6}$

Triangular distribution gives equal weight to each estimation while beta distribution gives higher weight to the most likely estimate by multiplying it with 4. Therefore, activity duration in beta distribution comes closer to the most likely estimate.

> PERT estimation can be used for time and cost estimates.

So, although we have seen this technique in estimate activity durations process, it can be used when determining required budget for an activity as well.

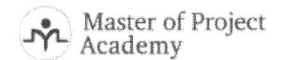

It is better to provide activity standard deviation and activity variance as well.
Activity standard deviation is calculated by dividing the difference of pessimistic and optimistic estimates to 6.

> Activity Standard Deviation $= \dfrac{P-O}{6}$

Activity variance is calculated by taking the square of activity standard deviation.

> Activity Variance $= \left(\dfrac{P-O}{6}\right)^2$

Since an estimation is provided for an activity during Estimate Activity Durations process, estimations can be given in a range instead of one exact estimation. This range is given with the help of estimated activity duration and standard deviation.

> EAD + SD → end of range
> EAD − SD → start of range

After the activity duration estimates are completed, project duration is estimated by sum of estimated activity durations in the critical path of the project. Standard deviation of the project will give a range for the project duration as well. Standard deviation of a project is calculated by taking the square root of sum of activity variances in the critical path of the project.

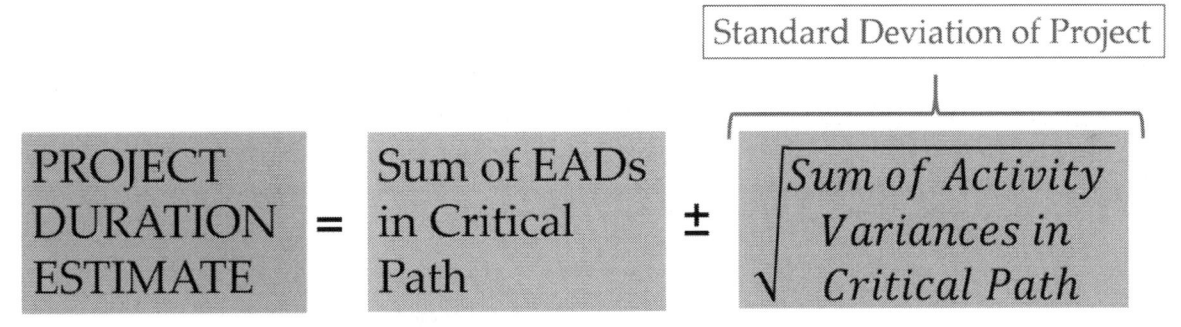

$$\text{PROJECT DURATION ESTIMATE} = \text{Sum of EADs in Critical Path} \pm \underbrace{\sqrt{\text{Sum of Activity Variances in Critical Path}}}_{\text{Standard Deviation of Project}}$$

For a well-defined and clear activity with no or very little risk, we expect to see pessimistic and optimistic estimates will be closer. Because, activity is clear, there are no ambiguities and estimator expects no high surprises during performing the activity.

> Higher activity ranges, standard deviations and variances show the risk level of activities.

If there are unclear points, so much ambiguities or risks with an activity, estimator will consider all these when providing estimate for the pessimistic value, and this will cause a higher standard deviation, variance and activity range respectively.

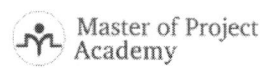

Three Point Estimating PERT Analysis Example

Assume that you are the project manager of a software project. You ask a software developer in your team about his estimation on the development of a specific screen. He gave the PERT estimates as following and after you get these estimates for an activity, estimated activity duration is calculated in next step.

Most Likely	Optimistic	Pessimistic
7 days	5 days	15 days

So, what is triangular and Beta distribution PERT estimates, standard deviation and activity range for the development of this screen?

Triangular distribution was calculated by taking the average of three estimates optimistic, most likely and pessimistic. When these values are substituted in the equation, we find the estimate of the activity as 9 days in triangular distribution.

- Triangular Dist. $= \frac{O+M+P}{3} = \frac{5+7+15}{3} = 9$ days

Beta distribution was giving more weight to the most likely estimate by multiplying it with 4 during calculation. When we substitute the optimistic, most likely and pessimistic values of the activity, we find the beta distribution estimation as 8 days.

- Beta Dist. $= \frac{O+4M+P}{6} = \frac{5+4*7+15}{6} = 8$ days

As you see from the results, beta distribution estimated activity duration is closer to the most likely estimate since beta distribution gives more weight to most likely estimate in the equation.

Standard deviation is found by dividing the difference of pessimistic and optimistic estimates to six. When we substitute the values in the equation, result is 1.67 days.

- Standard Deviation $= = \frac{P-O}{6} = \frac{15-5}{6} = 1.67$ days

Finally, activity ranges are defined with the help of estimated activity duration and standard deviation.
- Activity Ranges
    - Triangular: 9 +/- 1.67 days = [7.33, 10.67] days
    - Beta: 8 +/- 1.67 days = [6.33, 9.67] days

Estimate Activity Durations Process Example

Typically, one technique is chosen and used for all activity duration estimations in a project. In our Estimate Activity Durations process example, we used Beta Distribution of PERT analysis.

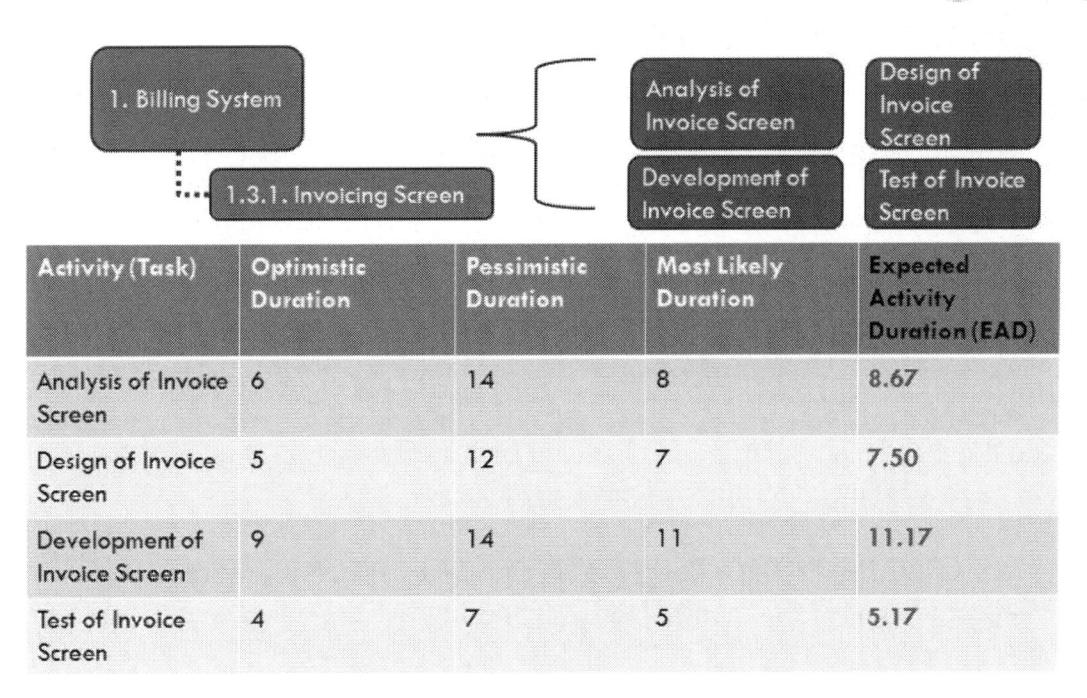

Activity (Task)	Optimistic Duration	Pessimistic Duration	Most Likely Duration	Expected Activity Duration (EAD)
Analysis of Invoice Screen	6	14	8	8.67
Design of Invoice Screen	5	12	7	7.50
Development of Invoice Screen	9	14	11	11.17
Test of Invoice Screen	4	7	5	5.17

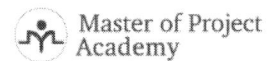

As you see in the screen, optimistic, pessimistic and most likely activity duration estimates for each activity are taken from the estimator. When we substitute these optimistic, pessimistic and most likely values in the beta distribution formula of PERT analysis,

- Estimated activity duration for analysis of invoice screen is 8.67 days.
- Estimated activity duration for design of invoice screen is 7.50 days.
- Estimated activity duration for development of invoice screen is 11.17 days.
- Estimated activity duration for test of invoice screen is 5.17 days.

These estimated activity durations are used to calculate the total project duration and complete the schedule of the project as well.

Reserve Analysis

Although the project manager aims to eliminate project risks, such as mitigating, transferring, some risks may still exist and these risks might be managed appropriately to reach the project's goals and objectives in the end. However, extra costs and time that need to be associated to overcome the risk if it occurs must be planned during estimation.

- **Estimating must be connected to risk management:** Consider that there is an activity that would take normally 5 days. But if there is a risk that might occur during that activity and can cause to delay the activity for 2 days, this must be considered during estimation since the final schedule of the project will be determined based on the estimations.

- **Estimating will help determining risks, and completing risk management, which will reduce the range of time and cost estimates:** Because during estimation, possible risks that can cause an activity to take longer will be considered. While estimators are providing activity duration estimates, they will think about possible risks, which can cause delays in activity completion. This will help determining risks respectively.

- **Risk management saves time and money:** This is very important. Because, with the risk management, you are evaluating any unexpected things that can happen during the project and take appropriate actions upfront. If any risk happens, since you are prepared and have an appropriate risk response plan, the risk will affect your project less compared to be caught unprepared. Consider that there is a risk that one of your project resources might resign in near future. Since you know this, you asked from project resources to prepare a handover document and keep them up to date, which will include their list of activities and how they performed them. In case risk happens, in other words the resource resigns, a new project team member will be able to handover his activities easily. However, if you do not make these kinds of risk planning, your new project resource might get lost on what to do and how to do once he starts to project.

- **Project management must have reserve to accommodate risks if there are any remaining risks after completion of risk management activities:** As we described earlier, you cannot transfer or mitigate all risks of a project. If there are risks, you might have reserves to accommodate those risks to minimize the impacts of risks when they occur.

There are two types of reserves:

- **Contingency Reserve:** Contingency reserves are time reserves or buffers. For instance, in a software project, if a software developer is estimating a screen development activity as 5 days, but stating that it might take up to 8 days due to risks, extra 3 days here is contingency reserve. Because, risks will cause activity completion delays respectively.

- **Management Reserve:** Management reserves are extra funds for unseen risks. Consider that in a construction project, estimations show that groundbreaking will cost around $200,000. However, due to the geological area of the project, you might hit big rocks and that would cause to cost up to $240,000. The extra $40,000 will be your management reserve to accommodate the risk of hitting big rocks during groundbreaking activity.

Develop Schedule Process

Develop Schedule process is the 5th process of Schedule Management Knowledge Area. In previous schedule management knowledge area process we have seen until now, activities have been determined, activity relationships were described, activities were put in sequence, activity resources and activity durations have been estimated. During develop schedule process; outputs of previous process are organized to produce the final schedule of the project.

- **Develop Schedule process is process of analyzing activity sequences, durations, resource requirements, and schedule constraints to create the project schedule model.** At the end of this process, you will have a finalized project schedule that will include start and end dates of each project activity, relationship of activities, resource of activities, total duration of the project etc.

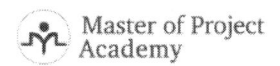

- **Develop Schedule process generates a schedule model with planned dates for completing project activities.** After activities are put in order, resource and activity relationships are defined in the schedule, all planned start and completion dates of project activities will be determined in the project schedule.

In project schedule, estimates are time based (in days, or in hours, or in weeks, or in months). For instance, for a software project, similar activities and their estimations will be as:
- Installation of database is 5 days
- Front-end development of the login screen is 2 days
- Back-end development of the login screen is 3 days, etc.

Project Schedule is calendar based. After all activities are put on schedule in an organized way, start and end, dates of activities will be determined. Start and end dates of each activity will be visible on schedule respectively. For instance,
- Activity A will start of 13th of February, will end on 15th of February and performed by Jane.

What do you need to develop a project schedule?

- **Project scope statement:** Project scope statement is at the top of the list, no doubt. Because, your project's main goal is completing the project scope on agreed time and budget with the agreed quality. Therefore, project scope statement plays a vital role in developing a project schedule.
- **Activity list:** Activity list shows the individual activities that needs to be performed to complete work packages and respectively the overall project scope. In the end, project schedule includes the ordered and organized project activities. Therefore, activity list is a critical input for develop schedule process.
- **Network diagram:** Network diagram shows the flow of project activities from the start of the project till end. Therefore, while defining the interrelationship of activities in develop schedule process, it will be critical to have network diagram in hand.
- **Activity duration estimates:** Activity duration estimates provide the time estimates of each activity. After interrelationship of activities are put on project schedule, once the time estimates are defined in each project activity, start and end dates of each activity will be determined respectively.
- **Activity resource requirements:** Activity resource requirements will help to show what materials will be needed to complete an activity or which project team member or supplier etc. will be performing an activity.
- **Resource calendars:** Resource calendars show the availability schedule of a project resource. For instance, a software developer might be going for a vacation during your project, or one of your project resources might be working part-time. In order to define exact planned start and end dates of each activity, you need to consider the resource calendars of your team.
- **A company calendar (working/non-working days):** And the last thing we will list here is Company calendar. Company calendars generally include working and non-working days

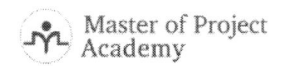

of a company annually. It also includes public holidays as well. Alternatively, if there is a special info day or conference day that whole company will not work, these are defined in the company calendars. When completing the project schedule, company calendars must be considered.

- **Develop schedule is iterative and can occur many times during project.** Because, based on the actual results, you need to update your schedule. For instance, consider that estimation was to complete an activity in 5 days. However, during execution, it took 8 days to complete. You need to update this in the project schedule and all remaining activities must be updated accordingly to see the new project schedule. Otherwise, schedule will be misleading.

Alternatively, if you have an approved change request, you need to put regarding project activities for that change request into your project schedule, and they will extend your project duration.

Once the schedule is complete, schedule network analysis can begin and may take one of the following forms:

- **Critical Path:** Critical path method is the most important schedule network analysis technique. It shows the shortest duration that a project can be completed. We will see it in detail with examples during our further notes.
- **Schedule Compression:** Schedule compression will help you to compress the project activities and complete the project in a shorter duration.
- **What-if Scenario Analysis:** What if Scenario analysis helps to simulate what could happen based on some parameters and generally simulated by computer programs.
- **Resource Leveling:** Resource leveling is used to produce a resource-limited schedule. Although some activities in project are not technically related with others, you might need to wait to start a new activity since there is not any available resource. Resource leveling will help to optimize resource usage in a project and complete the project in the shortest time.
- **Critical Chain Method:** It is another method we will be seeing in our further notes.

Critical Path Method (CPM)

As we mentioned in our previous heading, Critical Path Method, which is abbreviated as CPM, is one of the most popular schedule network analysis technique. This technique relies on determining the longest path in the network diagram.

> Critical Path Method determines the longest path in the network diagram.

After schedule network of the project has been finalized, you will have start and end dates of each activity from the beginning of the project until end. Activities of the project will be completed in order depending on the relationship between them. Critical path method aims to determine the longest path of activities from start of the project until end. Because this will give us the project duration.

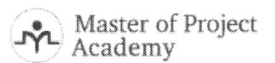

Critical Path is the longest duration path through a network diagram and determines the shortest time to complete the project. In other words, once you determined the critical path, you will have the project duration.

Critical Path is determined by identifying all paths of activities from beginning of the network diagram until end of the network diagram. After all alternative paths of activities are identified, longest path that goes from the beginning until end will be critical path.

The closest path to critical path in terms of duration is called as near critical path. Say that your project's critical path is 18 months. If the nearest path that is close to 18 months in the network diagram is 17 months, then near critical path will be this one.

It is better to describe Float here.

> ❈ Float, also called as Slack, is the amount of time that an activity can be delayed without causing project delays or causing delays in other activities.

There are three types of float. We will see each of them one-by-one.

1. **Total Float:** Total Float is the amount of time an activity can be delayed without delaying the project end date or an intermediary milestone. Consider that a project activity is not on critical path. Since it is not on critical path, delay on this activity can be compensated. However, there is a limit here. If it is delayed too much, you will exceed the critical path duration and this will cause project delay. Float here helps you to see how long you can delay an activity, without affecting the project duration.

2. **Free float:** Free float is the amount of time an activity can be delayed without delaying the early start date. Early start date of an activity shows the earliest data that an activity can be started. Because, an activity will depend on other activities, constraints etc. Therefore, it will have an early start date. Free float is the amount of time that an activity can be delayed, without delaying the early start date.

3. **Project Float:** This is the amount of time an activity can be delayed without delaying externally imposed project completion date.

> ❈ Critical path activities should have zero float.

This is because the critical path activities show the longest path of the project to complete, and therefore any activity on the critical path will have zero float. Any delay on a critical path activity will cause project delays respectively.

Float of an activity can be calculated in two ways.

> ➤ Float = Late Start – Early Start (LS – ES)
> ➤ Float = Late Finish – Early Finish (LF – EF)

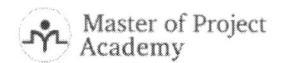

How do we calculate the Early Start, Early Finish, Late Start and Late Finish of an activity? This figure gives us a way to do this calculation.

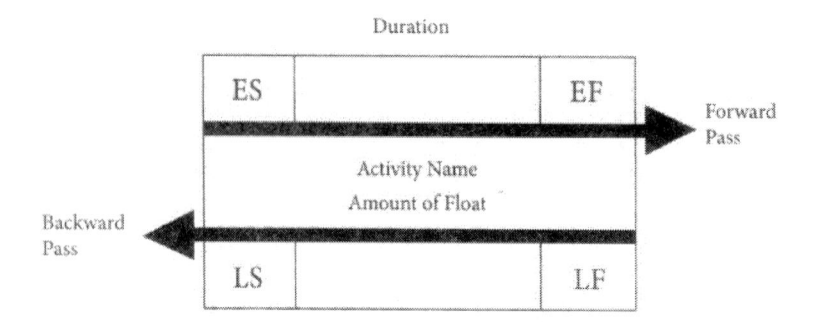

```
                    Duration
         ┌──────┬──────────┬──────┐
         │  ES  │          │  EF  │
         ├──────┴──────────┴──────┤──► Forward Pass
         │     Activity Name      │
         │     Amount of Float    │
◄── Backward ───────────────────────┤
    Pass │  LS  │          │  LF  │
         └──────┴──────────┴──────┘
```

> When calculating Early Start/Finish, you have to start from beginning and move towards end.
> When calculating Late Start/Finish, you have to start from end and move towards beginning.

Critical Path Method (CPM) Exercise

We will go through the activity list you see in this figure, define the relationship of activities, create the network schedule, determine the critical path, and calculate the floats of two activities.

Activity	Successors	Duration (days)
A	F	6
B	---	5
C	---	8
D	E,F	4
E	G	8
F	B,G	7
G	H	5
H	C	7

As you see on the screen, there are eight activities in the project, and these are:
- Activity A and its successor is F. Its duration is six days. This means activity A will be followed by activity F.
- Activity B does not have any successor, and its duration is five days.
- Activity C has not any successor as well, and its duration is eight days.

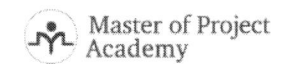

- Activity D is followed by activity E and F, and its duration is four days.
- Activity E is followed by activity G, and its duration is eight days.
- Activity F has two successors B and G, and its duration is seven days.
- Activity G has one successor, which is activity H, and its duration is five days.
- Finally, the last activity, activity H is followed by activity C, and it takes seven days.

Here in this exercise we will find the critical path of the project, and float of activities E and F. In order to find the critical path, first we will draw the network diagram. Then we will define each possible path in this network diagram from start of the project until end, and then we will define the longest path in this network diagram, which will give us the critical path. After finding the critical path, we will find the float of activities E and F, respectively.

Activity	Successors	Duration (days)
A	F	6
B	---	5
C	---	8
D	E,F	4

In order to draw the network diagram, first, we will define the relationships of each activity.

➢ First row says that, activity A is followed by activity F, and its duration is six days. To draw this relationship, A is followed by activity F; we define a finish to start relationship. In addition, we reflect the duration of activity on the F side of the arrow.
➢ Similarly, we have to define activity B's relationship. Since, it has not any successors, it must be one of the latest activities in the project and project should end after these activities.
➢ Similarly, activity C is also the last activity of the project and its duration is eight days.
➢ In addition, for activity D, it is followed by two activities, activity E and F. Its duration is four days.

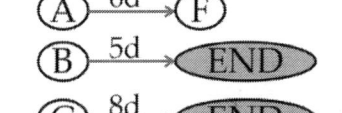

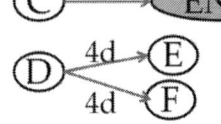

Now, we will draw the relationship of the last four activities.

Activity	Successors	Duration (days)
E	G	8
F	B,G	7
G	H	5
H	C	7

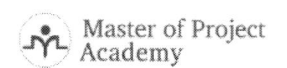

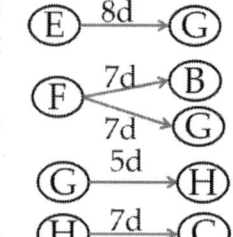

- First, we draw the relationship of activity E and G, as can be seen on the screen. Activity E is followed by activity G, and its duration is eight days.
- Activity F has two successors B and G, and activity F's duration is seven days.
- Activity G is followed by activity H, and its duration is five days.
- Finally, activity H has a successor activity C, and its duration is seven days.

We have completed to define the interrelationship of eight activities.

Next step is, connecting these relationships with each other to construct the overall network diagram of the project.

In addition, once it is done, you will reach this network diagram. As you see, it includes all activities, duration of activities, and relationship of activities from start of the project until end. It also includes all possible activity paths from start until end of the project to complete the project. We will go over these paths one-by-one now to identify critical path of the project.

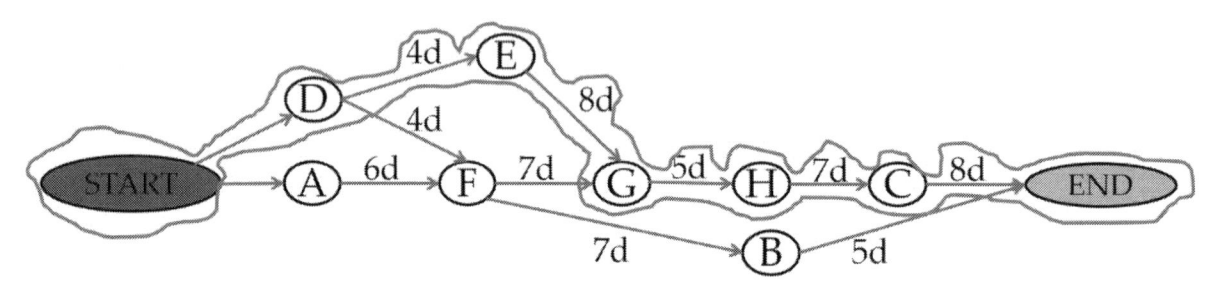

PATH 1 = 4+8+5+7+8 = 32d

This is our first path. As you see, the green sketch shows our first path from beginning of the network diagram until end. Activities of this Path 1 are D, E, G, H, and C, respectively. Now, if we calculate the duration of each activity in this green path, it gives the path duration as 32 days.

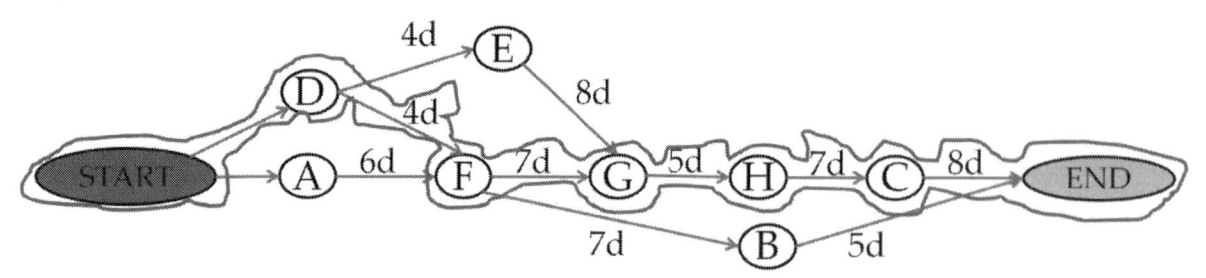

PATH 1 = 4+8+5+7+8 = 32d
PATH 2 = 4+7+5+7+8 = 31d

Second path is this one. In this path 2, we have activities D, F, G, H, and C, respectively. If we calculate the durations of the activities in this path, we will have 31 days as the duration of Path 2.

PATH 1 = 4+8+5+7+8 = 32d
PATH 2 = 4+7+5+7+8 = 31d
PATH 3 = 6+7+5+7+8 = 33d

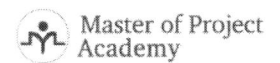

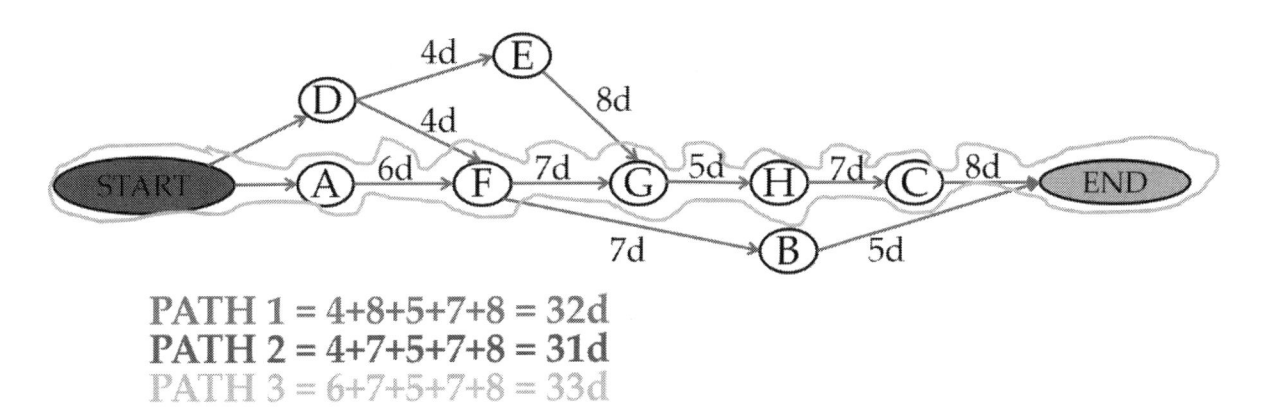

Moreover, the next path is this yellow path, and in this path, we have activity A, F, G, H, and C, respectively. When we aggregated the durations of each activity in this Path 3, we find the duration of Path 3 as 33 days.

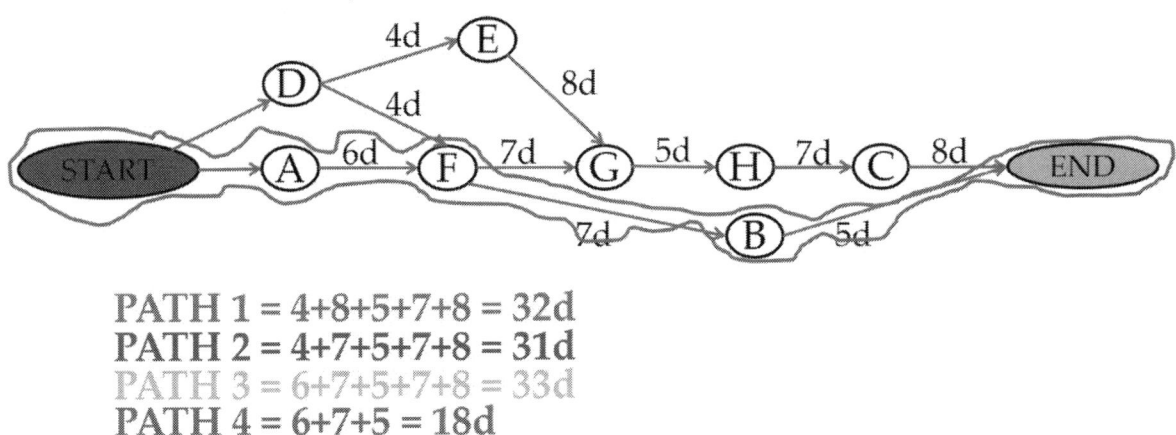

PATH 1 = 4+8+5+7+8 = 32d
PATH 2 = 4+7+5+7+8 = 31d
PATH 3 = 6+7+5+7+8 = 33d
PATH 4 = 6+7+5 = 18d

In addition, the last other possible path from beginning of the network diagram until end is Path 4, which is the purple path, and in this path, we have three activities which are A, F and B respectively. When we sum up the activity durations in this purple path, we find duration of Path 4 as 18 days.

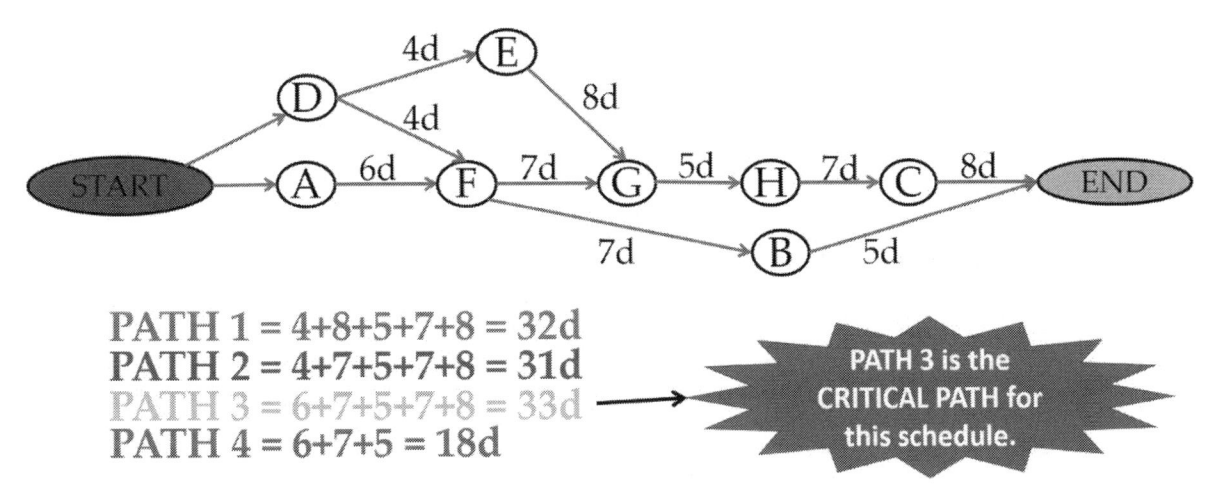

PATH 1 = 4+8+5+7+8 = 32d
PATH 2 = 4+7+5+7+8 = 31d
PATH 3 = 6+7+5+7+8 = 33d
PATH 4 = 6+7+5 = 18d

→ **PATH 3 is the CRITICAL PATH for this schedule.**

As you see here, over the four possible paths, from the beginning of the network diagram until end, **the longest path is Path 3. Therefore, Path 3 is the critical path of this network diagram.** In other words, this project can be completed in 33 days.

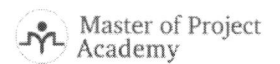

Since activities A, F, G, H, and C are on critical path, any delay on these tasks will have direct impact on the project duration. Therefore, these critical path tasks have zero float.

Now, we will calculate the float of activity E. Here, if you remind the calculation of float, when we were calculating the early start and early finish values, we were moving from start point to the end point of a network diagram. When we were calculating the late start and late finish values, we were starting from the end point of the network diagram and moving towards the start point of network diagram.

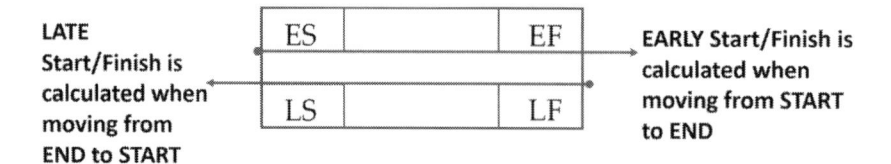

ES		EF
LS		LF

LATE Start/Finish is calculated when moving from END to START

EARLY Start/Finish is calculated when moving from START to END

Now we will calculate the float of activity E. We will use late finish and early finish values to calculate the float. In order to calculate early finish, I will start from the beginning of network diagram and sum up the activity durations till Activity E is completed.

In order to finish Activity E, Activity D must be finished first, and then Activity E must be completed. Therefore, the earliest finish duration for Activity E is 12 days.

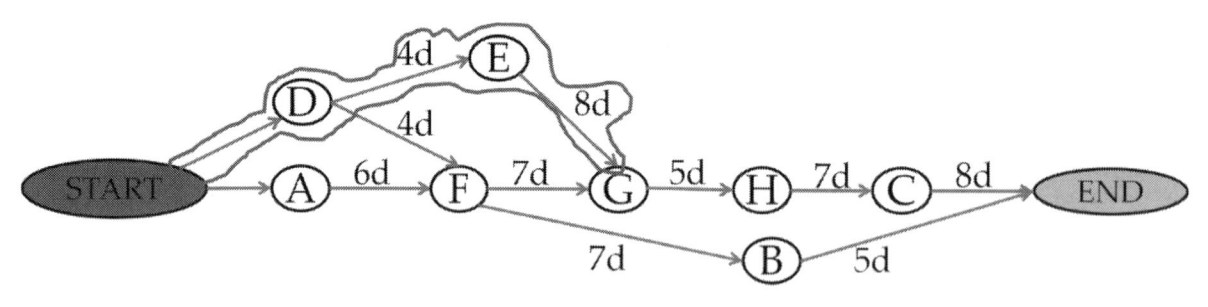

EF = 4 + 8 = 12d

In addition, in order to calculate late finish, we will start from the endpoint of the network diagram and subtract the activity durations until end of activity E.

In order to finish the project, activity G, H, and C must be finished after Activity E. When we subtract the duration of these activities from the project duration, which is 33 days, we will find the late finish value of Activity E as 13 days. In other words, in order to complete the project on time, Activity E must have been finished 13 days before the project completion date.

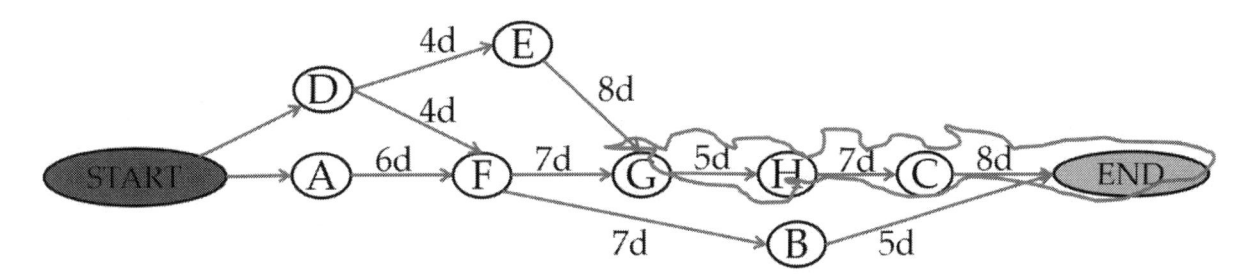

EF= 4+8 = 12d
LF= 33-8-7-5 = 13d

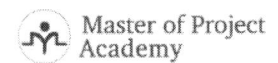

Now, we have late finish and early finish values for Activity E.
If we substitute these values in the formula, float of activity E will be found as 1 day. This means Activity E can be delayed only for 1 day without effecting the project duration.

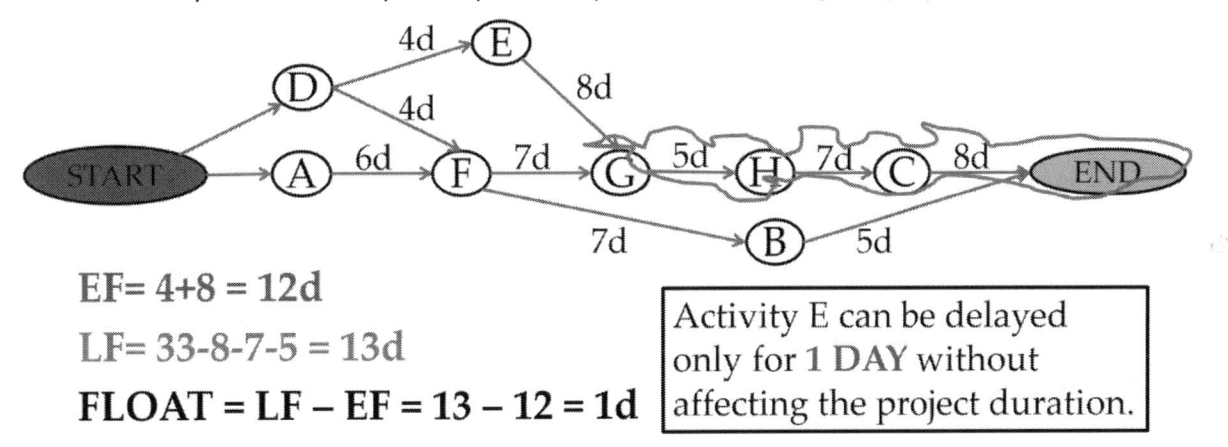

EF= 4+8 = 12d
LF= 33-8-7-5 = 13d
FLOAT = LF − EF = 13 − 12 = 1d

Activity E can be delayed only for 1 DAY without affecting the project duration.

During this heading, we have seen creation of network diagram over an activity list, defining relationship of activities, creation of network diagram, determining critical path and calculation of float over a sample project scenario.

Notes about Critical Path Method

Critical Path Method is a very important topic. It is widely used in project management world and in real-world projects as well. Therefore, it is better to stress important notes about critical method in this heading.

- **There can be more than one critical path in a project:** If there are more than one critical path, which have same duration, then, you need to focus on all of these critical paths to monitor the project duration.
- **Having several critical pats or having several near critical paths mean project has high risk:** Because, instead on only one critical path, your project schedule depends on several critical paths. Respectively, your project schedule performance will be depending on activities on those several critical paths. Several critical project activities will bring higher risks respectively.
- **Critical path of the project can change over time:** Consider that you determined the critical path of the project of our sample scenario in previous heading. Near critical path was 32 days and critical path was 33 days. If an activity is completed 2 days earlier in the

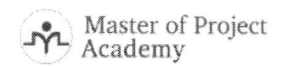

critical path during execution, your near critical path can be the new critical path of the project. Therefore, actual results must be updated on the project plan frequently, and up to date critical path must be monitored to reach project deadlines.

- **There can be negative float in a project:** This means schedule of the project is behind than the planned value. Normally, if everything is going as planned, float of an activity must be zero or positive. Only critical path activities will have zero float. However, if the project is delaying, some activities might have negative floats because the previous project duration is no longer valid.
- **If there is negative float, you should compress the schedule:** Negative float means project is behind the schedule. In order to meet the agreed deadline, you must complete the remaining activities in shorter time and this is achieved by schedule compression. We will see schedule compression in our further notes.
- **If you need to cut an activity duration in critical path, cut the earlier activity's duration:** Because, when you are closing to the finish of the project, you will have less room to accommodate surprises or risks. Nevertheless, if you shorten the duration of an earlier activity, even if you experience any risk or surprise with that activity, since you will have more time, it will be better to deal with it.

Schedule Compression (Fast Tracking & Crashing)

No matter how better you plan a project; actual results will differ from what you have planned. In terms of schedule, actual durations of tasks can take longer than what is planned. In order to meet the project deadline, you need to take corrective actions to get back on track. Schedule compression techniques are applied if a project is behind the schedule.

> Objective of schedule compression is to try to compress the schedule without changing project scope.

Because, if a project scope has not changed, and if the project is behind schedule, you can meet the planned deadline only by compressing the remaining schedule of the project.

There are two approaches for schedule compression:

1. **Fast Tracking:** In fast tracking technique, <u>critical path activities are performed in parallel instead of series</u>. This is possible only the activities are not in mandatory dependency. Because, if two activities are depending on each other by nature, for instance, you cannot start testing of a screen before completing development, you cannot do these two activities in parallel. If critical path activities are depending on each other because of resource dependency or if there is discretionary dependency, you can fast track those activities to complete remaining activities faster.

   Let us visualize fast tracking over a sample. Consider that there are three activities that needs to be completed each other: activity #1, activity #2 and activity #3. If you are aiming to finish the project faster, you can perform activity #2 and activity #3 in parallel after completing activity #1. This is called fast tracking.

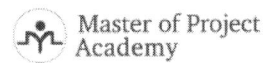

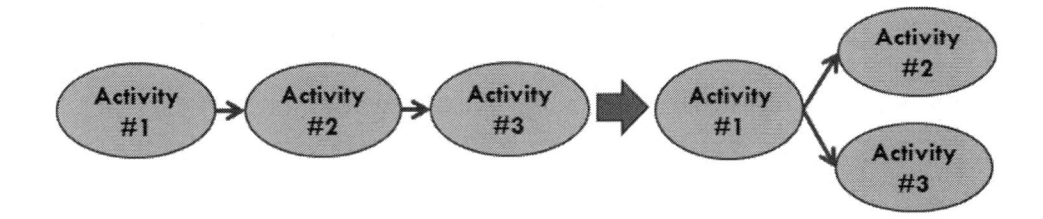

2. **Crashing:** In crashing technique, there is a trade-off between cost and schedule. If the scope is same and project is behind schedule, another option for compressing the schedule is <u>putting extra resources on remaining activities of the project.</u> Because if it is possible to assign more than one resource on an activity, activity duration will decrease respectively. This will help to complete the project faster. However, since these extra resources were not in the initial plan, there will be additional cost that must be bear if crashing is used for schedule compression.

If a project is behind the schedule, there are 5 major steps that must be followed in sequence.

1. **Check risks and re-estimate:** Because, for the remaining activities, if the risks that were considered during planning are no longer valid, re-estimation of the remaining activities can result in shorter activity durations. Re-estimation will show how long it will take to complete remaining activities of the project.
2. **Fast-track the project:** If re-estimation results in a later deadline for project completion, Fast-tracking the project must be considered. Remaining critical path activities are evaluated and possible activities that can be performed in parallel can be done to shorten the duration of the project. Fast-tracking is preferred over crashing because fast-tracking does not bring extra cost to project.
3. **Crash the project:** Extra resources are planned and extra budget is allocated to accommodate the increasing costs. Since more resources will work on remaining activities of the project, it is expected to finish the project on time.
4. **Reduce scope:** Reducing the scope can help to reduce the remaining activities in the project and if customer agrees, reducing the scope can help to complete the project on time.
5. **Cut quality:** Achieving a certain level of quality means cost and time. If customer agrees to decrease its quality expectations, cutting quality can help you to complete project faster.

Note that, fourth and fifth steps are not recommended course of actions in a project.

What-if Scenario Analysis

What-if scenario analysis is another schedule network analysis technique.

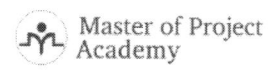

- **What-if scenario is actually analysis of "what if X changes, would it produce shorter schedule?":** There are lot of parameters and factors that can affect project schedule. Risks, experience of the activity assignee, number of resources etc. These parameters and factors are analyzed in what-if scenario analysis to check whether a shorter schedule can be produced.
- **Assumptions for each activity changes in a project:** And this affects the activity durations as well. During what-if scenario analysis, assumptions are put into play to check the schedule results as well.

One of the most popular what-if scenario analysis technique is Monte-Carlo analysis. Monte-Carlo analysis uses computer software to simulate outcome of a project with three-point estimates: Since there are several factors and parameters that can affect a project, doing this analysis manually will be impossible. Therefore, parameters and factors are put into a computer program, and alternative outcomes are simulated through the computer program.

After inputs are provided to the Monte-Carlo analysis program, simulation tells:
- **Probability of completing the project on a specific day:** For instance, the simulation will give you an outcome like: possibility of completing the project on 1st of January is 80%, possibility of completing the project on 1st of February is 90% and possibility of completing the project on 1st of March is 95%. The later the date, the more probable to finish the project on that date.
- **Probability of completing the project for a specific cost:** For instance, the simulation will give you an outcome like: possibility of completing the project with 1-million-dollar budget is 80%, possibility of completing the project with 1.2-million-dollar budget is 92% etc.
- **Probability of any activity actually being on the critical path:** It is also derived from the Monte-Carlo analysis. It also provides the overall project risk.
- **Monte-Carlo analysis converge multiple paths into one or more activities, thus brings extra risk to project:** This is because of the nature of the analysis technique. Brings an extra risk to the project as well.

Resource Leveling

- **Resource leveling technique is used to produce a resource-limited schedule.** Although there is not a mandatory dependency between the project activities, since you have limited resources, these activities can depend on your project resources.

- For instance: development of login screen and development of category page are two independent activities in a software project. However, if there are limited software engineers in the project, and if the same software engineer will work on these two development tasks, they must be completed one after each other. This is achieved by resource leveling.

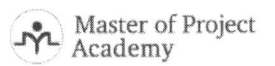

- **Resource leveling allows to see peaks and valleys in resource usage in a project.** For instance, 10 engineers in 1st month of the project, 7 engineers in 2nd month of the project etc. Now, let us go over a sample to understand resource leveling better. Assume that there are three activities that must be completed in a project. Tom and Sue will work on Activity A for 1 day, Sue will work on Activity B for 1 day and after Activity A and B finishes, Activity C can start, which will be performed by Tom.

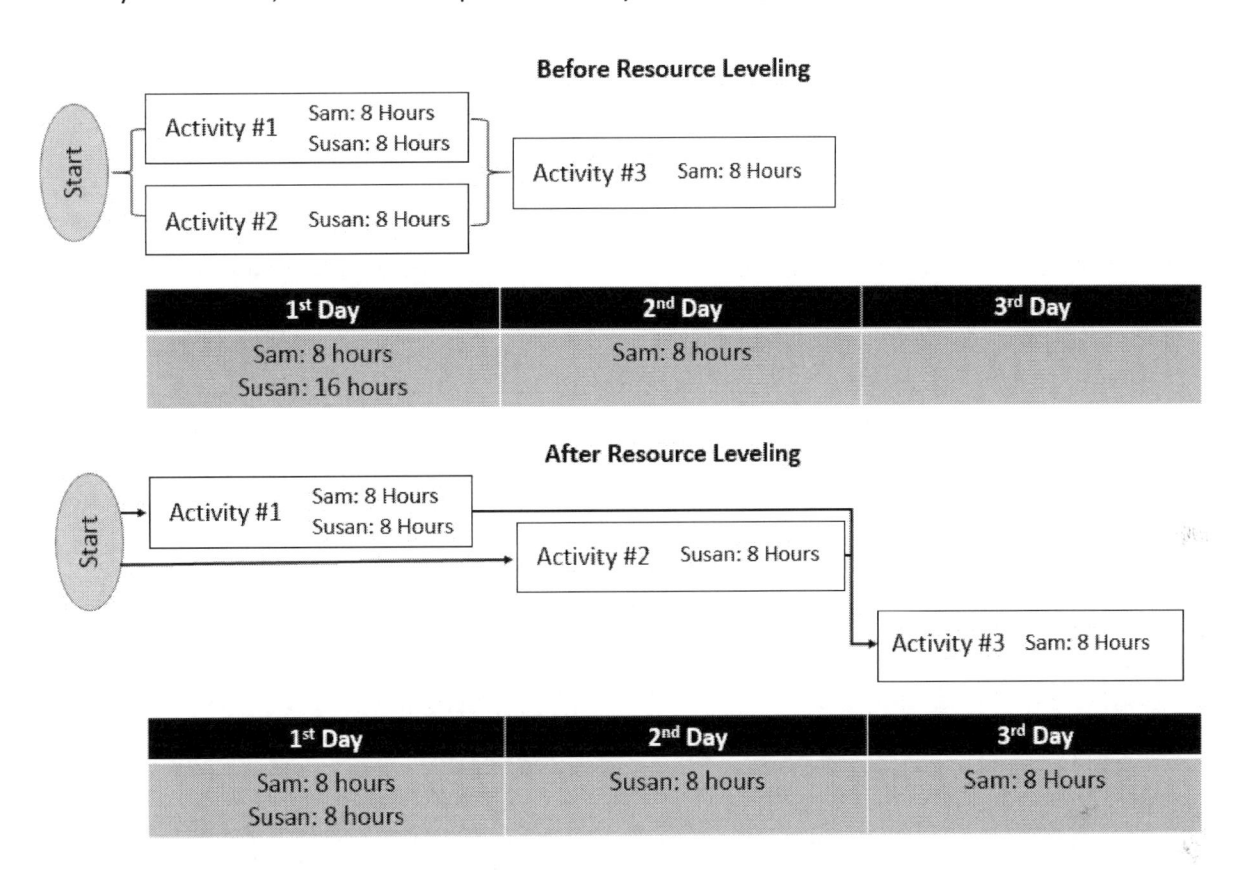

Before Resource Leveling

Start → Activity #1 (Sam: 8 Hours, Susan: 8 Hours), Activity #2 (Susan: 8 Hours) → Activity #3 (Sam: 8 Hours)

1st Day	2nd Day	3rd Day
Sam: 8 hours Susan: 16 hours	Sam: 8 hours	

After Resource Leveling

Start → Activity #1 (Sam: 8 Hours, Susan: 8 Hours) → Activity #2 (Susan: 8 Hours) → Activity #3 (Sam: 8 Hours)

1st Day	2nd Day	3rd Day
Sam: 8 hours Susan: 8 hours	Susan: 8 hours	Sam: 8 Hours

As you see, Activity A and Activity B are not depending on each other. Normally, these tasks can be performed in parallel. However, since Sue cannot work on Activity A and Activity B at the same time, first, Activity A must be finished. Then, Sue should start to work on Activity B on next day. After Activity A and B finishes, Tom can start to work on Activity C on third day. This is resource leveling.

Critical Chain Method

Critical Chain method is the last schedule network analysis technique we will go through. If you remember the critical path method, we have defined the relationship of activities, and then connected these activities to create network schedule of the project. Then determine the longest path to find critical path. Critical Chain method approaches in a different way.

1. A network diagram is created, and then schedule is developed by assigning each activity to occur as late as possible to still meet the end date.
2. **Resource dependencies are added and the critical chain is calculated.** Because as we discussed in our previous heading, you will not have unlimited project resources in a

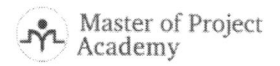

project. Even if there is not a mandatory dependency between the activities, if same resource will perform the activities, there is a resource dependency. This must be considered in critical chain method as well.
3. **Then, buffers are added to critical tasks.** Because if there are risks that may cause project activities to take longer, these must be reflected in planning to create a realistic and attainable schedule.

Agile Release Planning

Agile release planning is another tool used in develop schedule process.

- **High-level summary timeline of the release schedule (3-6 months):** Agile release planning provides a high-level summary timeline of the release schedule. This timeline is generally from three to six months. Product is aimed to be developed in releases. For instance, four release is planned to be done during the project, and at the end of each release, a working feature set of the final product must be ready to be tested.

- **Determines the number of iterations or sprints in the release:** These releases are planned by iterations. Therefore, agile release planning determines the number of iterations or sprints in the release. For instance, six iterations complete an iteration. Moreover, in each iteration, a number of features are developed through user stories. Let us go through an example to understand this.

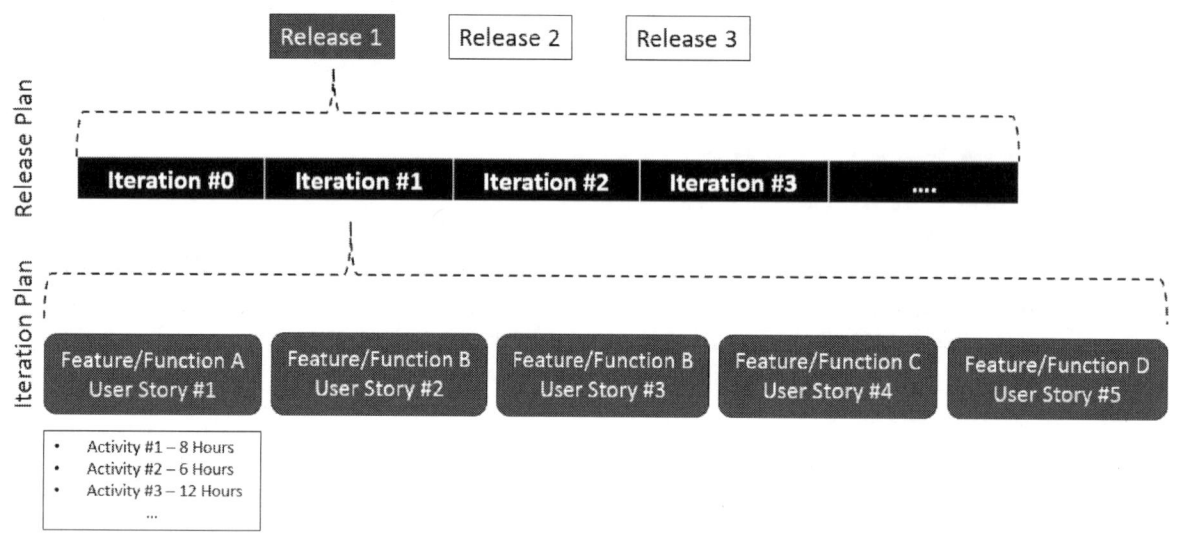

This figure shows the relationship of releases, iteration and features. As you see, product of the project is aimed to be completed in three releases. Product vision determines the product roadmap and how it will evolve. Product roadmap drives the release plans. Each release plan is completed by a number of iterations. Iteration plans accomplish the feature development of the product. In each feature, there are a number of activities and once they are completed, one feature, function or user story is accomplished.

Consider this as a website of a corporate customer. First release can be completing the admin screens of the website to manage users etc. In first iteration of the first release, you can plan to complete admin login feature, admin change password feature, forgot password feature etc. Each feature can be completed in several tasks.

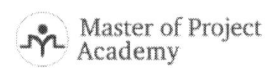

Project Schedule

Until now in schedule management knowledge area, we have seen determination of project activities, defining their interrelationship, creation of network diagram, schedule network analysis etc.

- **Project schedule is the end result of the schedule network analysis and previous planning processes.** Project schedule shows, which project activity, will start and finish when, who will perform which activity, which activity depends on which activity etc. Overall project duration can be determined after finalization of the project schedule.

- **Project schedule can be shown with or without dependencies.** For instance, testing of a project activity depends on the completion of regarding development activity first. But, project schedule may or may not show this dependency. However, these kinds of relationships in the network diagram will affect and determine the start and end dates of each activity and project schedule must show these dates respectively.

- **Project schedule is represented in three common formats in a project.**
  - Network Diagram
  - Milestone Charts
  - Bar Charts (or Gantt charts)

We have seen the network diagram in detail. So, we already know about network diagram in detail.

- o **Milestone charts show the critical dates of a project on timeline.** We have described in our previous notes that milestones have zero duration and represents a specific and important moment in project. Generally, milestones do not have assignee as well.

ID	Milestone	December	January	February	March	April
1	Start					
2	Requirements Gathered	● 12/14	● 12/31			
3	Design Complete			● 1/17		
4	Coding Complete			● 2/15		
5	Testing Complete				● 3/15	
6	Implementation Complete					● 4/4
7	End					● 4/15

As you see in this example, there are seven milestones for this software project. Start of the project, completion of requirements gathering, completion of design, completion of coding, completion of testing, completion of implementation and completion of the project. In a software project, there will be several project activities to complete, but as can be seen, milestone chart only shows seven major steps of the project and dates for these milestones as well.

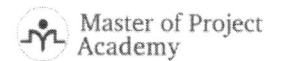

Milestone charts are similar to bar charts or Gantt charts, only difference is, milestone charts show only significant events of a project.

- Bar charts or Gantt charts show activity ID, activity name, duration, start and end dates of project activities in a list. In this example, there are 10 project activities and their duration, start and end dates are listed in the chart respectively.

ID	Activity Name	Duration	Start	Finish	September 8/18	8/25	9/1	9/8	9/15	9/22	October 9/29
1	Start	0 days	Mon 8/26	Mon 8/26							
2	D	4 days	Mon 8/26	Thu 8/29							
3	A	6 days	Mon 8/26	Mon 9/2							
4	F	7 days	Mon 9/2	Tue 9/29							
5	E	8 days	Fri 8/30	Tue 9/10							
6	G	5 days	Wed 9/12	Wed 9/17							
7	B	5 days	Wed 9/12	Wed 9/17							
8	H	7 days	Wed 9/18	Thu 9/26							
9	C	8 days	Fri 9/27	Tue 10/8							
10	Finish	0 days	Tue 10/8	Tue 10/8							

Gantt charts are weak planning tools. Because they are, activity specific and do not show the relationship of activities or critical path of a project as network diagrams do.

Gantt charts are effective for progress reporting and control. For instance, in order to show which activities are completed, which activities are in progress and which activities are remaining to be completed can be listed with Gantt charts. Project team can see start and end dates of each activity from Gantt charts as well.

We have seen three types of project schedule reports. However, which format is useful when?

Schedule Format	When to use
Network Diagram	For showing interdependencies of activities.
Milestone Chart	For reporting to senior management.
Bar Chart (Gantt Chart)	To track progress and report to team.

Network diagrams show critical path of a project and interdependency of activities with each other. Therefore, if you would like to stress these, network diagram will be a good option.

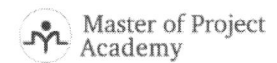

Milestone charts show only critical moments of a project. Therefore, if you are preparing a report for senior management, high-level information will be more relevant for them instead of activity by activity detail.

Gantt charts are used to track progress and report to team. For instance, if you would like to show completed activities, activities in progress or activities of the coming weeks etc., Gantt charts will be a better option for this type of reporting.

Briefly, you need to use appropriate format of reporting depending on which stakeholders you will be reporting and what you will be reporting.

Schedule Baseline

- **Schedule baseline is an approved version of a schedule model that can be changed only through formal change control procedures.** After project has been developed, a baseline needs to be taken. Because, actual results will not go as planned in the beginning and during monitoring and controlling, actual results will be compared with the schedule baseline to determine variation. Based on the variation, corrective and preventive actions need to be taken to get back on track.

- Schedule baseline of the project will include start and end dates of each activity; therefore, actual results for each activity will be checked with the help of the schedule baseline.

- **In order to check schedule performance of the project, schedule baseline will be used as a reference point to compare actual results versus planned values.** For instance, if an activity was planned for 5 days, but took 8 days to complete during execution, there is a 3 days' variance. If this activity is in critical path, it will cause 3 days of delay in over project schedule.

- Note that, this is just an example for a single activity. If you think that there will be several activities in a project, comparison of actual results with the schedule baseline will give an overall indication about project schedule performance. If the project schedule is behind the planned values, appropriate schedule compression techniques must be applied to complete the remaining activities of the project in a shorter time to complete project on time.

Develop Schedule Process Example

In our previous process examples, we have gone through our billing system project. We have gone through these four tasks under invoicing screen work package to give you an insight about how these processes are executed. At the end of the develop schedule process, you will have an end-to-end flow of project activities with start and end dates.

For our sample project, project schedule will be as following.

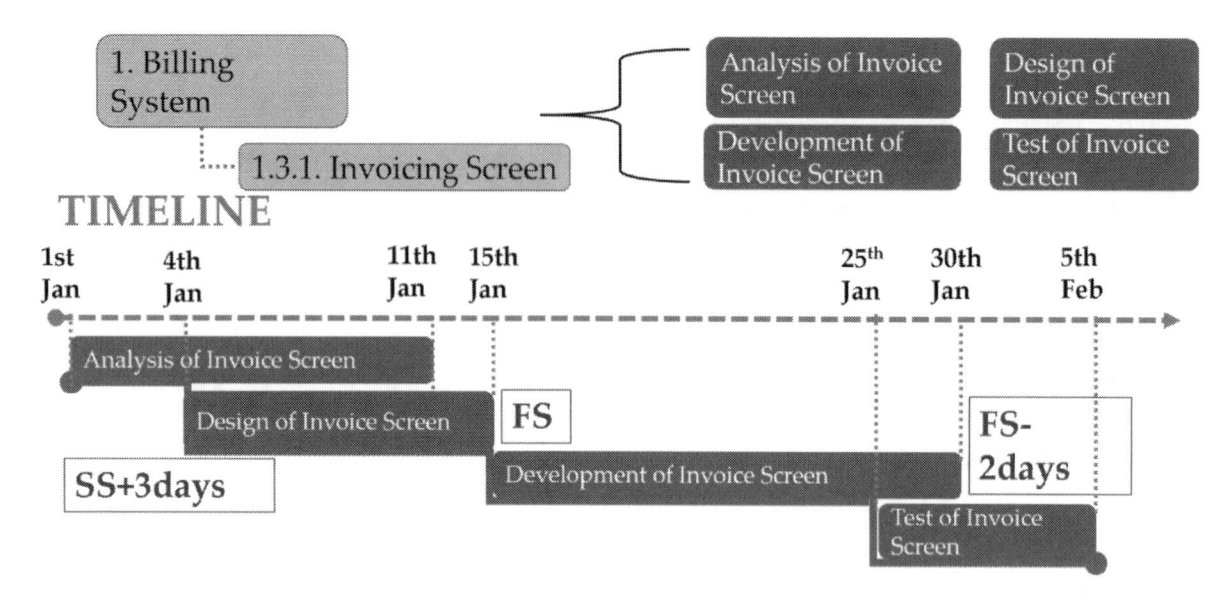

```
1. Billing System
  └─ 1.3.1. Invoicing Screen
       ├─ Analysis of Invoice Screen
       ├─ Design of Invoice Screen
       ├─ Development of Invoice Screen
       └─ Test of Invoice Screen
```

TIMELINE

| 1st Jan | 4th Jan | 11th Jan | 15th Jan | 25th Jan | 30th Jan | 5th Feb |

- Analysis of Invoice Screen
- Design of Invoice Screen
- SS+3days
- FS
- Development of Invoice Screen
- FS-2days
- Test of Invoice Screen

Analysis of invoice screen will start on 1st of January. Moreover, 3 days after analysis of invoice screen started, design of invoice screen will start on 4th of January. There is a *start-to-start + 3 days'* relationship between these two activities. Because, in order to start design, analysis of the screen must have come to a certain level before.

Design of invoice screen is completed on 15th of January. Right after that, development of invoice screen starts. There is a finish-to-start relationship because in order to start development, technical design of the screen must be complete and clear.

In addition, the last task, test of invoice screen, starts just 2 days before the completion of development of invoice screen. Ideally, test should start after development is completed. However, in real-world project schedules, testing of a development activity starts after the development reached around 80% completion level. This is done to shorten duration of the project. This is how it is planned in our example as well. Testing finishes of 5th of February.

Control Schedule Process

Control schedule is the last process of schedule management knowledge area. We have determined the project activities, defined the relationship of activities, estimated the duration of activities and finally reached a project schedule. This schedule must be controlled throughout the project whether actual results are aligned with the planned values.

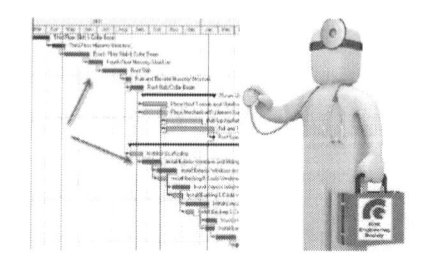

- **Control schedule is the process of monitoring the status of the project activities to update project progress and manage changes to the schedule baseline to achieve the plan.** After develop schedule process is complete, you will have the project schedule and it will include start and end dates of each project activity. During project execution, actual results of the project will differ from the planned values. While some activities could be completed earlier than planned, some activities will take longer to complete. During control schedule process, actual results of the activities will be compared against the schedule baseline to determine any variances.

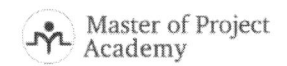

- **Project managers must measure against the plan and control the project.** If there is a variance based on the schedule performance control, and if the project cannot be completed on time, corrective actions must be planned and taken. For instance, schedule compression can be planned to complete the remaining project activities earlier than planned to complete the project on time.
- **During project execution, if factors causing many changes are found, these factors must be eliminated to prevent the root cause of changes.** If they cannot be eliminated, impact of these factors must be minimized by taking preventive actions.

What are the activities in control schedule process?

- **Re-estimation of the remaining components of a project.** During planning of the project, all future activities of the project are estimated based on very limited information on hand. While project progresses, unclear points will be cleared, project team will have more information about the project and by this way, remaining activities will be estimated healthier respectively. Therefore, re-estimation for the remaining activities of the project is done during control schedule process to check whether the target project completion date will be achieved.
- **Conduct performance reviews.** Actual results of each activity will be measured against the planned values in the schedule baseline. Based on the performance review, whether the project is on track is determined. If project is behind the schedule, appropriate actions must be taken to get back on track.
- **Future parts of the project must be adjusted to deal with delays.** For instance, schedule compression techniques like fast tracking or crashing can be applied for a project behind the schedule.
- **Measure variances against schedule.** We will see the schedule performance index in our next section. Schedule variance and schedule performance index of the project will show how far behind is the project from the planned values. For instance, if the project duration is 12 months, and if the schedule variance is 1 month, this means project will be completed in 13 months with a 1-month delay. Alternatively, if schedule performance of the project shows 0.90, this means, 90 percent of the planned activities could have been completed to date. Therefore, there is a delay for the remaining part and project is behind the schedule. We will see this performance analysis during our further notes.
- **Level resources to distribute work.** Based on the actual results of the project, some remaining activities of the project may cause overload on some project resources. In order to offload the project activities to available resources, resource leveling can be done during control schedule process.
- **Continue to play "what if..." to better optimize.** Planning is an iterative process in project management as we mentioned previously. Therefore, during control schedule process, if there are any alternatives to shorten the duration of the remaining project activities, these must be identified and applied respectively.
- **Adjust progress and project reports.** During project progression, you need to report to project stakeholders about the status of the project. Depending on the stakeholders, you

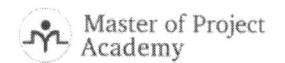

are reporting to, you need to adjust appropriate reports. For instance, if you are reporting to executive managers, you need to prepare high-level milestones in your report and if you are preparing for your project team, you need to prepare detailed report showing status of activities, remaining activities etc.

- **Utilize change control process.** Once project schedule is complete, schedule baseline is taken, and it can be changed only if there is an approved change request in the project. Change requests are evaluated by change control board in a project and if approved, appropriate changes must be aligned in the project plan to accommodate this change. For instance, in order to implement change request, new project activities need to be added to project schedule and maybe the critical path of the project will change. During control schedule process, it is ensured that changes are applied through change control process and only approved change requests are applied.
- **Identify need for change requests.** What is the reason for the change request? Is it because an improper planning or is it a new requirement coming from the customer? As a project manager, you have to avoid unnecessary changes in your project. These are analyzed during control schedule process as well.

Re-estimating

Re-estimate the remaining components of project at least once over the life of project to make sure you can still meet deadline, budget, and objectives.

In the planning phase of your project, you have planned the project activities appropriately. You have a cost baseline, you have a schedule baseline and you have project management plan to execute the project. With these baselines and plan, you know what to deliver at what time and at what cost. However, during the execution of your project, the actual values of these activities might be different from what you planned in the beginning.

Based on your actual values, you have to do frequent re-evaluations, frequent reviews, and frequent re-estimation on your project to check whether you will be able to still meet your project schedule and whether you will be able to still meet your target budget at the end of your project.

And if there are problems, for instance if there is any variance, that are showing that you will exceed your budget or that you will exceed the agreed end date of the project, then, you have to take corrective actions to meet the schedule baseline and to meet the cost baseline of your project.

In order to detect these variances and then take corrective actions respectively, you have to do re-estimating in your project frequently, and these should be determined in the beginning of your project. For example, you might say that, I will be doing re-estimating each month or I will be doing re-estimating in every two weeks. Because re-estimation will take a time and you need to determine appropriate frequency for re-estimating. Moreover, based on this frequency, you have to do re-estimating and check whether you are still meeting the baselines of your project.

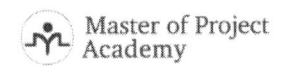

Quiz – Section 5

1- All of the Schedule Management processes belong to planning process group EXCEPT:
A) Define Activities Process
B) Estimate Activity Durations Process
C) Develop Schedule Process
D) Control Schedule Process

2- Which of the following is major output of Plan Schedule Management Process?
A) Schedule Management Plan
B) Time Management Plan
C) Delivery Plan
D) Requirements Management Plan

3- Schedule Management Plan will help to answer following questions EXCEPT:
A) How will I create the schedule?
B) Reserves planned for risks
C) How will I go about planning the schedule for the project?
D) How will I manage schedule variances?

4- Schedule Management Plan includes all of the following EXCEPT:
A) Establishment of a schedule baseline
B) Planning for how schedule variances will be managed
C) Metrics of internal tests
D) Scheduling software to be used

5- All of the following are outputs of Define Activities process EXCEPT:
A) Activity List
B) Activity Attributes
C) Milestones
D) WBS

6- Which of the following is NOT true about milestones?
A) Milestones must be assigned to a specific project team member
B) Milestones represent a specific moment in time
C) Milestones have zero duration
D) Milestones are included in project charter

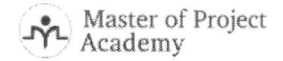

7- Sequence Activities process is identifying and documenting relationships among the project activities. Which of the following is key result of this process?
   A) Schedule Plan
   B) Time Plan
   C) Network Diagram
   D) Activities List

8- All of the following are correct about Network Diagrams EXCEPT:
   A) Shows dependencies of activities
   B) Shows start and end dates of activities
   C) If durations are included, also shows critical path
   D) Shows successor of activities

9- You have just taken over an ongoing software project from a resigned project manager in your company. When you looked to the Network Diagram, you noticed that development task of a screen has a finish-to-start dependency to analysis task of same screen. This means that:
   A) Development of a screen can start with analysis of same screen
   B) Development of a screen can start only after analysis of same screen finishes
   C) Development of a screen can finish only after analysis of same screen finishes
   D) Development of a screen does not have any dependency to analysis of same screen

10- After you have planned your project activities, your team member John had 3 activities to complete in sequence. However, due to a delay in predecessor activity of John's first activity, you asked John to do his second activity. Dependency between John's activities are an example of:
   A) Project Dependency
   B) External Dependency
   C) Mandatory Dependency
   D) Discretionary Dependency

11- In your project plan, testing of a screen can start 3 days before development of same screen finishes. This is an example of:
   A) Risk Time
   B) Delay
   C) Lead Time
   D) Lag Time

12- You are working as a project manager in a social project. In scope of project, 1000 trees will be planted in a park in your district. Disinfecting the trees can start 15 days later after planting trees. This is an example of:
   A) Risk Time
   B) Delay

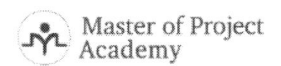

C) Lead Time
D) Lag Time

13- Network diagrams can be used to do all of the following EXCEPT:
A) Show risks regarding activities
B) Aid in planning, organizing and controlling
C) Show interdependencies of activities
D) Show project progress

14- There are some important points about estimating in projects. Which of the following is NOT true about estimating?
A) Historical information from previous projects is very important
B) Risks of activities do not affect estimation for an activity
C) Project manager must meet any agreed-upon estimates
D) Estimation of an activity should be done by the performer of the activity

15- All of the following causes padding in Estimate Activity Durations process EXCEPT:
A) Ambiguities about the activity
B) Unclear points about the task
C) Unclear roles & responsibilities
D) Estimator does not have sufficient information regarding an activity

16- All of the following are techniques used in Estimate Activity Durations process EXCEPT:
A) Direct Estimating
B) One-Point Estimate
C) Parametric Estimating
D) Analogous Estimating

17- You are managing a software project and Nelly is a software developer in your project team. When you asked her estimation about a module that she needs to develop during the project, she said "I developed a similar module in my previous project, and it took 5 days. It should take 5 days in this project as well". This is an example of:
A) Heuristics
B) One-Point Estimate
C) Parametric Estimating
D) Analogous Estimating

18- You are a project manager of a software project and in your project, each software developer will develop three screens. During your analysis, you found out that developers finished their screens 20% faster in their 2nd screen, and 30% faster in their 3rd screen. This can be explained by:
A) Regression Analysis

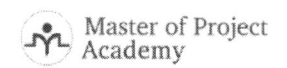

B) Learning Curve Effect
C) Subject Matter Expertise
D) Process Excellence

19- You are working in a software company. Your company estimates analysis estimations of tasks as 25% of the development tasks. This is an example of:
A) Heuristics
B) Pre-judgment
C) PERT Analysis
D) Percent Estimate

20- You use triangular distribution of PERT estimation in your project. An estimator gave 5 days as optimistic, 6 days as most likely and 10 days as pessimistic estimate. What is the estimated activity duration?
A) 6 days
B) 6.5 days
C) 7 days
D) 8 days

21- An estimator gave 4 days as optimistic, 6 days as most likely and 14 days as pessimistic estimate. What is the activity duration if beta distribution is used?
A) 6 days
B) 7 days
C) 8 days
D) 9 days

22- As a project Manager, you need all of the following during Develop Schedule process EXCEPT:
A) Activity List
B) Network Diagram
C) Resource Calendars
D) Organizational Structure of your company

23- All of the following about Critical Path are true EXCEPT:
A) Longest path in the network diagram
B) All activities in the critical path have zero float
C) Critical Path activities can be delayed without changing end date of project
D) There can be several critical paths in a project

24- All of the following are true EXCEPT:
A) Near critical path is the second critical path of a project

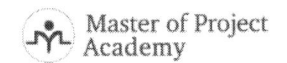

B) There can be negative float
C) Critical Path of a project can change over time
D) Having several critical paths mean project has high risk

25- You noticed that your project is getting delayed. In order to complete a critical path activity earlier, you assigned an additional team member to the activity. This is an example of:
A) Fast Tracking
B) Crashing
C) Monte-Carlo Analysis
D) Team Spirit

26- Resource Leveling is done in projects in order to:
A) Complete project earlier
B) Complete project cheaper
C) Reduce project risks
D) Distribute tasks uniformly to resources

27- Your company's vice president requires a 15-minute project briefing in every month. Which of the following will be useful reporting format?
A) Network Diagram
B) Milestone Chart
C) Bar Chart
D) Project Chart

28- All of the following activities are done during Control Schedule Process EXCEPT:
A) Re-estimation of remaining activities
B) Applying schedule compression techniques
C) Leveling resources
D) Measuring variances

Answers

1 – D	16 – A
2 – A	17 – D
3 – B	18 – B
4 – C	19 – A
5 – D	20 – C
6 – A	21 – B
7 – C	22 – D
8 – B	23 – C
9 – B	24 – A
10 – D	25 – B
11 – C	26 – D
12 – D	27 – B
13 – A	28 – B
14 – B	
15 – C	

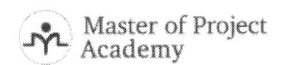

Mapping Game – Section 5

The output of Plan Schedule Management	the critical path
the durations which the team works toward completion of a goal.	False
Milestones are always one day long. True or False?	Near Critical Path
Duration estimates do not include any lags. True or False?	Schedule management plan
sequence of activities that represents the longest path through a project	Fast Tracking
Amount of time an activity can be delayed without delaying the early start date.	True
doing critical path activities in parallel instead of series	time-boxed period
Closest path to critical path in terms of duration	PERT Analysis
Three Point Estimating	Free Float

Answers

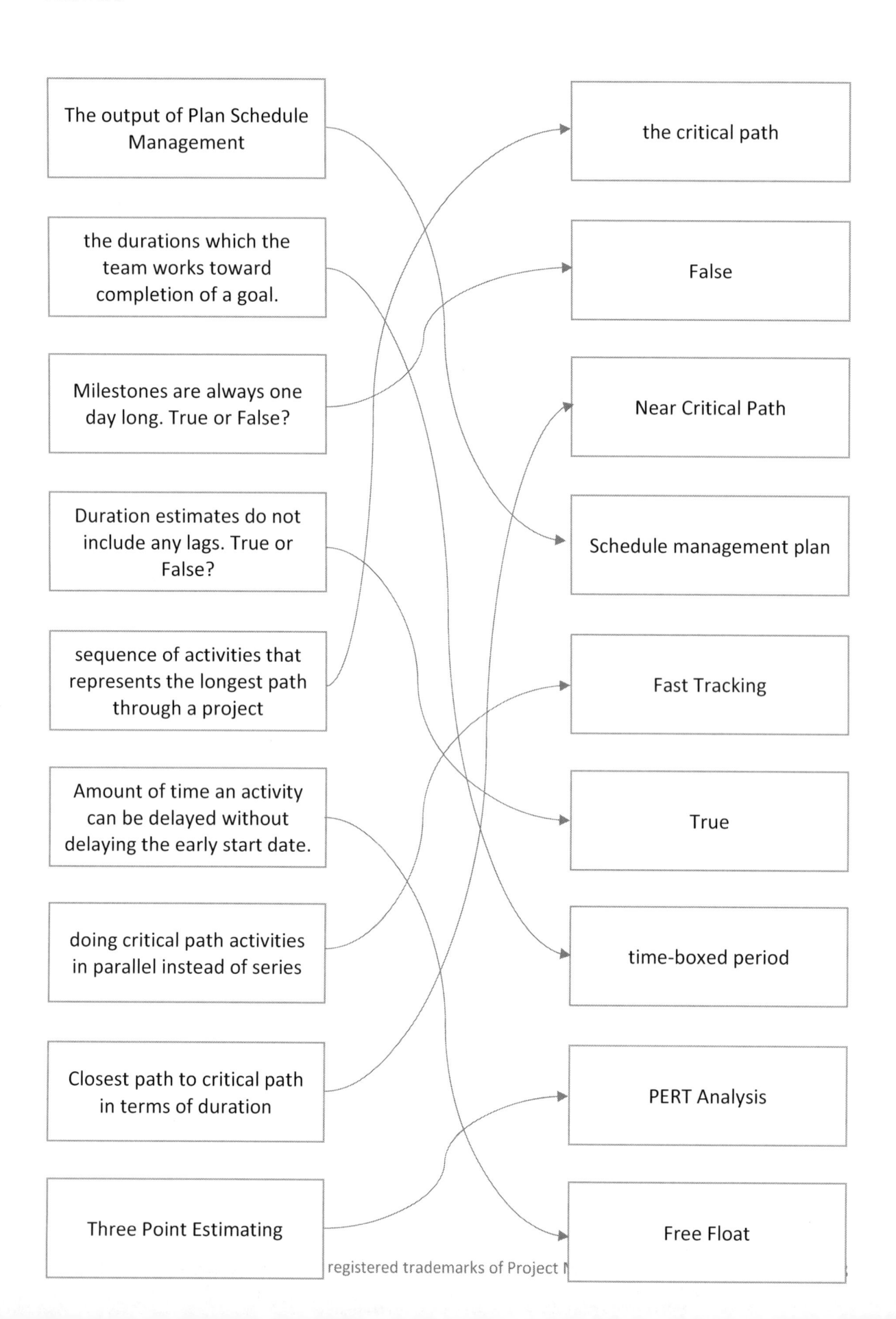

Left	Right
The output of Plan Schedule Management	Schedule management plan
the durations which the team works toward completion of a goal.	time-boxed period
Milestones are always one day long. True or False?	False
Duration estimates do not include any lags. True or False?	True
sequence of activities that represents the longest path through a project	the critical path
Amount of time an activity can be delayed without delaying the early start date.	Free Float
doing critical path activities in parallel instead of series	Fast Tracking
Closest path to critical path in terms of duration	Near Critical Path
Three Point Estimating	PERT Analysis

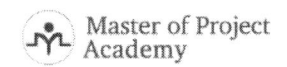

Section 6

Cost Management

Section 6 – Cost Management

Cost Management is another knowledge area of the project management. There are several activities in a project, several project resources work on project activities and several materials, tool and equipment are used to complete the project scope. All these require a budget to be allocated. Because you need to purchase tools, materials, and the company must pay salaries of the project personnel etc. Briefly, cost management knowledge area plans how to manage expenses and budget of a project, monitor and control the status of the project and measures budget performance. During this section of the book, we will go over the content and processes of cost management knowledge area.

What will be the agenda of the cost management knowledge area section?

- **Overview of Cost Management:** First, we will go over the cost management briefly. We will describe the important definitions, major outputs and processes of cost management knowledge area.
- **Plan Cost Management Process:** First process of cost management knowledge area is, plan cost management process. In this process, how to determine budget, estimate costs and manage the expenses throughout the project are planned. We will go over the plan cost management process in detail.
- **Cost Management Plan:** Cost Management plan is the primary output of the plan cost management process. It describes how to manage the project costs and budget. We will go over the details of cost management plan.
- **Life Cycle Costing:** Life cycle costing is an important term in project management. Everything that is produced has a lifetime. Do you still use your first cell phone? Most probably no. Because in today's world, most of the technological products have at most 2 years of lifecycle. We will go over this concept in our further notes.
- **Value Engineering:** Value engineering is performing same work with a less costly way. For instance, if you need a bulldozer for your construction project only for 2 months, most probably, leasing the bulldozer will be less costly than buying a bulldozer if you won't use it in your future project works. We will go over this concept in detail in our further notes.
- **Estimate Costs Process:** Estimate costs process is the second process of cost management knowledge area. We will go over this process in detail. Cost estimation for each project activity and tools, materials, equipment are done in this process. Based on these estimations, overall project budget is estimated.
- **Types of Costs:** There are different types of costs in a project. For instance, office rent for a project is a fixed cost. Regardless of how many project resources will work, you need an office, and this cost will be in your project budget. On the other hand, material costs, expenses for project personnel etc. will be variable depending on the amount of people or materials. We will see these different types of costs in detail.
- **Inputs to Estimating Costs:** Inputs to estimating costs are important. Because, all cost estimation is based on the inputs. We will see these inputs.
- **Estimating:** We will go over estimating activities in a project.
- **Accuracy of Estimates:** Accuracy of Estimates is an important concept. If you need a crispy clear estimation, you will need to work more on planning to reach a more accurate

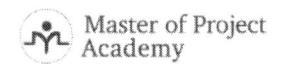

estimation. Depending on the accuracy necessity, estimation is must be planned accordingly.

- **Determine Budget Process:** Determine Budget Process is third process of cost management knowledge area. After estimations are done, all cost estimations are combined during this process and overall project budget is determined. We will go over this process in detail in our further notes.
- **Project Budget Components:** Project Budget will have components. After activity cost estimates are complete, there will be contingency reserves on top of these estimates such as activity contingency, management reserve etc. to accommodate any risks if they occur during the project.
- **Control Costs Process:** Control costs is the fourth and last process of the cost management knowledge area. This process mainly aims to control the project expenses and complete the project on determined budget. We will go over this process in detail in our further notes.
- **Progress Reporting:** Progress reporting for cost management is crucial as well. Because, based on the previous expenses and track, whether the remaining activities will be completed with the remaining budget must be assessed frequently. These must be reported to relevant stakeholders.
- **Earned Value Management:** Earned Value Management is a critical part of cost management knowledge area. Earned Value calculations show whether you are ahead of budget or under budget. These calculations are critical to evaluate whether project will meet the schedule and cost targets. We will see earned value management calculations in detail with examples.

Overview of Cost Management

- **Cost Management includes processes required to complete the project within the approved budget:** With its processes, cost management knowledge area aims to determine the required budget to complete the project, and then aims to monitor and control the project costs to meet the determined budget.

- **Major output of the cost management knowledge area is Project Budget:** After the project scope is clear and project activities are determined, each project deliverable and each project activity will have an associated cost. Because, project resources will perform activities, and they have costs to projects such as expenses, salary etc. There will be tools, materials or equipment that need to be used during the project as well. These will require a budget as well.

- **Cost management knowledge area primarily concerns with the cost of resources needed to complete the project activities.** After the budget is determined, cost management will keep on measuring and monitoring the cost performance of the project to meet the agreed budget.

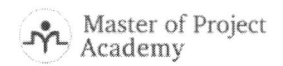

- **Cost Management has four processes.** Three of these processes belong to planning process group, and one of them belongs to monitoring and controlling process group. These processes are:
    1. Plan cost management,
    2. Estimate costs,
    3. Determine budget and
    4. Control costs.

Plan Cost Management Process

Plan cost management process is the first process of cost management knowledge area.

- **Plan cost management is the process of establishing policies, procedures, and documentation for planning, managing, expending and controlling project costs.**

    There will be several project resources in a project. Several and different type of materials will be needed. In addition, there might be tool and equipment necessity as well. Plan cost management process aims to plan, manage and control of these expenses in a project.
    For instance, for a construction project, several civil engineers, construction workers will work. Several materials such as cement, wood, steel etc. will be used and tools and equipment like trucks, bulldozer, hammers etc. will be needed. Cost management process mainly aims to determine cost of each activity, and determine the budget of the project. Then, management and control of the project budget to complete the project on the determined budget respectively.

- **Cost Management Plan provides guidance and direction on how the project costs will be managed throughout the project:** For instance, you will be able to see how much money you will need in a certain phase of the project with the help of plan cost management process.

- **Major output of the plan cost management process is Cost Management Plan:** Cost management plan briefly describes how to estimate costs, how to determine budget, and after the budget is determined, how to manage and control costs are outlined in the cost management plan

Cost Management Plan

As many management plans, cost management plan is also part of the project management plan which helps to meet the project goals and objectives as a whole.

Cost Management Plan answers two main questions:

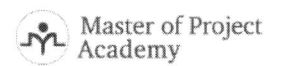

- **"How will I go about planning cost for the project?"**: Cost management plan will guide you on how to estimate costs for each activity, each deliverable and how to construct the overall project budget respectively.
- **"How will I manage the project to the cost baseline?"**: After the budget of the project is determined, cost baseline is taken. Cost baseline shows the initial cost estimate of the project. If nothing changes in the project, or if there will not be any approved change requests, it is expected that the determined project budget will be met. Cost management plan will guide you on when to spend on what throughout the project and ensure you meet the determined project budget.

Cost Management Plan includes:

- **Units of measure (days, km, liters, m² ...etc.)**: You will estimate costs based on the amount you need from a material. These units might change depending on the country or project. For instance, in UK, or US generally inches are used for length or foot-square is used for the area of a space. However, in European countries, meters are used for length and meter square is used for the area of a space. Since units of measure is a critical aspect to determine and estimate the cost, it must be included in the cost management plan.
- **Levels of precision (rounding up or down: $100.49 to $100 or $101)**: Levels of precision must be included in cost management plan as well. For instance, what will be the number of decimal places during calculations? This might come to you a trivial point. Nevertheless, if you consider the mega projects, millions of materials are used, and the level of precision might cause significant variances in total.
- **Control thresholds (amount of variation before taking action, e.g. $20.000)**: Control thresholds must be included in the cost management plan as well. For instance, what will be the amount of budget variance to take action to get back on track? If you are managing a 1 million-dollar project, and if you set $20,000 as control thresholds, this means, you need to take corrective actions if you are more than $20,000 behind the schedule.
- **Rules of performance measurement (EVM technique % completion method for activities)**: Rules of performance measurement such as earned value management technique or percent completion method for activities must be included in the cost management plan. Earned value management is the most common technique used to measure cost performance of a project, and abbreviated as EVM. Either EVM or any other method that will be used in performance measurement must be mentioned in the cost management plan. Percent completion method for activities must be included in the cost management plan as well. For instance, how do you consider an activity in progress? Generally, there are three assumptions for activities in progress. First approach considers them as not started. Second approach considers them as 50% complete. Third approach considers them as 100% completed. How activities in progress will be considered must be included in the cost management plan.
- **Reporting formats (format and frequency for cost reports)**: Reporting formats must be included in the cost management plan. How frequent will you be reporting about cost performance of the project? What will be the format for cost reporting? For instance, you will report a brief high-level cost report to senior management in every 2weeks, and a detailed report in every month. These must be cleared out in the cost management plan.
- **Additional details**: Additional details such as strategic funding choices, cost recording procedure etc. must be included in the cost management plan as well. In case you need

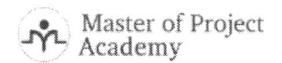

additional budget for your project, how to find sources should be mentioned in the cost management plan. If there are corporate tools or application that keep track of costs and expenses in a project, these must be described in the cost management plan as well.

Life Cycle Costing & Value Engineering

Life cycle costing and value engineering are two important concepts in cost management.

- **Life Cycle Costing:** Life cycle costing is looking at the cost of whole life of product, not just the cost of the product in the project. You might be buying a tool or equipment to use in your project. While buying it, your company must consider the life cycle cost of the product, not just the cost in the project. It is better to describe this concept over an example.

  Consider that, you will need a pressing machine for your project. However, your company plans to use this machine in future projects after your project is completed. Therefore, your company will buy the pressing machine instead of leasing it. There are two options for pressing machine. Low quality and high quality.

Quality Level	Cost of Product	Cost of Maintenance (After Project Completion)	Total Cost (Product+Maintenance)
Low	$80.000	$40.000	$120.000
High	$100.000	$10.000	$110.000

  Low quality pressing machine is $80,000 but it is expected to pay around $40,000 afterwards during maintenance in next years. So total lifecycle cost is $120,000 for low quality pressing machine. High quality pressing machine is $100,000. Expected maintenance costs for the next years is $10,000. Therefore, in total, life cycle cost of the high-quality pressing machine is $110,000.

  Now, if you consider only project costs, buying low quality pressing machine is more feasible. However, your company plans to use it in future projects, therefore, lifecycle cost must be considered and high-quality pressing machine must be purchased.

- **Value Engineering (or Value Analysis):** Value engineering is also known as value analysis. Value engineering is, briefly, finding less costly way of the same work. Please do not confuse this with reducing scope or decreasing quality to deliver project work with a lower cost. Value engineering aims to do the exact work with a less costly way. If a team is trying to decrease the costs with same scope, they are performing value analysis. In order to describe value engineering, I will go over a sample scenario.

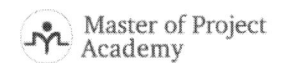

Consider that you need 5,000 meters' cube of wood for your construction project. You need the first 2,500 meters' cube in the beginning of the project and the next 2,500 meters' cube 3 months later. However, your wood supplier tells you that, if you buy all 5,000 meters' cube at once, he can make 25% discount from the list price. You will need total 5,000 meters' cube wood anyhow in your project, and buying all wood at once at the beginning of the project is less costly.

Here in this scenario, total amount of the material that will be purchases is same, but you reduce the cost by buying all required amount at once. This is an example of value engineering.

Estimate Costs Process

Estimate costs process is the second process of cost management knowledge area.

- **Estimate costs is the process of developing an approximation of the monetary resources needed project activities.** If you remember from schedule management knowledge area, activity duration of each project activity was estimated. Now in estimate costs process, cost of each activity is determined. After that, these estimations are used to bottom-up all estimation values and create an overall project budget.

- **Estimates for each project activity are done during Estimate Costs process.** This is critical because you need to determine an overall project budget to complete the project. If you estimate the costs for each project activity, this will increase accuracy and precision during cost estimation.

- **Estimate costs process determines the amount of cost required to complete the project work.** For instance, consider that you are managing a construction project, and one of the project activities is, painting a room of the building. Assume that the paining will be completed in 1 day, and two painters will work.

- **Costs are estimated for all resources that will be charged to the project:** When estimating costs for this project activity, you need to consider the cost of the painters such as wages, insurance policies, clothes etc. and the material they will be using such as brushes, dye etc. Costs of other project activities are estimated and a total project budget is determined at the end of this process. Costs are estimated for all resources that will be charged to the project. These costs include labor that will be paid to project resources, materials that will be used when performing that particular project activity, equipment that will be used and any contingency reserves to accommodate delays or risks in that project activity.

- **Estimating costs are similar to the estimating done in Time Management.** Each activity is evaluated by the project resources, tools, materials etc. that will be used in that activity are considered, and a cost estimation for each project activity is determined in the end. After cost estimation for each activity is completed, overall project budget can be determined respectively.

Let us go through important points about estimating again. As you remember, we have gone through important points about estimating during our previous notes in Time Management knowledge area. The list is similar; therefore, we will not give a detailed explanation for each bullet again. Since these points are crucial, it is better to go over once again for cost management.

- **Cost Estimation should be based on WBS to improve accuracy.** Work Breakdown Structure of a project shows the hierarchy of project deliverables. Therefore, if estimation is done starting from the smallest part of work, it will be easier to sum up the cost of each work package to find the total cost of the project through the help of WBS.

- **Estimation of an activity should be done by the person doing the work.** Because he knows the details of the project activity, what he will be using as an equipment, and amount of material needed to complete the project activity. Therefore, estimation must be done by the assignee of the work.

- **Historical information from past projects is key!** Because, if your organization has done a similar project activity in past projects, it will give a very good insight about the activity in new project. For instance, if a 10 meter-square room has been painted with a $200 cost in past project, this will be a critical input for painting tasks of new project as well.

- **Cost baseline should be taken in the beginning and should not be changed except change requests.** Because cost baseline of a project will show your initial project cost estimation for a project. During the rest of the project, you need to meet these estimations to complete the project on budget. In order to measure cost performance of the project with the actual costs, you need to consider baseline values to check whether you are under budget or over budget. Therefore, as long as there is not a change request that will cause an increase in the project budget, cost baseline should not be changed in order to ensure healthy cost performance measurements.

- **Changes should be requested when cost problems occur.** Because, if the project is exceeding the agreed budget, you will need additional funding resources to fund remaining activities of the project.

- **Project manager may periodically recalculate the estimate to complete, which is abbreviated as ETC.** Estimate to complete value shows the required budget to complete the remaining activities of the project, based on the cost performance of the project achieved until now. Therefore, if cost performance of the project was worse than the planned, your ETC will show that you need a higher budget to complete the remaining activities of the project respectively. The vice versa is, if you completed the previous activities of the project with a smaller budget than the estimated, then, you will need a smaller budget to complete the remaining activities of the project.

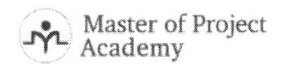

- **There is a process for creating the most accurate estimate.** This process must be followed for an accurate and attainable project budget.

- **Project manager must meet any agreed-upon estimates.** Therefore, if the project budget has been determined as 1 million dollars, project manager must complete the project with this budget as long as there is not a new change request that will increase the budget necessity.

- **Estimates can be decreased by reducing risks.** Because, during estimation of each activity, a contingency reserve is planned if there is any risk associated with the activity. If these risks are eliminated or reduced, contingency reserves planned to accommodate the impacts of these risks will be reduced respectively. This will help in reducing the estimates for the project activities.

During estimation, cost of all work needed the complete the project is estimated. These costs include:

- **Cost of quality efforts.** Quality has a cost. You cannot produce a high-quality product with small budget. Therefore, depending on the quality requirements of the project, your costs will differ.

- **Cost of risk efforts.** Negative risks may cause delays and extra costs to project. For instance, consider that you are managing a construction project in an area, which has high earthquake risk. In case of an earthquake, your construction will be affected, and you might need to fix hampered part of your construction after an earthquake. Therefore, risks of a project affect the contingency reserves to accommodate risks of the activities, and this affects the total project budget respectively.

- **Cost of project manager's time.** Depending on the project complexity, number of resources and nature of the project, project manager will spend effort for the project. This will bring a cost for the project as well.

- **Cost of project management activities.** Project management activities include planning, estimation, project meetings, etc. These activities will need a certain amount of time in the project. Therefore, these activities will have a cost respectively.

- **Costs directly associated with project (training, paper, pencils... etc.).** Depending on the project and industry, you will need materials to complete the project. For a construction project, you will need trucks, cement, steel, wood etc. For a software project, you will need development environment, testing equipment, PCs, etc. These materials will bring a cost to the project as well.

- **Cost of office expenses.** In order to bring project resources into a same place, you need to reserve a room in the company, or rent an office outside. In either case, reserving a room as a project working space will be a project cost.

- **Profit when applicable.** Projects are done to provide a positive output for the company or for commercial purposes. For instance, a smartphone manufacturer produces a new version to sell to consumers to make profit.

- **Overhead costs, such as management salaries, general office expenses etc.** CEO of a company does not work actively in a project, right? However, he has a salary so he has a cost to the company. Similarly, security guards of the company do not work on projects. However, they are cost to the company. These kinds of overhead costs of the companies are considered when calculating costs of each project. This does not mean that the cost of the CEO is placed into a particular project budget. Nevertheless, overhead costs of a company are considered with the all projects of a company, and when making calculations, these costs are considered in projects with a reflection of these overhead costs to the project.

Types of Costs

There are 4 main types of costs in a project.

1. Variable Cost
2. Fixed Cost
3. Direct Cost
4. Indirect Cost

1. **Variable Cost:** Variable costs change with amount of production or work. For instance, wages of the employees, cost of materials that will be used in the project are variable costs. Total wages you will be paying for the personnel will increase with the number of project resources respectively. Similarly, the more material you use in a project, the more you will spend for the materials.

2. **Fixed Costs:** These costs do not change as production changes. For instance, set-up cost of an equipment, or rental cost of an office. In your project, you will need an office to gather your project team members in same place. It does not matter whether there will be 5 team members or 10 team members, rental cost of the office is same.

3. **Direct Costs:** Direct costs of the project are directly attributable to the work on project. For instance, wages of the project resources, materials that will be used in the project are direct costs. Because, these will be input to the project in order to produce project deliverables.

4. **Indirect costs:** Overhead items or costs incurred for the benefit of more than one project are indirect costs. For instance, CEO of the company does not actively contribute to the projects of a company. However, his salary, compensation packages etc. are all cost to the company. Similarly, security guard of the building will not be working on the project, but his salary is a cost for the company. Therefore, when considering costs in project management, these costs are reflected to the direct costs of the project generally. This

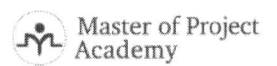

concept is more about finance but corporate companies calculate the costs of company and reflects these costs per revenue generating resource. For instance, cost of a software developer in a project will include the overhead costs of the company as well.

Inputs to Estimating Costs

During cost estimation, you will need several inputs in order to determine the overall project budget of the project.

- **Scope baseline:** Scope Baseline is one of the inputs. Scope of a project shows what will be delivered throughout the project, therefore, it is directly related with the amount of work that will be delivered and affects the costs.
- **Project Schedule:** Project schedule is an important input to the estimating costs.
    - **Timing of something you buy affects its costs.** For instance, for a construction project, costs of the materials might be increasing during summer since construction works are speeding during summer. Alternatively, if you are purchasing materials with a foreign currency, currency fluctuations overtime might affect your costs. Since project schedule will show which activity will be started and completed when, it will be a critical input for estimating costs.
    - **You need to develop a time-phased spending plan.** Consider that your project budget is 1 million dollars. Since you will not be using this budget at the day one of the project, you need to create a time-phased spending plan. For instance, you need to come with a monthly spending plan.
- **Human Resource Plan:** Human Resource Plan is a critical input for estimating costs as well. We will see human resource plan during human resource management in detail. Human resource plan of a project includes rewards, labor rates, qualifications, and quantity of resources. For instance, each project resource that will work throughout the project will be in the human resource plan, and their costs and qualifications will be listed in the human resource plan as well. Therefore, these costs will be determining project budget.
- **Risk Register:** Risk Register is another input for Estimating costs. We will go through risk register during Risk Management knowledge area. Risk Register of a project includes risks of the project, their probability of occurrence, impacts of risk when it occurred, and risk response strategies to overcome the impacts of risks when they occurred.
    - **Risks are input and output for "Estimate Costs" process:** Since risk register will include detailed information about risks, budget that needs to be allocated to overcome the impacts of risks are also included in the risk register of the project. Therefore, risks are input and output for "Estimate Costs" process.
    - **Costs for Risk Control:** Apart from the impact of risks, there will be risk control costs. For instance, you will need periodic risk reviews, re-evaluation and monitoring risks throughout the project. All these will bring cost to the project.
- **Policies on estimating templates, processes, procedures, lessons learned and historical information:** Policies are also input to estimating costs. For instance, if there is a specific procedure or process to provide estimates for the projects in a company, these must be considered during estimating costs.
- **Company culture and existing systems:** Company culture and existing systems about estimation must be used during estimating as well. For instance, if there is a specific tool

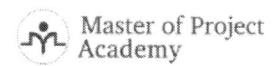

or application that is used during estimation of project activities, these must be used during cost estimation. Some corporate companies have tools or applications that calculate the materials or resource costs based on provided inputs. These must be used as inputs during projects.
- **Project Management costs will be an aspect of the project budget as well.** Project manager will spend time for creating and sending status reports, change analysis, managing project team etc. All these mean a cost for the project as well.

Estimating

There are some tools and techniques used in cost estimation. These tools and techniques used in Estimate Activity Durations process can be used in Estimate Costs process as well. We will list the tools and techniques used in activity duration estimates here, but since we have gone through these techniques in detail during previous notes, we will not go through these tools and techniques in detail.

- **One-point estimate technique:** One-point estimate technique is one the techniques used in cost estimation as well. Project activity details and information are provided to the assignee of the project. The assignee provides a one-point estimate for the work. For instance, for the installation of a database in a software project, the resource that will perform the activity can tell that the cost of the activity will be $2,000. Similarly, other project activity costs will be estimated, and overall project budget will be determined in the end.

- **Analogous Estimating technique:** Analogous Estimating technique is used to compare a similar activity that was performed in a previous project. For instance, if a similar development task cost $1,500 in previous project, this value can be considered when providing estimation for the similar activity in the new project.

- **Parametric estimating technique:** Parametric estimating technique calculates projected costs for an activity based on historical records, from previous projects or other info. It is actually a mathematical approach to find the cost estimation of a project activity. Parameters that might affect the duration of a project activity are determined, and based on these parameters, project activity durations are estimated.
For instance, for a construction project, you might get a parameter like "construction of a 1 meter-square area costs $2,000". Based on this parameter, overall construction project cost can be determined with the total space of the construction project.

- **Three-point estimate technique:** Three-point estimate was using three estimates for an activity. Pessimistic, most likely and optimistic estimates. Based on these estimates, an estimation of the activity is determined by taking average of these three estimations. Weight of each estimate can depend on the approach that will be used in three-point estimate technique. Triangular approach takes the average of three estimates, and beta distribution gives more weight to most likely estimate in calculation

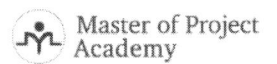

- **Bottom-up Estimating Technique:** This is a new technique for cost estimating.
    - **Detailed estimation is done for each activity or work package:** Because, project will be completed with the completion of these smaller pieces of work. Estimating the cost of a smaller piece will ease the estimation process and improve accuracy as well. After each activity or work, package cost is estimated.
    - **The estimates are rolled up to control accounts:** Several pieces of work and work packages constitute a control account if you remember from our work breakdown structure notes. Therefore, costs of each activity or work package will be summed up to find the total cost of a control account.
    - **Then into overall project estimate:** Third and the last step in Bottom-up Estimating is costs of control accounts are rolled up to the overall project estimate. Because several control accounts in a WBS hierarchy will construct the overall project scope. When costs of control accounts are rolled up, total project cost will be found. Note that, bottom-up estimating requires an accurate WBS. Because, cost of each piece in the WBS is estimated first, and then these costs are rolled up to the higher level in the WBS to find the costs of a work package, control account and the overall project respectively.

> A successful cost estimate requires an accurate WBS for sure.

Contributors to Creation of Estimates

We have seen how cost estimation is done in a project. During estimation, there are several contributors to the estimation process. We will list the most of important contributors to estimation process in this heading.

- **Project Management Software (can speed up calculations):** First contributor is Project Management Software. Depending on the industry, organization and dynamics of the project, several project management software applications can be used during cost estimations. For instance, Microsoft Project is the most popular project management software used by the project managers around the world. PPM product of the HP is used in corporate organizations for project, program and portfolio management. These software applications keep track of costs, ease calculation of overall project costs and speed up calculations.

- **Determining Resource Cost Rates:** Determining resource cost rates is another contributor to the estimation process. For instance, what is the man/hour rate of a subject matter expert? What is the monthly cost of a software developer who will be working in your project? These are important factors that will affect your cost calculations. Because, depending on the amount of work they will provide to the project, respective cost will be accrued to the project.

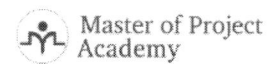

- **Reserve Analysis:** Reserve analysis is another contributor to the estimation process. Reserves are planned to accommodate unanticipated costs and risks in a project. If there are risks for an activity in the project, depending on the probability and impact of the project, reserves must be planned accordingly. For instance, if there is a risk of 2 days' delay for a certain project activity in the project, additional cost that will be caused by this delay must be planned as reserve and included in the cost estimation respectively.

- **Cost of Quality:** The last important contributor to the estimation process is Cost of Quality. Each project will have quality requirements as well. Depending on the quality requirements of a project, cost of activities will differ respectively. For a higher level of quality, it is expected that a higher amount of budget will be needed to meet those quality requirements respectively. Therefore, quality requirements of the project will be a critical aspect affecting project costs.

Accuracy of Estimates

Accuracy of estimates is a critical issue in project management. Because, after cost estimation is complete, necessary budget to run the project must be aligned by the management. This budget will be used to complete the project work throughout the project. If actual costs of the activities exceed the planned budget, you, as a project manager, might need to find additional source of funds to complete the remaining activities of the project.

- **Estimates in early phases of a project are less accurate than those made later in the project:** Because, in the beginning of the project, you do not know that much about the future of the project and risks are at the highest level. Therefore, uncertainties and ambiguities might cause higher deviances in future respectively. However, as the project progresses, you will have the actual results of project and you will get a better level of know-how about the project. Uncertainties and ambiguities will be cleared out in the meantime, and this will ensure more accurate estimation respectively.

- **Estimates must be in a range in a project:** For instance, for a screen development activity in a software project, duration estimate can be as 5 days' -/+ 1 day. This means, this activity can be completed in 4 to 6 days. Similarly, cost estimation must be in a range as well. Cost estimation for this activity can be $4,000 -/+ 10%. This means, the activity will cost somewhere around $3600 to $4,400.

- **These ranges are wider in the beginning of the project and will narrow as more information is determined during the project.** Estimator gives these estimations in a range because he does not have all information available in the beginning to make an accurate estimate for an activity. As time passes, activities are completed, unclear issues are cleared out, risks are eliminated or probability of occurrence decreases. All these factors help to narrow the estimate ranges respectively.

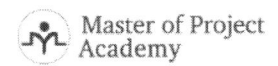

Typically, there are three types of activity estimation ranges. We will go over these three types of estimates one-by-one.

1. **Rough Order of Magnitude (ROM) Estimate:** First one is Rough Order of Magnitude estimate, which is abbreviated as ROM.
    a. **Rough Order of Magnitude estimate is used during the initiating phase of a project** when there is less information about the project, when there are high number of risks, ambiguities and uncertainties.
    b. **Rough order of Magnitude estimate provides an estimation in the range of "-25% to +75%" from actual values.** For instance, if an activity will cost $100, rough order of magnitude estimate gives a range from $75 to $175 respectively.

2. **Budget Estimate:** Second type of estimation range is Budget estimate.
    a. **Budget estimate is usually used during planning phase of a project.**
    b. **Budget estimates of an activity are in the range of "-10% to +25%" from actual values.** For instance, if an activity will cost $100, budget estimate gives a range from $90 to $125 respectively.

3. **Definitive Estimate:** Third and last type of estimation range is Definitive estimate.
    a. **Definitive estimates are used later during the project**, when things are clearer and when there is more information available about the activities.
    b. **Definitive estimates of an activity are in the range of "-10% to +10% or -5% to +10%" from actual values.** For instance, if an activity will cost $100, definitive estimate gives a range from $90 to $110 respectively.

These ranges are used during the project depending on the information available for an activity. Result of estimate cost process is having activity cost estimates and basis for those estimates. So, the main result, main output of the estimate cost process is, you will have the costs associated for each specific activity. With these cost estimates of each activity, when they are rolled up, you will reach the total cost of the project respectively.

Determine Budget Process

Third process of the cost management knowledge area is Determine Budget process.

> Determine Budget process is the process of aggregating the estimated costs of individual activities or work packages to establish an authorized cost baseline.

During estimate costs process, cost estimations of project activities and work packages are determined. With these estimates, overall project cost is found by rolling up the costs of project activities and work packages to control accounts. This is done during Determine Budget process. Once the cost of activities and overall project cost is determined, a baseline is taken.

- **Determines the cost baseline.** Cost baseline of a project shows the planned cost of each activity and work package in a project. Cost baseline is an important input during monitoring and controlling. Because, actual costs of the project will be compared against planned costs to measure the cost performance of the project.

- **Project budget refers to the total cost of the project.** You might be hearing project budget and project cost frequently. These actually refer to same thing and represents the total amount of money that needs to be spent on project activities to complete and deliver agreed project scope.

- **Budget defines how much money the company should have available to complete the project.** Based on the determined project budgets, organizations or companies align required amount of money to fund projects.

- **Project estimate cannot be completed without risk management activities and inclusion of reserves.** Because, when providing cost estimate of an activity, risks associated with the activity are considered and money that will be spent to overcome the impacts of risk when it occurred are planned in the project budget respectively. These costs planned to overcome the risks are called as reserves.

There are two types of reserves.

1. **Contingency reserves.** Contingency reserves are used to address the cost impacts of remaining risks. For instance, consider that you are managing a construction project. Cost of the construction of the main frame of the building is $1,000,000. However, due to bad weather conditions, workers might not progress as planned and this can cause additional $100,000 to this activity. In this example, $100,000 is the contingency risk for the bad weather conditions risk.

2. **Management Reserves:** Management reserves address the cost of any unforeseen risks. Although you followed the project management processes properly, and listed the possible risks that might affect the project, there might be unforeseen risks during the project. For instance, a regulatory impact, a strike in the company, natural disaster etc. For these kinds of unforeseen risks or changes, management team of the company plans an additional budget on top of the project cost. For instance, if the project budget is $10,000,000 for a construction project, management team of the company might plan a 5% management reserve for this project. This means, they reserve additional $500,000 budget for any unforeseen risks that might occur in the project.

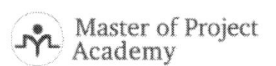

> ✦ The main difference between the contingency and management reserves is, contingency reserves are planned for identified risks while management reserves are for unforeseen risks.

Moreover, another difference is, contingency reserves are included in the project activity cost estimates while management reserves are put on top of the project's total cost.

Determine Budget Process Example

We have seen the determine budget process in our previous heading.

During Estimate costs process, cost estimations of each project activity and work package are determined. This is an example work breakdown structure and costs associated with each activity, work package and control account respectively.

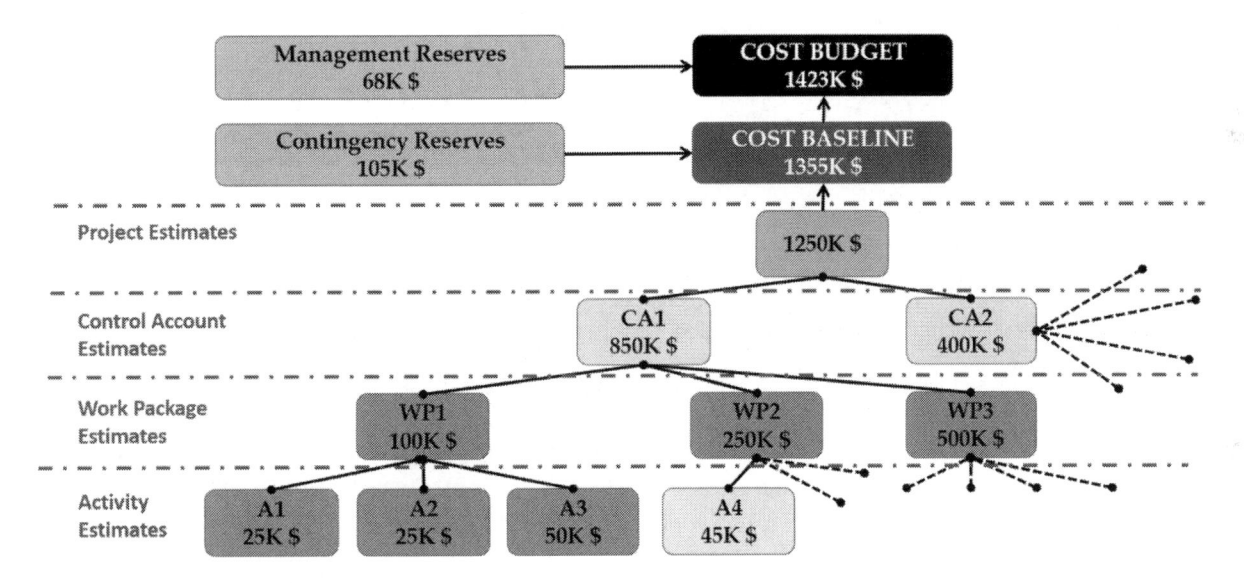

```
Management Reserves        COST BUDGET
68K $                      1423K $

Contingency Reserves       COST BASELINE
105K $                     1355K $

Project Estimates                          1250K $

Control Account            CA1                        CA2
Estimates                  850K $                     400K $

Work Package        WP1                 WP2           WP3
Estimates           100K $              250K $        500K $

Activity       A1      A2      A3       A4
Estimates      25K $   25K $   50K $    45K $
```

As you see, activity estimates are at the bottom of the WBS. Cost of activity #1 and activity #2 are $25,000. Cost of activity #3 is $50,000 and cost of activity #4 is $45,000. These cost estimates of activities are rolled up to find the cost estimates of work packages. As you see, work package #1 consists of activity #1, activity #2 and activity #3. Therefore, cost of work package #1 is total of the cost of activities belonging to it. Similarly, costs of the other work packages are found by rolling up the costs of activities belonging to regarding work package. Work packages are grouped under control accounts. Costs of work packages will determine the total cost of control account respectively. For instance, for control account #1. There are three work packages under this control account, and total cost of these work packages is $850,000, which is the total cost of control account #1.

Overall project estimate is found by aggregating the costs of control accounts in a project respectively. In this example, total project estimate is $1,250,000. However, this cost does not include the costs reserved for risks. Therefore, contingency reserves must be added on top of project estimates to find the total cost baseline. In this example, contingency reserves for the identified risks in the project is $105,000 and when this is added on top of the project estimates, cost baseline is found as $1,355,000.

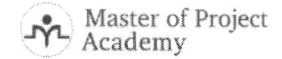

Cost baseline is under the management of project team and this is the planned amount of money that will be spend to complete the agreed project scope. However, there can be unforeseen risks in the project. Management reserves are planned by the organization or company management on top of the cost baseline. These reserves are used in case of any unplanned or unforeseen risks occur. For this example, management reserves are $68,000 for unforeseen risks. This amount is added on top of cost baseline and overall cost budget is found as $1,423,000. This means, in order to execute and complete this project successfully, company or organization must spare $1,423,000 funds for this project.

Cost Baseline & Project Budget Components

Cost baseline of a project represents funds authorized for project manager to manage and control. Project activities are determined and then cost estimations for each activity are completed. Estimated costs are aggregated to find the total cost of the project. Contingency reserves to accommodate risks of the project when they occur also planned in the cost.

After overall costs are determined, this will be cost baseline of the project. Assume that cost baseline of a project has been determined as one million dollars. This will include contingency reserves to minimize the impacts of risks when they occurred. Project manager will be using this budget to manage the project activities and complete the project successfully.
On the other hand, management team of the company or organization will put reserves for the project as well. As we mentioned in the previous notes, this is called as management reserves, and this is not in direct control of the project manager. Management evaluates projects in the organization and determines a reserve for the project for unanticipated costs that may arise during the project.

Cost Baseline + Management Reserves = Cost Budget

Cost baseline under the control of the project manager and management reserve put by the management of the company together constitute the total cost budget for a project. In other words, cost budget is the total amount of money that a company allocated for a project.

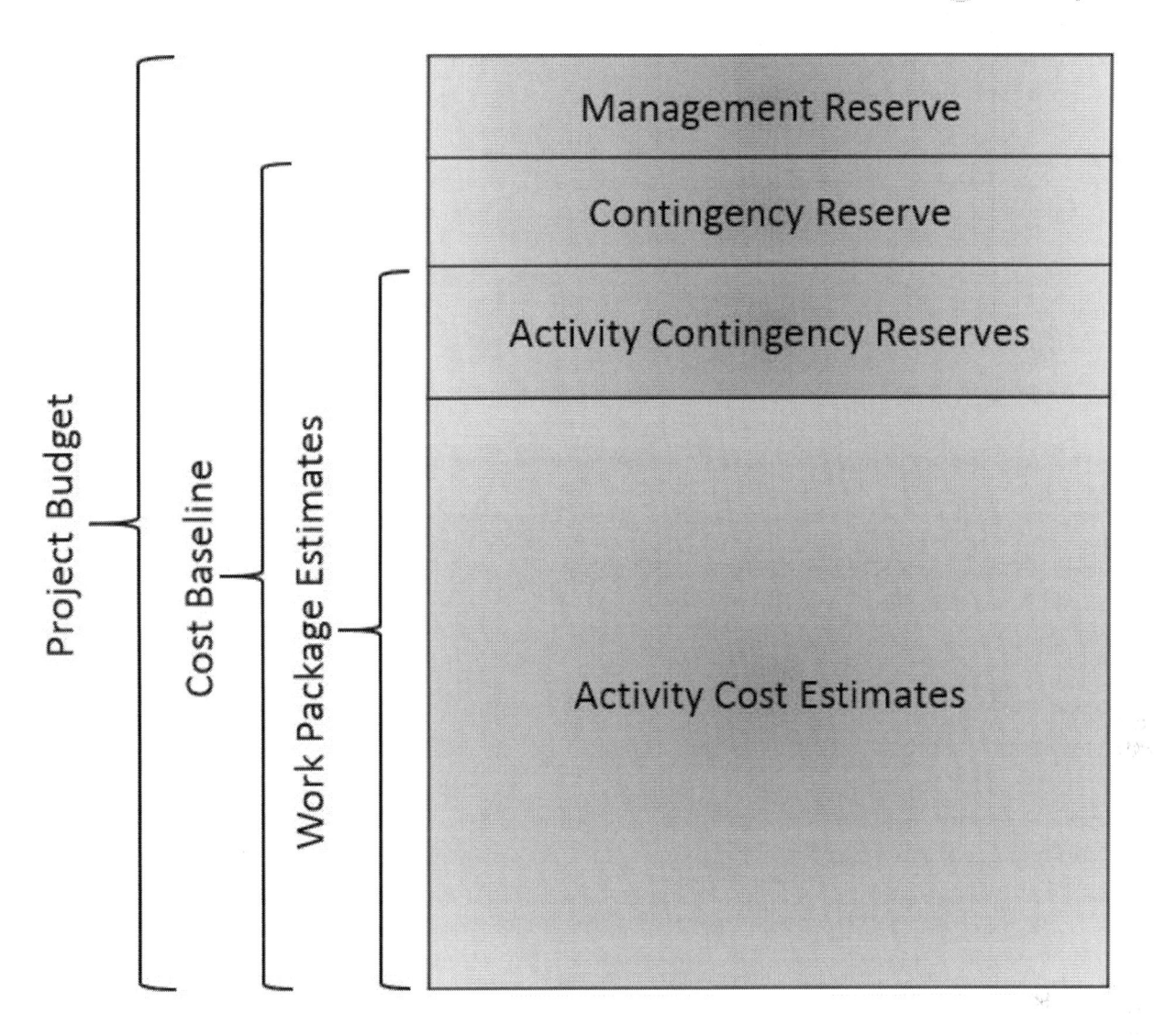

Project Budget ⎯ {
  Cost Baseline ⎯ {
    Work Package Estimates ⎯ {
      Activity Cost Estimates
      Activity Contingency Reserves
    }
    Contingency Reserve
  }
  Management Reserve
}

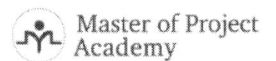

This figure shows how project budget is constituted clearly.

Note that, cost budget is also referred as project budget. As we have seen, cost baseline and management reserve together constitute the project budget. Cost baseline is constituted with the costs of control accounts. If you remember the work breakdown structure, we were aggregating the costs of each control account to find the cost bassline. Control accounts have work packages and estimates of the work packages with their contingency reserves bring us the cost of control accounts. The lowest level of a work breakdown structure is activities. Cost estimates of activities and their contingency reserves will constitute the cost of work packages.

It is better to summarize here again. Order of project budget estimation is as in the following five steps:

1. Estimate activity costs and contingency reserves
2. Aggregate activity cost estimates and contingency reserves to find work package costs
3. Aggregate work package costs and contingency reserves to find control account costs.
4. Aggregate control account costs to find cost baseline and this will be the total amount of money that will be managed by the project manager to complete the project activities.

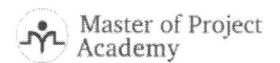

5. Determine management reserve, which is estimated by the management of the company, and add on top of cost baseline to finalize the project budget, or cost budget.

What to Do After Determine Budget

Project team members completed their activity estimations, and then costs of activities, work packages and control accounts have been aggregated. Project budget is now determined. What is next?

- **After cost baseline and cost budget are determined, estimators will make sanity check for their estimates.** Because, during cost estimations, each activity is assessed and evaluated by project team members. Once the overall project budget is determined, this needs to be re-checked by the estimators. Because, the total cost of work packages or control accounts in the work breakdown structure might give different insights to the estimators to revise their estimations.

- **Then, cash flows are defined to make sure that funding will be available when you need in your project.** For instance, consider that you determined the project budget as one-million dollars. However, the company or organization you work for will not give this total amount of money you will be spending at day one of your project. Therefore, a spending plan must exist and cash flow in and out of the project must be present. For instance, you should be able to state that $40,000 will be spent in first month, $100,000 will be spent in second month and $50,000 will be received from sales at the end of second month etc. This kind of cash flow will help your company's or organization's finance team to be prepared to provide necessary funds to your project.

- **Check constraints about the cost in project charter.** If you remember from our previous notes, constraints of a project were listed in project charter. For instance, if the sponsor can spare only one-million dollars for this project, this is a budget constraint and needs to be checked after you determined the budget of your project.

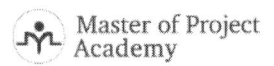

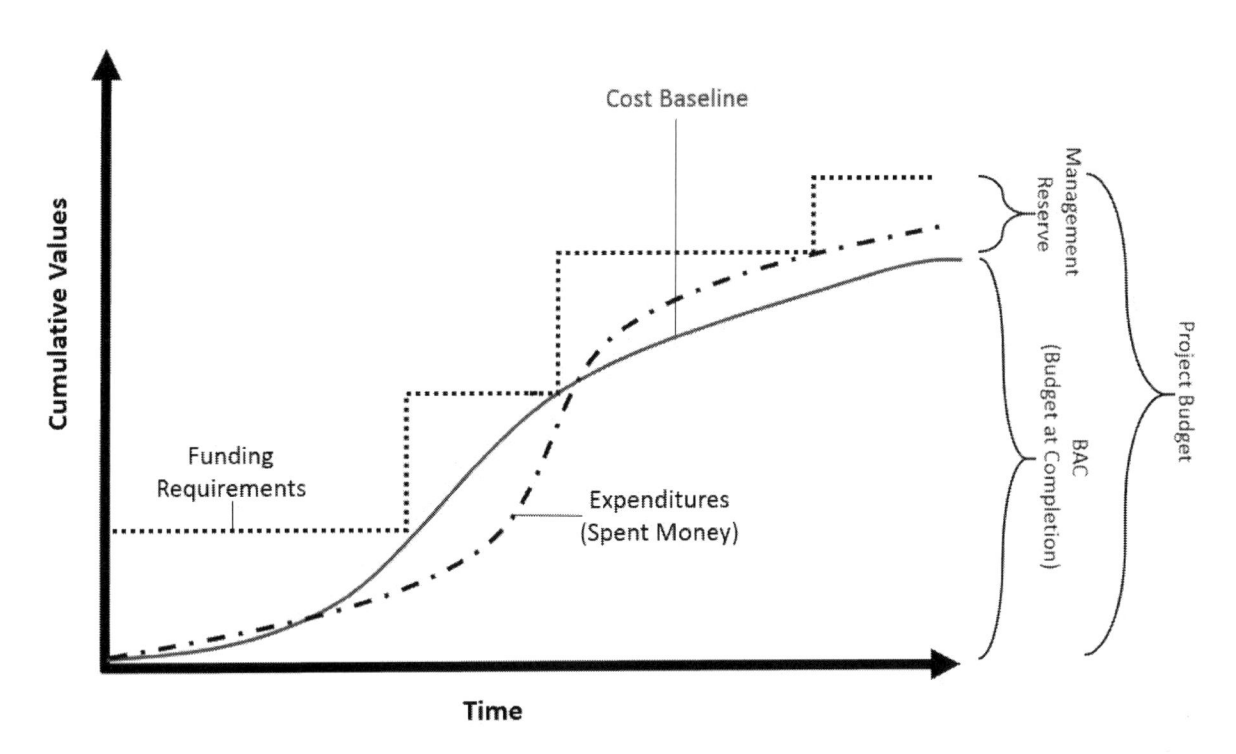

This figure shows the cost baseline, expenditures, and funding requirements in a project. Let us go through this figure to understand how project costs will be changing throughout the project.

Cost Baseline and Expenditures: As you see, the cost baseline is the middle curve in this figure and expenditures are the dotted line lying under the cost baseline. Therefore, this figure shows that expenditures are below the planned cost baseline until a time during the project. At some level later in the project, it exceeds the cost baseline.

Funding Requirements: And if you look to the funding requirements, we see a staircase model and this shows that funding will be provided for the project step-by-step. So, each increase in this dotted funding requirement staircase line represents a new cash flow into your project.

Management Reserve: The top of the figure shows the management reserve. Right end of the figure shows that; expenditures will exceed the budget at completion value, which is actually the initially determined project budget. Therefore, the management reserve will be used in this project.

Control Costs Process

Control costs is the last process of cost management knowledge area. We will go through the details of this process, and see the earned value management topic, which is a very important concept that is widely used in cost management of projects.

- **Control Costs is the process of monitoring the status of the project to update the project costs and managing changes to the cost baseline.** After the determine project budget process, you will have a cost baseline and this will show the total amount of money you will be spending to complete the project. During the project, you will be spending money for the materials that will be purchased, costs of employees, equipment that will be used etc. While you are spending money, you need to monitor progressively that you will be able complete the project with the determined project budget. This is done in Control Costs process.

- **Control Costs process provides the means to recognize variance from the plan.** Because you will be monitoring the expenditures, you will be doing throughout the project and you have the cost baseline of your project in hand as well. Assume that, in 2nd month of your project, you have spent $220,000 although you have planned to spend $180,000. Therefore, you exceeded $40,000 according to cost baseline. You need to assess this variance and take corrective actions to prevent any future variances respectively.

- **Any changes to the project should be prevented since changes will bring extra cost to the project.** One of the main responsibilities of the project manager is, preventing unnecessary changes in a project. We have seen this in our previous notes. If there are many change requests popping up in a project, you need to find the root causes of these changes and prevent them as soon as possible. Each change will bring additional activities to your project or rework. This means additional cost respectively.

Progress Reporting

Progress reporting is a critical activity that every project manager does throughout the project. You need to inform relevant stakeholders about the progress of your project.

- **Project progress is used to check whether project is on track.** When you check your project progress, if there are things going wrong, for example, if your project is behind schedule or over budget, you have to take corrective action in order to get back on track in your project. If the schedule is behind or over budget, you need to take corrective actions to get back on track and this need to be reported to project stakeholders appropriately. Otherwise, stakeholders might panic whether the project will be accomplished successfully.

- **Earned Value Management is one of the techniques used for progress tracking.** There are tools and techniques used for checking project progress in projects and earned value management is one of the most common techniques used for progress tracking. We will be going over the details of the terms used in earned value management in our following notes. We will go through sample scenarios and calculating the cost performance of the projects as well.

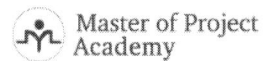

- **How much % of the work is accomplished is determined by asking the % complete to the performer of the activity.** The fundamental point of progress reporting in a project is, determining how much percent of a task is completed. How much percent of the work is accomplished is determined by asking the percent complete to the performer of the activity in projects.

  For example, during your project progress check, in order to determine the overall completion of the project percentage, you have to ask each resource of your project at what percent he or she is in his or her task, because this percent completes of each task constitute the overall percent complete of the project. This is generally done by asking to each resource of a project at what percent he or she is in his specific task or specific time tracking or task tracking tools may be used to collect this info from project resources.

Assume that you are the project manager of a software project and a software developer is working on a task, which was estimated as ten days. In the fifth day, if you go and ask him at what percent he is on his task, and if he says that I'm at 40%. Then, you should consider that this activity is a little bit behind the schedule since he might have completed the 50% since it is in the middle of estimated duration. Alternatively, if he says I am at 60% of the task on the fifth day, and then you might say that, okay, he is a little bit ahead than the planned. This kind of progress checks are generally done by asking the percent complete of each activity to the performer of the activity in projects. This method may be easier to manage in smaller project teams. You can check with each project team member about the status of his tasks. However, assume that there are hundreds of project team members in a project. It will be insane to check the percent completion of each task with the project team members and it will be unhealthy though.

If percent complete cannot be guessed by performers, then following approaches can be applied. There are three approaches for percent completion rates of activities in a project.
1. **50/50 rule:** In this approach, an activity is considered 50% complete when it begins and 50% credit for when it is finished. Therefore, in this approach, when an activity is started, by default, it's marked as 50% complete and when it's finished it's marked as 100% complete.

2. **20/80 rule:** An activity is considered 20% complete when it begins and 80% credit for when it's finished. Therefore, if you are using this approach, when an activity is started, you mark it as 20% complete and once it's finished, you mark it as 100% complete.

3. **0/100 rule.** In this approach, an activity is considered 100% complete when it finishes. Therefore, in this approach you do not mark any percent complete for an activity when it has started, so it is still 0%. You mark an activity as 100% complete only when it is completed.

Note that, these approaches are easier to apply and collect in projects. However, task durations must be shorter respectively. Otherwise, consider a task duration of 20 days. If you consider it as 100% complete or 50% complete in first day, this might lead to unhealthy progress calculations if you consider many other tasks in the project.

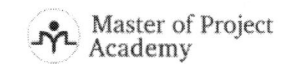

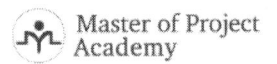

Earned Value Management

Earned Value Management, abbreviated as EVM, is a very important concept to measure the performance of a project. It is widely used in many industries. Earned Value Management is very important for project management world as well.

- **Earned Value Management is used to measure project performance against scope, schedule and cost baselines.** Scope, cost and schedule are critical aspects of a project. Therefore, earned value management plays a vital role in measuring performance of projects.

- **Earned Value Management is constituted around three fundamental terms.** These are:

    - **Planned Value (PV):** Planned value is the estimated value for the work planned. Assume that during estimation, an activity has been estimated as 10 days of work effort and $10,000 cost. These are actually planned values for this activity. Planned value for the schedule is 10 days, and planned value for the cost is $10,000.

    - **Earned Value (EV):** Earned Value is the estimated value of the work actually accomplished. Consider the previous activity. 10 days of work and $10,000 of cost were planned values. During project execution, these planned values will not be as planned. For instance, this activity might be completed in 9 days, and with a cost of $11,000. In this case, although you completed the work in 9 days, its earned value is 10 days from schedule perspective. From the cost perspective, although you spent $11,000, it was planned as a $10,000 valued activity. Therefore, your earned value will be $10,000 from cost perspective.

    - **Actual Cost (AC):** Actual cost is whatever it would take or cost about an activity during project execution. For instance, we have told that activity has been completed in 9 days, and cost $11,000 in our previous case. These are actual values for this activity. Actual cost from schedule perspective is 9 days, and actual cost from the cost perspective is $11,000.

Earned Value Management Exercise

Let us go through an earned value management exercise to understand this concept better. Here is our example scenario. You started a house renovation project. You planned to spend $100,000 in total for the project, and to finish the project in 100 days. Today is 20th day after starting to the project. Based on your plans, you should have spent $20,000 and completed 20% of the total work in the 20th day of your project. However, you spent $17,000 and completed 18% of the total work.

What is the planned value, earned value and actual cost for this scenario? See them one-by-one.

Now first look at the planned value of this example scenario. You should have spent $20,000 and completed 20% of the total work in 20th day of your project. This was your initial plan. Therefore, your planned value is 20 days from schedule perspective, which is formed by 20% multiplied by 100 days or time related calculations. Your planned value is $20,000 for cost related calculations, because you have planned that you should have spent $100,000. Therefore, your planned value is $20,000 from cost perspective for this scenario.

> Planned Value is 20 days (20%*100 days) for time related calculations.
> Planned Value is $20,000 for cost related calculations.

What is the earned value for this scenario?

You spent $17,000 and completed 18% of the total work. Therefore, earned value is 18 days from schedule perspective because you have completed 18% of the overall 100 days of total project work. It gives us earned value of 18 days for time related calculations.
Earned value is $18,000 for cost related calculations because, similarly, 18% of the total work has been completed, and since our total work was at $100,000 cost, 18% of it makes $18,000 as earned value.

> Earned Value is 18 days (18%*100 days) for time related calculations.
> Earned Value is $18.000 (18%*$100,000) for cost related calculations.

Now we will look to the actual cost of the project. Today is 20th day after starting to the project, but you spent $17,000. So actual cost is 20 days from schedule perspective because are at the 20th day of the project.
Actual cost is $17,000 for cost related calculations, because we have actually spent $17,000 in this project.

> Actual Cost is 20 days for time related calculations.
> Actual Cost is $17,000 for cost related calculations.

Variances in Earned Value Management

Variance in project management are critical indicators to find out whether a project is on budget and on track in terms of schedule. Schedule and cost performance of the project is measured and variances are determined accordingly. Based on the extent of variances, appropriate actions must be taken to get back on track if the project is behind schedule. Similarly, if the project is over budget, necessary actions must be taken to either find necessary funds or future activities must be reconsidered to not exceed the planned budget. Now, let us go over the variance terms that help us to find out whether a project is ongoing healthy.

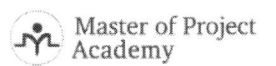

- **Schedule Variance (SV):** Schedule variance is abbreviated as SV and it is the measure of schedule performance. It is calculated by subtracting the planned value from the earned value.

$$SV = EV - PV$$

Consider that an activity was planned as 10 days during planning. If this activity is completed in less than 10 days during project execution, it will be ahead of schedule. If it is completed in more than 10 days during project execution, since it will take more than the planned time it will be behind schedule. Because, earned value of this activity will be 10 days.

Briefly,
- if SV < 0 , then, the project is behind schedule
- if SV = 0, then, project is on track as planned because activities are completed in their planned duration
- if SV > 0, then, the project is ahead of schedule. Because, you are completing the activities earlier than their planned values.

In summary, the greater the schedule variance is, the better project schedule performance you have.

- **Cost Variance (CV):** Cost Variance is abbreviated, as CV. Cost Variance is the amount of budget deficit or surplus. Briefly, it shows whether a project is under budget or over budget. Cost variance of a project or activity is calculated by subtracting the actual cost of from the earned value.

$$CV = EV - AC$$

Assume that an activity has an earned value of $10,000. During project execution, if this activity will cost more than $10,000, it will be over budget. If it is completed for less than $10,000, the activity will be under budget.

Briefly,
- If CV < 0, then, the project is over budget.
- If CV = 0, then, the project is on budget as planned.
- If CV > 0, then, the project is under budget.

In summary, the greater the cost variance is, the better project cost performance you have.

- **Schedule Performance Index (SPI):** Schedule performance index is, abbreviated as SPI, the measure of schedule efficiency. Schedule performance index, or SPI, is calculated by dividing the Earned Value of an activity or project to its planned value.

$$SPI = \frac{EV}{PV}$$

This means, if earned value is greater than the planned value, schedule performance index will be over 1. Assume that a project activity was planned as 10 days. If this activity is completed in less than 10 days, SPI will be over 1, and if it is completed in more than 10 days, its SPI will be less than 1.

Briefly,
- if SPI < 1, then, the project is behind schedule.
- if SPI = 1, then, the project is on track.
- if SPI > 1, then, the project is ahead of schedule.

In summary, the greater the schedule performance index is, the better project schedule performance you have.

- **Cost Performance Index (CPI):** Cost performance index is abbreviated as CPI. Cost performance index is actually the measure of cost efficiency of the project. Cost performance index, or CPI, is calculated by dividing the earned value of the project or activity to the actual cost.

$$CPI = \frac{EV}{AC}$$

This means, if the earned value of an activity or project is greater than the actual spent amount for that activity, CPI of the project will be greater.

Briefly,
- if CPI < 1, then, the project is over budget.
- if CPI = 1, then, the project is on budget as planned.
- if CPI > 1, then, the project is under budget.

In summary, the greater the cost performance index is, the better project cost performance you have.

Variances in Earned Value Management Exercise

We have seen the formula of variances and how variances are interpreted in the previous heading. Now, we will calculate the variances of our sample project scenario we have seen in previous notes.

- **Schedule Variance (SV) Calculation:** Let us calculate the schedule variance of the previous scenario. 18% of the work was complete in 20th day of the project. Therefore, earned value was 18 days, and planned value for the 20th day was 20 days of work should have been completed.
    - SV = EV – PV = 18 days – 20 days = - 2 days
    - SV < 0 → *Project is behind schedule.*

Therefore, we conclude that project is behind the schedule.

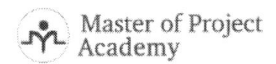

- **Cost Variance (CV) Calculation:** Let us calculate the cost variance now. 18% of the work has been completed and this was valued as $18,000 in 20th day of the project. For this, $17,000 has been spent. Therefore, earned value was $18,000 and actual cost was $17,000 for the project.
    - CV = EV – AC = $18.000 - $17.000 = $1000
    - CV > 0 → *Project is under budget.*

  Cost variance is greater than zero, therefore, project is under the budget.

- **Schedule Performance Index (SPI) Calculation:** We will calculate the schedule performance index now. Earned value was 18 days and planned value was 20 days.
    - SPI = EV / PV = 18 days / 20 days = 0.9
    - SPI < 1 → *Project is behind schedule.*

  Schedule performance index is less than 1, therefore project is behind the schedule.

- **Cost Performance (CPI) Calculation:**
    - CPI = EV / AC = $18.000 / $17.000 = 1.06
    - CPI > 1 → *Project is under budget.*

  Cost performance of the project is greater than 1. Therefore, project is under budget. In other terms, you are spending less than what you planned, which is good. This is actually same conclusion when we interpreted the cost variance results.

Forecasting in Earned Value Management

One of the critical aspects of project management is forecasting. You need to check always whether the remaining funds will be sufficient to complete the remaining activities in the project. If there is a huge variance, then, you need to take corrective actions to fix the variance. Otherwise, you will be short of funds in future and this will cause the project failure. We will be going over forecasting terms used in earned value management during this heading and show the formulas about how to calculate those terms for a project.

- **Budget at Completion (BAC):** First term is Budget at Completion. Budget at Completion is abbreviated as BAC. Budget at completion value shows the total project budget that is planned to be spent throughout the project. We have seen in our previous notes how to determine the project budget. Budget at completion is actually the output of that process.

- **Estimate at Completion (EAC):** Estimate at Completion is abbreviated as EAC. Estimate at completion value of a project shows the total cost of completing all work. It includes the sum of all actual cost to date and the estimate to complete. Assume that you determined the project budget as one million dollars during planning. When you accomplished the 20% of the work, you know more about the details of the project and based on the tasks that have been performed, you might conclude that remaining activities of the project can be costlier or less costly. Therefore, estimate at completion value might be more or less than the budget at completion value depending on the performance of the project. Estimate at completion is a critical term. Because, if you planned to complete the project with one-million-dollar budget, and if your new estimate at completion value shows that it would take $1,100,000 million dollar, you need to be prepared to find additional $100,000 budget to complete the project.

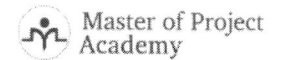

$$EAC = AC + Bottom\ Up\ ETC$$

Bottom-up ETC is actually a forecast about how much the remaining activities in the project will cost. Bottom-up ETC value can be found by estimating the work remaining to be completed. You can get the new estimation of project resources for the remaining activities in the project and they can revise their previous estimations based on their experience in the project and this will give more realistic and up-to-date estimate at completion value respectively.

- **Estimate at Completion (EAC) can be found by three different approaches using EV, SPI and CPI values:** Estimate at completion value can be found by the existing project performance values as well. In this way, you will not need to ask each project team member to revise his estimate. Because, if you go back to re-estimation frequently during the project, you will be spending a significant amount of time for re-planning instead of performing the project work. Therefore, generally, existing project performance values are used to calculate estimate at completion value. There project performance values are used to calculate estimate at completion. These are earned value, schedule performance index and cost performance index. Let us go over three approaches for calculating estimate at completion one-by-one now.

    o **1st Approach:** all future remaining work in the project are assumed that they will cost as they planned in the beginning. Moreover, cost of this remaining work is found by subtracting the earned value achieved until now from the budget at completion value. This is summed up with the actual cost to find total estimate at completion value.

$$EAC = AC + (BAC - EV)$$

    o **2nd Approach:** the cost performance achieved till now is expected to continue in the future. In other words, assume that you spent 20% more than what you planned until now. This approach assumes that you will be spending 20% more from the planned value for the remaining activities in the project as well. Therefore, formula uses the cost performance index to estimate at completion value estimate at completion is found by dividing the budget at completion value to cost performance index achieved till now. This assumes that, cost performance index achieved until now will be persistent until end of the project.

$$EAC = \frac{BAC}{CPI}$$

    o **3rd Approach:** estimate to complete work will be performed at an efficiency rate that considers both the cost and schedule performance indices. Formula of the 3rd approach is in this part. Actual cost is summed up with the estimate to complete value, which is calculated by using budget at completion, earned value, CPI and SPI. Actually, budget at completion value minus earned value (*BAC – EV*) gives the total remaining work as planned in the beginning of the project. By dividing this to *CPI x SPI*, cost and schedule performance of the project is considered. The better the cost and schedule performance are, the less estimate to complete effort will come out of this equation.

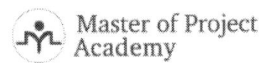

$$EAC = AC + \frac{BAC - EV}{CPI \times SPI}$$

- **Estimate to Complete (ETC):** Estimate to complete value is abbreviated as ETC and it is the expected cost to finish all the remaining project work. We have seen in previously, that different approaches can be used to calculate estimate to complete value.

$$ETC = EAC - EV$$

By this way, completed work's earned value is subtracted from the new estimated project completion budget calculated based on the performance of accomplished tasks. This result gives us estimate to complete value for the remaining activities in the project. Estimate to complete work can be re-estimated as well. At a certain point in the project, you can work with the project team members to revise their estimations for the remaining activities in the project. This will give the cost of remaining work in the project as well.

- **Variance at Completion (VAC):** Variance at completion is another term used in forecasting in earned value management. Variance at completion is abbreviated as VAC, and it is amount of budget deficit or surplus expressed as the difference between BAC and EAC.

$$VAC = BAC - EAC$$

This variance will show how much you will exceed your planned budget or how much you will complete the project under the budget.
    - if VAC < 0, project will be completed over the planned budget.
    - if VAC = 0, project will be completed on the planned budget.
    - if VAC > 0, project will be completed under the planned budget.

The last term we will be seeing in this heading is, to-complete performance index. To-complete performance index is abbreviated as TCPI. TCPI is a measure of the cost performance that is required to be achieved in order to meet budget. In other words, TCPI shows how likely to complete a project on budget at completion value or estimate at completion value.

- **To-complete Performance Index (TCPI):** TCPI is calculated in two ways. First way is, checking whether completing the project at BAC value will be achievable.

$$TCPI = \frac{BAC - EV}{BAC - AC}$$

If you look at the nominator, it gives us the cost remaining work, because it is the result of cost of the overall project minus accomplished work's earned value.

If you look at the denominator, it gives us the remaining budget after your expenditures. Because, it is the result of project budget minus actual cost. With these insights, if you spend more than the earned value of the completed activities in a project, TCPI will moving over 1. In addition, TCPI will go below 1 if earned value of the project is greater than the actual cost.

Note that, this formula can be applied when budget at completion is still valid. However, things might change during the project, and achieving budget at completion value might not be possible!

$$TCPI = \frac{BAC - EV}{EAC - AC}$$

In this case, a new estimate at completion value is calculated and project team aims to complete the project on new estimated budget. TCPI formula slightly changes when BAC value is no longer viable in a project. Instead of budget at completion value in the denominator, estimate at completion value is placed. The interpretation is similar in both of the TCPI calculations.

- If TCPI < 1, then, it is easier to complete the project in BAC or EAC value.
- If TCPI = 1, then, you will complete the project on planned BAC or EAC respectively.
- If TCPI > 1, then, it is harder to complete the project in BAC or EAC value.

Forecasting in Earned Value Management Exercise

We will be going our project scenario example we have gone through before, and calculate each forecasting value one-by-one.

Budget at Completion value was actually the planned budget to spend to complete the project activities. Since the scenario was telling that $100,000 was planned, budget at completion value is $100,000 respectively.

Let us calculate the estimate at completion (EAC) value now. There were three approaches to calculate estimate at completion value. We will be going over each approach and calculate EAC values one-by-one.

In 1st approach,
    EAC = AC+(BAC-EV)=$17,000+($100,000-$18,000)
    EAC = $99,000

As you see, since earned value of the completed work is more than the spent cost, estimate at completion value is less than the budget at completion value.

In the 2nd approach,

$$EAC = BAC/CPI = \$100,000/1.06$$
EAC = $94,340

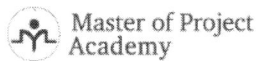

Since the current cost performance of the project is good, this performance is assumed to be achieved during the rest of the project. Thus, the estimate at completion value is lower than the one we calculated with the 1st approach.

In the 3rd approach,
$$EAC = AC+[BAC-EV]/[CPIxSPI]$$
$$EAC = \$17,000+[\$100,000-\$18,000]/[1.06x0.9]$$
EAC = $102,954

As you see, estimate at completion value with this approach is greater than the budget at completion value. Because, although the cost performance of the project was good, schedule performance of the project was bad. When the cost and schedule performance of the project is considered together to find the estimate at completion value, result is greater than the budget at completion value.

Estimate to Complete (ETC) Calculation:
$$ETC = EAC - EV = \$102,954 - \$18,000$$
ETC = $84,954

This means, with the new estimate at completion value, you will be spending $84,954 for the remaining activities of the project according to forecasts.

Note that, we used the estimate at completion value we found by 3rd approach in this case. Depending on the estimate at completion value you will be using, estimate at completion will vary as well.

Variance at Completion (VAC) Calculation
$$VAC = BAC - EAC = \$100,000 - \$102,954 = -\$2,954$$
VAC = -$2,954

As you see, project is going over budget according to forecasts. However, if we have used the estimate at completion values we found with the 1st or 2nd approach, VAC will be greater than zero and indicating that project will be completed under budget.

To-complete Performance Index (TCPI) Calculation (based on BAC)
First, we will calculate the TCPI based on BAC.
$$TCPI = [BAC-EV]/[BAC-AC]$$
$$TCPI = [\$100,000-\$18,000]/[\$100,000-\$17,000]$$
TCPI = 0.988

TCPI is less than 1, therefore, we can conclude that it will be easier to complete the project on planned budget at completion value. This is actually the result of completing works that brought higher earned value than their costs.

To-complete Performance Index (TCPI) Calculation (based on EAC):
When we use the second approach of TCPI, we will be placing EAC on the denominator instead of BAC. In this case, we put the EAC we found by 3rd approach.
$$TCPI = [BAC-EV]/[EAC-AC]$$
$$TCPI = [\$100,000-\$18,000]/[\$102,954-\$17,000]$$
TCPI = 0.954

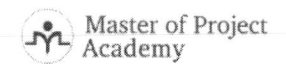

TCPI based on EAC (0.954) is less than TCPI based on BAC (0.988). Thus, it will be easier to complete the project at new EAC value than to complete the project at BAC value.

Important Notes About EVM

We will be going over important points about earned value management that will help you to understand and interpret earned value management values better.

- **Earned Value(EV) comes first in formulas.**
  In variance formulas, *EV comes first, then PV, AC etc. comes after the earned value.*
    - *For instance;* ***CV = EV – AC***
  Index formula, earned value(EV) will be in nominator of the formula.
    - *For instance,* ***CPI = EV / AC***

- **If formula is related about calculating cost forecast, then, you should use Actual Cost (AC).**
    - *For instance;* ***CPI = EV / AC***

- **If formula is related about calculating schedule forecast, then, you should use planned value (PV).**
    - *For instance;* ***SPI = EV / PV***

- **For variances, negative is bad, positive is good:** If you are interpreting a variance formula result, negative variance is an indication of bad performance, and positive variance is an indication of good performance.

- **For indexes, if it is greater than 1, it is good. (except TCPI):** If you are interpreting an index formula result, if it is greater than 1, it is an indication of good performance. This is valid except TCPI. For TCPI, results less than 1 are indication of good performance.

- **For indexes, if it is lower than 1, it is bad. (except TCPI):** If you are interpreting an index formula result, if it is less than 1, it is an indication of bad performance. For instance, CPI less than 1 means project is over budget, and SPI less than 1 means, project is behind schedule. This is valid except TCPI. For TCPI, results greater than 1 are indication of bad performance, and shows that it will be less likely to complete the project on budget at completion or estimate at completion value.

Now, let us see the earned value data for a project over budget and behind schedule on this graph.

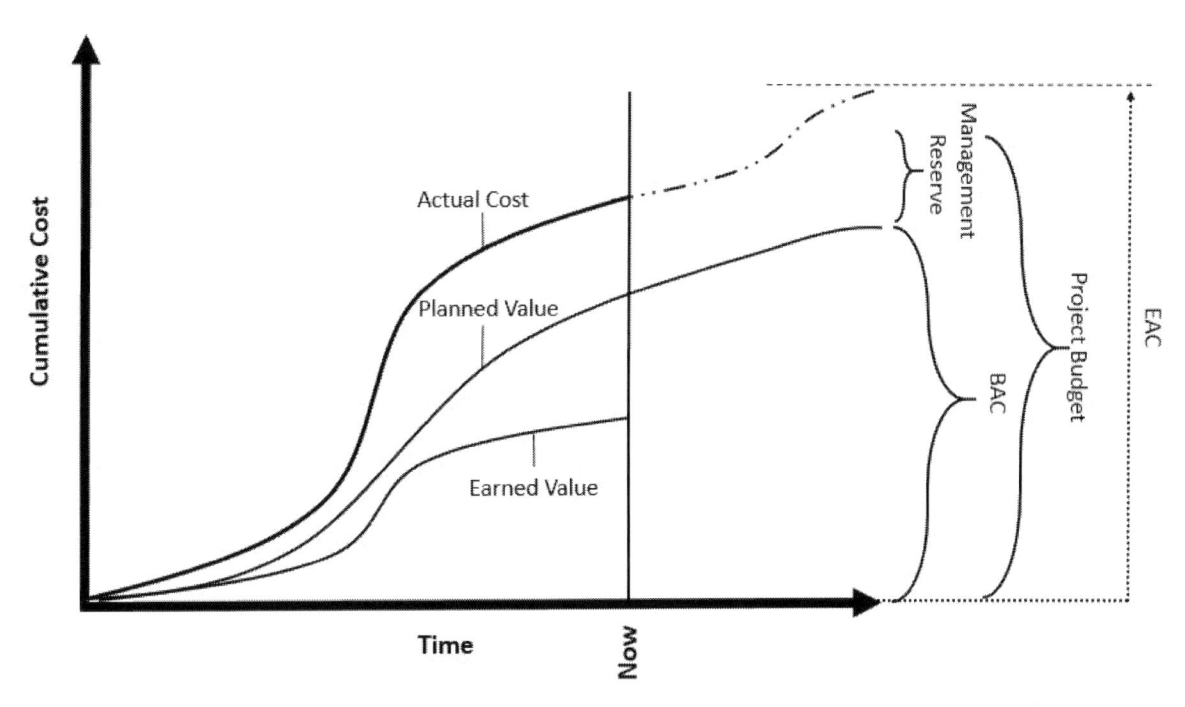

As you see on the graph, planned value line shows the planned project expenditures over time. Vertical line shows the current time. Earned value line is below the planned value line. Therefore, this project is spending more than what it brings as earned value. Respectively, actual cost line is above the planned value. In summary, for the moment, the project is over budget and spending more than what is planned. Based on forecasts, Estimate to completion line drives to a higher value than budget at completion. Therefore, estimate at completion will be greater than the budget at completion. Most probably, management reserve put this project will be spent for this project to accommodate the exceeding planned budget amount.

- **Earned value is an effective tool for measuring performance and determining the needs to request changes.** For instance, you might be behind schedule, or over budget compared to the initial plans. In this case, you need to take corrective actions to get back on track on the project. Otherwise, your project will miss the deadlines, and you will be spending more than the planned budget. This will cause project failures.
- **Control Costs process will result in change requests including corrective and preventive actions.** Control costs process comes into play at this stage. Based on the results of control costs process, if there is a negative variance in the project, corrective and preventive actions must be taken to get back on schedule and on budget. For instance, if the project is behind schedule, fast tracking or crashing can be evaluated to shorten the duration of remaining activities in the project. If the project is over budget, cost of remaining activities can be reconsidered whether any saving would be possible. Alternatively, additional sources of funds must be found to feed the project financially.

Quiz – Section 6

1- All of the following are processes of Cost Management Knowledge area EXCEPT:

   A) Estimate Costs

   B) Determine Budget

   C) Control Costs

   D) Explore Funds

2- Which of the following are major outputs of Plan Cost Management process?

   A) Cost Management Plan

   B) Project Budget

   C) Cost Control Professionals

   D) Cost Variances

3- All of the following are included in Cost Management Plan EXCEPT:

   A) Units of Measure

   B) Levels of Precision

   C) Cost Control Professionals

   D) Control Thresholds

4- You need a winch for your construction project. Price of winch is 300.000USD and yearly maintenance cost is 10.000USD. Yearly leasing fee for this winch is 180.000USD and your project is expected to finish in 2 years. Which of the following is best decision?

   A) Buying the winch

   B) Leasing the winch

   C) Subcontracting regarding part of the work to another company

   D) Information provided is not sufficient to take a decision

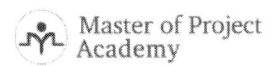

5- You need 10.000 liters of fuel for your vehicles in your project. You planned to buy 5.000 liters of fuel in the beginning and 5000 liters of fuel in the second half of the project. Since fuel supplier offered a 5% discount if all fuel need is purchased in the beginning, you bought 10.000 liters of fuel from the supplier when project started. This is an example of:

A) Value Engineering

B) Market Value

C) Life Cycle Costing

D) Cost Reduction

6- You are in the process of determining the amount of cost required to complete project work. In this process, you will do all of the following EXCEPT:

A) Estimates for each activity are made

B) Labor costs are estimated

C) Costs of organizations' other projects are estimated

D) Costs of materials that will be purchased are estimated

7- Cost planning of the project is done during planning. Project Manager may periodically recalculate the amount that needs to be spent for the remaining work. This will give:

A) Estimate to Terminate

B) Estimate to Complete

C) Project Budget

D) Cost of Risks

8- Cost of all work needed to complete the project is estimated including all of the following EXCEPT:

A) Cost of quality efforts

B) Cost of office expenses

C) Profit of the project

D) Cost of terminated projects

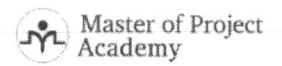

9- Project costs have different types. All of the following are examples of variable costs EXCEPT:

A) Wages of team members

B) Cost of materials used during project

C) Cost of compensation packages provided to project team members

D) Rental fee of project office

10- All of the following are inputs to Estimate Costs process EXCEPT:

A) Schedule Variances

B) Scope Baseline

C) Project Schedule

D) Risk Register

11- During Estimate Costs process of your project, you have completed detailed estimation for each activity, rolled up the estimations to control accounts and found the overall project estimate. This technique is called as:

A) One-point Estimate

B) Analogous Estimating

C) Bottom-up Estimating

D) Parametric Estimating

12- Estimates in early phases of a project are less accurate than those made later in the project. During initiating process group, you made your estimations in the range of -25% to +75% from actual values. This is an example of:

A) Wide Estimate

B) Rough Order of Magnitude (ROM) Estimate

C) Budget Estimate

D) Definitive Estimate

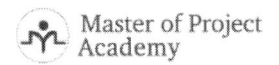

13- Determine Budget is the process of determining an authorized cost baseline. All of the following about Budget is true EXCEPT:

A) Defines how much money will be spent for each activity

B) Defines how much money the customer will pay for the project

C) Defines how much money or funds the company should have available

D) Includes costs regarding risks

14- Cost Baseline of a project includes all of the following EXCEPT:

A) Costs of Control Accounts

B) Costs of Work Packages

C) Contingency Reserves

D) Management Reserves

15- Monitoring the status of the project to update the project costs and managing changes to the cost baseline is done during:

A) Estimate Costs Process

B) Determine Budget Process

C) Control Costs Process

D) Manage Costs Process

16- During a performance analysis of your project, you found out that you spent 20.000USD although you should have spent 25.000USD. What is the cost variance of the project?

A) 5.000USD

B) -5.000USD

C) 20.000USD

D) 25.000USD

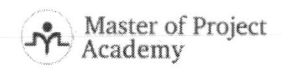

17- During a performance analysis of your project, you found out that 80 days of project work has been completed although 100 days of work should have been completed. What is the schedule variance of the project?

A) 20 days

B) -20 days

C) 80 days

D) 100 days

18- You are managing a construction project. During your project performance reviews, you found out that 1,100 man days of work has been completed while 1,000 days of work had to be completed based on initial plan, and 250,000 USD has been spent although 200,000 USD should have been spent when you checked the completed work. What are the SPI and CPI of the project respectively?

A) SPI: 0,91, CPI:1,25

B) SPI: 1,25, CPI:0,91

C) SPI: 0,8, CPI:1,1

D) SPI: 1.1, CPI:0,8

19- During Determine Budget Process of your project, you concluded that the project budget will be 100.000USD. After you have spent 20.000USD in your project, when you re-estimated the remaining work to be completed, you found out that you will need 90.000USD more. What is the Estimate at Completion (EA C) for this project?

A) 90.000USD

B) 100.000USD

C) 110.000USD

D) 120.000USD

20- You are managing a software project. Your project budget is 500.000USD. During performance analysis, you concluded that earned value is 160.000USD and Actual Cost is 200.000USD. If current cost performance is assumed to be continuing in the future, what will be the Estimate at Completion Value?

A) 625.000USD

B) 500.000USD

C) 400.000USD

D) 540.000USD

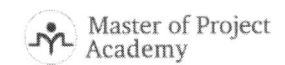

21- Initial budget estimate of a project is 100.000USD. During execution of the project, Estimate at Completion (EAC) of the project has been found as 120.000USD. If earned value of the project is 20.000USD and CPI is 1.0, what is the TCPI of the project?

A) 0,8

B) 1,0

C) 1,2

D) 1,4

22- During your cost performance analysis, you concluded that Variance at Completion value is 50.000USD. If your project budget was 250.000USD, what is Estimate at Completion?

A) 300.000

B) 250.000

C) 200.000

D) 50.000

23- Earned value of a project is 200.000USD, actual cost of the project is 250.000USD and schedule variance is 10 days. What is the status of the project?

A) Over Budget, Behind Schedule

B) Over Budget, Ahead of Schedule

C) Under Budget, Behind Schedule

D) Under Budget, Ahead of Schedule

24- When you conducted an analysis for your project, you realized that CPI of the project is 1.2 and SPI of the project is 0.9. What is the status of your project?

A) Over Budget, Behind Schedule

B) Over Budget, Ahead of Schedule

C) Under Budget, Behind Schedule

D) Under Budget, Ahead of Schedule

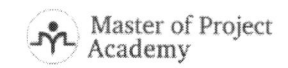

25- During execution of your project, you re-estimated the remaining work to be completed and found a new Estimate at Completion (EAC) value. When you calculated the TCPI of the project, you found that TCPI is 0.89. What is the conclusion?

A) It is harder to complete the project at new BAC value

B) It is easier to complete the project at new BAC value

C) It is harder to complete the project at new EAC value

D) It is easier to complete the project at new EAC value

Answers

1 – D	16 – A
2 – A	17 – B
3 – C	18 – D
4 – A	19 – C
5 – A	20 – A
6 – C	21 – A
7 – B	22 – C
8 – D	23 – B
9 – D	24 – C
10 – A	25 – D
11 – C	
12 – B	
13 – B	
14 – D	
15 – C	

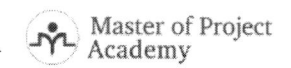

Mapping Game – Section 6

Left	Right
provides guidance and direction on how the project costs will be managed	cost baseline
the value of the work completed to date	Plan Cost Management process
Cost management plan	Planned Value
the realized cost incurred for the work performed on an activity	The output of Plan Cost Management
cost baseline	Earned Value
determines the monetary resources required for the project	"Estimate Costs" process
a measure of cost performance on a project	The summation of the control accounts
approved version of the time-phased project budget	Cost Variance (CV)
the value that you should have earned as per the schedule	Actual Cost

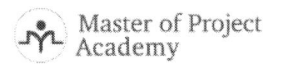

Answers

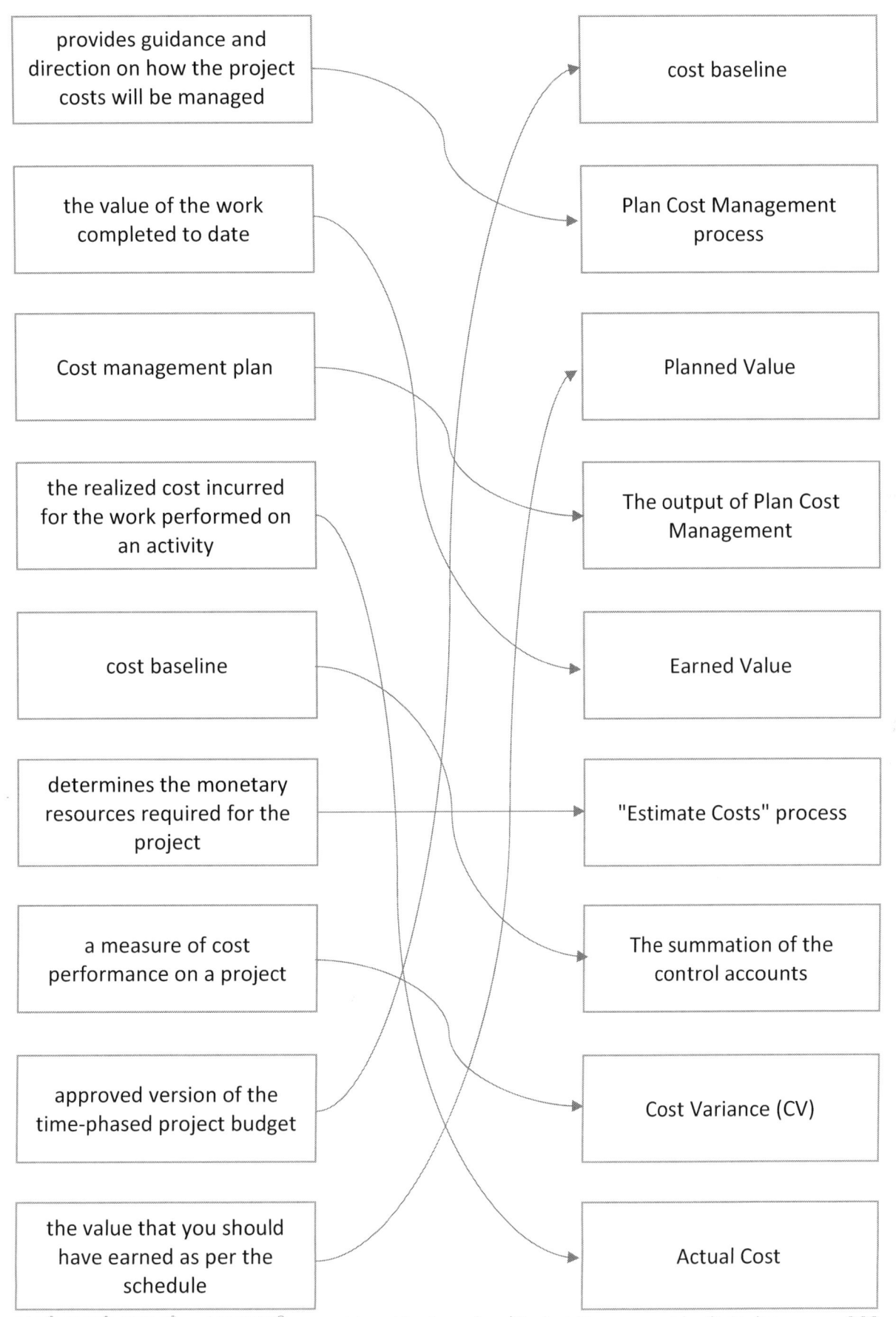

Left	Right
provides guidance and direction on how the project costs will be managed	Plan Cost Management process
the value of the work completed to date	Earned Value
Cost management plan	The output of Plan Cost Management
the realized cost incurred for the work performed on an activity	Actual Cost
cost baseline	The summation of the control accounts
determines the monetary resources required for the project	"Estimate Costs" process
a measure of cost performance on a project	Cost Variance (CV)
approved version of the time-phased project budget	cost baseline
the value that you should have earned as per the schedule	Planned Value

Section 7

Quality Management

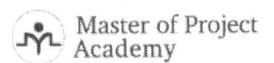

Section 7 – Quality Management

We will go through the Quality Management knowledge area throughout this section. Quality management is a critical aspect of a project. Because, a certain level of quality will be available only if you spend required amount of money to reach that quality.

Assume that you will be buying a car with $40,000 budget. Can you buy a Ferrari with this budget? Of course not. That is why the quality is in the 3rd angle of famous time-cost-quality triangle of project management.

However, you can manage your budget to get the best quality you can afford to get. Approach is similar in the project management. You have a scope, deadline and budget to complete the project. Quality requirements of the project must be aligned with the other aspects of the project accordingly. Quality management in a project aims to reach the negotiated quality requirements with its tools and processes.

What is the agenda of this section?

- **Overview of Quality Management:** First, we will go over the overview of quality management. What does it aim? What is the definition of quality management? We will answer these questions
- **Quality Management Processes:** We will see the quality management processes. There are 3 processes of quality management knowledge area. These are plan quality management, manage quality and control quality. We will be going through each process in detail in our further notes.
- **Terms and Concepts in Quality Management:** We will see the terms and concepts in quality management. We will go through the definition of quality, grade, precision, accuracy and other important terms about quality.
- **Plan Quality Management Process:** We will step into first process of quality management: plan quality management process. This is the process of where quality approach and activities of a project is determined.
- **Tools and Techniques Used in Quality Management Processes:** We will go over the tools and techniques used in quality management processes. We will see five different techniques at this stage. These are cost benefit analysis, cost of quality, benchmarking, design of experiment, and statistical sampling. We will go over each technique in detail.
- **7 Basic Quality Tools:** Then, we will see the seven basic quality tools. These quality tools are very important to check whether the produced results in a project meet the quality requirements that were agreed initially.
- **Manage Quality Process:** Then, we will go through the second process of quality management knowledge area: manage quality. This process mainly checks whether the produced results meet the agreed quality requirements with the customer. Therefore, this process belongs to executing process group and performed by the project team.
- **Tools and Techniques Used in Manage Quality Process:** We will see the tools and techniques used in manage quality process. These are quality audits, process analysis and quality management and control tools.

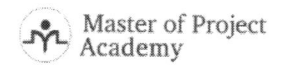

- **Control Quality Process:** Finally, we will go over the control quality process of quality management knowledge area. This is part of monitoring and controlling process group, and generally, quality specifications of the project deliverables are checked by the customer at this stage.
- **Concepts of Control Quality Process & Tips about Quality Management Processes:** We will go through concepts of control quality process and we will finalize the section with tips about quality management processes.

Overview of Quality Management

We will go through the overview of quality management in this heading.
Let us see the definition of quality management at first step.

- **Quality management includes processes and activities of the performing organization that determine quality policies, objectives and responsibilities.** Briefly, quality management of a project will ensure that you will reach the quality requirements that were set in the beginning of the project. Otherwise, customer may not accept the final product, and your project might fail as a result.

- **Quality management ensures that the project requirements, including product requirements, are met and validated.** For instance, if the customer is proposing 10 critical quality requirements to consider a project as successful, quality management activities, policies and processes will ensure to meet these requirements at the end of the project.

- **Lack of attention to quality will result in more rework or defects.** Because, performing an activity at first attempt is easier than going back and revising the completed work for the second or third time. Because, the performer has to remember the past work or re-start from the beginning when a correction is required for an activity he has already completed. Therefore, project activities must be completed with great attention and rework must be minimized.

- **In order to meet quality requirements of a project we need to know acceptable quality, how it will be measured and what we will do to make sure we meet those requirements.** Let us go through each of these three points one-by-one.

    - We need to know acceptable quality because the customer will seek this as acceptance criteria at the end of the project. For instance, if customer expects a web page to be loaded in less than 2 seconds at the end of the project, this must be considered when performing project activities to ensure that this quality requirement will be met.

    - We need to know how a quality requirement will be measured. For instance, Google's Web Developer console is a tool for software developers and test engineers to measure page load time. If this will be used, we need to know this, and before demonstrating the end result of the project, we should use this tool to verify whether our page load times will meet the requirements.

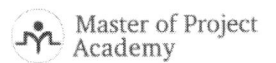

- o The most important part is for sure, we need to know what we will do to make sure we meet those requirements. In order to ensure that the page load will be less than 2 seconds, you need to minify the page content, improve loading mechanisms etc. In addition, several other technical actions might be needed from a developer to load a page in less than 2 seconds. These must be planned and performed accordingly to meet the customer's requirement.

- **There are three processes of quality management knowledge area.**
  These are:
  - Plan Quality Management Process (Planning)
  - Manage Quality Process (Executing)
  - Control Quality Process (Monitoring & Controlling)

Terms About Quality

Let us go through critical terms about quality. First term we will go through is "quality" itself.

- **Quality is the degree to which a set of inherent characteristics fulfill requirements.** Each project and product have unique quality requirements. For instance, loading a web page in less than 2 seconds, restarting a server in less than 5 minutes, building a "A+" house are examples of quality expectations. These kind of quality requirements must be met during projects in order to complete a project successfully.

- **Gathering requirements in scope management, and defining project statement accordingly is very important to quality.** Because, customer requirements must be gathered and these requirements must be negotiated with the customer at the beginning of the project. After that, project activities, estimations and the rest of the project is planned based on the negotiated requirements. Therefore, setting quality expectations at the beginning of the project is crucial.

- **Grade is the second term we will see about quality. Grade as a design intent a category assigned to deliverables having the same functional use but different technical characteristics.** There are several models of cars in the market. Consider two car models, BMW and Renault. Renault has several models and BMW has several models. However, you cannot compare BMW seven series, which is the highest level or highest-grade model of BMW, with Renault Clio. Because, Clio is a lower level or lower grade model of Renault. Therefore, grade here defines the number of features on the set of features or specifications for a product. In addition, remember that a low-grade product will be at high quality. For example, BMW 1 series have limited number of features or specifications compared to a BMW seven series car, but even that BMW one series are meeting the quality standards or quality requirements of the customers. So even that BMW's one series are high quality products.

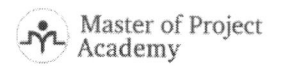

- **Precision is a measure of exactness.** It shows the detail of your measurement. For instance, "one dot three zero" is more precise than "one dot two zeros". Because, the first measurement shows a more detailed result compared to second one.
- **Accuracy is an assessment of correctness.** If the measured value of an item is very close to the true value of the characteristic being measured, the measurement is more accurate. It is better to describe accuracy with an example.

  Assume that you aim to produce 10 cm sticks. It will not be possible to produce exactly 10 cm sticks each time. Some of them will be slightly shorter and some of them will be slightly taller than 10 cm. Consider two sticks as an output of this process. One of them is 9.98 cm and the other one is 10.03 cm. In this case, we can say that 9.98 cm stick is more accurate. Because, it is closer to 10 cm which is the target length for sticks.

Quality Theorists

We will see the three most important quality theorists in this heading.

- **Joseph Juran:** First quality theorist is Joseph Juran.
    - **Joseph Juran developed the 80/20 rule we have seen in our previous notes.** This theory states that 80% of the problems are caused by the 20% of the root causes. By this way, when approaching to solve the problems, first, the most important problems that will eliminate the majority of the issues are targeted.
    - **Joseph Juran defined the quality as "fitness for use".** This means if your product is used properly, or user friendly for your customers, then you meet the quality requirements of your project and your product has a good quality.

- **W. Edwards Deming:** Second quality theorist is Edwards Deming.
    - **Edwards Deming developed the 14 steps to total quality management and Plan-Do-Act-Check as the basis for quality improvement.** PDCA cycle is a very famous cycle in many industries. It aims to improve quality continuously in any process and organization.

- **Philip Crosby:** Third and the last quality theorist is Philip Crosby.
    - **Philip Crosby popularized the concept of the cost of poor quality.** Cost of poor quality means the overhead costs that will be resulting due to low product quality. If a low-quality product is produced, maintenance and support costs of the product can be very high. Therefore, when producing a product, lifecycle cost of the product must be considered. Cost of poor quality might be higher than producing a better-quality product in the beginning.
    - **Philip Crosby believes that the quality is conforming to requirements.** This means, if customer requirements are met, expected quality level would be achieved respectively as well. Because, customer lists the expectations from a project. If these requirements are achieved throughout the project, customer will be happy with the end result respectively.

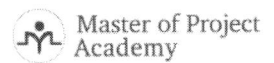

Concepts of Quality Management

We will be going over six different quality management concepts during this heading.

- **Gold Plating:** Gold plating is giving extras to customer such as higher functionality or better quality although it is not in the project requirements. Let us go over our website page development example. Assume that the customer requires a web page to be loaded under 2 seconds. If the page is loading in 1.8 seconds and if a project developer is still trying to optimize the web page to make it open under 1.5 seconds, this is an example of gold plating. Because, although the customer requirements are met, project resource is trying to do more to achieve a better result. This will cause additional cost to the project.

- **Prevention over inspection:** This concept states that you have to define your activities, your steps, your policies, your tools and procedures to manage your quality in your project. Focusing only on the project requirements without considering quality aspects and doing quality inspection in the end may cause lots of rework in the project. Therefore, project activities must cover to meet project's quality requirements as well.

- **Marginal Analysis:** Marginal analysis concept is looking for the point where the benefits or revenue to be received from improving quality equals the incremental cost to achieve quality. Think of a product that you will be able to sell in the market for $50 and it will cost $30 to produce for your company. Therefore, there is $20 of profit per product.
Assume that new functionalities can be added to this product or quality can be increase and this would cost $15. Therefore, new cost of the product with the added functionalities will be $45. However, based on market analysis, your company realizes that you can sell this new product for $60. In the end, you extended the features or quality of the product but new price and profit per product is not advantageous as before. Therefore, **marginal analysis concept proposes to stop at the point where more quality does not add value.**

- **Continuous Improvement (Kaizen):** Continuous Improvement concept is proposed by Kaizen and proposes looking for small improvements continuously. Big steps or big changes in a project or product can affect the ongoing processes drastically. Therefore, small improvement points must be determined and executed to improve a product continuously. This will be a safer path to increase the overall quality of the product.

- **Just In Time (JIT):** Just in Time is a concept having materials or products whenever is needed and this concept reduces the stock costs. Let me explain this concept with a real-life example. Wing mirrors of cars are provided just seven minutes before assembly in Nissan factories in United Kingdom. By this way, Nissan does not plan any warehouse or any store in order to place these wing mirrors. This enables to reduce the stock costs of materials or products, but this brings additional risk to the suppliers. For example, assume that there has been a problem during delivery of these wing mirrors and they did not arrive on time to the assembly line. In this case, the car production might stop. Therefore, in Just in Time concept, generally suppliers are pushed into very strict conditions and contracts. For example, they might have penalties if they cannot deliver the products on time to the assembly line or to the factory.

- **Total quality management (TQM):** Total quality management is a philosophy that encourages organizations and employees to focus on finding ways to continuously improve the quality of their business practices and products. Therefore, by the help of this philosophy, all employees, all parts of an organization, look for the improvements in their tools, in their processes, in their practices. Therefore, with this philosophy, organizations aim to reach a better level of quality management.
- **Responsibility for quality:** Responsibility for quality is another concept about quality management. This concept proposes that entire organization has responsibilities relating to quality. Therefore, achieving a level of quality is not under the responsibility of a group or department in an organization. From security guard waiting in front of the building up to the CEO has their own responsibilities relating to quality.
    - From project management perspective, project manager is responsible for the quality of the product of the project and meeting the quality requirements of a project.
    - This can be achieved if each team member checks his or her work whether it meets the quality requirements.
- **Impacts of poor quality is the last concept we will be seeing in this heading.** A lower cost of production can be achieved by producing low-quality products. However, there are several impacts of poor quality. We will go over each impact one-by-one.
    - **First impact is increased costs.** If a product is not meeting the quality requirements, customer will issue defects and in order to solve these defects, your team will have to rework on completed project tasks and these rework means additional cost for the project.
    - **Another impact of these reworks is, low morale in the project team**. Can you imagine that you go back to revise a completed project work several times? This will be very discouraging for a project team member.
    - **Low customer satisfaction is maybe the biggest impact of poor quality.** At the end of the project, if customer raises several defects regarding a produced product, this will affect the customers' perception about your work. These kind of low customer satisfactions can even cause loss of business in the market.
    - **Increased risk, rework and schedule delays are other impacts of poor quality.** If there are many defects to be solved, these will require additional time to solve as well. This means additional time and project delays.

Differences of Quality Management Process

We will be going over three quality management processes in our following notes. Before diving into these processes, it is better to see differences of each process.

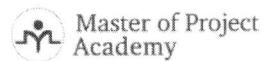

Plan Quality Management	Manage Quality	Control Quality
What is quality? How will we ensure?	Are we following standards?	Are we meeting standards?
Find existing standards and requirements	Use measurements from control quality	Measure quality
Create additional project-specific standards	Perform continuous improvement	Identify quality improvements
Determine what work you will do to meet the standards	Quality audit	Validate deliverables
Determine how you will measure	Find good practices	Complete checklists
Balance the needs of quality, scope, cost, time, risk, resources and customer satisfaction.	Share good practices with others in the organization.	Submit change requests
Create a Quality Management Plan		Update lessons learned

- We will go through this table and explain each process one-by-one. Plan quality management process answers the "what is quality?" and "how will we ensure?" questions. Manage quality process answers the "are we following standards?" question. Control quality process answers the "are we meeting standards?" question.

- Let us go through what is done under each process now. First, we will go through the activities of plan quality management process.
    - Existing standards and requirements are found first. If there are tools, procedures and policies of the company regarding quality management, these must be used during plan quality management process.
    - After checking existing standards and requirements, if there will be need for any project-specific standards these must be planned in plan quality management process.
    - Specific activities that will ensure to meet the quality requirements of the project are determined during plan quality management process.
    - After project deliverables are produced, they must be checked whether they meet the quality requirements. How to measure quality requirements of the project must be planned in plan quality management process.
    - There is a balance between the quality, scope, cost, time, risk, resources and customer satisfaction. How to construct this balance must be considered and planned in plan quality management process.
    - Finally, quality management plan of the project is produced at the end of the plan quality management process.
- Now, we will go through the activities of manage quality process.
    - Measurements from control quality process will be used in this process. These measurements will show where to focus and what to fix or improve respectively.
    - Continuous improvement is under the scope of manage quality process. Activities that will ensure continuous improvement of the product will be performed in manage quality process.
    - Quality audit is done in manage quality process. Quality audits shows whether the produced outputs are aligned with the project's quality requirements.

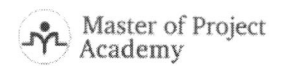

- Good practice of doing an activity or process are explored during manage quality process and these good practices are distributed among the organization for the use of other departments or employees.
- Third and at the last stage, we will see the activities of control quality process.
    - Quality measurement is done in control quality process. Outputs of the project are measured with the tools and methods that were determined in plan quality management process.
    - Based on the results of quality measurements, rooms for improving quality are analyzed. Project deliverables are validated during control quality process and if there are any quality checklists to approve a deliverable, these checklists are filled in during control quality process.
    - If a deliverable needs update or if customer is coming with a new feature request, customer submits a change request in control quality process after his or her checks. At the end of the control quality process, lessons learned documentation is updated and stored in the company archive for future reference.

Plan Quality Management Process

First process of the quality management knowledge area is plan quality management process.

- **Plan quality management is the process of identifying quality requirements and/or standards for the project and its deliverables, and documenting how the project will demonstrate compliance with relevant quality requirements.** How to define quality requirements of the project are planned during this process and how to meet the project quality requirements are documented in plan quality management process.

- **Plan quality management process provides guidance on how quality will be managed and validated throughout the project.** There will several project deliverables and outputs throughout the project. When these deliverables and outputs are ready, project team and customer must check whether these are aligned with the negotiated project quality requirements. How to check quality requirements on a deliverable and how to validate a deliverable or output is defined during plan quality management process.

- **Major output of the plan quality management process is quality management plan.** Quality management plan of a project shows how to define quality requirements, how to meet quality requirements, how to measure quality requirements and how to control and validate a deliverable as well.

- There are common quality standards for each industry. We listed the most popular ones here. The United Nations Convention and Contracts for International Sale of Goods, which is abbreviated as CISG, ISO 9000, and Occupational safety and health administration

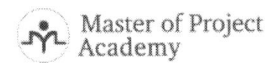

(OHSA), are just a few examples of common quality standards. If an organization is obliged to meet these common quality standards, project requirements must be aligned with these standards and how to meet the requirements of these standards must be documented in the plan quality management process as well.

- **Planning must be done to meet customer requirements.** Quality management plan should include steps for how to reach customer's quality requirements in the project.
- **Once existing standards are defined, additional standards needed by project are created.** Consider that a company is applying ISO 9000 as quality standard. They must be meeting the guidelines of ISO 9000 when producing a product in the project. However, if the project has additional quality requirements, these must be added to the list as well.
- **When doing this, it is important that new standards cannot violate other relevant standards.** For instance, if a new quality requirement is not aligned with ISO 9000 guidelines; this quality requirement cannot be accepted.
- **After standards are defined, Plan Quality management process involves determining the work that needs to be done to meet those standards.** Plan quality management process involves how to meet project quality requirements, how to measure project deliverables, and how to validate project deliverables as well.

Tools & Techniques Used in Quality Management Processes

Quality requirements of a project are collected, planned and measured respectively. There are tools and techniques used in quality management processes. We will be going over five common tools and techniques one-by-one during this heading.

1. **Cost Benefit Analysis:** First technique is cost benefit analysis. Cost benefit analysis technique weighs benefits versus the costs of meeting quality requirements. Remember the marginal analysis concept that we have seen in previous notes. There is a cost of quality in projects, and this generally increases by the level of quality. In order to increase the quality level of your product, you have to spend extra money. However, after some point, even if you spend extra money to meet quality, you might not get back relevant benefit from that product. After some point, even if you create more quality, this might not bring you additional benefit. Therefore, this cost benefit analysis analyzes the benefits of meeting quality requirements with the costs of meeting quality requirements.

2. **Cost of Quality (COQ):** Second technique is Cost of Quality. Cost of quality is abbreviated as COQ and helps to make sure that the project is not spending too much to assure quality. You need to spend money; you need to spend effort in order to meet a defined quality level in your project. Nevertheless, you should not spend too much money in order to meet the quality standards. Cost of quality helps you to not to spend too much money in order to meet an identified level of quality in your projects.

    o **Cost of conformance should be lower than costs of non-conformance.** Cost of conformance is the money spent during the project to avoid failures. Cost of non-conformance is the money spent during and after the project because of failures.

Cost of Conformance	Cost of Nonconformance or Failure
Prevention Costs (for building a quality product) • Training • Documenting Processes • Tools & equipment	**Internal Failure Costs (found by project team)** • Rework • Scrap/Hassles
Appraisal Costs (for testing the quality) • Tests • Loss during tests • Inspection	**External or Customer Failure Costs** • Penalties/liabilities • Warrantee/Guarantee costs • Losing business/competition
Money spent during the project to prevent failures	Money spent during and after the project because of the failure of the project product/service

Therefore, if you spend money in order to meet the quality standards, quality requirements of your project, there is a cost of this, and this is mentioned as cost of conformance. If you do not plan any quality activities or if you do not spend enough money in order to meet the quality requirements, quality standards of your project, then, this will bring you a cost of non-conformance.

First, we will start with the cost of conformance. There are two headlines under cost of conformance.

- **Prevention Costs:** Prevention costs is the first one. This is the cost spent in order to build a quality product.
    - **Training:** For example, training of your employees. If you train your employees, then they will know better about a concept, better about a product or process. Therefore, during your project, they will execute their activities, their tasks with a specific set of knowledge, and this will increase the quality of your product.
    - **Document processes:** If you document, if you record all your processes, what kind of activities, what kind of steps that will be followed in order to meet a defined level of quality, these will increase the quality of your project.
    - **Equipment:** Equipment, for example, if there will be a specific tool, specific equipment in order to measure the quality of your product, then, you will reduce the risk of non-conformance of your requirements. For instance, a test-automation tool for a software development project can be given as an example.
    - **Time to do it right:** Time to do it right is the last example of prevention cost of cost of conformance. Each activity has a specific sequence in the project and each activity must be performed at the right time during the project.

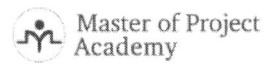

- **Appraisal Costs:** Appraisal costs is the second heading of cost of conformance.
  - **Testing:** And this is the cost of assessing the quality, for example, testing. Think that you are working on a software project. After you have developed your screens or your application, you have to test it internally first, in order to check whether it really meets the requirements of your customer.
  - **Destructive testing loss and Inspections:** Destructive testing loss and inspections are also under appraisal costs, and contributor to the costs of conformance.

What are the headings of cost of non-conformance?

- **Internal Failure Costs:** First, one is internal failure costs. These are the failures found by the project team, during your internal checks. Maybe, your quality control department might find these.
  - **Rework or Scrap:** And if these failures are found internally in your project, you have to either do a rework or scrap in your project. In either case, you have to spend extra time, extra money in order to overcome these failures and in order to meet the standards, the requirements of your project.

- **External Failure Costs:** And the second heading of cost of non-conformance is external failure costs, and these are the failures found by the customers.
  - **Liabilities:** And if these failures are found by your customers, if they find that end product is not conforming to their initial requirements, then this can cost you liabilities. For example, if you cannot meet the requirements of your customers and if there is a penalty regarding this in your contract, your company might be obliged to pay that penalty since you could not meet the requirements of your customer.
  - **Warranty work:** Warranty work, is another example of cost of non-conformance. If your company is applying a warranty period for the end product that you have delivered to your customers and if a failure has been found during this period, you have to fix that defect for free since it has been found during warranty period. Although you fix it free for your customer since you are in the warranty period, it still costs additional time and money for your organization. Therefore, it is a cost of non-conformance.
  - **Lost Business:** And the last contributor of cost of nonconformance is lost business. If there are many failures at the end of your project, regarding product of your project, the customer might not be choosing you in their next project since you could not meet their quality requirements. Therefore, it is important.

3. **Benchmarking:** Looking at past projects to get ideas for improvement on the current project, and provide a basis to use in current project. Benchmarking, as we have discussed previously in our previous notes, can be done within the same organization or among the

different organizations in the same market. Moreover, when you are doing benchmarking, you look for the better alternatives, better options that are applied within a specific area, and you try to apply those best practices in your current project. For instance, Samsung might look at Apple's screen technology to get insights about improvement points in its products and this is an example of benchmarking.

4. **Design of Experiments (DOE):** Design of experiments is abbreviated as DOE. Design of experiments is experimentation to statistically determine what variances will improve quality. Therefore, this technique guides you to identify what are the best options, what are the best combinations of variances that will produce better quality in your project.

    - DOE allows finding which combination of factors have least impact on the project. Therefore, by evaluating different alternatives, different parameters or different options in a project, it helps you to find the least impact on the project.

    - DOE is faster and more accurate since all variables can be changed at the same time rather than changing a variable at a time. For example, this method is used generally in automotive industry to find the best suspension and tire combination. Design of experiment is generally done by the assistance of computer software. Assume that there are ten parameters affecting the driving quality in a car. DOE technique helps you to find which alternatives, which combination of these ten parameters will produce the best results, best quality, in terms of driving quality.

5. **Statistical sampling:** Statistical sampling technique involves choosing a part of a population for investigation. Because, investigation of whole population will take too long, cost too much, and be too destructive. For example, assume that you are working in a pen factory, and your factory produces 1 million pens a day. If you want to make quality assessment, quality control in all pens that are produced, it will take too long, it will cost too much and it will be too destructive to repair all defects that you might find.
    - There will be a huge quality cost in your project if you try to do quality audit on all produced items. Therefore, in this kind of a situation, you might do a statistical sampling. For example, you might choose one thousand pens of 1 million pens that are produced in a day and you can make quality assessments, quality controls on that sample population that you have chosen. By this way, your quality control or your quality inspections will take shorter and it will be less costly as well.
    - **Sample size and frequency is determined as part of plan quality management process.** Sampling is done in manage quality process. Consider our pen production example. We said, one thousand pens of the one million pens produced a day can be assessed. One thousand pens we defined here is sample size and determined during plan quality management process.
    - Assume that each 1.000th pen coming out of the assembly line will be controlled. This defines the frequency of your measurements. This frequency is also determined in plan quality management process. However, choosing that each 1.000th pen at the end of your assembly line for quality control is done in perform quality management process.

The 7 Basic Quality Tools (7QC Tools)

Seven quality control tools or seven QC tools is very popular across many industries that are doing quality management. We will be going over seven quality control tools one-by-one during this and following heading.

1. **Cause-and-effect Diagrams:** First, one is the cause-and-effect diagrams, also known as fish bone or Ishikawa diagrams.
    - **Cause-and-effect diagrams help to find both how to repair a defect and get the root cause of the problem and it is a creative way to look at the cause of a problem.** Assume that you have a problem and you suspect from several reasons or several root causes about this problem. Cause-and-effect diagram will help you to find out possible reasons of the problem.
    - **Cause-and-effect diagrams help stimulate thinking, organizes thoughts, and generates discussion.** Since cause-and-effect diagrams generate discussion among the team about the possible reasons or about the possible root causes of a problem, it will help you to find what the root cause of the problem is.
    - **Cause-and-effect diagrams can be used to explore factors that will result in a desired future outcome.** Since this tool stimulates thinking, it will help you to find new factors that might affect a problem to occur. Therefore, it helps you to list all possibilities and take appropriate actions for each reason accordingly.

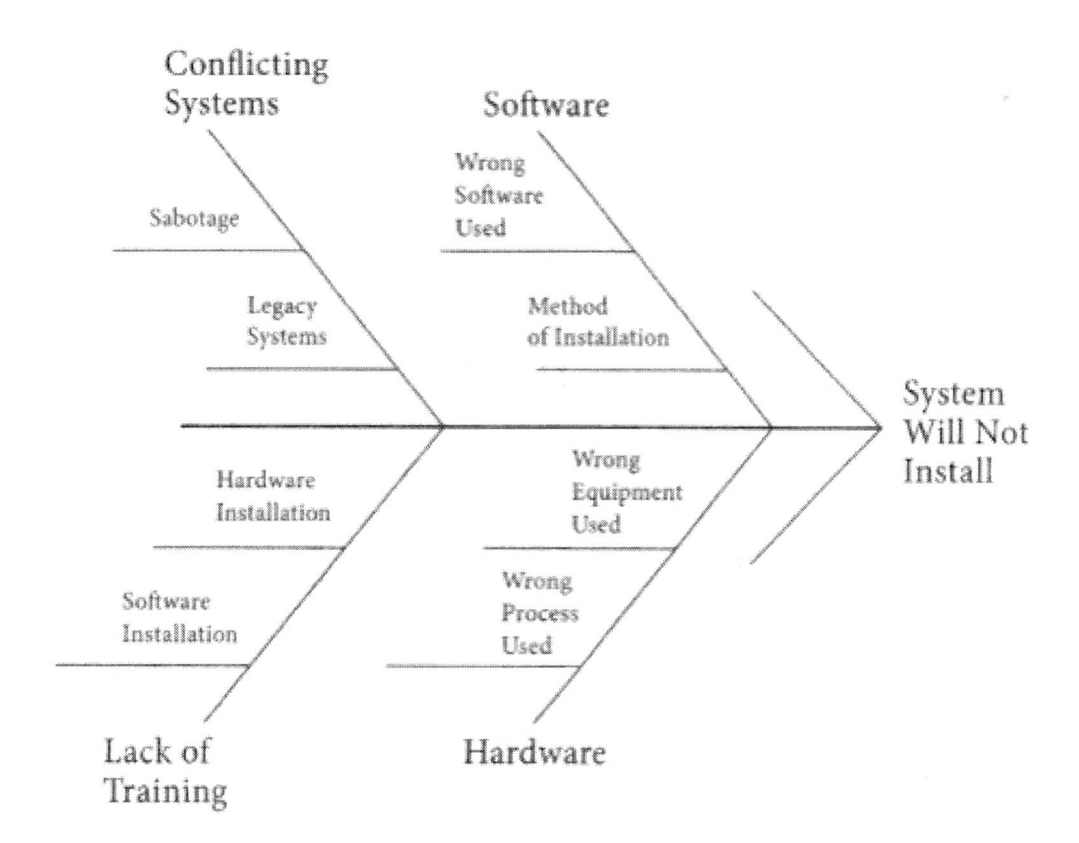

Here we see a sample cause and effect diagram. As you see the problem or the possible problem is system will not install and as can be seen there are four high level headings, which are high-level problems that might cause that "system will not install" problem.

In addition, under these four high level headings, you see low-level reasons or root causes that might cause this "system will not install" problem. For example, under conflicting systems you will see sabotage and negative systems. Under Software, you see Wrong Software Used and Method of Installation. Under Hardware, you see Wrong Processes Used, Wrong Equipment Used. Finally, under Lack of Training you see Hardware Installation and Software installation. As you see, these are high level and low-level root causes of the problem of "system will not install". When this problem is faced, this diagram will guide you to find possible reasons easily.

2. **Flowcharts (Process Maps):** Flowcharts are the second tool we will explore. Flowcharts are also referred as process maps and these show how process or system flows from beginning to end. In addition, how the elements are interrelated with each other. Therefore, it defines the interrelations of steps, which steps you will need to follow, which actions you need to take, in order to complete a specific process in a project. Flowcharts can be used in Control Quality process to analyze problems.

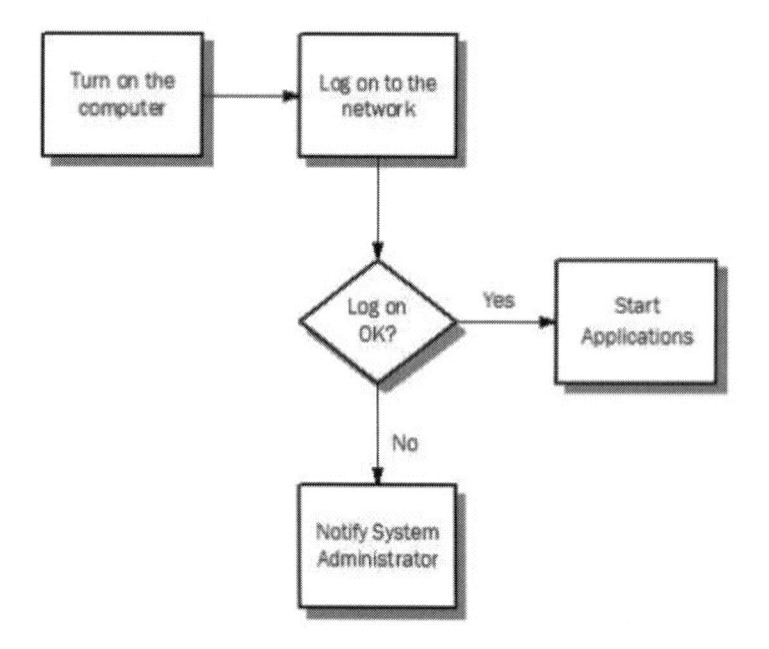

In addition, here, we see an example of flowcharts. This is a very simple example, as can be seen; the first box says turn on the computer. After you turn on the computer, you log on the network by typing your ID and password and if logon is successful here, you see a decision node, yes or no. If the logon is successful, then you can start applications in your PC or in your computer. The other option of logon is not successful and, in this case, you have to notify your system administrator. This is a very simple process of starting your computer in your company for example.

These kind of flowcharts or process maps can be used in your projects. However, depending on your product, these flowcharts might be too complex and might include several decision nodes, several processes, and several activities respectively.

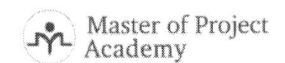

3. **Checksheets or tally sheets:** Checksheets are used as a checklist when gathering data. Checksheets enable effective collection of useful data about a potential quality problem. With the help of checksheets, data about a problem is collected in a structured method.

Type of Defect	Count	Score
Dirty	|||| |||| ||	12
Broken stitching	|||| |||| |||| |||| |||| |||| |||| |||| ||	42
Inconsistent margin	|||| |||| ||||	15
Wrinkle	|||| |||| |||| |||| |||| ||||	30
Long thread	|||| ||||	10
Padding shape	|||| |||	8
Off center	|||| |||| |||| |||	18
Stitch per inch	|||| |||| |||| |||| ||||	24
Others	|||| |||| |||| |||| ||	22
	Total Defects:	**181**

Here you see a check sheet example. On the first column, you see type of defect, on the second column, you see the count of defects, and on the last column, and you see the total score, the total count of the defects. If you look at the check sheet, padding shape defect frequency has the least frequency with eight occurrences. Broken stitching defect was seen 42 times and the is the most frequent defect. Therefore, it might be better to look at this defect first since it has the highest score. These kind of check sheets can be used in your project in order to define the problems and frequency of problems during your quality control.

4. **Pareto diagrams or Pareto Charts:** Pareto diagrams are a special form of vertical bar chart and they are used to identify the root cause of the most frequent problems that make the greatest impact on quality. Since Pareto diagrams have to define the most frequent problems that make the greatest impact on quality, these charts enable you to focus on those most frequent and important problems first. By this way, if you fix the most impacting problem, you will take a great step to improve the quality in the project. Therefore, Pareto diagrams enable you to find the most important problems and respectively enable you to find alternatives or options in order to overcome these problems in your project.

Pareto diagram helps focusing attention on most critical issues. It prioritizes potential causes of the problems and it separates the critical few problems from non-critical many. There might be several problems in a project. If you try to deal with all of them in the project, you might not control the problems properly. Pareto diagrams will guide you to focus on which problem first therefore, help you to focus on fixing the most important problems first.

Customer Complaints

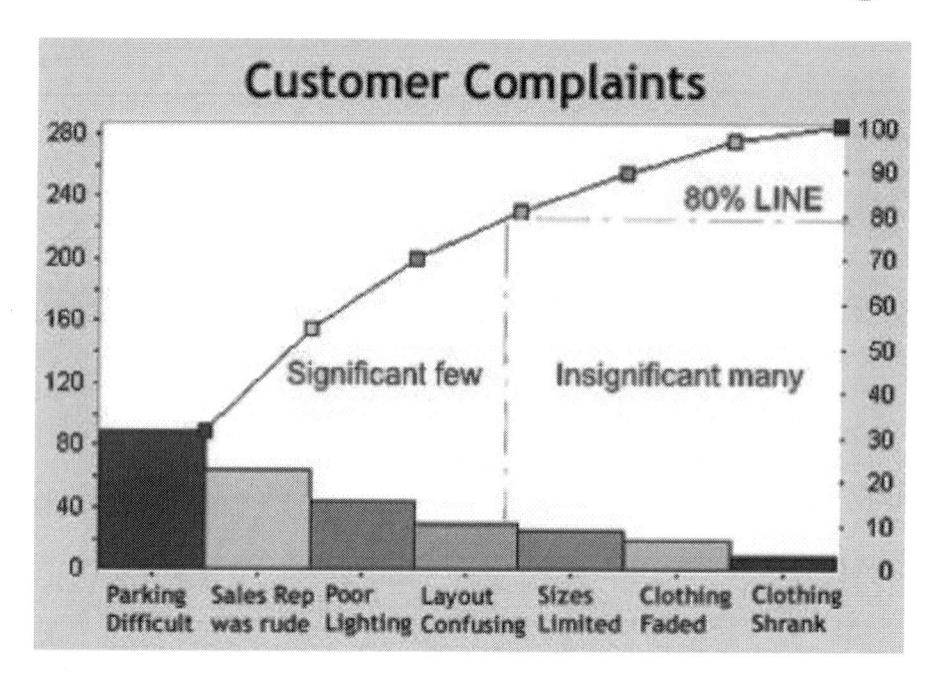

Here in this figure we see the customer complaints received by a store. As you see, the most frequent problem is "parking is difficult" for the store and the second one is "sales representative was rude". The third most important problem is poor lighting and the fourth most important problem is layout confusing.

As you see, these first four problems constitute the 80% of the customer complaints. Although there are seven types of customer complaints, if you first focus on the first four ones, you will be eliminating the 80% of your customer complaints. After you fix these first four problems you can focus on next three problems, and you can aim to decrease your customer complaints to 0%.

5. **Histograms:** Histograms are special form of bar chart and are used to describe the central tendency, dispersion, and shape of a statistical distribution. A problem or occurrence is analyzed in a XY chart. One dimension of the chart shows the frequency while the other dimension shows another attribute of the problem. We will be understanding histograms better with an example. Here you see a sample of histogram.

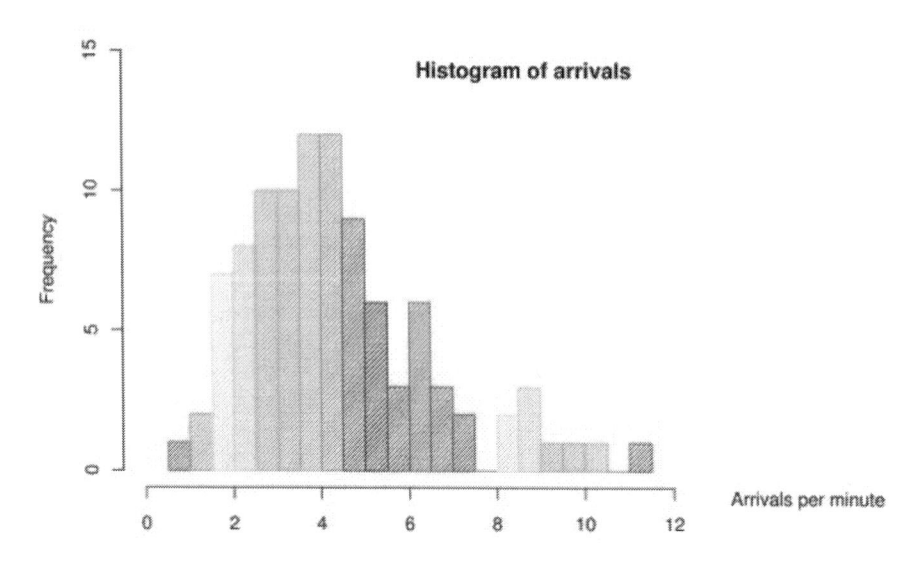

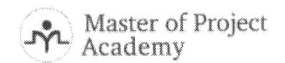

As you see, this figure defines the arrivals per minute in an airport. The highest frequency is seen at 4 minutes. Therefore, it shows that the central tendency of this histogram is four.

6. **Scatter diagrams:** Scatter diagrams track two variables to see if they are related. These two variables can be different. For instance, number of workers and speed of construction are two sample variables that can be tracked for a construction project. Number of defects and experience of software developers can be two variables that can be tracked for a software development project.

   Direction of correlation might have three alternatives:
   - **Positive Correlation (Proportional):** First alternative is, positive correlation or proportional. In this case, if you increase one variable, then, the other variable, which is in positive correlation with this variable, will increase as well. Alternatively, if you decrease this variable, the other variable will decrease as well.
   - **Negative Correlation (Inverse):** Second type of correlation is negative correlation or inverse correlation. In this type of correlation, if you increase one variable, the other variable in negative correlation with this variable will decrease. Alternatively, if you decrease the variable, the other variable will increase.
   - **Zero Correlation:** Third and last type of correlation is zero correlation. After your analysis, you might find zero correlation, which means that, two variables that you are analyzing are not related with each other.

   At the end of your analysis, if you can find that there is a correlation, then a regression line can be plotted. With the help of the regression line, you can estimate how a change on one variable will affect the other variable.

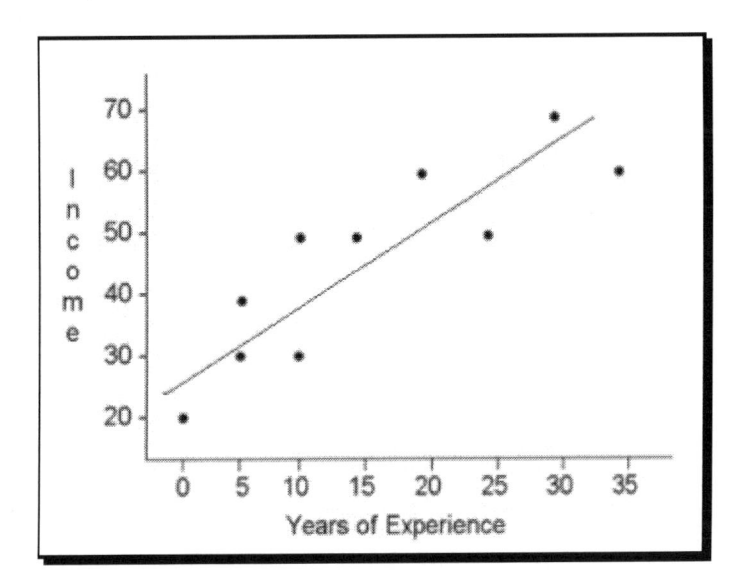

Here is an example of a scatter diagram. Two variables are years of experience and income level graph. Assume that this graph represents the income level of people working within the same industry. As you see, the dots are representing the years of experience versus the level of income. After ten samples have been collected, a positive correlation between years of experience and income level had been established. This correlation helps us to draw the regression line. Now, you can easily estimate what will be the income level of specific years of experience in this industry.

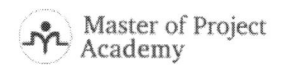

7. **Control Charts:** Seventh and last QC tool is Control charts. During this heading, we will be going over control charts in detail. Control charts are used to determine whether a process is stable or has predictable performance. Control charts are generally used to check whether your production or whether your output, the deliverable or work package of the project is meeting the quality standards of your customer or your project.
    - Control charts help to monitor production and other processes to see whether processes are in acceptable limits, or if any action required. So, based on the analysis on your control charts, if you see that the outputs of your project are not in line with the quality requirements of your project, you have to take corrective action in order to fix the problems in your project. See the features and details of control charts now.

    Now we will see some terms and concepts about control charts.

    - **Upper and Lower Control Limits:** First, we will see the upper and lower control limits. Upper and lower control limits define the acceptable range of variation for a process. For example, assume that you are producing wood sticks in your project. Your quality standards of your project or quality requirements of your customer says that the produced sticks must be in the length of 10 +/- 0.03 centimeters. In this case, 10 +/- 0.03 centimeters represent a range actually. Moreover, 9.97 centimeters is here the lower control limit of this range, and 10.03 centimeters represents the upper control limit of this range. Data points in this range are referred as in control. Therefore, as long as the produced sticks of your project are between 9.97 centimeters to 10.03 centimeters, you can say that you are producing your sticks in control, so you are meeting the quality standards of your project. However, if data points are out of this range, the process is out of control. For example, assume that one of the sticks that you have produced is 10.05 centimeters, which is greater than the upper control limit. Alternatively, another stick is in length of 9.95 centimeters, so it is lower than the lower control limit. Therefore, in these cases, you have to check why this variation occurred, and this represents that your process is out of control. In addition, you have to analyze why these variances occurred, why this process has gone out of control. Respectively, you have to take corrective actions in order to meet the quality standards of your project back again.
    - **Mean or average:** Mean or average is indicated by a line in the middle of the control chart, and it shows the middle of the range of acceptable variations of the process. So, let us remember that our quality standards from our previous example was saying that we have to produce our sticks in the range of 10 +/- 0.03 centimeters. Therefore, the middle of this range is ten centimeters. Therefore, we can say that for this example, our mean or average is ten centimeters and represents the middle of our control chart.
    - **Specification Limits:** Specification limits are the customer expectations or contractual requirements for performance quality and quality on the project. Therefore, these limits are defined by the customer. If you cannot stay in line with

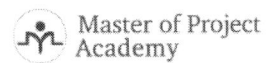

these limits, you will have acceptance problems with your customer in the future. Specification limits are inputs from customer, since these are required as quality requirements of your customer. Let us go through our wood stick production example. For example, if your customer says that the produced sticks in your project must not be shorter than 9.97 centimeters and must not be taller than 10.05 centimeters, these are the requirements of your customers. These represent the specification limits for the produced sticks in your project.

- **Control Limits:** The last bullet points out an important concept about the interrelation of specification limits and control limits. Companies' control limits must be stricter than specification limits to meet specification limits of the customer. What does this mean? Assume that your specification limits are stricter than the control limits of your project. In this case, when you are checking your product or your deliverable internally during quality controls of your project, even if you meet the control limits of your project, when you come to the customer acceptance, if the produced outcome is falling between the control limits and specification limits, customer may not accept it since your control limits are lighter than the specification limits of customer. Let us go through an example to illustrate this better. Assume that your control limits represent that the produced sticks must be between 9.95 centimeters to 10.05 centimeters. However, your specification limits of customer say that the produced sticks must be between 9.98 centimeters to 10.02 centimeters. Assume that, during your internal checks of these produced sticks, you found that one of your stick's length is 9.96 cm. Since it is in control limits of your project, you can say that it is okay, it is meeting the quality standards of the project, and you can go to your customer for demonstration. However, 9.96 cm is below the lower specification of the customer, which is 9.98 cm and customer will not accept it. Therefore, always control limits of a project must be stricter than the specification limits of the customer.

- **Out of control:** The process is out of a state of statistical control if a data point falls outside of the upper or lower control limit. Therefore, if there is any output which is greater than the upper control limit or lower than the lower control limit, this point is out of control and should be investigated. In addition, if there are seven consecutive points that are above or below the mean, these should be investigated since this also represents a process, which is out of control. Out of control here represents the lack of consistency and predictability in the process. Therefore, you have to analyze the root causes of the problems that pushed your process out of control. Otherwise, you might have quality problems in the future because of these out of control data points in your project.

- **Rule of seven:** Rule of seven indicates nonrandom data points grouped together in a series that total seven on one side of the mean in a control chart. Assume that there are seven consecutive data points, which are between the lower control limit and the mean of the control chart. Alternatively, there are seven consecutive data points above the mean, but lower than the upper control limit. If you look to these seven data points individually, they all fit into the range between upper and lower control limits. So, they individually meet the quality standards of a project.

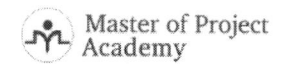

However, since these seven consecutive points are either above or below the mean, this can cause problems in the future. Therefore, this represents that the process is out of control, and these data points should be investigated.

- **Assignable cause or special cause variation:** Assignable cause or special cause variation proposes that, data points or rule of seven that requires investigation to determine the cause of variation. Therefore, if there is a case of rule of seven in your project, or if there is a data point which is greater than the upper control limit or lower than the lower control limit, you have to determine the cause of variation. This is referred as the assignable cause, or special cause variation. In addition, after you have found the cause of the problem, you have to fix it in order to get back in line with your quality requirements of your project.

Now, we will see a control chart example for our stick production project example.

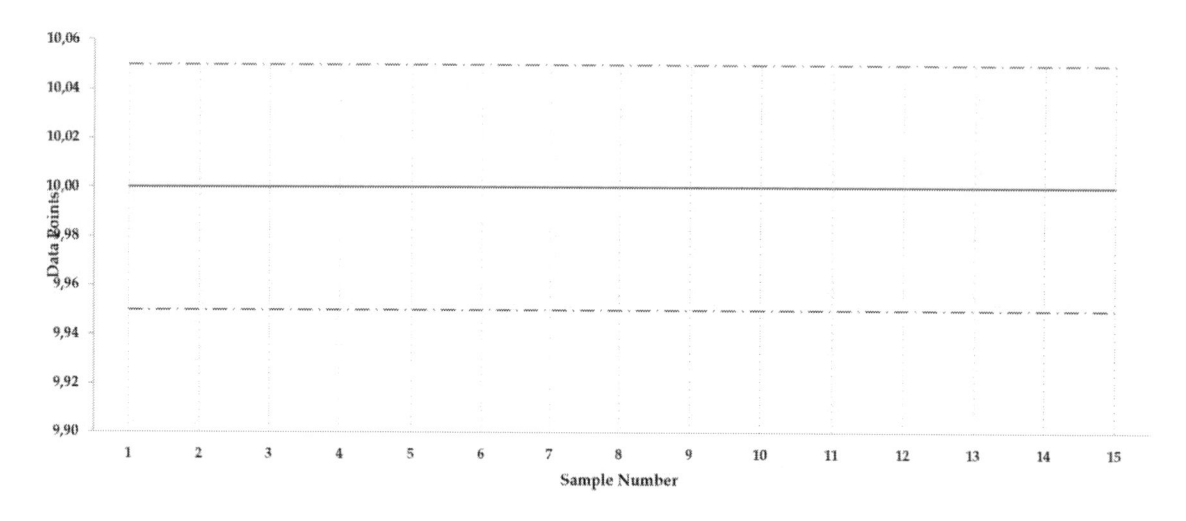

As you see, line plotted at "10" here represents the mean or average of our control chart, which is the blue line. The first dotted line, which is plotted at the 9.95 cm level, represents the lower specification limit of the customer. Therefore, it states that the produced sticks must not be lower than 9.95 cm in our project. The second line on the upside of the chart represents the upper specification limit of the customer. It states that the produced sticks must be lower than the 10.05 cm. In summary, customer states that, as a quality requirement, the produced sticks must be between 9.95 cm to 10.05 cm.

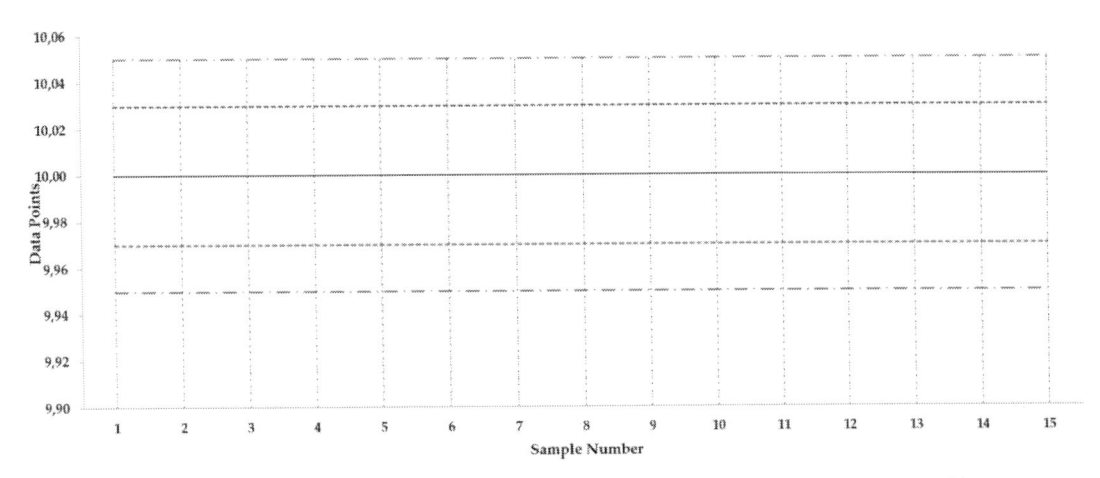

Moreover, these blue dotted lines represent the upper and lower control limits. As you see, the first blue dotted line represents the lower control limit, which is at 9.97 cm. The second blue dotted line on the upside of the chart represents the upper control limit of the project, and it is at 10.03 cm.

Briefly, after your internal checks, you have to verify that each produced stick must fit between 9.97 cm to 10.03 cm in order to meet the quality standards of your project.
Here we see the example data points for this example. Dots on the graph represent the lengths of each produced stick. There are 15 produced sticks, and the length of each of these produced sticks are plotted on this control chart.
The third, fourth, fifth, sixth, seventh, eighth, and ninth produced sticks are all between the mean and the lower control limit of the project. Therefore, if you look individually to each data point of these seven consecutive data points, they are all in between the mean of the control chart and the lower control limit of the project. So, if you look individually to each of these data points, they are in line with the quality standards. However, since all these seven lines are consecutively lower than the mean of the control chart, you can say that this process is out of control. You have to analyze the reasons why this process has gone out of control.

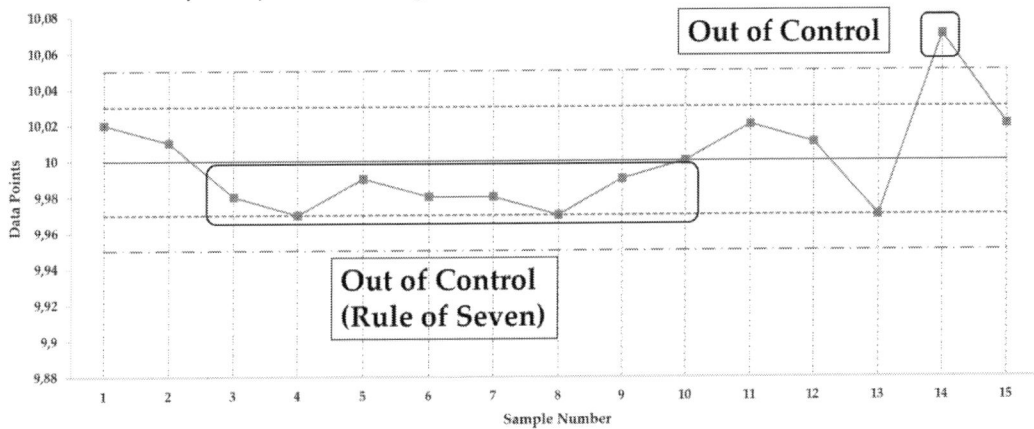

We have another data point, which is out of control. As you see the 14th produced stick's length is 10.07 cm, which is above the 10.05 cm, which is the upper specification limit of the customer. Since it is greater than the specification limit of the customer, customer will not accept this 14th produced stick. Therefore, you have to analyze the reasons of this variation, the reasons of this problem. Then, you have to fix and correct your processes accordingly.

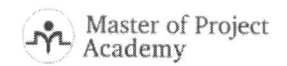

Outputs of Plan Quality Management Process

We have gone through the details of plan quality management process in our previous notes. What are the outputs of plan quality management process?

- **Quality Management Plan:** The major output of this process is quality management plan, and as we said in the beginning, it defines how you will define quality requirements, how you will ensure quality requirements in the project, how you will measure and validate the quality as well.
- **Quality Metrics:** Quality metrics are also included in the outputs of plan quality management process, and these define availability of the product, reliability of the product, defect frequency, failure rate, test coverage etc.

  For example, if you are delivering a telecommunication product to a customer of your company, which is the telecom operator, and if your operator requires that the produced product must be 99.99% reliable, you have to meet this quality requirement of your customer.

  Defect frequency might be another quality metric for a project. Assume that customer proposes that a specific web page in a software development project must not exceed five defects. In this case, you should not exceed the defects received for that specific web page in your project.

  Similarly, there might be other quality metrics such as failure rate and test coverage as well.
- **Quality Checklists:** Quality checklists might be another output of the plan quality management process. What are the set of required steps? What are the specifications, specific activities that you need to complete in order to meet the quality standards, quality requirements of your project? These are mentioned in the quality checklist of the project, and this is an output of plan quality management process.
- **Process Improvement Plan:** Another output of the plan quality management process is process improvement plan. In this plan you define how you will improve your processes. How you will get better results in each project activity in your project. These are all defined in process improvement plans of your project.
- **Project Documents Updates:** And finally, you update your project documents accordingly as an output of plan quality management process.

Manage Quality Process

Second process of quality management knowledge area is Manage Quality Process.

- **Manage Quality is the process of auditing the quality requirements and the results from quality control measurements to ensure that appropriate standards and operational definitions are used.** During plan quality management process, standards and policies that will be used, metrics that will be used and how to measure quality is determined. In

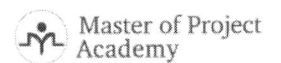

manage quality, results are checked whether they meet the determined quality standards and metrics.
- **In other words, manage quality process answers "Are we using standards?" and "Can we improve standards?" questions.** Assume that, your company is adapting ISO 9000 as a quality policy in entire organization. During manage quality process; it's checked whether the project's outputs are aligned with the ISO 9000 standards. If there are project specific quality standards as well, these are checked during this process respectively. Improvement areas to improve quality are assessed during manage quality process as well.
- **Manage quality process facilitates the improvement of quality processes.** Therefore, it helps how you can improve the quality processes, how you can produce better results continuously in your project.

The Tools and Techniques used in Manage Quality process

What are the tools and techniques used in Manage Quality process?

- **Quality Audits:** Quality Assurance Department needs to check whether your project is using standards, processes, and procedures of company, best practices, etc. If you are working in a corporate company, your organization should have a quality assurance department. There are several policies, standards and guidelines of a company. Quality assurance department checks whether these are followed by the departments and people in the organization.
    - **In terms of project management, quality assurance department will check whether the organization's policies, quality standards and guidelines are followed by the project team.** Assume that ISO 27001 is used in the organization for information security. Quality assurance department will audit the projects to check whether project team members follow the guidelines of this standard.
- **Process analysis:** Process analysis is actually part of continuous improvement. It will be better to describe this technique over an example.
Assume that there will be 100 PC installations in scope of your project. During each installation, project team is preparing their lessons learned documentation as well. Actually, installation of PC is a repetitive process in the project and requires predetermined steps to be followed in sequence. However, there can be better ways to do the installation or alternatives to complete the installation faster. If you check the lessons learned after each 10th PC installation, you might see weak points of the process and improve PC installation process for the next installations. This is called process analysis.

- **Quality Management and Control Tools:** As you see in the screen, there are seven tools here. We will not go over the details of each tool here. It will be sufficient to know that there are some quality management and control tools used in manage quality process.
    - These are Affinity Diagrams, Process Decision Program Charts, which is abbreviated as PDPC, Interrelationship Digraphs, Tree Diagrams, Prioritization Matrices, Activity Network Diagrams, and Matrix Diagrams.

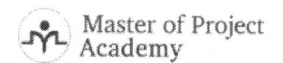

The Outputs of Manage Quality process

What are the outputs of manage quality process?

There are two major outputs:

- **Change requests:** Assume that ISO 9000 is the company wide standard for quality in your organization. Quality Assurance Department inspected your project and they have found that some points of the ISO 9000 are not applied appropriately in the project. In this case, quality assurance department might raise change requests and you should take corrective actions to apply ISO 9000 standards in your project.
- **Project Management Plan and Project document updates:** Project Management Plan and Project document updates are common outputs of many processes. Based on the steps and activities of manage quality process, project management plans and documents must be updated respectively.

Control Quality Process

Control quality is the third and last process of quality management knowledge area.

- **Control quality is the process of monitoring and recording results of executing the quality activities to assess performance and recommend necessary changes.**

    In this process, you check whether the produced outcome and the output of your project is in line with the quality requirements of your project. If you remember our previous example, the produced sticks must be between 9.97 cm to 10.03 cm as per the customer requirements. Briefly, in this process, you check whether your produced sticks are in this range of length. In other words, produced outputs are checked whether they meet the quality requirements.

- **Identifying the cause of poor process or product quality and recommending and/or acting to eliminate them.** If there are any out of control situations or if there are any quality problems regarding the output of your project, this can be in a deliverable or a work package of your project, you have to analyze the reasons of this poor quality. Then, you should take corrective actions to repair the problems and you should take preventive actions in order to eliminate the problems that might occur in the future again.

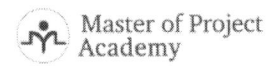

- **Validating that project deliverables and work meet the requirements specified by key stakeholders necessary for final acceptance.** Say that you produce sticks in scope of your project. You have to check whether the produced sticks are in line with the quality requirements of your project. This check is performed by the project team first. Then, if the sticks pass the internal checks and if they are okay in your internal checks, you have to meet with your customer to get the interim acceptance for the produced deliverables of your project. Therefore, it is important to validate the project deliverables or work packages of your project. This is part of control quality process.

- **Control quality includes ensuring a certain level of quality in a product or service.** Certain level is defined here by the quality standards of your organization or your company, and the specification limits of your customer or the quality requirements of your customer.

- **Control = Measure.** This means, in order to control the quality of your project or the output of your project, you have to measure whether it really fits with the requirements of your project.

- **Quality control departments may measure quality in large organizations and send change requests or reports to project manager.** If you are working in a small organization or in a small project environment, quality measurement can be performed within the team. For example, assume that you are working in a project team with eight people. In this case, the quality control might be performed by two test engineers, which are working on your project team. However, if you are working in a very large organization, then, there might be specific functional departments, which are checking the quality of the outputs of several projects. For example, testing department for Software Company might check the outputs of several software projects ongoing in an organization. Based on their checks, they can send their change requests or reports to project managers for their related projects.

- **Control quality process answers two main questions. "Are we meeting standards?" and "What changes should be considered?".** First question, "Are we meeting standards" will answer whether the company wide standards, like ISO 9000, are followed, and quality requirements of the customer are met. Second question, "What changes should be considered?" is related with the answer of first question. If the company wide standards are not followed, or if the project outputs do not meet the quality requirements of the project, corrective and preventive actions might be taken. By this way, any deviation from quality requirements will be fixed respectively.

Terms & Concepts About Control Quality Process

We will go through important terms and concepts about control quality process during this heading.

- **Mutual Exclusivity:** This concept defines that two events are mutually exclusive if they cannot occur in a single trial. For example, if you toss a coin, the outcome cannot result head and tails at the same time. It can be either head or tail. This is an example of Mutual Exclusivity.

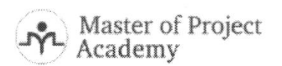

- **Probability:** Probability defines the likelihood of something to occur. For example, if you toss a coin, the probability of turning a head as an outcome is 50%, or 0.50. Probability shows the possibility ratio of an event or result to happen in a project.

- **Normal Distribution:** Normal Distribution is the bell curve used to measure variations. If there are several characteristics of a data, it is expected to see a normal distribution or bell curve in distribution of the data. For instance, consider the income level of a country. We would expect that the majority of the population will be close to average income level and this will result in a normal distribution curve.

- **Statistical Independence:** Statistical Independence defines that the probability of one event does not affect the probability of another event. For example, probability of turning head as a result of a coin toss is statistically independent from the probability of turning a tail on next toss. Therefore, these two cases are statistically independent from each other.

- **3 or 6 Sigma:** 6 Sigma or 3 Sigma is a quality concept, which defines a certain level of quality that should be met in the production processes or in the production outcomes of the organizations. Different sigma levels refer to different quality levels.

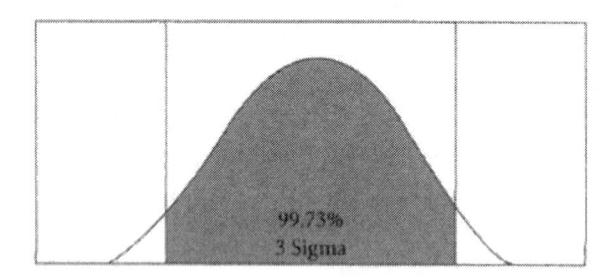

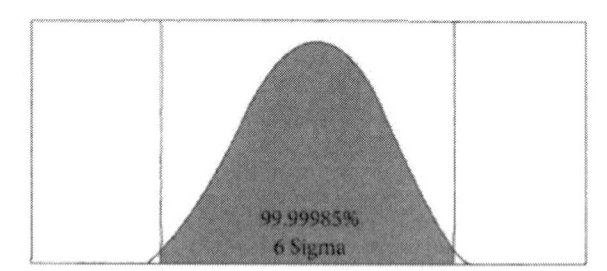

For example,

- 3 Sigma refers 2,700 items out of 1 million can be faulty (0.27%x1,000,000)

- 6 Sigma refers 1,5 items out of 1 million can be faulty (0.00015%x1,000,000)

Assume that you are working in a pen factory and if the pen factory is applying 3 Sigma standards and if there are one million pens produced a day, only 2700 items of these pants can be faulty and this is the acceptable limit.

Consider our pen factory example. If you are producing one million pens a day and if your company is adapting 6 Sigma, only 1.5 of the pens can be faulty. Can you imagine how sharp 6 sigma quality level is? That is why several companies achieved to save billions of dollars by applying six sigma quality standards.

- **Standard Deviation (Sigma):** Standard Deviation is the measure of how far you are from the mean. And 3 or 6 Sigma is also another name for standard deviation. 3 or 6 Sigma represents the level of quality that a company has decided to try to achieve. There are several processes, several concepts that should be applied under 3 or 6 Sigma in order to meet a certain quality level in the production processes of the company. This is a very deep area that should be look into further if you are related to the quality management or with the production processes.

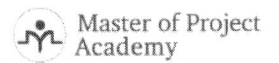

However, from the project management point of view, it is enough to know that 6 Sigma or 3 Sigma represents a certain level of quality that should be met by an organization. In addition, the faulty levels, the acceptable faulty levels of the 3 or 6 Sigma should be known.

Outputs of Control Quality Process

What are the outputs of control quality process?
- **Measurements:** In order to check whether you are meeting the quality standards or the specification limits of your customer, you have to measure the produced outcomes of your project. Remember, control equals to measure. If you cannot measure the deliverables of your project, you cannot manage quality.
- **Validated Changes:** Validated changes are another output of control quality process. If you have received a defect repair or a change request from your customer, and if you have implemented this change request or fixed a defect in your project this is an example of validated change.
A validated change should be retested in order to check whether it has been delivered as planned in the beginning and whether it meets the quality requirements.
- **Change requests:** Change requests might be the output of control quality process. Assume that during the tests of your customer, they have found a defect in your product. Alternatively, you have figured out an out of control data point during your internal tests. In these cases, you have to fix the defects. After the test of the customer, customer might come with a completely new requirement that needs to be delivered in your project. In this case, change request must be evaluated by the change control board, and if approved, it must be implemented in the project respectively.
- **Validated deliverables:** Validated deliverables are another output of control quality. Based on your quality checks, or based on the acceptance tests of the customer, if the produced deliverable or the outcome of the project is meeting the quality standards and quality requirements of the customer, it is validated and marked as passed in your project. Briefly, deliverables or produced items passing the quality control process are marked as validated deliverables.
- **Project Management Plan and Project Documents updates:** And finally, as an output of your control quality process, you have to update your project management plan and project documents in your project. As you know, this is a common output of many processes.

Tips About Quality Management Processes

We will go over three important tips about quality management processes in this heading. These tips will be about reminding whether a situation is related to plan quality management process, manage quality process or control quality process.

- **If the situation is <u>looking forward</u> in time, it is most likely a planning function (Plan Quality Management):** Because you plan something that will occur in the future. For instance, if you are determining the quality standards you will be using, quality metrics and how to measure quality in future, these are all part of plan quality management process.

- **If it is <u>looking back</u> in time <u>at standards</u>, it is most likely part of quality assurance (Manage Quality):** For instance, if you are checking whether the determined quality standards are applied properly in a project, this is part of manage quality process. There might be companywide standards such as ISO 9000, and there might be project specific quality standards. In either case, manage quality process ensures that the determined standards are followed.

- **If it is <u>looking back</u> in time <u>at results</u>, it is most likely a part of quality control (Control Quality):** For example, if you are checking whether you have met the quality requirements of your customer, then you are doing an activity, which is belonging to quality control. For instance, remember our wood stick production project. If you are checking whether the produced sticks are in line with the quality requirements, you are in control quality process.

Quiz – Section 7

1- As a project manager, you need to know all of the following about quality EXCEPT:

A) Acceptable quality

B) How it will be measured

C) Actions to meet quality requirements

D) Requirements of all Quality Standards

2- All of the following about grade and quality are true EXCEPT:

A) A product meeting quality requirements cannot have a low grade

B) Quality is the degree to which a set of inherent characteristics fulfill requirements

C) Grade is a category assigned to deliverables having the same functional but different technical characteristics

D) A low-grade product can have a high quality

3- You are trying to determine precision level of your project during quality measurements. Which of the following has highest precision?

A) 1,0 cm

B) 1,00 cm

C) 1,000 cm

D) 1,0000 cm

4- All of the following are quality theorists EXCEPT:

A) Joseph Juran

B) Edwards Deming

C) David McClelland

D) Philip Crosby

5- Which of the following is an example of Just in Time (JIT) Environment?

A) Checking for small improvements in every new car production in a car factory

B) Providing hand-brakes of a bicycle 3 minutes before assembly in a factory

C) Encouraging entire company to find better practices in order to increase quality

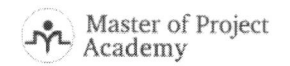

D) Providing more than the requirements of customer in projects

6- All of the following are processes of Quality Management EXCEPT:

A) Determine Quality

B) Plan Quality Management Plan

C) Manage Quality

D) Control Quality

7- All of the following about Plan Quality Management process is true EXCEPT:

A) Planning must be done to meet customer requirements

B) Project specific standards can be created after existing standards are defined

C) Project specific standards can violate existing standards if they conflict

D) Plan Quality Management process involves determining the work that needs to be done to meet quality standards

8- There is a cost of conformance to requirements in projects. All of the following are examples of cost of conformance EXCEPT:

A) Training for project team

B) Testing

C) Inspections

D) Rework

9- During customer acceptance tests of your project, your customer found that application could not meet 99% reliability in a day. Based on the liabilities put in the contract, you had to pay penalty to your customer. This is an example of:

A) Prevention Cost

B) Appraisal Cost

C) Internal Failure Cost

D) External Failure Cost

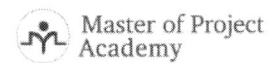

10- You are working on a construction project. Parameters affecting the strength of a building are:

- Cement type
- Steel type
- Column structure

In order to find best combination of these factors, your team is conducting tests by changing all these three variables at the same time. Which technique is used by your team?

A) Design of Experiment

B) Benchmarking

C) Cost of Quality

D) Statistical Sampling

11- You used statistical sampling technique in your project. All of the following are the reasons for using statistical sampling EXCEPT:

A) Investigation of all population takes too long

B) Investigation of all population costs too much

C) Investigation of all population will generate unreliable results

D) Investigation of all population can be too destructive

12- In your airplane-manufacturing project, your team noticed a problem in avionics part of the airplane and you need to find the root cause of the problem. Which of the following tools will be BEST option to find the root cause of the problem?

A) Flowcharts

B) Ishikawa Diagrams

C) Checksheets

D) Process Maps

13- All of the following are benefits of using Pareto Diagrams in projects EXCEPT:

A) Helps focusing attention on most critical issues

B) Prioritize potential causes of the problems

C) Separate the critical few problems from the uncritical many problems

D) Show the root causes of most critical problems

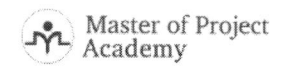

14- You are using Control Charts as a quality tool in your project. All of the following are true about Control Charts EXCEPT:

A) Data points between upper and lower control limits are in control

B) Middle point of upper and lower control limits defines mean of the control chart

C) Specification limits might be customer requirements in a project

D) Specification limits can be stricter than control limits in a project

15- During your internal tests in your project, your team realized that seven consecutive points regarding a measurement are between the mean and upper control limit. What should be the BEST action?

A) This is a rule of seven and requires investigation

B) This is a rule of seven but points are in limits, there is not a problem

C) Data points are within the specification limits, thus, there is not a problem

D) Tests should be re-executed since this indicates a problem

16- All of the following are outputs of Plan Quality Management process EXCEPT:

A) Quality Management Plan

B) Quality Metrics

C) Quality Measurements

D) Process Improvement Plan

17- Main target of Manage Quality process is:

A) Performing acceptance tests

B) Auditing whether defined standards are used during project

C) Measuring quality

D) Determining assignable cause for the problems

18- During your project, you have to ensure that a certain level of quality in a product or service is achieved. This is mainly done in:

A) Plan Quality Management Process

B) Manage Quality Process

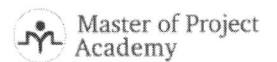

C) Control Quality Process

D) Measure Quality Process

19- Your company uses 6 Sigma standards. Your project will produce 2.000.000 electronic devices. What is the allowable fault count based on 6 sigma standards?

A) 10.000

B) 5400

C) 3

D) 1,5

20- All of the following are outputs of Control Quality process EXCEPT:

A) Measurements

B) Validated changes

C) Validated deliverables

D) Process Changes

Answers

1 – D	11 – C
2 – A	12 – B
3 – D	13 – D
4 – C	14 – D
5 – B	15 – A
6 – A	16 – C
7 – C	17 – B
8 – D	18 – C
9 – D	19 – C
10 – A	20 – D

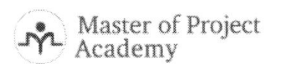

Mapping Game – Section 7

keeping errors out of the process	Tolerances
the most expensive approach of quality management	Inspection
giving extras to customer	Kaizen
Money sent during and after the project because of failures	Let the customer find the defects
specified range of acceptable results	Cost of Non-Conformance
Money spent during the project to avoid failures	Gold plating
check on the effectiveness of the quality processes	Recurring retrospectives
keeping errors out of the hands of the customer	Prevention
looking for small improvements continuously	Cost of Conformance

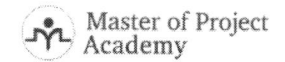

Answers

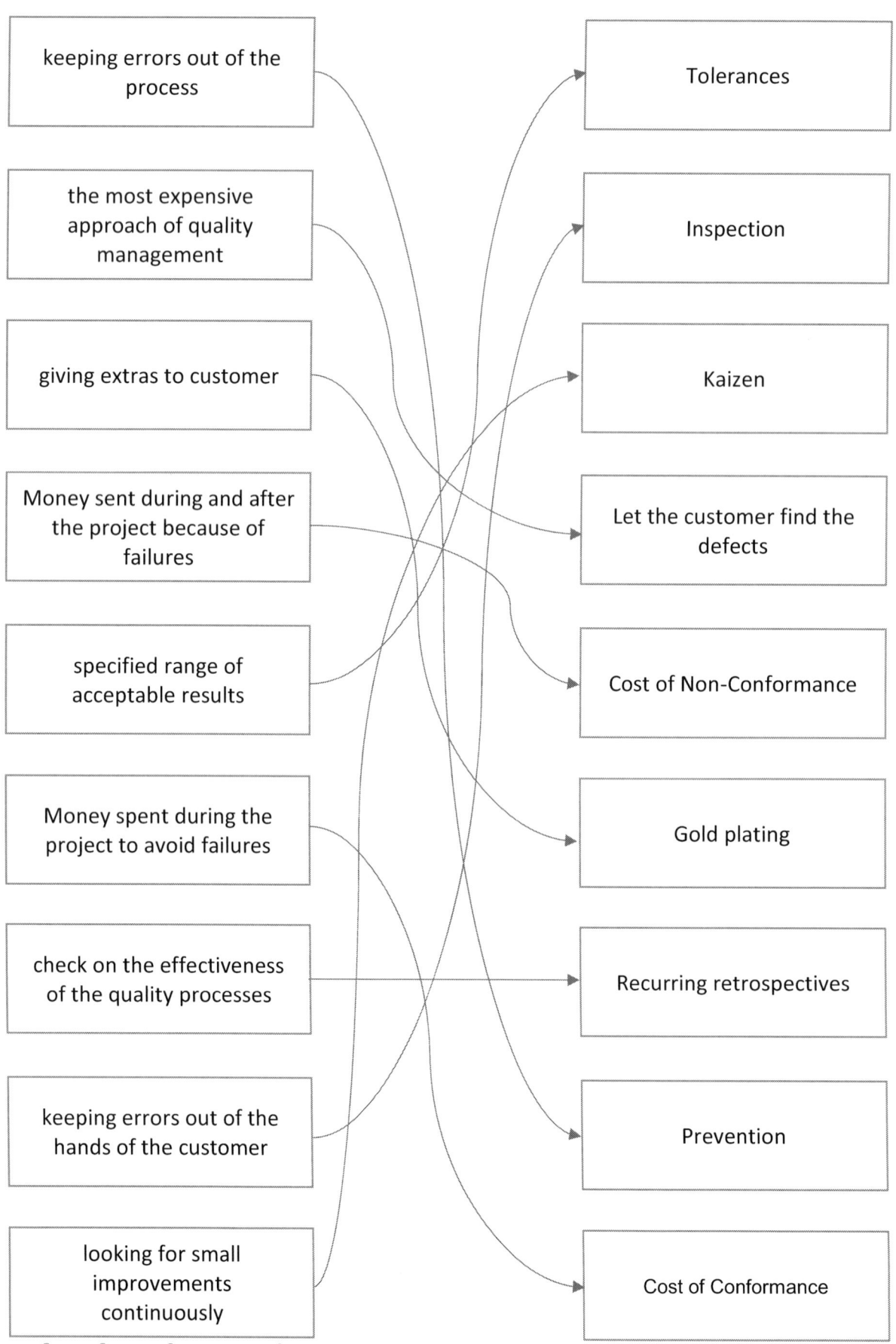

Left	Right
keeping errors out of the process	→ Prevention
the most expensive approach of quality management	→ Let the customer find the defects
giving extras to customer	→ Gold plating
Money spent during and after the project because of failures	→ Cost of Non-Conformance
specified range of acceptable results	→ Tolerances
Money spent during the project to avoid failures	→ Cost of Conformance
check on the effectiveness of the quality processes	→ Recurring retrospectives
keeping errors out of the hands of the customer	→ Inspection
looking for small improvements continuously	→ Kaizen

Section 8

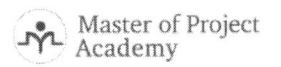

Resource Management

Section 8 – Resource Management

Resource management is another critical knowledge area of project management. Resource management knowledge area is related with people management. In order to complete your project activities, you will need project team. For instance, for a construction project, you will need architects, civil engineers, construction workers etc. For a software development project, you will need business analysts, software engineers, test engineers etc.

Resource management knowledge area mainly deals with the management of the people resources in a project team. Let us go through the agenda of this section now.

- **Overview of Resource Management:** First, we will go through the overview of Resource Management knowledge area. We will describe the concept of resource management and then we will go through the important points about project team performance and people management.
- **Resource Management Processes:** Then we will go through the processes of Resource Management knowledge area. There are 6 processes of Resource management knowledge area. We will see these process and which project management process group they belong to respectively.
- **Roles & Responsibilities:** We will go over roles and responsibility. There are different roles in a project. Stakeholders, project team, project sponsor, program manager, portfolio manager, functional manager etc. Each of these roles have different responsibilities respectively. We will go over the roles & responsibilities in detail.
- **Plan Resource Management Process:** Then, we will step into first process of resource management knowledge area Plan resource management process. Team formation, organization structure of the team, reporting hierarchy, rewards and recognition system etc. are all planned during plan resource management process. We will go through this process in detail.
- **Resource Management Plan:** Major output of the plan resource management process is resource management plan. Resource management plan includes roles and responsibilities of the project team members, organization charts, recognition and rewards system etc. We will go through the content of resource management plan in detail.
- **Staffing Management Plan:** Staffing management plan is another output of plan resource management process. Staffing management plan includes plan for staff acquisition, resource calendars, staff release plan, training needs of the project team members etc. We will go over the staffing management plan in detail.
- **Estimate Activity Resources:** Second process of the resource management knowledge area is Estimate Activity Resources process. In this process, which activity will require how many resources, how many materials, tools, equipment etc. are determined.
- **Acquire Resources Process:** Third process of the resource management knowledge area is Acquire resources process. Acquire resources process verifies the required resources are available and obtains the required people to the project team.

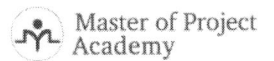

- **Develop Team Process:** Fourth process of resource management knowledge area is develop team process. Main objective of this process is ensuring a well-performing project team. Develop team process includes activities about improving teamwork, skills of the project team members, performance etc.
- **Manage Team Process:** Fifth process of resource management knowledge area is Manage team process. This process deals with the tracking team member performance, providing feedback, resolving issues and managing team changes. We will be seeing the manage team process in detail.
- **Conflict Management:** Conflict management is a critical aspect of project management. Several conflicts may arise in the project. These can be either in the project team or among other stakeholders. As a project manager, you need to solve these conflicts as soon as possible. Otherwise, project performance might be hampered from the conflicts. We will go over the conflict resolution techniques in detail.
- **Theories About Motivation:** At the last part of the section we will go over the theories about motivation. We will see Mc Gregor's Theory of X and Y, Maslow's Hierarchy of needs, David McClelland's theory of needs and Herzberg's theory.
- **Control Resources Process:** Sixth and the last process of resource management is Control Resources Process. During this process, it is checked whether the planned resources are available and used as planned. Deviances from planned values are monitored and necessary corrective actions are taken.

Overview of Resource Management

Before diving into the resource management, let's go through the overview of the resource management first. What is the definition of resource management?

- **Resource management includes processes that organize, manage, and lead the project team and resources.** There will be many project activities in your project. These activities will be performed by the project team members. In order to complete the project successfully, project team members must be managed appropriately, their motivation must be good and activities must be performed in an organized manner. This is achieved by the help of the resource management knowledge area.

- **Involvement of all team members in project planning and decision making is beneficial.** Because your project team, your team members will actually perform the project activities or project tasks. Therefore, you have to do your project planning with your project team. They should define the specific activities of a project. They should give the estimations, because they will be the actual performers of your tasks and activities in your project. If you do this, you will ensure the team buy-in. Since they were in the planning phase, they will be motivated to complete the tasks they planned.

- **Participation of team members during planning adds their expertise to the process and strengthens their commitment to the project.** If you involve the project team members during the planning phases, during the planning processes, then you will have their commitment. Think about the opposite case. If you do the planning with other resources and assign these activities to different project team member, they might not be committed to the project activities that they did not estimate.

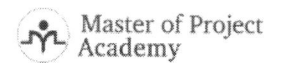

Let me describe this through an example. Consider a web page development activity in a software project. One of the senior engineers in the planning phase estimated that this activity can be completed in 10 days. However, during project execution, you assigned this activity to another developer who does not think that activity can be completed in 10 days. This will cause a big commitment and motivation issue. Therefore, participation of team members during planning is crucial.

- **Recognition and rewards system must be applied in resource management of a project.** If there are desired behaviors of your project team members, you must recognize and give rewards to improve their commitment and motivation. For example, if there is an over performing team member in your project, you have to recognize him in front of project team. By this way, the other project team members will see that the desired behavior or the over performing people are recognized in the company or in the project and this will increase the overall project team performance respectively. You should also give rewards for the over performing employees. These can be a weekend holiday in a hotel, bonus salary, a gift card etc.

- **Project managers should improve team member's competencies.** Competency means the knowledge or the skills of a project team member. For example, experience of Java programming language for a software developer is a competency. Similarly, designing a skyscraper, or designing a bridge is a competency for a civil engineer. Therefore, when team members enroll in your project for the project execution, you should improve their competencies during your project. This can be achieved by organizing training for the project team members or encouraging knowledge sharing among project team members. Improving competencies of project team members is not only good for the project, but also for the organization or company. Because, in next project, the project team member will have improved skills and expertise.

- **Resource management is done in executing phase.** Because actual work, actual tasks are delivered to the customer in the executing process group. Since majority of the project team is working in the executing process group, resource management is done in executing process group.

- **Projects are planned by the team but coordinated by project managers.** If you remember from our previous knowledge areas, project activities, project cost and time estimations were planned together with the team. Therefore, during planning, all project team should give inputs to the planning processes. However, after your project planning is complete, during execution phase, the project plan is coordinated by project manager. This includes tracking the status of project activities, monitoring team members' performance, making forecasts etc.

- **In big projects, some of the team might have project management activities.** This team is called as project management team or core executive or leadership team. Let us describe this through an example. Assume that you are working on a project where you have 100 software engineers in the project team. You have 10 different software development teams. In order to make better coordination, you assign a team leader to each software development team. Therefore, each software developer is assigned to a team leader and these ten team leaders are assigned to you.

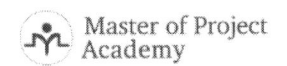

- **These 10 team leaders might help to the project manager in some of the project management activities like performance reporting, performance monitoring etc.** In this scenario, these ten team leaders plus you, as a project manager, constitute the project management team.
- **Project manager must track team member's performance.** When you assign a task or when you assign an activity to a team member, you have to evaluate his or her performance. For example, if you assign a project activity to a specific software developer in your project and if the initial plan or the initial time estimate for the activity was five days for the activity, you have to evaluate whether the developer will complete that activity in five days. If he could not complete on time, you have to evaluate whether there was a performance problem or even if he finished early, you have to check whether he over performed or whether there was a problem with the initial estimate of the activity. Therefore, you have to always evaluate the team members' performance in your project. This is crucial for timely completion of the project.
If there are problems with the performance of your project team members, you have to take corrective actions or find alternative ways to motivate your project team members better in your project.
- **There are six processes in Resource Management knowledge area.** Two of them belong to Planning process group, three of them belong to Executing process group and one of them belongs to Monitoring & controlling process group. These processes are:
    - Plan Resource Management,
    - Estimate Activity Resources,
    - Acquire Resources,
    - Develop Team,
    - Manage Team and
    - Control Resources.

We will be going over these processes one-by-one in our following notes.

Roles & Responsibilities

Before going further into the processes of resource management knowledge area, we will summarize the roles and responsibilities that are too often to see in a project.

- **Project management must clearly show the roles and responsibilities of management, team members and other stakeholders.** Otherwise, if you could not clearly show the roles and responsibilities of your resources in the project, then, most probably, you will have conflicts in your project. The team members might have conflicts about what to do, whom to report, who should be responsible of what etc. if you could not clearly define the roles and responsibilities of each team member.
- **When assigning roles and responsibilities to resources in a project, Responsibility Assignment Matrix can be used.** In addition, there is another form of this Responsibility Assignment Matrix; we just call this RACI matrix. RACI stands for responsible, accountable, consulted, and informed. We will see RACI matrix later in this section.

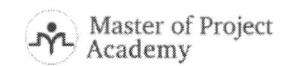

Role of the Project Sponsor (Initiator)

The main role of the project sponsor is providing financial resources for project. Project sponsors are powerful people in an organization and main supporter of the projects. They are the initiators of the project and they support project financially to complete the project successfully. Role of the project sponsor changes in different phases of a project. See the role of the project sponsor in each phase now.

- **During Initiating Phase:** What are the roles of project sponsor during initiating phase?

    - **Has requirements that must be met:** project sponsor states his expectations from the project and high-level requirements of the project are gathered.
    - **Spokesperson of the project:** Acts as the spokesperson of the project in the organization. He or she follows the processes of the organization in order to initiate a project.
    - **Provides funding:** Project sponsor is responsible for providing funding. Generally, in corporate companies, project sponsors have budgets under their control, and they assign project budgets from their overall budget. For instance, Vice President of Technology in a software vendor can have one hundred-million-dollar annual budget. From this budget, he can preserve forty-five million dollars for the new software projects. When a new project required funding, he will be able to allocate required budget respectively.
    - **Provides project statement of work:** Another critical role of the project sponsor in initiating phase is, providing project statement of work. Project statement of work is a short brief of project scope and describes what will be done throughout the project. Project sponsor, as the initiator of the project, will define the high-level requirements of the project and provide project statement of work.
    - **Provides info about initial scope of project:** In initiating, Project Sponsor also provides information about initial scope of the project. Later in planning, this initial scope is detailed into detailed requirements and detailed scope. Based on these detailed scope and requirements, project activities are defined in the planning process.
    - **Determines priorities among constraints:** Project sponsor determines priorities among constraints in initiating phase. Assume that, there is a time constraint and if there is a cost constraint in the project. If sponsor requires this project to be completed in six months instead of one year, most probably, he should spend extra money. Then, he should define whether the time constraint or the cost constraint is more important in the project. Based on these priorities among constraints, the project is planned accordingly.
    - **Gives authority to project manager (in charter):** Project sponsor gives authority to the project manager, and this is achieved by authorizing project charter if you remember from our previous notes. Once the project charter is signed by the project sponsor, project becomes official in the organization and this gives the authority to the project manager in a project.
    - **Set priorities between projects:** Project sponsor set priorities between projects. For example, a critical resource might be required by two projects at the same time in an

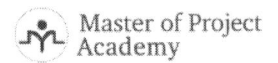

organization. In this case, one of the projects should have higher priority over the other one. Otherwise, there will be conflict between the project managers of two projects. Therefore, project sponsor must clearly define the priorities between projects.

- **During Planning Phase**: What are the roles of project sponsor in planning phase?

    o **Provides project team with time to plan:** He provides project team with time to plan. Project sponsor states is his time requirements. For example, what he expects at specific milestones or specific deliverables. For example, the project sponsor can require the project to be delivered in one year and he can expect the first phase completion at the end of third month. These are examples for time requirements of the project sponsor. These are given by the project sponsor to the project manager in the planning phase.
    o **Supplies the list of risks:** Project sponsor supplies the list of risks. If there are risks associated with the project that the sponsor is aware of, the sponsor provides these risks. Project manager must consider these risks during planning to accommodate impacts if they occur.
    o **Provides expert judgment:** Project sponsor provides expert judgment if you need special information about a topic. For example, there might be a new regulation proposed by the government that may affect your project. You may consult to the project how this new regulation will affect your project.
    o **Approves final project management plan:** Project sponsor approves final project management plan. If you remember, once you completed all of your plans for the project, you should have got the agreement from the project sponsor. Because, project sponsor is the ultimate owner, ultimate buyer of the project. He provides the funding, he spends money; therefore, you should get the final project management plan approval from the project sponsor.

- **During Executing, Monitoring and Controlling Phases:** What are the roles of project sponsor during initiating phase?

    o **Protects project from outside influences:** In these phases of a project, project sponsor protects project from outside influences. Assume that a new project that will be initiated soon might affect your project. For instance, new project might delay some of your project activities. In this case, project sponsor takes the responsibility and protects your project from the outcomes of the other project in your organization.
    o **Resolve conflicts:** Conflicts are inevitable in a project. These conflicts can be either between project team members or between the project managers of the organization or functional managers. If the conflict is between project managers or between a project manager and functional manager, project sponsor might be involved to resolve the conflict. Because, project sponsor has the power in the organization and he or she can affect both project managers and functional managers.
    o **Approves or reject changes (as part of CCB):** Project sponsor approves or rejects changes as part of Change Control Board. If you remember from our previous notes, when there was a change request in a project, these change requests were being escalated to the change control board, and after evaluation of the impacts of the change request, Change control board was deciding whether to accept this change. If

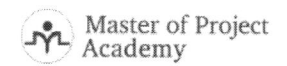

project sponsor is part of the Change Control Board, then he approves or rejects changes since he is a member of the Change Control Board in a project.
- **Clarifies scope questions:** Project sponsor clarifies scope questions because he is the owner of high-level requirements in a project. He is the initiator of a project and source of the high-level requirements. Therefore, if there are problems or if there are questions about scope, project sponsor can clarify this ambiguity.
- **Works with project management to monitor progress:** Project sponsor works with project management to monitor progress. You, as a project manager, planned your project and got the final approval from your project sponsor. After the milestone dates and deliver dates have been shared with the project sponsor, you must share progress reports with the project sponsor. Project sponsor must know whether the project is in progress. If there are problems in the project, for instance, project might be behind schedule; in this case, additional funding might be needed to add additional resources to the project to complete the project on time. At this point, project sponsor should find the additional funding if contingency and management reserves do not satisfy the required amount.

- **During Executing, Monitoring and Controlling Phases:** What are the roles of project sponsor during closing phase?

  - **Provides formal acceptance of deliverables:** Project sponsor provides formal acceptance of deliverables in closing phase. If you remember from the previous notes, the interim deliverables were being delivered during project and these were validated by the customer whenever they were finished during execution of the project. However, the formal acceptance of the final deliverables or the final project approval is done by the project sponsor. Note that, this is not the validation or the acceptance of all interim deliverables. Project sponsors are busy and executive people. The cannot dive into the tiny details of projects. The formal acceptance here means the final acceptance of the overall project. Generally, these interim validations or interim checks are done by other people in the organization and by the customer.
  - **Supports collection of historical info from past projects:** Project sponsor supports collection of historical information from past projects. Once you complete your project, you have to conclude your lessons learned documentation. During this phase, you can ask your sponsor to give inputs about lessons learned for this project.

Role of the Project Team

Before we see the role of the project team, let us define what "project team" is first. Project team is group of people who will complete the work on project. If you consider a software development project, business analysts, software engineers, test engineers are all part of the project team. Each project team member can have individual project activities or they may work together on some project activities.

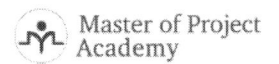

- **One of the roles of this project team is creation of WBS.** After your scope is defined, the high-level deliverables or work packages are defined by the team members, in other words, project team. Once these work packages and high-level deliverables of the project are defined, you construct your WBS in the project. If you remember from the previous notes, WBS was one of the fundamental bricks of a project and shows the work package and project activity hierarchy in a project.
- **Time and cost estimation.** Time estimates for each project activity are collected from the project team members who will perform the task. Therefore, these time and cost estimations are done by the project team. Each individual who will perform a specific activity or specific task in the project will make the estimation.
- **Completion of activities and determination of variances.** Once you have completed your planning, you will assign each activity to an individual in your project team. These individuals will perform their activities or their tasks in the project. Project team members will determine the variances as well.

  For example, you might tell a software developer to complete a specific web page in ten days. Software developer might complete this task in 12 days with 2 days delay. In this case, he should notify you that he completed his activity two days later. Alternatively, if he sees that he will exceed the time estimate he did in the planning phase of the project, he should notify you upfront, before he finishes his work. By this way, you can take preventive and corrective actions to accommodate delays.
- **Identifying and involving stakeholders.** During planning or later in the execution phase of the project, team members might identify new stakeholders. In addition, whenever they identify new stakeholders, they should share this information with you and you should involve those stakeholders in your project.

  For instance, in your software project, one of your software developers might come to you and tell that he notified another software developer from another project working on the same database. In this case, you should coordinate your project activities with the other project in order to not interfere each other.
- **Identifying requirements:** Project requirements are collected from several stakeholders. As an internal stakeholder of the project, project team members might identify new requirements. These should be considered during project management.
- **Identifying constraints and assumptions:** During project planning and later in the project execution, project team members might identify new requirements or assumptions. For instance, one of the construction workers in a construction project might come and warn the project manager about weather conditions that might hamper the project.
- **Identifying dependencies between activities.** For example, if a specific activity will start after another activity finished, this means a finish to start dependency. These types of mandatory or discretionary dependencies should be defined by the project team during planning.
- **Recommending changes to project.** Whenever a project team member sees a better way of completing a specific activity, he should give input to the project manager. On the other hand, if there are deviations, for example, if a specific activity is behind schedule, then, if the project team member has ideas about how he can correct this variance, he should share his ideas with the project manager.

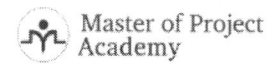

Role of the Stakeholders

A project stakeholder is anyone who can positively or negatively influence the project. Basically, project team members, project sponsor, customer are all parts of the project stakeholder. Power and influence of each stakeholder vary on a project. Therefore, specific stakeholder management strategy for each stakeholder must be developed. We will see this in our further notes.

- **Stakeholders might be in creation of project charter and project scope statement as well.** As an affected party from the project outcomes, project stakeholders express their requirements and expectations during project charter creation and project scope state development. These requirements are evaluated and finalized by the project team under the supervision of the project manager.
- **Stakeholders might be part of the change control board and approve or reject changes.** For instance, manager of a functional department might be part of the change control board and during evaluation of a change request, he might express his thoughts on the change.
- **Stakeholders validate scope. Stakeholders express their requirements and expectations from a project.** Once the project deliverables are ready, stakeholders check the results and validate the scope. For instance, customer checks the end product whether it meets its expectations.
- **Stakeholders may become risk response owners at the end of the risk management planning.** We will see in risk management section that each identified risk will have a risk response owner. Moreover, in case that risk occurs, risk response owner should act to accommodate impacts of risks.

Role of the Functional Manager

Functional managers manage and own the resources in a specific department.

For instance, software development manager manages the software developers under his line. Alternatively, test department manager manages the test engineers reporting to him or her. In other words, functional managers direct technical work of resources.

For example, Software Development Manager in a company directs the technical work; technical software development works in a company. He assigns technical tasks that needs to be done to his team members and checks whether there are any technical issues in their progress. In case the team needs help, he assists and guides on solving problems.

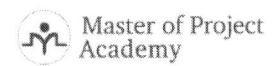

- **Assign resources to projects.** When resources are needed for the projects, functional managers assign resources to projects. For instance, if a project needs two software developers for his project, he needs to contact with the software development manager to assign developers to his project.
- **Functional managers provide subject matter expertise.** Functional managers are generally high-skilled technical people. Therefore, they provide subject matter expertise in projects if needed.

  For example, we expect a Software Development Manager to have a significant software development experience. Therefore, if there is a technical issue in the project or if there is a topic that needs to be illuminated by a subject matter expert, functional managers can assist at this point.
- **Functional managers approve final schedule and project management plan.** Because once the project plan is complete, the project manager will have what kind of resources he or she will need and when they are required as well.

  For instance, after a software project plan is complete, project manager might state that he will need two software developers in March 4 software developers in April and three software developers in May. Functional manager will assign resources to the project based on the project plan. Therefore, he needs to be aware of the plan to assign resources to the several projects of an organization respectively. If you do not get the approval of functional manager, you might have difficulties in finding resources you need when the time comes to get resources.
- **Functional manager manages activities in his functional area.** For example, marketing department manager in a company manages the marketing activities, the operational work related to marketing the company and they assist problems on their team faces.
- **Functional managers assist problems about team member performance.** Assume that a software engineer has been assigned to your project, and you are suffering performance problems about this individual. After you tried to identify the reasons of his underperformance, you could not find anything. You can ask to his functional manager about his underperformance in order to find the real cause, real problem about his underperformance. In these cases, functional managers can assist to find the problems about team member's performance.
- **Functional managers improve staff utilization.** It is better to first explain what utilization is. Say, there are 20 working days in a month and if a resource is working in a project or working in another assignment for 18 days of this month. In this case, 18 over 20, which makes 90% is the utilization ratio for this resource.

  Since there are several requirements, several resource requirements coming from several projects in an organization, functional manager evaluates these requests and tries to increase the staff utilization in his department. Generally, functional managers have utilization targets in corporate companies. For example, they have an average utilization target of 80%, which means in average, each resource might be charged or might be assigned to a project in 80% of the working days in a year.

Role of the Project, Portfolio & Program Manager

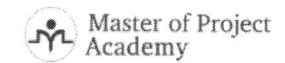

We have seen the project, program, portfolio and their interrelationship with other. During this heading, we will be seeing the role of project manager, portfolio manager and program manager briefly.

What is the role of the project manager?

- **Project manager manages the project to meet project objectives.** There are many roles for the project manager in a project. I said, we need to keep it brief here. Here, I listed the most important role of the project manager in a project. Because we have covered the other roles of the project manager during the other sections.
As a project manager, you have to meet schedule objectives, cost objectives, quality objectives, etc., in your project in order to complete your project successfully.

What is the role of the portfolio manager?

- **Portfolio manager is responsible for governance at an executive level of the projects or programs that make up a portfolio.** If you remember from our previous notes, portfolio was consisting of projects or programs. However, projects or programs under a portfolio might not be entirely related with each other. Important point here is, projects and programs under the same portfolio must assist to attain a strategic goal in a company.
- **Portfolio managers manage various projects or programs that might be unrelated to each other.** As we discussed already, there might not be any interrelation between the programs or projects under a portfolio.
- **Portfolio managers work with senior management for providing support to projects.** Since portfolio managers aim to achieve a strategic goal of a company, they work with the senior management of the company. Because senior management of the company directs the company and sets the strategic goals that needs to be achieved with the portfolios, programs and projects.
- **Portfolio manager gets the best return from resources invested.** Generally, portfolio managers look on the financial and strategic side of the project or programs under their portfolio. They take actions to get the most possible output from a resource invested

What is the role of the program manager?

- **Program manager manages a group of interrelated projects.** If you remember from the previous notes, interrelated projects with each other were grouped under programs. Program manager manages these interrelated projects.
- **Program manager supports and guides individual project managers.** Since interrelated projects are grouped under program and since there are project managers associated with each project under the program, these project managers are reporting to program manager. Therefore, program managers support and guide these individual project managers.

Plan Resource Management Process

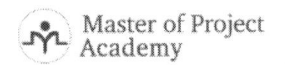

Plan resource management is the first process of resource management knowledge area.

Plan resource management is the process of identifying and documenting project roles, responsibilities, and required skills, reporting relationships, and creating a staffing management plan.

> Briefly, plan resource management process will guide on who will report to who and who will be responsible of what in a project.

- **Plan resource management process establishes project roles and responsibilities, project organization charts and staffing management plan.** Project roles and responsibilities will clear out who will do what in a project. For instance, software development lead might be responsible of checking the outputs of other software engineers from technical point of you. Test engineer can be responsible of conducting test activities of the project.
- **Project organization chart shows the hierarchy of the team.** For instance, a software engineer can be reporting first to the software development lead, and software development lead can be reporting to the project manager. These kinds of project hierarchical relationship are shown in project organization chart.
- **Staffing management plan includes who will work when, resource calendars, staff release plan, training needs etc.** We will go over staffing management plan in detail in our further notes.

Inputs for Plan Resource Management Process

First input for plan resource management process is enterprise environmental factors. As you remember, one of the main aspects of enterprise environmental factors was company culture and existing systems. During plan resource management process, following questions are answered.

- **What organizations will be involved in project?** For example, which departments of your company will be related with this project? Which department should support this project? Whether there will be other companies which will be working with your organization on a specific project. These are all defined as a factor under enterprise environmental factors.
- **Are there any hidden agendas?** If there are specific dates, if there are specific "off" days, if there are specific target dates for the company, these are all defined as an input of the enterprise environmental factors in plan resource management process.
- **Is there anyone who does not want project?** This is important. Because, if there are stakeholders that do not want your project to reach success, and if these stakeholders have high influence and power in the organization, you need to be very careful when managing the project. For example, let us say you are delivering a new technology project to a customer, and once your project is successfully delivered, some of the employees who are using old technology will be fired, or pushed to relocate to another department. In this case, most probably those people who do not know the new technology, and accustomed to work with old technology, will not want your project to be completed successfully. This should be highlighted in plan resource management. This case will be even more critical if your project needs support from this group of people.

- **What is the availability of training for the team members?** If there are specific skills, specific competencies that will be needed for your project team, these should be evaluated in plan resource management process. For example, let us say you will be managing a software development project and at the end of your project you are aiming to build a webpage for your customer. If your customer requires the project to be completed in "Sprint" technology, which is a web development technology in software development, and if your resources have little knowledge about this "Sprint" technology, you might need to organize a training for your resources in your project to teach them "Sprint". Therefore, these kinds of evaluations, whether your resources will require a training, should be done in plan resource management process.
- **Organizational process assets are another input for the plan resource management process.** Organizational process assets are the processes, procedures, and historical information about project. For example, if you have a common template for roles, or responsibilities for similar projects in your organization, then these templates for roles and responsibilities can be used in repetitive projects, or in similar projects. Therefore, these common templates can be used as an input to your plan resource management process.

Organization Charts & Position Descriptions

It is very important to show roles and responsibilities to the project team in a transparent way. This is done with the help of organization charts and position descriptions.

There are several ways to show roles and responsibilities in a project. Most of the common formats are in the following three forms:
- Hierarchical,
- Matrix and
- Text-oriented.

1. **Hierarchical-Type charts:** Hierarchical-type charts are used to show positions and relationships in a graphical top-down format. Positions or departments in the lower level hierarchy are connected to the upper level positions or departments with lines and positions that are connected to a box reports to that position owner or department. Example for these hierarchical-type charts are organizational breakdown structure, OBS, and resource breakdown structure, RBS. We will be going over each of them one-by-one.

    - **Organizational Breakdown Structure (OBS):** This chart is an example for organizational breakdown structure.

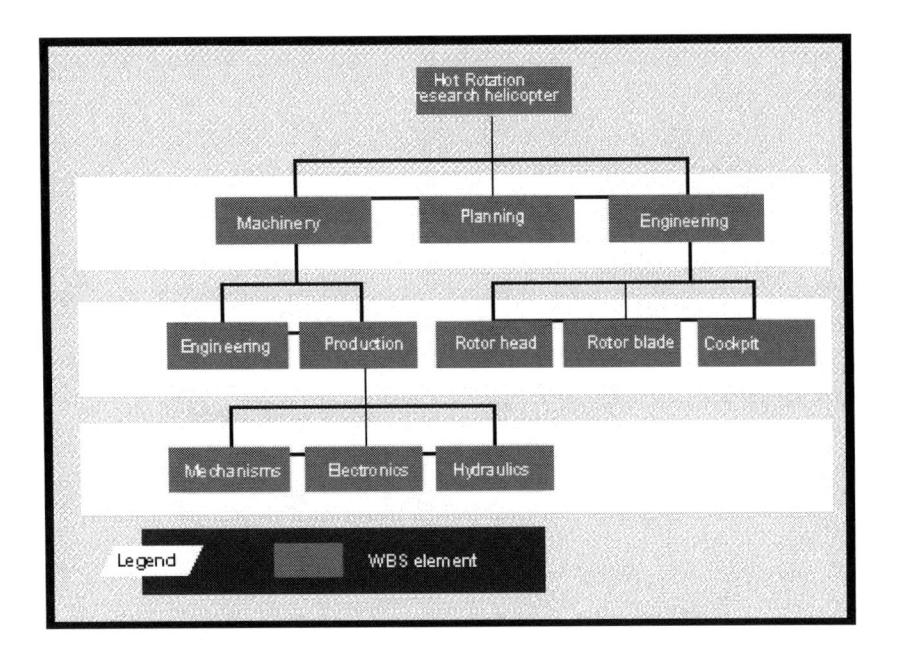

As you see, it shows the responsibility by department. This is an OBS for hot rotation research helicopter project. As you see, there are three departments, machinery, planning, and engineering. Machinery department will do the engineering work and the production work. The engineering department will do the rotor head, rotor blade, and cockpit parts of the project. There are other levels under production work as well.

- **Resource Breakdown Structure (RBS):** It breaks down the work by type of resource.

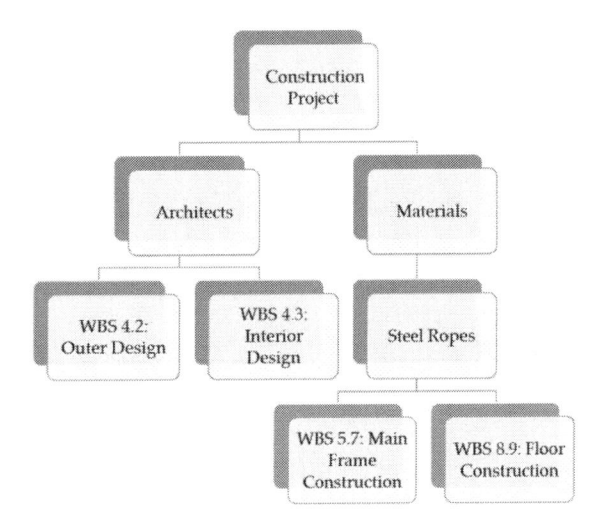

For example, we have a construction project and architects will do the WBS 4.2 Outer Design, and WBS 4.3 Interior Design. Second branch of the project is materials box. Note that human resources and the materials, tools, equipment are resources of a project. Steel ropes are resources of your project belonging to materials based on this chart. Under the steel ropes box, we see two work packages: WBS 5.7 frame construction and WBS 8.9 floor construction.

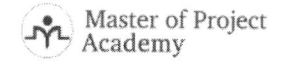

As you see, which type of resource will be used in which work is identified in resource breakdown structure.

2. **Matrix-Based Charts:** These are used to show who is responsible for what in a project. The two common types of these matrixes are Responsibility Assignment Matrix, RAM, and RACI Matrix. RACI stands for responsible, accountable, consulted and informed respectively. Actually, RACI is a more detailed version of responsibility assignment matrix.

    o **Here we see an example of responsibility assignment matrix, RAM.**

Activity	Team Member			
	Jess	Paul	Erica	Jude
A	P		S	
B		S		P

Key: P = Primary responsibility, S = Secondary responsibility

We see two activities in the chart. Activity A and activity B. We see four resources, Jess, Paul, Erica, and Jude. As you see, activity A is on responsibility of Jess primarily and it is under responsibility of Erica secondarily. Therefore, the primary responsible of activity A is Jess and the secondary responsible of activity A is Erica. Similarly, for activity B, primary responsible is Jude and the secondary responsible is Paul.

    o **An example for RACI Matrix.**

RACI Chart	Project Team Members				
Activity/Task	Ryan	Sue	Bill	Jack	Emily
List activities	I	A	R	C	C
Gather stakeholder requirements	A	C	I	I	R
Prepare coding environment	A	R	I	I	I
Create test scripts	I	A	R	R	C

This is actually a detailed form of RAM matrix. As you see for each activity, who is responsible, who is accountable, who is consulted, and who is informed are defined in the matrix. For example, let us look at gather stakeholder requirements activity as example to examine. Bill and Jack is informed for this activity. Therefore, we should give information to them about the outputs, about the change of this activity. Ryan will be accountable for this gather stakeholder requirements activity. Therefore, Ryan is the reporting person about this activity. Emily is the responsible person for gathering stakeholder requirements, so, Emily will be performing this activity. Sue is consulted for the gather stakeholder requirements activity, which means, you can ask, you can consult to Sue on how you can gather requirements; how you can do specific activities under collect requirements etc.

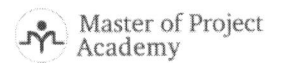

- **Text oriented formats:** These are used to show responsibility in detailed descriptions. Text-oriented formats include information about responsibilities, authority, competencies, and qualifications.

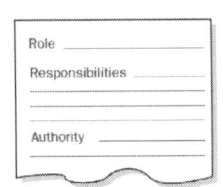

    - **Responsibilities:** Responsibilities define what you will do and what your activities are in a project.
    - **Authority:** Authority defines your decision level. What kind of initiatives you can take on your own without asking to an upper person in the organization? Authority clarifies this.
    - **Competencies:** Competencies define what a person knows about a topic. For example, team-leading, contract management, risk management etc. are all examples of competencies for a project manager. Similarly, other resources in the project will have relevant competencies. For instance, a software developer might have database programming skills, web development skills etc.
    - **Qualifications:** Qualifications define the specific skills required for a role. For example, if you will be assigning a project manager and PMP certification is required for this role, then you should list in the qualifications area of this text-oriented format in your project.

Resource Management Plan

- **Output of Plan Resource Management process:** The major output of the plan resource management process is resource management plan.
- **Part of project management plan:** As all other management plans, resource management plan is also part of the project management plan.
- **Provides guidance on how project resources should be defined, staffed, managed and eventually released:** Resource management plan provides guidance on how project resources should be defined, staffed, managed and eventually released. From project start till end, resource management plan describes how you should determine the project resource requirements, how you will train the project team, how you will recognize and reward well performing team members, how you will release when the activities of a project team member are complete etc. Briefly, resource management plan is a complete guide on how to manage people in a project.
- **Roles and responsibilities:** Resource management plan includes roles and responsibilities. Here, we will describe four important terms one-by-one: role, authority, responsibility, and competency.

- **Role:** Role is the function assumed by or assigned to a person in the project. For example, civil engineer, analyst etc. Actually, it is the title, it is the position for the resource in the project. Generally, title or role of the resource is same in the organization as well.
- **Authority:** Authority is the right to apply project resources, make decisions, sign approvals, accept deliverables, and influence others to carry out the work of the project. In summary, authority defines the decision level of the person or the level of taking initiatives on her own or on his own in a project. For instance, project charter gives authority to project manager to execute the project, spend budget allocated for the project, assign activities to the resources in the project etc.
- **Responsibility:** Responsibility is assigned duties and work to a team member. For example, John will perform tasks A, B, C. It defines actually who will perform what task in a project.
- **Competency:** Competency is the skill and capacity required to complete project activities. For example, software developers must know web development technology Sprint. Project manager must have an experience of software project management. These are examples of required competencies for a software project.

Resource management includes:

- **Project Organization Charts:** We have seen different types of organization charts in previous notes. Once you defined which type of chart you will use, these organization charts should be included in your resource management plan. These will define who will report to who in your project or work organization in the project.
- **Staffing Management Plan:** Staffing management plan is another output of plan resource management process. Staffing management plan is part of resource management plan, and it describes when and how project team members will be acquired and how long they will be needed in the project. We will be seeing staffing management plan in detail in our next heading.

Staffing Management Plan

We have seen in our previous heading that, staffing management plan is part of resource management plan. During this heading, we will be going over what staffing management plan includes.

- **Plan for Staff Acquisition:** Staffing management plan includes plan for staff acquisition. For example, whether your HR, human resource department, will hire new employees for the project or whether they actually exist in your organization and you will be contacting with functional managers to get required resource for the project. In some cases, subject matter experts might be needed in the project, and these resources might be outsourced from another organization. These plans for staff acquisition should be mentioned in your staffing management plan.

- **Resource Calendars:** Resource calendar is also included in staffing management plan. Resource calendars contain information about who will be available when. For example, if there are specific resources, which will go for annual leave during execution of your project, you have to consider these "off days" of these resources when you are developing your project schedule. Therefore, resource calendars are important. Similarly, if there is a part-time resource who will be working in your project, you should know his or her "off days" in a workweek in order to make proper schedule your project.

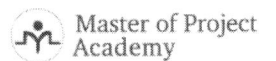

- **Staff Release Plan:** Staff management plan also includes staff release plan. How you will release resources once their activities in your project have been accomplished is covered in the staff release plan. For instance, you might need one software engineer for 6 months and one software engineer for 3 months. These release plans should be included in the staffing management plan.

- **Training needs:** Training needs of the resources are also part of staffing management plan. Say a specific training about a specific topic is needed for your resources because they are not well equipped for this topic. In this case, you have to organize training for your resources, and these training needs for your resources should be mentioned in staffing management plan.

- **Recognition and Rewards:** Recognition and rewards is very important. If a resource in your project is over performing or showing a desired behavior, you should recognize him or her in a visible and transparent way in your project, and this recognition should be done in front of the project team. Because recognitions and rewards motivate well-performing resources and encourage the project resources to perform better. Rewards for the project resources can be a gift card, 2-day holiday, bonus salary etc. These are outlined in the policies of human resources department of the company as well.

- **Compliance:** Compliance means how you are in line with the regulations of your company or with the labor law in a country. For example, if there are specific rules that you cannot exceed a limit of overtime in a country, this should be mentioned in staffing management plan. Say, if you cannot exceed four hours of overtime for a project resource in a week in the country where you are managing your project, you should be compliant with this labor law.
- **Safety:** Safety component of the staffing management plan covers how you will ensure the safety of your project team resources. For instance, in a construction project, all project resources must wear helmet when they are in the construction area.

Resource Histogram

Resource histogram is part of the staffing management plan.

> Resource histogram shows required number of hours that will be needed from each department or person for each week or month during the project.

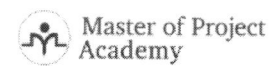

Let us go through an example resource histogram

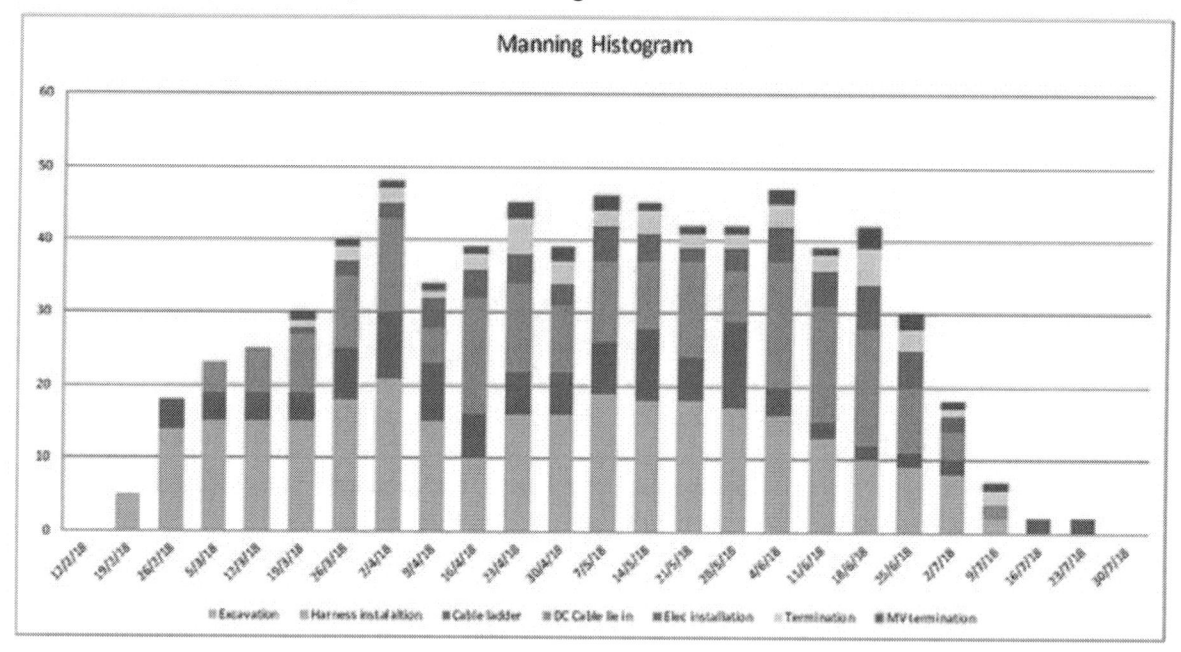

Manning Histogram

Here, we see the number of personnel working in a project and their distribution by specialties week by week. For instance, on 19th of Feb 2018 week, around five people from excavation team will be working. Peaks of the number of personnel who will be working on the project will be on 2nd of April and 4th of June weeks. Nearly 50 personnel will be working on the project during these weeks.

Recognition & Rewards Systems

As we have seen in the previous notes, recognition and rewards system is critical aspect of a project. Desired behaviors and over performers must be recognized and rewarded in the project to encourage all project team. This should be done with a transparent recognition and rewards system.

- **Part of Staffing Management Plan:** Recognition and rewards systems is part of staffing management plan. We have seen how to recognize and give rewards to project resources in previous notes. We will be going over the details of a recognition and rewards system in this heading.

- **Project managers must be able to motivate the team.** Because if you motivate the team and if your resources are motivated to work, then you will have the maximum output from your project team. In the end, this will ensure the to meet the project goals and objectives.

- **Recognition and Rewards System may include:**
    - say "thank you" more often to your project team members,
    - award prizes such as "member of the month", or
    - The most successful or the most performing person of the project must be awarded.

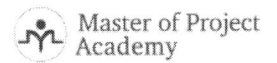

We will see in the further notes that good salary and compensation packages are hygiene factors. As long as they are over an acceptable limit, more salary will not motivate the resources as must as a good recognition or reward. Therefore, well performers must be recognized and awarded in a project. By this way, they will be motivated better and produce better results respectively.

Prizes can be a two-day holiday, bonus salary, sending to a special event, gift card etc. Note that, prizes must be in line with the human resources department policies.

Recognition and rewards system may include:

- **Sending notes to team member's manager about over performers.** Because, if you are working in a matrix organization, the end year performance review will be done most probably by the functional manager of the resource, and in order to consider his over performance in a project, you should send notes to the functional manager of your resources if they over performed in the project.

- **Plan milestone parties.** Once you passed a specific milestone in your project, you should celebrate this with your project team and these parties will increase the belonging of the project resources to the project team and motivate the resources. For instance, once you completed software development phase of a project, you can organize a milestone party.

- **Acquire training for members.** Resources might be motivated by attending in trainings in the areas they are interested in. For example, a software developer might be interested in learning machine learning skills. As a reward for this project resource, you can send him or her to a machine learning course.

Estimate Activity Resources Process

Estimate activity resources process briefly helps to assign which resources in the project will do which project activities.

- **Estimate activity resources is the process of estimating the type and quantities of material, human resources, equipment, or supplies required to perform each activity.** In order to complete a project activity, you will need performer of the task, for instance software developer for a software project or civil engineer for a construction project. Materials that will be used to produce the project deliverable. For instance, cement, wood, steel etc. will be used during construction. Equipment will be used such as trucks, cranes to lift and place the materials. Estimate activity resources process provides the estimation of all these in a project.

- **Once the activities are sequenced, the type and quantity of needed resources are determined.** For instance, how many construction workers, how many civil engineers you will need for the construction project and the amount of the cement, steel, wood etc. that will be used during the project are determined during the Estimate activity resources process.

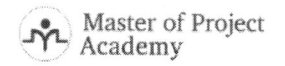

What is involved in the Estimate Activity Resources process?

- **Reviewing resource availability.** Some of the needed project resources might not be present in your company. For instance, for a niche software development project requiring specific set of skills, your company might not have any software developer meeting the requirements. In this case, alternatives such as outsourcing the required resource or hiring a new software developer must be planned.

- **Reviewing WBS and Activity List.** Since activity resources will be estimated for the project activities, and these activities belong to the WBS and part of activity list, WBS and activity list must be reviewed during the Estimate Activity Resource Process. Necessary resource estimations will be done for each activity in the activity list respectively.

- **Identifying potentially available resources.** If it is possible to allocate who will do a specific project activity, these must be identified during estimate activity resources process.

- **Reviewing historical info about reuse of resources.** If there had been a similar project in the organization, that would be very useful for you to check what kind of resources have been used. Because, most probably, you will use similar resources in your project as well.

- **Reviewing organizational policies on resource usage.** There might be policies and guidelines on how to request a resource, how to assign a task, how to monitor etc. For instance, many corporate companies use PPM tool of HP. This tool helps to monitor project phases, assign activities to project team members and time reporting. These kinds of organizational policies on resource usage must be followed during the estimate activity resources process.

- **Expert judgement on what resources are needed and available.** Based on the project activities, what kind of competence and experience must be looked in the project team member candidates can be obtained from subject matter experts. The outputs of the experts will guide you on how to form project team respectively.

- **Analysis of alternatives whether they are better to utilize resources.** For instance, if you will need a graphic designer for your project and this team member will work only 2 days a week, it will not be a good solution to dedicate this resource completely on the project. This can be outsourced to a vendor and required work might be acquired from them respectively. This will be less costly than hiring a new graphic designer or dedicating a resource 100% on the project.
- **Make or buy decisions are taken during estimate activity resources process.** Assume that you need a crane for your construction project and you will need this only for 2 months and this is not a tool that your company uses in other projects. If the cost of the crane is $500,000 and rental cost of the crane for 2 months is $100,000, it will be a good decision to rent the crane. These kinds of make or buy decisions are taken during estimate activity resources process.

- **Breaking down the activity further if it is still complex to estimate.** Although WBS is created and activity list is composed, some activities might be still large enough to estimate. In this case, further breakdown of an activity can be done during the Estimate Activity Resources process.

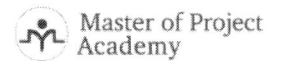

- **Quantify resource requirements by activity.** If you are managing a software project, you know that you will need analysts, software architects, software engineers, testers etc. However, do you know how many from each of these roles you will need? Estimate activity resources process will help to quantify resource requirements by activity.

- **Create a hierarchical structure of resources.** Actually, this is Resource Breakdown structure and abbreviated as RBS. For instance, if you have four software engineers in the software project and three of them are reporting to one lead software engineer, this must be highlighted during estimate activity resources process.

- **Develop plan as to what type of resources will be used.** As we expressed already, roles you need in the project team, their hierarchy, skills and competence must be highlighted during estimate activity resources process.

- **Update Project Documents.** As in many other processes, activities done in the estimate activity resources process require update of project documents as well.

Estimate Activity Resources Process Example

During this heading, we will go over our billing system project example and show you how estimate activity resources process can be for this sample project.

We have determined the activities of invoicing screen in our previous notes. There are four activities: analysis, design, development and test.

During Estimate Activity resources process, these activities are assigned to project team members, their role, experience and skills are mentioned as well.

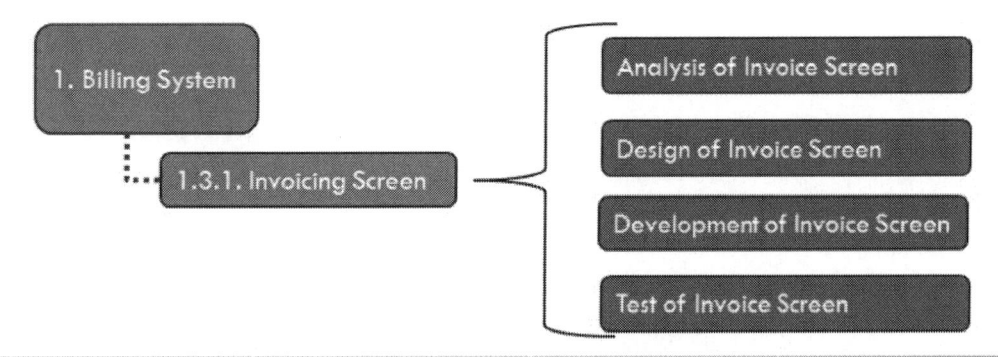

Activity (Task)	Assignee	Role	Experience
Analysis of Invoice Screen	David Sea	Analyst	10+
Design of Invoice Screen	Emily Lee	Designer	5+
Development of Invoice Screen	Jon Huyton	Software Developer	8+
Test of Invoice Screen	Ed Liu	Test Engineer	7+

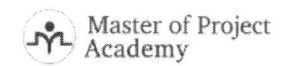

As you see in the table below, analysis of the invoice screen is assigned to David Sea and he is Analyst in the project team. He has over 10 years of experience. Design of the invoice screen is assigned to Emily Lee and he is designer in the project team. He has more than 5 years of experience. Development of invoice screen is assigned to Jon Huyton and he is software developer with more than 8 years of experience. Finally, test task is assigned to Ed Liu, test engineer with over 7 years of experience. Note that, this sample shows only human resources. Normally, if there would be any tool, equipment or material that will be used during an activity, these must be placed in the plan as well. For instance, if test engineer will use a test automation tool, this must be planned during estimate activity resources process as well.

Acquire Resource Process

- **Acquire resources is the process of confirming resource availability and obtaining the team necessary to complete project activities.** You do project planning, plan activities, schedules, resource requirements and determine which resources will work on your project. For instance, how many analysts or engineers will work on your project or for how long they will work. After this, you need to acquire required resources for your project.

- **This is actually acquiring the final project team.** In this process, you actually get the final resources of your project who will perform your project activities. See the inputs of the acquire resource process

Inputs of Acquire Resource Process

- There are three inputs for this process, Resource Management Plan, which was the output of plan resource management process, Enterprise Environmental Factors and Organizational Process Assets.

- **Resource management plan** shows how you will request project resources, who to contact and how to manage getting resources to your project. Enterprise Environmental Factors and Organizational process assets are input to this project as they were input in other processes. If there is a hiring policy of the company, this must be followed when hiring a new project resource to the project. Alternatively, if there is a resource request tool used to ask for resources from functional managers in the company, this must be used in this process as input.

- **Acquire resource process involves knowing pre-assigned resources and their availability.** We will see what pre-assignment is in our further notes. If there are scarce resources in your organization, for example, if there are resources having a very niche skill set, and if these resources might be required from several other projects at the same time, this should be planned and organized properly in order to not have a problem in the projects of your organization. Therefore, the pre-assignment should be done for these scarce resources or the resources that require a better, precise planning.

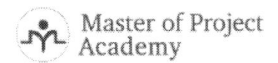

- **Hiring new employees.** If a specific skill set could not be found in a resource in your organization, then, you might need to acquire new resources to your company for your project. In this case, you need to hire new employees for your project.

- **Outsourcing from another organization.** Assume that you need a software developer in your project only for two months, then, hiring a new employee might not be feasible in this case. Therefore, you might ask for an external organization to send a consultant for your project. This is called outsourcing.

- **Require project team process also involves managing the risk of resources becoming unavailable.** For example, you could not find a resource who does not know a niche skill set. What will you do in this case? Assume that, you will need a database administrator who knows Oracle, and you could not find it within your organization. What would be your risk response for this case? Whether you will outsource this work completely to an Oracle database administration company, or look for other alternatives? These must be considered during acquire resources process.

Tools & Techniques Used in Acquire Resources Process

We will go through the tools & techniques used in acquire resources process during these headings. First one is Pre-assignment. We have actually defined this briefly in our previous notes.

- **Pre-assignment:** Pre-assignment is selecting project team members in advance. Pre-assignment generally happens if the project depends on specific resources or expertise. Since these specific resources or expertise are very rare in organizations and if these resources are required for many projects in the organization, then, these should be organized and planned properly. Otherwise, you cannot have the scarce resources you need in your project.

- **Negotiation:** Second technique is negotiation. Staff assignments are negotiated on many projects because in order to acquire the project resources to your team, you need to negotiate with other departments, other organizations, other companies, etc. To do this, project managers may need to negotiate with functional managers.
For example, if you are working in a matrix organization, you might need to ask for the functional managers of related departments for the resources, or other project management teams. Assume that a resource you need is working for another project. His or her task has been delayed and he could not come to your project at the time you planned in the beginning. In order to overcome these kinds of problems, you will need to speak with other project managers in your organization.

- **Project managers may need to negotiate with external organizations, vendors, suppliers, or contractors as well.** For example, assume that you are receiving materials from a supplier for your project. In order to agree the deadlines or time plan for the delivery of the materials you need, you have to negotiate with them.

- **During negotiations, Project Manager should know the needs of the project and its priority for the organization.** For example, if you do not know what material you will need or what skill set you need for a resource, then, you will not be able to define your requirements to your organization. In addition, knowing priority of your project for your organization is important. Assume that a resource is needed at the same time for your project and for another project. In this case, that resource should be provided to the project, which has higher priority in the organization. Because there is only one resource, but two projects need that resource at the same time. In order to overcome these kinds of conflicts in an organization, prioritization of the projects should be known by project managers.

- **Project managers should not ask for the best resources if it's not needed.** Assume that you need a software developer for an activity in your project, which can be performed by a junior developer. If you ask for a senior developer for this activity, then, although you could have completed or performed this activity at a cheaper cost, you have chosen to do it with a more expensive resource, which is senior developer. Therefore, if you do not really need a very skilled resource or very senior resource for your project, you should not ask for it. They will increase costs in your project.

- **A project manager should build relationships with the resource managers since you can ask their expertise when needed.** Resource managers or functional managers in an organization do not only provide resources for your project. They also help you when you have problems with the project resources, since they are the line managers or functional managers of your resources. Even if you do not face any problem with the resources, you might have specific technical issues, technical problems in your project. These resource managers or functional managers are generally the most experienced resources of a company on a specific topic. For example, software development manager is expected to be one of the most experienced developers in an organization. Therefore, if you are managing a software development project and if you have a specific software development issue or problem in your project, you might ask these problems, these issues to software development manager in your project in order to overcome these issues.

- **Acquisition:** Acquisition is another technique used in acquire resources process. If required resources cannot be found within an organization, acquisition takes place. Assume that, you require a resource with a specific skill set to work in your project.

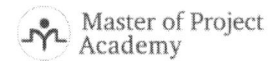

However, you could not find it in your organization, and then you should acquire it from another place.

- o **You can outsource individual consultants:** You can outsource individual consultants if you could not find a specific resource in your organization. For example, you can look at consultancy firms and you can hire, outsource consultants to your project for a limited period. Once your project is complete or once the assigned activity for these outsourced consultants have finished, you can release those resources.

- o **Another option is, you can subcontract a part of your work completely to another organization.** Assume that, you are working in an automotive company and you might say that electrical components of the car will be done by Company Z. Once electrical components of the car are ready, it can be integrated with the car during the project. This is an example of subcontracting a part of your work in your project.

Virtual Teams

Virtual team is a benefit came to the business with the globalization. Virtual teams are groups of people with a shared goal who fulfill their roles with little or no time spent meeting face to face. Therefore, virtual team is in summary, having people contributing to team from different geographical areas.

- **For some sectors, virtual teams are not possible to work with.** Can you do a virtual team for a construction project? No, because the work should take place in the construction site. Virtual teams are popular especially in IT sector. For instance, in a software project, software architects can be in Belgium while software developers in India and test engineers are in Bulgaria. This is an example of virtual team.
- **Generally, communication is done with emails, teleconference, social media, or web-based meetings**, since these people are working in different countries.
- **Virtual team model enables to form teams of people in widespread geographic areas.** We gave an example of this already. Different sub-teams or individuals of a project can work from different locations of the world. Their work is delivered and merge in online environments generally.
- **Virtual team adds special expertise to a project team even though the expert is not in the same geographic area.** Assume that you are working in a company and a very niche specific guru in a specific topic lives in Sweden. With the help of virtual team formation, you can have the expertise of this guru, although he lives in Sweden. You can have his opinions by enabling a virtual team in your project, and by the help of virtual team, you can get the required consultancy from this guru in your project.
- **Virtual team incorporates home office employees.** With the help of home office practices in companies, generally, the office fees, rental fees of offices and other administrative

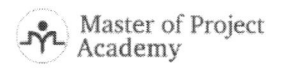

costs that are associated with the employees and buildings are reduced. Virtual team formation supports home office practices.
- **Virtual team also forms teams who work different shifts or days.** For example, in my previous job, there were three locations for giving support to customers for our telecommunication products all over the world. One geographical location was in India. The second geographical location was in Spain, and the other location was in South America. It was in Brazil. Since these locations have eight hours of difference from each other, this model was called, "follow the sun" which was ensuring 24 hours ongoing support for a ticket or for a problem raised by a customer.

  For example, when a customer raised a problem or raised a ticket about a product, it was received by an Indian engineer in India, and when he finished his working time in the evening, Spanish engineer comes to work and he can start to deal with the ticket until evening. If he could not resolve the issue until evening, then, and the last shift was in Brazil, so the Brazilian engineer was taking over the problem. By this way, by these shifts, the company was enabling 24 hours support for all tickets received by the customers.
- **Virtual team also enables, including people with mobility limitations or disabilities.** Because virtual team brings the flexibility that, everybody can work from everywhere. Therefore, if there are disabled people, or if there are mobility-limited people, you can have them in your team.
- **It reduces travel costs.** Since you can enable working in a virtual team environment, there will be no need or there will be very limited number of needs for travels, which will reduce your travel costs.

We have seen the benefits of virtual teams but there is other side of the coin as well. What are the disadvantages of virtual team model?

- **There is possibility of misunderstanding.** Always, the best way to communicate with another people is speaking or communicating face to face. However, in virtual team model, people communicate through emails, teleconference, or through web-based platforms and this can cause misunderstandings between the resources of a project team.
- **Feeling of isolation.** Assume that you are a home office employee working in your home but belonging to a company and working in a project. Since you are working always at home and contributing to a project in a virtual team model, this might cause you to lose your belongingness to your company because you are always working from home and you do not breath the company environment.
- **Another disadvantage of virtual team model is difficulties in sharing knowledge within a team.** Since the people in a virtual team are spread over different geographical areas, the sharing knowledge or the sharing experiences between the different team members in a project becomes more difficult. Sharing knowledge and experience is easier in a regular face to face working project team.
- **Cost of appropriate technology.** Assume that you require a teleconference system for enabling virtual team for your project and this might cost you an additional technological equipment needed for your project. Alternatively, other specific tools and environments might be needed to ensure cooperation of virtual teams.

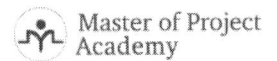

Halo Effect

Halo effect theory defines that promoting a well performing resource to a new position that he or she is not qualified can cause schedule, cost, and quality problems.

It was a given fact of the business world not more than a decade ago that, well-performing employees were promoted to a supervising or managerial position. However, a well-performing technical person may not be a well-performing supervisor or manager. If he or she is not qualified with his or her new position, this may cause problems.

Assume that you have a software developer working very well in your organization. In the next project, this software developer is assigned as a project manager in your organization. He might be a very good software developer in previous projects and he might have over performed in his activities. However, this does not mean that he is a good project manager or this does not mean that he fulfills the requirement or qualifications of project management position. Therefore, you might have problems in his project. This is called Halo Effect.

Develop Team Process

Develop Team is the process of improving competencies, team member interactions, and overall team environment, and enhance project performance.

In order to reach project goals and objectives, you must have a motivated and well-performing team.

Key benefits of this process are:
> improved teamwork,
> enhanced people skills and competencies,
> motivated employees,
> reduced staff turnover rates, and
> improved overall project performance.

These benefits will not only ensure a successful project completion but also increase the belongingness of the employee to the organization.

How do we develop a project team?

- **As a project manager, you should use many soft skills like mentoring, leadership, empathy, communication to your project team members.** Project manager is not only a person who assigns the tasks and monitors the health of the project. Project manager is the captain of the ship. Crew will like to get mentoring and leadership insights from the project manager.

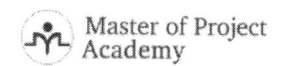

- **You must encourage teamwork because teamwork develops a project team. There is a limit of what you can do on your own.** You cannot do everything on your own. A specific resource can be perfect, but this does not mean that he or she can do all project work on his or her own. Therefore, you should encourage teamwork. Project is delivered with the project team and project team must work in a well harmony to complete the project successfully.

- **Communicate honestly to the project team.** You should not hide information or necessary information from your project team. For instance, if the project is behind schedule or if the customer is not happy with the deliverables, you should share these with your team in an appropriate manner.

- **Establish trust.** If project resources are not trusting to you, then you will have problems managing them. In order to establish trust, you must be transparent and fair in distributing activities. You must not do favor for a project resource that will demotivate another resource.

- **Collaborate with team.** You should always ask the opinion of the team when planning or when executing. If you make project decisions on your own, you might lose the motivation of your project team. If a decision will affect the project team or any individual project resource, you should make decisions in collaboration.

- **You must motivate your project team.** These can be recognitions, rewards or other forms or motivational activities. For instance, you can organize a social activity where all project team will attend.

- **You should establish ground rules.** We will define what ground rules are in our further notes. Briefly, ground rules define what is allowed and what is not allowed in project. For instance, you can prohibit checking emails or touching smart phones during team meeting to increase interaction. This is an example of ground rules.

Team-Building Activities

Team-building activities define forming the project team into a cohesive group for the best interest of the project, to enhance project performance. Briefly, team-building activities improve resources motivation and performance. This contributes to complete the project successfully.

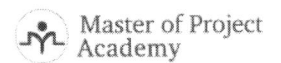

- **For example, WBS creation is a team-building tool.** Because, it shows the overall project work that needs to be completed by project team. It shows the project deliverables in a logical hierarchy. Since the project team sees what needs to be done during the project and how their work contributes to the completion of the project, WBS increases the motivation and dedication to the project.

- **Team building should start as early as possible in a project.** Because from initiation until closure, project resources will work in the project. If team building starts early, better performance can be achieved earlier in the project.

- **If the project team does not trust to the project manager, the project will suffer.** Because, if the project manager is not trusted, then, his assignments or management in a project will not be regarded as trustworthy by the project team members. This will cause de-motivation and suffer the delivery of the project respectively.

> Tuckman Ladder defines the formal stages of formation and team development in a project.

- **Tuckman proposes that a team follows five stages when team members work together in a project.** Tuckman Ladder defines the formal stages of formation and team development in a project.
    1. **Forming:** In this stage, people are brought together as a team. Therefore, this is the first stage and team members start to meet with each other. Because a team is formed in the beginning of the project.
    2. **Storming:** Since people start to work with each other, they start to know each other in a better way. In this stage, disagreements may arise as people learn to work together. These disagreements are important and may hamper the team's productivity. Disagreements must be moderated and resolved by the project managers when they arise.
    3. **Norming:** In this stage, team members start to build good working relationships with each other. After disagreements and negotiations, team members will know the boundaries and characteristics of other teammates. Good working relationships will be ensured respectively.
    4. **Performing:** In this stage, teams become efficient and work together. This is the stage where a team performs the best. Team members know each other in detail and they perform at their best since everybody knows each other well.
    5. **Adjourning:** In this stage, project ends, and the team is disbanded or the resources of the project are released.

Note that these stages are the regular stages for formation of the team development in the project. However, in some cases, teams can skip some stages of the Tuckman ladder and proceed with the other stages. For instance, if the resources of a project know each other from previous projects, then, first two or three stages can be skipped and project can start directly from the fourth stage. Therefore, depending on the project, depending on the people who know each other, these stages can be skipped in projects.

- **Team-building activities can be enrolling in trainings together with the project team.** For instance, if there is a technical or soft skill training that team needs to attend, enrolling in that training will be a team-building activity. During the training, resources will be interacting with each other and this will improve team collaboration.

- **Milestone celebrations are another example of team building activities.** Whenever you complete a milestone in your project, you can celebrate this with your project team. Milestone celebrations will encourage people in your team to accomplish other milestones and deliver your project successfully. Therefore, it is important.

- **Holidays and birthday celebrations are examples of team-building activities as well.** For instance, giving a one-day off to the team after a successful delivery or celebrating birthdays of each resource in project team are good practices of team-building activities.

- **Outside-of-work trips can contribute to team building as well.** For instance, going to picnic or trekking as a team can improve your projects performance since team members will interact with each other in a social environment.

- **As we have seen in the beginning, WBS is a team-building activity as well.** Because, it defines the hierarchy of project work that needs to be completed. Since project team can see the completed and remaining work in the WBS, it acts as a motivation figure. WBS also enables to see how a project team member's activity fits into the overall project work.

Tools & Techniques Used in Develop Team Process

During this heading, we will be going through tools and techniques used in develop team process.

- **Training:** Training is the first technique. All activities designed to enhance the competencies of the project team members are called as training. These can be soft skill trainings like effective communications, effective team leading, or they might be also technical trainings like software development, web development, etc. These training activities enhance the competencies of project resources.

    These trainings can be classroom trainings, online trainings, computer-based trainings, or on-the-job trainings. On-the-job training is a very trending training in recent years. In this training model, a new joiner to a company is accompanied by an existing or a senior resource in the company. While they are doing work together, the new joiner learns the job from the senior resource of the company.

    Training costs will be included in project budget if a training is required for a project. If a specific training is required, which is specific to your project, and if this skill or this knowledge will not be used by your resource in other projects in the organization, then, the cost of this training can be included in your project budget.

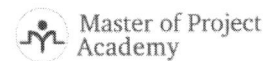

- **Ground Rules:** We have seen what a ground rule can be in previous notes. Here, we will give some examples about ground rules and we will give an official description of ground rules.

  Ground rules establish clear expectations regarding acceptable behavior by project team members. Ground Rules define what is acceptable and what is not acceptable in a project. In other words, it defines the project rules. For example, here, there are two examples of ground rules in a project.

  What is the way of interruption in a team meeting?
  Ground rule for this can be; you should wait until a team member finishes his sentences or you can dive in the middle of his sentences if he is talking about your activities. Is using phones or laptops are allowed in meeting? If you think that open laptops and smartphones distract your team members, then, you can establish a ground rule and disallow your resources to use their phones, laptops during your meetings.

- **Colocation or Tight Matrix:** Colocation is placing many or all of the most active project team members in the same physical location to enhance their ability to perform as a team.

  Assume that you are the project manager of a software development project. If all of your analysts, software engineers, test engineers and you work in same room, this will be an example of colocation. Colocation is referred as tight matrix as well. In some organizations, at critical stages of a project, project team comes together in a meeting room and works together. This is called as war room as well.

  This increases the productivity of your project team because they work in the same location. Sharing knowledge and sharing information will be easier. Instead of emailing or calling through phone, they will be able to talk interactively on about an issue. Therefore, this colocation technique in projects decreases conflicts, because, face-to-face communication always takes place in the war room. This increases performance of your project team.

- **Recognition and Rewards:** Recognition and rewards are planned in plan human resource management process. How you will recognize a team member, or what kind of rewards will be given to over performers are all defined in plan human resource management process. When you notice an over performer in your project team, these over performers are recognized and rewarded in develop project team process. Because, you have to see your project team in action to evaluate the resources' performance and this happens in execution stage.

  When giving recognitions or rewards to your project team members, cultural differences should be considered. For example, if you are working in the Middle East in a Muslim country, you cannot give a fifty-year-old wine as a prize to a Muslim team member. Because, as you know, alcohol is not allowed in their religion. Therefore, your Muslim team member can consider it as an abuse and this can distract not only his performance but also your relationship with him.

- **Team Performance Assessments:** In team performance assessments you look at the teams' effectiveness, how your team is operating, how they are working as a team, whether their productivity is at the required levels when you consider the overall team project performance etc. Performance of a successful team is measured in terms of technical success. For example, whether your project team is achieving the quality levels, which were planned in the beginning. Whether your project team is meeting the budget, you planned in the beginning. Whether your project team is meeting the deadlines of your project. These are all measured to evaluate team performance in a project.

Manage Team Process

This is the process of tracking team member performance, providing feedback, resolving issues and managing team changes to optimize project performance. In other words, this is actually day-to-day management of people. During project execution, you will assign project activities to your resources and they have to complete those activities in order to complete overall project work.

If there are problems in the activities or if there are performance problems in your project resources, you have to evaluate the reasons of the underperformance and you have to find solutions for these problems. You have to motivate these underperforming resources and this is critical for project success

> In other words, Manage Team Process is actually day-to-day management of people.

- **Manage Team process involves encouraging good communication.** Because good communication increases productivity in a project team. If you use inappropriate language to the resources, they will be demotivated and this will hamper the project.
- **Working with other organizations is part of manage team process.** For instance, if you are project manager of a construction project, you will contact with the suppliers during procurement. If you are project manager of a software project, then, you may need to contact with other vendors for acquiring a specific consultant to your project.
- **Using negotiation skills is a major aspect of manage team process.** Because, there will be conflicts in the project. In order to keep stakeholders engaged to the project, you need to solve conflict without demotivating a stakeholder. This requires negotiation skills.
- **Using leadership skills is required in manage team process.** In order to influence your project team members, you should use your leadership skills. Because you are managing them, and in order to direct them, in order to manage them to perform their activities,

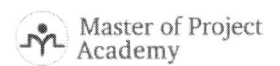

you should show your leadership skills. Do not forget that, project resources will look for leadership and mentoring from a project manager.
- **You should use issue logs during manage team process.** Issue logs define waiting topics or actions, expected actions from resources, reporting date of an issue, when an issue is opened, when it is closed etc. in detail. We will see an example of issue log in our next headings.
- **Making good decisions is also a part of manage team process.** During project execution, there will be plenty of situations that you need to make a decision. You should have required analytical reasoning skills in order to evaluate a situation and make optimum decisions.
- **Being a leader is critical in project management.** You are the captain of the team, and you have to lead your project team in order to reach project success.
- **Looking for conflicts and resolving them is part of manage team process as well.** Conflicts are inevitable in a project, but the important thing is how you resolve these conflicts. Because in most of the cases, even when you are thinking that you are resolving a conflict, you might be creating another conflict in your project. Assume that, there are two alternative solutions to fix a problem in the project. One of your resources are supporting one alternative while the other resource is in favor of another solution. While evaluating these alternatives and making a decision, you should not lose the commitment and engagement of resources.

Tools & Techniques Used in Manage Team Process

During this heading, we will be going over the tools & techniques used in manage team process.
- **Observation and Conversation:** First technique in manage team is observation and conversation.
  - **This technique is used to stay in touch with the work and attitudes of project team members.** In order to evaluate the motivation of project resources, you have to be in touch with the project team members. You have to talk about their activities, impediments, or issues that cause lower performance. The best way to get information about an activity in a project is going into conversation with the project team members.
  - **Project management team tracks how project work is done.** If you remember from our previous notes, project management team consists of project managers and team leaders. Project management team is responsible for monitoring how project work is done. For instance, software team leader of a project team must watch out the quality of the produced code, whether the software developers can finish the project work on time etc. The project manager must monitor the overall deliverables of the project, whether the projects is on track, on budget etc.
- **Project performance appraisals:** Project performance appraisals are another technique used in manage team process. Project performance appraisals are inputs about individuals' performance in project. These show whether a project resource performed as expected or not. It includes technical and soft skills evaluation of the project resources.

- o **Project performance appraisals can be provided by coworkers, subordinates or supervisors.** If a project resource is evaluating another project resource in a similar hierarchical level in the project, this is an example of coworker project performance appraisal. If a project resource is evaluating his team leader or project manager, this is an example of subordinate project performance appraisal. If a project manager or team leader is evaluating a project resource reporting to himself or herself, this is an example of supervisor project performance appraisal.
  - o **Team Performance Assessment & Project Performance Appraisals:** Note that we have seen two terms until now about performance. Team performance assessment and project performance appraisals. Team performance assessment is actually a team evaluation. In team performance assessment, you evaluate the productivity performance of the overall project team, whether your project team is achieving your project targets or project goals. However, in project performance appraisals, you are evaluating your team members' individual performance. Therefore, they are different.

- **Issue Log:** We have described the issue log previously. Here, we will see an example of issue log. Many project managers keep a log of issues to be resolved in the project. Actually, this is a must to not get lost in lots of actions that needs to be tracked in a project.

ID	Description	Date Raised	Issue Owner	Impact	Recovery Plan	Update	Status
1	No space to set up project office	10/07/2011	Ellie	High	Locate space	17/7/11: Ellie sourced alternative building for project office. Moving in early August.	Closed
2	Budget for Phase 2 has not yet been approved	11/07/2011	Claude	High	Prepare strategy paper for Project Board meeting explaining scope of Phase 2 and budget forecast.	In progress	Open
3	Test data will not be available until October. This will delay the testing phase and the eventual go live date	30/07/2011	Marylin	Medium	Discuss with test manager and replan team's activities to enable a smaller set of data to be used for testing	1/8/11: Marylin is meeting with the test manager this week	Open

For example, here in this issue log sample, there are three issues. First one is "no space to set up project office" is already closed.

Look at the second issue tells, "Budget for phase two has not yet been approved". The issue owner is Claude. In addition, you see the date of issue or date raised, July 11th, 2011, and we see the recovery plan for this issue. Therefore, it clarifies what will be the next action if this issue is not resolved on time. We also see the impact of this issue if it does not happen. It is classified as a "high" priority issue.

There is also an update column and a status column in the issue log. As we see, it is still open and assigned to Claude. Therefore, this issue needs to be resolve or managed by Claude.

You can have several other columns in an issue log depending on your project dynamics. We have just given an example of project issue log to illustrate this concept better.

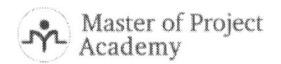

Powers of the Project Manager

You can use different types of power when getting cooperation from the team and stakeholders.

Mainly, there are 5 different types of power in project managers. We will be going over each type of power one-by-one.

- **Formal (Legitimate):** First one is formal or legitimate power. Legitimate power of the project manager comes with the nature of the project manager's position. Project resources report to the project manager, and resources must to do what project manager assigns in a project.
You see an example here. *"You need to listen to me, I am in charge!"* Here, you are using your position. You are emphasizing to project team member that you are the project manager and the team member should listen to you. Therefore, this is an example of using formal power.

- **Reward:** Second type of project manager power is Reward. Reward power of the project manager stems from giving a reward. For example, you can say to a project team member, "based on your performance, you will code the screen you want as next assignment". Therefore, you are rewarding him that if he performs well in his current activity, he will have the preference to select the screen he will code as next assignment. There can be alternative rewards to motivate team members as well

- **Penalty (Coercive):** Third type of project manager power is Penalty or coercive power. Penalty power of project manager gives the authority to penalize the team members. For example, you can state that "team members overdue in their tasks will not attend to company party". Catching deadlines in a project is crucial for project success. If the project resources are overdue in their assignments and if you ask the overdue task owners to not to attend company party, this will be an example of penalty or coercive power.

- **Expert:** Fourth type of project manager power is Expert. Expert power of project manager actually comes from being technical or project management expert. Project managers should have work and project management experience. Knowledge is power, and in case a project team member needs help about an issue, project manager must guide the resource, show leadership and mentorship respectively.

- **Referent:** Fifth and last type of project manager power is Referent. Referent power of the project manager comes with charisma and fame. This generally comes with the appreciation, admiration or designation in the company. In a project management office, there will not be a position like "best project manager" officially. However, when it is asked who the best project manager of this PMO is, we would expect to hear 2-3 people based on their experience and performance. Referent power comes from these kinds of charisma and fame.
For example, the best project manager of the company, Nelly states, *"we should change the scope statement template of our company"*. Here, the person who is saying what Nelly told about the scope statement template of our company is admiring Nelly. Therefore, this sentence comes with an influence that *"if Nelly says that scope statement template should*

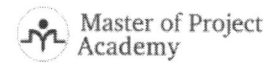

change, there should be a problem with it". This is an example of referent power of project managers.

Let us wrap up what we learned about the powers of the project manager until now.

- **Expert and reward are best form of power.** In expert power, you demonstrate your knowledge and expertise. In reward power, you motivate your team members in order to ensure better performance in the project.

- **Penalty is the worst choice**, because, you penalize your project team members and this can cause demotivation in your project. No one wants to get a penalty in a project, right?

- **Formal, reward, and penalty powers are derived from the project manager's position in the company.** In other words, project resources report to the project manager. Therefore, project manager will be able to give rewards to the resources for their desired behavior and penalize the resources if there are problems with their tasks, which are caused by the project resource.

- **Finally, expert power is earned on your own.** Because, expert power was coming from the knowledge of project management or a technical knowledge in a specific area. This is owned only by getting experience in specific areas.

Conflict Management

- Conflicts are inevitable in a project environment. There are three main reasons of why the conflicts are inevitable in a project.

- **Nature of projects requires needs and requirements of many stakeholders:** As you remember from our previous notes, several stakeholders have several requirements from a project. There should be a balance of these stakeholder needs in the project. Generally, this is not easy. One stakeholder requirement might be competing with another stakeholder's requirement. In this case, you have to solve this conflict in a way that fits best for the project goals and objectives. If the conflict resolution will be in favor of one stakeholder over another's, this will create problem in the project.
- **Limited power of project manager:** Second reason of why conflicts arise in projects is the limited power of project managers. Although you might be the project manager for the project, you might not have the ultimate authority in the company. You can have a limited level of making decisions or a limited level of taking initiatives. For the decisions that you cannot make on your own, or for the problems that you cannot solve on your own, you have to escalate the issue to the upper management. Therefore, these might cause conflicts in projects.
- **Necessity of obtaining resources from functional managers:** Third reason of conflicts in projects is obtaining resources from functional managers. Assume that you need a specific resource under a functional department for your project. If that resource is not available for the project, or even if he was available, if functional manager cannot assign him to your

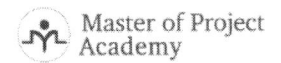

project for some other reasons, this might cause conflicts between you and that functional manager.

These are advice to avoid or minimize conflicts in your projects.

- **Project Manager should show where project is headed.** You should show the clear direction of the project, where we are aiming, where we are going, what is our target. Project goals and objectives must be clear. Deadlines, scope and targets must be visible to all project stakeholders.

- **You should inform stakeholders about constraints and objectives.** For instance, if completing the project by end of the year is an objective, this must be informed to the all project stakeholders. Similarly, project constraints must be informed to the stakeholders as well. For instance, if the end product of the project is a building, its strength against an earthquake will be a constraint. This must be informed to the stakeholders.

- **Inform contents of project charter.** If you remember, project charter was containing high-level economies, high-level risk, and high-level scope of the project. Therefore, if you inform the contents of the project charter to your project team, they will have the high-level information about your project. What is expected from this project? What is the initial scope? What are the high-level requirements and high-level risks of the project? These questions will be clear for stakeholders if you inform the stakeholders about the content of the project charter. Therefore, they will have higher commitment and this will avoid conflicts in the project.

- **You should inform all key decisions to your project team, and you should inform about changes.** If there is a change and this affects the activities in a project or if the change affects how the team will perform activities in the project, in order to avoid future conflicts, you should inform the project team about the changes in your project.

- **You should assign works as clearly.** Otherwise, if team members start to make assumptions for an activity that you have assigned to them, they might go in different directions than you planned in the beginning. Therefore, you should assign work, tasks, and activities in your project clearly to your project resources.

- **Follow good project management and planning practices.** Discrepancies in project management processes and planning practices will cause conflicts in your project. This can cause even project failures.

7 Common Sources of Conflicts

There are seven common sources of conflicts in projects. We will go over each conflict source one by one.

- **Schedules:** First one is the schedules. For example, if customer is requiring you to complete the project by the end of year, and if there are delays in the project and if you cannot meet that deadline, then, this might cause conflict between you and your customers in your project.

- **Priorities:** Priorities between projects is another source of conflict. Depending on the priorities of projects in an organization, requirements of one project might be more important than another project. This might cause conflicts in projects. For instance, if a scarce project resource is required both by your project and for another project at the same time, this is a conflict and priority of the projects in the organization will resolve it.

- **Resources:** Third one is resources. For instance, a resource working in your project might have departmental works as well. In this case, if project resource is doing departmental works and if this is causing project delays in your project, you can have conflicts with the functional manager of the resource.

- **Technical opinion:** Technical opinion can be a source of conflict in projects as well. For instance, if there are alternative ways of solving a technical issue in the project, and if one of the project resources is opting for one solution while another project resource is option for another solution, there will be a conflict between two resources.

- **Administrative procedures:** Administrative procedures might be a source of conflict as well. Annual leave forms, applications for ID cards, or how to create a support ticket etc. are examples of administrative procedures.
- **Cost:** Cost can be a source of conflict in projects as well. For instance, if your customer expects you to finish a project with a one-million-dollar budget and if your calculations show that the project requires 1.2-million-dollar budget, this will be a conflict between you and your customer respectively.
- **Personality:** Finally, personality can be a source of conflict as well. Can you image a team full of troublemakers? It will be impossible to negotiate on a topic and proceed with project actions.

Conflict Resolution Techniques

As we discussed before, conflicts are inevitable in a project. The important thing is, how you manage conflicts. If you cannot manage conflicts in a project properly, they can cause demotivation and bad performance in your project respectively. There are common ways to deal with conflicts in a project. We will go over five common conflict resolution techniques one-by-one.

- **Withdraw/Avoid:** First one is withdrawing or avoiding. This technique is postponing the issue to be better prepared or to be resolved by others. In other words, you do not take an action for the conflict at the moment. You address the conflict to a later date and expect to be in a better position regarding the conflict.

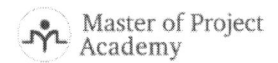

- **Smooth/Accommodate:** Second conflict resolution technique is Smoothing, or accommodating. This is emphasizing areas of agreement, rather than areas of difference. Therefore, in this technique, two parties might have different views or different solutions for a problem. However, you emphasize the common parts of their areas, the common parts of their methods, in order to find an agreement. This is called smoothing or accommodating.

- **Compromise/Reconcile:** Third technique for conflict resolution is compromising or reconciling. In this technique, both parties will have limited satisfaction. Since both parties do not have all they want, this is a lose-lose situation.

- **Force/Direct:** Fourth technique for conflict resolution is forcing or directing. This is pushing one's viewpoint at the expense of others. This is a win-lose situation because only one person's wish or request will happen and the others become unhappy. Because, their viewpoint, their decision or opinion is not accepted.

- **Collaborate/Problem Solve:** Fifth and the last common technique for conflict resolution is collaborating or problem solving. The parties incorporate multiple viewpoints in order to lead to consensus, and this is leading to win-win situation in projects. Because, you brainstorm about the possible ways, possible methods to solve a problem or to resolve a conflict in this technique. Since you lead to a consensus, since everybody agrees at the end of this technique, this leads to win-win situation.

Important Terms & Topics

Now we will see important terms, topics, and theories about motivation and people management.

- **Expectancy Theory:** First one is expectancy theory; this theory implies that employees who believe their efforts will lead to effective performance and expected to be rewarded. In other words, this theory says that everybody thinks that I am perfect and I will be rewarded. Isn't it the case in your projects? Everybody thinks that he or she is performing well and he or she will be recognized and awarded.
- **Arbitration:** Second term is Arbitration. Arbitration is a neutral party evaluates a dispute. So, if there is a problem between two parties, then, a referee comes to solve a problem, in order to have a neutral viewpoint to the problem. For instance, if two technical resources are arguing about a problem in the project, a technical subject matter expert can be the arbitrator to evaluate reasoning of resources to find a solution to the conflict.
- **Perquisites (Perks):** Third term is Perquisites or Perks. Some employees receive special rewards. For example, free parking, executive dining, etc. Depending on the grade in the organization, or depending on the years of experience in the company. Some employees may receive special rewards and this is called perks or perquisites.

- **Fringe Benefits:** Fourth term is fringe benefits. Fringe benefits are standard benefits given to all employees. For example, tickets for lunch, shuttle service for employees, or insurance. If these are given or provided to all employees in the company, then these are called as fringe benefits.
- **Motivation Theory:** Fifth and the last term we will describe is motivation theory. There are different theories for motivation. These are McGregor's theory of X and Y, Maslow's hierarchy of needs, David McClelland's Theory of Needs, and Herzberg's theory. These theories classify employees or people and guides on how to approach each employee or people in each category to motivate them better. During the next headings, we will be going over each theory one-by-one.

McGregor's Theory of X and Y

This theory states that all workers in a project or organization fit into one of two groups, X or Y.

McGregor X - Y Theories

Theory X	Theory Y
* people need close supervision	* people want independence in work
* will avoid work when possible	* people seek responsibility
* will avoid responsibility	* people are motivated by self-fulfilment
* that they desire only money	* people naturally want to work
* people must be pushed to perform	* people will drive themselves to perform

- **Theory X states that these people need close supervision, will avoid work when possible, will avoid responsibility, and they desire only money and these are people that must be pushed to perform.** In other words, for the resources fitting in the X category, you have to do close management. Because, they will avoid work when possible. You have to monitor their tasks and activities closely. In case of any loaf, you should warn these resources. You should not give critical responsibilities to the resources that fit into X category because they only work for money and you need to push them to work.

- **Theory Y states that, people fit into this category want independence in work, seek responsibility, are motivated by self-fulfillment, naturally want to work, and will drive themselves to perform.** For resources fitting into Y category, you should assign tasks and activities and do not look back again. Because they are self-motivated and they look for responsibility. Once you assign a task to these people, they will perform their best to accomplish the task. You will not need to push them to work. Since they are self-motivated and look for responsibility, they will not like close monitoring of a project manager.

Maslow's Hierarchy of Needs

This theory states that people are not motivated to work by security or money. Many employers or organizations thinks that if they pay enough to an employee, he or she will be motivated to work for the organization. However, Maslow states that, as long as an employer pays enough, more money will not motivate the employee. Instead, they will look for other motivational factors. **Maslow proposes a hierarchy of needs pyramid.**

- **Highest motivation is to contribute and use their skills (self-actualization):** According to Maslow's theory, one of the most importance motivational factors is, contributing and using skills in work. For instance, a software engineer will look for optimum software development conditions to produce the best code. A civil engineer will look for the best construction conditions to show his skills to build a facility.
- **People cannot ascend to next level, without fulfilling a previous level in Maslow's pyramid.** Because, the next level in the pyramid is most comfortable and better than the previous level.

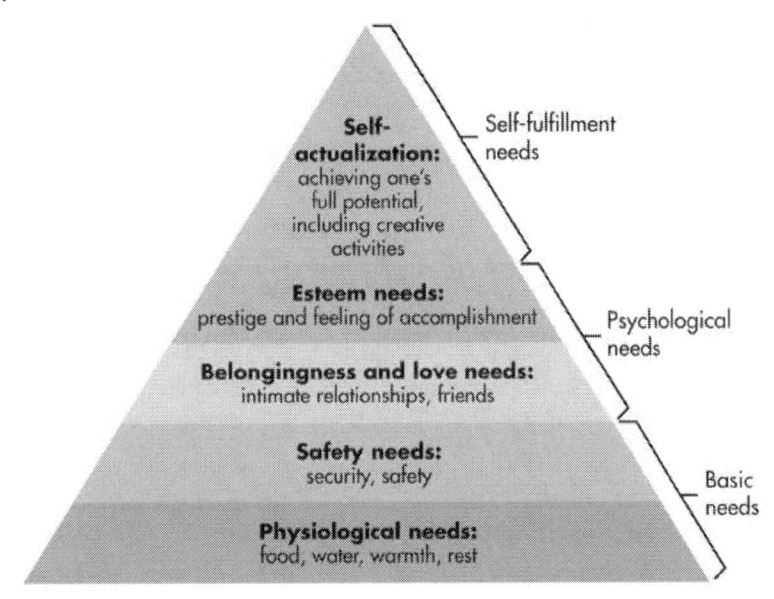

![Maslow's Hierarchy of Needs pyramid showing from bottom to top: Physiological needs (food, water, warmth, rest), Safety needs (security, safety) — Basic needs; Belongingness and love needs (intimate relationships, friends), Esteem needs (prestige and feeling of accomplishment) — Psychological needs; Self-actualization: achieving one's full potential, including creative activities — Self-fulfillment needs.]

Here, we see the Maslow's Hierarchy of Needs, or Maslow's pyramid. We will go over each level in this pyramid one-by-one.

- **Physiological needs:** As you see, bottom level represents the physiological needs. Food, water, warmth and rest. First, a person needs food, water, warmth and rest in order to live, in order to survive in the life. You cannot survive without food and water. Therefore, this is the first step.

- **Security:** Then, he needs security, safety in order to protect himself from the external dangers. If he cannot protect himself, his life will be in danger.

- **Belongingness and Love:** And once psychological needs and safety of the people are provided, people need belongingness and love in the third step of Maslow's pyramid. Therefore, they seek for intimate relationships, friends, social network, etc. Do not forget, human is a social creature by nature.

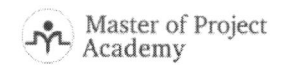

- **Esteem Needs:** In the fourth step of Maslow's pyramid, they need prestige and feeling of accomplishment. They need to be recognized by their colleagues or by their friends in this stage.

> A person cannot pass to a next step in Maslow's pyramid unless he fulfills the requirements of previous level.

- **Self-Actualization:** Fifth and the last level of the Maslow's pyramid is self-actualization. When a person achieves this level, he discovers his full potential, including creative activities. For instance, a software engineer developing a worldwide famous app can be in this last stage of Maslow's pyramid.

David McClelland's Theory of Needs

This theory states that people are motivated by one of the three needs:
- Achievement,
- Affiliation and
- Power.

People looking for achievement desires to accomplish a work. People look for affiliation needs help and cooperation when completing a work. People looking for power looks for leading roles.

- **Based on David McClelland's theory, each person falling into different group should be managed different from each other.**

- **People falling into achievement group, likes recognition and rewards.** They are motivated by successful results. They look for recognitions once they succeeded a work. In order to motivate this group of people, you should assign them challenging but reachable projects. They want to work independent if possible.

Achievement	• Likes recognition • Challenging but reachable projects motivate
Affiliation	• Seeks approval rather than recognition. • Works best when cooperating
Power	• Likes organizing and influencing others • Should be allowed to manage others

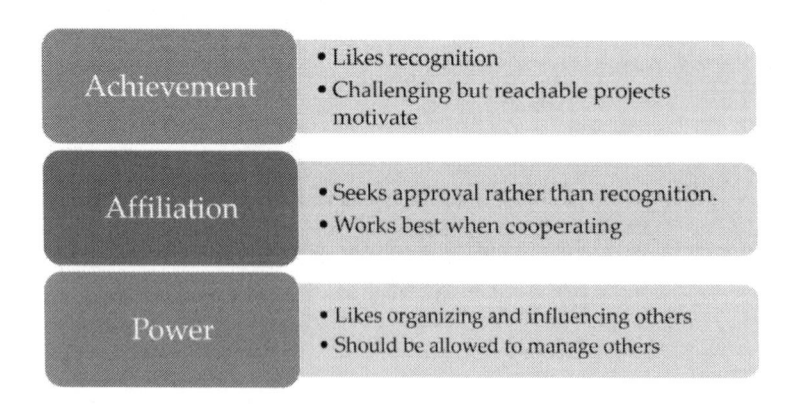

- **People falling into the second group, affiliation, seeks approval rather than recognition.** They do not want to take initiatives or they do not want to make any decision. They will be happy if their task is clearly defined and they will ask for confirmations when they are

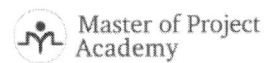

doing activities in a project. These people work best when cooperating. They cannot work on their own because they need always another person assisting them.
- **The last group looks for power. These people like organizing and influencing others.** These people should be allowed to manage others. People falling into this category are motivated by management positions. Therefore, you should give those leading roles or management roles in projects or in an organization. For instance, if a senior software engineer is fitting into this category in your project, you should assign him as a team leader of other software engineers. He will be motivated with these kinds of leading roles.

Herzberg's Theory.

This theory mainly deals with two factors, hygiene factors and motivating agents. We will be describing each of these terms one-by-one.

> Hygiene factors are factors that inexistence of these factors may destroy motivation, but improving these hygiene factors may not increase motivation.

- **Hygiene factors:** Hygiene factors are factors that inexistence of these factors may destroy motivation, but improving these hygiene factors may not increase motivation. **Working conditions, salary, relationships at work, security are examples of hygiene factors.** Assume that you are working in a reputable company, you have a good office, office is in a shining skyscraper and you have good friendships at work. However, your employer pays low than what you need. This will demotivate you. Because salary is a hygiene factor, and inexistence will cause demotivation. Similarly, even if all of these factors are ok for you, improving your office environment or a better salary will not motivate you. You might think that the better salary will motivate everyone but this is what Herzberg says. After enough salary, people look for additional motivational factors in a job.

- **Motivating Agents:** Second factor of Herzberg's Theory is motivating agents. This factor states that, the work itself motivates the people. **Responsibility, self-actualization, professional growth, recognition and similar factors motivate people.** For example, if people are seeing a carrier path in their current organization. This will be a motivational factor for them. On the other hand, if you give responsibility to senior people in your organization, this will motivate them. Similarly, if people see that a professional growth can be achieved in their organization, they will be motivated to work.

Control Resources Process

Control resources is the last process of resource management knowledge area. The main purpose of control resources process is ensuring that resources are allocated for the project are available as planned.

- **Assume that you make a project plan that will take two years to complete.** There are several work packages, several activities and several resources need to be planned. During planning, you can assign resources that are planned to be executed one year later however, when the time comes to execute that task, which available resource might not be available, or he might have resigned from the company etc. Therefore, control resources process continuously checks whether the planned resources are available.
- **This includes monitoring the planned versus actual utilization of resources.** For instance, based on your planning, you might have planned an architect to work for three months in the project. However, during the project, you might need one additional work from the architect. With the help of the control resources process, these kind of planned versus actual utilization of resources are monitored.
- **Outputs of this process can be update of resource management plan, schedule baseline or cost baseline.** Resource management plan was including the overall resource availability, resource plans of the project. Therefore, if any resource availability or plan changes, resource management plan needs update respectively.
- **Based on the resource availability changes, schedule and cost of the project can change as well.** For instance, if one of the resources resigns, until you find a suitable resource and handover the work, you might lose time and this can cause delays. Besides, new resource replacing the old one can be cheaper or more expensive and this can require cost baseline updates respectively.

Briefly, control resources process monitors the resource availability of the project. It helps project manager to see deviations and take corrective actions regarding resource management when necessary.

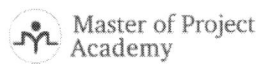

Quiz – Section 8

1- All of the following about Resource Management is true EXCEPT:

   A) Recognition and rewards system must be applied

   B) Project managers should improve tea member's competencies

   C) Projects are planned together with the team

   D) Resource Management is done mainly in planning

2- All of the Resource Management processes belong to executing process group EXCEPT:

   A) Plan Resource Management

   B) Acquire Resources

   C) Develop Team

   D) Manage Team

3- You are managing a satellite launch project. More than 80 engineers are working in the project and for better coordination, project team has been divided into 8 groups. There are team leaders of each group who are doing project management activities. These team leaders are reporting to you. These team leaders and you, as a project manager, can be called as all of the following EXCEPT:

   A) Core Team

   B) Executive Team

   C) Supervising Team

   D) Leadership Team

4- All of the following are role of the Project Sponsor EXCEPT:

   A) Provides funding

   B) Manages day-to-day activities of a project

   C) Provides project statement of work

   D) Set priorities between projects

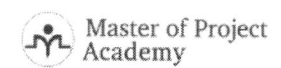

5- Project team is referred as group of people who will complete the work on project. All of the following are roles of project team EXCEPT:

A) Creation of WBS

B) Time and cost estimation for activities

C) Identifying stakeholders

D) Ensuring payment for purchased materials

6- Functional manager manages the resources in a specific department in an organization. All of the following are roles of functional manager EXCEPT:

A) Performing tasks of a team member leaving the team.

B) Assigning resources to projects

C) Providing subject matter expertise

D) Approving final schedule of project

7- Plan Resource Management process establishes all of the following EXCEPT:

A) Project roles and responsibilities

B) Activity assignment of each project team member

C) Project organization charts

D) Staffing management plan

8- There common formats to show roles and responsibilities in a project. All of the following are examples of these common formats EXCEPT:

A) Hierarchical

B) Matrix

C) Resource Based

D) Text-oriented

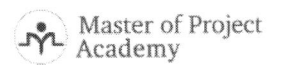

9- In your Plan Resource Management process, it has been decided to show responsibility by department in a top-down format. Which of the following format is appropriate?

A) Responsibility Assignment Matrix

B) RACI Matrix

C) Organizational Breakdown Structure

D) Resource Breakdown Structure

10- Which of the following statements describe competency?

A) Function assigned to a person

B) Right to apply project resources, make decisions and sign approvals

C) Assigned duties and work to a team member

D) Skill and capacity required to complete project activities

11- Resource Management Plan is major output of Plan Resource Management Process and includes all of the following EXCEPT:

A) Costs of Team Members

B) Project Organization Charts

C) Staffing Management Plan

D) Recognition and Rewards Information

12- You have just taken over a project from another project manager in your organization. You wanted to check for how long the resources will be needed and when are their annual leaves. You need to check:

A) Resource Management Plan

B) Staffing Management Plan

C) Resource Time Plan

D) Resource Leave Plan

13- Staffing Management Plan includes all of the following EXCEPT:

A) Resource Calendars

B) Plan for funding employee salaries

C) Plan for Staff Acquisition

D) Training Needs

14- You are planning your resource needs for your project. Functional managers of your organization wanted to see required number of hours that will be needed for your project. Which of the following is appropriate for this?

   A) Resource Histogram

   B) Resource Fluctuation

   C) Staffing Management Plan

   D) Resource Time Plan

15- You are confirming human resource availability for your project in your organization. This is done in which of the following processes?

   A) Plan Resource Management

   B) Acquire Resources

   C) Develop Team

   D) Manage Team

16- Acquire Resources process involves all of the following EXCEPT:

   A) Knowing pre-assigned resources

   B) Hiring new employees

   C) Outsourcing

   D) Tracking progress of activities on project team members

17- Which of the following BEST describes pre-assignment?

   A) Assigning tasks of resources before project starts

   B) Outsourcing unavailable resources

   C) Selecting project team members in advance

   D) Assigning a subject matter expertise in a project

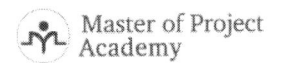

18- You are managing a telecommunication product development project. Software engineers of this project are working from India, analysts are located in Italy and testers will work from Sweden. This is an example of:

A) Virtual Team

B) Distance Delivery

C) Halo Effect

D) Acquisition

19- All of the following are advantages of Virtual Team model EXCEPT:

A) Decreases possibility of misunderstanding

B) Reduces travel costs

C) Includes disabled people

D) Enables forming teams of people in different locations

20- Develop Team is the process of improving competencies, team member interaction, and overall team environment. Which of the following is not a benefit of this process?

A) Improved Teamwork

B) Motivated Employees

C) Reduced staff turnover rates

D) Increased staff utilization

21- You have started to a construction project 1 month ago. Project team members started to learn each other and you observe disagreements between team members in some cases. In which Tuckman stage is your project team?

A) Forming

B) Storming

C) Norming

D) Performing

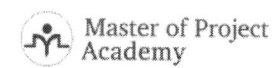

22- Team-building activities should be done during a project in order to enhance project performance. Which of the following is NOT a team-building activity?

A) Organizing a training for whole team

B) Celebrating an accomplished milestone

C) Providing fringe benefits of team members on time

D) Creating WBS

23- You have declared in the beginning of your project that all cell phones must be switched off and laptops should not be open during project status meetings. This is an example of:

A) Ground Rules

B) Project Rules

C) Team Respect

D) Resource Responsibility

24- Your project team will be developing software for a bank. Based on customer requirements, your project team will be delivering project on customer premises. For this purpose, all project team has been placed in a meeting room during project. This is called as:

A) Colocation

B) Virtual Team

C) Customer Team

D) Tight Team

25- Performance of team members are tracked during Manage Team process. In this context, Project Performance Appraisals can be provided by all of the following EXCEPT:

A) Coworkers

B) Subordinates

C) Team mates from previous project

D) Supervisors

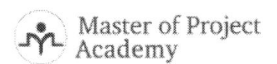

26- Project managers have different types of power. In your project, you declared to your team members that best performing team member will be awarded with a 2-day weekend holiday. This is an example of which type of power?

A) Coercive

B) Reward

C) Referent

D) Organizational

27- Conflicts are inevitable in a project but Project Managers can avoid conflicts by doing all of the following EXCEPT:

A) Informing changes

B) Assigning works clearly

C) Showing where project is headed

D) Taking all key decisions within core team

28- You are managing a software project. Currently, your team is in analysis phase and in your project team meeting, two team members started to discuss server type that will be used in the project and they have different ideas. You stopped the discussions and mentioned that there is still time to take this decision and this can be discussed two weeks later. Which of the following conflict resolution techniques did you use?

A) Withdraw

B) Smooth

C) Reconcile

D) Collaborate

29- Which of the following group needs independence when performing their work and seek responsibility?

A) Junior Resources

B) Affiliation

C) Theory X

D) Theory Y

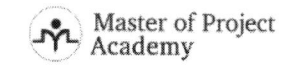

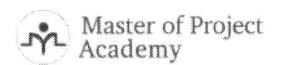

30- All of the following about Maslow's Hierarchy of Needs is true EXCEPT:

   A) People are not motivated to work by security or money

   B) Highest motivation level is self-actualization

   C) Working environment is primary driver of motivation

   D) People cannot ascend to next level in the pyramid without fulfilling previous level

31- Which of the following motivation theories deal with hygiene factors?

   A) David McClelland's Theory

   B) Herzberg's Theory

   C) Maslow's Hierarchy of Needs

   D) Mc Gregor's Theory

32- Which of the following processes of resource management mainly aims to monitor the availability of planned resources and tracks the resource utilization?

   A) Plan Resource Management

   B) Acquire Resources

   C) Manage Team

   D) Control Resources

Answers

1 – D	21 – B
2 – A	22 – C
3 – C	23 – A
4 – B	24 – A
5 – D	25 - C
6 – A	26 – B
7 – B	27 – D
8 – C	28 – A
9 – C	29 – D
10 – D	30 – C
11 – A	31 – B
12 – B	32 – D
13 – B	
14 – A	
15 – B	
16 – D	
17 – C	
18 – A	
19 – A	
20 – D	

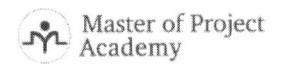

Mapping Game – Section 8

Left	Right
validates the scope	Functional Manager
directs technical work of resources	Competence
creates the WBS	Program Manager
the team that functions with an absence of centralized control	Collaborate/problem solve
The skill and capacity required to complete assigned activities	Resource Requirements
identify the types and quantities of resources required for work packages	Stakeholders
manages related projects	Project Team
provides financial resources for project	Self-organizing team
conflict resolution method can result in a win-win situation	Project Sponsor

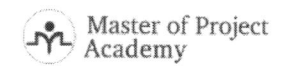

Answers

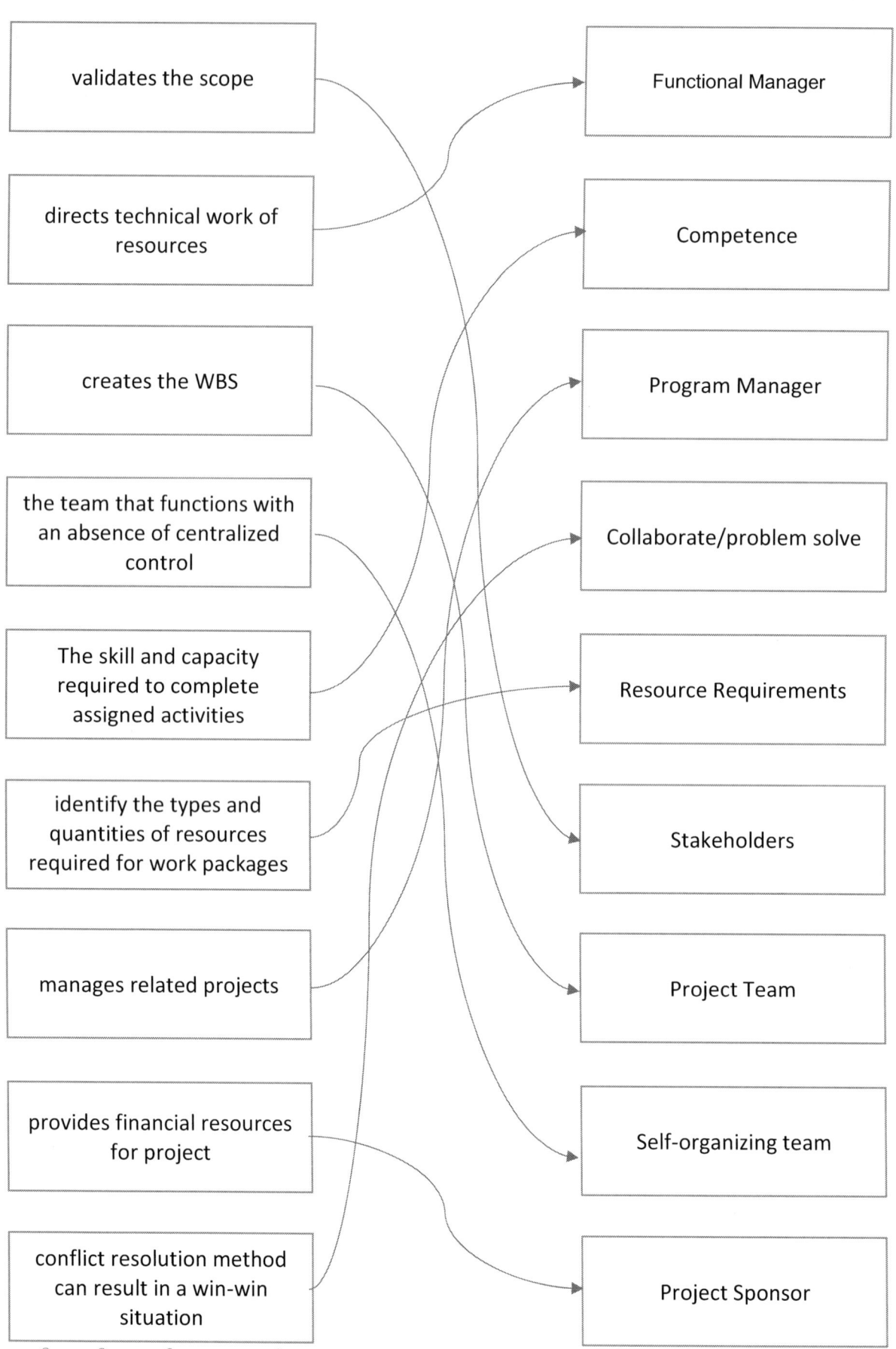

Left	Right
validates the scope	→ Project Team
directs technical work of resources	→ Functional Manager
creates the WBS	→ Project Team
the team that functions with an absence of centralized control	→ Self-organizing team
The skill and capacity required to complete assigned activities	→ Competence
identify the types and quantities of resources required for work packages	→ Resource Requirements
manages related projects	→ Program Manager
provides financial resources for project	→ Project Sponsor
conflict resolution method can result in a win-win situation	→ Collaborate/problem solve

Section 9

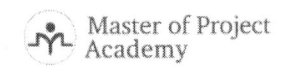

Communications Management

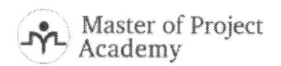

Section 9 – Communications Management

Communication skills of a project manager is crucial. Based on statistics, a project manager spends around 90% of his or her time for communications. These include emailing, meetings, face-to-face communication with project team members, presentations to management, meetings with customer, reporting etc. Therefore, many employers assess the communication skills of a project manager critically during job interviews.

- **Overview of Communications Management:** In communication management section, first we will see the overview of communications management. We will see the definition of the communications management and we will list the processes of communications management knowledge area as well.
- **Processes of Communications Management:** There are three processes of communications management knowledge area.
    - Plan Communication Management Process
    - Manage Communications Process
    - Monitor Communications Process
- **Dimensions of Communication:** Then, we will go over dimensions of communication. There are various dimensions of communication. Formal, internal, external, vertical, horizontal, official, written, oral etc. We will go over these dimensions.
- **Effective Communication Skills:** We will go over the effective communication skills. We will go over the tips about better communication in project management. These include active listening, questioning, coaching, motivating, persuading etc.

Overview of Communications Management

Communications management knowledge area includes processes that are required to ensure timely and appropriate planning, collection, creation, distribution, storage, retrieval, management, control, monitoring, and the ultimate disposition of project information.

> The main purpose of communications management knowledge area is to ensure the best communication, effective and efficient communication within a project.

- **Throughout the project, lots of information, reports, and documents will be sent, received and shared among stakeholders.** There will be several meetings organized at different levels as well. Communications management knowledge area mainly aims to control and coordinate the flow of information throughout the project. How you will get information from several stakeholders, or how you will get information from several parties. How you will collect them, how you will organize them. Moreover, if you need to distribute or dispose any information from your project to the other stakeholders of your project, how you will do this, through email, through phone, etc. These are all defined in communications management knowledge area.

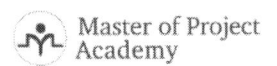

- **Project managers spend most of their time with communication.** On a research that I have read two or three years ago, the project manager was spending almost 90% of his time doing communication. This might be either through phones, through e-mails, through meetings. This shows the importance of communications management in a project.

- There are three processes in communications management knowledge area.
    - Plan Communications Management (Planning)
    - Manage Communications (Executing)
    - Monitor Communications (Monitoring & Controlling)

We will be going over these processes one-by-one in our further notes.

Potential Dimensions in Communications Management Processes

Before going into processes of communications management knowledge area, we will see some basic concepts and terms about communications.

Potential Dimensions in Communications Management Processes:

- **Internal and External:** One of the communication dimensions can be either internal or external. For example, there might be information that you are sharing with your project team. Alternatively, a project team member might come to notify you about the risk, about the problem that he is facing. This is an example of internal communication. In addition, there might be external communication. For example, you might send an email to a subcontractor of your project or to another organization that you are doing your project together. This is an example of external communication.

- **Formal (reports, minutes) and informal (emails, ad-hoc discussion):** Another communication dimension is formal or informal communication. Formal communication includes reports or minutes. For example, if you are producing progress reports frequently, for example, each week or in every two weeks, or if you are sending minutes of the meetings that you have organized, these are examples of formal dimension in communications.
In addition, there might be informal communications. For example, if you are sending an email regarding a usual task in the project, this is an example of informal dimension.
If you are speaking about a topic, speaking about a problem with a project team member in your project, this is an example of ad-hoc discussion. These are examples of informal dimensions in communications management.

- **Vertical and horizontal (in organization):** Another dimension is vertical and horizontal in organization. For example, if you are sharing an information with your manager or with an executive manager of your company, this is an example of vertical dimension. Because you are sending or sharing information with a person who has a higher level in the organization hierarchy in your company. Therefore, this is an example of vertical dimension.

On the other hand, you might be sharing information with your colleague. For example, if you are working in the project management office, PMO, and if you are sharing the information with another project manager in your department, this is an example of horizontal dimension. Because your colleague and you are, peers and you have the same level in organization hierarchy.

- **Official (newsletters, annual report) and unofficial (off the record communications):** There might be also official and unofficial dimensions. Official dimensions can be newsletters and annual report. For example, newsletters include monthly or quarterly news about a company. Therefore, this is an example of official dimension. Moreover, annual report of a company includes the financial standing or the financial summary of the previous year of the company. Therefore, this is an example of official dimension.

  Unofficial dimension is off the record communications. For example, any conversation that is happening between team members or between you and a team member on a verbal basis might be an example of unofficial dimensional communication.

- **Written and oral, and verbal (voice inflections) and nonverbal (body language):** The last communication dimension we will list here is written and oral, and verbal and non-verbal dimensions. For example, sending an email is an example of written dimension. However, if you speak the same content with your project team member, this will be an example of oral communication.

  Verbal communication dimension occurs with voice inflections. For instance, you can stress an important point during your meetings with the tone of your voice. You might use your body language as well when you are sending or influencing a person in your project. This is an example of nonverbal body language dimension.

Effective Communication Skills

We will see effective communication skills during this heading. However, these skills are not specific to project management field.

Actually, these communication skills are generic and can be applied in almost all areas.

- **Listening actively and effectively:** This skill is crucial in order to understand the topics or concerns better from the other side, from the other party that you are communicating with. You need to listen actively. If you do not listen, you cannot understand the details of the topic or the problem clearly.
- **Questioning and probing ideas to better understand:** During your discussions or conversations, if there are parts or if there are sections that you could not understand clearly, you should question those parts in order to clarify, in order to eliminate unclear

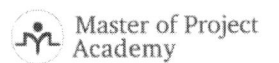

parts for the sections that you could not understand. Otherwise, there will be problems when addressing the problems if you could not understand the issues clearly.

- **Educating to increase team's knowledge:** Each project team member, including you as project manager, must learn new things from the project. At the end of the project, he must have gained new aspects in terms of professional experience. As a project manager, you have to ensure a learning project team environment and encourage project team members to learn new things while you deliver your project work.
- **Fact-finding to identify or confirm information:** There might be rumors or incorrect information disseminating among project stakeholders. Before you act against an information you received, you must validate what you learned.
- **Setting and managing expectations:** For example, as a project manager, you have to set and manage expectations of your stakeholders. There might be competing requirements of stakeholders in your project. You need to balance those needs of stakeholders in your project in order to ensure a successful delivery of your project. This is an example of setting and managing expectations.
- **Persuading a person, a team or an organization to perform an action:** During your project, you need to assign activities; assign tasks to people in your project team. You might face situations that the project team member is not willing to take an activity or task. You have to persuade him. You might need to persuade a functional manager as well. Assume that, you need a specific project resource from a department in your project. However, the functional manager wants to assign a different resource. In order to convince the functional manager, you have to use your convincing skills.
- **Motivating to provide encouragement:** In order to improve performance of your project team, you need to provide encouragement. You need to motivate the project team to ensure your project team produces the best output. This will help you to reach your project goals.
- **Coaching to improve performance:** Project management is not only assigning tasks, following the status of the project and ensuring the project success. You need to coach you project team members and you need to show them how to approach a problem, how to approach to deliver an activity, a task in your project. Project manager must have leadership skills and coaching is one of them. A coaching project manager will motivate the project team better.
- **Negotiating between parties:** As a project manager, you may need to negotiate with several parties. For example, for your resource needs, you need to negotiate with functional manager of regarding departments. For materials, you may need to negotiate with suppliers of your organization. If you are subcontracting a part of your project work, you need to negotiate with the subcontractor. To coordinate this communication between several parties, negotiation is a critical effective communication skill.
- **Resolving conflict:** There might be conflicts arising in your project. Conflicts may arise in the project team or between other stakeholders. For instance, two software developers might argue about the best method to solve a technical problem and this is a conflict. Two executive managers of the company might be asking for competing requirements in the project and this is a conflict as well. Conflicts in the projects must be solved without hampering the relationship among stakeholders and this requires conflict resolution skills in project manager.
- **Summarizing, recapping, and identifying next steps:** And the last bullet of the effective communication skills is, summarizing, recapping, and identifying next steps. This is very

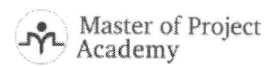

important if you are finalizing a meeting. You need to summarize the outcome of the meeting and you need to summarize or mention the next steps that will be taken after the meeting.

Plan Communications Management Process

Plan communications management is the first process of communications management knowledge area.

- **This is the process of developing an appropriate approach and plan for project communications based on stakeholder's information needs and requirements.** Therefore, the main purpose, of this plan communications management process is, providing a basis for which information will be delivered to who, when, and in what format. Should you send every detail about your project status to an executive manager? Of course, no, you have to provide a brief summary and critical points about the project to the executive manager. However, a detailed report might be required for your project team.

> Plan communications management process organizes how relevant information will be delivered to relevant stakeholders in a project.

- **Plan communications management process identifies and documents the approach to communicate most effectively and efficiently with stakeholders.** One of the main purposes of this process is ensuring effective and efficient communication to project stakeholders.

- **Effective communication:** Effective communication is providing information in the right format, at the right time, to the right audience, and with the right impact. For example, if you are meeting a Vice President of your company, you should not give every single detail of your project. Because, Vice President or Executive Manager of a company will not be dealing with every single detail of your project. They are generally interested in the overall progress of the project, if there are any high risks or high problems, in the project.
Therefore, the information should be provided in right format. You have to prepare a brief progress report, which shows the progress of the project, high-level problems and what you expect from the executive management. This is an example of effective communication. You should give information at the right time. For example, if you are giving progress reports every week or in every two weeks, there is no need to take progress reports or some progress reports between these predefined times. Therefore, providing information at the right time is important.Providing information to right audience is important. For example, if you are producing a project progress report for the technical managers of your company, then this might not be relevant with the human resources department. Even if you share your report with the human resources department, it will not have any impact on them. Therefore, providing information to the right audience and with the right impact is important.

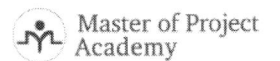

- **Efficient Communication:** Efficient Communication is providing only the information that is needed. In my professional life, I have seen many project progress reports that is including hundreds of pages and too many information. Most of the stakeholders even do not read or even do not check the attachments of these project progress reports. Therefore, we should give the information that is really needed by the relevant stakeholders in a project. You should not provide less information and you should not provide more information than needed.

Number of Communication Channels

Number of potential communication channels is another aspect of communications in project. Number of communication channels in a project represents the complexity level of your communication in your project.

If there are N stakeholders in a project, following formula gives the total number of communication channels,

$$\frac{N(N-1)}{2}$$

If your potential number communication channels is higher, then, the project will require more detailed planning in communications management and, if your potential communication channels is low, then, you will need less time during communications management planning.

Let us go through an example.

If there are four stakeholders in your project, what is the number of potential communication channels for our project?

$$\frac{N(N-1)}{2} = \frac{4(4-1)}{2} = 6 \text{ communication channels}$$

Now we can justify this example through a visualization.

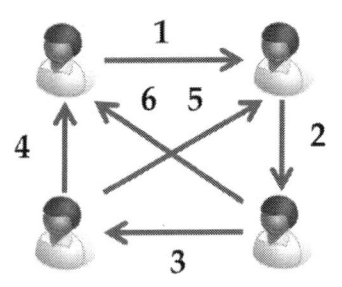

As you see, we have justified the formula. We have drawn each communication channel for each stakeholder for a project, which has four stakeholders. Formula gave us six as total number of communication channels as well.

Communication Technology

Communication technology defines how to communicate in a project. In other words, which medium you will use for communication. For example, whether you will communicate through telephone, through email, or if you are in the same environment with the party that you will communicate, face-to-face etc. These are all examples of communication technology.

Following factors affect choice of communication technology in a project:

- **Urgency of the need for information.** For example, if you need a very urgent information from the other party, instead of emailing, or instead of faxing, you might want to call the other party directly, and get the information from him.
- **Availability of technology.** For example, if you do not have an internet connection in a customer premise, then, you may want to use phone conversation with the other party.
- **Ease of use.** For example, if you will tell a very long history to your manager, then emailing all the scenarios, all the problems, and topics through an email might not be efficient. Because there might be several things that you may want to tell to your manager and emailing this may take hours. Instead of this, you may prefer a phone call and tell your opinions or tell problems to your manager in minutes, with use of telephone.
- **Project environment.** For example, if you are working in a virtual team environment, then, face-to-face communication will not be possible with your project team members who are working in different geographic locations. In this case, you might want to use emails, or phone conversations, or conference calls with the project team.
- **Sensitivity and confidentiality of the information.** For example, emails might be hacked or distributed out of control. Therefore, financial information or very confidential information about a company should not be distributed through emails. In this case, you may want to deliver these kinds of confidential information by hand to the other party or in an encrypted email with a password. This is an example of how to deliver a sensitive and confidential information.

Communication Models

The basic communication model consists of two parties, sender and receiver. Sender encodes the message and transmits to the other side. Other party or the receiver decodes the message and acknowledges. Then, after he decodes it and acknowledges the message, he also tells his opinions, his ideas to the other party as a feedback message and this communication is handled over a medium.

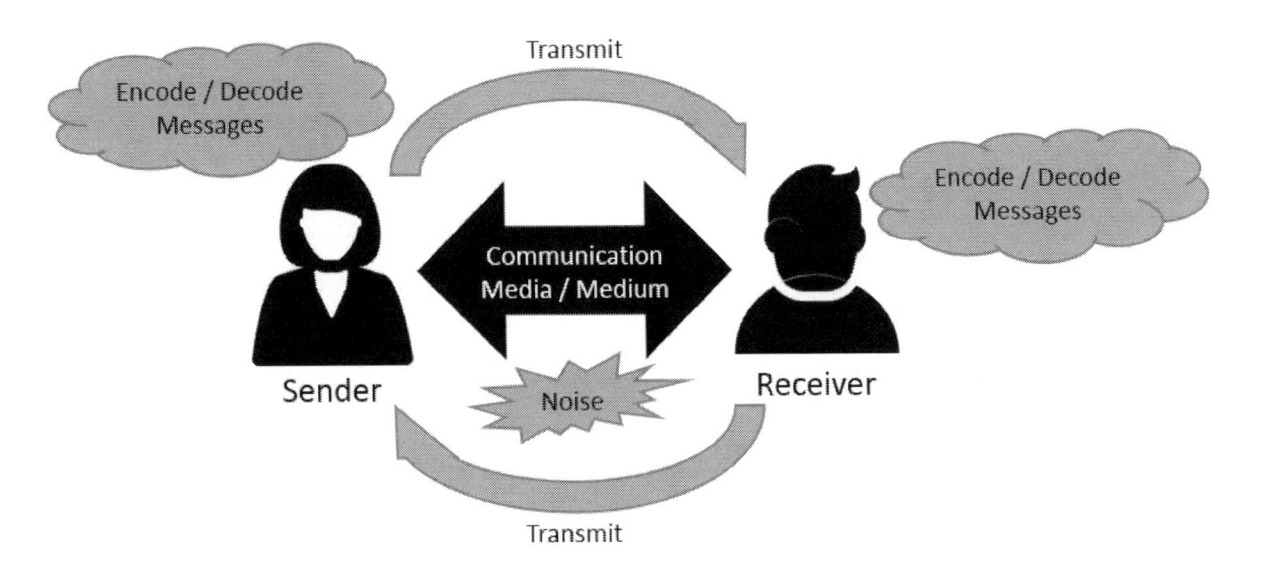

Actually, here, the medium is the technology used for communication. It can be email, telephone, fax, etc. that we saw previously. Now, we will see these steps in communication model one-by-one.

1. **Encoding.** Thoughts or ideas are translated, encoded, into language by the sender. So, the sender speaks or writes his message to the other party.

2. **Transmit Message.** Information is sent by sender using the medium. Medium is as we said, the communication technology used. It can be email, phone, etc. When the message is transmitted, culture, education, experience can compromise the message. For example, a higher educated professional might use different tone compared to a primary school graduate. This is an example of education compromise in communication.

3. **Decode.** When the other party receives a message, it is translated by receiver back into meaning thoughts or ideas. Therefore, when a receiver receives the message, he decodes the thoughts and ideas of the other party and understands the message.

4. **Acknowledge:** Upon receipt of the message, receiver signals or acknowledges that the message is received, but this acknowledgement does not mean that the receiver agreed with the message. Therefore, when the receiver signals that the message is received, this does not mean that "I agree with your opinion" or "I agree with your thoughts". This only means that I received your message.

5. **Feedback/Response:** Finally, feedback or response is sent back to the sender. Upon decoding and understanding, receiver encodes thoughts and ideas into a message and then transmits this to sender. The receiver got the message, he acknowledged and he wanted to give his or her feedbacks or responses to the sender. After he developed his thoughts or ideas in his mind, he encodes his feedback or response message and sends it back to the sender. These are five steps of a basic communication model between two parties.

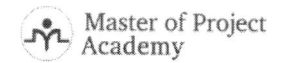

Communication Methods

We have seen communication technology and communication models. Now, we will see communication methods. There are three communication methods:

- **Interactive Communication:** This is a reciprocal and multidirectional information exchange. For example, conversations, meetings, conference calls are examples of interactive communication. During a team meeting, you may want to discuss a problem that you are facing in your project. After you asked the opinion of your project team members, everybody can propose his or her idea about the resolution options of the problem. During this information exchange, everybody will listen to each other and everybody will evaluate the opinions or thoughts of each other. This is an example of interactive communication.

- **Push Communication:** This is a one-way stream communication method. Sender sends the message and does not ensure that it is received by other parties. For example, emails, reports, faxes, or blogs are examples of push communication. Assume that you produced a project progress report that you should prepare each week. You send it to many stakeholders in your project, but you will not be sure whether the recipients of this email will read all you have written in your project progress report. So, you do not ensure that your message is received by the parties that you have sent the information. This is an example of push communication.

- **Pull communication:** It is the last communication method used for large volumes of information delivery. Information is placed into a central place and recipients collect the message from the central place. For example, intranet, e-learning, lessons learned databases are examples of pull communication. Assume that you want to share analysis documents or design documents of your project with your project team members. If the total size of these documents are more than 100 Megabytes, it will not be possible to send these documents through email because most of the email programs or most of the corporate organizations email standards do not allow sending emails more than 10 Megabytes. In this case, you may want to place these documents into corporate knowledge base or into an intranet site, and everybody who will need these documents may download these documents or information, from the central place that you placed your information. This is an example of pull communication.

Communications Management Plan

Communications Management Plan is the major output of Plan Communication Management Process.

- **Communications management plan describes how project communications will be planned, structured, monitored and controlled.** This plan actually defines, which information will be provided to which stakeholder in what frequency and in what format.

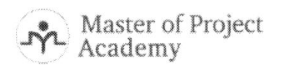

For instance, what kind of information will be available to project team members, which confidential information will be delivered to who in what format. What will be the frequency of project progress reports? What will be the content of executive reports? These are all defined in Communications Management Plan.

- **Part of the project management plan:** As all other management plans Communications Management Plan is also part of the project management plan.

- **Communications management plan may include stakeholder communication requirements.** For example, a functional manager might require getting project progress reports in every month and a vice president in your organization may want to see project progress reports in each quarter. PMO department manager may want to see master reports. On the other hand, your customer may want to see project progress reports weekly and in a more detailed format. Therefore, these different stakeholders may need different levels of details in their information requirements. What kind of information will be available to which stakeholder and the information format will be included in communications management plan.

- **Information to be communicated, format, content and level of detail can be included in the communication management plan.** As we discussed in the above bullet, information that will be delivered to stakeholders, what kind of information will be delivered to who, in what frequency, in what format and level of detail are all defined in Communications Management Plan.

- **Time and frequency for distribution of the required information.** For example, you may want to deliver your project progress reports to your stakeholders in every month. On the other hand, your customer may want to see the project progress reports weekly. So, these time and frequency requirements may change from stakeholder to stakeholder and depending on the requirements of your stakeholders, you will need to define time and frequency for distribution of required information.

- **Person responsible for communicating the information.** For example, a specific progress report may be provided by a team leader or by team members working as a project management team in your project. On the other hand, the high-level information about the project can be delivered only by you to the executive vice president of the company. Therefore, who will be responsible for delivering which kind of information and to who are all defined in Communications Management Plan.

- **Person responsible for authorizing the release of confidential information.** For example, your company's confidential information, like shareholding structure or seller information, personal details of the employees etc. are confidential information of your company. When you are delivering this kind of confidential information to the relevant parties, you need to be so sensitive and use appropriate and secure communication technology. Communication way of this kind of confidential information should be defined and who will be responsible for delivering this information should be defined in communications management plan.

- **Communications Management Plan may include also glossary of terminology.** For example, depending on your project, there might be specific terms regarding you project and in order to familiarize the project team members or all project stakeholders with the terminology of the project, this glossary of terminology might be included in your communications management plan.

- **Person or groups who will receive information about your projects should be included in the communication management plan.** For example, functional managers, stakeholders, any other departments in your company etc. can be stakeholders of a project. If they are interested in your project, they should be included as person or groups who will be receiving information in Communications Management Plan.

Manage Communications Process

Manage communications process is the second process of communications management knowledge area.

- **Manage communications is the process of creating, collecting, distributing, storing, retrieving, and the ultimate disposition of project information.** Actually, in plan communications management process, you define how you will create project information, how you will deliver the information, who will be responsible for delivering what kind of information and the frequency of delivery of information. In manage communications process; you execute what you planned in plan communications management process.
For example, if you planned to send weekly reports to your project team members and monthly reports to your executive management team of your company, in manage communications process, you will prepare these reports and send to relevant stakeholders respectively.

- **Manage communications process enables an effective communication between stakeholders.** Therefore, depending on your communications management plan, you will manage your communications to relevant stakeholders in your project. Moreover, as long as you go in line with your communications management plan, you will be able to ensure efficient and effective communication between stakeholders. When you identified problems or conflicts in your communication management plan, you should immediately take a corrective action to correct the problems in the communications of your project.

Monitor Communications Process

Third and the last process of communications management knowledge area is monitor communications process.

Monitor communications process is the process of monitoring and controlling communications throughout the entire project life cycle, to ensure that the information

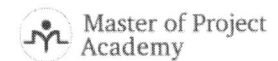

needs of project stakeholders are met. So, the main purpose of monitor communications is checking whether you follow your communication management plan. You have plans to deliver, store, retrieve and send your project information to several parties, several stakeholders in your project. In monitor communications process, you check whether the relevant stakeholders receive relevant information as planned in plan communications management process. If there are deviations or if there are problems that you could not follow the communications management plan, these should be investigated and corrected in manage communications process respectively.

Monitor communications process ensures an optimal information flow among all communication parts. The main purpose of this process is ensuring the effective and efficient optimal information flow among all communication participants and all project stakeholders.

Quiz – Section 9

1- All of the following are processes of Communications Management knowledge area EXCEPT:

   A) Plan Communications Management

   B) Manage Communications

   C) Monitor Communications

   D) Distribute Communications

2- All of the following are examples of formal communication EXCEPT:

   A) Ad-hoc discussions

   B) Meeting Minutes

   C) Project Reports

   D) Executive Reports

3- Effective communications skills are crucial in project environment. All of the following are effective communication skills EXCEPT:

   A) Resolving Conflict

   B) Negotiating between parties

   C) Delegating tasks to team members

   D) Coaching to improve performance

4- All of the following about Plan Communications Management process are correct EXCEPT:

   A) Process of developing an appropriate approach and plan for communications

   B) Distributes information to relevant stakeholders

   C) Identifies approach for effective communication

   D) Identifies approach for efficient communication

5- There might be several stakeholders in a project and different stakeholders may need different level of information. This can be ensured by:

   A) Effective Communication

   B) Efficient Communication

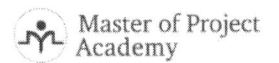

C) Stakeholder Communication Plan

D) Reliable Communication

6- You are project manager of a software project. There are 4 software developers, 1 analyst and you as a project manager currently in the project. Next week, 2 test engineers will join the team. What will be the total number of communication channels in the project?

A) 13

B) 15

C) 21

D) 28

7- Communication technology defines how to communicate with other party. All of the following factors affect choice of communication technology EXCEPT:

A) Urgency of the need for information

B) Ease of use

C) Team member motivation

D) Project Environment

8- All of the following about communication models is true EXCEPT:

A) Sender encodes thoughts or ideas

B) Sender transmits the message to receiver

C) Receiver decodes the message

D) Receiver agrees the message

9- Your project team is working in a virtual team environment. After you created the project plan, you placed it into corporate knowledge base and team members can download it from there. This is an example of:

A) Pull Communication

B) Push Communication

C) Interactive Communication

D) Virtual Communication

10- Communications Management Plan is major output of Plan Communications Management process. All of the following can be included in Communications Management Plan EXCEPT:

A) Time and frequency for distribution of required information

B) Roles & responsibilities of team members

C) Stakeholder communication requirements

D) Information to be communicated

Answers

	1 - D	
	2 - A	
	3 - C	
	4 - B	
	5 - B	
	6 - D	
	7 - C	
	8 - D	
	9 - A	
	10 - B	

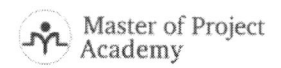

Mapping Game – Section 9

Left	Right
information provided at the right time, to right audience, with the right impact.	Effective Communication
Reports, formal meetings, meeting agendas and minutes	examples for push communication
conversations, meetings, conference calls	Project management information systems (PMIS)
information is sent by sender using medium	examples to formal communication
providing only the information that is needed	Project reporting
a set of standard tools to capture, store, and distribute information	examples for pull communication
e-mails, reports, faxes, blogs	examples for interactive communication
The act of collecting and distributing project information	Efficient Communication
intranet, e-learning, lessons learned databases	Transmit Message

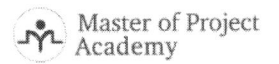

Answers

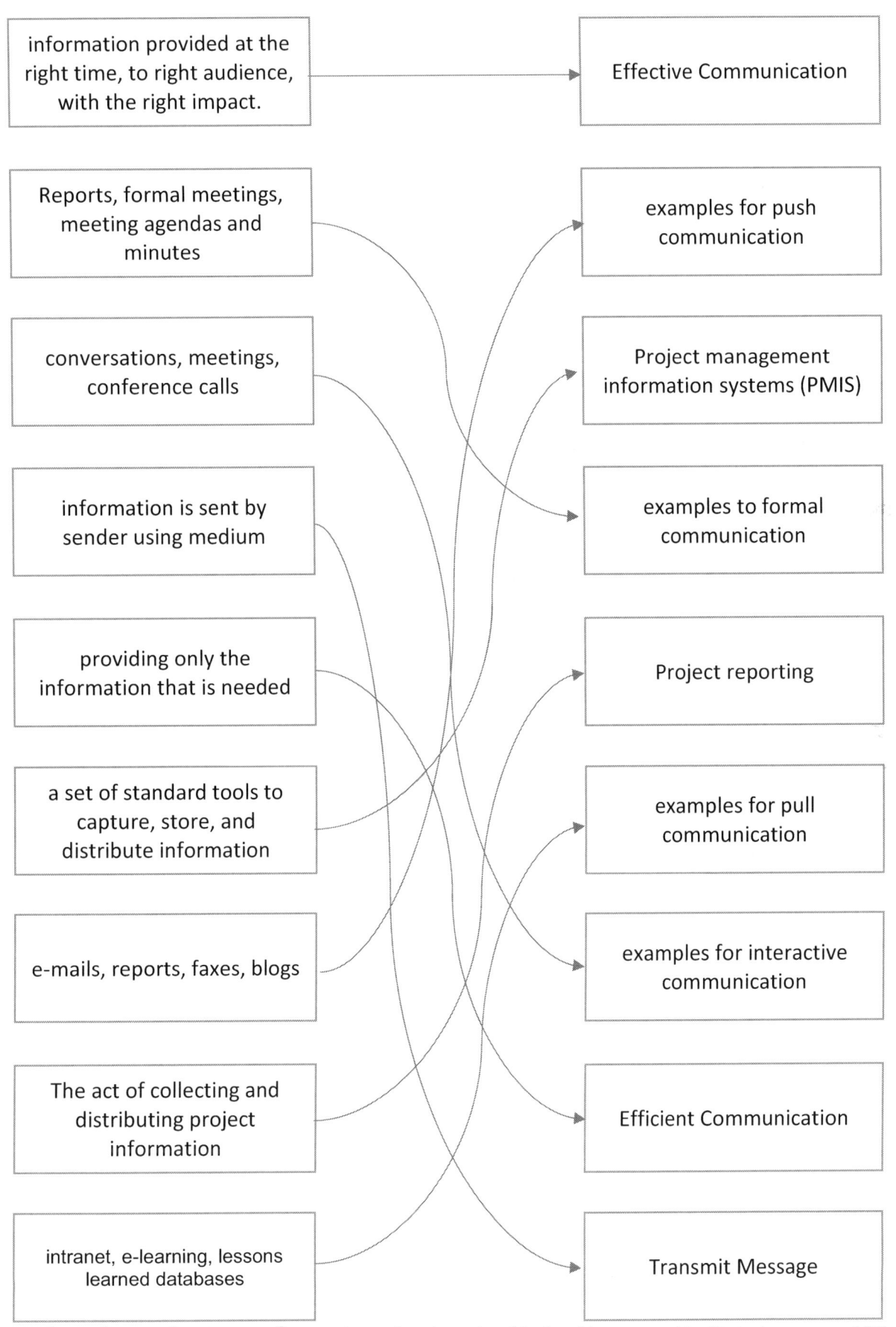

Left	Right
information provided at the right time, to right audience, with the right impact.	Effective Communication
Reports, formal meetings, meeting agendas and minutes	examples to formal communication
conversations, meetings, conference calls	examples for interactive communication
information is sent by sender using medium	Transmit Message
providing only the information that is needed	Efficient Communication
a set of standard tools to capture, store, and distribute information	Project management information systems (PMIS)
e-mails, reports, faxes, blogs	examples for push communication
The act of collecting and distributing project information	Project reporting
intranet, e-learning, lessons learned databases	examples for pull communication

Section 10

Risk Management

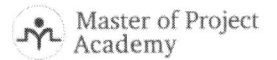

Section 10 – Risk Management

Risk Management knowledge area is another critical knowledge area in project management. There is a common misconception about risks in project management field. Risks are considered as threats to the projects. However, opportunities that will bring benefits to the projects are considered as positive risks in a project. During this section, we will be going through Risk Management in detail.

- **Overview of Risk Management:** First we will look on risk management briefly. We will define what risk is and what risk management knowledge area focusses on.
- **Risk Management Processes:** Then we will be going through the Risk Management knowledge area processes. There are seven processes of Risk Management knowledge area and we will be going over these one by one.
- **Risk Management Concepts:** We will be going over Risk management concepts. These are threats, opportunities, uncertainty, risk factors, risk averse, risk tolerances and risk thresholds.
- **Plan Risk Management Process:** After that, we will start with the first process of Risk Management Knowledge area Plan Risk Management Process. This is the process of how you plan to manage the threats and opportunities of the project.
- **Risk Management Plan:** Risk management plan is produced at the end of Plan Risk Management Process. We will be going through the Risk Management plan as well.
- **Risk Categories:** Risks are categorized for better coordination and management. We will be seeing risk categories.
- **Identify Risks Process:** Then, we will go through identify risks process. In this process, opportunities and threats of the project are listed to take proactive actions against the threats while improving the chance of opportunities to happen.
- **Risk Register:** After the risks are identified, they are listed in the risk register document. Risk register document includes the details about the risk, impact if it occurs, accountable of the risk and who will act once it occurs etc.
- **Perform Qualitative Risk Analysis Process:** Then, we will go over Perform qualitative risk analysis process. This process is the subjective analysis of risks in a project. Project resources and subject matter experts provide their opinions about the risk in this process.
- **Perform Quantitative Risk Analysis Process:** Next, we will see perform quantitative risk analysis process. This is objective and numerical analysis of risks in the project. Impact of risk, possibility to occur etc. are analyzed mathematically in this process.
- **Plan Risk Responses Process:** After risks are analyzed qualitatively and quantitatively, risk responses must be prepared to reduce the impact of threats and increase the benefits of opportunities. This will help us to figure out how to act for a risk when it occurred.
- **Risk Response Strategies:** Risk response strategies will be an output of plan risk responses process. There are different risk response strategies like avoiding, transferring, mitigating, etc. We will be seeing these strategies during plan risk responses process.
- **Implement Risk Responses:** Implement Risk responses is next process of Risk Management knowledge area. Determined risk response plans are implemented during this process.
- **Monitor Risks:** Finally, we will see the last process of risks management knowledge area, which is monitor risks process.

Overview of Risk Management

Defining Risk management knowledge area is best entry for risk management overview. Risk management includes processes of conducting risk management planning, identification, analysis, response planning, and controlling risk on a project. Briefly, risk management knowledge area deals with how to identify risks, how to plan responses for those risks, how to monitor risks, how to allocate reserves for those risks, etc.

- **Main purpose of risk management is increasing the likelihood and impact of positive events.** By this way, if there is any probability of positive events to occur and if those events occur, then your project will be affected in a good way and benefits that will come with the project will increase as well.

- **In addition, the other purpose of risk management is decreasing the likelihood and impact of negative events.** If you decrease the probability of occurrence of these kinds of negative events in your projects, then you will decrease the possibility of affecting your project in a bad way.

- **Project managers should focus on preventing problems.** If you remember, the main role, the main purpose of project manager should be preventing root cause of changes, preventing problems before they occur. Of course, the project managers must take corrective actions after a problem occurred or after a risk happened. However, the most important thing for project manager is to prevent bad things before they happen. Actions that are taken to prevent threats or bad things to happen are called as preventive actions, and project manager should focus on preventing these problems before they occur.

- **Risk management saves time and money.** Because, if you are better prepared for a risk that is probable to happen in your project, you will have a plan to act against the impacts of the risk. Since you have risk response plans, since you know how to act, how to overcome what the risk brought to project, you will have a plan to act and this will save you time and money. If you do not have a plan, you will struggle to overcome with the impacts of risk and most probably, you will lose more time and more money.

- **There are seven processes of risk management knowledge area.** These are:
    - Plan Risk Management (Planning)
    - Identify Risks (Planning)
    - Perform Qualitative Risk Analysis (Planning)
    - Perform Quantitative Risk Analysis (Planning)
    - Plan Risk Responses (Planning)
    - Implement Risk Responses (Executing)
    - Monitor Risks (Monitoring & Controlling)

This shows that, risk management is critical during planning phase of a project. Risk management activities are focused more on planning, because you plan how to act, how to react and how to overcome problems that will be outcome of risks in your project.

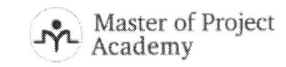

Risk Management Concepts

Before we start to see Risk Management knowledge area processes, we will define risk management concepts during this heading.

- **Threats and Opportunities:** First concept we will be seeing is threats and opportunities.

    - **Threat is a negative risk.** For example, if a flood happens in your project server's location, servers might be damaged and this might cause you to lose your project work. Because, in a software development project, software developers store their codes on servers, so, your project work is stored in servers. If flood happens, if servers are damaged, then, you might lose some of your work and this is an example of threat.

    - **Opportunity is on the other hand, a positive risk.** For example, if you buy 20 components at once in your project, you will pay 20% less in total for those components. This might be a promotion generated by a supplier, if you buy a bulk items or bulk materials in your projects. If the supplier makes you promotion due to your bulk buying, this might be an opportunity or positive risk in your project since you will be purchasing the materials needed for your project for a lower cost.

- **Up to 90% of the threats identified in risk management can be eliminated.** Therefore, it is important to conduct risk management activities and risk management planning in your projects. If you go through your risk management processes, you will be able to identify 90% of the threats that might be happening in your project in future. If you can identify those risks, you will be able to be better prepared for those risks, if they happen in your project. Once the risks occur, you will have prepared risk response plans and you will go through these planned responses to minimize the impacts of risk.

- **Uncertainty:** Uncertainty is another concept about risk management. Uncertainty is lack of knowledge about an event that reduces confidence in conclusions. You plan the project however; you never know what will happen exactly until it happens in time. Generally, there is less information available during the early phases of a project. So, if you are uncertain or if there is less information about the topic, about the problem, then it will reduce your confidence in conclusion. Can you make any decision; can you make any conclusion about an event, about a topic that you do not know about? Of course, you cannot. This is called uncertainty.

- **Risk Factors (attributes):** Risk factors are actually attributes of risks.

    - **Probability of its occurrence:** For example, probability of its occurrence is a risk factor. For instance, if the project team calculated possibility of the flood to happen during your project and if it is 15%, this is actually the probability of flood risk to happen.

    - **Range of possible outcomes:** Range of possible outcomes is another risk factor. These actually explain what the expected results of risks are. For example, if most experienced team member resigns, the project might be delayed. Alternatively, if a fault happens, reworks might be needed which will result in exceeding costs. These are examples of possible outcomes of risks.

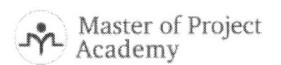

- o **Expected timing:** For example, if you can say that a risk might happen in following month or during execution of your project or at a specific time in your project, these are references to the expected timing of your risk.

- o **Anticipated frequency of risk events from that source:** If there is a recurring risk that is expected to happen in your project, frequency of reoccurrence is a risk factor. For instance, if you migrate your data in your servers at the end of each month, and if there is a risk of losing data during this process due to a technical issue, frequency of this risk is one month.

- **Risk Averse.** Someone who does not want to take risks are called risk averse.

- **Risk Tolerances.** These are the areas or limits of risk that are acceptable or unacceptable. For example, if your company says that any risk that affects company reputation is not tolerated, then you cannot take any risk that would affect the brand or reputation of your company in your project. Alternatively, if there are any risks that can cause to lose your company reputation, you must do everything to eliminate that risk to happen in your project. If you cannot eliminate, you should discuss it with management whether to proceed with project or not.
- **Risk Thresholds define the point where a risk becomes unacceptable.** Therefore, this is the up limit of a risk. For example, maximum acceptable delay time is two weeks for our project or maximum over budget limit is $100,000. These are examples of risk thresholds.
- **If you have a good risk management plan, there are no huge fires to put out every day.** Because if a risk happens, you know what to do, how to act, how to follow your risk response steps. You will have a risk response planning and by this way, you will be able to overcome the outcomes of risks in a planned way, in a methodological approach and this will save you time and money.
- **Risks are brought up in every meeting before they happen.** Since risks are discussed in meetings before they happen, everybody can say their opinion, their solving methods for those risks and this will generate better ideas, better plans to deal with risks in projects.
- **If the risk event happens, there is a plan to act.** If you do not have a risk management plan and if you are caught to a risk without a plan, it will take time to figure out how to eliminate the outcomes of the risk. This will take more time than overcoming with a risk with having a proper risk response plan. Therefore, there must be risk response plans for every identified risk in a project.
- **Risk can be identified at any time in a project.** Although most of the risk management activities are focused on planning process group, new risks can be identified during later phases of a project once more information is available about the project. Once new risks are identified, these must be worked and appropriate response plans must be prepared respectively.
- **Risk management process is very iterative.** Because, although you plan your risk management activities during planning process group, some risks might be outdated or

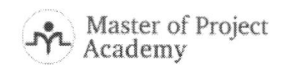

the probability of a risk might decrease over time during the project. Opposite of this can happen though that, probability of a risk to happen can increase over time as well.

Plan Risk Management Process

Plan risk management is the first process of risk management knowledge area.

- **This is the process of defining how to conduct risk management activities for a project.** Therefore, this process defines your steps, your approach and your methodologies that you will use in your risk management activities.
- **Major output of the plan risk management process is risk management plan.** Briefly, risk management plan draws the steps that needs to be taken to list, monitor and manage risks of a project. We will be going over risk management plan in detail throughout this heading.
- **Risk management plan includes methodology to manage risks of a project.** This includes approaches, tools, and data sources that will be used to perform risk management on the project. For instance, if there is a risk management tool that you will be using in the project, this will be part of methodology. Similarly, your roadmap to manage risks is under methodology umbrella. These are all defined on the methodology section of risk management plan.
- **Roles and responsibilities are also part of the risk management plan.** Who will do which risk management activities in a project? For example, if a risk happens, what will be the money source for the cost effects of the risk? Alternatively, who will be dealing with each activity in order to overcome the outcomes of a risk? These are all defined in roles and responsibilities.
- **Risk management plan includes budgeting as well.** Cost of risk management activities go under the budgeting. If you remember from our cost management knowledge area, we were defining contingency reserves for our activities or for our work packages. After we defined our budget, management was giving a credit for unforeseen risks in the projects as well. Under the budgeting section of risk management plan, how contingency and management reserves will be managed are defined.
- **Timing:** When and how often the risk management processes will be performed during project are determined under timing section. For example, will you be checking the last status of your risks each month, in every two weeks or weekly? This must be determined under timing area of risk management plan.
  Because the probability and impact of a risk might change during the execution of a project. Therefore, you have to process your risk management activities based on a predefined frequency during your project.
- **Risk Categories provide the means for grouping potential causes of risks.** Project management offices or companies should have standard lists of risk categories that can be applied in all projects to help identify risks. For example, cost risks, schedule risks, or analysis risks, development risks are examples for categorization.
  Assume that you are working in a software vendor. Sample risk categories might be analysis risks, development risks, design risks and test risks that are actually representing

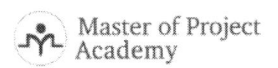

the phases of a software development lifecycle. These are different ways of categorizing risks in risk management plan.

- **External Risks:** External risks can be regulatory, environmental, government, or market shifts that are affecting your project. For example, if you are executing a project and if there is a law which will be published by the government that is affecting your project, and due to that regulation which will be published by the government, if you have to apply new processes, new activities in your project, this might cause extra cost, extra time in your project. This is an example of External risk.
- **Internal Risks:** Internal risks can be time, cost, or scope changes, inexperience, poor planning, people, etc. For example, if you have a junior resource in your project or an incompetent project resource that you assigned to a project activity, there might be reworks in their works, which will cost your extra money, and time in your project. Similarly, wrong planning can cause to waiting times or delays in project, which can affect the project schedule and costs respectively. These are examples of internal risks.
- **Technical Risks:** Technical risks can be caused by changes in technology. During execution of your project, a change might happen in technology and this might affect your project in a way that you have to revise your adopted technology in your project. In addition, you might have to do a rework in your project.
- **Unforeseeable risks:** Unforeseeable risks are actually a small portion of the risks. As we have seen before, almost 90% of the risks are identified during the management activities, and about 10% of the risks are unforeseeable for a project. You should have reserves for unforeseen risks as well and you must tackle with them once they happened.
- **Risks can be categorized by the source of the risks, or generator of the risks as well.** Sources or generators of the risks can be customer. For instance, if the customer cannot give the requirements of the project clearly, this will make the scope of the project unclear. In future, this might bring risks during acceptance tests that will be run by the customer.
- **Lack of project of management effort can cause risk.** If there is only a very limited time to plan a project although it needs more detailed planning, this will be risky. Details of the project might not be seen during planning which can cause risks to occur in future.
- **Lack of knowledge of project management is a risk generator.** Can you think of a project manager who does not know project management? This will be the top risk of the project for sure!
- **The customers and customer's customers might be the source of risks**. Because, you will deliver your work to your customer and your customer will use your project's product or outputs to serve its end customer. Therefore, customer's customer can generate risks for your project.
- **Suppliers can be source of your risks as well.** For example, if you are waiting materials, tools, equipment from your suppliers, and if they are delivering their deliverables late to your project, this will cause delays in your project respectively.
- **Resistance to change can bring risk to your project.** Generally, the organizations or companies are reluctant to change. This means, people generally do not want to change their behaviors or actual working behaviors, if they are used to do their work in a regular pattern. If a project is bringing a new methodology, a new approach or new technology to a company, then, people working in the company might resist to that change.
- **Cultural differences between the team members, between stakeholders might be a risk.**
- **Risks also can be categorized by source, for example schedule risks.** Here, there is an example. If John cannot finish on time, two engineers will start waiting to finish. Assume

that there are two successors of John's activity. Thus, if John cannot finish his task on time, then, two engineers will start to wait for John to finish his activity first. Otherwise, two engineers will remain idle and this will mean additional cost to the project since they will wait with no output.

- **Let us go over a cost risk.** If you buy the steel before spring, we will have 25% cost advantage. This is an example of positive risk. Due to seasonal changes in markets, prices of materials might change depending on the season you purchase. In this case, there will be a cost advantage if the steel is purchased before the spring.
- **Here is an example for quality risk.** Planning a training about the technology use in the project may decrease the number of defects in end-product. Because, the resources who are developing the end product will have more knowledge about the project after training and this will increase the quality of the end product, which will in consequence decrease the number of defects that will be received from the customer acceptance tests.
- **Scope can be a source of risk as well.** For example, if the analysis document is not clear enough to develop the software, then software engineers will have trouble when developing their codes. It will take time to clarify each requirement in the analysis document, this will cause additional time and cost in the project respectively. This is an example of scope risk.
- **Resource Risks:** If we cannot find an engineer who knows software architecture, project will be delayed. If you cannot find competent resources or required skills for your project on time, this will be risk for your project. This is an example of resource risk.
- **Customer satisfaction:** If we cannot provide a mature output, this will cause customer dissatisfaction during acceptance tests. Because, customer accepts a viable product when you come to the customer acceptance tests. If you demonstrate a product with lots of bugs, customer will be unhappy. Therefore, this is an example of customer satisfaction risk.

Risk Management Plan

Major output of the plan risk management process is risk management plan. Briefly, risk management plan draws the steps that needs to be taken to list, monitor and manage risks of a project. Risk management plan includes:

- **Definitions of Risk Probability and Impact:** Different levels of risk probability and impact can be defined that are specific to project. Therefore, probability and impact of risk can change from project to project. Same risks impact can be different for different projects. For example, an earthquake risk can have a higher impact for a construction project, compared to a software project. Because major output of a construction project is buildings, bridges, etc. If an earthquake happens, and if those buildings, bridges are damaged, project team will have to construct the damaged parts.
  However, if an earthquake happens, a software project will be affected less compared to a construction project. Because, in a software project, you are developing codes and those codes might be backed up in tapes or in external storage devices. If an earthquake happens, those work, those codes, those applications can be transferred from external devices, from external storage to new servers again. You will still need time and money to recover your work however; it will be not as much as in a construction project.

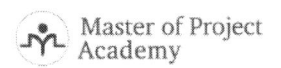

> A risk can have different levels of probabilities and impacts for different projects.

- **Stakeholder Tolerances:** For example, which stakeholder can accept which risk, and which stakeholder is risk averse etc. If there is a specific risk which is not accepted by a vice president, or if there is a specific risk which is not accepted by a functional manager, these should be noted under stakeholder tolerances.
- **Reporting Formats:** Reporting Formats define how the outcomes of the risk management process will be documented and communicated. For example, what will be the format of risk register document? What kind of information will be included in risk reports? What will be the detail level of these reports? These are all defined under the reporting formats section.
- **Tracking:** Tracking is the last section we will be seeing that can be part of the risk management plan. How risk activities will be recorded and how risk management processes will be audited are documented under tracking section.

Identify Risks Process

Identify risks is the second process of risk management.

- **Identify risks is the process of determining which risks may affect the project and documenting their characteristics.** In this process, you will identify the risks of your project. You will categorize the risks e.g. high impact, low impact, highly probable or low probable risk etc. Risk identification will help you to see all known threats and opportunities of your project.

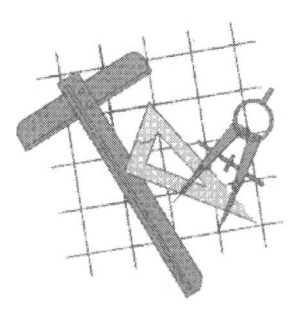

- **Identify risks process covers the documentation of existing risks, knowledge, and ability it provides to the project team to anticipate events.** Therefore, by listing your risks that might happen in your project, you will be able to identify their impact, their probability of occurrence. In addition, by identifying these risks, later in risk management activities, you will be able to create risk response plans for these risks. These response plans will help you to be prepared to minimize the impact of risks when they occurred.
- **Project risks are identified during the identify risks process and everyone should be involved in risk identification phase of a project.** From your project resource to vice president or general managers of your company, everybody can provide you input during risk identification in your project. Because, risks can hamper the project's success.
- **Risk identification is done first in initiating. At this stage, high-level risks of the project are outlined and these are put in project charter respectively.** Detailed risk identification then starts in planning phase of the project. However, new risks can come up or may be identified at any stage of a project.
- **Later during project, new risks can be identified since more information will be available about the project in later phases.** Similarly, impact or probability of occurrence of a risk

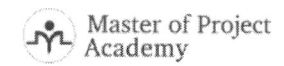

can change over time during project progress. Therefore, risk management is an ongoing process in projects.

Tools & Techniques for Risk Identification.

Risks are important factors that can affect a project's success. There are several tools and techniques used in identify risks project. We will be going over the tools and techniques used in risk identification one-by-one.

- **Documentation Reviews:** In this technique, project documentation is analyzed and possible risks are outline from the available information. Project charter, contracts, planning documents, assumptions etc. are documents of projects, and these are reviewed to check whether there are risks in the project. For example, an obligation in contract might be a risk for your project. Another risk example can be, if your planning is weak, if you could not allocate enough time for project planning, this might be risk of your project.
- **Information Gathering Techniques:** Which are used in Collect Requirements process can be used for identifying risks as well. These are Brainstorming, Delphi Technique, Interviewing, and Root Cause Analysis. We will see these techniques one by one.
    - **Brainstorming:** Goal of brainstorming is to obtain a comprehensive list of project's risks. You might have heard of brainstorming a lot. This is a very generic term not specific only to the project management. Project resources, stakeholders, executive team or other related parties express their ideas about the risks of the project.
        - Ideas about project's risks are generated and categorized. In this technique, a group of people starts to generate these ideas. Then, ideas are evaluated by the participants of the meeting and evaluated respectively. Then, the ideas are finalized by the participants' consensus.
    - **Delphi Technique:** It is a way to reach a consensus of experts, project risk experts participate in this technique anonymously. In Delphi technique, risk experts participate through a questionnaire or survey, and their opinions about a project are asked anonymously. After each expert provided his or her opinion about the risks of a project, these are combined together and results are sent back to the risk experts again for their review. This loop is continued until every project risk expert reaches a consensus, and then the overall risk list is announced to the project risk experts who participated in the survey.
    - **Interviewing:** Experienced project stakeholders, subject matter experts can be interviewed to identify risks of a project. Because, these professionals have past experience from similar project or expertise on a specific area. If you conduct an interview with these people, they will be highlighting the potential risks of the project.
    - **Root Cause Analysis:** It is a specific technique used to identify a problem. Similarly, we can use this technique in order to identify risks for a project as well. The main issue or generator of a risk or problem is tried to be found in this technique.
- **Checklist Analysis:** Risk identification checklists are developed based on lessons learned. If your company, organization, or your project management office has already a checklist for the risks identification, then, you can follow this list to identify risks associated with your project. Moreover, these lists are updated at the end of each project as well. Because,

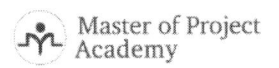

during that project a new risk might be identified through a different pattern, and that new identified pattern must be also listed in the checklist of the company as well.
- **Assumptions Analysis:** This technique explores the validity of assumptions as they apply to the project. During project execution, some assumptions that you have done in the beginning of the project might come true or may not come true. These are analyzed during Identify Risks process.
- **Diagramming Technique:** Tools and techniques used in Quality Management can be used under Diagramming Technique umbrella as well. If you remember, we have seen cause and effect diagrams, which were referred as Ishikawa or Fishbone diagrams as well, system or process flow charts and influence diagrams in our previous notes. These can be used for Risk Identification as well.
- **SWOT Analysis:** It is another technique used in risk identification. SWOT stands for Strengths, Weaknesses, Opportunities and Threats. SWOT analysis is not specific to project management world. This technique is widely used in marketing and strategy field as well to assess the feasibility of a market. This technique identifies strengths and weaknesses of projects, and this helps to identify the risks of the project respectively.
- **Expert Judgement:** Experts on a topic may directly identify risks of a project. For example, assume that you are working on a construction project. An expert in construction projects might identify the possible risks of your project directly. Because, he has several years of experience in constructions and his expertise will let him to see possible risks of a project.

Risk Register

Risk register is one of the most critical project documents belonging to risk management area.

- **Risk register is the output of identify risk process, and in this document risk information of the project is kept.**
- During identify risks process; project risks are determined with the risk identification tools and techniques. Determined risks are categorized, their probability to occur, impact if they occur etc. are all recorded in risk register document. Since risks' impact or probability to occur can change over time, risk register document is updated accordingly as well.
- **Risk register document includes the list of identified risks.** Generally, risk register document includes the risks in two different expression formats.

    EVENT may occur causing IMPACT
    (e.g. if _steel_ doesn't arrive on time, there will be _delays_)

    If CAUSE exists, EVENT may occur leading to EFFECT.
    (e.g. if _John resigns_, Project will be _deprived of his expertise_ and this can cause _demotivation._

First one is events may occur, causing impact. For example, if steel does not arrive on time, which is the event of this expression, there will be delays, and this is the impact of the risk if it occurs. Event is followed by the impact in this first expression format.

Second expression format is if cause exists; event may occur leading to effect. For example, if John resigns, project will be deprived of his expertise, and this can cause demotivation. John's resignation is the cause of this expression that will trigger the risk. Loss of expertise is the event that will occur if this risk occurs, and the demotivation is the effect of this risk if it happens. Risk register document of a project will include these kinds of expressions.

- **List of potential responses:** These are also included in the risk register document. We will go through the risk response strategies in our further notes. Risk responses define the actions or to do is to minimize the impact of a risk in a project. If a response for a risk is ready, it is documented in the risk register document as well.
- **If identified already, root causes of risks are also covered in risk register document.** Root cause of a risk shows the main reason or generator of the risk.
- **Updated risk categories are also covered in risk register document.** For example, if you have identified a new risk category that you could not identify in the planning process of your project, then, this new risk category should be updated in risk register document of your project.
- **If you just started the project, risk register will only have identified risks.** Because, generally, limited information is available in the beginning of a project. Therefore, you might have only the identified risks in the beginning and you might not have the risk responses, impacts, probability to occur etc.
- **As the project progresses, more information will be available and risk response, plans will be added to this document.** By this way, risk register will include what to do in the case of a risk occurs. This will help you to be better prepared to minimize the impacts of project risks.
- **If a risk response is already known at this stage, it can be documented in risk register.** During identify risk process, although you are in the planning process group, you might already know how to act or what to do in order to overcome the outcomes of a possible risk. In this case, you can document the risk response actions or plans in the risk register document respectively.

Perform Qualitative Risk Analysis Process

During previous processes of risk management, risk management plan is produced to draw how to conduct risk management activities in a project and then project risks are identified in identify risks process.

The next step is doing risk analysis. There are two types of analysis processes in risk management: qualitative and quantitative. We will be going over perform qualitative risk analysis process in this heading.

- **Perform qualitative risk analysis is the process of prioritizing risks for further analysis or action by assessing and combining their probability of occurrence and impact.** Briefly, two parameters of a risk are considered in this process when prioritizing a risk. These are probability of occurrence and impact of risk. Risk prioritization is critical because a high impact risk with high probability of occurrence will need a good risk response plan since it can push your project to failure easily.

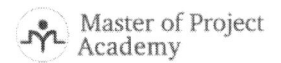

- **Perform qualitative risk analysis process enables project managers to reduce the level of uncertainty and focus on high priority risks.** Consider a risk that has a high impact and high probability of occurrence in your project. There is another risk that has low impact and low probability of occurrence. Which one would you focus first? Of course, the first one. Therefore, this risk prioritization helps project managers to focus on high priority risks first.

- **Qualitative analysis is actually subjective analysis of risks identified during planning.** This does not mean that any stakeholder can say his subjective idea about the risk. There is still a process to follow when prioritizing risks in this process and we will see it during this heading.

- **Risk probability and impact assessment is one of the techniques used in perform qualitative risk analysis process.** Risk probability means the likelihood that each specific risk will occur in the project. For instance, most probably, the most experienced software developer in the project team might resign during the project. This is an example of high probable risk in the project. A percentage or grade can be given to reflect the probability of the risk as well. For example, John, the most experienced software of the team might resign soon and the probability of this risk is 70%. Risk impact is potential effect on a project objective. Generally, these impacts are on project cost, schedule, quality etc.
  For example, if John resigns, we have to find a new experienced software developer and do the handover that will take around 3 weeks and $40,000 cost in total. You see that schedule and cost impact of the risk is stated in this example.

- **Risk probability and impact can be assessed in interviews or meetings.** During interviews or meetings with your project team or your project stakeholders, you can ask the opinion of the participants about the probability of risk and impact of risk if they occur.
  During these meetings or interviews, risk probability and impact are rated according to definitions in the risk management plan. These rates will help you to classify and prioritize project risks and focus on the most critical risks first respectively.

- **Probability and impact matrix is used to sort risks in a project.** Risks are put in a matrix with their probability of occurrence and impact. The matrix shows the most probable and high impact risks respectively. Company or project management office department of the company should standardize this matrix. Otherwise, each project will have its own matrix and this will decrease the uniformity of risk categorization in the company and will reduce the risk perception of the project stakeholders respectively.
  Probability and impact matrix makes this process more repeatable between projects. If how to produce the probability and impact matrix of a project can be documented and standardized, then, each project will follow the same steps when categorizing the risks of the project. This will help project stakeholders to evaluate impact of risks and their probability easily since they will be using same matrix structure in each project.

Probability	Threats Risk Score = Probability x Impact					Opportunities High (RED) / Med (YEL) / Low (GRN)				
0.90 Very Likely	0.05	0.09	0.18	0.38	0.72	High	High	High	Med	Low
0.70 Likely	0.04	0.07	0.14	0.28	0.56	High	High	Med	Med	Low
0.50 Possible	0.03	0.05	0.10	0.12	0.40	High	High	Med	Low	Low
0.30 Unlikely	0.02	0.03	0.06	0.12	0.24	High	Med	Med	Low	Low
0.10 Very Unlikely	0.01	0.01	0.02	0.04	0.08	Med	Low	Low	Low	Low
	0.05	0.10	0.20	0.40	0.80	Very High	High	Med.	Low	Very Low

Example Impact Definitions – May Be Tailored to Each Project Objective
Impact on an Objective (e.g. Cost, Schedule, Scope, Quality)

Here, we see an example of probability and impact matrix. On the vertical side, we see the ratings for the probability, and on the horizontal side, we see the ratings for the impact. Depending on the probability and impact of a threat or opportunity, these probability rating and impact rating is multiplied to find the risk rating of that specific risk. For example, assume that there is a risk, which is very less probable to happen in your project, and its probability rating is 0.10. On the other hand, its impact if it happens is very high, and it is 0.80. Since its probability is very low, although its impact is very high, as can be seen its risk rating is 0.08.

Similarly, if a risk probability is very high which is 0.90 and its impact is very high as well, which is 0.80, and then the risk rating will be the highest, which is 0.72. Based on this risk probability and risk impact assessments, you will have the risk ratings of each risk in your project. Based on these risk ratings, you should prioritize your risks in your project.

Risks that will be falling in red or darker area will have high priority while risks that fall in light green or lighter area will have less priority. When focusing on these risks, risk prioritization will be critical. High priority risks must be focused in detail since they might hamper the project worse compared to the other risks

- **Risk Data Quality Assessment is another perform qualitative risk analysis tool.** This technique evaluates the degree to which the data bout risks is useful for risk management. There might be several information about a risk of the project. However, not every data or detail might be useful for risk management activities. Risk Data Quality assessment technique helps you to collect and organize relevant information about risks of a project. This technique may include determining following for each risk:
  - ➢ extent of understanding of the risk,
  - ➢ data unavailable about the risk,
  - ➢ quality of data and
  - ➢ reliability and integrity of data.
    - ○ **Extent of the understanding of the risk** is an important parameter. An important risk might not be considered critical by some critical stakeholders of the project. If

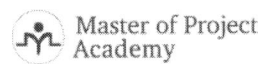

there is a misunderstanding or underestimation about the criticality of a risk, this is a big issue and must be fixed to focus on the risk at the needed level.
- **Data unavailable about the risk:** When the beginning of the project, there will be little information about future tasks and risks of a project. This is related with the data unavailable about the risk parameter. You might not have detailed and enough information about a risk in your project.
- **Quality of the available data** is important when performing qualitative risk analysis. If the available information is precise and accurate, you will have the chance of evaluating risks properly. If the quality of the data you have is not good enough, your risk analysis and evaluations might not be healthy.
- **Reliability and Integrity of Data:** Reliability means the credibility of the data. You have a data about a risk that might or might not happen in future. Your data about the risk might be true or might not be true as well. Reliability of data refers to credibility of data in this respect. Integrity of data refers whether the available data draws a comprehensive evaluation about the risk. Because, a standalone data might not be useful for some cases and integrity of data with other data might be critical to assess the risk.

- **Risk Categorization** is an important technique to categorize risks of a project. Categorization can be done in different ways.

  Risks to project can be categorized by sources of risk, the area of project affected, or other useful categories. For instance, if you are managing a software development project, it will have phases like analysis, development, testing, integration, deployment etc. These phases can be used as a categorization medium. For example, risks about software development can be grouped under development risks.
    - **Risk Categorization helps to determine the areas of project most exposed to the effects of uncertainty.** For example, if you have several risks in the development phase for a software development project, you will be able to identify that project is most exposed to the effects of uncertainty in the development phase of the project. Therefore, this will enable you to focus on the development phase with a special focus. This will help you to minimize the impact of risks that might happen in future.
    - **Risk Categorization may help to eliminate risks by eliminating one cause.** So, if you can categorize your risks, you will be able to identify the root cause of these risks by their category, and by eliminating the root cause of that risk, you will be able to eliminate all risks which are under that category as well.

- **Risk Urgency Assessment** is an important technique to classify risks and prioritize them.
    - **Risks requiring near term responses may be considered more urgent to address.** Assume that you have two risks in your project. One of the risks might happen in the next month. The other risk might happen in next 6 months. Since the first risk might occur sooner, risk response plans must be addressed first for that risk.
    - **Urgent risks are moved more quickly through the process than others.** Because, since there is little time left for the expected time of risk occurrence, if they happen, you may not have enough time to overcome with those risks.
    - **In some qualitative analysis, urgency is combined with risk rating coming from probability and impact.** If you remember, in our previous sub-sections, we have

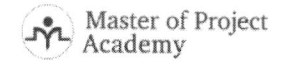

defined risk rating for each risk by multiplying the probability and impact scores for each risk. In some qualitative analysis, urgency of the risk can be combined when calculating the risk rating for a risk and this can give another approach to the risk rating in risk management.

Outputs of Perform Qualitative Risk Analysis Process

What are the outputs of perform qualitative risk analysis process?

Risk register: Risk register updates is the major output. Now, let us go over what can be updated in risk register after this process.

- **Assessments of probability and impacts for each risk:** Since you have scored probability and impacts for each risk, you can update risk register document with these values of the risks. This will help to prioritize risks in the risk register document.

- **Risk ranking or scores:** We have seen that risk probability, impact and urgency can be used to calculate the risk ranking or score. Once these ratings are determined, they can be updated in the risk register document respectively.

- **Risk urgency information can be updated in the risk register document as well.** Urgent risks might be addressed sooner than the less urgent ones.
- **Risk categorization classifies the risks based on their sources, affecting area or phase etc.** This risk categorization can be updated in risk register document.

- **Watchlist actually includes non-critical or non-top risks in the project.** Watchlist is part of risk register document. Watchlist may include low probability or low impact risks of a project. Although these risks are not that much critical, they must be watched since their probability or impact may change over time.

Assumptions Log: When assessing risks, assumptions might be done. During risk analysis, assumptions might change and this must be reflected in the assumptions log updates respectively.

Perform Quantitative Risk Analysis Process

Perform quantitative risk analysis process is analytical approach to risk assessment. Perform Quantitative Risk Analysis is **the process of numerically analyzing the effect of identified risks on overall project objectives.** In this process, effect of risks to the project are calculated and numerical results are produced.

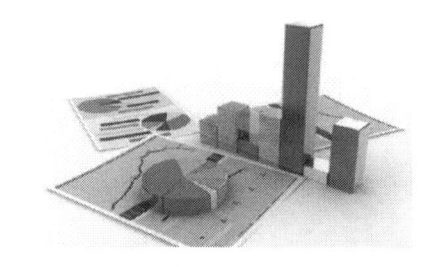

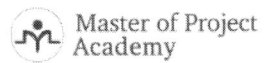

- **This process produces quantitative risk information to support decision making, in order to reduce project uncertainty.** At the end of this process, you will have analytical outcomes about how much the risk will cost to your project or how much it will delay etc. For instance, resignation of the senior developer might cost $40,000 and 3 weeks delay. This shows the numerical effect of the risk. Since it provides quantitative results, it helps to make a decision as well. Moreover, the analytical outcomes of the quantitative risk analysis reduce the ambiguity about the project that might come with the project risks.
- **Perform quantitative risk analysis process determines which risks warrant a response.** There might be several risks of a project. While some of these risks are so critical, some of the risks might be trivial and have very low impact to the project. Since you will have analytical outputs about the effect of a risk to the project, this process helps you to determine which risks warrant a response respectively.
- **This process determines the quantified probability of meeting project objectives.** For instance, you can have a probability of completing a project at a specific date with a specific budget at the end of perform quantitative risk analysis process. For example, we have a 90% chance of delivering project in 8 months, 95% chance of delivering project in 9 months and 98% chance of delivering project in 10 months. Similar calculations can be done for budget or other objectives as well. For example, we have an 85% chance of delivering this project with an $800,000 total budget.
- **This process also determines cost and schedule reserves.** For the risks that you could not avoid or eliminate, you need to allocate cost and schedule reserves to overcome the impact of risk when it occurred. These reserves will help you to overcome the impact of risks if it happens. Since the perform quantitative risk analysis process assesses the impact of a risk, it helps to determine the schedule and cost reserves of risks as well.
- **This process identifies risks acquiring most attention.** At the end of perform quantitative risk analysis process, you will have the impacts of risks to the project if they occur. This will help you to prioritize risks. For instance, the risk with a high probability to happen and high cost and schedule impact will require more focus than other risks.
- **Note that the previous process, perform qualitative analysis, is always done in projects, and actually it was subjective.** This means, it was depending on the opinions, thoughts or the experience of the people or the parties.
- **However, perform quantitative analysis may be skipped depending on the project.** In other words, this process is not a must that needs to be followed in risk management activities.
- **Another difference of quantitative analysis from qualitative analysis is, this process is objective, so it is not changing from person to person, or it is not changing from an expert to the other.** Because it generates numeric and statistical outputs of the impacts and probabilities of risks.
- **If your project is short and if you do not have many risks, you might skip perform quantitative risk analysis process in order to save effort.** Assume that you are managing a very short project, and you do not have many risks in your agenda, and even if those risks occur, it will not cost you too many time or too many cost. If you do this process, maybe you will spend more time or more cost compared to the effort and money that you would be spending when those risks occur. Therefore, in these kinds of cases perform quantitative analysis process might be skipped.

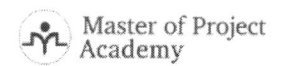

Tools & Techniques for Quantitative Risk Analysis

What are the tools and techniques used for Quantitative Risk Analysis?

- **Interviewing:** Interviewing relies on experience and historical data to quantify the probability and impact of risks on project objectives. As we have seen in our previous notes, in interviewing technique, a subject matter expert or an experienced project resource who participated in a similar project before is interviewed. His thoughts and experiences are gathered to do analysis in new project.

  Information can be gathered as in three-point estimation technique. We have seen this technique before. Optimistic, pessimistic and most likely estimates of a risk is collected. Let us go through an example.

WBS Element	Low	Most Likely	High
Plan	$3M	$3.5M	$4.2M
Develop	$15M	$19M	$23M
Test & Deploy	$7M	$9M	$9.5M
Total Project	$25M	$31.5M	$36.7M

Here, we see an example of interviewing technique. Assume that your project has three phases: plan, develop and test & deploy. You asked the interviewee budget estimate for each of these phases: lowest estimate, most likely estimate and highest estimate. Based on his experience, interviewee provided his estimations. In the end, total project estimation is calculated by summing up the budget estimate provided for each phase.

- **Probability distributions:** Probability distributions is another technique used in quantitative risk analysis process. Continuous probability distributions represent the uncertainty in values such as durations of schedule activity and costs of project components. In probability distribution graphs, you see the possibility of a project value cost, schedule, etc. to happen with its likelihood to happen in that value. See it over the graphs.

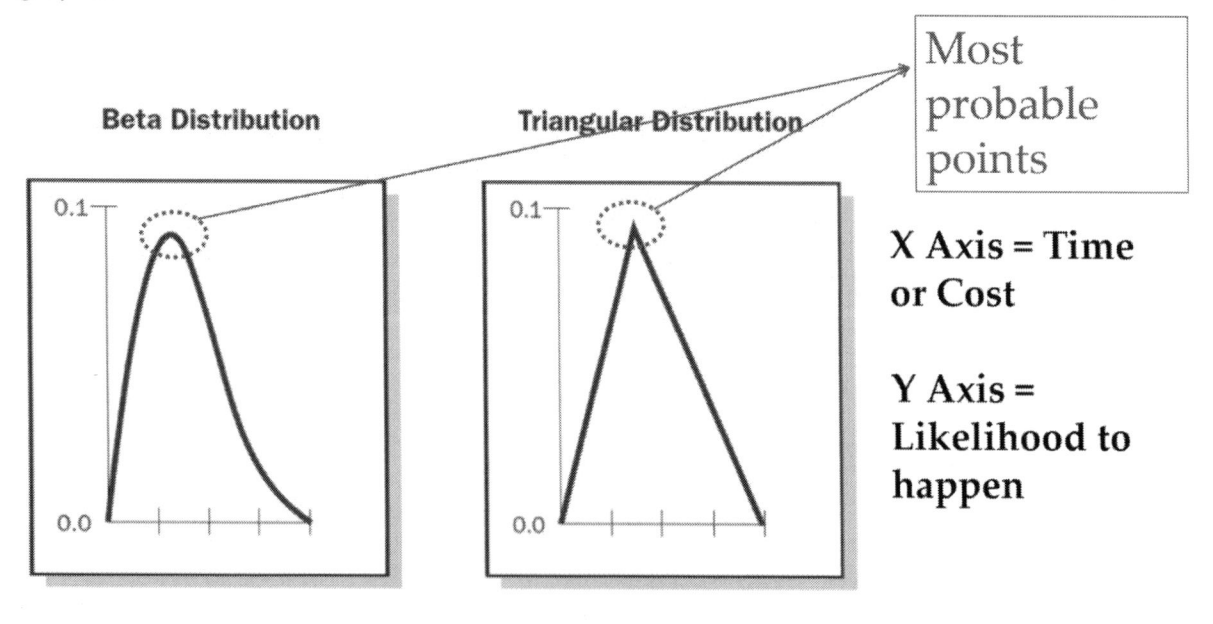

Beta Distribution **Triangular Distribution** → Most probable points

X Axis = Time or Cost

Y Axis = Likelihood to happen

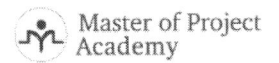

Here in this figure, we see two distributions, beta distribution and triangular distribution. In these figures, x-axis represents time or cost values and y-axis or the vertical axis represents the likelihood to happen for that value.

These top points or peak points of these graphs represent the most probable points to happen. In other words, an activity cost, a project budget or a risk impact will be most probably at these cost or time values.

- **Sensitive Analysis:** Sensitive Analysis is another quantitative risk analysis technique. This analysis helps to determine which risks have the most potential impact on the project. At the end of the perform quantitative risk analysis project, you will have the numerical or analytical results of what the risk impact will be. Sensitivity analysis technique visualizes the impact of risks in an understandable way. One typical display of sensitive analysis is tornado diagram. See an example of tornado diagram.

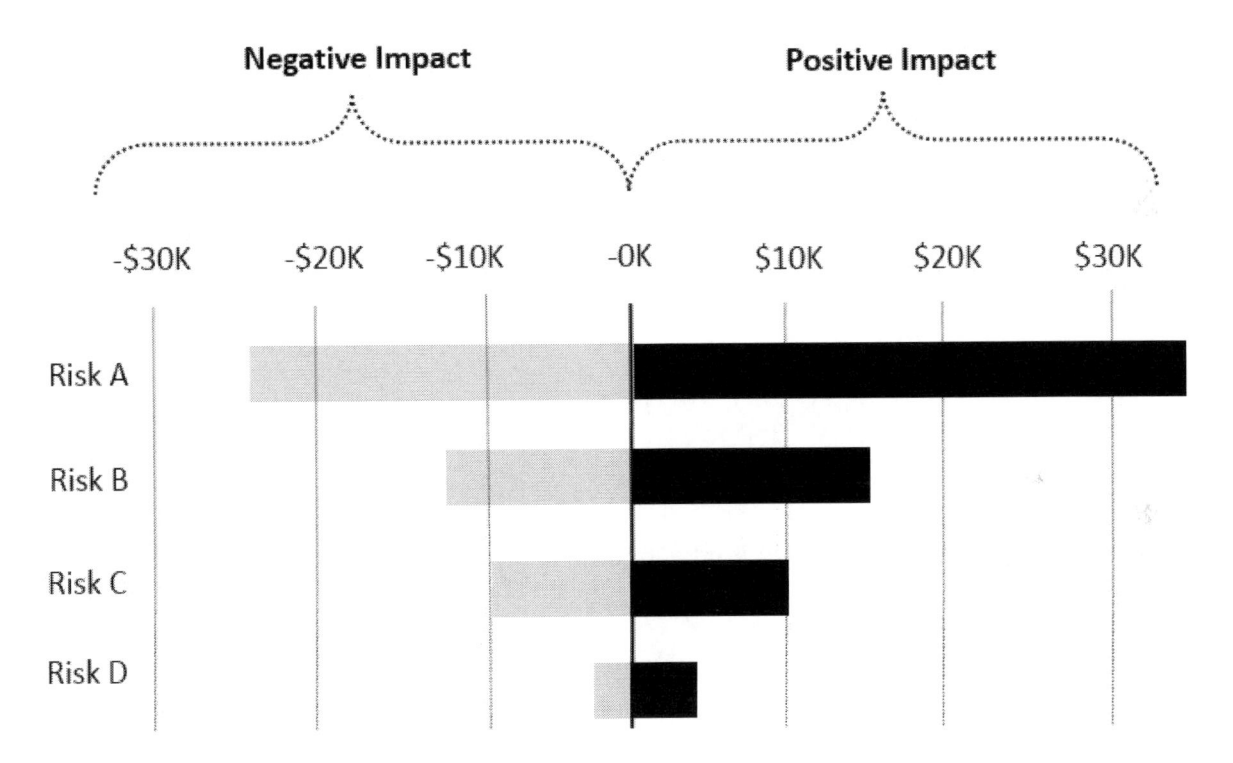

Here we see an example of tornado diagram. As you see, risk A has the highest impact for the project and the other risks are listed respectively from the most potential impact to the least potential impact. In this order, risk D has the least potential impact on the project. This graph shows the negative and positive impacts of risks as well. For example, if you look to the risk A, its positive impact is above $30,000 and its negative impact is around $25,000. This means that, if this risk happens in a positive way, it will bring $30,000+ value to the project. Alternatively, if this risk happens in a negative way, it will cause additional $25,000 to your project.

- **Expected Monetary Value (EMV) Analysis:** Expected Monetary Value or EMV Analysis is an important technique that we have seen in our previous notes. This technique is actually a statistical concept that calculates the average outcome when the feature includes scenarios that may, or may not happen. Basically, this technique calculates the impact of a risk in difference cases if it happens. Output of the expected monetary value analysis have two types of values. Opportunities generate positive values and threats generate negative values. Because, opportunity generates a benefit for the project, thus positive value reflects the benefit. However, threat hampers the project, thus negative value means additional cost or time to the project.

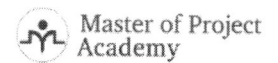

Expected monetary value of a project is calculated by multiplying the value of each possible outcome by its probability of occurrence and then adding these products or values together. Assume that the possible outcome of a risk, if it happens, is $100,000 and probability of its occurrence is 50%. Then, in order to calculate the expected monetary value for this risk, you need to multiply $100,000 outcome with the 50% probability and you will have $50,000 result as expected monetary value. We will go through a sample scenario to understand expected monetary value concept better.

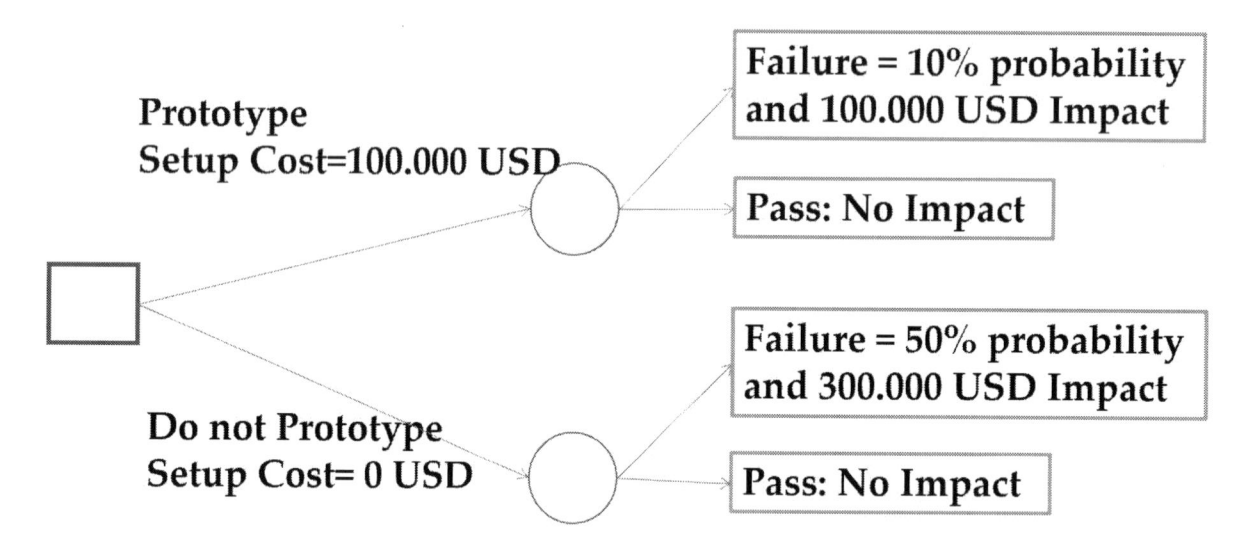

Prototype
Setup Cost=100.000 USD

Failure = 10% probability and 100.000 USD Impact

Pass: No Impact

Do not Prototype
Setup Cost= 0 USD

Failure = 50% probability and 300.000 USD Impact

Pass: No Impact

A common form of expected monetary value analysis is decision trees. We will see the possible outcomes of building a prototype or not building a prototype in a project. Let's go through the sample scenario.
First scenario is building a prototype in order to get the customer feedbacks in the project to reduce reworks that might happen in future. Setup cost for prototype is $100,000. If this prototype passes the tests, there is no impact. However, if it fails, failure probability is 10% with a $100,000 impact.
On the other hand, if you do not prototype, you will have zero cost for setup, because we do not have any prototype. However, possibility of failure is 50% with a $300,000 impact. Now we will calculate the expected monetary value of each case.

Expected Monetary Value of prototyping is $100,000, which was the set-up cost for prototype plus 10% probability of failure in case of prototyping multiplied by $100,000 impact, which may occur in case of prototyping. This equation gives us $110,000 as expected monetary value for prototyping. In order to calculate the expected monetary value of not prototyping, we need to multiply the impact of not prototyping, which was $300,000 by the 50%, which was the probability of failure in case of not prototyping. This equation gives us $150,000 as expect monetary value of not prototyping.

To conclude, since the expected monetary value of prototyping is cheaper than not prototyping, it is better to make prototyping. Because, it has a lower impact, or a lower expected monetary value compared to not prototyping. Prototyping is a better decision for this decision tree.

- **Modeling and simulation:** Modeling and simulation is another technique used in quantitative risk analysis. In this technique, specified detailed uncertainties of the project are simulated to find their potential impact on project objectives. There might be several risks and uncertainties in the project. Calculation of each scenario by hand or manually will be impossible. With the help of this technique, you will have the potential impact of these each risk on the overall project objectives.

  These modeling simulations are generally done by the aid of computer programs. Because, many parameters are considered when calculating the impact of risks on project objectives. Doing a manual calculation will be impossible.

  For example, Monte Carlo analysis is the most commonly used technique for this modeling and simulation technique.

  Modeling and simulation technique provides probability of completing the project on a specific date and cost. For example, at the end of simulation, you will have values like: probability of completing this project on June next year is 80% and probability of finishing this project with $1 million budget is 90%. You will have these kinds of results at the end of modeling and simulation.

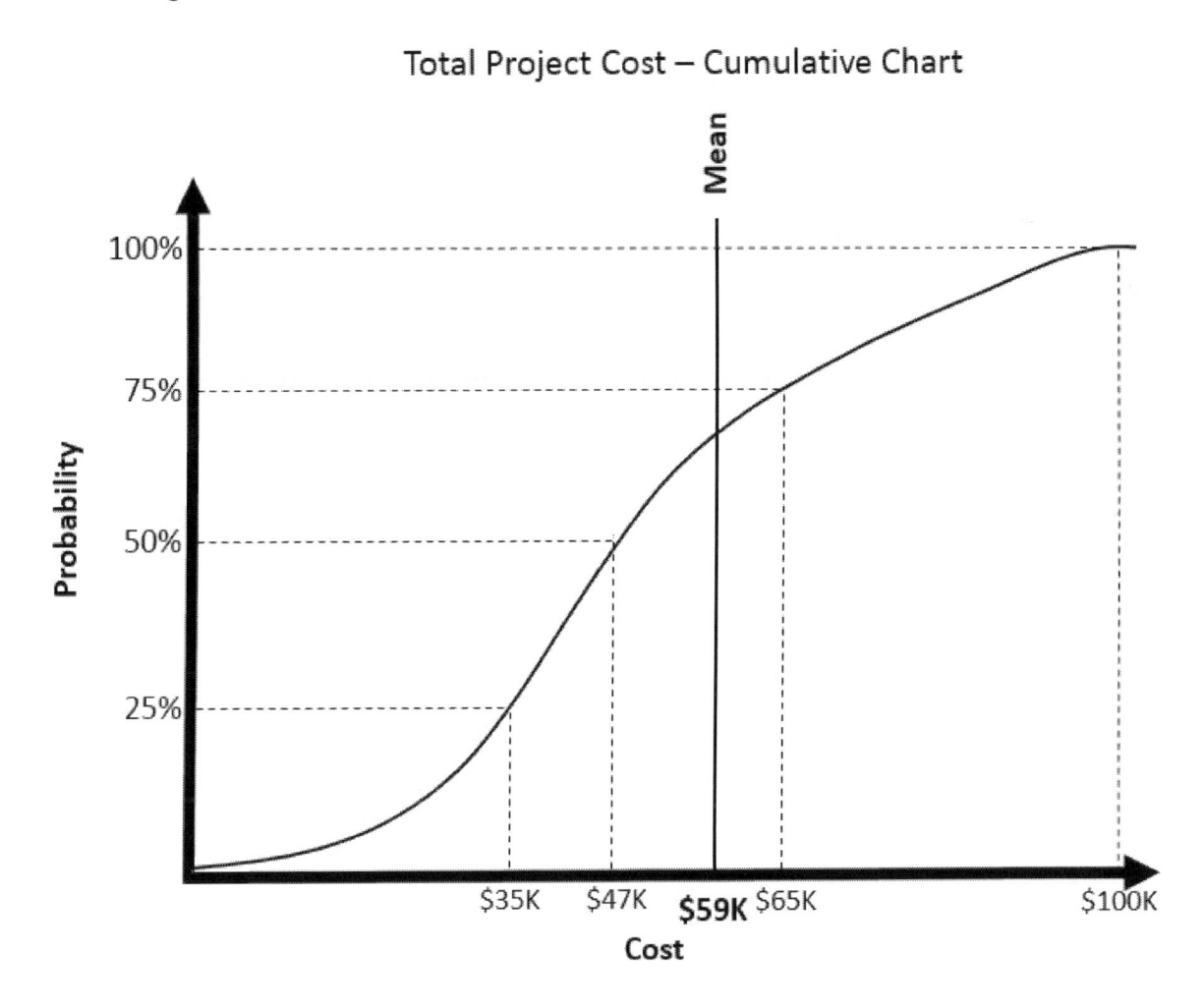

Total Project Cost – Cumulative Chart

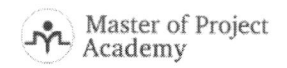

For example, here we see an example outcome of these simulations. In this graph, there are different probability levels for different costs. This graph represents the probability of finishing a project at what cost.

For instance, finishing this project with $35K budget is 25%, so it has a very low probability. Most probably, it will not be completed with $35K. Finishing this project with $65K budget is 75%. If you look to the 100% probability, you will see that the project will be completed with $100K budget. As you see, at the end of this kind of modeling or simulation techniques or Monte Carlo analysis, you will have probabilities for completing the project on specific dates and specific costs.

- **Expert judgement:** Expert judgement is the last technique we will be seeing in quantitative risk analysis. In this technique, experts define potential cost and schedule impacts of risks with their probability based on their experience. These experts are generally subject matter experts, which have several years of experience in their niche or field. We have seen this technique in detail in our previous notes, thus we will not go in detail here again.

Outputs of Perform Quantitative Risk Analysis

What are the outputs of perform quantitative risk analysis process? During quantitative risk analysis, analytical assessment of the risks is completed and these must be reflected in the risk register document respectively.

Risk Register Updates: During quantitative risk analysis, analytical assessment of the risks is completed and these must be reflected in the risk register document respectively.

- **Probabilistic analysis of the project, for instance possible completion dates, costs with their confidence levels etc. are updated in risk register document.** Because, at the end of quantitative risk analysis, you will have probability of completing the project at specific dates and at specific budgets. This information should be updated in the risk register document as well.
- **You should also update the probability of achieving cost and time objectives.** For example, probability of finishing the project with 41-million-dollar budget is 12%. These kinds of updates should be done in risk register document as well.
- **Prioritized list of quantified risks is updated in risk register document.** After quantitative analysis of risks, financial and schedule impact of the risks, if they occur, are determined. These results will help to sort greatest threats or opportunities respectively. A risk that has a big impact and high probability to occur must be focused first to address with a proper risk response plan.
- **Trends in quantitative risk analysis results also should be updated in risk register document.** Impact and probability of occurrence of risks can change over time. Therefore, quantitative risk analysis is a repetitive activity. For example, in the planning processes you might have identified a risk with a medium priority. However, during the execution of the project, this medium priority risk might climb up to a higher potential risk. These kinds of trends of risks for all risks should be included in risk register document. Because, you will conduct risk management activities regularly during your project. These updates and trends of risks should be updated in risk register documents as well.

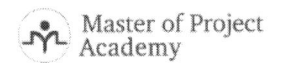

Plan Risk Responses Process

In previous processes of risk management, risks are determined, evaluated, and qualitative and quantitative analysis are performed to prioritize the risks and focus on the risks based on their priority and urgency. Next step is developing risk responses for these risks to overcome them when they occurred. This happens in plan risk responses process.

- **This is the process of developing options and actions to enhance opportunities and to reduce threats to project objectives.** Opportunities increase the chance of reaching project objectives and threats reduce the chance of reaching project objectives. Plan risk responses process aims to enhance opportunities while decreasing the threats to the project.
- **Plan risk responses process addresses the required resources and activities into the budget**. Each risk response will require a special budget or additional time to overcome the impacts of risk if it occurs. Once the risk response plans are determined, resources that will be working on response actions when the risk occurred and budget and time reserves for each risk must be reserved as well.
- **Briefly, plan risk responses answers what are we going to do about each top risk?** Risk response action owners, budget and time reserves, processes to follow etc. are all in scope of risk response plans and determined during plan risk responses project.
- **Plan risk responses aims doing something to prevent threats before they occur and doing something to make sure, the opportunities happen.** The main purpose of project management activities is reaching project objectives. As a project manager, you have to prevent threats before they occur. Similarly, you have to ensure that opportunities will happen.
- **If you cannot prevent threats or if you cannot make sure that opportunities will happen then you might look for decreasing the probability or impact of threats and increasing the probability or impact of opportunities.** Therefore, the first step is preventing threats or making sure that opportunities will happen. If you cannot do this, you should decrease the probability of bad things or risks or threats. Similarly, you should increase the probability or impact of opportunities or positive risks.

- **For remaining or residual threats that cannot be eliminated, you must have backup plans to overcome the impact of risk when it happened.**

    > **Contingency plans:** Contingency plans are executed once the risk occurs. These plans try to minimize the impact of the risk. It can include a budget to overcome the impacts or bad effects of the risk as well.
    > **Fallback Plans:** If contingency plans are not effective, you will need a second plan. This is called fallback plan. Although you have prepared a contingency reserve and

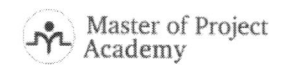

plan to overcome the impacts of a risk, your contingency plan might not work. In this case, you must have a fallback plan to deal with the impacts of the risk.

Risk Response Strategies for Negative Risks

We will see different Risk Response Strategies in this heading. Risk response strategies are divided into two groups: strategies for negative risks and strategies for positive risks. There are four different strategies for each group. Four common strategies for negative risks or threats are avoiding, transfer, mitigate, and accepting. Strategies for positive risks or opportunities, are exploit, enhance, share and accept.

As you might have noticed already, "escalate" and "accept" are strategies that can be applied for both negative risks and positive risks.

- **Escalate:** This strategy is appropriate if the risk is outside the scope of the project or proposed risk response would exceed the project manager's authority. For instance, if you are managing a project, which is under a program, and if another project's outputs are affecting your delivery, any delay risk of the other project is risk of your project. However, you cannot control the other project. In this case, you must escalate this risk to the program management level and program manager must take actions to avoid any delays that will be caused from regarding project.

- **Avoid:** This strategy is about eliminating the threat or protect the project from the impact of risk. For example, if there is a very risky work package, or if there is an incompetent resource in your project that will affect the outcomes of your work, you can remove the related work package from your scope. Similarly, if the incompetent resource will affect your project outcomes' quality in a bad way, you can look for replacement opportunities with a competent resource. These are examples of avoid risk response strategy.

- **Transfer:** Transfer is another strategy for negative risks. Transfer is shifting the impact of a threat to a third party, together with ownership of the response. This strategy involves payment of a risk premium to the taking party. For instance, using insurance, subcontracting a riskier part to a third party are examples of transfer strategy.
  For example, in a construction project, fire is a risk. In case of fire, you might lose your building or you might lose the components that you have completed during your construction project. By using insurance, or making insurance for your project, actually you do not completely remove the risk of fire. However, in case of fire, you will have an insurance payment that will cover your loss in the project.
  With the extra money that will be provided by the insurance company, you can rework or you can heal the problematic parts that might have happened because of fire.
  Subcontracting a riskier part of the project is also a sample transfer strategy. For example, if your project has riskier parts or components that need to be developed in a very short time and with a limited budget, and if you see that you cannot complete these activities

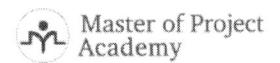

with the proposed schedule with provided project resources, you can subcontract these parts to another vendor or another supplier. For instance, car manufacturers work with suppliers for completing some components of cars. For example, the manufacturer does not produce wipers. They agree with a supplier and wipers are integrated in the car factory. This is an example of risk transfer.

- **Mitigate:** Mitigate risk response strategy is reducing the probability of occurrence or impact of a risk. For example, conducting more tests in your project will decrease the probability of customer rejection. Therefore, if you conduct more tests, you will have higher probability of getting customer acceptance easier.
  Choosing a more stable supplier is an example of mitigate strategy as well. If you will choose a more stable supplier, you will most probably have your deliverables; or your materials on time in your project. This will reduce the schedule delays in the project respectively. Similarly, prototype development can reduce rework risks in a project. For example, if you are developing a prototype and presenting this prototype to your customer before going in full production, you will have the feedbacks of your customer before delivering the final product. This will decrease the probability of rejection and reworks in the project.

- **Accept:** Accept is the last strategy we will be seeing for negative risks. Accept strategy is the acknowledgement of risk and not taking any action unless the risk happens. Actually, this strategy states "I know that there is a risk but I do not have any plan. If that risk happens, it happens."
  Best example of accept strategy is establishing contingency reserves such as time, money and resources, to handle risk when it happens. Therefore, in this strategy, you know that there is a risk that has probability to happen in your project and for that risk, since you could not eliminate, you plan extra time or extra money in order to deal with that risk when it happens.

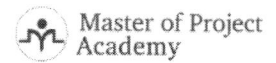

Risk Response Strategies for Positive Risks

Now we will see the strategies for positive risks or opportunities.

- **Escalate:** If there is an opportunity which is outside the project scope or if the response exceeds the project manager's authority, escalate strategy is appropriate. Opportunity is escalated to the program or portfolio management of the organization or other related parties of the organization to get maximum benefits out of the opportunity.

- **Exploit:** Exploit strategy is ensuring that opportunity is realized. In exploit strategy, necessary actions are done to ensure that opportunity will happen.
  For example, assigning the most talented resources to reduce time is an example of exploit strategy. If you assign most talented resources to your project team or most experienced resources of your organization to your project team, you will most probably decrease the schedule of your project respectively.
  Using new technologies to reduce cost is an example of exploit strategy as well. If new technologies enable your resources to deliver project work in a cheaper way or with a less effort, then, using new technologies might reduce cost of your project.

- **Enhance:** Enhance strategy is increasing the probability and, or the positive impacts of an opportunity. For example, adding extra resources to an activity to finish early is an example of enhance strategy. If you remember from our previous notes, this is an example of crashing technique and if you add extra resources to an activity, you can finish that activity earlier.

- **Share:** This strategy is allocating some or all of the ownership of the opportunity to a third party. Partnerships, teams, and joint ventures are examples of risk sharing. For example, Sony is an electronical manufacturer giant in the world and Ericsson is a telecommunication products manufacturer giant in the world. Sony and Ericsson were joint ventures in smartphone sector. This is an example of share strategy. In order to bring their expertise on telecommunication and electronics, they did a venture to produce better smartphones to the market.

- **Accept:** As we mentioned before, accept is a strategy for negative risk as well. Accept strategy is willing to take advantage of opportunity if it happens, but not actively pursuing it. In this strategy, you know that there is an opportunity or positive risk that will happen in your project. However, you do not take any action in order to make sure that it will happen.

Contingent Response Strategies

Contingent response strategies are designed for use only if certain events occur. Instead of risks, certain events or trigger points are monitored to execute contingent response strategies.

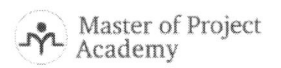

- **Events that trigger contingency response should be defined and tracked.** A schedule under performance level or a budget underperformance level can be the trigger point for executing a contingent response strategy.
- **These risk responses are called contingency plans or fallback plans.** An example of contingent response strategy is given here.
  If SPI falls down to 0.9, add extra one more resource to the project. If SPI falls down to 0.9, this means that you are behind schedule. If this is a risk trigger, our contingent response is adding one more resource to the project. With extra one resource, it is expected to complete remaining activities in a shorter time compared to the planned values. This will help to get back on track and complete the project on schedule respectively.
- **Knowledgeable parties express their opinions on actions need to be taken if a risk happens.** As in other processes, subject matter experts or the gurus in their areas can mention their opinions or thoughts about risk responses that can be taken for the risks of a project. These responses can be evaluated during meetings, and can be selected as a proper risk response.

Outputs of Plan Risk Responses Process

What are the outputs of plan risk responses process?

Project management plan updates:

- **At the end of plan risk responses process, you might need to update several project management plans such as schedule management plan, cost management plan etc.** Because, risk response plan actions might be correlated with the actions in the management plans.
  For instance, a risk response plan might require two weeks of additional effort to overcome the impacts of risk when it happened. In this case, this two weeks' time must be planned in the schedule management plan.
  Similarly, a risk response plan might require $60,000 additional budget to overcome the impacts of a risk when it happened. In this case, cost management plan might include this contingency reserve in the budget.

- **Other plans might require relevant updates depending on the actions that need to be taken to overcome the impacts of risks.** Besides, scope baseline, schedule baseline and cost baseline might require updates accordingly.

Risk register updates:

- **Residual risks must be included in the risk register document.** Even if you have tried to eliminate all risks of the project, some risks might remain that cannot be eliminated. These remaining risks should be updated as residual risks in the risk register document.

- **For the risks that could not be eliminated, we should have contingency plans or fallback plans.** In other words, if these risks happen, we should have time reserves, cost reserves etc. in order to accommodate the impacts of these risks. These contingency or fallback plans are included in the risk register document as well.

- **We should also identify and mention the risk response owners in risk register document.** If the risk happens, who is accountable to overcome the impacts of risk? Who will take regarding actions to overcome the risk? These are listed in risk register document.

- **Secondary risks are updated in risk register document as well.** A risk response can generate another risk for your project and those risks should be included in the risk register document. For instance, if adding an extra resource is a risk response to overcoming a delay in an activity, cost of this extra resource can generate the risk of exceeding project budget. There should be risk responses for secondary risks as well. Secondary risks with their responses must be included in the risk register document.

- **Risk triggers are the events that are triggering contingency plans.** For instance, a specific underperformance level can be a trigger for a risk response plan. These triggers are updated in the risk register document.

- **Contracts:** If some part of the project work has been given to a supplier or vendor, contracts with those vendors and suppliers might be updated in the risk register document as well.

- **Reserves for residual risks must be documented in the risk register.** Risks that could not be eliminated will require time and budget contingency reserves. These must be documented in the risk register document.

Project documents might require update as usual as it was in other processes.

Important Notes about Plan Risk Responses

We have gone through several points about plan risk responses process till now. It will be good to do a recap of what we learned during these headings. Now we will go over some important notes about plan risk responses process.

- **First one is contingency reserves are put for known risks.** If you remember from our previous notes as well, contingency reserves are allocated for the risks that we could not eliminate. We know that these risks might happen in project, and we will need additional budget or time to overcome the impacts of risks. For this reason, we plan time reserves, or cost reserves to minimize the impacts of risks when they occurred.

- **Management reserves are put for unknown or unforeseen risks.** Even if you do proper risk planning, you never know what exactly will happen in future. Although you determined the possible risks that might occur in a project, another risk that was not in your risk register might happen in your project. When these unknown risks happen, you will have to overcome the impacts of these risks as well. Management reserves are used for minimizing the impacts of unknown risks.

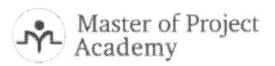

- **Non-critical risks are documented in watchlist and then visited periodically.** After risk analysis, risks are categorized; their impact and probability to happen are evaluated. After these analyses, risks are prioritized. A high impact and high probable risk is focused first compared to a risk that has low impact and low probability to happen. After this prioritization, non-critical risks are placed in watchlist and monitored periodically. Impact and probability of risks can change over time. For instance, a non-critical risk might be critical due to other progresses in the project. Therefore, watchlist must be monitored periodically.

- **More than one response strategy can be chosen for a risk.** We have seen different response strategies for risks in our previous notes. You can choose several strategies in order to overcome a particular risk in your project. It is not a must that you should apply only one strategy per risk.

- **Most important item to address in project meetings is risk.** As we have seen previously, risks impact, probability and urgency can change over time. A risk might be eliminated completely while a low priority risk might turn into a critical risk. Last status of risks are discussed in project meetings to keep the risk information up to date.

- **Risks are addressed with three major questions in meetings.**

    o **What is the status of risks?** Last status of the risks are discussed. Impacts, probabilities to happen and risk responses are re-evaluated whether they are up-to-date. Because, you will have more information about the project and risks as the project progresses, and this can change the parameters of risks respectively.

    o **Do we expect a new risk to happen in near future?** As we discussed already, although you do proper risk management, some lists might not be determined during identify risks process. There is always a room for new risks to happen in a project. In meetings, if there are new risks that might happen in near future, these are discussed and risk responses for these risks are determined.

    o **Are there any changes in probabilities and impacts of risks?** Probabilities and impacts of risks might change over time in a project based on completed events or other factors that affected the project. These changes must be discussed in project meetings as well.

Implement Risk Responses Process

Implement risk responses is the next process of risk management knowledge area and belongs to executing process group.

- **During implement risk responses process, agreed-upon risk response plans are implemented**. For instance, if transfer risk response strategy has been determined for a threat, and exploit risk response strategy has been determined for an opportunity, implement risk responses process is the process of where these strategies will be executed.

- **Implement risk responses process aims to minimize the effects of threats and maximize the benefits of opportunities.** With the help of this process, threats of the project are eliminated or the negative impacts of the risks are reduced. Similarly, opportunities are increased or positive outcomes of the opportunities are increased.

What are the outputs of implement risk responses process?

- Two major outputs are change requests and project document updates.

    - **Change Requests:** If implementing any risk response strategy causes a scope change, budget change, schedule change etc., this must be aligned with the project management plan. This is done through change requests.

    - **Project Document Updates:** As usual, processes require project document updates and based on the outputs of implement risk responses process, issue log, lessons learned register, team assignments, risk register and risk report documents may require updates.

Monitor Risks Process

Monitor risks is the last process of risk management knowledge area.

- **This is the process of tracking identified risks, monitoring residual risks, identifying new risks and evaluating risk process effectiveness throughout the project.** If a risk happens in a project, risk response plan prepared for that risk is executed in implement risk responses process. Risks in the risk register document are monitored and updated periodically in scope of monitor risks process.

- **New risks might appear in project.** These new risks are identified with the help of monitor risks process. Evaluation of the overall risk management of the project is done in monitor risks process as well.

What are the tools and techniques used in Monitor Risks Process?

- **Risk Reassessment:** Identification of new risks, reassessment of current risks and closing outdated risks are done in scope of risk reassessment. Risk reassessment should be done regularly and scheduled in the project. Because, impacts, probabilities, urgencies, risk responses, risk owners etc. might change over time. These must be updated respectively to have an up-to-date risk plan.

- **Risk Audit:** Risk audit is examining and documenting effectiveness of risk responses, root causes of risks and risk management processes. In the Risk Audit, you evaluate whether your risk responses will really overcome the impacts of a risk. Root causes of the risks are analyzed in risk audits as well. If you can eliminate the root cause of a risk, you can eliminate the risk as well.

    Other thing that risk audit does is, evaluating the effectiveness of risk management processes. Weaknesses of risk management processes are identified by the help of risk audits and corrective actions are taken respectively for a better risk management in the project.

- **Variance and Trend Analysis:** Variance analysis is done to compare the planned results to the actual results.

    For example, you might have planned ten days as time reserve and $10,000 as cost reserve for a particular risk in the project to overcome the impacts of risk when it occurred. Assume that, that risk occurred, and you spent eight days and $12,000 to overcome the impacts of risk. There is a two days of time reserve variation and $2,000 of cost reserve variation of this contingency response. These kinds of variance analysis are done with the help of Variance and Trend Analysis technique.

    Trends in project's execution should be reviewed using performance information. Are the probability of occurrence of risks is increasing or decreasing? Are the impacts of risks increasing during time or decreasing over time? These questions are answered with the help of trend analysis technique.

- **Technical Performance Measurement:** It is, comparing technical accomplishments to the schedule of technical achievement. For example, weight, transaction times, number of delivered defects, storage etc.

    Assume that you are delivering a software project. You did not receive any defects in last six months. Normally, planned date or the desired date for delivering that software was four months. It is good that you have delivered a very quality software, which did not receive any defects. However, you are exceeding the desired plan date for the project. Therefore, achieving this quality level is not feasible since it causes to exceed the project due date. This kind of Technical Performance Measurement should be done in Monitor Risks Process.

- **Reserve Analysis:** Reserve Analysis is assessing the amount of the contingency reserves for the remaining risks. For example, you might have planned ten days as time reserve and $10,000 as cost reserve in order to accommodate a particular risk that might happen in your project during planning processes.

    However, during execution, after you reassessed this risk, you might have seen that if you can reserve five days and $5,000 as contingency reserve for that risk, it will be sufficient. Since impact of risks if they occur might change over time, reserve analysis should be done in order to re-evaluate your reserve needs for your remaining risks in your project.

    After reserve analysis, if probability of a risk to happen reduced to 0%, or in other words, if that risk will not happen anymore, reserves planned to overcome the impacts of that risk is returned to company. Because, you will not use that contingency reserve any more.

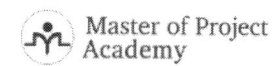

- **Meetings:** Project risks must be a major topic in project status meetings. You should go over the remaining risks and update their information based on last status. If there are new risks upcoming in near future, risk responses must be discussed. Briefly, risks must be evaluated and updated in project meetings.

What are the outputs of Monitor Risk Process?

- **Work Performance Information.** What was the planned value of an activity? What is the actual value? What have you planned as a contingency reserve for a risk and what is the actual time you spent or actual money you have spent in order to overcome that risk? This kind of work performance information are outputs of Monitor Risk Process.

- **Change Requests, recommended corrective actions and preventive actions can be outputs of Monitor Risks Process.** For instance, you might find a way to reduce the probability of a risk in your project. In order to reduce the probability, you might need to add new tasks to the project, which means a change request. This is an example of how change requests can be output of monitor risks process.

- **Project Management Plan updates, Project Documents and Organizational Process updates are also outputs of Monitor Risks Process.** Since these are outputs of many processes, we will not go over these in detail. We already know that when things change in a project, documents and plans need an update.

Quiz – Section 10

1- All of the following are purposes of Risk Management activities EXCEPT:

   A) Conducting risk management planning

   B) Increasing likelihood and impact of positive events

   C) Decreasing likelihood and impact of negative events

   D) Allocating reserves for risks

2- All of the Risk Management processes belong to planning process group EXCEPT:

   A) Identify Risks

   B) Monitor Risks

   C) Perform Quantitative Risk Analysis

   D) Perform Qualitative Risk Analysis

3- Risks have several factors. All of the following are risk factors EXCEPT:

   A) Probability of its occurrence

   B) Expected Timing

   C) Management Reserves

   D) Range of possible outcomes

4- During your project planning, it has been decided that maximum budget exceeding can be 100.000 USD. This is an example of:

   A) Risk Threshold

   B) Risk Averse

   C) Risk Tolerance

   D) Risk Reserve

5- Risk Management Plan is major output of Plan Risk Management Process. All of the following are included in Risk Management Plan EXCEPT:

   A) Project Organization Chart

   B) Risk Categories

   C) Budgeting

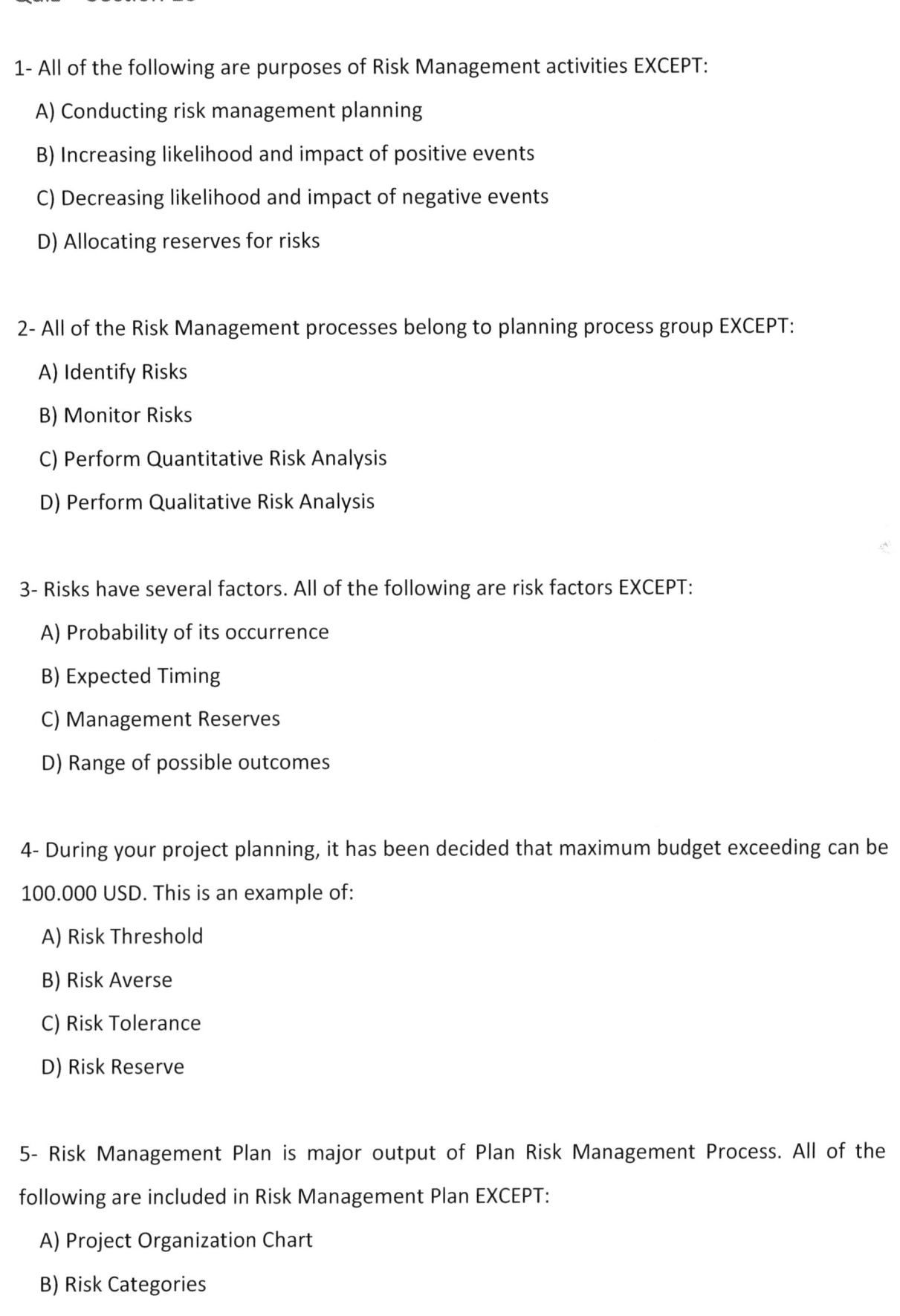

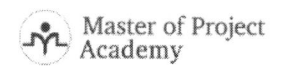

D) Roles and Responsibilities

6- All of the following about Identify Risks process are true EXCEPT:

A) Project risks are identified

B) Characteristics of risks are identified

C) Project risks are identified only by project management team and sponsor

D) Existing risks are documented

7- You will be starting to a new hospital construction project. Your company completed a similar project in past and you scheduled a meeting with a team member of previous project in order to ask risks of previous project. You used which of the following techniques of Identify Risks process?

A) Documentation review

B) Interviewing

C) Root Cause analysis

D) Brainstorming

8- SWOT analysis is a technique used in Identify Risks process. SWOT stands for:

A) Strict, Weighting, Opportunities and Threats

B) Straight, Weaknesses, Opportunities, Tight

C) Strengths, Weaknesses, Opportunities and Trust

D) Strengths, Weaknesses, Opportunities and Threats

9- Which of the following documents include information about risks?

A) Schedule Baseline

B) Scope Baseline

C) Risk List

D) Risk Register

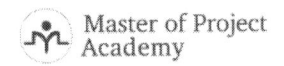

10- Agreed-upon risk response strategies are executed in which of the following risk management processes?

A) Perform Quantitative Risk Analysis

B) Identify Risks

C) Implement Risk Responses

D) Monitor Risks

11- All of the following about Risk Register document is true EXCEPT:

A) Created in initiating and finalized in planning process group.

B) Includes list of identified risks

C) Includes list of potential responses

D) Includes root causes of risks

12- All of the following about Perform Qualitative Risks Analysis process is true EXCEPT:

A) Risks are prioritized

B) Reduces the level of uncertainty

C) Objective analysis of risks is done

D) Enables to focus on high-priority risks

13- All of the following are benefits of using Probability and Impact Matrix EXCEPT:

A) Sorts risks based on their importance

B) Eliminates several risks

C) Can be used as a standard in entire company

D) Enables the prioritization process repeatable in other projects

14- Some risks that might occur in near-term need to be addressed first. In order to do determine near-term risks, which of the following should be done?

A) Risk Data Quality Assessment

B) Risk Urgency Assessment

C) Risk Categorization

D) Risk Response Planning

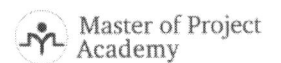

15- All of the following about Perform Quantitative Risk Analysis Process is true EXCEPT:

A) Numerically analyzes the effect of identified risks

B) Determines which risks warrant a response

C) Subjective analysis and cannot be skipped in a project

D) Determines cost and schedule reserves

16- There are several techniques that can be used in Perform Quantitative Risk Analysis process. In your project, you want to see most probable and affect point for a risk. Which technique is BEST for this purpose?

A) Interviewing

B) Sensitivity Analysis

C) Expected Monetary Value Analysis

D) Probability Distribution

17- In your project, you are evaluating whether to make insurance or not for your construction project. Probability of an earthquake to happen during your project is 2% and if earthquake happens, it will cost a 1.000.000 USD rework in your project. What is the expected monetary value of this threat?

A) 20.000 USD

B) 200.000 USD

C) 1.000.000 USD

D) Information provided is not sufficient

18- During risk management activities, options and actions need be planned in order to enhance opportunities and to reduce threats. This is done during:

A) Plan Risk Responses

B) Identify Risks

C) Perform Qualitative Risk Analysis

D) Perform Quantitative Risk Analysis

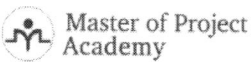

19- Which of the following risk response strategies can be applied both for opportunities and threats?

   A) Avoid

   B) Exploit

   C) Mitigate

   D) Escalate

20- You are managing a project. A part of your project has a very risky work package. In order to decrease the risk of your project, you removed the regarding work package from your project after negotiating with customer. Which response strategy did you choose for this risk?

   A) Avoid

   B) Transfer

   C) Mitigate

   D) Accept

21- A customer has requested a device, which can locate their vehicles via GPS technology and an application for tracking the vehicles. Your company has an experience on hardware design and decided to get the software application from another company, which is expert on software development. This is an example of which risk response strategy?

   A) Exploit

   B) Enhance

   C) Share

   D) Accept

22- During your risk management activities, you have avoided, transferred or mitigated several risks. There are still 4 risks remaining. Which of the following is the BEST action?

   A) Removing regarding work package from scope

   B) Planning contingency reserves for remaining risks

   C) Shifting the risks to another party

   D) Reducing probability of occurrence of risks

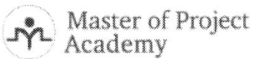

23- Which of the following is an output of Plan Risk Responses process?

A) Scope Baseline

B) Schedule Baseline

C) Cost Baseline

D) All of the above

24- During your risk management activities, you can eliminate several risks. After risk management activities, remaining risks are called as:

A) Reserve

B) Risk Response

C) Risk Register

D) Residual Risks

25- Your project is behind schedule. In order to get back on track, you added extra resources to delaying activities in your project. However, this response plan can cause you to exceed your project budget. This is an example of:

A) Secondary Risk

B) Contingency Reserve

C) Management Reserve

D) Inevitable Risk

26- During risk management activities of your project, you determined that if project's schedule performance index (SPI) falls below 0.9, you will put extra resources to your project. Fall of SPI below 0.9 is an example of:

A) Risk Starter

B) Risk Action

C) Risk Trigger

D) Risk Register

27- All of the following about Risk Management is true EXCEPT:

A) Non-critical risks are monitored in watchlist document

B) Only one best response for a risk can be chosen

C) Contingency reserves are put for "known" risks

D) Management reserves are put for "unknown" risks

28- Which one of the following is the most important item to address in project status meetings?

A) Upcoming milestones

B) Risks

C) Current progress

D) Accomplished tasks

29- In your project, you want to compare the planned results with the actual results regarding risks. Which of the following technique would you use?

A) Risk Audits

B) Meetings

C) Reserve Analysis

D) Variance and Trend Analysis

30- All of the following are outputs of Control Risks process EXCEPT:

A) Planning response strategies for risks

B) Work Performance Information

C) Project Document Updates

D) Change Requests

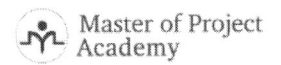

31- You planned a contingency reserve for a residual risk in your project during planning process group. Later in execution process group, you discovered that risk that you planned a contingency reserve will not happen. What would you do the contingency reserve allocated for that risk?

A) Add extra resources to finish project earlier

B) Allocate for other risks

C) Return to company

D) Wait for end of the project

Answers

1 – D	21 – C
2 – B	22 – B
3 – C	23 – D
4 – A	24 – D
5 – A	25 – A
6 – C	26 – C
7 – B	27 – B
8 – D	28 – B
9 – D	29 – D
10 – C	30 – A
11 – A	31 – C
12 – C	
13 – B	
14 – B	
15 – C	
16 – D	
17 – A	
18 – A	
19 – D	
20 – A	

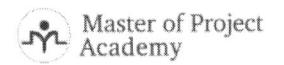

Mapping Game – Section 10

The Point where a risk becomes unacceptable	Risk breakdown structure (RBS)
Uncertainty exists about some key characteristics of a planned event or activity	Management
lack of knowledge about an event that reduces confidence in conclusions	Ambiguity risk
hierarchical representation of potential sources of risk	Risk Threshold
Eliminating the threat or protect the project from its impact	Share
Proposed risk response would exceed the project manager's authority	Avoid
allocating some or all of the ownership of the opportunity to a 3rd party	Uncertainty
The reserves are put for "known" risks.	Variability risk
The reserves are put for "unknown" risks.	Contingency

Answers

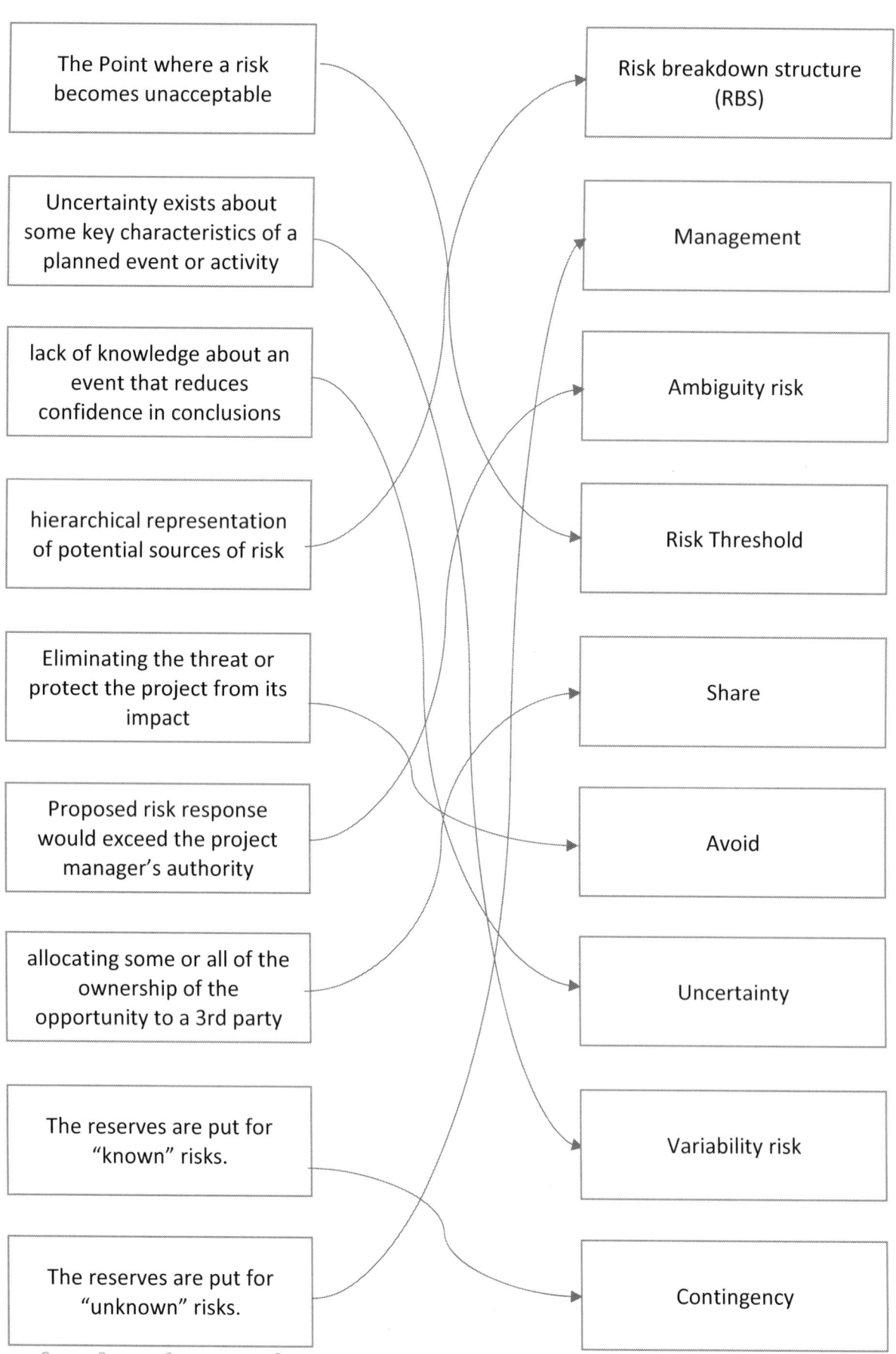

Left	Right
The Point where a risk becomes unacceptable	→ Risk Threshold
Uncertainty exists about some key characteristics of a planned event or activity	→ Variability risk
lack of knowledge about an event that reduces confidence in conclusions	→ Ambiguity risk
hierarchical representation of potential sources of risk	→ Risk breakdown structure (RBS)
Eliminating the threat or protect the project from its impact	→ Avoid
Proposed risk response would exceed the project manager's authority	→ Management
allocating some or all of the ownership of the opportunity to a 3rd party	→ Share
The reserves are put for "known" risks.	→ Contingency
The reserves are put for "unknown" risks.	→ Uncertainty

462

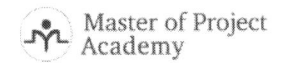

Section 11

Procurement Management

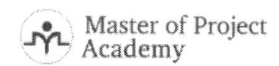

Section 11 – Procurement Management

Dictionary definition of procurement is the action of obtaining or procuring something. Similarly, in project management, you will need human resources, materials, tools, equipment and other items to deliver the project scope. For instance, in a construction project, you will need wood, steel, cement, vehicles etc. to complete the project.

> Procurement management knowledge area mainly deals with preparing contracts with regarding parties to obtain necessary items for the project.

What will be the agenda of this section?

- **Overview of Procurement Management:** What it covers and what this knowledge area aims to succeed in a project.

- **Procurement Management Processes:** There are four processes in procurement knowledge area. We will be describing the role of each process briefly.

- **Procurement Concepts:** We will define what the buyer and what the seller is. We will give tips about procurement and define the role of the project manager in procurement. We will describe the two types of contracting which are decentralized and centralized contracting as well.

- **Plan Procurement Management Process:** We will see the first process of procurement management knowledge area: plan procurement management process. This process mainly deals with how the procurement management activities will be managed throughout the project.

- **Types of Contracts:** We will see the different types of contracts. Fixed price contracts, cost reimbursable contracts, and time and material contracts. There are also different variations of these contracts. We will be going over different types of contracts.

- **Terms and Concepts about Contracts:** If there will be any dispute between the buyer and seller, and if this cannot be resolved, contract terms will be determining to solve the issue in justice.

- **Procurement Management Plan:** Procurement management plan will define how to conduct procurement during the project. For instance, when you need a material or equipment, which type of contract will be used or which supplier must be contacted etc. are all defined in procurement management plan.

- **Conduct Procurements Process:** It is the execution part of procurement. When you will need to purchase tools, equipment or material, you will follow the steps defined in procurement management plan. Procurement is executed during conduct procurements process.

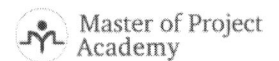

- **Control Procurement Process:** It checks whether the procurement occurs as planned in the project. For instance, if you have agreed with a supplier to provide steel for your construction project, in control procurements process, you will check whether the supplier meets the contract terms and conditions. For example, you will check whether the supplier delivers the material on time, in agreed quality and whether your company as the buyer pays appropriately to the supplier. After the contract conditions and terms are met, for instance if the supplier delivered the agreed materials, tools and equipment and if the buyer paid for these, contract is closed in this process as well.

Overview of Procurement Management

Procurement Management includes processes necessary to purchase or acquire products, services, or results needed from outside the project team. As we have seen in the previous heading, you will need materials, tools and equipment to deliver the project scope. To do this, you have to deal with the vendors and suppliers.

- **Procurement management knowledge area helps to plan, manage and control procurement of these products, services or other things from these suppliers or vendors.** This is ensured with the help of the contract management processes. In our further notes, we will be going over each procurement knowledge area process in detail.

There are mainly three processes of Procurement Management knowledge area.

1. **Plan Procurement Management (Planning):** This process plans how the procurement will be done throughout the project. Types of contracts, how to prepare contracts, how to procure items, preferred suppliers etc. are planned during this process.

2. **Conduct Procurements (Executing):** In this process, planned procurement steps are executed.

- **Control procurements (Monitoring & Controlling):** Signed contracts, terms and conditions are monitored in this process. For instance, whether the suppliers deliver on time with the agreed quality is checked in this process. Once the contract terms and conditions are met, for instance if the supplier provided the products and services as required, contract is closed in control procurements process as well.

Procurement Concepts

There are special terms and concepts specific to procurement. We have to learn these concepts. We will be going over the procurement concepts in this heading.

- **Buyers and sellers:**

- **Seller:** Seller is actually company or person who provides services or goods. We frequently mention contractors, subcontractors, vendors, service providers or suppliers during our notes. Actually, these organizations or companies are sellers to a buyer organization. For example, you give a part or a work package of your project work to a subcontractor so they are providing a work package to you, so they are seller. Alternatively, you might be acquiring some of the materials, some of the goods, some of the products that you will be using in your project from a specific supplier, so they are selling goods. They are seller to your project as well.

- **Buyer:** Buyer is actually company or person who purchases the services, goods or materials. For instance, if you are hiring outsource personnel from a consulting company for your software development project, you are buyer in this case.

> In the exam, unless the otherwise is stated, assume that you are in a buyer organization.

- **Seller is not supplying people to adjunct the buyer's team.** Assume that you are working in an automotive company. You are working on production of a new car model. Your company agreed with a vendor to provide the wipers of the car. In this case, people working on the production of wipers are not considered as your project team. Because, wipers are belonging to the seller's team and once they will be ready, the supplier will provide them to you to implement in your new car model.

- **Seller remains external to project team.** Because, although they are delivering materials for your project or delivering a part of your project work, they are external to your project team. They are not part of your project team.

Now we will see important tips about procurement.

- **Contracts require formality.** Because if there will be a dispute, if there will be a problem throughout the project, and if the parties cannot resolve the dispute, it must be solved in courts. In this case, terms and conditions of the contract will be binding which side is right or wrong. Therefore, requirements, terms and conditions of contracts should require formality and should be protected by laws of the regarding company or should be protected by international laws.

- **Project requirements should be documented in contract.** If there are schedule requirements, cost requirements, quality requirements, these should be documented in contract. For example, project must be completed in one year. Project must not exceed one million dollars of cost. Maximum number of defects that can be received by the software application that will be developed as an output product of the project must not exceed 100. These might be requirements of your project and these all should be documented in contracts.

- **If something is not mentioned in contract, change control process should be started.** If there is a new request coming from the customer, which is not mentioned in the contract, this will be a change request. Change requests should go through integrated change control process, and if it is accepted, first, it should be changed in contract that new change request should be added to the scope of the project. After the changes in scope and update in the contract, change can be implemented.

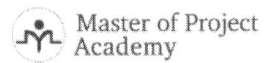

- **Contracts are legally binding.** This means, if there would be a problem when meeting requirements, or meeting deliverables, which are mentioned in contracts, these might be problems between the buyer and seller. If there is a dispute between parties, contracts will determine how to proceed. Contracts are under the protection of laws. If the parties are operating in different countries, there might be international laws protecting the contracts.

- **Contracts should help diminish the project risk.** Can you think that you agreed with a supplier to provide your materials but you did not sign any contract? During the project, if this supplier cannot provide the materials, tools or equipment on time, this can cause project delays. In this case, if you do not have a contract, you will not have any power to push the supplier to deliver the materials on time. Respectively, project risks will increase. Therefore, contracts help diminish the project risk.

- **In case of a dispute that could not be negotiated between parties, parties meet in court.** As we said, contracts are legally binding and if there are disputes, if there are problems that parties could not negotiate with each other, these contracts are protected by laws, and in order to resolve disputes, parties can meet in courts and justice can give a decision about their problem.

Project Manager's Role in Procurement

What is the Project Manager's Role in Procurement?

- **Project Manager must know procurement process.** The project manager should know which procurement actions will be followed and which procurement processes should be followed in which sequence. For example, what is the source selection criteria for a supplier? What are the payment terms for the vendors? What are the terms and conditions of the contract? These are all should be known by the Project Manager.

- **Project Manager must understand contract terms and conditions.** Because, contract terms and conditions are legally binding and defining the obligations of parties. Either you are a buyer or a seller; you should know the obligations that you have to meet to the other party. For instance, what is the payment conditions when a supplier provided materials for the project? What is the payment period? Thus, it is important to understand contract terms and conditions.

- **Project Manager must make sure contract contains all scope and regarding information.** As we mentioned already, contracts require formality and they are legally binding. Therefore, all scope, all project work that will be delivered to the other party should be stated in the contract. Because, if there will be a dispute between the parties, contract will come into play to resolve the dispute.

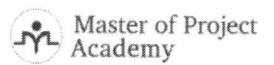

- **Project Manager must identify risks and document allocation of risks.** Risks associated with the project and contingency reserves for those risks must be identified and documented in the contracts. If there are assumptions about the risks, these must be documented in the contract as well. For example, if risk A happens, we are planning to spend ten days of effort with $10,000 cost. These kinds of risks, assumptions and their contingency reserves must be included in the contract since these reserves will be used in case the regarding risk occurs in the project.

- **Project Manager must be involved in negotiations.** Either if you are a buyer or seller, you should be present in negotiations in order to know the history of procurement. Because, the project manager is ultimate accountable of the project and must be aware of the procurement history, terms and conditions. To have this knowledge, project manager must be present in negotiations.

- **Project Manager must protect the integrity of the project.** So, the cohesive whole of the project should be related with the other parts of the project. You might sign a contract with different vendors or suppliers to deliver different parts of the project. However, these must be completing each other to protect the integrity of the project.

- **Project Managers must make sure that all work in contract is done.** Therefore, if you are buyer, you must be sure that the supplier, seller or vendor have completed all work that they have to deliver to your project. On the other hand, if you are seller, you have to be sure that you have delivered all project work to the buyer and received the appropriate payments from the buyer.

- **Do not make anything that does not exist in contract, unless regarding change is done in contract.** For example, you have delivered your project work to your customer or you have delivered all contract items, terms and conditions in you project. If customer comes with a change request to you and if it is not reflected in the contract, this should not be executed right away. First, contract should be changed or revised. The new scope or new change request should be updated in the scope part of the contract, and then the change should be implemented.

- **Project Managers work with procurement manager to manage changes to the contract.** We will see different types of procurement departments. There are centralized procurements and decentralized procurements. Depending on the organization type of the company, one of these procurement organization types is adapted.

- **Project Managers might not be expert in procurements.** Procurement is actually a different profession that is handled by the procurement professionals. Therefore, Project Manager must work together with procurement manager to manage changes to the contract. Because there are specific laws, specific terms and conditions regarding procurement and Project manager might not be aware of these. Therefore, Project Manager needs the assistance of the procurement manager.

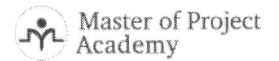

- **Project Manager must be assigned to the project before awarding the contract.** This is important for project manager in order to be involved in the negotiations with the seller or buyer. Project Manager is responsible for the success of the project and contract binds what needs to be done in detail. Therefore, before awarding the contract, project manager must be aware of what is negotiated and what is involved in the contract. Thus, the project manager should know the history of the changing terms and conditions, scope of the contract from the beginning. Therefore, Project Manager must be assigned before awarding the contract.

Centralized-Decentralized Contracting

Now we will see two types of contracting in Organizations. There are two common types of contracting in organizations. First one is Centralized Contracting. In this type of organizations, procurement managers belong to the procurement department.

- **Centralized Contracting:** In centralized contracting, procurement managers deal with different contracts of different projects. For example, project number one, project number two, project number n. There will be several projects going on in an organization and procurement managers will be dealing with the contracts of each project.
  When project managers need assistance about the contract they assist or ask questions about procurement of their projects to the procurement managers.

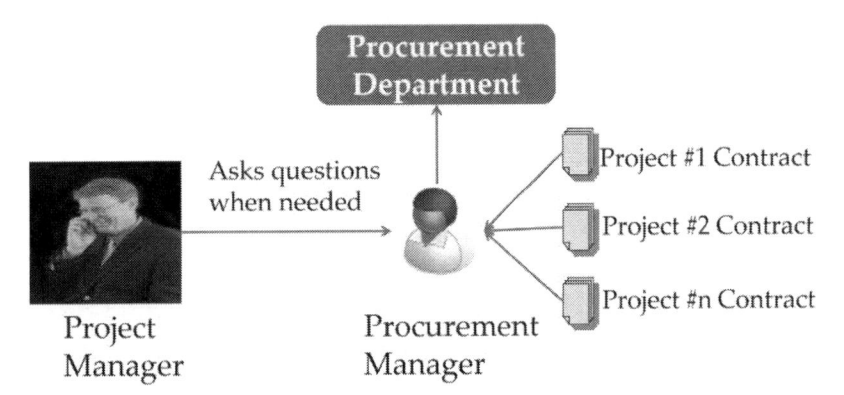

- **Decentralized Contracting:** In this type of contracting, project manager deals with project and there is a procurement manager dedicated to the project manager. The dedicated procurement manager will be dealing with the project contract mainly which he or she is assigned to. The procurement manager will be under direct provision of the project manager.

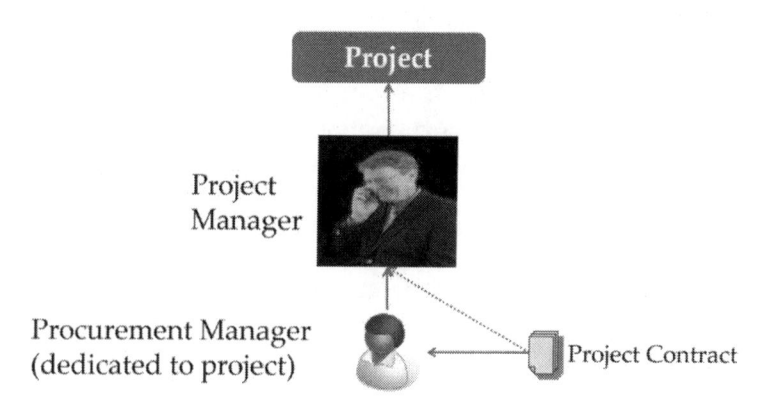

Plan Procurement Management Process

Plan procurement management is the first process of procurement management knowledge area.
Plan procurement management process is the process of documenting procurement decisions, specifying the approach and identifying potential sellers.

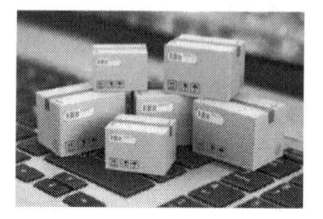

- **This process defines how you will acquire the products or services or how you will outsource a specific part of your project work to a vendor.** What will be the payment conditions? What will be the source selection criteria for potential sellers? These are all defined and planned in plan procurement management process.

- **This process determines and answers the following questions:**

    o **Do we need outside support?** Depending on the nature of the project, you may need a specific skill for your project. For instance, you might need a subject matter expert who has knowledge and experience on a niche area and you might need to outsource this personnel from a consultancy company.

    o **How do we acquire?** What will be the contract type? You might pay a fixed price for the materials or service you will be purchasing. In some cases, especially when getting a consultancy service, efforts of the experts are charged per day. How the acquisition will take place must be planned.

    o **How much is needed?** For example, how much steel will you need for your construction project? How many trucks will you need? These must be planned in plan procurement management process.

    o **When do we need to acquire?** Time you will need the procured items are also important. Because the vendors or suppliers will be planning on their side to meet the delivery time. Assume that you are managing a construction project. Getting all materials from day one of the construction is not feasible. Most probably, you will have storage problems to place the whole materials. If you plan when you will get which materials and the amount as well, it will be easier both for you and for the seller as well.

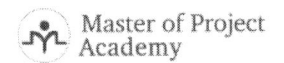

- **Contract Types:** There are different contract types. Actually, they are grouped under three main categories for contract types.
  - Fixed Price (FP)
  - Cost Reimbursable Contracts (CR)
  - Time and Material Contracts (T&M)

Fixed Price Contracts

In these types of contracts, a fixed total price is set for a defined product, service, or result to be provided. Buyer defines what they require from the project. Seller clarifies the buyer's requirements and prepares a proposal. If buyer and seller agree on the price, buyer awards to project to the seller. Seller takes all risks of project and delivers the project scope and final product for the agreed price. Upon successful deliveries, buyer pays the agreed amounts to the seller.

- **Sellers under fixed contracts are legally obligated to complete contracts.** Therefore, no matter the conditions, seller must provide the detailed project work, which is mentioned in the contract. If the seller cannot meet the terms and conditions of the contract, buyer can bring the dispute to the court.
- **Buyer needs to precisely specify the product or services being procured.** Seller will evaluate the buyer's requirements and work on a solution to provide these requirements. These requirements will determine the project cost and the project price that will be requested by seller as well. Therefore, buyer must be clear and concise when defining their project requirements. Otherwise, several changes might arise during project work.
- **Changes in scope can be accommodated with an increase in contract price.** Because, seller proposes the fee based on the buyer requirements. If new requirements come up or the buyer requests changes, these must be updated in the contract first and an additional fee must be paid to the seller to accommodate the cost of the changes.

Firm Fixed Price Contracts (FFP):
First type of fixed price contract is firm fixed price contract, and this is abbreviated as FFP. Actually, Fixed Price Contracts are the most common used contract types in the market.

- **The buyer has the best cost risk because additional cost that might occur is the responsibility of the seller.** During negotiations, buyer defines details of the work, product or material that they will acquire from the sellers. Based on the requirements of the buyer, seller proposes a price. If the buyer and seller agree, seller provides the required work or required materials to the buyer for a fixed price. Any risk that might increase the cost of the project must be bear by the seller since the contract is signed as fixed price. Therefore, buyer has the best cost risk.

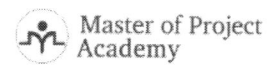

- **Buyer should define specifications and requirements precisely.** Otherwise, if buyer could not define the requirements of the work or requirements of the materials precisely, then, these might cause change requests later in the project. For all these change requests, contract must be updated and all these changes will be charged additionally to the buyer. Therefore, in order to go with firm fixed price contracts, buyer must have defined their requirements precisely and concisely.

- Here, we see an example of firm fixed price contract.

> **Fixed Price Contract**
> Contract = $800.000

After buyer tells what is needed in their project, seller evaluates the requirements of the work or the requirements of the material that will be provided. Then, the seller proposes a price offer to the buyer. For example, $800,000.

Unless the scope of work or the scope of the materials that will be delivered by the seller change, this price will not change. The buyer will pay this price to the seller based on agreed conditions.

Fixed Price Incentive Fee Contracts (FPIF):
Second type of fixed price contracts is fixed price incentive fee contracts. This is abbreviated as FPIF.

- **In these types of contracts, a price is set; however, based on performance of the seller, additional incentives can be paid additionally.** Generally, incentives are related to cost, schedule or technical performance.

- Here, we see an example of fixed price incentive fee contracts.

> **Fixed Price Incentive Fee Contracts**
> Contract = $800.000 + $10.000 for every early month

Contract says that, for the project work that will be delivered, the total price is $800,000. However, if the project is completed earlier than the planned date, for every month that the project has been completed earlier, the seller will get extra $10,000.

In this example, incentive has been set for early delivery. Incentives can be set for quality of the product, reduced costs or other metrics as well. These incentives will push seller to complete the project with a better performance.

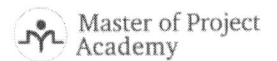

Fixed Price with Economic Price Adjustment Contracts (FP-EPA):

Last type of fixed price contracts is fixed price with economic price adjustment contracts. This is abbreviated as FP-EPA.

- **This type of contract is used when seller's performance is spread over a period of years or in long-term relationships.** Consider a shopping mall construction project that will take four years to complete. Even if the requirements are clear, you cannot know the future changes that will affect the cost of materials, wages and other parameters of the project. Therefore, future economic conditions must be reflected in the contract to change the contract price if economic conditions change.

- **Future economic conditions that might change the contract price can be inflation, cost increases or decreases of the materials.** There can be other parameters such as strike, embargo etc. as well.

- **Fixed Price with Economic Price Adjustment contracts protect both buyer and seller from external conditions beyond their control.** Therefore, in long-term contracts, this contract can be used.

- Here is an example for this type of contract:

> Fixed Price with Economic Price Adjustment Contract = $800.000 + 2nd year inflation increase

Contract price is $800,000. However, 2nd year inflation increase will be applied to the price.

Cost Reimbursable Contracts

Second type of contracts we will be seeing is cost reimbursable contracts. These types of contracts are used if the scope is uncertain and costs cannot be estimated correctly. In some cases, buyer may not know the project scope exactly. However, the buyer might want to start the project. In this case, sellers cannot provide a fixed price for the project since they cannot determine the costs of the project. Because, scope is uncertain and costs may vary depending on the changes in scope. In these cases, cost reimbursable contracts are preferred.

- **Buyer has the most risk in this type of contracts since total costs are unknown.** The scope is uncertain. This means, project scope might increase over time. Due to this change, additional costs will rise in the project. Since the seller accepted the project, seller must bear the costs of these risks.
- **All costs incurred for the completed work plus a figure representing seller profit is reflected in these contracts.** For instance, if the total price for the work that will be completed by the seller is $100,000, a fee, which is representing the profit of the seller, might be added to this price. For example, the fee will be $20,000 and in total $120,000 is paid by the buyer to the seller.

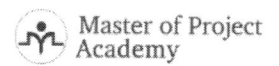

- **This type of contracts may include financial incentives based on seller performance**. For example, based on the schedule performance, cost performance or quality performance of the seller, buyer might pay additional fees to the seller to improve the project results. The buyer can provide special incentives to seller in context of these contracts.

Cost Plus Fixed Fee Contracts (CPFF):

First type of cost reimbursable contracts is Cost Plus Fixed Fee Contracts. This is abbreviated as CPFF. **All costs for performing the contract work and a fixed fee payment is paid by the buyer.** For example, you have estimated the cost of the project as one-million-dollar. Seller requires $200,000 as fee or in other words profit for this project. In this case, you, as a buyer, have to pay $1.2 million dollars as the total project price to your seller.

- **Generally, fixed fee is calculated as a percentage of the initial estimated project costs.** For example, if your total project cost is one-million-dollar and if the seller requires a 20% profit, in this case, you will pay $200,000 profit or fee to your seller.

- Here we give an example of Cost Plus Fixed Fee contracts.

> **Cost Plus Fixed Fee Contracts (CPFF)**
> Contract = Cost + $100,000

- In these types of contracts, as we said, you add the fee or profit of the seller to the total cost of the project and this defines the total price that will be paid by the buyer to seller.

Cost Plus Incentive Fee Contracts (CPIF):

Second type of cost reimbursable contracts is Cost Plus Incentive Fee Contracts, and these is abbreviated as CPIF. All costs for performing the contract work and a predetermined incentive fee based on achieving certain performance is paid by buyer. Incentives can be dependent on the cost performance, schedule performance, quality performance or about the product performance that will be produced as the outcome of the project.

- **If final costs are less or greater than original estimates, buyer and seller share cost from the departures based on pre-negotiated cost-sharing formula.** For instance, a sample sharing ratio can be 80% to the buyer, and 20% to seller. For instance, you have assumed that the total project cost is one-million-dollar. At the end of the project, seller has delivered this project for $900,000 costs. Therefore, they have actually completed the project for a cost, which is $100,000 less than the initial estimates. If you have an 80% to buyer and 20% to seller cost-sharing formula, $80,000 of this cost saving will be remaining in the buyer and $20,000 will be paid as incentive to the seller based on their cost performance that they have achieved in delivery of the project.

- Here we give an example for cost plus incentive fee contracts. The total project price is calculated by total cost of the project, plus 80 to 20 sharing from the targets. Here 80% for the buyer, and 20% for the seller.

Cost Plus Incentive Fee Contracts (CPIF)
Contract = Cost + 80/20 sharing from targets

Below are the cost values of a project that has been managed under a cost plus incentive fee contracts. Initial targets of the project say that, target cost of the project will be $210,000. Target fee or profit for the seller will be $25,000. The target price of this project will be $235,000. Sharing ratio for the cost savings will be 80 to 20. If there will be cost savings, 80% of the savings will be remaining to buyer and 20% will be remaining to seller.

- Target Cost: 210,000 USD
- Target Fee : 25,000 USD
- Target Price : 235,000 USD
- Sharing Ratio: 80/20 → 80% to buyer, 20% to seller

Assume that, when the project is complete, it cost $200,000 to your company.
- Actual Cost: 200,000 USD
- Target Cost – Actual Cost = 10,000 USD

We have completed this project $10,000 cheaper compared to our initial target cost.

When we use our sharing ratio in order to find the remaining values from these cost savings to buyer and seller, we multiply 80% sharing ratio of the buyer with $10,000 cost saving and we find $8,000 to buyer.

Moreover, if we multiply 20% sharing ratio of the seller, with $10,000 cost saving, we find $2,000 to the seller as incentive.
- 10,000x80% = 8,000 USD to Buyer, 10,000x20%=2,000 USD to seller

Finally, if we calculate the total price of the project, the actual cost of the project was $200,000 plus we will also pay the fee of the seller, which was defined as $25,000. We will also give the incentive that the seller deserved from the cost savings, which is $2,000. The total price of the project makes $227,000
- Total Price= 200,000 + 25,000 + 2,000 = 227,000 USD

Cost Plus Award Fee Contracts (CPAF):
The last type of cost reimbursable contracts we will go over is, cost plus award fee contracts, and this is abbreviated as CPAF. All costs for performing the contract work is paid and the majority of the fee is earned only based on broad subjective performance criteria of the seller. Since the majority of the fee depends on the subjective evaluation of the buyer, this is not a common type of contract.

- **An award is determined in advance in these contracts so the seller is motivated to deliver the project work accordingly.**

- **The performance of the seller is evaluated subjectively by the buyer.** In previous types of contracts, if there will be awards or incentives that will be paid by the buyer to the seller, these were being evaluated by the objective performance criteria like schedule performance or cost performance. However, in these types of contracts, performance of the seller is evaluated mainly based on the subjective performance criteria of the seller.

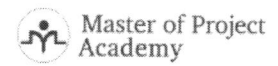

- For example, we see an example of Cost Plus Award Fee Contracts.

> **Cost Plus Award Fee Contracts (CPAF)**
> Contract = Cost + $5,000 every month if production exceeds 10,000 units. Max Award= $50,000

Cost plus $5,000 every month will be paid to the seller, if production exceeds 10,000 units. Maximum award amount that will be paid to the seller cannot exceed $50,000. This is an example of Cost Plus Award Fee Contract.

Time & Material Contracts

Third type of contracts we will be seeing is time and material contracts. These contracts are actually hybrid type of contracts and they contain aspects of cost reimbursable and fixed price contracts.

- **Time and material contracts are generally used for staff augmentation, acquisition of experts and any outside support when a work could not be precisely described.** If you will acquire consultants or subject matter experts to your project from an external organization, you might use time and material contracts. Assume that you are managing a software project. For a specific technology, you need an expert and the required resource is not in the company. In this case, needed consultant or expert must be outsources from a consultancy company or vendor. Time and material contracts are used in these cases. Based on the consultants or experts' effort, buyer pays a daily rate or hourly rate for the time the consultant spends on the project. Similarly, if buyer buys materials frequently from a supplier, time and material contract can be set for this case as well. For instance, you might be purchasing wood, steel, or other materials for your construction project from a supplier. Since you will need these materials frequently, a time and material contract can be prepared and a price for each unit of materials can be agreed between the buyer and seller. As long as the buyer needs new materials, seller can provide those from the agreed unit prices.

- **Buyers pays on a per hour, per day, per month, or per item basis in these types of contracts.** For example, if you are acquiring a subject matter expert to your project or a consultant from an outsourcing company, generally their rates are agreed by per hour, per day, or per month in contracts. Alternatively, if you are buying an item or buying goods from suppliers like wood, iron, steel, for a construction project, these are actually defined per item. For example, per metric cube for wood or per ton for iron.

- **These types of contracts are used for small works and short-lasting works.** Assume that you need a subject matter expert for your project. Most probably, it is required for a short amount of time and since hiring that resource will be more expensive, outsourcing will be more feasible. Therefore, that resource is acquired with a time and material contract.

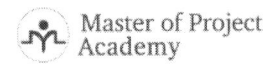

- **In these types of contracts, there should be a "not-to-exceed" clause.** Assume that you will acquire a Java coding expert for your project, and you negotiated with the outsourcing company that the rate of this expert will be $1,000 per day. However, there should be a statement in the contract that, the payment for this resource to the seller will not exceed $20,000. So, in this case, if the expert stays in the project more than 20 days, or if he works overtime, with this clause, you will protect yourself that you will not exceed the $20,000 of price that you will be paying to your seller or to the outsourcing company. These kinds of clauses also help you to not to exceed your cost targets in your project.

- Here we gave an example of time and material contracts.

> **Time and Material Contracts (T&M)**
> Contract = 100$ per hour + expenses + material costs

- $100 per hour plus expenses of the resource plus material costs. This is an example of time and material contracts.

Terms & Concepts about Contracts

Now, we will see some terms and concepts about contracts.

- **Incentives:** Incentives are used to bring the seller's objectives in line with the buyer's. These are actually bonus for sellers. Buyers make projects to produce a product, add a new feature to an existing product etc. Sellers provide services and products for the buyers to make money. In order to provide a healthy business between the buyer and the seller, seller's objectives must be in line with the buyer's. For example, if the seller delivers the project better than the planed values, buyer might pay additional bonus to the seller. Buyer wants the projects to be completed faster, with a lower cost and with high quality. If buyer and seller agree on incentives that will be paid to the seller in case the project is completed with better performance, for instance with a lower cost, earlier delivery time etc., this will bring the buyer's objectives in line with the seller's.

- **Payment Schedule:** Contracts mention when is done to seller. This is important especially for long projects. Assume that you are executing a project for two years. You cannot wait for two years to get the payment from your customer. Because you cannot financially justify the expenditures of your employees without getting any payment for two years. Therefore, the cost of the project should be charged to the customer periodically. For example, depending on the contracts, there might be monthly or quarter-based payments of the buyer. Another option can be paying to the seller based on interim deliverables or milestones. These are all planned and mentioned in procurement documents and this is done in plan procurement management process.
Project managers must ensure the funds will be available to make the payments. If you are working as a project manager in a buyer organization, you have to be sure that you will be paying the sufficient money to your suppliers when the time for the payment comes and if the seller met the contract terms and conditions.

- **Trade-offs within the different contract types:**

Contract Type	Priorities (Least to Most Important)
CPFF	Cost, Time, Performance
CPAF	Cost, Time, Performance
CPIF	Time, Performance, Cost
T&M	Performance, Time, Cost
FPIF	Time, Performance, Cost
FFP	Cost, Time, Performance

First column describes the contract type and the second column describes the priorities from the least to the most important. For example,

> For Cost Plus Fixed Fee contracts, cost is least important, time is medium level important, and performance is most important.
> For Cost Plus Award Fee contract, the priorities are the same as in Cost Plus Fixed Fee contracts.
> For Cost Plus Incentive Fee contracts, time is least important and cost is the most important parameter.
> For Time and Material contracts, performance is least important, time is medium level important, and cost is more important parameter.
> For Fixed Price Incentive Fee contracts, time is least important, performance is medium level important, and cost is the most important parameter.
> For the last type of contract, Firm Fixed Price contracts, cost is the least important, time is medium level important, and performance is most important parameter.

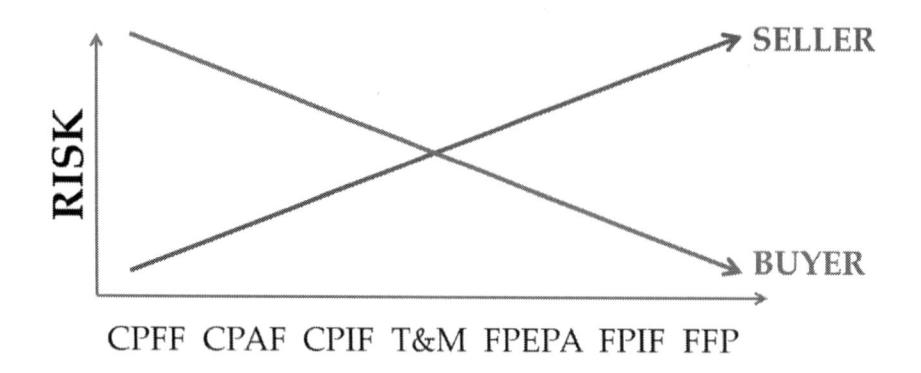

```
                                    → SELLER
     ↑
     RISK        ╲     ╱
                   ╳
                 ╱     ╲
                                    → BUYER
     
     CPFF  CPAF  CPIF  T&M  FPEPA  FPIF  FFP
```

In this graph, we see the different types of contracts in the horizontal side of the graph, and we see the risk level changing for seller and buyer on the vertical side of the graph.
As you see for cost reimbursable contracts, risk of the seller is at the lowest level and it increases when contracts are changing towards Time and Material and to Firm Fixed Price. The highest risk happens for the seller, if it is a Firm Fixed Price contract. Because if the scope is clearly mentioned in the Firm Fixed Price contract, all additional costs will be under the responsibility of the seller. Therefore, seller has the highest risk in Firm Fixed Price.

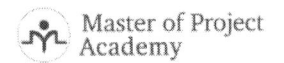

From the buyer perspective, Cost Plus Fixed Fee has the highest risk because in these types of contracts, there are many uncertainties in the scope of the work that will be required. Due to these uncertainties, there might be several change requests during the project. This can cause increases in the cost of the work that is being acquired or in the cost of materials that are being acquired.

As you see, the risk of buyers is at the highest levels for Cost Plus Fixed Fee contracts, and it has the lowest risk level for the Firm Fixed Price. Because if the scope of the work is clear, then, buyer addresses the risk to the seller. Buyer pays only the negotiated price to the seller and all risks that might arise during the project must be addressed by the seller.

- **Price:** Price is the amount the seller charges to the buyer. For the work delivered or for the materials that is acquired from the seller, you have to pay charges. Price covers the cost of the materials, which is known by the seller and profit of the seller as well.

- **Profit or Fee:** Profit or Fee is actually the planned profit of the seller included in the price. For example, if the total cost of the project is $800,000 and if the profit of the seller is $200,000, then buyer will be paying one-million-dollar as a price for the project. $800,000 of this amount will be gone to the costs and only $200,000 remain as profit to the seller.

- **Cost:** Cost actually refers the items costs to sellers. Seller has to spend money when delivering project or providing materials to the buyer as well. This is actually cost of seller.

- **Target price:** Target price represents the initial price objective of the project. For instance, if the seller and buyer agreed to complete the project for one million dollar, this is the target price and buyer must pay this amount to the seller if the project goes successfully. The target price is used to compare the result with what was expected. For instance, although you have planned to complete the project for one-million-dollar price, you might exceed this amount with change requests that will bring additional cost to the project. In this case, actual cost will be compared with the target price to evaluate the deviation from the target.

$$Target\ Cost + Target\ Fee = Target\ Price$$

Target price is calculated by aggregating the target cost with target fee or target profit that will be paid to the seller.

- **Sharing Ratio:** Sharing ratio defines the sharing proportion of the buyer and seller over cost savings. For example, if there will be a cost saving during the project, what percent of the savings will be remaining for the buyer? What percent of the savings will be remaining for the seller? The sharing ratio defines how to distribute these amounts to the seller and buyer.

- **Ceiling Price:** Ceiling Price defines the highest price the buyer will pay to the seller. For example, if you say that the ceiling price is one million dollar, then the total amount or total price that you will be paying the seller cannot exceed the ceiling price.
This is actually a cost protection for the buyer. Although you have negotiated the price of the project with the seller, price might increase with new change requests. In order to

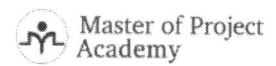

prevent buyer from increasing price, a maximum amount that can be paid by the buyer can be set.

- **Point of Total Assumption (PTA):** PTA only applies to Fixed Price Incentive Fee contracts. Point of total assumption is a cost level that if it is exceeded, project is assumed to be mismanaged. Although you have done cost estimations appropriately, actual values can exceed the planned costs. However, there is a level for this and if it exceeds that level, it is assumed that the project was mismanaged. Point of Total Assumption is calculated by:

$$PTA = \frac{Ceiling\ Price - Target\ Price}{Buyer's\ Sharing\ Ratio} + Target\ Cost$$

Assume that say ceiling price of the project is $220,000. The target price of the project, which is actually the initial price objective that will be paid to the seller is $200,000. Buyer's sharing ratio is 80% which means that if there will be any cost savings or exceeding, 80% of these savings or exceeding will be remaining to buyer.
The target cost of the project is $180,000. This is actually the amount that the seller will be spending to deliver the project.
- Ceiling Price = 220.000 USD
- Target Price = 200.000 USD
- Buyer's Sharing Ratio = 80%
- Target Cost = 180.000 USD

Now, if you substitute the values in the Point of Total Assumption formula, we will find the PTA value.
We subtract the $200,000, which is target price, from the $220,000, which is the ceiling price.
Then, we divide this to the buyers sharing ratio, which is 80% and this is referred as 0.80 in the denominator of the formula.
This makes $25,000 and then we add target costs to this result, which is $180,000.

$$PTA = \frac{220.000 - 200.000}{0.80} + 180.000$$

$$PTA = 205.000\ USD$$

Final result of this formula gives us PTA as $205,000.
To summarize, target cost for this project is $180,000 and Point of Total Assumption, PTA, is $205,000. If you exceed the $205,000 of cost in your project, this will be considered or assumed as management's mistake. Therefore, even if there will be risks or additional costs in the project, you should not exceed the $205,000 total cost value for this project.

Tools & Techniques Used in Plan Procurement

Now we will go over tools and techniques used in Plan Procurement Process.

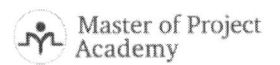

- **Make-or-Buy analysis:** Make-or-Buy analysis is actually the determination of whether a particular work can be accomplished by the project team or should be purchased from outside sources. You have a project budget to deliver a project scope. If you do everything with your project resources or if you purchase all tools or equipment although you need them for a short time, your budget will be too much to complete the project.

  > In Make-or-Buy analysis, you are evaluating some part of your project work can be executed by your project team or it is better to outsource to an external party.

- **Buying decreases risks since the work is outsourced.** If you outsource a part of your project work and if you can identify the work you are requiring from the seller clearly and precisely, then, all risks can be transferred to the company or to the subcontractor that will be delivering the regarding project work.

- **It is better to make instead of buying in a project:**

    - **if there is an idle plant or workforce.** Assume that there are resources or there are team members waiting idle in your company and if you are making Make-or-Buy Analysis, instead of buying, you can choose making this part of your project work. Because, you have an idle force and they are sitting and they are waiting for new work or new projects. Therefore, in this case, it might be better to make instead of buying. Because buying will require additional payment while making will be free since that workforce is idle.

    - **if you want to retain the control of the work.** Because, if you are making a project work or a work package, you will have better control, better management of that regarding work in your project since the project resources will be under your control.

    - **if the work requires or involves proprietary information or procedures.** For instance, if you are delivering a very confidential project including trade secrets, this will be crucial for your company. In this case, even if making will be costlier, it might be better to make it with company resources. Assume that Coca-Cola is working on a project about its taste and formula. Would it be wise for them to work with a outsource company? For sure, it will be better to do in-house to keep the secrets of formula and taste.

- Let us go over a Making-Or-Buying analysis example.
  Assume that we have an opportunity to lease a vehicle or buy a vehicle for our project.
  Leasing the vehicles price is $120 per day.
  If you buy the vehicle, sales price is $1,200 as initial cost. There will be a $20 cost per day for maintenance as well.
    - Leasing a vehicle: $120 / per-day
    - Buying the vehicle: $1200 sales price+ $20 / per-day

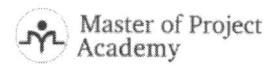

Now, we will make the break-even point analysis.

Break-even point describes the number of days, where leasing the vehicles equals to the buying the vehicle in terms of costs of buying or leasing. In order to do this break-even point calculation, we will multiply the cost of leasing a vehicle per day with the number of days that we will be leasing. Therefore, it constitutes the left side of the equation as $120 multiplied by X days.

On the right side of the equation, we will substitute the initial cost of the buying vehicle, which is $1,200 plus $20 per day multiplied by each day.

$$120 \times X \, days = 1200 + 20 \times X \, days$$

In this equation X is the break-even point where buying and leasing will be same cost. If you go through the rest of the formula, you will see that our break-event point is 12 days.

$$120X = 1200 + 20X$$
$$100X = 1200$$
$$X = 12 \, days$$

It means that, if you need this vehicle for more than 10 days, it is better to buy. However, if you will need this vehicle less than 10 days in your project, then it is better to lease instead of buying.

- **Expert judgement:** Experts can provide information about procurement. For example, evaluation of seller proposals, terms and conditions of the contract etc. Expert Judgement is actually a technique used in many processes during project management. Experts are generally subject matter experts or professionals, who are expert or have many years of experience in a special topic and they can give information about the procurement.

- **Market Research:** Market Research is another tool or technique for plan procurement management process. This is actually an examination of industry and specific vendor capabilities in order to decide which vendor or supplier is more suitable. If you have decided to purchase a material, a tool or if you have decided to subcontract a part of your project to an external source or external company, you may want to do a market research about which company can deliver this part of your project work in the optimum way or which company is most capable of delivering the required work.
  Therefore, in that case, a market research will be a good technique to find the best seller that will fit with your expectations in the market.

- **Meetings:** In these meetings, information between sellers and buyers can exchange. Buyers might tell the required work or the required material that will be purchased from the external sources and sellers might ask questions about the unclear parts, unclear points about the procurement. With the help of the meetings, the unclear points or questions of the sellers might be concluded in a faster way.

Procurement Management Plan

Procurement management plan is the output of plan procurement management process. We will be going over what it covers in detail. Briefly, procurement management plan describes how the procurement will be done in a project.

- **After decision is made for outside resources, management of these procurements should be documented in procurement management plan.** After evaluating whether to make or buy, if the decision is buying, how to make purchasing is documented in the procurement management plan.

- **What is the material you will be purchasing? What is the amount needed and time plan for the need? What is the selection criteria?** These and similar other questions are answered in procurement management plan.

What does procurement management plan cover?

- **Procurement management plan may include types of contracts to be used.** For instance, if you have a clear scope that you can share with the potential sellers, it might be better to use fixed price contract. Because you will decrease the cost risk if you can agree on fixed price contracts. Depending on negotiations, other type of contracts may be used as well. This must be covered in the procurement management plan.

- **Risk management issues are covered in the procurement management plan.** How will you be handling the risks that might occur in your project, what are your contingency reserves, in what conditions will you be using your resource, are all mentioned in procurement management plan.

- **Standardized procurement documents are included in procurement management plan.** If you already have standard processes, standard act of ways of how procurement should be handled, these are already included in the procurement management plan. For instance, a template for RFP or Bidding may be standardized procurement document.

- **Managing multiple suppliers can be in scope of the procurement management plan.** If you have several suppliers in your project, for example, if you are buying steel from a supplier, buying wood from another supplier, and buying iron from a third supplier, managing these several suppliers that you are in contact during your procurement should be mentioned in procurement management plan. For instance, prices agreed with each supplier must not be visible to each other.

- **Coordinating procurement with other project aspects can be included in the procurement management plan.** Scheduling can be an example for this. For instance, what is the amount of steel and wood that is needed for your construction project and when will you need them?
  For example, 2,000-meter cubes of wood will be purchased in March. Two tons of steel will be purchased in April. These kinds of procurement items should be detailed in procurement management plan with the other project aspects like scheduling.

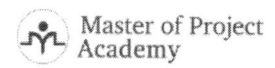

- **Any constraints and assumptions that could affect planned procurements should be listed in procurement management plan.** For instance, if you are working in a tough climate, transfer of materials might be impossible during Winter. Inability to transfer materials during winter is a constraint and must be included in the procurement management plan.

- **How to make or buy decision should be mentioned in Procurement Management plan.** In what cases you would be making, or in what cases you would be purchasing from an outside seller. These should be defined clearly in Procurement Management Plan.

- **Procurement Management plan may include also setting scheduled dates for each deliverable.** For example, if you are executing a very large project and if there are interim deliverables that you are requiring from your seller to deliver in specific days, these days should be mentioned and defined clearly in procurement management plan. For instance, you might expect the 10,000 bricks to be delivered on 10th of March, 20,000 bricks to be delivered on 25th of March and 15,000 bricks to be delivered on 7th of April. These kind of detailed delivery dates must be outlined in the procurement management plan.

- **Identifying requirements for performance bonds is covered in procurement management plan.** In which cases you will be making payments to sellers, what the acceptance criteria are, what the performance requirements are to give performance bonds to your seller should be identified clearly in procurement management plan.

- **Identifying pre-qualified sellers is covered in procurement management plan.** Pre-qualified sellers are determined based on a checklist or evaluation steps depending on the buyer's expectations. When a material or item will be needed, these pre-qualified sellers are preferred first to purchase materials.

- **Procurement metrics to be used to manage contracts and evaluate sellers should be included in procurement management plan as well.** What kind of metrics, what kind of categories will you be using in order to evaluate the potential sellers? Which category, which metric is more important compared to others? For example, technical capability of the seller might be more important, the financial capacity of the seller might be more important, or the past performance of the seller in similar projects might be more important. These kinds of evaluation criteria, and their importance are mentioned in procurement management plan.

Procurement Statement of Work

We will see the procurement state of work in this heading.

- **Procurement Statement of Work defines the scope of work to be done in each procurement.** It describes what will be purchased and the conditions of the purchase from the other party. Based on this procurement statement or work, sellers propose their bids and solutions for this procurement statement of work document. For instance, if an automotive company will outsource the wiper development of the cars to an external company, features and requirements about the wiper are detailed in procurement statement of work document.

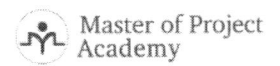

- **Scope baseline is broken down to works, and purchased from sellers.** Scope baseline covers the overall project scope about what needs to be done in the project. Some part of this work might be done by external companies. In this case, related part of the scope is outlined in the procurement statement of work and asked from seller to provide the regarding scope.
For example, work package number one might be purchased from seller one. Work package number two might be purchased from seller two. Other work packages in the project might be executed by your project team.

- **Procurement statement of work must be as clear, complete and concise as possible, and describe all works that seller must complete.** Because, based on the procurement statement of work, sellers will make their bids and price will be determined based on the procurement statement of work. If there will be unclear points or ambiguities in the procurement statement of work, seller will place additional reserves to accommodate unclear parts. This will cause price increase in sellers' offers. Therefore, procurement statement of work must be clear.

Procurement (Bid) Documents

What are the procurement or bid documents?

> After the contract type is selected and procurement statement of work has been created, the buyer can put together the procurement documents, which describes their needs from seller.

- After you have defined contract type, whether you will use fixed-price contracts, cost reimbursable contracts, or time material contracts, and after you have defined the procurement statement of work, which describes what you will be acquiring, what you will be purchasing from the seller, this information can be put together in procurement documents. These documents actually describe your requirements from the potential sellers. There are three common forms of procurement documents. We will be going over each one-by-one.

- **Request for proposal (RFP):** RFP is detailed information about the work that needs to be done. It actually defines the scope of the work that you will be purchasing from the outside company or from the subcontractor. Based on the requirements documented in the RFP, seller works on a solution and proposes their solution with a price offer. Buyer evaluates the proposals of buyer and picks the optimum one.

- **Invitation for bid (IFB) or Request for Bid (RFB):** Actually, RFB stands for request for bid. Buyers invite potential sellers to bid for their purchasing request. This is done with IFB or

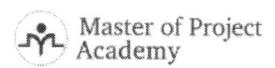

RFB. Buyer expects from seller to bid on requested purchasing request with their price offer.

- **Request for Quotation (RFQ):** It is actually a request for the price for an item, per-hour, per-meter, etc. For instance, for your construction project, if you will be purchasing goods, then, you might ask for a request for quotation for the potential sellers of what their price will be for per meter cube of wood. What will be the price for a ton of steel, or per brick etc.? Price offers of the sellers are prepared and returned to the buyer. Buyer evaluates and selects the optimum seller respectively.

- **Request for Information (RFI):** RFI is not a procurement document actually. However, this information document might be used by the buyers to retrieve information from the sellers in order to use at any time. For instance, an automotive company can ask detailed information from a wiper manufacturer and wiper manufacturer can provide its catalog to show different types of wipers they produce, their features, metrics etc. Note that, this is not a procurement document, and RFIs can be used to get detailed information from potential sellers at any time.

- **RFP, IFB or RFB are to buy something from seller.** If you will be purchasing or acquiring a part of your project work, you can use RFP, IFB or RFB, in order to define what you will be acquiring, what you will be purchasing, and what the details of the work are that you will be purchasing in these documents.

- **Before signing contracts, documents are reviewed and sellers might make suggestions.** Assume that you have prepared your procurement documents and you will be conducting procurement in order to select the best possible seller for your project.

- **Before signing contracts, these procurement documents are reviewed by the sellers.** Sellers might come with recommendations at this stage to revise the documents. For instance, they can propose a better way of doing same work that can reduce costs. Recommendations of the sellers must be evaluated and considered during procurement.

Source Selection Criteria

What is source selection criteria?
Source selection criteria defines the features or capabilities of the seller that buyer expects to see.

- **Source Selection Criteria is actually included in procurement documents to give information to sellers, whether they will bid or make a proposal.** For example, in your Source Selection Criteria, if you have defined that a company which has less than 50 employees cannot bid or cannot be a possible seller, then, if the potential seller has less than 50 employees they will be seeing that they will not be able to sell or give the required project work. Therefore, defining the source selection criteria is important. Another example, if you are requiring from your sellers to have ISO 9000 certificate, which describes a certain quality level in a company, and if there are potential sellers, which do not have this certificate, then those companies will not be able to bid for your procurement. Therefore, defining your source selection criteria in procurement management is important.

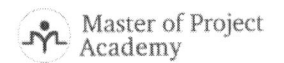

- **In Conduct Procurement process, source selection criteria will be basis when buyer is evaluating bids or proposals.** Buyer will evaluate the potential sellers based on source selection criteria when evaluating to which company they will award the contract.

- Here, there is a list of some possible metrics that can be included in Source Selection Criteria. Note that, these might be extended as well.

    - **Understanding of need:** You might be ranking the sellers based on the understanding level of your need. For example, if a particular seller has understood you well or understood better compared to another seller, you might select that seller over the others.
    - **Overall or life-cycle cost:** Based on the proposed bids, based on the proposed price offers, cheapest proposal might be the winning one.
    - **Technical capability**: You might be assessing which company is more capable when delivering the required project work compared to others.
    - **Warranty:** For example, if warranty is important in your procurement, you might be selecting the company, which will be providing a longer warranty period for the delivered work.

- **If the financial power of the seller is important for your procurement, you might be assessing the financial capacity of the potential sellers.** In some projects, vendors may need to deliver work before getting payment. In this case, company must be financially viable to deliver the required work.

- **Business size and type might be important when selecting a seller.** For example, if you are working in a banking project and if you will be selecting a software vendor, which has a banking software project development experience, then, you might be assessing the potential sellers for having a similar project experience.

- **Past performance of sellers can be a good indication for sellers.** If you had a contract or if you have already purchased some items, some project work in the past from the sellers, you might be assessing their past performance in order to evaluate next procurement.
- **References can be critical for first time contracts.** You might be asking from the potential sellers for the references of these sellers for their previous business. For example, you might be asking from a potential seller to provide you a reference letter from a previous customer that they worked with.

- **Intellectual property rights and proprietary rights is also important.** Project work that will be under procurement can be a trade secret or it can include confidential information of the buyer. In this case, buyer will assess the sensitivity of the sellers to this confidentiality and this will be source selection criteria as well.

Other Terms & Concepts About Procurement

We will go over other terms and concepts about procurement.

- **Non-disclosure Agreement:** Many procurements have great confidentiality. Projects are executed to have a better position in the market, produce a new product or improve the features of an existing product etc. Therefore, procurements in these projects will require confidentiality.
  Buyer will want to keep their work information confidential. Because, in procurements, buyer will share information about the details of the project to the seller. Seller must know these details in order to be able to bid appropriately. Therefore, non-disclosure agreements make sure that either party of the contract will not give any secret information or confidential information of the other party to another third party.
- **Teaming Agreement or joint-venture:** Two sellers work together for one procurement for buyer. For instance, if a buyer requires a project work or items that need to be provided by sellers and if two sellers see an opportunity to go in a joint-venture in order to provide that required project work for the buyer, two companies can come together or go in joint-venture to provide better performance for procurement. This is called teaming agreement. For example, a construction company might ask to deliver the doors of the building from a seller. A door manufacturer and door handle manufacturer can come together to bid for the procurement of the buyer. This is called teaming agreement or joint-venture.
- **Standard Contract:** If similar works are done in projects, similar contracts which have been agreed on past procurements might be used in new procurements as well. For example, assume that you are working as a project manager on a construction project. You are purchasing materials like steel, wood, iron and bricks frequently from a seller that you know very well. In this case, instead of making a new contract in each time, you can sign a standard contract and use this contract in each purchase or in each new project.
  However, special provisions or special conditions might be edited on standard contracts. After reviewing standard contracts, project managers may want to add special conditions. For instance, if you are buying materials from a supplier through a standard contract and if you want to add additional penalty conditions for the cases if supplier cannot provide the materials on time, then, these kind of special provisions or special conditions might be added to standard contracts.

Now we will go over terms and conditions which are important in contracts. Terms and conditions exist in contracts and these describe the points of work.

- **Arbitration:** Arbitration describes third parties involvement for disputes. Although there is a signed contract between the seller and buyer, there might be disputes between two parties. Going to court can be a long way to solve the issue. It can take long time and hamper both parties. For these cases, a third party can be determined in contract to act as referee for the disputes that might arise between the seller and buyer.
  Arbitration is faster and better than courts. For example, if buyer and seller could not agree on a contract term, and if this has caused dispute or conflict between buyer and seller then third party agreed by the seller and buyer can come to evaluate the dispute in an objective way as a referee. This is called arbitration.

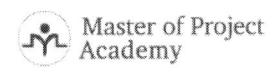

- **Bonds:** Bonds are payment done to the seller based on performance. Bonds protect buyer from claims of nonpayment by seller.

- **Breach or Default:** Breach or default occurs when one of the parties cannot meet any obligation of the contract. For example, if the seller could not provide the materials or tools on time, or if the seller could not deliver the required project on time, then this is an example of breach or default. Similarly, if the buyer could not pay to the seller on time for the payment that has been agreed on the contract, this is also an example of breach or default.

- **Force Majeure:** Force Majeure is allowable excuse for either party for not meeting contract requirements. This is actually act of God in a project. For example, you do not have control of a fire, storm, earthquake, or war. In these cases, contracts conditions and terms might not be legally binding because this is an act of God. You can take preventions for natural disasters however they may not be sufficient. In order to protect buyer and seller from the obligations of the contract, force majeure can be added in contracts to state that contract conditions might not be binding if there will be a natural disaster or war etc.

- **Retainage:** Retainage is amount of money, for example 5% or 10%, which is withheld from each payment to ensure completion. This is a condition that protects buyer from seller to leave the contract or work incomplete. For instance, once the seller completed the 20% of the project, buyer can pay 15% of the over price and 5% can be reserved as retainage. This keeps seller stick to the contract since the buyer owes them for the delivered work. Retainage amount is paid after the project is completed if there is not any issue with the delivery of the seller.

What is letter of intent?

- **Signing contract requires many approvals, controls, processes in real-life.** I know from some of my projects that it took from six months to one year to sign an official contract between buyer and seller. Because, contracts include several obligations of both parties and it takes a long time to negotiate on conditions of the contract. After negotiation, approval process takes time as well.

- **In order to start some activities of the project before signing contract, seller might ask a letter of intent from the buyer to ensure that they will sign the contract.** Because, seller takes a risk here and they want to minimize the risk with letter of intent. Seller starts to deliver materials or some part of the project before the contract is signed. If there will be any dispute between the buyer and seller, since there is not any contract, seller will not be able to look for its rights in law. Therefore, letter of intent will minimize the risk of seller in these cases.
For example, hiring people or buying items can be started by sending a letter of intent by the buyer to seller. The important point of letter of intents are they are not legally binding.

- **Letter of Intent is not legally binding:** If you are providing items or if you are providing resources to your buyer as a seller and if there is a dispute or if there is a problem between your buyer, then, this letter of intent is not legally binding. You will not be able to protect your rights in front of law or in front of courts.

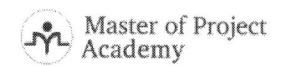

- **Privity:** Privity is actually contractual relationship between two parties. Assume that there are three companies, Company A, Company B, and company C.

```
Company A  —Signs Contract→  Company B  —Signs Contract→  Company C

COMPANY A CANNOT CONTACT COMPANY C
```

Company A signed a contract with Company B for a procurement. Company B signs another contract with Company C for another procurement.

In this case, company A cannot contact company C. Because, they do not have a contractual relationship. There is company B, between company A and company C.

Noncompetitive Forms of Procurement

- **If there is one seller in the market that sells the items or service you will be acquiring, or if you want to buy from a specific company, there is no need to go through whole procurement processes.** Because, you have to negotiate and purchase from the determined seller. In a regular procurement, you define the requirements and sellers propose their offers for your procurement. Then, you evaluate the offers and award the contract to the best seller based on your source selection criteria requirements. However, this is a process and if there is one seller or you want to buy only from one seller, you do not need to go through these steps.

- **There will be procurement SOW.** Procurement statement of work must be prepared by the buyer and seller must propose their price offer and solution for the requirements of the buyer respectively. Procurement statement of work is critical since it defines the context of procurement in detail. Even if there is one seller, it must be documented.

- **Noncompetitive forms of procurement might save time since it does not go through all procurement processes.** Since you should follow some processes and steps in regular procurement processes, it might save you time if you have already identified your seller.

- **There are two types of noncompetitive forms of procurement:**

    o **Single Source:** There are potential sellers in the market, but seller wants to work with only one of them. Assume that you need smartphones, which has android operating system for your project. There are several brands like Samsung, LG, Sony and more in the market. However, if you want to purchase from Samsung, this is an example of single source procurement. Because, although there were other options in the market, you opted for Samsung.

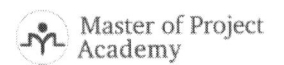

- **Sole Source:** In this case, there is only one potential seller regarding the work or item that needs to be outsourced. For instance, if seller has a specific pattern or specific product which does not exist in another company in the market, then you have to buy that item or work from that seller, and this is an example of sole source of procurement. For example, you need smartphones which has iOS operating system for your project. There is only one company around the world which produces smartphones with iOS operating system. That is Apple. So, you must purchase iPhones. This is an example of sole source procurement.

Conduct Procurement Process

Conduct Procurement is another process of procurement management knowledge area. Conduct procurements is the process of obtaining seller responses, selecting a seller and awarding a contract. Therefore, in previous process, plan procurements management process, you have defined how you will purchase, what source selection criteria you will use, preferred sellers etc.

- **In conduct procurement process, you will be executing those steps that have been defined in procurement management plan.** You will be evaluating potential sellers based on the defined source selection criteria. Then, you will select a seller and award a contract with that seller.
- **This process provides alignment of stakeholder expectations through established agreements.** In order to be able to meet project requirements, tools, materials and equipment will be needed throughout the project. This process ensures the purchasing of required materials for the project through contracts.
- **Bids and proposals are received based on provided procurement statement of work, and appropriate sellers matching to predefined selection criteria are evaluated and selected.** During plan procurements management process, you have prepared your procurement statement of work, your source selection criteria and your terms or steps you will be following in procurements management. After you have prepared your procurement documents, you have sent these documents to the potential sellers. Based on the sellers' evaluations, they have given their bids and solutions or proposals for the work that you will be acquiring or for the materials, tools that you will be purchasing. During conduct procurement process, you will be evaluating the potential sellers that provided their price bids, and select one seller or more sellers and award contract with the selected sellers.

Tools & Techniques Used in Conduct Procurements Process

In this part, we will go over tools and techniques used in conduct procurements process.

- **Bidder Conferences:** These are meetings between the buyer and prospective sellers prior to submittal of a bid or proposal. During plan procurement management process, you have defined, you have prepared your procurement documents. In those documents, you have actually defined what you will be purchasing, what you will be looking in potential sellers, etc.

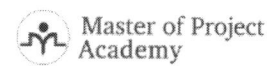

- **Based on the evaluation of these procurements documents, sellers will provide their bids, their price offers to the buyer.** However, there might be unclear points about the procurements documents or there might be questions of the sellers regarding the procurement statement of work. In bidder conferences, buyers come together with the potential sellers to illuminate them on the questions or on the unclear points of procurement documents.

- **Sellers clarify the unclear points about the work:** Sellers clarify the unclear points about the work by asking questions about the unclear parts of the procurement statement of work.

- **Questions and answers during these conferences are recorded in procurement documents.** This is to include or to illuminate the unclear parts for everybody or every potential seller in the conference.

- **Seller Proposal, Price Quota, or Bid:** Sellers send their responses to procurement documents. After you have prepared you procurement documents at the end of your plan procurements management process, you will be sending your procurements statement of work and other procurement documents to potential sellers. After potential sellers evaluate the work, materials or tools you will be purchasing, they will be sending their responses to your procurement documents. Proposals are sent for request for proposal, price quota is sent for RFQ, and bid is sent for IFB of buyers.

- **Proposal Evaluation or Review:** After reviewing proposals, buyer selects seller based on predefined criteria in Plan Procurements Management. During Plan Procurements management process, you have defined the categories and the metrics that you will be using to evaluate potential sellers in conduct procurements process. In this process, after you have received the bids of the potential sellers or the price offers or the proposals of potential sellers, you will be evaluating them based on the source selection criteria and other metrics that you have defined in the Plan Procurements Management process.

  - **Criteria are measurable and provide a basis to quantitatively evaluate proposals.** This is important to make an objective selection of a seller. For instance, past performance of the seller, technical capability, financial capability, references etc. can be assessed during this stage to select the best seller.

  - **Choosing methods might be varying from procurement to procurement.** Because, even if the organization is same, requirements of the projects might be varying. Depending on the requirements, choice method for sellers can change as well.

- **Weighting System:** In this technique, buyers select the seller by weighting the source selection criteria. Seller is evaluated from different aspects and marks are provided for each category. Each category will have a different weight in scoring as well. Depending on the weight and score in each category, seller will have a final score and this will be the main score when evaluating different sellers.

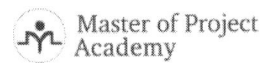

For example, here, there are three categories for source selection criteria: Ability, Sector Experience, and Price. Weight of these categories while evaluating sellers are 40%, 30%, and 30% respectively.

Criteria	Weight	Seller Score (1-10)	Seller Score
Ability	40%	8	3.2
Sector Experience	30%	6	1.8
Price	30%	9	2.7
		Total Seller Score	7.7

In the third and fourth column of this table, we see the Seller Score respectively. For example, when we are evaluating Ability of a seller, we have scored 8 out of 10 for a potential seller and when we are evaluating the seller, we have given 6 out of 10 for Sector Experience. We can say that, this seller does not that much experience in sector.

And we are evaluating the Price of the seller, we have given 9 out of 10. We can say that they have given a very competitive price compared to other potential sellers. In order to find the Seller Score for each category, we have multiplied the Weight of the category with the Seller Score.

For example, for Ability category, we have multiplied the 40% with 8 and we have found the Seller Score for Ability category is 3.2.

We have found the Sector Experience Seller Score is 1.8 and we have found the Price category Seller Score as 2.7 respectively.

When we have aggregated these Seller Scores for these three criteria, we have found Total Seller Score as 7.7.

Note that this is a Seller Score example for one potential seller. Similar evaluations should be done for other sellers as well and the seller, which will get the highest score, should be awarded with a contract.

- **Independent Estimates:** Procuring organization may prepare its own independent estimate or have an estimate of costs prepared by an outside professional estimator. Because, as a buyer, you will be purchasing a service, tool or material. If you do not know how much it will cost roughly, it is best to have an independent estimate. Otherwise, sellers might intend to charge more than a service or material worth.

    o **These independent estimates are used to benchmark seller proposals.** These kinds of independent estimates are used in order to evaluate whether you will be purchasing cheaper or more expensive. For instance, assume that you have conducted an independent estimate work for the items that you will be purchasing or for the project work that you will be outsourcing. You have concluded that the independent estimates say that the cost of this project work, or the cost of these materials should be around $900,000 to one million dollars. After you have gotten the bids of your potential sellers, you will be evaluating the bids of the sellers against this independent estimate to benchmark whether the seller proposals are matching with your independent estimates. The correlation of independent estimates with the bids or quotations of sellers indicate the clarity level of procurement statement of work. For instance, if you receive seller bids similar to the range of independent estimate, you can conclude that your procurement statement of work is clear.

- o **Significant differences in proposals and estimates are indications of unclear procurement statement of work or sellers did not understand the procurement statement of work well.** Assume that you have conducted an independent estimate and if you have found that your project work or the items that you will be purchasing should be costing around $900,000 to one million dollar. If your sellers are giving bids ranging from $500,000 to $1,500,000 or from $100,000 to $800,000, then, these significant differences show that either you could not clarify the project work that you will be purchasing or the potential sellers could not understand your procurement statement of work very well.

- **Expert Judgment:** Expert Judgment is also a technique for this process as well. Evaluation of seller proposals might be done by experts. These experts might be coming from different areas such as contracting, legal, finance, engineering, design, research, sales, etc. Based on the experts' expertise, they might be giving their opinions, they might be giving their thoughts about selecting a potential seller over several proposals.

- **Advertising:** Potential sellers can be expanded by advertisements in newspapers, magazines, Internet, etc. After you have defined what you will be purchasing in procurement statement of work and prepared your procurement documents, you can give advertisements in newspapers, magazines, Internet to get more bids, more proposals for your procurement statement of work.

    - o **Some government jurisdictions require public advertising of certain types of procurement items.** This is important because many of the government procurements require announcements of purchases or announcements of procurements to the public to ensure fair competition between potential sellers. Therefore, in some countries, if government will be purchasing tools, materials, or if government will be going in a tendering process about the project, they must be announcing this to public channels through special government portals or through special government websites.

- **Screening System:** Screening System eliminates sellers who do not meet minimum requirements. For example, if ISO 9000 is a quality requirement or company size is a requirement in your selection criteria or if there is a requirement of past experience in your selection criteria, then, screening system will help you to eliminate the sellers which will not meet these requirements.

- **Past Performance History and Presentations:** These are also other techniques used in conduct procurements. Past Performance History is valid only in case of the buyer has relationship with the seller from past projects. Based on the past performance of the seller, buyer can select a seller, if they performed well in previous projects. If the past performance of the seller is not good, buyer will eliminate regarding seller during conduct procurements process. Presentations might be done by the potential sellers to the buyers in order to provide how they understood the procurement statement of work. These presentations may include seller's solution, strengths, and capability to deliver regarding procurement statement of work. In these presentations, sellers actually define how they will be fitting or how they will be meeting the requirements of procurement.

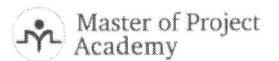

- **Procurement Negotiations:** Procurement Negotiations clarify the structure, requirements, and other terms of the purchases so that mutual agreement can be reached. There might be several requirements of a procurement. These must be finalized and agreed during meetings and negotiations between the seller and buyer.

    o **Negotiations conclude with a contract document.** Contracts are legally binding and if the seller and buyer falls into a dispute that they cannot resolve between them, contract terms and conditions will define the conclusion with respective laws.

    o **Project managers may not be the lead negotiator on procurements.** However, it is recommended that the project manager must be present in all procurement negotiations between buyer and seller. During these negotiations, the payment terms, the acceptance criteria, payment scheduling, etc. will be all negotiated between the buyer and seller. After negotiations concluded, these negotiated items will be written in contract. Negotiations can be managed by contract manager, purchasing specialist etc. However, project manager must be aware of the contractual terms and conditions.

    o **In Procurement Negotiations, scope, schedule and price are negotiated in sequence in a contract.**
        1. **Scope:** Scope of a contract defines what you will be delivering, what you will be purchasing from a seller. These should be defined in scope part of the contract.
        2. **Second, schedule is negotiated.** What you will be requiring to be delivered when if you are a buyer? For example, if you will be requiring a specific part of the project to be delivered on a specific date, then, these dates should be mentioned in contract. Additionally, regarding penalties if these dates could not be met should be defined in contract. For instance, 1,000 wipers must be delivered to Frankfurt campus of Mercedes-Benz until 15th of January. If these wipers cannot be delivered on time, $50,000 penalty will be paid to Mercedes-Benz for each day after 15th of January.
        3. **After you have negotiated the scope and schedule, then you should negotiate the price.** Because, scheduling might be changing the price of the contract. For example, if you have a very aggressive schedule in your project, then you will have a higher price in consequence most probably. Therefore, you should negotiate scope, schedule and then price respectively.

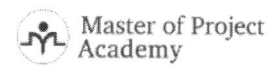

- Other things to negotiate are responsibilities, authority, applicable law, project Management processes to be used, payments schedule, etc.
  For example, if you are working in same country with the seller then you might be using the law of the country that you are operating. However, if your seller is from another country, then, international laws might be applicable in your contracts, and these should be agreed during negotiations and finalized in contracts.

- **Payments schedule also should be negotiated.** Amount of payments, schedule and conditions to make payment must be clearly defined in contracts.

- **After negotiations are complete, if both buyer and seller agree, then, contract is awarded.**

Outputs of Conduct Procurements Process

What are the outputs of conduct procurements process?

- **Selected sellers:** Main output is selected sellers. Based on the techniques and tools we have gone through, best sellers are evaluated and selected.

- **Agreements:** After the seller is selected, negotiations start and if both buyer and seller agree, contract is awarded to the seller.

- **Resource calendars:** Resource calendars are clarified during conduct procurements process. Because, delivery dates and scheduling are documented in contracts. To define scheduling, resource calendars must be available.

- **Change requests:** If buyer is coming with a new feature or request which was not put in contract, this will be a change request. While the seller is working on delivering the scope of the contract, change requests may arise.

- **Project Management Plan updates:** As usual in all other project management processes, project management plans are updated accordingly based on the activities done during conduct procurements process.

- **Project Documents updates:** Project documents might be updated as well as an output of conduct procurements process.

Control Procurements Process

Control procurements is another process of procurement management knowledge area. Control procurements is the process of managing procurement relationships, monitoring contract performance, and making changes and corrections to contracts as appropriate. After awarding a contract to the seller, contract terms, conditions, delivery schedule and similar other conditions must be monitored. This is done during control procurements process.

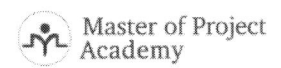

- **Control procurements process ensures that both seller and buyer meet procurement requirements.** Contract between the buyer and seller will determine the liabilities and obligations of each parties. During control procurements process, obligations of each party are monitored and controlled.

- **A project that receives too many changes should be re-evaluated and re-negotiated.** During plan procurements management process, you have prepared procurement statement of work, procurement documents and these documents have been shared with potential sellers. Based on the procurement statement of work, the sellers evaluated what you will be acquiring, what you will be purchasing and they have given their bids or their proposals based on your procurement documents.

    During conduct procurements process, you have selected the best matching, the optimum seller based on the source selection criteria that you have defined in plan procurements management process. After you have awarded a contract to the seller at the end of conduct procurements process, you have started to execute your project with the selected seller. Now, during control procurements process, you will monitor the relationship, the terms and conditions and the procurement statement of work defined in procurement management plan. You will check whether the delivery of purchased items or service is really done in accordance with the contract. In summary, during control procurements process, you are actually evaluating and monitoring whether the negotiated and agreed points in the contract are really met by the buyer and seller.

    Note that, if you could not negotiate in the details of the contract, you might be receiving too many changes regarding your project. If your scope was not clear in the beginning, or if you could not clearly identify what you will be acquiring from the seller in your procurement statement of work, this might cause many changes later in your project. In that case, it would be better to re-evaluate or re-negotiate with the seller and restart the contract from the beginning.

- **Payments to the seller based on the works accomplished are monitored during control procurements process.** In contracts, payments to the seller are defined clearly to terms and conditions. For example, at the end of the milestone one, 10% of the total cost of project will be paid to the seller. At the end of the second year of the project, if 90% of the project has been accomplished, one million dollar will be paid to the seller. Actually, these are examples of payment conditions, amounts and schedules in contracts. These kind of payment details documented in the contract are monitored during control procurements process.

- **Performance of the seller to meet procurement requirements is evaluated.** For example, if there are cost performance targets or schedule performance targets, these are evaluated by the buyer. Especially, if you are working with incentives in contracts, the performance of the seller will be important to determine how much incentive you will be giving to your seller. Therefore, the performance of the seller is evaluated in control procurements, and then the incentive amount and the payment that will be given to the seller based on the performance is determined during control procurements process.

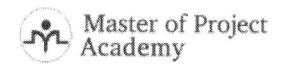

Tools & Techniques Used in Control Procurements

Now we will go over Tools & Techniques Used in Control Procurements process.

- **Contract Change Control System:** This system defines the process by which the procurement can be modified. After the contract is signed, depending on the progress of the project, updates might be needed for the contract. Contract change control system ensures to keep the track of changes in contracts and helps to do changes in a controlled way.

    - **Paperwork, tracking systems, dispute resolution procedures are parts of Contract Change Control System.** For instance, if the organization has a contract system that keeps the history of changes to a contract, who modified last, last update, update context etc. this is an example of contract change control system.

    - **These systems are integrated with integrated change control system.** We have seen integrated change control system during integration management knowledge area, which was actually checking and tracking the effects of a change to the other components of a project. If there will be a change in the contract, this must be updated in other parts of the project respectively. Therefore, contract change control system must be operating in line with the integrated change control system.

- **Procurement Performance Reviews:** These are structured reviews of seller's progress to project scope and quality within cost and on schedule. After you award the contract to the seller, you must check whether the seller meets the agreed requirements in the contract.
    - **Structured review of seller's progress to deliver:** So, in this kind of Procurement Performance Reviews, you are actually checking whether the seller is delivering your project scope, your materials or your tools according to the predefined quality, within the pre-negotiated cost and within the pre-negotiated schedule. Deviations from the negotiated cost, schedule, quality and scope are all checked and recorded in order to evaluate the performance of the seller.

- **Inspections and Audits:** Inspections and Audits are required by the buyer and supported by the seller as specified in contract.

    - **Verification of compliance in the seller's work/deliverables:** Because, these inspections and audits are actually verification of compliance in the seller's work and deliverables. Assume that you asked from a seller to develop a shopping website for your company. During the project, there will be interim checkpoints to check whether the seller is developing the site based on requirements. These inspections and audits will prevent huge deviations from project scope, cost and quality. Therefore, both seller and buyer must be intending to do inspections and audits throughout the project.

- **Performance Reporting:** Work performance data and reports supplied by sellers are evaluated against requirements. For example, you have given a part of your project to a supplier or to a consultant company. They will be sending progress reports about the project or about the work that they are delivering to you and you will be checking whether their schedule performance, cost performance, and quality performance are meeting the requirements that you have pre-negotiated with the seller in the contract.

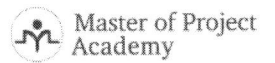

- o **Performance Reporting technique provides management with information about how effectively the seller is achieving the contractual objectives.** Performance reporting from the seller will give information about the completed work, planned work, spent budget etc. Therefore, it helps the buyer to see whether the contractual terms and conditions are met by the seller.

- **Payment Systems:** After delivered work is authorized by the buyer, then, payments to the seller are processed by the accounts payable system of the buyer. After the buyer authorized that the work or that the items delivered are meeting the contractual requirements, buyer should make payment to the seller. Approved payments are generally done by the accounts payable system of the buyer.

- **Claims Administration:** Contested changes are those requested changes where the buyer and seller cannot agree on compensation for the change. Although there can be a contract between the buyer and seller, parties may not agree on some topics throughout the project.
  - o **These are called as claims, disputes or appeals.** When there is a dispute between the buyer and seller, first approach must be solving the issue in peace with negotiations. If this will not be possible, claims are progressed through contract life cycle in accordance with the terms of the contract.
  - o **If buyer and seller cannot agree, respective laws will be deciding factor when solving disputes.**

- **Records Management System:** Documents, mails, pictures, etc. should be recorded and archived during contract management in a project. When needed, these recorded documents, mails, pictures, etc. can be checked. Therefore, records management system will help to control procurement in a project as well.

Closing a Procurement

We have seen how to control a contract. What about closing a procurement?

After the terms, conditions and obligations of a contract has been met by the seller and buyer, contract must be finalized and contract must be closed. For instance, if the seller delivered the required materials to the seller on time as agreed and if the buyer made the all agreed payments, a contract can be closed.

- **Agreements and related documentation are documented for future reference.** In this process, after you have completed all procurements, procurement documents such as procurement statement of work, negotiation emails, contract etc. must be stored in company archives. In future, these might be needed.

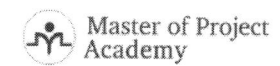

- **Control Procurement process supports the close project or phase process by ensuring contractual agreements are completed or terminated.** Assume that you are purchasing materials, tools, or if you are purchasing a specific work package of your project from a seller. If the seller has completed that package, then, regarding phase or regarding work package, should be closed in your project. Respectively, the contractual part, the procurement part of the regarding work should be closed as well.

- **Contract Termination can be a result of three reasons:**

    - **Mutual agreement by both parties:** If both buyer and seller agree to terminate the contract, the contract can be closed. In this case, for the work that has been delivered or for the items that have been supplied by the supplier or by the seller, buyer have to make payment.

    - **Default of one party:** For example, if seller could not meet the requirements of a contract, or if buyer could not make the negotiated payments to the seller, these can be reasons of termination of the contract.

    - **Convenience of the buyer if provided in the contract:** In some contracts, buyer might be mentioning that they can terminate the contract in convenience. This means, buyer can terminate the contract without giving a reason to the seller. This does not mean that if a buyer is terminating the contract in convenience, the buyer will not pay anything to the seller. Actually, after termination of the contract, buyer has to make all necessary payments to the seller for the accomplished work. However, termination of a contract by the convenience of the buyer can be done only if it is provided in the contract with special terms and conditions.

- **Procurements are closed in two cases:**

    - **If a contract is complete.** If seller has delivered all items or all work that they have to deliver to the buyer, contract is complete, all procurements, all payments are complete, and contract can be closed.

    - **If a contract is terminated before work is complete:** This might be due to default, convenience, or mutual agreement that we have defined already in previous sub-sections.

> Procurement closure is done before project closure.

Because, first, you have to make sure that all required work and procurement statement of work has been delivered by seller to the buyer, and you have to be sure that the buyer paid all regarding payments for the delivered work of the seller. Only then, you can close the project. Therefore, procurement closure comes before project closure in projects.

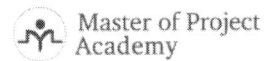

Key Outputs of Procurement Processes

Now, we will summarize the major components of procurement process.

- First procurement process was plan procurements management process. Main output of this process is procurement management plan, which is defining how we will be making purchases. Procurement management plan covers the source selection criteria, buy-make analysis process, steps to follow during procurement management etc.

- Another output is procurement statement of work and this was actually defining the scope of the work, scope of the materials or tools that will be acquired from the sellers. It is defining in detail what will be acquired from a potential seller.

- The last major part in plan procurements is procurement documents. Negotiation documents, meeting notes, contracts, RFP, RFI etc. are all procurement documents. How these documents will be and how they will be managed is determined during plan procurements.

PLAN PROCUREMENTS
- Procurement Management Plan
- Procurement SOW
- Procurement Documents

→ **CONDUCT PROCUREMENTS**
- Signed Contract

→ **CONTROL PROCUREMENTS**
- Substantial completion
- Change requests
- Project Management Plan Updates
- Formal acceptance
- Closed procurements

- After you have planned your procurements management, you enter to the conduct procurements process. Based on the source selection criteria that you have defined in procurement management plan, you will be evaluating the proposals and bids of the sellers.

- Seller, which matches best to the source selection criteria, is elected and awarded with contract. Major output of conduct procurements is awarding contract.

- After you have signed the contract, the procurements start. Therefore, the seller starts to deliver your project work or provide materials or tools to your project.

- Outputs of this process are substantial completion of the required work that has been defined in procurement statement of work, change requests and management plan updates. When the project is progressing, seller will complete the contractual terms and conditions. Buyer might come with new requests during project and if these changes are approved and agreed between the seller and buyer, contract must be revised. After contract revision, change request can be applied and necessary project management plan updates must be done accordingly as well.

- Finally, after all procurements have been completed and all deliverables have been delivered by the seller and payments are done by the buyer to the seller, closing procurements start. At this stage, formal acceptance of the procurements or formal acceptance of the deliverables are done by the buyers.

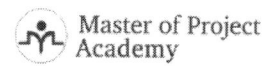

- Once all payments are done successfully by the buyer to seller and once the buyer accepts that all deliverables that have been mentioned in procurement statement of work have been delivered by the seller in accordance with the contract, the procurements are closed in projects.

Quiz – Section 11

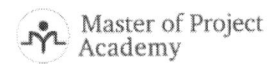

1- Processes necessary to purchase or acquire materials are included in which of the following knowledge areas?

   A) Sales Management

   B) Purchasing Management

   C) Acquisition Management

   D) Procurement Management

2- All of the following are Procurement Management Knowledge Area processes EXCEPT:

   A) Terminate Procurements

   B) Plan Procurement Management

   C) Conduct Procurements

   D) Control Procurements

3- Which of the following statements about Sellers Is TRUE?

   A) Material suppliers cannot be sellers

   B) Sellers are part of the project team

   C) Contractors are examples of sellers

   D) Sellers provide people to adjunct the buyer's team

4- All of the following about procurement is true EXCEPT:

   A) Contracts require formality

   B) Contracts include only high-level requirements of the project

   C) Contracts are legally binding

   D) Contracts should help diminish project risk

5- All of the following are main contract types EXCEPT:

   A) Fixed Price

   B) Fixed Profit

   C) Cost Reimbursable

   D) Time and Material

6- All of the following about Firm Fixed Price Contracts are true EXCEPT:

A) Most commonly used contract type

B) Buyer has the best cost risk

C) Additional bonus is provided to seller based on performance

D) Buyer should define requirements precisely

7- Your company is trying to select sellers for its shopping center construction project. Requirements of the project are clearly mentioned. But project will last in 4 years. In order to protect buyer and seller, which of the following contract types should be used?

A) Fixed Price with Economic Price Adjustment

B) Fixed Price Incentive Fee

C) Firm Fixed Price

D) Fixed Price Plus Bonus

8- Your company is aiming to start a new project. Requirements of the project are unclear and scope is uncertain. But executive management wants to start project immediately. Which of the following contract types is BEST in this case?

A) Time and Material

B) Firm Fixed Price

C) Fixed Price

D) Cost Reimbursable

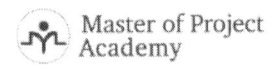

9- You are project manager of an airplane manufacturing project. You have outsourced the avionics systems part of your project to an external company with Cost Plus Incentive Fee Contract under following conditions:

- Target Cost: 2.000.000 USD
- Target Fee: 400.000 USD
- Sharing Ratio: 75/25 (75% buyer, 25% seller)

Outsource company finished the project with 1.900.000 USD cost. What will be the fee that should be paid to the outsource company?

A) 400.000 USD

B) 425.000 USD

C) 475.000 USD

D) 500.000 USD

10- Your company is in preparation to start a new software project. Since company does not have sufficient resources, your company has decided to acquire 2 new software developers from a consultant company for 750 USD per day + expenses. This is an example of:

A) Cost Plus Award Fee Contracts

B) Cost Reimbursable Contracts

C) Fixed Price Contracts

D) Time and Material Contracts

11- In which of the following contracts buyer does not know the profit of the seller?

A) Firm Fixed Price

B) Cost Plus Incentive Fee

C) Cost Plus Award Fee

D) Cost Plus Fixed Fee

12- In which of the following contracts buyer has the most risk in terms of cost?

A) Fixed Price Incentive Fee

B) Cost Plus Incentive Fee

C) Cost Plus Award Fee

D) Cost Plus Fixed Fee

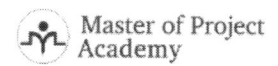

13- In your software project, you will use a specific testing tool to test your deliverables. Price of the tool is 1500 USD, and leasing cost is 100 USD per day. It is better to buy this tool if you will need this tool more than _____ days in your project.

A) 10

B) 13

C) 15

D) 20

14- Major output of Plan Procurement Management Process is Procurement Management Plan. All of the following are included in Procurement Management Plan EXCEPT:

A) Types of contracts to be used

B) Salary information that will be paid to your project team

C) Standardized procurement documents

D) Any constraints and assumptions that could affect planned procurements

15- Which of the following documents define scope of work to be done in each procurement?

A) Purchasing Statement of Work

B) Procurement Statement of Work

C) Project Statement of Work

D) Scope Baseline

16- Source Selection Criteria are included in procurement documents to give information to sellers whether they will bid or make a proposal. All of the following can be examples of selection criteria EXCEPT:

A) Personal relationships of project manager with the seller

B) Understanding of the need by the seller

C) Lifecycle cost of the proposed offer

D) References

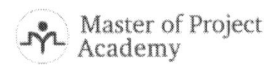

17- During preparation of your contract, you put following statement:

- In case of a natural disaster that will affect the operations of buyer and seller, conditions of this contract will be waived.

This is an example of:

A) Arbitration

B) Breach

C) Force Majeure

D) Retainage

18- You are working in a pharmaceutical company. In country that you are working, a chemical dangerous material is under control of a government agency, and there is not any other alternative channel to purchase this material. This is an example of:

A) Legal Source

B) Ultimate Source

C) Single Source

D) Sole Source

19- In which of the following Procurement Processes a seller is awarded with a contract?

A) Plan Procurement Management

B) Control Procurements

C) Select Seller

D) Conduct Procurements

20- All of the following are tools and techniques used in Conduct Procurements process EXCEPT:

A) Delphi Technique

B) Seller Proposal

C) Bidder Conferences

D) Proposal Review

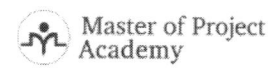

21- In order to use as a benchmark in Conduct Procurements process, after you created your procurement statement of work, you asked an internal department of your company to give estimation for this work. Which of the following technique did you use?

   A) Expert Judgment

   B) Weighting System

   C) Independent Estimate

   D) Internal Estimate

22- After you awarded the contract for a seller, your project started. Payments should be done to seller based on interim deliverables if they meet the terms and conditions negotiated in the contract. This is done during _____ process :

   A) Close Procurements

   B) Control Procurements

   C) Conduct Procuements

   D) Control Payments

23- After you selected a seller and awarded a contract, seller's progress to deliver negotiated project scope and quality is tracked. This is done by _____ technique.

   A) Payment Systems

   B) Procurement Performance Reviews

   C) Claims Administration

   D) Records Management System

24- All of the following are reasons for closing a procurement EXCEPT:

   A) Completion of all required work in contract

   B) Convenience of the buyer since it is stated in the contract

   C) Completion of several project milestones

   D) Default of the seller

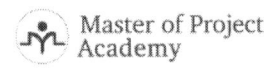

25- Interim deliverables of a project are accepted during project execution and substantial completion of contract requirements are done during _____ (1) process. Formal acceptance of the project is done during _____ (2) process.

   A) (1) Conduct Procurements, (2) Close Procurements

   B) (1) Close Procurements, (2) Control Procurements

   C) (1) Conduct Procurements, (2) Control Procurements

   D) (1) Control Procurements, (2) Control Procurements

Answers

1 – D	16 – A
2 – A	17 – C
3 – C	18 – D
4 – B	19 – D
5 – B	20 – A
6 – C	21 – C
7 – A	22 – B
8 – D	23 – B
9 – B	24 – C
10 – D	25 – D
11 – A	
12 – D	
13 – C	
14 – B	
15 – B	

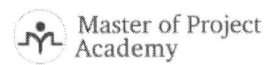

Mapping Game – Section 11

responsible to make sure all work in contract is done	Seller
company or person who purchases the services, goods or materials.	Firm-Fixed-Price
Document that request for the price of the work that needs to be done.	Buyer
100$ per hour + expenses + material costs	Cost Plus Fixed Fee Contracts
company or person who provides services or goods.	Project Manager
contract type has the highest risk for seller	Invitation for Bid (IFB or RFB)
Allowable excuse for either party for not meeting contract requirements	Time and Material Contracts
agreement which the buyer want to keep their work information confidential	Force Majeure
contract type has the highest risk for buyer	Non-Disclosure Agreement

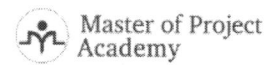

Answers

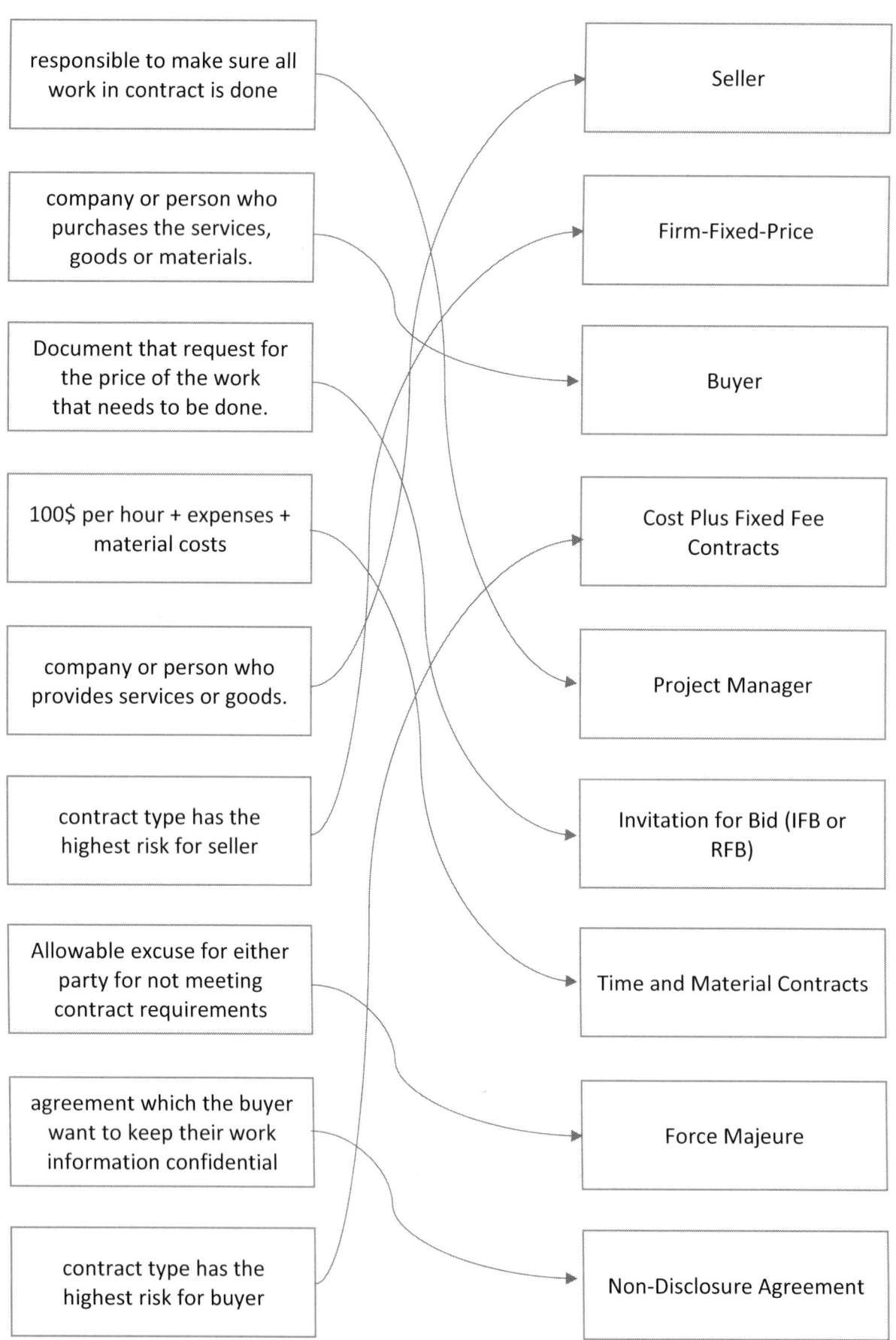

Left	Right
responsible to make sure all work in contract is done	Seller
company or person who purchases the services, goods or materials.	Firm-Fixed-Price
Document that request for the price of the work that needs to be done.	Buyer
100$ per hour + expenses + material costs	Cost Plus Fixed Fee Contracts
company or person who provides services or goods.	Project Manager
contract type has the highest risk for seller	Invitation for Bid (IFB or RFB)
Allowable excuse for either party for not meeting contract requirements	Time and Material Contracts
agreement which the buyer want to keep their work information confidential	Force Majeure
contract type has the highest risk for buyer	Non-Disclosure Agreement

Matches:
- responsible to make sure all work in contract is done → Seller
- company or person who purchases the services, goods or materials. → Buyer
- Document that request for the price of the work that needs to be done. → Invitation for Bid (IFB or RFB)
- 100$ per hour + expenses + material costs → Time and Material Contracts
- company or person who provides services or goods. → Seller
- contract type has the highest risk for seller → Firm-Fixed-Price
- Allowable excuse for either party for not meeting contract requirements → Force Majeure
- agreement which the buyer want to keep their work information confidential → Non-Disclosure Agreement
- contract type has the highest risk for buyer → Cost Plus Fixed Fee Contracts

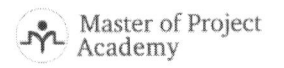

Section 12

Stakeholder Management

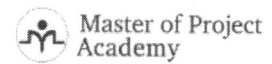

Section 12 – Stakeholder Management

Stakeholder management knowledge area is the last knowledge area of this book. Stakeholders are critical to the success of a project. Anybody who can affect the project or can be affected by the outcomes of the project positively or negatively is called stakeholders.

Project scope is determined with the requirements coming from project stakeholders. These requirements are negotiated and finalized together with stakeholders. At the end of the project, since customer will check the final outputs of the project, stakeholder management is critical throughout the project.

Here is the agenda of this section.

- **Overview of Stakeholder Management:** First, we will see the overview of stakeholder management knowledge area. What is the purpose of this knowledge are, what are the key benefits and what is the importance of stakeholder management knowledge area? We will be going over these.

- **Stakeholder Management Processes:** There are four processes in stakeholder management knowledge area. These processes belong to initiating, planning, executing, monitoring, and controlling process groups respectively.

- **Identify Stakeholders Process & Stakeholder Register:** Main output of this process is stakeholder register document, which includes stakeholders of the project and their details like position, department etc.

- **Plan Stakeholder Engagement Process & Stakeholder Engagement Plan:** After that, we will see second process, plan stakeholder engagement process that defines how stakeholder's, their expectations, conflicts, interests etc. will be managed during the project. Major output of this process is stakeholder engagement plan.

- **Manage Stakeholder Engagement Process:** Third process is Manage Stakeholder Engagement process and mainly includes execution of the Stakeholder Engagement plan in order to meet the desired level of stakeholder engagement to meet project goal and objectives.

- **Monitor Stakeholder Engagement Process:** Finally, we will go over 4th and last process of stakeholder management knowledge area, Monitor Stakeholder Engagement process. During this process, engagement levels of stakeholders are tracked and necessary actions are taken if some of the stakeholders are not engaged in the desired level. Especially key stakeholders must be engaging to the project at the desired level for successful project completion.

Overview of Stakeholder Management

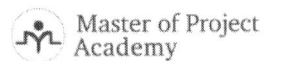

Let us look at the definition of stakeholder management first.

Stakeholder Management Knowledge area includes processes required to identify the people, groups, or organizations that could impact or be impacted by the project, to analyze stakeholder expectations and their impact on the project, and to develop appropriate management strategies for effectively engaging stakeholders in project decisions and execution.

- **Project stakeholders are people, group or organizations that might be affected positively or negatively from the decisions, activities, and outcomes of a project.** Stakeholders of a project have different level of interest, involvement and power. These stakeholders have different expectations from a project and their expectations might compete with each other as well. Main purpose of stakeholder management knowledge area is defining stakeholders and desired level of involvement of these stakeholders in a project, how expectations and requirements of these stakeholders will be managed and how to resolve conflicts when they arise.

- **Stakeholder satisfaction should be managed as a key project objective.** Because, satisfaction of stakeholders is key to successful completion of project goals and objectives. Let us think the project sponsor of your project. He will provide the high-level requirements of your project like project budget, deadline etc. If you cannot meet these negotiated requirements of your sponsor, who is one of the key stakeholders of a project, then it will affect your project success drastically.
  Similarly, let us think that you will need resources from different functional departments of your organization. You need to satisfy the requirements of the functional manager in order to have a good relationship with him and get the required resources for your project on time. Note that, functional managers do not only provide resources, they will provide subject matter expertise on technical issues you might face during your project. Therefore, their expectations and interests must be considered during the project in order to get their support when needed as well.

Stakeholder Management Knowledge area has four processes:

- **Identify Stakeholders (Initiating):** First process is Identify Stakeholders process and belongs to initiating process group. During this process, all relevant stakeholders of a project are identified and their roles, positions etc. are defined in stakeholder register document.

- **Plan Stakeholder Engagement (Planning):** Second process is Plan Stakeholder engagement process and belongs to Planning process group. During this process, how stakeholders and their requirements will be managed, how conflicts will be resolved if they arise between stakeholders are defined in stakeholder engagement plan document.

- **Manage Stakeholder Engagement (Executing):** Third process is Manage stakeholder engagement process and belongs to Executing process group. During this process, actions and steps planned in stakeholder engagement plan is executed in order to meet desired level of stakeholder engagement and satisfaction.

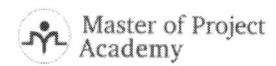

- **Monitor Stakeholder Engagement (Monitoring & Controlling):** Last and fourth process is Monitor Stakeholder Engagement process and belongs to Monitoring and controlling process group. During this process, planned involvement levels of stakeholders are compared with the actual involvement levels. If there are deviations, necessary actions are taken to reach desired level of involvement from stakeholders.

Identify Stakeholders Process

Identify Stakeholders is the process of identifying the people, groups or organizations that could affect or be impacted by outcomes of the project.

- **Main purpose of this process is defining who will be affected positively or negatively from the decisions, activities or outcomes of the project.** For example, if your company is constructing a dam in a lake, examples of stakeholders can be residents living close to lake area, team members of the project, sponsor of the project etc. However, stakeholders can be groups or organizations as well. For instance, if you need to get permissions for the construction project from the municipality or government agencies, these are stakeholders of your project as well and need to be identified during Identify Stakeholders Process.

- **Key benefit of the process is identifying the appropriate focus for each stakeholder or group of stakeholders.** Because, each stakeholder has varying levels of involvement and authority in projects. Let us think that you are working in a software vendor and your customer is a bank and your project will be delivering a software application. In this scenario think of the executive vice president of your company, project sponsor in the bank, a software developer in your project, and security department of the bank that will approve your entry requests to the bank premises. Do you think that all these stakeholders need same focus and treatment? Of course, no! For sure, these stakeholders have different levels of involvement and authority to affect your project. Therefore, appropriate focus for each stakeholder must be set during Identify Stakeholders process.

- **Project Stakeholders are individuals, groups or organizations who might affect or be affected by the outcomes of the project.** Actually, this is what we mentioned already. Project stakeholders are the people, group, organizations who might be affected by, or affecting a project positively or negatively.

- **Stakeholders may be at different levels within the organization and might have varying authority levels.** As we discussed already, a vice president and a software developer or security personnel can be project stakeholder. But, their interest to the project and especially authority or power will be different as you can consider. Therefore, these different stakeholders need different stakeholder management strategies.

- **Identifying stakeholders early in the project and analyzing their interest and expectations is crucial for project success.** Because, it is easier to change or affect a project during early phases of a project compared to later phases in a project. Therefore, especially key decisions, high level plans, actions and steps need to be agreed upon stakeholders early in the project. Let us think that you made your plans and resource planning without getting agreement from functional managers who will provide your resources. When you need resources for your project later, since you did not agree with the functional managers before, they might not be able to provide necessary resources for your project. Therefore, involving stakeholders early in the project and getting agreement of all stakeholders on the decisions taken and plans created is crucial for project success.

Tools & Techniques Used in Identify Stakeholders

Now, we will go over tools and techniques used in Identify Stakeholders process.

Stakeholder Analysis: First and the most important technique is Stakeholder Analysis.

- **This technique identifies all stakeholders related to a project and systematically gathers and analyzes whose interest should be considered.** Because, as we discussed already, each stakeholder has different levels of involvement and different levels of authority. Therefore, depending on the interest level of stakeholders, which stakeholders need to be managed closely are analyzed and identified in Identify Stakeholders process.

- **This process also defines, how, what, when to communicate with each stakeholder.** For instance, executive vice president of your company will not need every single detail of your project in your project report. Therefore, he might want to see a milestone report in each month to see the high-level progress of your project. On the other hand, primary responsible of your project in your customer might want to see a detailed report each week. Thus, these communication requirements of stakeholders, frequency of delivery, format and content of the information that will be delivered need to be analyzed.

- **There are certain steps that need to be followed in stakeholder analysis:**

    1. **Identify all potential stakeholders and relevant information (e.g. roles, departments, interest, knowledge, influence, authority etc.):** First, potential stakeholders and relevant information regarding stakeholders are identified. For example, James is a stakeholder of a project and sponsor of the project. He is head of software development department and his position is director. He has one of the highest levels of interest to the project and he has one of the most powerful stakeholders of the project. This kind of stakeholder information is identified for all stakeholders in first step of stakeholder analysis technique.

    2. **Analyze the potential impact or support of each stakeholder:** Since stakeholders have different levels of interest and power, their impact and attitude on the project will vary as well. Can you think that your project sponsor is not supporting your project at the desired level? Most probably, your project will fail because he is the spokesperson of the project and need to protect from internal and external influences. On the other hand, a stakeholder who has low level of interest and authority in your project will not affect your project

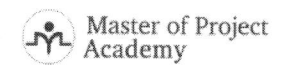

significantly. However, this does not mean that he or she should be ignored. All necessary actions and steps need to be taken to get his or her support in the project as well.

3. **Assess how key stakeholders are likely to react in various situations:** For instance, what will be the reaction of project sponsor if your project is delayed or goes over budget during execution? Alternatively, what will be the preference of a functional manager when you and another project manager need same resource for projects? This kind of stakeholder reactions in various situations need to be analyzed in order to be prepared for the reactions of stakeholders when they occur in the project.

Stakeholder Analysis Models: Now, we will see different stakeholder analysis models in this part. There are four models:

1. **Power Interest Grid model:** In this model, stakeholders are grouped based on their authority or power and their level of concern or interest to the project.
   Here, we will see an example for Power Interest Grid model. As you see, horizontal side of the grid reflects the interest of the stakeholder and vertical side of the grid reflects the power of the stakeholder.
   If a stakeholder has a high level of authority or power and high level of interest to the project, this stakeholder can impact your project severely. Therefore, as can be seen in the right above corner of the grid, these stakeholders must be managed closely and their support needs to be taken in order to complete project successfully. If their expectations and requirements are not met in your project, your project can even fail.
   If a stakeholder has high level of power and low level of interest to the project, this stakeholder must be satisfied, their expectations and requirements need to be met in the project.
   If a stakeholder has low level of power and high level of interest to the project, this stakeholder must be informed. It is of course better to satisfy requirements and expectations of this stakeholder as well but even if you cannot satisfy, since he has a relatively low level of power, he will not be affecting your project drastically.
   Finally, if a stakeholder has a low level of power and low level of interest, this stakeholder will have very low impact on the project but it is better to monitor this stakeholder.

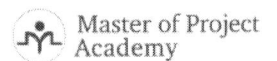

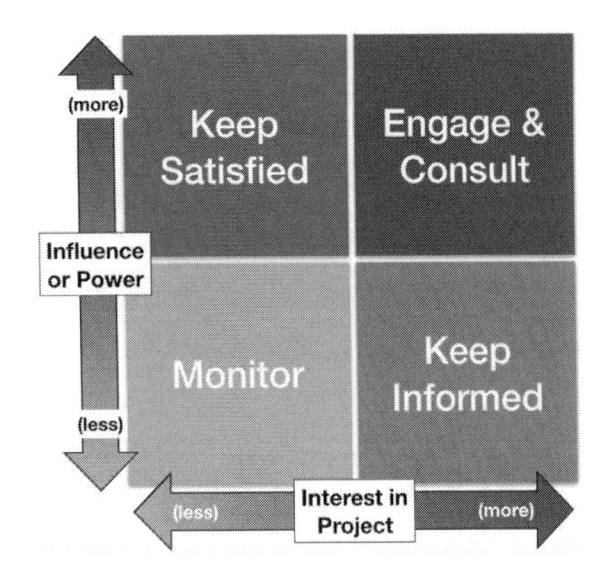

2. **Power Influence Grid model:** In this model, stakeholders are grouped based on authority or power and their active involvement or influence in the project.

3. **Influence Impact Grid model:** In this model, stakeholders are grouped based on involvement or influence and their ability to affect or impact the project.

4. **Salience Model:** In this model, stakeholders are described based on their power, urgency and involvement in the project.

- **Expert Judgment:** In expert judgment technique, stakeholders of a project can be identified by taking assistance of an expert and these experts can provide their opinion on who or which organizations can be stakeholder of a project.

- **Meetings:** And in meetings technique, with the participation of regarding people and parties, power, authority, influence, involvement etc. of stakeholders can be discussed during meetings.

Stakeholder Register

Stakeholder Register is the main output of Identify Stakeholders process. As an output of Identify stakeholders, you will have all related stakeholders of your project and relevant information about your stakeholders. These stakeholders and their relevant information are kept in Stakeholder Register document.

- **Stakeholder Register document contains details of identified stakeholders:** This document includes
    - **Identification information** like name, organizational position, location, role contact info etc. For instance, Nelly is the functional manager of software development department, works in San Francisco office, and her role in the project is providing software developers and subject matter expertise for problems. Contact info for Nelly is nelly@masterofproject.com

- o **Assessment information** about a stakeholder is also included in Stakeholder Register document. This information can be major requirements, main expectations, potential influence in the project etc. Think Nelly again. She was functional manager of software development department. Her major requirements and expectations are seeing staffing management plan at least 2 months before project starts in order to provide sufficient resources for the project. Her potential influence is, if she cannot provide project resources on time, project can get delays.
- o **Stakeholder classification** is another content that is included in Stakeholder Register document. This classification info includes whether the stakeholder is internal or external which means if stakeholder is directly involved in your project it is internal, if not external. For example, project manager, sponsor, team members are internal stakeholders. If there is a government or municipality agency as a stakeholder in your project, these will be external stakeholders. In addition, stakeholder engagement level can be included as supporter, neutral, resistor etc. in stakeholder register document. If we give this classification information over Nelly again, she is an internal stakeholder and she is supporter since she does her best to provide your project resource on time in order to complete project successfully.
- **Stakeholder register must be updated regularly since new stakeholders might be added, change during the project.** First, you create stakeholder register document during initiating process group. However, stakeholders of a project can change over time, during later phases of your project, new stakeholders can be identified and these need to be updated in stakeholder register document. In addition, some stakeholders may resign or leave their roles, positions. In these cases, new people might be assigned to their roles, positions and for a reason these changes need to be reflected in Stakeholder Register document respectively as well.

Plan Stakeholder Engagement Process

Plan Stakeholder Engagement is the process of developing appropriate strategies to effectively engage stakeholders throughout the project life cycle. Because, managing stakeholders' requirements and expectations are crucial in project success. Especially when there are competing requirements or expectations of different stakeholders, these need to be balanced properly and to do this you need to have an appropriate stakeholder management strategy. These strategies are developed during Plan Stakeholder Engagement process.

- **Key benefit of the process is that it provides a clear, actionable plan to interact with stakeholders.** If you do not have this plan, you might interact with the stakeholders in a way that they did not require or expect. Their dissatisfaction can cause failure or problems in your project. Also, a generic plan for how to engage stakeholders is not possible since every stakeholder will have different requirements and expectations. Therefore, different requirements, different expectations, and different engagement levels of stakeholders require individual stakeholder management strategies for each stakeholder.

- **This process generates the stakeholder engagement plan, which contains detailed plans on how effective stakeholder management can be realized.** This plan needs to be followed during managing stakeholders in order to have a better management of all stakeholders and to be prepared for reactions of different stakeholders in different situations. For example, what will be the reaction of project sponsor if project exceeds budget and goes behind schedule. How this information should be communicated to sponsor through meeting, through mail, by executive management? What is the likely response of stakeholder? Will he be so angry, over reactive? Will he be supportive or blaming? What are your preplanned steps to overcome this situation? These kinds of evaluations are done and a proper stakeholder engagement plan is prepared during this process. If you do not have these prepared plans, you might have troubles when managing stakeholders especially in critical points if you are caught unprepared.

Tools & Techniques of Plan Stakeholder Engagement

Now, we will go over tools and techniques used in plan stakeholder engagement process.

- **Expert Judgment:** In order to determine the required engagement level of stakeholders, expert opinion can be taken. For example, senior stakeholders must be highly engaged at the beginning of the project.

- **Meetings:** Meetings can be organized in order to determine engagement level of stakeholders with relevant participants as well. During these meetings, desired engagement level for each stakeholder is discussed and determined by the participants.

- **Analytical Techniques:** This technique involves comparison of engagement levels of all stakeholders with the planned engagement levels. For instance, you might have planned high level of involvement of project sponsor. However, this might not be possible during the project and he might have a low level of involvement. Since sponsor is a critical stakeholder, his engagement level is also crucial. Therefore, these planned and actual engagement levels are compared in analytical techniques. Then further actions need to be taken especially if key stakeholders are engaging to the project lower than the desired or planned engagement level.

    o **Stakeholder engagement throughout the life cycle of the project is critical to project success.** Because during project life cycle, you might need different level of engagement from different stakeholders in each phase for example. Then, you need to monitor the actual engagement level of a stakeholder and compare it with the desired level of engagement in each phase. If there is a deviation, then you need to take actions to increase the level of engagement of stakeholders.

    o **Stakeholders are classified based on their engagement level in a project.** There are five common engagement levels: unaware, resistant, neutral, supportive and leading. Now, we will see each level respectively.

- **Unaware:** Unaware stakeholders are unaware of project and potential impacts. Probably they did not hear even about the project or even if they heard, they do not think that they will be affected by the project.

- **Resistant:** Resistant stakeholders are aware of project and potential impacts and resistant to change. These stakeholders must be managed properly especially if they have high authority and influence to the project. Because, they can even have hostile attitude to your project and this can cause your project to be unsuccessful. For instance, if your project is bringing a new technology to your customer and employees who work with existing technology will be either replaced or fired after introduction of new technology, then people knowing this existing technology might be resistant to your project. You might not get adequate support, information from them or even they might show additional hostile actions in order to drive your project to failure. Therefore, these stakeholders need special care and management.

- **Neutral:** Neutral stakeholders are aware of the project, but they neither support nor resist to your project. If these stakeholders have high authority, it might be better to take actions to get their support on your project since it will affect the project in a good way.

- **Supportive:** Supportive stakeholders are aware of the project and potential impacts and they are supportive to change. These stakeholders are your brother in arms and they will work with you to deliver the project successfully. You need to be careful when managing the stakeholders that you should not lose their motivation or support. Otherwise, you might lose a wing carrying your project.

- **Leading:** Leading stakeholders are aware of project and potential impacts and they are actively engaged in ensuring the project is a success. These stakeholders can be executives of your company, project sponsor etc. These stakeholders are actually locomotive of your project. Therefore, their support and involvement are crucial in your project that if they are not involved in desired level, your project can even fail.

Stakeholder Engagement levels can be shown in Stakeholders Engagement Assessment Matrix. C represents the current engagement level of a stakeholder while D represents the desired or planned engagement level.

Stakeholder Engagement Assessment Matrix					
Stakeholder	Unaware	Resistant	Neutral	Supportive	Leading
Sam		C		D	
John				C	D
Debbie	C			D	
Hillary				C - D	

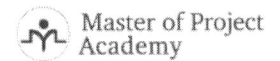

As you see in the table, Sam's current engagement level is resistant. So, he is resisting for the project since he thinks that the project will affect him or his situation negatively. However, his desired engagement level is supportive. Here there is a great gap! You need to take necessary actions to increase stakeholder engagement level to supportive.

John's current engagement level is supportive while his desired engagement level is leading. Thus, also necessary steps need to be done in order to increase engagement level of John.

Debbie's current engagement level is unaware although she should be supporting the project! Debbie should be informed about the project outcomes and her support should be acquired.

Hillary's current and desired engagement levels are both supportive. This stakeholder is engaged at the planned level so you need to monitor this stakeholder that she should keep this level of engagement as he is already engaged at the planned level.

Stakeholder Engagement Plan

Stakeholder engagement plan is component of the project management plan and major output of plan stakeholder engagement process. This plan defines how you will manage stakeholders of your project, balance their requirements, expectations, what you should do in order to increase engagement level of stakeholders if they are below the desired level of engagement etc. This plan is prepared in planning process group in order to manage stakeholders during execution of the project.

- **Stakeholder engagement plan can be formal, informal, highly detailed or broadly defined depending on the needs of the project.** Think of two projects. First project is a construction project, which will take around 4 years, includes over 1000 team members, and includes involvement of government, municipality and ministry agencies.
Second project is a new project initiated after completion of your first project; one software developer will work to implement new simple features requested by your customer.
For sure, formality or detail level of the stakeholder engagement plans of these projects will differ. Thus, depending on the project needs, formality and detail level of stakeholder engagement plan can change.

Stakeholder engagement plan includes:

- **Desired and current engagement levels of stakeholders.** As we mentioned already, if a stakeholder, especially if he has a high level of authority and influence, has lower level of actual engagement than the desired level, then all necessary actions need to be taken to increase his or her engagement level.

- **Stakeholder communication requirements** are included in stakeholder engagement plan. Each stakeholder might have varying communication requirements. For example, an executive of your company might require a 15-minute high-level progress meeting each month, while your project sponsor requires a detailed report each week and by mail. These kinds of different format, content, frequency requirements of stakeholders are determined in stakeholder engagement plan and information is coordinated accordingly with these stakeholders.

- **Information to be distributed** to stakeholders may also vary. Information required to be delivered regarding your project for a project team member and head of human resource department will vary for sure. Therefore, as we discussed before in communications management knowledge area, efficient and effective communication must be ensured when distributing information to stakeholders.

- **Time frame and frequency for the distribution of information** is also included in stakeholder engagement plan. Some stakeholder might require frequent updates while others do not. Information needs to be delivered based on frequency requirements of stakeholders.

- **Method for updating stakeholder engagement plan:** Stakeholder engagement plan is created in planning process group. However, since stakeholders of a project might change during project life cycle, methods for updating stakeholder engagement plan should be included in stakeholder engagement plan as well. For instance, what should be the steps for defining a management strategy for a new stakeholder? How will this be updated in the document? These should be written down in stakeholder engagement plan.

Manage Stakeholder Engagement Process

Manage stakeholder engagement is the process of communicating and working with stakeholders to meet their need and expectations. During identify stakeholder's process, you identify project stakeholders and during plan stakeholder engagement process, you define how to manage your stakeholders and document these plans in stakeholder engagement plan. In manage stakeholder engagement process, you execute your stakeholder engagement plan in order to meet the requirements and expectations of your stakeholders in order to meet project goals and objectives and finish the project successfully.

- **Key benefit of this process is increasing support and minimizing resistance from stakeholders and increasing the chances to achieve project success.** Because if key stakeholders do not support the project at the adequate level, there might be problems when achieving project success. So, if a stakeholder's engagement level is lower than the planned value, necessary actions to increase his or her engagement level is taken during manage stakeholder engagement process. In addition, resistant stakeholders are danger for project success and their hostile or inappropriate behaviors must be suppressed as much as possible to increase the chances of success in project.

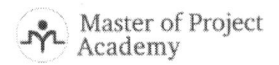

- **Ability of stakeholders to influence the project is highest during the initial stages and gets progressively lower as the project progresses.** Because, as a project nature, uncertainties are higher during early stages of a project and planning activities or taking decisions regarding critical points or actions direct the future of a project higher during early stages. During these early stages, relevant parties or relevant stakeholders have highest level of influence. Therefore, especially key stakeholders' engagement level is crucial during early stages of project when taking critical decisions about the project.

- **Active management of stakeholder involvement decreases the risk of the project failure.** Especially if the supportive and leading stakeholders are performing their roles as planned, this will decrease the risk of project failure. Therefore, if a stakeholder is engaging to the project in a lower level than the planned level, then necessary actions, necessary steps need to be done in order to increase his or her engagement level to the desired level.

Manage stakeholder engagement process includes:

- **Engaging stakeholders to obtain or confirm their commitment to success of the project.** As we mentioned already, stakeholders should be involved in a project at their planned level of engagement in order to complete project successfully. If actual engagement levels are, lower than the desired or planned values, necessary actions need to be taken.

- **Stakeholder expectations are managed during manage stakeholder engagement process.** Stakeholders have different requirements and expectations from a project. Meeting all stakeholder expectations and requirements is impossible. Nevertheless, especially key stakeholders must be satisfied and if there are competing stakeholder requirements, these need to be balanced and a solution needs to be found before these conflicts create major problems for the project.

- **Manage stakeholder engagement process also includes ensuring project goals are achieved.** Since stakeholder expectations and requirements are managed and realized during this process, project goals are achieved respectively as well.

- **If there are conflicts between stakeholders, these might cause future problems in your project.** Therefore, these conflicts between stakeholders must be resolved as soon as possible in a project.
- **Manage stakeholder engagement process also includes that the stakeholders understand the project goals, objectives, benefits and risks.** Because, before starting to project, every stakeholder must be on same page and need to agree on the taken decisions about the project. If there are stakeholders that were not present during taking decisions about a project, then these stakeholders might create problems in future since they were not involved during taking decisions, which might be related with their area.

Monitor Stakeholder Engagement Process

Monitor stakeholder engagement is the process of monitoring overall project stakeholder relationships and adjusting strategies and plans for engaging stakeholders. During plan stakeholder engagement process, you defined which stakeholder should be engaged in what level to the project. During monitor stakeholder engagement process, current engagement levels of stakeholders are assessed. If there are stakeholders who have lower levels of engagement levels than their planned levels, then these stakeholders should be managed to achieve the desired level of engagement levels in manage stakeholder engagement process.

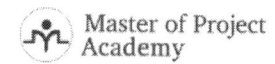

- **Monitor stakeholder engagement process maintains or increases the efficiency and effectiveness of stakeholder engagement.** If there are gaps or weaknesses in stakeholder engagement plan, these are monitored and tracked during monitor stakeholder engagement process as well. Then, necessary updates and corrections are done to stakeholder engagement plan respectively.

Quiz – Section 12

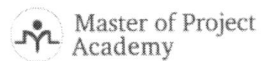

1- Requirements, expectations, needs of stakeholders are managed main in which of the following knowledge area?
   A) Procurement Management
   B) Resource Management
   C) Communications Management
   D) Stakeholder Management

2- All of the following are processes of Stakeholder Management knowledge area EXCEPT:
   A) Determine Stakeholders
   B) Identify Stakeholders
   C) Manage Stakeholder Engagement
   D) Monitor Stakeholder Engagement

3- Your company will construct a new hospital in a district. Which of the following are stakeholders of this project?
   A) Team members of the project
   B) Residents living closer to hospital
   C) Doctors that will start to work in this hospital
   D) All of the above

4- All of the following about stakeholders are true EXCEPT:
   A) Stakeholders are affected by project
   B) Stakeholders might affect the project
   C) Stakeholders can be only individuals
   D) Stakeholders need to be managed

5- All of the following techniques are used in Identify Stakeholders process EXCEPT:
   A) Stakeholder Analysis
   B) Brainstorming
   C) Expert Judgment
   D) Meetings

6- You want to classify your project stakeholders based on their power and interest or concern to the project. Which of the following classification model is appropriate for this?
   A) Power/Influence Grid
   B) Power/Interest Grid
   C) Influence/Impact Grid
   D) Salience Model

7- Stakeholder Register document is the major output of Identify Stakeholders process. Stakeholder Register document includes all of the following information about stakeholders EXCEPT:
   A) Personal details
   B) Identification information
   C) Assessment information

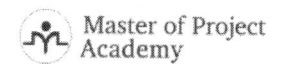

D) Stakeholder classification

8- Stakeholders' expectations and requirements must be balanced and managed properly. For this purpose, management strategies for stakeholders are prepared during _____ process.
   A) Identify Stakeholders
   B) Plan Stakeholder Strategy
   C) Plan Stakeholder Engagement
   D) Manage Stakeholder Engagement

9- You are managing a software project. Project sponsor actively monitors status of the project, protects the project from internal and external influences and also participates in critical meetings when taking decisions. His engagement level is:
   A) Pushing
   B) Neutral
   C) Supportive
   D) Leading

10- Stakeholder Management Plan includes all of the following EXCEPT:
   A) Desired and current engagement levels of stakeholders
   B) Stakeholder communication requirements
   C) Frequency for information distribution
   D) Method for how to ignore weak stakeholders

11- During Monitor Stakeholder Engagement process, you noticed that a stakeholder is involved in the project at neutral level although he should have involved as supportive. What is the NEXT action you should do?
   A) Take actions to increase his engagement level to supportive
   B) Reevaluate the Stakeholder Register document
   C) Ignore the stakeholder and put maximum effort on other supportive stakeholders' management
   D) Wait for him for another 1-2 months to see whether he will be supportive

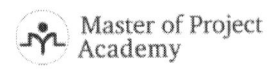

Answers

1 - D	11 - A
2 – A	
3 – D	
4 – C	
5 – B	
6 – B	
7 – A	
8 – C	
9 – D	
10 – D	

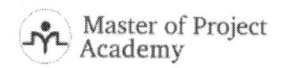

Mapping Game – Section 12

Left	Right
"Managing stakeholder expectations" activity is part of which process?	Salience Model
Analysis Model where groups based on authority and their level or concern	Stakeholder Identification Information
name, organizational position, location, role, contact info etc.	Monitor Stakeholder Engagement
Analysis Model based on Stakeholders' authority and their involvement	Identify Stakeholders
Project charter is input of which process?	Power/Interest Grid
Analysis Model based on Stakeholders' power, urgency and legitimacy	Power/Influence Grid
major requirements, main expectations, potential influence in the project etc.	Monitor Stakeholder Engagement
Maintains or increases the efficiency and effectiveness of stakeholder engagement	Manage Stakeholder Engagement
Work performance information is output of which process?	Stakeholder Assessment Information

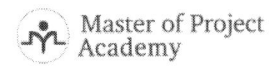

Answers

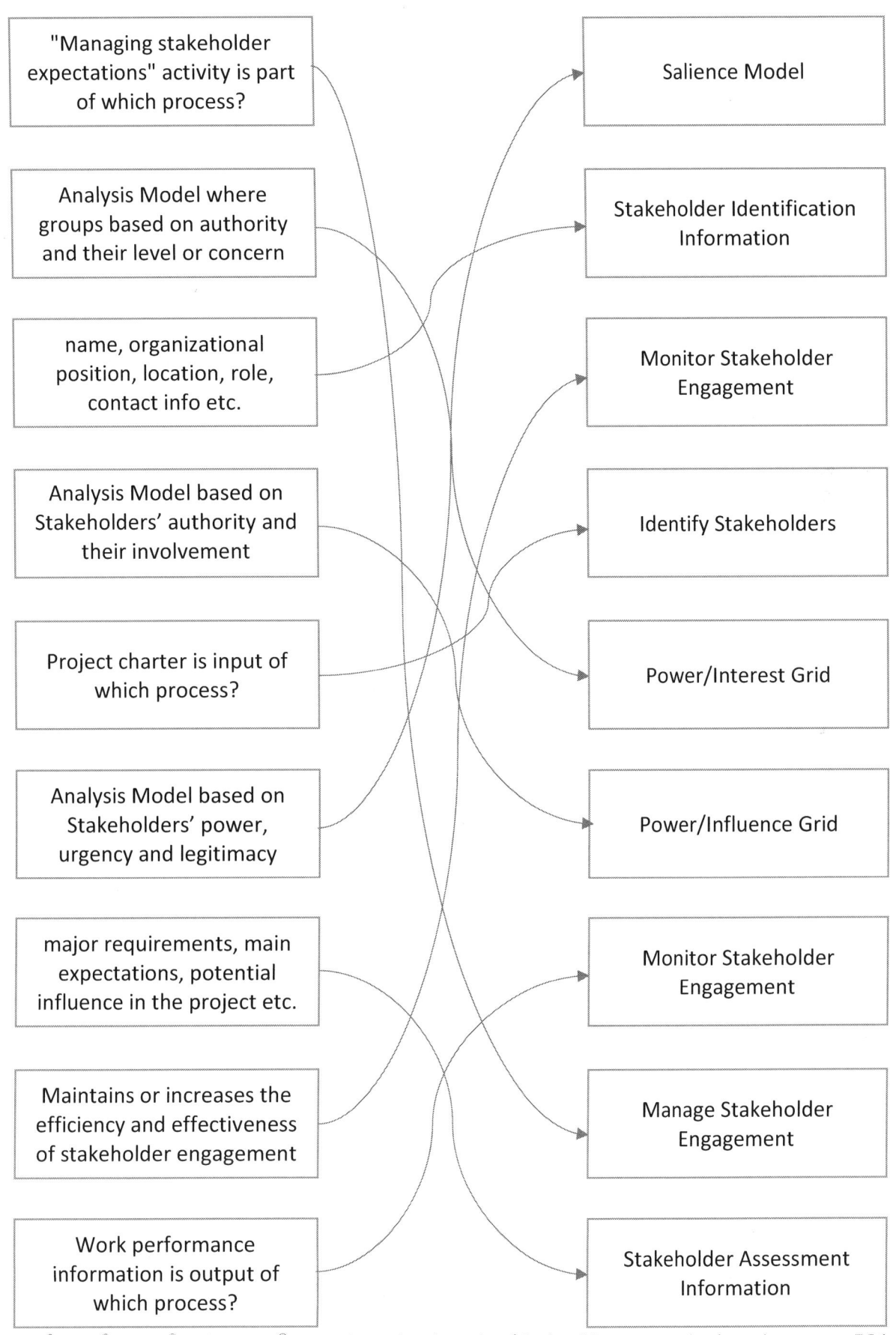

Left	Right
"Managing stakeholder expectations" activity is part of which process?	→ Manage Stakeholder Engagement
Analysis Model where groups based on authority and their level or concern	→ Power/Interest Grid
name, organizational position, location, role, contact info etc.	→ Stakeholder Identification Information
Analysis Model based on Stakeholders' authority and their involvement	→ Power/Influence Grid
Project charter is input of which process?	→ Identify Stakeholders
Analysis Model based on Stakeholders' power, urgency and legitimacy	→ Salience Model
major requirements, main expectations, potential influence in the project etc.	→ Stakeholder Assessment Information
Maintains or increases the efficiency and effectiveness of stakeholder engagement	→ Monitor Stakeholder Engagement
Work performance information is output of which process?	→ Monitor Stakeholder Engagement

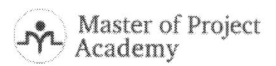

Section 13 – Sample PMP® Practice Exam

1. A contract obligates the seller to provide the specified product and obligates the buyer to pay for it. In this context, which of the following is a mandatory feature of a contract?
   A-) Legally binding
   B-) Complicated
   C) Very detailed statement of work
   D-) Signatures of senior leadership of the buyer

2. After the project schedule is created, a project manager should use schedule control for all of the following EXCEPT:
   A-) Influencing the factors that create schedule changes
   B-) Determining that the project schedule has changed
   C-) Determining planned start and finish dates for project activities
   D-) Managing actual schedule changes as they occur

3. You have recently assumed charge of a project from another project manager. You want to know what kind of information you should provide to different stakeholders and what methods to adopt for this purpose. You will find this information in the:
   A) Communications management analysis
   B) Performance reports
   C) Project records
   D) Communication management plan

4. You had earlier worked as a project manager in a firm specializing in manufacturing semi-conductor chips. Now that you are working with a competitor,
   A) You should not use the knowledge gained in the first company to improve the competitor`s product quality
   B) You can use the knowledge gained in the first company to improve your present company`s product quality
   C) You should get your first company`s approval before doing anything that may adversely impact them
   D) You should do nothing by way of competing with or undermining the products of the first company

5. There are two projects:
   Investment in project A is $ 1,000,000 and its NPV is $ 100,000
   Investment in project B is $ 1,200,000, its net cash inflows are $ 2,000,000, and net cash outflows are $ 1,900,000
   Which project should be selected if net present value(NPV) criterion is used for selection?
   A) Project A

B) Project B
C) The information in the question is inadequate
D) Either project A or project B

6. You have completed the process of developing options and actions to enhance opportunities and to reduce threats to project objectives. What is your NEXT step?
    A) Determine which risks may affect the project and document their characteristics.
    B) Implement risk response plans, track identified risks, and monitor residual risks.
    C) Define how to conduct risk management activities for a project.
    D) Assess the priority of identified risks using their probability of occurrence.

7. As a project manager, you are using the configuration management system to centrally manage approved changes and baselines within the project. What are the configuration management activities that you will include in the integrated change control process?
    A) Configuration accounting and verification and audit
    B) Configuration identification, status accounting, and configuration accounting
    C) Configuration identification, status accounting, and verification and audit
    D) Configuration verification, configuration identification, and risk forecast

8. During Plan Quality process, you are going to use Design of Experiments (DOE) to determine which factors might influence specific variables. Which variable can be used in your analysis?
    A) Dollars
    B) Pounds
    C) Weight
    D) Meters

9. All the following statements about a project life cycle are correct EXCEPT:
    A) All project life cycles are usually identical.
    B) The level of risk is highest at the start of the project and decreases as the project progresses.
    C) The ability of the stakeholders to influence the final characteristics is highest at the start and gets progressively lower as the project continues.
    D) Cost and staffing requirements usually peak during the intermediate phases.

10. There has been a change in the scope of your project, which may adversely impact the project schedules and cost. You have updated the technical and planning documents. All the requested changes and recommended corrective actions will now be processed through:
    A) Impact request statements
    B) Change control system
    C) Integrated Change Control process
    D) Changes to the scope management plan

11. You are working as a project manager in a software vendor. Your company signs a contract with a customer to develop a Questionnaire Software. Your manager Wayne

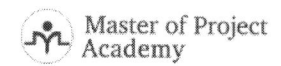

brings you to the meeting with customer. In the meeting you realize that automation tool will be developed for marketing department of the customer and all financial resources will be provided by Marketing Director, Linda. You also meet with the technical manager of the project in customer, David, who will assist you to execute your project and project manager of customer Lily. Who is the sponsor of the project?
A) Wayne, Your Manager
B) David, Technical Manager of Customer
C) Lily, Project Manager of Customer
D) Linda, Marketing Director

12. You would like to obtain information, quotations, bids, offers, or proposals from sellers as part of the Conduct Procurements process. In this process, which of the following is the most critical?
A) Determine whether a product should be purchased or manufactured in-house.
B) Ensure that prospective sellers clearly understand the technical and contract requirements.
C) Clarify the structure and requirements of the contract.
D) Prepare an independent estimate to verify the proposed price structures of the seller.

13. You are the project manager of an educational company. You know that the technical writing team starts editing the project document 15 days after they start writing it. This waiting time can also be referred to as:
A) Lead time
B) Project float
C) Constraint
D) Lag

14. You have recently conducted a variance analysis of your project and found that the project is 25% over-budget. This is a very important issue, which you would like to discuss with your project stakeholders. What communication method should you use?
A) War room discussion
B) Face-to-face meeting
C) Formal report
D) Telephone calls and electronic mail

15. A project manager disclosed some crucial information to a prospective seller. Which aspect of PMI Code of Ethics and Professional Conduct did he violate?
A) Maintain and satisfy the scope and objectives
B) Prevent conflict of interest
C) Provide accurate and truthful representations
D) Refrain from offering or accepting inappropriate payments, gifts, etc.

16. You are given the following four projects. Which project will you select?

A) Project A with an opportunity cost of $ 100,000
B) Project B with a benefit-cost ratio of 0.75
C) Project C with an IRR of -2%
D) Project D with NPV of $ 100,000

17. You have geographically dispersed team members, from whom you would like to anonymously obtain expert opinion on the project you are managing. Which information gathering technique should you use?
    A) Brainstorming
    B) Delphi technique
    C) SWOT analysis
    D) Checklists

18. A project manager has to manage conflict in an organization. Which of the following could be the source of least conflict in an organization?
    A) Weak matrix structure with multiple managers to report to
    B) Low position in the organization hierarchy
    C) Roles that are not well defined
    D) Work pressure and high stress

19. You are working as a project manager in an automobile company. Recently the government has amended the regulations to enforce stricter emission requirements for automobiles. As a project manager, you are concerned that your project quality norms may not satisfy the revised quality standards. So, you do an audit and try to remedy this problem through:
    A) Quality assurance
    B) Quality planning
    C) Quality control
    D) Modifications to quality management plan

20. Almost all projects are planned and implemented in a social, economic, or environmental context, and have intended and unintended positive or negative impacts. In this context, which of the following statements about enterprise environmental factors is NOT true?
    A) Neither promote nor hold back the project management processes
    B) May restrict the project management processes
    C) May promote the project management processes
    D) May either promote or hold back the project management processes

21. After collecting requirements, one of your tasks as a project manager is to prepare a scope statement for your project. The scope statement provides:
    A) Authorization to the project manager for using organizational resources for project activities.
    B) Documentation of how the project scope will be managed and how scope changes will be integrated into the project.
    C) Definition for work breakdown structure

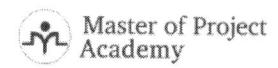

D) A documented basis for making future project decisions and for confirming or developing a common understanding of the project scope among the stakeholders.

22. You have been given a high priority task that needs to be completed within a short time frame. Since you know what has to be done, you assign tasks to different team members and tell them when and how the tasks should be completed. The management style that you are following is:
    A) Directing
    B) Laissez Faire
    C) Delegating
    D) Task-oriented

23. A contract is legally binding in all the following cases EXCEPT:
    A) The seller is not able to produce goods as part of the contract.
    B) The signatory to the contract leaves the company.
    C) The buyer is not able to satisfy financial obligations.
    D) The contract violates the law of the land.

24. Please refer to the table below:

Task A --> Optimistic:5, Pessimistic:9, Most Likely:7

Task B --> Optimistic:8, Pessimistic:14, Most Likely:10

Task C --> Optimistic:4, Pessimistic:7, Most Likely:5

If these three tasks (i.e., Tasks A, B, and C) are not part of the critical path of a project, what is the PERT estimate for the duration of the project?
    A) 22.5
    B) 10.33
    C) 32
    D) Cannot be determined

25. All the following statements relating to communications management are correct EXCEPT:
    A) Communication planning involves determining the information and communication needs of the stakeholders.
    B) Communicating is the most critical skill for a project manager.
    C) Project managers spend more than 90% of their time communicating.
    D) To be effective, a project manager should control all communication channels.

26. While reviewing the performance reports of your project, you notice that the Cost Performance Index (CPI) is 1.2 and Schedule Performance Index (SPI) is 0.8. In this case you should:
    A) Make changes to the performance baseline to improve the SPI
    B) Evaluate options to crash or fast-track the project
    C) Inform the management why the project got delayed
    D) Tell the team-members that they have no option but to meet the target dates as stated in the project schedule

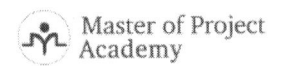

27. Which project will be selected from the following options?
    A) Project A: internal rate of return of 12%, opportunity cost $0
    B) Project B: internal rate of return of - 2%, opportunity cost of $ 20,000
    C) Project C: benefit cost ratio of 0.5, payback period of 6 months
    D) Project D: internal rate of return of 0%, opportunity cost of $ 200,000

28. During Plan Risk Responses process, you realize that there is a critical risk which may have a high impact on the project completion. So, you create a fallback plan which could include any of the following conditions EXCEPT:
    A) Subcontracting the project to an outside vendor
    B) Developing fallback options
    C) Allocating contingency reserves
    D) Reviewing risks driven by strategies

29. A technological advance, legal requirement, or social need refers to:
    A) Issues that need to be managed in the project plan
    B) Environmental factors that usually have detrimental effect on the project
    C) Risks that have to be managed by the project manager
    D) Factors contributing to the creation of the business case

30. After quality planning, you have created a component-specific tool to verify that the required steps have been performed to test your product. This can also be referred to as:
    A) Checklist
    B) Operational definition
    C) Quality management plan
    D) Design of experiments (DOE)

31. In a kick-off meeting for your project, you provided information to your team members about the different process groups to be followed in the project. According to PMI, which are the project management process groups?
    A) Conceptualizing, Initiating, Executing, Monitoring and Controlling, and Closing
    B) Initiating, Planning, Executing, Monitoring and Controlling, and Closing
    C) Initiating, Verifying, Executing, Monitoring and Controlling, and Closing
    D) Initiating, Planning, Executing, Controlling, and Administrative Closure

32. As a project manager, you wish to review the detailed description of work packages and control accounts. In which document would you find this information?
    A) Work performance measurements
    B) RBS
    C) Work performance information
    D) WBS dictionary

33. As a project manager, you are interested in the personal activities of team-members. Other than working with you on the project, the team members love to go out with

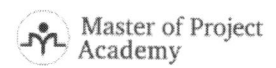

you for lunch or play an occasional game of golf. The power that you have over the team members is:
A) Penalty power
B) Expert power
C) Legitimate power
D) Referent power

34. In your project, you wish to manage procurement relationships, monitor contract performance, and make changes and corrections as needed. For this, you use all of the following EXCEPT:
A) Contract
B) Work performance information
C) Approved change requests
D) Project schedule

35. In your project team, you have developed a rule of thumb that scarce resources will have to be allocated first to the critical path. This rule of thumb can also be referred to as:
A) Constraints
B) Assumptions
C) Best Practices
D) Heuristics

36. During critical negotiations on outstanding issues arising out of a contract, you should pay close attention to which form of communication?
A) Oral formal
B) Oral informal
C) Non-verbal
D) Written formal

37. When the contract is halfway through, the buyer requests you to incorporate some additional requirements which were not defined in the original contract. Since satisfying the buyer is important, you go ahead and incorporate those requirements as part of the project. According to PMI, this action is a violation of which aspect of Code of Ethics and Professional Conduct?
A) Responsibility to maintain and satisfy the scope and objectives
B) Responsibility to ensure that a conflict of interest does not compromise legitimate interests
C) Responsibility to provide accurate and truthful representations
D) Responsibility to cooperate with PMI concerning ethics violation and the collection of related information

38. Your business partner is ready to invest $ 110,000 in your company one year from now. The interest rate used in your company to calculate Present Value (PV) of expected yearly benefits and costs is 10%. What is the PV of this investment?
A) $112,000
B) $100,000

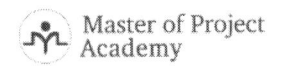

C) $80,000
D) $70,000

39. As a project manager, you estimate that, in your project, there is:
    - 50% probability of earning $ 40,000 profit
    - 50% probability of incurring $ 25,000 loss

    What is the expected profit/loss for the project?
    A) $32,500
    B) $25,000
    C) $7,500
    D) -$7,500 (i.e. loss of $ 7,500)

40. In the process of directing and managing the project work, your project team may request changes to expand or modify project scope, policies, procedures, project cost, or budget. Which of the following is NOT a request for a change?
    A) Direct or indirect
    B) Externally or internally initiated
    C) Optional or legally mandated
    D) Formal or informal

41. As a project manager, you are aware that quality has costs associated with it. Which of the following statements is NOT related to cost of quality?
    A) Cost of appraising the product or service for conformance to requirements
    B) Cost of rework
    C) Costs incurred by investment in preventing non-conformance to requirements
    D) Cost of evaluating alternative projects

42. Which of the following is NOT a characteristic of a project life cycle?
    A) Stakeholder influence, risk, and uncertainty are highest at the start of the project.
    B) Ability of the stakeholders to influence final characteristics of the project's product increases as the project progresses.
    C) The project life cycle determines which transitional actions at the beginning and end of the project are included, so that the project can be linked to the ongoing operations of the performing organization.
    D) Stakeholder influence, risk, and uncertainty decrease as the project progresses.

43. When you encounter constraints as a project manager, in which document will you record the information about these constraints?
    A) Project scope statement
    B) Risk register
    C) Issue log
    D) Change management plan

44. In your project, you would like to document team member roles and responsibilities. You have documented project roles as responsible, accountable, consult and inform. A good way to depict the information is through:

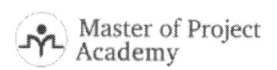

A) RBS (resource breakdown structure)
B) RAM (responsibility assignment matrix)
C) Text-oriented format
D) WBS (work breakdown structure)

45. In a fixed price contract, the buyer decides to increase the scope of work to make the product better. In this case, which of the following can the buyer NOT do?
    A) Issue a contract change request
    B) Start another fixed price contract to do the additional work
    C) Start another cost reimbursable contract to do the additional work
    D) Cancel the existing contract and start a new contract

46. You are in the test phase of your software project, and the project sponsor has requested a definitive estimate of when your project will be completed. The most likely estimated duration is 30 days. Which of the following duration estimations will you give to your sponsor?
    A) 29 - 31 days
    B) 24 - 36 days
    C) 20 - 40 days
    D) 15 - 45 days

47. You, as the project manager, are planning to document relevant information on interest, involvement, and impact of the stakeholders on the project success. Which of the following processes should you follow?
    A) Monitor Stakeholder Engagement
    B) Plan Communications Management
    C) Manage Stakeholder Engagement
    D) Identify Stakeholders

48. As a PMI Certified project manager, you are responsible for all of the following EXCEPT:
    A) Maintaining the confidentiality of sensitive information that you have access to
    B) Managing situations wherein conflict of interest arises
    C) Ensuring the integrity of your team members
    D) Refraining from offering and accepting inappropriate payments and gifts

49. While doing monitoring and controlling for your project, you notice that the cost variance is negative, but schedule variance is positive. This indicates:
    A) Cost and schedule are not dependent on each other
    B) Project is under budget and behind schedule
    C) Project is over budget and ahead of schedule
    D) Crashing may be recommended to make the cost variance positive

50. Since you know the importance of risk management, you always include it as an agenda item in your weekly status meetings and spend ten minutes discussing the risks. Some of your project team members complain that since none of the risks are actually happening, discussing risk management issues in status meetings is a waste of time. What should you do?

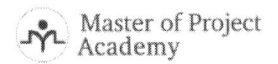

A) Talk to your team members about the importance of risk management and why the project team needs to be aware of all risks at all points of time.
B) Agree with your team members and mention to them that henceforth, no more time would be spent on discussing risks in the project status meetings unless required in the future.
C) Call a meeting with your project sponsor and project management team to discuss potential training requirements for your project team members so that they can appreciate the benefits of risk management.
D) Escalate to your management that some of your team members do not agree with your risk management practices.

51. The aggregation of the processes, tools, techniques and methodologies to manage a project is referred to as:
A) Project management system
B) Change Control System
C) Organizational process assets
D) Project management information system

52. After performing quality control using checklists, the completed checklists should become part of the:
A) Organizational process assets updates
B) Project document updates
C) Project management plan updates
D) Lessons learned documentation

53. You are responsible for the development and launch of a NASA satellite. Your role is that of a:
A) Project Manager
B) Project Coordinator
C) Program Manager
D) Functional Manager

54. In your project, while doing scope verification of the product, the customer points out that a particular work component performed by a team member is not as per specification. You review the project WBS and confirm that the customer is correct. What would be your NEXT step?
A) Put the particular requirement through the change control process
B) Call a meeting of your project team to discuss this requirement
C) Escalate the issue to your project sponsor
D) Review the requirement and talk with the team member who implemented the requirement

55. You are the blue-eyed boy of your vice chairman who appreciates the way in which you work in projects. She also consults you during performance appraisals. This helps you in managing interpersonal relationships with your team members, because you have the following power:
A) Legitimate

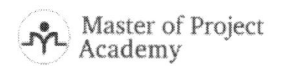

B) Expert
C) Penalty
D) Referent

56. In your project, you would like to use the `Conduct Procurements` process to obtain quotations for subcontracting your work. All the following tools can be used to facilitate this process EXCEPT:
    A) Bidder conferences
    B) Contract types
    C) Advertising
    D) Procurement negotiations

57. Since you are in the preliminary stages of your project, you estimate that your project may be completed in one year. However, the optimistic estimate is 6 months and pessimistic estimate is 18 months. This type of estimate is also called:
    A) Definitive
    B) Capital cost
    C) Order of magnitude
    D) Feasibility

58. As part of Project Communications Management, you are collecting and disseminating information to stakeholders about resources used to achieve project objectives. This is done as part of:
    A) Plan Communications
    B) Distribute Information
    C) Report Performance
    D) Administrative closure

59. You have earned a doctorate from MIT and are currently working with a leading chip manufacturer. A seller you met at a vendor conference requested you to be their part-time consultant to design an innovative automobile component. At MIT, you did a similar project and are inclined to participate in the venture, as there is no conflict of interest involved. In this context, it is advisable that you should:
    A) Decline the seller's offer, because it could be construed as conflict of interest by your company
    B) Ask your senior management whether you can participate in this venture
    C) Leave the company and take up the seller's offer, because it interests you
    D) Accept the seller's offer and inform senior management

60. The value of work actually accomplished is also known as:
    A) Planned Value
    B) Earned Value
    C) Actual Cost
    D) Budgeted Cost for Work Scheduled (BCWS)

61. You are the project manager of a software company developing a new banking software product. You would like to obtain information from various experts about the

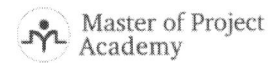

risks associated with your project. You decide to use the Delphi technique because this keeps any one person from having undue influence on the outcome of the Identify Risks process. The Delphi technique also has the added advantage that it:
A) Finds out a problem, discovers the reasons that led to it, and develops preventive actions.
B) Helps reduce bias in the data.
C) Examines the project from each of the SWOT perspectives to increase the breadth of the identified risks.
D) Provides a qualitative assessment of risk.

62. You are preparing a document using project statement of work, business case, contract, enterprise environmental factors, and organizational process assets. These are valid inputs for:
A) Develop Project Management Plan
B) Direct and Manage Project Work
C) Develop Project Charter
D) Perform Integrated Change Control

63. Quality management complements project management, as both recognize the importance of:
A) Exceeding customer expectations using additional features
B) Providing customer satisfaction
C) Decreasing total scope of ownership of the project
D) Decreasing risks associated with outsourcing

64. You are working as a project manager. You are in the process of defining and documenting stakeholders' needs to meet project objectives. What documents are you going to use for this purpose?
A) Project charter
B) Requirements documentation
C) Stakeholder register
D) Project charter and stakeholder register

65. The customer and project manager need to validate the scope of the deliverables. This will help to:
A) Ensure proper project selection
B) Create WBS
C) Obtain customer's acceptance of the project deliverables
D) Mitigate project risks

66. According to Herzberg's theory, the absence of hygiene factors can create job dissatisfaction, but their presence does not motivate or create satisfaction. Which of the following can be categorized as a hygiene factor?
A) Recognition
B) Responsibility
C) Advancement in career
D) Interpersonal relations

67. In your project, the process of obtaining seller responses, selecting a seller, and awarding a contract is performed as part of :
   A) Control Procurements
   B) Plan Procurements
   C) Conduct Procurements
   D) Close Procurements

68. Please refer to the chart given below:

Task	Preceding Activity	Estimate in Months
Start	-	0
1	Start	3
2	1	4
3	Start	2
5	3	5
4	Start	7
5	4	1
End	2	3
End	5	4

What is the slack of task 3?
   A) 1
   B) 0
   C) 2
   D) -1

69. In your project, as part of Manage Communications process, you have created an information retrieval system, which helps team members and stakeholders to share information. What will you do next?
   A) Create a communications management plan
   B) Perform stakeholder analysis to develop a methodical and logical view of information needs
   C) Determine methods of accessing information for scheduled communications
   D) Conduct regular status review meetings to exchange information on the project

70. You are in the closing stage of the project. While reviewing the product, you have come to know that the tolerance is .05 microns more than what was specified in the project requirements. This is a very minor deviation, and you know that your customer will not notice it during product delivery. Also, it will not adversely impact your customer when the product is put to actual use. What should you do in this situation?
   A) Inform the customer about the deviation
   B) Change the project documents to allow for small deviations

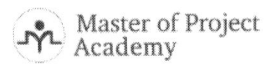

C) Ask your project team to make changes to the product
D) Create a change request to make changes in the product

71. The following are the details of a project: Payback: $2,000 Profit: $1,000 Project cost: $800 Life cycle cost: $1200 What is the Benefit Cost Ratio for this project?
    A) 2.50
    B) 1.25
    C) 1.67
    D) 0.83

72. In Plan Risk Responses process, you are developing options and actions to reduce threats to your project's objectives. When you show the results to your project sponsor, she is not comfortable with the risks in the project and suggests that the project scope should be decreased. This is an example of:
    A) Risk acceptance
    B) Risk avoidance
    C) Risk mitigation
    D) Risk transfer

73. You are in the process of developing a project charter for your project and would like to use organizational process assets as inputs for the purpose. In this context, which of the following statements about organizational process assets is NOT correct?
    A) Organizational process assets do not include organization communication requirements.
    B) Any and all the process related assets that are used to influence the project's success can be drawn upon from any or all of the involved organizations.
    C) Organizational process assets represent the lessons learned by the company from previous projects.
    D) Organizational standard process, policies, and standardized process definitions are used in the organization.

74. In your organization, 3 sigma quality processes have been implemented. That means all measurements should be within ____ % of the target value.
    A) 99.99
    B) 99.7
    C) 95.4
    D) 68.2

75. You are the project manager in a company, which has a balanced matrix organizational structure. Who do you report to?
    A) Functional Manager
    B) Program Manager
    C) Manager of Project Managers
    D) Portfolio Sponsor

76. You have recently joined as the project manager of ABC Company. You notice that the customers are getting frequent change requests implemented by informally

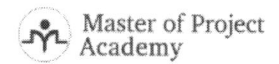

approaching the team members. This has resulted in work disruption and discontent among team members. What should be your FIRST priority to remedy the situation?
A) Create a detailed project scope statement
B) Align the project objectives with the organizational goals
C) Ensure proper project scope control
D) Call a meeting of all the project stakeholders to resolve any outstanding issues

77. As a project manager, you are in the process of creating a list of all the project team members, their roles, and communication information. This information should reside in:
A) Project plan
B) Project team directory
C) Performance reports
D) Responsibility assignment matrix

78. In your company, you are in the process of deciding whether to buy a product or to make it in-house. All the following statements related to make-or-buy analysis are correct EXCEPT:
A) Make-or-buy analysis is part of the Conduct Procurements process that can be used to determine whether a particular product can be produced cost effectively by the performing organization.
B) A make-or-buy analysis should consider all related costs.
C) Budget constraints may influence make-or-buy decisions.
D) Buy-side of the analysis includes both the actual out-of-pocket costs to purchase the product, as well as the indirect costs of supporting the purchasing process.

79. An activity has an optimistic estimate of 10 days, pessimistic estimate of 16 days, and most likely estimate of 13 days. What is the Beta PERT estimate for the task?
A) 13 days
B) 10 days
C) 16 days
D) Cannot be determined with available information

80. In your project, you actively manage stakeholders' expectations. This is helpful for all of the following reasons EXCEPT:
A) Chances of stakeholders' acceptance of the project goals increase.
B) Expectations of stakeholders are influenced and negotiated to achieve and maintain project goals.
C) Stakeholders' awareness of all project details is ensured
D) Concerns are uncovered and discussed.

81. You are doing a project under cost-reimbursable contract where the target price was $ 1,200,000. Your project is nearing completion and CPI is currently 1.4. You are concerned that you will be losing money by billing for less. In this context, you should:
A) Tell your buyer about the CPI as it stands today and explain the reasons for the deviation from the plan.

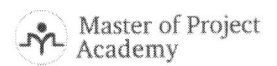

B) Invoice for $ 1,500,000 because there are chances for costs being higher in a subsequent project.
C) Tell the bad news to the buyer and suggest charging more from the customer.
D) Add some extra features to cause "customer delight".

82. Calculate the to-complete performance index of your project, based on EAC, when the actual cost of your project is $200,000, cost variance of your project is $25,000 and the budget at completion of your project is $350,000.
    A) 1.125
    B) -1.4
    C) 1
    D) -1

83. In your new project the objective is to develop a new drug. After doing financial analysis, your finance manager provided you with these statistics:
    - 30% probability of success with benefits of $ 700,000
    - 70% probability of failure with loss of $ 300,000

    Based on this information, you:

    A) Suggest that the project should proceed.
    B) Suggest that the project should be stopped.
    C) Communicate to your senior management that you cannot take a decision whether to proceed with the project or not.
    D) Start working on the project and ask your finance manager for additional information.

84. The customer communicates a request for a change in your project plan. What should be your first step towards addressing the change request?
    A) Talk with team members to understand implications of the change.
    B) Communicate the change to the management to get their inputs.
    C) Open up a change control.
    D) Implement the change and communicate to the customer.

85. Your company manufactures bearings for the automobile industry. You have historical information on the identified errors and defects, and you would like to use this information to determine future performance. An appropriate tool which you can use is:
    A) Scatter diagram
    B) Statistical sampling
    C) Control chart
    D) Trend analysis

86. Your director has appointed you as a portfolio manager in the company. Your responsibility as a portfolio manager is to:
    A) Select and support projects or program investments

B) Manage groups of projects in a coordinated way
C) Create a unique product, service, or result
D) Ensure that customer requirements are satisfied through progressive elaboration of projects

87. As part of decomposing, you break down the project work that needs to be accomplished in the near term at a low level of WBS. However, the work planned in the future is broken down at a relatively high level of WBS. This technique is called :
A) Procrastination
B) Delaying tactics
C) Futuristic planning
D) Rolling wave planning

88. In your software project, you have a programmer, who constantly professes to know all about project management and keeps challenging his superiors. The programmer is playing the role of:
A) Aggressor
B) Conflict maximizer
C) Devil`s Advocate
D) Dominator

89. You will use the Conduct Procurements process to receive bids or proposals and apply the selection criteria for selecting a provider. Which of the following tools and techniques can be used for the Conduct Procurements process?
A) Procurement negotiations, bidder conferences, and independent estimates
B) Procurement negotiations, contract types, and bidder conferences
C) Procurement negotiations, make-or-buy analysis, and independent estimates
D) Performance reporting, advertising, and independent estimates

90. Float is the amount of time an activity can be delayed without delaying the project finish date. It is also called:
A) Slack
B) Free float
C) Path float
D) Critical path

91. The processes used in Project Communications Management are:
A) Plan Communications Management, Manage Communications and Monitor Communications
B) Plan Communication, Report Performance, and Integrated Change Control
C) Plan Communication, Administrative Closure, Report Performance, and Distribute Information
D) Identify Stakeholders, Manage Communications, and Monitor Communications

92. You recently took over the responsibilities of a project manager from another person. While reviewing the project cost, you realize there has been an item of $120,000

waiting to be paid, which, you think, is a disputed item. Your project CPI is 1.1. In this case:
A) Since this is a small amount compared to the total project value, it can be paid ignoring all objections.
B) Since the project CPI is greater than one, you do not have any difficulties with the cost of the project. You can, hence, bury the payment in contingency account and move on with the project.
C) You should inform your manager and ascertain the facts of the matter before making the payment.
D) You must refuse the payment.

93. In your project, you have reasons to believe that the current variances occurred because of extraneous factors, and you do not expect similar variances to occur in future. What should be the estimate at completion (EAC) for your project?
- BAC = $ 300,000
- AC = $ 100,000
- EV = $ 150,000
- CPI = $ 1.5

A) $ 250,000
B) $ 220,000
C) $ 280,000
D) $ 200,000

94. Workarounds differ from contingency plans in that:
A) Contingency plans are planned in advance and workarounds are not planned in advance.
B) Workarounds are planned in advance and contingency plans are not planned in advance.
C) Contingency plans include plans for force majeure events, e.g. natural calamities, but workarounds are the residual risks in the project.
D) Workarounds only include plans for force majeure events, e.g. natural calamities

95. As a project manager, you know that project plan development is an important element to manage projects. Develop Project Management Plan is done as part of:
A) Initiating
B) Planning
C) Executing
D) Controlling

96. You are working as a research assistant studying the growth of bacteria under different environmental conditions. Based on your experiments, you conclude that the longevity of bacteria increases as the temperature increases. What type of diagram can you use to illustrate your observation?
A) Control chart
B) Run chart
C) Scatter diagram
D) Histogram

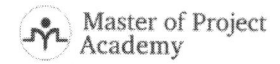

97. A project manager is responsible for managing project costs and human resources. Factors like cost and staffing level for a project:
    A) Increase with duration of the project
    B) Decrease with duration of the project
    C) Are low at the start, peak as the work is carried out, and drop rapidly as the project draws to a close
    D) Cannot be determined, as they are specific to the project

98. In your project, you are preparing the requirements management plan to define and document stakeholders' need to meet the project's objectives. All of the following are components of the requirements management plan EXCEPT:
    A) Traceability structure
    B) WBS
    C) Requirements prioritization process
    D) Product metrics

99. Among the various conflict resolution modes (Confrontation, Compromise, Withdrawal, Forcing, and Smoothing), which conflict resolution mode is most preferred or least preferred by project managers (answer format: most preferred, least preferred)?
    A) Compromise, Withdrawal
    B) Confrontation, Withdrawal
    C) Confrontation, Forcing
    D) Smoothing, Withdrawal

100. In your project, the seller is worried that the CPIF contract is reaching the point of total assumption. What is meant by the point of total assumption?
    A) Point where share ratio becomes irrelevant
    B) Point where risk registers need to be updated
    C) Point where buyer assumes all the risk
    D) Point where seller decides not to do the project any more

101. An activity has an optimistic estimate of ten days, pessimistic estimate of sixteen days, and most likely estimate of thirteen days. Assuming a normal distribution, what is the probability that the task will be completed within 10 to 16 days?
    A) 99.99 %
    B) 99.73 %
    C) 95.46 %
    D) 68.26%

102. You are a procurements manager and are responsible for managing complex procurement contracts. In this context, which of the following is the most effective means of handling complex communications?
    A) Formal oral
    B) Formal written
    C) Informal written
    D) Informal oral

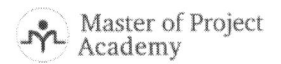

103. You realize that you are not able to concentrate on your work due to an actual or potential conflict of interest situation. Which out of the following should you NOT do, in this context?
    A) Disclose the facts to the affected stakeholders
    B) Prepare a mitigation plan
    C) Seek stakeholders' consent to proceed further
    D) Engage in decision-making activities related to the conflict of interest situation

104. Resource calendars provide information on a specific resource or a category of resources. They show how a project team member might be unavailable (on vacation or in a training program) or how a labor contract can limit certain workers to certain days of the week. Resource calendars are valuable inputs to:
    A) Develop an approximation of the monetary resources needed to complete project activities.
    B) Aggregate the estimated costs of individual activities or work packages to establish an authorized cost baseline.
    C) Manage the actual changes when and as they occur.
    D) Monitor work performance against funds expended.

105. In risk management, you deal with processes concerned with conducting risk management planning, identification, analysis, responses, and monitoring and control. In this context, all the following statements related to processes used in risk management are correct EXCEPT:
    A) Processes interact with each other.
    B) Processes always have discrete elements with well-defined interfaces and never overlap.
    C) Risk management processes interact with processes in other knowledge areas.
    D) Each process generally occurs at least once in every project, and occurs in one or more project phases, if the project is divided into phases

106. You are in the initiating phase of your project and are involved with creation of the project charter. Which of the following statements relating to the project charter is NOT correct?
    A) Includes or references the business need and product description.
    B) Provides authority to the project manager.
    C) Formally authorizes a project.
    D) Authorized only by the project sponsor.

107. You are trying to determine the cost and schedule trade-off, which will be most appropriate for determining the ride quality of a car. You classify factors like tire pressure, suspension, height of vehicle, etc., which have to be optimized to improve ride quality. A tool you can use to facilitate making the decision is:
    A) Cost of quality
    B) Cause-and-effect diagrams
    C) Design of experiments
    D) Network diagrams

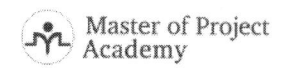

108. In your project, you are coordinating people and resources as well as integrating and performing activities of the project in accordance with the project management plan. This is performed during:
    A) Initiating Process Group
    B) Executing Process Group
    C) Planning Process Group
    D) Monitoring Process Group

109. In your project, you are subdividing major project deliverables into smaller, more manageable components. This will be done as part of:
    A) Create WBS
    B) Scope Verification
    C) Work Authorization System
    D) Product Analysis

110. During manage team process, a project manager performs all the following activities EXCEPT:
    A) To observe and converse to stay in touch with the work and attitudes of project team members
    B) To perform appraisals to clarify roles and responsibilities, develop training plans, etc.
    C) To negotiate for assignment of appropriate project members to the team.
    D) To maintain an issue log to document persons responsible for resolving specific issues by a target date.

111. The scope of your project is very well defined and you have completed all the work described in the contract to your satisfaction, but you think your buyer is not happy with the work. What should you do (select the best answer)?
    A) Go through arbitration proceedings to ensure that disputes are resolved
    B) Talk with senior management about changing the scope of the project to accommodate requirements that would satisfy the customer
    C) Ask customer for inputs and get her advice on changes that need to be made
    D) Move to contract close-out

112. In which of the following processes is decomposition used as a tool?
    A) Define Activities
    B) Sequence Activities
    C) Estimate Activity Resources
    D) Estimate Activity Durations

113. In your project, a team member is not performing well. Best way to handle issues of poor performance is through:
    A) Informal written communication
    B) Informal verbal communication
    C) Formal written communication
    D) Formal verbal communication

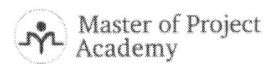

114. You are managing a team consisting of members from four different countries; you realize that some cultural differences among your team members are hampering the progress of your project. In this context, what should you do?
    A) Conduct team building activities in which most of the team members can participate actively.
    B) Train your team members on project objectives.
    C) Train your team members on the broad objectives of your organization.
    D) Provide training to your team members regarding cultural diversities among different countries along with training on project objectives and the company culture.

115. In your project, you have determined the planned quantity of work to be performed. Luckily, a similar project was successfully completed three months ago, and historical information from that project is readily available. To get a cost estimate for your project, you multiply the planned quantity of work in your project with the cost per unit obtained from the previous project. This is a classic example of:
    A) Analogous estimating
    B) Determining resource cost rates
    C) Bottom-up estimating
    D) Parametric estimating

116. In your project, you are about to complete Plan Risk Responses process. Completion of certain tasks marks the end of the process. Which one from the following is NOT that task?
    A) People have been identified to take responsibility for each agreed-to and funded risk response.
    B) High priority risks are addressed in detail in the risk register.
    C) Low priority risks are included in the risk mitigation plan if they occur.
    D) Negative risks have been considered for avoidance, transference or mitigation.

117. A non-governmental agency authorizes a project to provide potable water systems, latrines, and sanitation education to low-income communities. The need for the project arose due to:
    A) Market need
    B) Business need
    C) Social need
    D) Legal requirement

118. A description of how a project management team should implement the overall intention and direction of an organization with regard to quality (as articulated by top management) is available in:
    A) Operational definitions
    B) Quality management plan
    C) Checklists
    D) Quality policy

119. Earlier you were working at the helpdesk of ABC company managing a team. Your job primarily involved handling customer queries, analyzing customer feedback, and supervising your team. You have recently been re-assigned to a new project involving integration of the helpdesk activities with an ERP (Enterprise Resource Planning) package. This project will improve efficiency in the company and help in integrating all inter-related activities. All the following could be the possible differences between helpdesk and the present project EXCEPT:
    A) The objective of the project is to meet strategic objectives of the company. The objective of the helpdesk was to sustain the business.
    B) A project has to be planned, executed, and controlled, and it is not so in the case of helpdesk.
    C) As part of the project, you are creating a new information system, but nothing unique was being created as part of the helpdesk activities.
    D) Unlike a project, helpdesk was an ongoing operational activity.

120. Inspection includes activities such as measuring, examining, and testing undertaken to determine whether results conform to requirements. The other terms used for Inspection are all of the following EXCEPT:
    A) Product review
    B) Audit
    C) Walkthrough
    D) Stage-gate

121. You are the manager of a project, which aims to start 15 more schools in your state. You have to deal with several non-government organizations, state agencies, sponsors, and other stakeholders. There are conflicts between stakeholders. In this context, you should know that maximum intensity of conflicts happens due to:
    A) Personality conflict, cost, and administration
    B) Risk management, status meetings, and Define Scope
    C) Schedules, priorities, and manpower
    D) Administration, technical issues, and procedures

122. In your project, you are preparing procurement documents to seek proposals from prospective sellers. All the following statements about procurement documents are accurate EXCEPT:
    A) The buyer structures the procurement documents to facilitate an accurate and complete response from prospective sellers.
    B) Requests to potential sellers to submit a proposal or bid is formally issued in accordance with the policies of the buyer's organization.
    C) With government contracting, some or all of the content and structure of procurement documents can be defined by regulation.
    D) The term `proposal` is usually used when the seller selection decision will be based on price.

123. An activity has an optimistic estimate of 10 days, pessimistic estimate of 16 days, and most likely estimate of 13 days. If your company has a quality requirement of Six

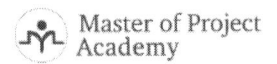

Sigma, what is the duration within which this task must be completed (consider beta distribution in PERT calculations)?
- A) 10 days to 16 days
- B) 7 days to 19 days
- C) 12 days to 14 days
- D) 11 days to 15 days

124. You are preparing the communications management plan for your project by using communication requirements analysis. All the following statements related to communication requirements analysis are accurate EXCEPT:
    - A) Requirements are defined by combining the type and format of information needed with an analysis of the cost of that information.
    - B) Project resources are expended on communicating information that contributes to success.
    - C) Project resources are expended on communicating information where lack of communication can lead to failure.
    - D) The intention is to prevent overloading stakeholders with minor details.

125. You and your sponsor are discussing the financial benefits of selecting between two similar projects - project A and project B. When evaluating the projects, you realize that project A will cause some amount of short-term environmental damage but minimal long-term environmental problems. In this context, what will be the best course of action?
    - A) Explain to your senior management about the potential environmental damage caused by project A and persuade them to discard the project.
    - B) Select the project A as there is only low probability of causing long-term environmental damage.
    - C) Try to find solutions to the environmental damage that may occur in the future because of project A.
    - D) Undertake the project A but try to minimize the environmental damage, if any.

126.

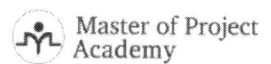

Tasks A, B, C and D are in the critical path of a project; all the tasks are estimated To require similar effort of 5 days each and cost $ 5,000 per task

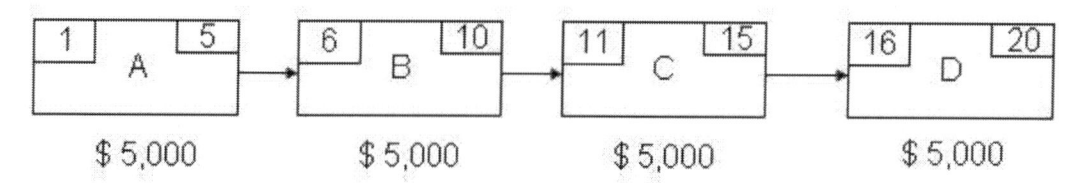

```
[1   5]      [6   10]      [11   15]     [16   20]
   A    →      B     →       C      →      D
 $5,000      $5,000        $5,000        $5,000
```

At the end of day 11, Task A and Task B are complete; Task C is 50% complete, and $ 13,000 has already been spent

Notation Used:

```
[Start        Finish]
 Date         Date
      Task ID
```

What is the Earned Value (EV)?
A) $ 5,000
B) $ 10,000
C) $ 11,000
D) $ 12,500

127. In your project, you have completed Identify Risks process to determine which risks may affect the project, and a risk register has been prepared. What should you do NEXT?
A) Risk probability and impact assessment
B) Avoiding, transferring or mitigating negative risks
C) Exploiting, sharing or enhancing opportunities
D) Risk audits

128. A new project manager has been appointed to manage a project which was terminated six months earlier because of funding related issues. The project manager wants to find out the exact reasons for the termination of the project. He also wants to know which deliverables were produced from the terminated project. Which of the following document(s) should the project manager refer to?
A) Final product, service, or result transition
B) Project files
C) Historical information
D) Project closure documents

129. You are the project manager of a car manufacturing company. You understand that there are costs associated with improvement in quality parameters. To justify costs required to improve quality, you find out the incremental increase in benefits for an incremental improvement in quality. This is an example of :
A) Parkinson's law

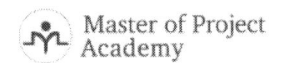

B) Learning Curve theory
C) Marginal analysis
D) Maslow's hierarchy of needs

130. Your construction company recently secured a project to build a new flyover on Interstate 10. You have been appointed as project manager for the assignment. Your company had successfully executed similar projects in the past, and you would like to refer to the past project documents. At what stage of the project should this be done FIRST?
A) Executing
B) Initiating
C) Planning
D) Monitoring and Controlling

131. You are the project manager of a software company involved in creating an anti-virus software product. You are in the execution phase of the project when you realize that a requirement was not included in the product. This is due to an omission in defining the scope baseline of the project. What should you do?
A) Issue a change request
B) Take corrective action
C) Add the requirements to your product and continue with execution
D) Take defect repair action

132. You are promoted to a new role in your company to replace someone who recently retired. To be an effective leader, which of the following should you do FIRST?
A) Enroll in appropriate training programs
B) Understand all the leadership theories
C) Find out your strong and weak areas
D) Take advice from the person who retired from the company

133. Your company (buyer) has entered into a few contracts recently that have not been successfully implemented. Your sponsor calls for a meeting to determine what should be the overall goal while you negotiate contracts. In this context, what should be the most important objective of a contract?
A) Protect the interests of the project
B) Ensure that negotiation is conducted as per legal statutes
C) Negotiate for the best price and protect interests of the buyer
D) Objective could vary depending on the type of contract

134. In your project, you wish to include certain significant events in the milestone list for the project based on historical information. Such milestones are:
A) Optional
B) Mandatory
C) Statutory
D) Authorized

135. All the following are valid inputs for "Identify Stakeholder" process EXCEPT:

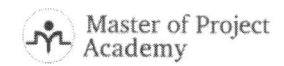

A) Enterprise environmental factors
B) Procurement documents(if project is done as part of a contract)
C) Project scope statement
D) Project charter

136. While managing a crucial project for your company, your sponsor reprimands you for not including an additional feature, beyond the project scope, which could have provided "customer delight". In this context, you should:
A) Resign from the project.
B) Give precedence to project and organizational objectives.
C) Complain against the sponsor to the customer.
D) Add the new feature to the product as requested by the sponsor.

137. In your project, you estimate the cost of individual activities or work packages, and then roll up the individual estimates for subsequent reporting and tracking purposes. This can be done using:
A) Bottom-up estimating
B) Analogous estimating
C) Parametric modeling
D) Top-down estimating

138. Being a diligent project manager, you understand the importance of identifying all project risks which can then be prioritized using Perform Qualitative and Quantitative Risk Analysis. In this context, which of the following tools and techniques can be used for Identify Risks process?
A) Documentation reviews, brainstorming, root cause analysis and checklist analysis
B) Assumptions analysis, probability and impact matrix, interviewing and Delphi technique
C) Expected monetary value, root cause analysis, influence diagrams and documentation reviews
D) Risk exploitation, assumptions analysis, influence diagrams and Delphi technique

139. While managing a project for a manufacturing company, you receive a change request from the customer for a minor alteration to the product configuration. In this context, which of the following is NOT a step you would take next?
A) Evaluate the impact of the change
B) Examine other options
C) Seek approval from change control board
D) Reject the change request as this would change the product configuration

140. You have successfully completed a project and the customer is happy with the product. From a project management perspective, when a service or a product meets customer expectations, it means that:
A) Cost of quality is low
B) Project is completed
C) Cost of quality is high
D) Quality is achieved

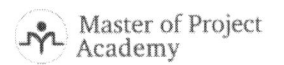

141. In your project, you use a specific set of processes and automation tools to manage contract and procurement documentation. This is referred to as:
    A) Claims administration
    B) Project documents
    C) Records management system
    D) Procurement document package

142. Please refer to the following diagram:

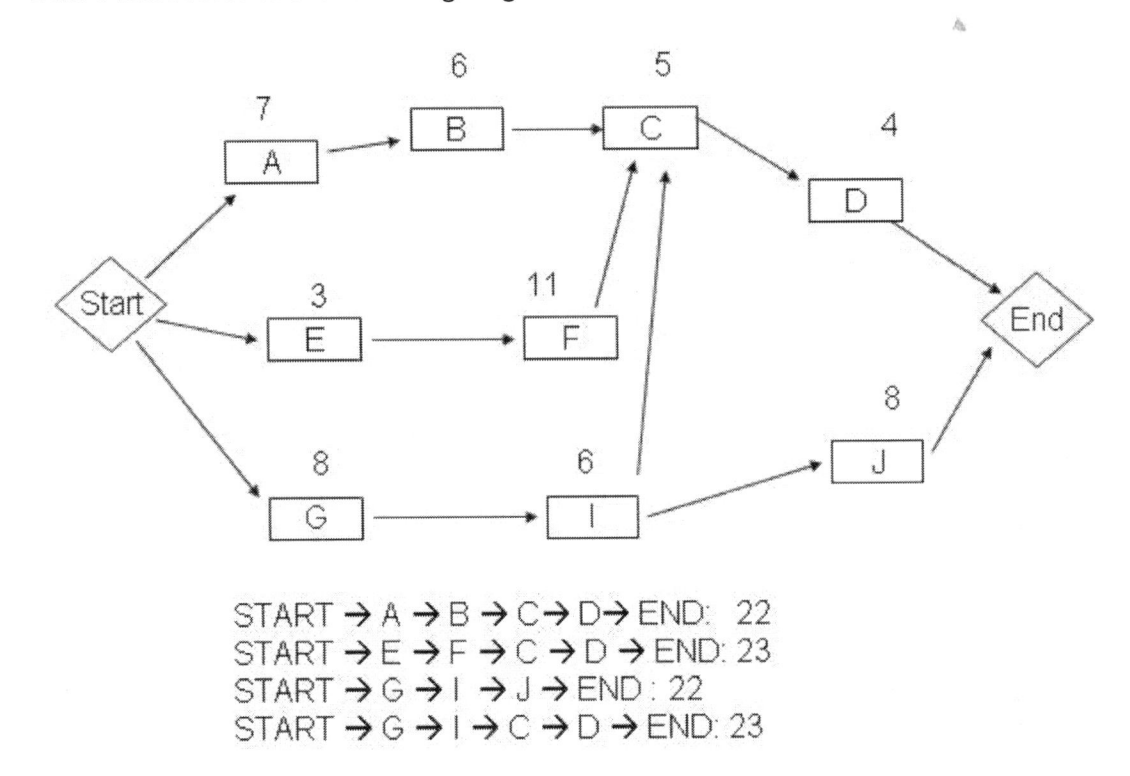

START → A → B → C → D → END: 22
START → E → F → C → D → END: 23
START → G → I → J → END : 22
START → G → I → C → D → END: 23

What is the effect on the project if the duration of task J is increased to 9 weeks?
    A) No effect since task J is not on the critical path
    B) Risk of the project will further increase
    C) The overall time-frame required to complete the project will increase by 1 week
    D) Project has to be fast tracked or crashed to prevent delay

143. In the recent status meeting, you discover that your project has a 65 percent chance of making a USD 100,000 profit and a 35 percent chance of incurring a USD 100,000 loss. What is the expected monetary value for the project?
    A) USD 100,000 profit
    B) USD 100,000 loss
    C) USD 30,000 profit
    D) USD 30,000 loss

144. As a project manager, your key responsibility is to:
    A) Prevent changes in the project
    B) Manage project core teams` appraisal
    C) Perform project integration and uphold the project`s interest
    D) Maintain good relationship with vendors

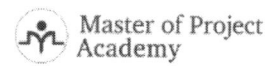

145. You are a project manager. During the quality audit, you find out that the team members have committed a number of minor mistakes. To determine whether the process is in control, the most helpful tool you use is:
    A) Ishikawa diagram
    B) Pareto chart
    C) Bar chart
    D) Control Chart

146. Your contract is nearing completion when the buyer mentions that there are some outstanding issues - this can be a potential dispute or conflict situation. In this context, what is the best way to deal with a dispute in a contract?
    A) Negotiation
    B) Change request
    C) Arbitration including mediation or alternative dispute resolution methods
    D) Litigation in courts

147. A project has a critical path of twenty-three weeks. What is the impact on the duration of the critical path if the management wants you to complete the project in twenty weeks?
    A) Increases by three weeks.
    B) Decreases by three weeks.
    C) Remains the same.
    D) Cannot be determined.

148. You are the project manager for a new software development project. A previously unidentified risk is discovered when the project is nearing completion. You realize that this risk may adversely impact the project's overall ability to deliver. As a project manager, what step do you take FIRST?
    A) Perform Quantitative Risk Analysis
    B) Inform the project sponsor and the stakeholders about the potential impact of the risk on the project
    C) Perform Qualitative Risk Analysis
    D) Mitigate the risk to reduce its impact

149. For a new project manager, who has never managed a project before, it is BEST to rely on which of the following to improve chances of project success?
    A) Advice from outgoing project manager in the company
    B) Your project management training
    C) Historical information
    D) Intuition

150. Recently, there have been quality related problems in your project and your sponsor has asked you to work on improving the quality parameters. In this context, all of the following statements on quality parameters are correct EXCEPT:
    A) Customer satisfaction refers to understanding and managing expectations so that customer requirements are met.

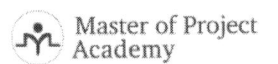

B) Customer satisfaction is a combination of conformance to requirements and fitness for use.
C) Quality should be planned and built in - not inspected in.
D) Cost of preventing mistakes is generally higher than cost of correcting them.

151. The process of identifying the product needs that can be met by acquiring products outside the project organization is done as part of:
A) Conduct Procurements
B) Administer Procurements
C) Close Procurements
D) Plan Procurement Management

152. You are in the process of identifying and documenting the relationships among the project activities. You want to ensure that every activity and milestone except the first and last are connected to at least one predecessor and one successor. Which of the following tools can you use for this purpose?
A) Scheduling tool
B) Decomposition
C) Schedule network templates
D) Schedule compression

153. You are in the execution stage of your project. For the information of the stakeholders, you have documents to highlight project status, lessons learned, issue logs, and outputs from other knowledge areas. These documents should be included in:
A) Project reports
B) Change logs
C) Lessons learned documentation
D) Performance Reports

154. In your project, the project manager believes in the superiority of his own race or ethnic background. This is an example of:
A) Monochronic
B) Polychronic
C) Ethnocentric
D) Egalitarian

155. In your project, you use the earned value technique (EVT) to measure:
A) Work performance and magnitude of variation
B) Work schedule
C) Risk responses
D) Activity duration

156. In your project, you are formalizing acceptance of the completed project deliverables. This is done during:
A) Perform Integrated Change Control
B) Validate Scope
C) Control Scope

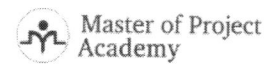

D) Report Performance

157. You have recently joined as a project manager of an equipment manufacturing company. Your project sponsor stresses the importance of obtaining stakeholders` formal acceptance of completed deliverables. This should be done:
A) At the end of the project
B) At the end of each project phase
C) After deliverables are completed and ready for review
D) After project milestones are defined

158. The project manager is trying to manage conflicting stakeholder requirements. The IT manager wants a new management information system. To lower costs, the system architect emphasizes technical excellence, and the programming contractor wants to maximize profits. To balance the needs of several stakeholders and achieve lasting resolution of conflicts, the most desirable conflict resolution technique is:
A) Confrontation
B) Smoothing
C) Withdrawal
D) Forcing

159. In your project, you notice that one of the team members is not following a company policy about reporting daily status in the company Project Management Information System. You also realize that by not following this policy, the team member is able to be more productive since he spends the extra time working on project deliverables. What will you do in this situation?
A) Do nothing since the team member is more productive
B) Ask the team member to follow the company policies and report daily status(even if it means lower productivity).
C) Modify the company policy to the requirements of the project.
D) Escalate this issue to senior management.

160. While performing variance analysis for your project, you refer to your status reports which show the following information:
- Planned value = $ 100,000
- Actual cost = $ 125,000
- Earned value = $ 90,000

In this context, all the following statements are true EXCEPT:
A) Schedule variance is - $ 10,000 and you are behind schedule
B) Cost variance is - $ 35,000 and you are over-budget
C) CPI is 0.5 and you are over-budget
D) SPI is 0.9 and you are behind schedule

161. You have acquired a team and assigned tasks for the selected team members of your project. This activity is performed during:

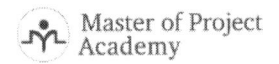

A) Planning
B) Monitoring and Controlling
C) Executing
D) Closing

162. While performing Scope Control process, you ensure that all requested changes and recommended corrective actions are processed through the Perform Integrated Change Control process. In this context, if a change is requested, what should the project manager do FIRST?
    A) Discuss the change in the next status review meeting
    B) Try to find out the financial implication of the change
    C) Evaluate the change and try to prevent unwarranted changes
    D) Involve the change control board

163. Managing conflicts is essential for successful implementation of a project. The conflict resolution techniques that are most frequently used in project management practice are:
    A) Withdrawal, Forcing, Compromising
    B) Withdrawal, Authoritative, Forcing
    C) Withdrawal, Authoritative, Compromising
    D) Withdrawal, Confronting, Legitimate

164. Patrick, a senior member of your team, brought to your notice a flaw in one of the project's deliverables. The team is now engaged in repairing it. In which of the following project management processes would this be performed?
    A) Direct and Manage Project Work
    B) Perform Integrated Change Control
    C) Close Project or Phase
    D) Monitor and Control Project Work

165. Your company manufactures bearings for the automobile industry. Control charts are used to determine whether or not a process is stable or has predictable performance. Specification limits help to determine:
    A) If process is within control limits
    B) Whether the product would be successful in the market
    C) Maximum and minimum values allowed
    D) Process improvement opportunities

166. In your contract, you can make pre-defined final adjustments to the contract price due to changed conditions like inflation, foreign exchange value fluctuations, and input cost variations. This provision is built into which of the following types of contracts?
    A) Cost Reimbursable contracts with escalation clauses
    B) Fixed Price with Economic Price Adjustment contracts
    C) Fixed Price Incentive Fee contracts
    D) Cost Plus Award Fee contracts

167. Please refer to the diagram given below.

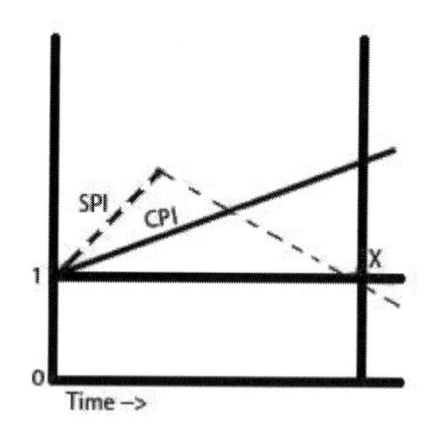

At time x, the project is :
A) Behind schedule, over-budget
B) Ahead of schedule, over-budget
C) Behind schedule, under-budget
D) Ahead of schedule, under-budget

168. You have created the Work Breakdown Structure (WBS) for your project. Major project deliverables have been divided into smaller more manageable components. What should you do NEXT?
A) Prepare a detailed project scope statement
B) Aggregate estimated costs of individual activities through cost budgeting
C) Develop project schedule
D) Identify specific activities that need to be performed to produce various project deliverables

169. Your current project has very limited information on activity durations. You wish to use the actual duration of a previous, similar activity as a basis for estimating the current activity duration. What should be your next step?
A) Create an activity list.
B) Calculate early and late start and finish dates for the unfinished project activities.
C) Conduct performance reviews to determine variances.
D) Subdivide project work packages into smaller more manageable components for better management control.

170. You are the project manager at an aircraft manufacturing company, where you use a wind tunnel to test how changes in different parameters like wind speed, temperature, humidity, etc. will impact the flight parameters of a prototype airplane. So, the project model is computed many times (iterated), with the input values chosen at random for

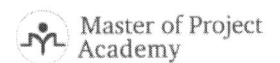

each iteration from the probability distributions of these variables. The technique used is:
- A) Monte Carlo simulation
- B) Expected monetary value
- C) Sensitivity analysis
- D) Probability distributions

171. In your project, you want to ensure that each requirement adds business value by linking it to the business and project objectives. This also provides a means to track requirements throughout the project life cycle, helping to ensure that requirements approved in the requirements documentation are delivered at the end of the project. A tool that you can use is:
    - A) Requirements documentation
    - B) Brainstorming
    - C) Requirements management plan
    - D) Requirements traceability matrix

172. All the project managers should be good at delegation because this helps them concentrate on leadership activities and delegate routine activities. In this context, which, out of the following, can a project manager delegate to her subordinates?
    - A) Long-range planning
    - B) Performance appraisals
    - C) Project monitoring and controlling
    - D) Personal matters

173. You are in the Close Project or Phase of the project. You finalize all activities across all the project management process groups to formally complete the phase. You also update documents, such as project management plan, scope management plan, cost management plan, etc. that are generated from project's activities. These documents are also referred to as:
    - A) Project or phase closure documents
    - B) Project plan
    - C) Historical information
    - D) Project records

174. In a scatter diagram, if points are close to the diagonal line, it indicates that:
    - A) Scatter diagram has some erroneous data
    - B) Three variables are closely correlated
    - C) Independent and dependent variables are related
    - D) No inference can be made from the analysis

175. In your project, you are creating documents which will be used to solicit proposals from prospective sellers. These can also be referred to as:
    - A) Procurement management plan
    - B) Procurement documents
    - C) Contract
    - D) Procurement statement of work

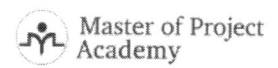

176. The actual cost of your project is $200,000, budget at completion is $325,000, and the cost variance is -$25,000. From the data above calculate the To-complete performance index of your project, given that, senior management did not agree to revise the estimate at completion based on current performance
    - AC = 200,000
    - BAC = 325,000
    - CV= -25,000

    A) 0.7
    B) 1.2
    C) 0.8
    D) 1

177. You are the project manager in a company where you have maximum authority. To which organizational structure does your company belong?
    A) Functional
    B) Weak Matrix
    C) Strong Matrix
    D) Projectized

178. You are managing a project. Your company has set a pre-defined budget for you to work with. In this context, a pre-defined budget is considered as a:
    A) Risk
    B) Assumption
    C) Constraint
    D) Stage point

179. In your project, you are in the process of determining the project roles, responsibilities and reporting relationships for your team members. Which of the following is not used for this process?
    A) Activity resource requirements
    B) Enterprise environmental factors
    C) Organizational process assets
    D) Team performance assessments

180. You are planning to award a contract and are evaluating sellers, using criteria like management approach, technical approach, life-cycle cost, and production capacity and interest. These criteria are called:
    A) Screening criteria
    B) Source selection criteria
    C) Evaluation criteria
    D) Contract selection methods

181. Which of the following statements related to precision and accuracy is correct?
    A) Precise measurements are always accurate
    B) Accurate measurements are always precise

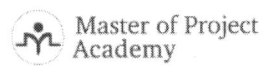

C) High precision measurements have little scatter
D) Accuracy means that measurements are clustered

182. Contracts are formal legal documents and can be amended at any time prior to contract closure by mutual consent, in accordance with the change control terms of the contract. In this context, you should be aware that:
    A) Contract administration is usually an integral part of project organization
    B) Contract administration is usually an administrative function separate from the project organization
    C) Contract administration is usually outsourced to an external agency or company
    D) Contract administration is always done alike in all organizations

183. You are the project manager of a project team that includes several new recruits. You notice that most of the team members possess "I am right mentality" and put forth their own ideas for consideration. In this context, your team is in which of the following stages of group development?
    A) Forming
    B) Storming
    C) Conflicting
    D) Performing

184. All the following statements about the activity list produced as an output from Define Activities process are true EXCEPT:
    A) The activity list must include all activities that will be performed on the project
    B) The activity list should include descriptions of major activities in sufficient detail
    C) The activity list should include activity duration estimates and scope of work description for each activity
    D) The activity list is obtained through decomposition of work packages.

185. In your project, during the planning process group, you will do all of the following EXCEPT:
    A) Develop options and actions to enhance opportunities and reduce threats to project objectives
    B) Identify and document project roles, responsibilities and required skills, report relationships, and create a staff management plan
    C) Monitor the status of the project to update the project budget and manage changes to the cost baseline
    D) Determine project stakeholder information needs and define a communication approach

186. You are an excellent technical architect. Your project sponsor believes that you can be an effective project manager. This is an example of:
    A) Halo effect
    B) Pygmalion effect
    C) Galatea effect
    D) Expert concept

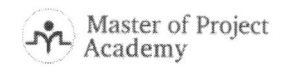

187. Which of the following organizational process assets cannot influence the Estimate Activity Durations?
   A) Historical duration information
   B) Project calendars
   C) Scheduling methodology
   D) Organization culture and systems

188. You have been appointed as a project manager to build a state-of-the-art flyover on Inter-state highway 10 which, when completed, helps reduce the traffic congestion by more than 40 percent. You have raised a request for bid and received many responses from prospective sellers, which you are now evaluating. During which of the following project management processes would you perform this activity?
   A) Plan Procurements
   B) Control Procurements
   C) Close Procurements
   D) Conduct Procurements

189. You are a project manager and you wish to distribute important project information that has accumulated since the beginning of the project to all the stakeholders. In this context, which of the following is NOT an information distribution tool?
   A) E-mail
   B) Press releases
   C) Project reports
   D) Electronic databases

190. While creating a network diagram, you wish to identify those activities that can be done in parallel where initiation of the successor activity depends on the initiation of the predecessor activity. Which diagramming method should you use for this purpose?
   A) PDM
   B) Schedule network analysis
   C) Simulation
   D) ADM

191. During Monitoring and Controlling phase of your project, you conduct regular meetings with your team to identify new risks, reassess current risks and close outdated risks. This is done through:
   A) Risk reassessment
   B) Variance Analysis
   C) Technical performance measurement
   D) Risk Audit

192. Which of the following exhibits greatest resistance to change?
   A) Business Requirements
   B) Technology
   C) People
   D) Environment

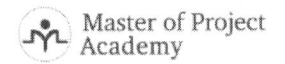

193. You are explaining the importance of Work Breakdown Structure (WBS) to your project team members. In this context, all of the following statements relating to Work Breakdown Structure(WBS) are correct EXCEPT:
    A) It is a hierarchical decomposition of work
    B) Planned work contained in the lowest level WBS components are also called WBS dictionaries
    C) WBS subdivides the project work into smaller, more manageable pieces of work
    D) WBS organizes and defines the total scope of the project work

194. You are managing the project for setting up an oil rig in the Pacific Ocean. Which of the following could be a valid constraint when you are doing human resource planning for your project?
    A) Weak matrix organization structure
    B) Unlimited budget, since the project is very critical to meet compliance needs
    C) Oil price increasing to more than $ 60 a barrel
    D) Oil price decreasing below $ 40 per barrel

195. It is estimated that 6 resources are needed to complete a certain task requiring 240 hours of work in 5 days, given that 1 resource can work 40 hours in 5 days. Which technique is used to arrive at this estimate?
    A) Parametric estimating
    B) Three-point estimates
    C) Reserve analysis
    D) Analogous estimating

196. In your project, you are behind schedule by 2 months, and you are under-budget by $ 50,000. In this context, your best course of action will be to:
    A) Talk with your sponsor to take some non-critical activities out of the project schedule
    B) Develop a new WBS
    C) Crash the project
    D) Fast track the project

197. In your pharmaceutical project, you would like to determine the duration required to complete a schedule activity. In this context, what should you consider FIRST that will help you in determining the duration estimates?
    A) List of activities and activity resource requirements
    B) Decomposition and templates
    C) Project schedule and schedule baseline
    D) Project scope management plan and project charter

198. Your company has decided to outsource one of its IT product developments to ABC IT Services through a contract. You clarify the structure and requirements of the contract so that mutual agreement can be reached prior to signing the contract. All the following statements on procurement negotiations are correct EXCEPT:
    A) You have to discuss technical and business management approaches, proprietary rights, overall schedule, payments, and price.

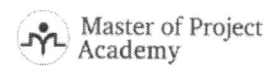

B) At the end of the procurement negotiations, you will have a contract document executed by both buyer and seller.
C) The project manager is the lead negotiator on the procurements.
D) Final contract language will reflect all agreements reached.

199. In Develop Schedule process, you create a distribution of probable durations for each activity and use it to calculate the distribution of probable results for the total project. The technique that you are using is:
A) Parametric estimating
B) Mathematical analysis
C) What-if analysis
D) Resource leveling

200. You are managing a critical project with virtual teams located in eight countries. At times, team members find it difficult to understand and interpret what others are communicating via tele-conferencing. From a communication management point of view, this difficulty in transmitting and understanding messages can also be referred to as:
A) Disturbance
B) Noise
C) Interference
D) Breakdown in encode-decode model

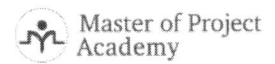

Section 13 – Sample PMP® Practice Exam Answers & Rationales

1. A. A contract is a legal relationship subject to remedy in the courts.
2. C. Option C is an activity performed as part of the Develop Schedule process. The remaining options are activities that are performed as part of Control Schedule process.
3. D. The communication management plan provides stakeholder communications requirements, information that need to be communicated, including language, format, content, level of detail, methods or technologies, etc.
4. B. Knowledge gained in one company is not proprietary information and can be used in subsequent jobs. This is acceptable as long as you do not unethically use any contacts or proprietary information belonging to the first company. Options A, C, and D are inappropriate, because they imply that knowledge and experience gained from the first company, if used in the present company might adversely impact the former company's business interests.
5. D. NPV of project A = $ 100,000 NPV of project B = $ 2,000,000 - $ 1,900,000 = $ 100,000 Both projects have the same NPV; therefore, either project may be selected, if NPV criterion is used.
6. B. Plan Risk Responses is the process of developing options and actions to enhance opportunities and to reduce threats to project objectives Monitor and Control Risks is the process of implementing risk response plans, tracking identified risks, and monitoring residual risks Please note that this process should follow Plan Risk Responses process. So, option B is the correct answer. The other options take place prior to Plan Risk Responses process.
7. C. Some of the configuration management activities included in the integrated change control process are: configuration identification, configuration status accounting, and configuration verification and audit.
8. C. Weight is the only variable here. All the other options refer to units of currency and measurement.
9. A. Although many projects may have similar phase names with similar deliverables, few are identical. Some will have only one phase..., Other projects may have many phases.
10. C. Controlling the project scope ensures all requested changes and recommended corrective or preventive actions are processed through the Perform Integrated Change Control process.
11. D. Project sponsor provides financial resources for project.
12. B. Bidder conferences (sometimes called contractor conferences, vendor conferences, and pre-bid conferences) are meetings with all prospective sellers and buyers prior to submittal of a bid or proposal. They are used to ensure that all prospective sellers have a clear and common understanding of the procurement (both technical and contractual requirements), and that no bidders receive preferential treatment.
13. D. A lag directs a delay in the successor activity.
14. B. Face-to-face meetings are the most effective means of communicating and resolving issues with stakeholders. When face-to-face meetings are not warranted or practical (e.g., international projects), telephone, electronic mail, and other electronic tools can be used for exchanging information.

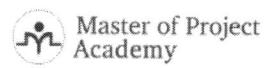

15. B. The project manager should maintain and respect the confidentiality of sensitive information obtained in the course of professional activities or otherwise where a clear obligation exists. Also, the project manager should ensure that a conflict of interest does not compromise legitimate interests of a client or customer, or influence professional judgments.
16. D. If Project B and project C are selected the company would suffer losses. Project A is not selected, because opportunity cost is not a project selection criterion. Project D is the only suitable option, because this project has a positive NPV and hence could be selected.
17. B. The Delphi technique is a way to reach consensus of experts. Project risk experts participate in this technique anonymously.
18. B. A low position in the organization could be the source of least conflict. Please note that Option A (Weak matrix structure with multiple managers to report to), Option C (Roles that are not well defined) and Option D (Work pressure and high stress) increase conflict in an organization
19. A. Quality Assurance is auditing the quality requirements and the results from quality control measurements to ensure appropriate quality standards and operational definitions are used.
20. A. Enterprise environmental factors may enhance or constrain project management options and may have a positive or negative influence on the outcome
21. D. Project Scope Statement. Narrative description of the project scope... and for confirming or developing a common understanding of project scope among the stakeholders.
22. A. In Directing, managers tell people what tasks will be performed and when and how they should be done.
23. D. A contract is a legal relationship subject to remedy in the courts.
24. D. Since the tasks are not on the critical path of the project, we cannot determine the PERT estimate for the duration of the project. The PERT estimate can only be calculated for the critical path of the project.
25. D. A project manager cannot control all the communication channels, because the number of such channels could be very large. Also, the number of communication channels is fixed. For N people, the number of communication channels is N * (N-1) / 2.
26. B. Since SPI is 0.8, the project is behind schedule. But since CPI is 1.2, you are under budget. Option B (Fast tracking or crashing) is the only alternative that helps solve the problem. They may increase costs but decrease the project timelines.
27. A. The only suitable option is option A, because the internal rate of return is positive, i.e., 12%. All other options exhibit unfavorable selection criteria. Opportunity cost is not a selection criteria.
28. A. Subcontracting the project to an outside vendor is a risk transference technique. It simply transfers the responsibility of managing the risk to the other party but does not eliminate the risk. So, we should not subcontract a critical risk unless it is explicitly mentioned that the seller has expertise in handling such risks. A fallback plan can be developed for implementation if the selected strategy is not fully effective or if an accepted risk occurs. Developing further fallback options, allocating contingency reserves, reviewing risks driven by strategies etc. should be contained in the fallback plan.

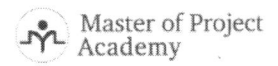

29. D. The business case is created as a result of one or more of the following: Market demand, Organizational need, Customer request, Technological Advance, Legal requirement, Ecological impacts, Social need
30. A. A checklist is a structured tool, usually component-specific, used to verify that a set of required steps has been performed.
31. B. The five process groups are Initiating, Planning, Executing, Monitoring and Controlling, and Closing.
32. D. The WBS dictionary provides more detailed descriptions of the components in the WBS, including work packages and control accounts.
33. D. The five interpersonal influences are: Legitimate Power: The ability to gain support, because project personnel perceive the project manager as being officially empowered to issue orders. Reward Power: The ability to gain support, because project personnel perceive the project manager as capable of directly or indirectly dispensing valued organizational rewards such as salary, promotion, bonus, and future work assignments. Penalty Power: The ability to gain support, because the project personnel perceive the project manager as capable of directly or indirectly dispensing penalties that they wish to avoid. Penalty power usually derives from the same source as reward power, with one being a necessary condition for the other. Expert Power: The ability to gain support, because personnel perceive the project manager as possessing special knowledge or expertise. Referent Power: The ability to gain support, because project personnel feel personally attracted to the project manager or her project.
34. D. Project schedule is an input to the Plan Procurement Management process; all the other options are inputs to Control Procurements process.
35. D. Heuristics (or rule of thumb), such as allocation of scarce resources to the critical path first, can be applied to develop a schedule.
36. C. Non-verbal communication forms more than 55% of the total communication and is important to pay attention to while negotiations are being conducted
37. A. Option A is violated because adding the requirement violates the contractual terms, which will impact project deliverables.
38. B. PV = 110,000 / (1 + 10/100) = 100,000
39. C. Expected Profit = Sum of (Probability X Profit) (for each alternative) = (0.50 x $ 40,000) + (0.50 x - $ 25,000) = $ 20,000 - $ 12,500 = $ 7,500
40. D. Requests for change can be direct or indirect, externally or internally initiated, and can be optional or legally/contractually mandated.
41. D. Cost of quality includes all costs incurred over the life of the product by investment in preventing nonconformance to requirements, appraising the product or service for conformance to requirements, and failing to meet requirements (rework)
42. B. Stakeholders` ability to influence the final characteristics of the project`s product, without significantly impacting cost, is highest at the start of the project and decreases as the project progresses towards completion.
43. A. Information on constraints may be listed in the project scope statement or in a separate log.
44. B. A responsibility assignment matrix (RAM) is used to illustrate the connections between work packages or activities and project team members. One example of a RAM is a RACI (responsible, accountable, consult, and inform) chart.
45. D. Cancellation of the contract has to be done by both the seller and the buyer (i.e., the buyer cannot unilaterally cancel the contract).

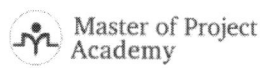

46. A. The different types of estimates are: Definitive: - 5% to +10% accuracy Budgetary: - 15% to +25% accuracy Order of magnitude: - 50% to +50% accuracy So, if -5% to +10% variation is allowable, only 29 - 31 days fits that criterion.
47. D. Identify Stakeholders is the process to identify all those (people or organizations) impacted by the project and document relevant information on their interests, involvement, and impact on the success of the project.
48. C. Although the project manager is responsible for ensuring the integrity of the project, she cannot be responsible for the integrity of her team members. However, she should definitely try to influence her team members to perform all project activities in an ethical manner and with integrity.
49. C. Positive schedule variance means the project is ahead of schedule; negative cost variance means the project is over-budget. Also, please note that crashing will increase costs and impact the cost variance adversely .
50. B. Project Risk Management should be an agenda item at periodic status meetings. The amount of time required for that item will vary, depending upon the risks that have been identified, their priority, and difficulty of response.
51. A. Project Management System: The aggregation of the processes, tools, techniques, methodologies, resources, and procedures to manage a project.
52. A. When checklists are used, the completed checklists become part of the organizational process assets updates.
53. C. A program is defined as a group of projects managed in a coordinated way to obtain benefits and control not available from managing them individually.
54. D. The best option is to first review the requirement, contained in the project WBS, with the particular team member who has implemented the requirement. Either the team member has not done the work properly or there might have been lack of clarity in defining the requirement in the WBS.
55. C. Penalty Power: The ability to gain support, because the project personnel perceive the project manager as capable of directly or indirectly dispensing penalties that they wish to avoid. Penalty power usually derives from the same source as reward power, with one being a necessary condition for the other.
56. B. Contract types are not tools or techniques used in Conduct Procurements process.
57. C. The different types of estimates are: Order of Magnitude: -50% to +50% Budget Estimates: -15% to +25% Definitive Estimates: -5% to +10%
58. C. Report Performance is a process of collecting and distributing performance information, including status report, progress measurements, and forecasts. Report Performance process involves periodic collection and analysis of baseline versus actual data to understand and communicate project progress and performance, as well as to forecast the project results.
59. B. Option B is the best choice. This is the first step that you should take. Once you inform the senior management, they may allow you to take the part-time assignment with the seller, if they see no conflict of interest. If, on the other hand, your company sees this as conflict of interest, you can go for
60. B. Earned Value is physical work actually accomplished.
61. B. The Delphi technique helps reduce bias in the data and keeps any one person from having undue influence on the outcome.

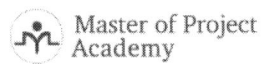

62. C. Project statement of work, business case, contract, enterprise environmental factors, and organizational process assets are inputs for the Develop Project Charter process.
63. B. Modern quality management complements project management, as both disciplines recognize the importance of customer satisfaction, prevention over inspection, continuous improvement, and management responsibility.
64. D. Project charter includes project goals and objectives. Stakeholder register includes needs and expectations of stakeholders.
65. C. Validate Scope is the process of formalizing acceptance of the completed project deliverables. Validating scope includes reviewing deliverables with the customer or sponsor to ensure that they are completed satisfactorily and obtaining formal acceptance of deliverables by the customer or sponsor.
66. D. Factors such as company policy, supervision, interpersonal relations, working conditions and salary are hygiene factors
67. C. Conduct Procurements is the process of obtaining seller responses, selecting a seller, and awarding a contract.
68. A. The lengths of the different paths are: Path1: Start -> 1 -> 2 -> End: 10 Path2: Start -> 3 -> 5 -> End: 11 Path3: Start -> 4 -> 5 -> End: 12 Since the longest path is Start -> 4 -> 5 -> End, this is the critical path. Length of the critical path is 12. Slack = 12(critical path duration) - 11(duration of path having task 3) = 1
69. D. Option D (communication methods like status review meetings) is one of the tools and techniques used for Monitor Communications process, which is performed after Manage Communications process.
70. A. It is the project manager's responsibility to maintain and satisfy the scope and objectives of professional services, unless otherwise directed by the customer. Option A: This is the correct answer. According to PMI, if there is any change in the project or product scope, it has to be explained to the customer, who can then make an informed decision.
71. A. BCR = Payback/Project Cost = 2000/800 = 2.50
72. B. Risk avoidance involves changing the project management plan to eliminate the threat entirely. The project manager may also isolate the project objectives from the risk's impact or change the objective that is in jeopardy. Examples of this include extending the schedule, changing the strategy, or reducing scope.
73. A. Organizational processes and procedures for conducting work include… organization communication requirements. The other organizational process assets that can influence the Develop Project Charter process include but are not limited to organizational standard processes, policies, and standardized process definitions for use in the organization, templates (e.g., project charter template), historical information, and lessons learned knowledge base, etc.
74. B. A standard normal distribution, which shows standard deviation (or sigma) as distance of the measurement from the mean (target) value. For 3 sigma, this is 99.7%
75. A. The project manager reports to the functional manager in a balanced matrix organization
76. C. Controlling the project scope ensures all requested changes and recommended corrective or preventive actions are processed through the Perform Integrated Change Control process. Project scope control is also used to manage the actual changes when

they occur and is integrated with the other control processes. Uncontrolled changes are often referred to as project scope creep.

77. B. Project team directory is a documented list of project team members, their project roles, and communication information.

78. A. Make-or-buy analysis is part of the Plan Procurement Management process. It is a general management technique used to determine whether particular work can best be accomplished by the project team or outsourced.

79. A. In a normal distribution, the PERT duration (also called mean) = {Pessimistic + (4* Most Likely) + Optimistic}/6 = {10 + (4 * 13) + 16}/6 = 13

80. C. Actively managing the expectations of stakeholders to increase the likelihood of project acceptance by negotiating and influencing their desires to achieve and maintain project goals. Addressing concerns that have not become issues yet, usually relates to the anticipation of future problems. These concerns need to be uncovered and discussed.

81. A. As per PMI Code of Ethics and Professional Conduct, you should assume: a. Responsibility to maintain and satisfy the scope and objectives of professional services, unless otherwise directed by the customer Option A: This is the correct answer, because it is ethical to inform the buyer about the CPI as it stands.

82. A. CV= EV-AC EV = CV + AC = 25,000 + 200,000 =225,000 CPI=EV/AC =225,000/200,000 =1.125 EAC= BAC/CPI =350,000/1.125 =311,111.11 TCPI=BAC-EV/EAC-AC =350,000-225,000 / 311,111.11-200,000 =125,000 / 111,111 = 1.125

83. C. Expected Value of the project = Expected Value of success (0.30 * $ 700,000) + Expected value of Failure (0.70 * - $ 300,000) = 210,000 - 210,000 = 0 Since the Expected Value is "0", you cannot take a decision whether to continue with the project or not.

84. A. Any time the customer requests for a change, you should: 1. Understand what kind of change is requested and talk with team members to assess the implication of the change. 2. Open up a change control if there is a formal change control mechanism. 3. Communicate the change to the management, and inform the customer about the impact of the change (e.g. increase in sizing, schedule, etc.). 4. Implement the change if it is accepted.

85. D. Trend analysis is performed using run charts and involves mathematical techniques to forecast future outcomes based on historical results. Trend analysis is often used to monitor technical performance - how many errors or defects have been corrected and how many remain uncorrected.

86. A. A portfolio refers to a collection of projects or programs and other work that are grouped together to facilitate effective management of that work to meet strategic business objectives.

87. D. Rolling Wave Planning: A form of progressive elaboration planning where the work to be accomplished in the near term is planned in detail at a low level of the Work Breakdown Structure, while the work far in the future is planned at a relatively high level of the work breakdown structure.

88. D. Dominator team member -Always tries to take over -Professes to know everything about project management -Tries to manipulate people -Will challenge those in change for a leadership role

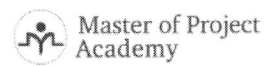

89. A. Procurement negotiations, bidder conferences, advertising, and independent estimates are some of the tools and techniques used in the Conduct Procurements process.
90. A. Float is also called slack.
91. A. Processes of Communications Management Knowledge Area are: Plan Communications Management, Manage Communications and Monitor Communications
92. C. Option C is the best answer because, as a project manager, you are supposed to deal with any issue or alleged unethical practice and not ignore it
93. A. Since current variances are atypical, Estimate at Completion, EAC = AC + BAC - EV = $ 100,000 + $ 300,000 - $ 150,000 = $ 250,000
94. A. Workaround. A response to a negative risk that has occurred. Distinguished from contingency plan in that a workaround is not planned in advance of the occurrence of the risk event.
95. B. Develop Project Management Plan process belongs to planning process group.
96. C. A scatter diagram shows the relationship between two variables. This tool allows the quality team to study and identify the possible relationship between changes observed in two variables. Dependent variables versus independent variables are plotted. The closer the points are to a diagonal line, the more closely they are related.
97. C. Cost and staffing level is lowest during beginning and closure of a project typically and highest during the project work is performed.
98. B. Components of the requirements management plan can include, but are not limited to... requirements prioritization process, product metrics that will be used and the rationale for using them; and traceability structure, that is, which requirements attributes will be captured on the traceability matrix and to which other project documents requirements will be traced.
99. B. The most preferred conflict resolution techniques adopted by project managers (in descending order of preference) are as follows: 1. Confrontation 2. Compromise 3. Smoothing 4. Forcing 5. Withdrawal
100. A. Point of total assumption refers to the point where the costs have to be incurred by the seller herself when they have exceeded the ceiling limits stipulated in the contract. Hence, share ratio ceases to exist.
101. B. In a normal distribution, the PERT duration (also called mean) {Pessimistic + (4* Most Likely) + Optimistic} / 6 = {16 + (4 * 13) + 10}/6 = 13 1 Standard Deviation (sigma) = (Pessimistic - Optimistic) / 6 = (16 - 10) / 6 = 1 If the task has to be completed within 10 days to 16 days, then the probability of completion within the timeframe is 99.73%(3 sigma)
102. B. The best way to manage complex communications, such as in contracts, is through formal written communication.
103. D. When you realize that you are in an actual or a potential conflict of interest situation, you should immediately withdraw from engaging in decision-making activities. Decisions taken in such situations might go against the interests of your current project and the employer company.
104. B. Determine Budget is the process of aggregating the estimated costs of individual activities or work packages to establish an authorized cost baseline. Resource calendars are inputs to this process.

105. B. The processes in risk management interact with each other and with the processes in the other Knowledge Areas... Each process occurs at least once in every project and occurs in one or more of the project phases, if the project is divided into phases. Although the processes are presented here as discrete elements with well-defined interfaces, in practice they will overlap and interact.
106. D. Projects are authorized by someone external to the project such as a sponsor, PMO, or portfolio steering committee. The project initiator or sponsor should be at a level that is appropriate to funding the project. They will either create the project charter or delegate that duty to the project manager.
107. C. Design of Experiments (DOE) is a statistical method for identifying which factors may influence specific variables of a product or process under development or in production.
108. B. The Executing Process Group consists of those processes performed to complete the work defined in the project management plan to satisfy the project specifications. This process group involves coordinating people and resources as well as integrating and performing the activities of the project in accordance with the project management plan.
109. A. Decomposition is the subdivision of project deliverables into smaller, more manageable components until the work and deliverables are defined to the work package level. (Decomposition is done as part of Create WBS process).
110. C. Option C (negotiation) is a tool and technique for Acquire Resources process. Option A (observation and conversation), Option B (project performance appraisals) and Option D (issue log) are tools and techniques for Manage Team process.
111. D. TAs stated in the question, the scope of your project is very well defined, and you have completed all the work described in the contract. You should now move towards contract close-out. Also note that `you think` that your buyer is not happy, but there is no mention of the buyer explicitly stating that she is not satisfied.
112. A. Decomposition is a tool used in the Define Activities process.
113. B. Informal verbal communication, such as in a face-to-face meeting, is the best way to handle issues of poor performance and resolve disputes among team members
114. D. When working with team members of different countries, to ensure that cultural diversities do not hamper the progress of the project, the project manager must provide training to her team members regarding cultural diversities among various countries, project goals, and the ethics and culture of the company.
115. D. Parametric estimating uses a statistical relationship between historical data and other variables to calculate an estimate for activity parameters, such as cost, budget, and duration. An example for the cost parameter is multiplying the planned quantity of work to be performed by the historical cost per unit to obtain the estimated cost.
116. C. Risks judged to be of low priority are included in a "watchlist" for periodic monitoring.
117. C. The business case is created as a result of... social need (e.g., a non-governmental organization in a developing country authorizing a project to provide potable water systems, latrines, and sanitation education to communities suffering from high rates of cholera).
118. B. The quality management plan describes how the project management team will implement the performing organization's quality policy.

119. B. Helpdesk work is an operational activity. Organizations perform work to achieve a set of objectives. In many organizations, the work performed can be categorized as either project or operations work. These two types of work share a number of characteristics as follows: a. Performed by individuals b. Limited by constraints including resource constraints c. Planned, executed, monitored and controlled Projects and operations differ primarily in that operations are ongoing and produce repetitive products, services, or results. Projects are temporary, and end.
120. D. Inspections are sometimes called reviews, product reviews, audits, or walkthroughs.
121. C. Source of conflicts in a project from highest to lowest respectively are: Schedules, Priorities, Manpower, Technical, Procedures, Personality, Costs
122. D. Terms such as bid, tender, or quotation are generally used when the seller selection decision will be based on price (as when buying commercial or standard items), while a term such as proposal is generally used when other considerations such as technical capability or technical approach are paramount.
123. B. In a normal distribution, the PERT duration (also called mean) = {Pessimistic + (4* Most Likely) + Optimistic}/6 = {16 + (4 * 13) + 10}/6 = 13 1 Standard Deviation (1 Sigma) = (Pessimistic - Optimistic) / 6 = (16 - 10) / 6 = 1 So, if the company has Six Sigma quality requirements, Mean - 6 Sigma = 13 - 6 * 1 = 7 Mean + 6 Sigma = 13 + 6 * 1 = 19 The task can be completed within 7 days to 19 days.
124. A. The analysis of the communication requirements determines the information needs of the project stakeholders. These requirements are defined by combining the type and format of information needed with an analysis of the value of that information.
125. A. Project managers, while making decisions regarding a project, should preferably select a project with no(or minimal) negative impact on the environment, community and society.
126. D. Earned Value (EV) = The sum of the approved cost estimates for activities completed during a given period = Estimated cost of work that is completed after day 11 = $ 5,000 + $ 5,000 + $5,000*.50 = $ 12,500 (because Tasks A and B are completed and Task C is 50% complete).
127. A. After Identify Risks process, the next step is Perform Qualitative Risk Analysis process. Risk probability and impact assessment is one of the tools and techniques for Perform Qualitative Risk Analysis process.
128. D. If the project was terminated prior to completion, the formal documentation indicates why the project was terminated and formalizes the procedures for the transfer of the finished and unfinished deliverables of the cancelled project to others. During project closure the project manager reviews prior phase documentation, customer acceptance documentation from Scope Verification and the contract, to ensure that all project requirements are complete prior to finalizing the closure of the project
129. C. Marginal analysis balances the additional benefits from an action against the additional cost. It is an acknowledgement that decisions should be made based on the incremental gains and losses that result from a decision.
130. B. Organizational Process Assets is an input to Develop Project Charter (which is in the Initiating Process Group).
131. A. Analysis of scope performance can result in a change request to the scope baseline or other components of the project management plan.

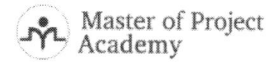

132. C. (Option C) Finding out your strong and weak areas helps determine how you can do the job better and become an effective leader. This may also result in identifying the needed training programs. Therefore, option A (enroll in appropriate training programs) and option B (learning all leadership theories) are not recommended. Option D (Taking advice from the person who retired from the company) is recommended, but this can be done after determining your strong and weak areas.
133. A. It is the project management team's responsibility to make certain that all procurements meet the specific needs of the project while adhering to organizational procurement policies.
134. A. A milestone list identifies all milestones and indicates whether the milestone is mandatory, such as those specified by contract, or optional, such as those based upon historical information.
135. C. Project scope statement is output of Define Scope process.
136. B. The PMI code of ethics and professional conduct mandates a project manager to maintain her professional demeanor at all times. Also, the project manager should always try to uphold project and organizational objectives.
137. A. Bottom-up estimating is a method of estimating a component of work. This technique is used to estimate the cost of individual work packages or activities at the greatest level of specified detail. The detailed cost is then summarized or rolled-up to higher levels for subsequent reporting and tracking purposes.
138. A. Option A: This is the correct answer as it has all the tools and techniques which are used for Identify Risks process.
139. D. Requests for a change can be direct or indirect, externally or internally initiated, and can be optional or legally/contractually mandated and can include corrective and preventive actions.
140. D. Quality refers to "the degree to which a set of inherent characteristics fulfill requirements."
141. C. Option C: This is the correct answer. Records management technique is a technique used in Control Procurements processes.
142. B. If the duration of task J is increased by 1 week, Start -> G -> I -> J -> End = 23 weeks; this also lies on the critical path (23 weeks). Since there are 3 critical paths now, a delay in any of the critical paths will delay the overall project; this increases the overall risk to the project.
143. C. Expected monetary value is calculated by the formula EMV = Probability x Impact. 0.65 x 100,000 = 65,000 0.35 x 100,000 = 35,000 EMV = 65,000 - 35,000 = 30,000
144. C. In the project management context, integration includes characteristics of unification, consolidation, articulation, and integrative actions that are crucial to project completion, successfully managing stakeholder expectations, and meeting requirements.
145. D. Control Chart is the BEST tool here as, in this process, the appropriate data is collected and analyzed to indicate the quality status of project processes and products. Control charts illustrate how a process behaves overtime and when a process is subject to special cause variation, resulting in an out-of-control condition.
146. A. In all procurement relationships, the final equitable settlement of all outstanding issues, claims, and disputes by negotiation is the primary goal. Whenever settlement cannot be achieved through direct negotiation, some form of alternative dispute

resolution (ADR) including mediation or arbitration may be explored. When all else fails, litigation in the courts is the least desirable option.

147. C. Duration of critical path = 23 weeks If the management wants to complete the project in twenty weeks, then the project float will be: 20 - 23 = -3 weeks The project float compares the critical path with an externally imposed date and may be negative. You may be forced to fast track or perform crashing to ensure that the project is completed on time as required by the management.

148. C. Perform Qualitative Risk Analysis is the process of prioritizing risks for further analysis or action by assessing and combining their probability of occurrence and impact. Organizations can improve the project's performance by focusing on high-priority risks.

149. C. Historical information and lessons learned information are transferred to the lessons learned knowledge base for use by future projects or phases. This can include information on issues and risks as well as techniques that worked well that can be applied to future projects.

150. D. One of the fundamental tenets of modern quality management states that quality is planned, designed, and built in - not inspected in. The cost of preventing mistakes is generally much lower than the cost of correcting them when they are found during inspection.

151. D. Plan Procurement Management is a process that identifies those project needs, which can best be, or must be, met by acquiring products, services, or results outside of the project organization, versus those project needs, which can be accomplished by the project team.

152. C. Sequence Activities is the process of identifying and documenting the relationships among the project activities. Schedule network templates are the tools used in this process.

153. A. Project reports include formal and informal project reports that describe project status, documents like lessons learned, issue logs, project closure reports, and outputs from other knowledge areas.

154. C. Some important definitions:

- a) Monochronic: Doing one thing at a time
- b) Polychronic: Doing many things at once
- c) Ethnocentric: Belief in the superiority of one's own race or ethnic background
- d) Egalitarian: Treating all the project team members equally
- e) Culture shock: Homesickness (in foreign assignments)

155. A. Earned value technique (EVT) is a specific technique for measuring the performance of work and used to establish the performance measurement baseline (PMB).

156. B. Validate Scope is the process of formalizing acceptance of the completed project deliverables.

157. C. Validate Scope is the process of formalizing acceptance of the completed project deliverables. Validating scope includes reviewing deliverables with the customer or sponsor to ensure that they are completed satisfactorily and obtaining formal acceptance of deliverables by the customer or sponsor.

158. A. Confrontation focuses on solving the problems. Leads to win-win situation for both parties. Therefore, it is the most desirable conflict resolution technique.

159. B. Project Managers should ensure that team members adhere to the company policies at all times.

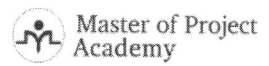

160. C. CV (Cost Variance) = EV - AC = $ 90,000 - $ 125,000 = - $ 35,000 (since this is negative, you are over-budget) CPI (Cost Performance Index) = EV/AC = $ 90,000 / $ 125,000 = 0.72 (since this is <1, you are over-budget) SV (Schedule Variance) = EV - PV = $ 90,000 - $ 100,000 = - $ 10,000 (since this is negative, you are behind schedule) SPI (Schedule Performance Index) = EV/ PV = $ 90,000 / $ 100,000 = 0.9 (since this is <1, you are behind schedule) The above calculations show that all options except option C are correct . Hence, option C is the right answer.
161. C. Acquire Resources is the process of confirming resource availability and obtaining the team necessary to complete project assignments. Project staff assignments is an output of "Acquire Team" process, which is a part of executing process group.
162. C. The project manager should always try to first evaluate the change and try to prevent unwarranted changes, which can adversely impact the project scope.
163. A. Most used conflict resolution techniques are: Withdrawal, Forcing and Compromising
164. A. Direct and Manage Project Work also requires implementation of approved changes covering corrective and preventive actions and defect repair. Corrective action. Documented direction for executing the project work to bring expected future performance of the project work in line with the project management plan.
165. C. Control charts are used to determine whether or not a process is stable or has predictable performance. Upper and lower specification limits are based on requirements of the contract. They reflect the maximum and minimum values allowed.
166. B. Fixed Price with Economic Price Adjustment contract (FP-EPA) is a contract type which is used whenever the seller's performance period spans a considerable number of years as is desired with many long-term relationships. It is a fixed-price contract, but with a special provision allowing for pre-defined final adjustments to the contract price due to changed conditions, such as inflation changes, or cost increases (or decreases) for specific commodities.
167. C. The diagram shows that at time x, SPI < 1 (i.e., behind schedule) and CPI>1 (i.e., under-budget). Please note that in earned value management calculations, ratios >1 is desirable.
168. D. Define Activities is the process of identifying specific actions to be performed to produce the project deliverables. This is done after Create WBS process.
169. B. If you are working on a project, which has very limited information, then when estimating durations... you should use the actual duration of previous, similar projects as the basis for estimating the duration of the current project. This is done as part of Estimate Activity Durations. Once we estimate the duration of the project, we should calculate the early and late start and finish dates.
170. A. A project simulation uses a model that translates the specified detailed uncertainties of the project into their potential impact on project objectives. Iterative simulations are typically performed using the Monte Carlo technique. In a simulation, the project model is computed many times (iterated), with the input values (e.g., cost estimates or activity durations) chosen at random for each iteration from the probability distributions of these variables.
171. D. The requirements traceability matrix is a table that links requirements to their origin and traces them throughout the project life cycle. The implementation of a requirements traceability matrix helps ensure that each requirement adds business value by linking it to the business and project objectives. It provides a means to track

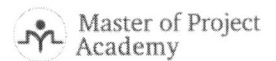

requirements throughout the project life cycle, helping to ensure that requirements approved in the requirements documentation are delivered at the end of the project.

172. C. A manager should not delegate long-range planning, performance appraisals, personal matters, or leadership activities to her subordinates. She can, however, delegate routine project monitoring and controlling activities.

173. A. The project or phase closure documents, consisting of formal documentation that indicates completion of the project or phase and transfer of the completed project or phase deliverables to others, such as an operations group or to the next phase.

174. C. A scatter diagram shows the relationship between two variables. This tool allows the quality team to study and identify the possible relationship between changes observed in two variables. Dependent variables versus independent variables are plotted. The closer the points are to a diagonal line, the more closely they are related.

175. B. `Procurement documents` is one of the outputs of Plan Procurement Management process, and is used to solicit proposals from prospective sellers.

176. B. EV=AC+CV EV= 200,000-25000 EV= 175,000 CPI=EV/AC =175,000/200,000 =0.875 TCPI=(BAC-EV)/(BAC-AC) =(325,000 - 175,000)/(325,000 - 200,000) =150,000/125,000 =1.2

177. D. Project Managers have maximum authority in a company with a projectized organizational structure.

178. C. Constraint: An applicable restriction or limitation, either internal or external to a project, which will affect the performance of a project or a process. For example, a predefined budget, any imposed dates, or schedule milestones that are issued by the customer or performing organization.

179. D. Team performance assessments is used to evaluate the performance of project team members during and after the project completion.

180. B. Source selection criteria are often included as part of the procurement solicitation documents. Such criteria are developed and used to rate or score seller proposals, and can be objective or subjective. Other selection criteria can be identified and documented to support an assessment for more complex products, services, or results. Some examples are: understanding of need, overall or life-cycle cost, technical capability, risk, management approach, technical approach, etc.

181. C. Precision and accuracy are not equivalent. Precision means the values of repeated measurements are clustered and have little scatter. Accuracy means that the measured value is very close to the true value. Precise measurements are not necessarily accurate. A very accurate measurement is not necessarily precise.

182. B. Due to varying organizational structures, many organizations treat contract administration as an administrative function separate from the project organization.

183. B. Stages of group development are as follows: -Forming: team members meet and agree on goals -Storming: team members put forth individual ideas ("I am right" mentality) and different ideas compete for consideration -Norming : team members adjust their behavior to work as a team ("we can work together" mentality) -Performing: team members are able to function as a unit as they find ways to do the job smoothly and effectively -Adjourning: team members are disbanded after the task is completed.

184. C. The activity list is a comprehensive list including all schedule activities required on the project.

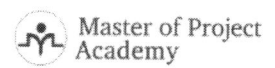

185. C. Control Costs is the process of monitoring the status of the project to update the project budget and managing changes to the cost baseline. (This is a part of Monitoring and Controlling Process Group).
186. A. Halo effect: Perception of a particular outstanding trait influences the overall perception of a person.
187. D. The organizational process assets that can influence the Estimate Activity Durations process include but are not limited to: historical duration information, project calendars, scheduling methodology, and lessons learned.
188. D. Conduct Procurements is the process of obtaining seller responses, selecting a seller, and awarding a contract. In this process, the team will receive bids or proposals and will apply selection criteria to select one or more sellers who are qualified to perform the work and acceptable as sellers.
189. C. Project reports describe project status and include lessons learned, issue logs, project closure reports, and outputs from other knowledge areas. They are not information distribution tools. E-mail, paper-based reports, and electronic databases are the tools used to distribute information.
190. A. PDM (Precedence diagramming method) includes... start-to-start - the initiation of the successor activity depends upon the initiation of the predecessor activity.
191. A. Risk Reassessment. Monitor and Control Risks often results in identification of new risks, reassessment of current risks, and the closing of risks that are outdated. Project risk reassessments should be regularly scheduled. The amount and detail of repetition that is appropriate depends on how the project progresses relative to its objectives.
192. C. People exhibit greatest resistance to change
193. B. The planned work is contained within the lowest level WBS components, which are called work packages. A work package can be scheduled, cost estimated, monitored, and controlled.
194. A. In a weak matrix organization structure, the project manager's role is more of a coordinator or expediter than that of a true project manager.
195. A. Parametric estimating uses a statistical relationship between historical data and other variables to calculate an estimate for activity parameters such as cost, budget, and duration. Activity durations can be quantitatively determined by multiplying the quantity of work to be performed by labor hours per unit of work.
196. C. Crashing: A schedule compression technique in which cost and schedule tradeoffs are analyzed to determine how to obtain the greatest amount of compression for the least incremental cost. Crashing does not always produce a viable alternative and may result in increased risk and/or cost.
197. A. Estimate Activity Durations process requires that the amount of work effort required to complete the activity is estimated, and the amount of resources to be applied to complete the activity is estimated; these are used to approximate the number of work periods (activity duration) needed to complete the activity.
198. C. The project manager may not be the lead negotiator on procurements.
199. C. What-if scenario Analysis: This is an analysis of the question "What if the situation represented by scenario `X` happens?". A schedule network analysis is performed using the schedule to compute the different scenarios...The most common technique is Monte Carlo Analysis, in which a distribution of possible activity durations is defined for each activity and used to calculate a distribution of possible outcomes for the total project.

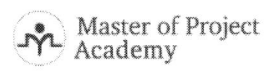

200. B. Noise is anything that interferes with the transmission and understanding of the message (e.g., distance).